HBJ TREASURY OF LITERATURE

Components

Harcourt Brace Jovanovich

Assessment Choices

Unit Skills Assessment and Teacher's Edition (1-8)
Tests that measure students' mastery of reading skills and strategies.

Unit Holistic Assessment and Teacher's Edition (1-8)
Literature passages and questions that assess students' progress in reading comprehension.

Unit Integrated Performance Assessment and Teacher's Edition (1-8)
Reading and writing prompts that model realistic literacy activities for authentic performance assessment.

Portfolio Assessment Teacher's Guide (K-8)
A resource guide for managing portfolio assessment.

Individual Inventory for Reading and Writing (1-8)
Reading passages that assess a student's reading and writing abilities for placement.

Group Placement Tests, Teacher's Edition with Copying Masters (1-8)
Primary, intermediate, and advanced tests for appropriate placement.

Computer Management System (1-8)
A technology aid for assessment (available for Apple and IBM computers).

Learning Technology

Laserdisc (1-8)
Dynamic full-motion videos and still images that build concepts, illustrate key vocabulary, and stimulate critical thinking—all easily accessed by bar codes. A teacher's guide is provided.

Reading Software (3-8)
A reading skills practice program with activities that reinforce vocabulary, comprehension, thinking, study, and language skills (available for Apple IIe, IIc, and IIGS computers).

Second-Language Support

Second-Language Support Manual (1-8)
Designed for use with *HBJ Treasury of Literature*, a valuable teaching resource guide with lesson-by-lesson strategies for helping second-language students build English language and reading skills.

Transition for ESL Students, Teacher's Manual (1-6)
Useful suggestions and strategies for helping ESL students make a comfortable transition to *HBJ Treasury of Literature*.

English as a Second Language (1
Colorful classroom posters and a helpful teacher's manual for developing English language skills.

For more information call:
1-800-CALL-HBJ (1-800-225-5425)

HBJ TREASURY OF LITERATURE

FEAST YOUR EYES

TEACHER'S EDITION · VOLUME TWO

SENIOR AUTHORS
ROGER C. FARR
DOROTHY S. STRICKLAND

AUTHORS
RICHARD F. ABRAHAMSON
ELLEN BOOTH CHURCH
BARBARA BOWEN COULTER
MARGARET A. GALLEGO
JUDITH L. IRVIN
KAREN KUTIPER
JUNKO YOKOTA LEWIS
DONNA M. OGLE
TIMOTHY SHANAHAN
PATRICIA SMITH

SENIOR CONSULTANTS
BERNICE E. CULLINAN
W. DORSEY HAMMOND
ASA G. HILLIARD III

CONSULTANTS
ALONZO A. CRIM
ROLANDO R. HINOJOSA-SMITH
LEE BENNETT HOPKINS
ROBERT J. STERNBERG

HARCOURT BRACE JOVANOVICH, INC.

Orlando   Austin   San Diego   Chicago   Dallas   New York

Acknowledgments appear on pg R110.

Printed in the United States of America.

ISBN 0-15-300447-9

2 3 4 5 6 7 8 9 10   059 96 95 94 93

DEAR EDUCATOR,

HBJ TREASURY OF LITERATURE, an integrated reading and language arts program, offers a wealth of literature to touch the hearts and minds of its readers. Readers grow in confidence with the turn of every page because the program is built on the following principles:

Reading is an interactive process of constructing meaning. Good readers are strategic readers. They learn, practice, and apply strategies as part of this dynamic process. Authentic literature provides a richness of opportunities for children to interact with concepts and ideas, setting the foundation for a lifelong love of reading.

Effective instruction is meaning-based and integrates listening, speaking, reading, writing, spelling, and thinking. Integrating language arts instruction across the curriculum enables students to make critical connections to all subject areas.

Emergent literacy activities build upon the language understandings that children bring from home. Immersing children in a print-rich environment allows teachers to capitalize on the children's natural curiosity about print and language.

Meeting individual needs in a classroom means access to a wide variety of instructional activities that provide for different learning modalities, varying language proficiencies, and individual learning styles.

Multicultural literature and activities, infused throughout the curriculum, enable children to appreciate cultural diversity, to grasp the concept that all groups have contributed to society, and to take pride in cultural heritage.

Assessment is an ongoing, natural part of the reading and language process. Whether formal or informal, it should help teachers determine, in a meaningful context, what students know and what they need to learn.

HBJ TREASURY OF LITERATURE offers your students a collection of trade books under one cover and sets the foundation for a lifelong love of reading.

SINCERELY,
THE AUTHORS

UNIT ONE/CONTENTS
....
CELEBRATIONS

UNIT TWO/CONTENTS
• • • • • • • • • • • • •
A N I M A L   T A L E S

UNIT THREE/CONTENTS
• • • • • • • • • • • • •
NATURE'S GIFTS

UNIT FOUR/CONTENTS
• • • • • • • • • • • •
D I S C O V E R I E S

UNIT FIVE/CONTENTS
••••••••••••
T R A V E L E R S

UNIT SIX/CONTENTS
. . . .
D R E A M E R S

CONTENTS
REFERENCE FILE

Feast Your Eyes

Reflecting on the Literature

Invite students to think about what they have read.

Ask students to look at the Contents for Units 1–3 on pages 4–9. Use questions such as the following to help them reflect on what they have read so far in *Feast Your Eyes*.

- Which theme was your favorite? Why?
- Which selection was your favorite? Why?
- Which author was your favorite? What makes his or her writing so special?
- Which was your favorite library or Bookshelf book? Why?

Help students preview the rest of the book.

Ask students to preview the Contents for Units 4–6 (pages 10–15). Have them examine the illustrations and the unit, theme, and selection titles. Encourage them to use this information to make predictions about the remaining literature in the Student Anthology. Remind students that the Handbook for Readers and Writers, the Glossary, and the Index of Titles and Authors appear at the back of the book, and ask volunteers to tell how they can use each resource.

Thinking About Classroom Management

Consider management options.

At this point, you may find it useful to ask yourself the following questions. Use the answers as you think about classroom management options for the last three units of *Feast Your Eyes*.

- What kinds of selections and which authors did my students find most enjoyable? How can I use this information to further "hook" my students on reading? (Additional Reading in the lesson plans and Bookshelf in the Student Anthology will help you gather a list of titles that will appeal to your students.)
- What kinds of activities worked well with my students? How can I use this information to help me plan classroom management for the rest of the year? (Managing the Literature-Based Classroom, Options for Reading, and cooperative reading suggestions offer a variety of alternatives from which to choose.)

HBJ TREASURY OF LITERATURE

FEAST YOUR EYES

SENIOR AUTHORS
ROGER C. FARR
DOROTHY S. STRICKLAND

AUTHORS
RICHARD F. ABRAHAMSON
ELLEN BOOTH CHURCH
BARBARA BOWEN COULTER
MARGARET A. GALLEGO
JUDITH L. IRVIN
KAREN KUTIPER
JUNKO YOKOTA LEWIS
DONNA M. OGLE
TIMOTHY SHANAHAN
PATRICIA SMITH

SENIOR CONSULTANTS
BERNICE E. CULLINAN
W. DORSEY HAMMOND
ASA G. HILLIARD III

CONSULTANTS
ALONZO A. CRIM
ROLANDO R. HINOJOSA-SMITH
LEE BENNETT HOPKINS
ROBERT J. STERNBERG

HBJ HARCOURT BRACE JOVANOVICH, INC.
Orlando Austin San Diego Chicago Dallas New York

Acknowledgments continue on page 590, which constitutes an extension of this copyright page.

Acknowledgments
For permission to reprint copyrighted material, grateful acknowledgment is made to the following sources:

Atheneum Publishers, an imprint of Macmillan Publishing Company: The Gold Coin by Alma Flor Ada, illustrated by Neil Waldman. Text copyright © 1991 by Alma Flor Ada; illustrations copyright © 1991 by Neil Waldman. Cover illustration from *The Big Tree* by Bruce Hiscock. Copyright © 1991 by Bruce Hiscock. Cover illustration by Nancy Oleksa from *The Chickenhouse House* by Ellen Howard. Illustration copyright © 1991 by Nancy Oleksa.

Avon Books: From pp. 9-21 in *The Plant That Ate Dirty Socks* (Retitled: "The Amazing Beans") by Nancy McArthur. Text copyright © 1988 by Nancy McArthur.

Black Butterfly Children's Books: "Grandma's Bones" from *Nathaniel Talking* by Eloise Greenfield. Text copyright © 1988 by Eloise Greenfield; illustrations © 1988 by Jan Spivey Gilchrist.

David Boxley: Illustrations by David Boxley from *Totem Pole* by Diane Hoyt-Goldsmith. Copyright © 1990 by David Boxley.

Bradbury Press, an affiliate of Macmillan, Inc.: Cover illustration by Clifford Faust from *Windcatcher* by Avi. Illustration copyright © 1991 by Clifford Faust. *Dream Wolf* by Paul Goble. Copyright © 1990 by Paul Goble.

Curtis Brown, Ltd.: "Last Laugh" by Lee Bennett Hopkins. Text copyright © 1974 by Lee Bennett Hopkins.

Curtis Brown Group Ltd., London: "Come on into My Tropical Garden" from *Come on into My Tropical Garden* by Grace Nichols. Text copyright © 1984 by Grace Nichols.

Carolrhoda Books, Inc., Minneapolis, MN: Cover illustration from *A Pianist's Debut* by Barbara Beirne. Copyright © 1990 by Carolrhoda Books, Inc. Cover illustration by Amy Johnson from *What Are You Figuring Now? A Story about Benjamin Banneker* by Jeri Ferris. Illustration copyright © 1988 by Carolrhoda Books, Inc.

Childrens Press: Kwanzaa by Deborah M. Newton Chocolate, illustrated by Melodye Rosales. Copyright © 1990 by Childrens Press®, Inc.

Clarion Books, a Houghton Mifflin Company imprint: Cover photograph by Peter Ziebel from *Greening the City Streets: The Story of Community Gardens* by Barbara H. Huff. Photograph copyright © 1990 by Peter Ziebel.

Cobblehill Books, an affiliate of Dutton Children's Books, a division of Penguin Books USA Inc.: Excerpted from *The Canada Geese Quilt* (Retitled: "The Very Special Gift") by Natalie Kinsey-Warnock. Text copyright © 1989 by Natalie Kinsey-Warnock.

Cobblestone Publishing, Inc., Peterborough, NH 03458: "Happy Vietnamese Holiday" by Tran Phuong Hoa and "Happy Holidays" from FACES: Happy Holidays, December 1990. Text © 1990 by Cobblestone Publishing, Inc.

CPP Belwin, Inc.: Lyrics from "Talk To The Animals," music and lyrics by Leslie Bricusse. © 1967 by Twentieth Century Music Corporation. Rights assigned to EMI Catalogue Partnership and controlled and administered by EMI Hastings Catalog Inc. International copyright secured.

Crown Publishers, Inc.: Cover illustration by Robert Andrew Parker from *Grandfather Tang's Story* by Ann Tompert. Illustration copyright © 1990 by Robert Andrew Parker.

Jackie Dodell, on behalf of Richard Williams: Cover illustration by Richard Williams from *Encyclopedia Brown Gets His Man* by Donald J. Sobol.

Dial Books for Young Readers, a division of Penguin Books USA Inc.: Cover illustration by Jerry Pinkney from *Yagua Days* by Cruz Martel. Illustration copyright © 1976 by Jerry Pinkney.

Doubleday, a division of Bantam Doubleday Dell Publishing Group, Inc.: "Sun Dancers" by Patricia Irving from *The Whispering Wind* by Terry Allen. Text copyright © 1972 by the Institute of American Indian Arts.

Farrar, Straus & Giroux, Inc.: Cover illustration from *Kneeknock Rise* by Natalie Babbitt. Copyright © 1970 by Natalie Babbitt. "The Drum" from *Spin a Soft Black Sun* by Nikki Giovanni. Text copyright © 1971, 1985 by Nikki Giovanni.

Sid Fleischman, Inc.: McBroom Tells the Truth by Sid Fleischman. Text copyright © 1966 by Sid Fleischman.

Four Winds Press, an imprint of Macmillan Publishing Company: Cover illustration by Ruth Chew from *Shark Lady: True Adventures of Eugenie Clark* by Ann McGovern. Copyright © 1978 by Ann McGovern.

Greenwillow Books, a division of William Morrow & Company, Inc.: Cover illustration by James Stevenson from *Georgia Music* by Helen V. Griffith. Illustration copyright © 1986 by James Stevenson. *Music, Music for Everyone* by Vera B. Williams. Copyright © 1984 by Vera B. Williams.

Harcourt Brace Jovanovich: The Great Kapok Tree by Lynne Cherry. Copyright © 1990 by Lynne Cherry. "The Marmalade Man Makes a Dance to Mend Us" from *A Visit to William Blake's Inn* by Nancy Willard, illustrated by Alice and Martin Provensen. Text copyright © 1981 by Nancy Willard; illustrations copyright © 1981 by Alice and Martin Provensen. Pronunciation Key from *HBJ School Dictionary*, Third Edition. Text copyright © 1990 by Harcourt Brace Jovanovich, Inc.

continued on page 590

HBJ TREASURY OF LITERATURE

Dear Reader,

A character in this book is asked in a dream, "If you destroy the beauty of the rain forest, on what would you feast your eyes?" The literature in this book will challenge you to make decisions as this character must. And you'll feast your eyes on many different kinds of people. As you read, celebrate their beauty—and yours!

Because our country is made up of people from many different places, we are able to enjoy a wide variety of celebrations. Perhaps you've wondered how some of these are alike and different. The literature in this book will transport you to some special times and different cultures. You'll be invited to join an African American family's Kwanzaa celebration. You'll see, hear, and even smell a Vietnamese New Year celebration. You'll share a Polish family's joy as they celebrate their arrival in America. You'll make connections between some of these celebrations and a holiday celebrated by Hispanics both in Mexico and in the United States.

We invite you to make *Feast Your Eyes* an important part of a wonderful school year. We invite you to laugh and cry with the characters, and to explore the wonders of the plant and animal kingdoms. Maybe you'll be moved to change the world for the better. Our invitation may best be stated in these lines by poet Grace Nichols:

> Come on into my tropical garden
> Come on in and have a laugh in
> Taste my sugar cake and my pine drink
> Come on in please come on in

Sincerely,
The Authors

FEAST YOUR EYES

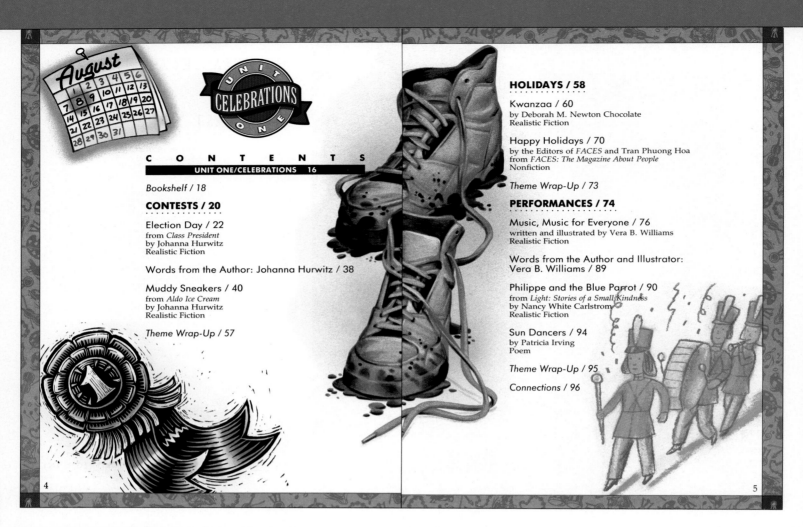

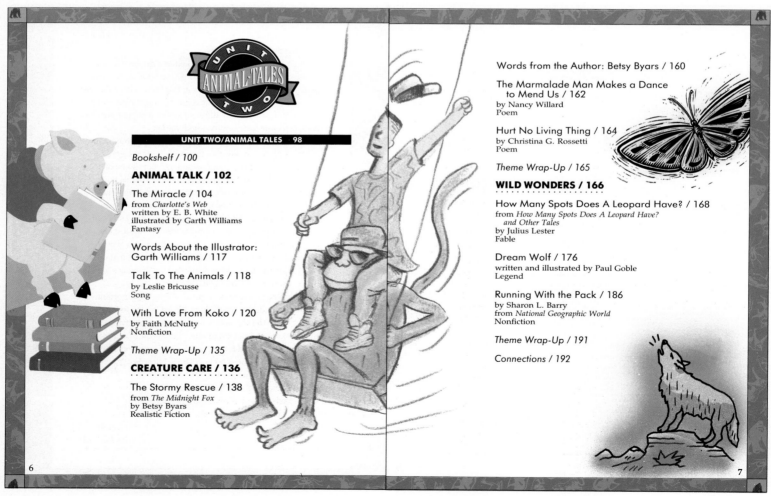

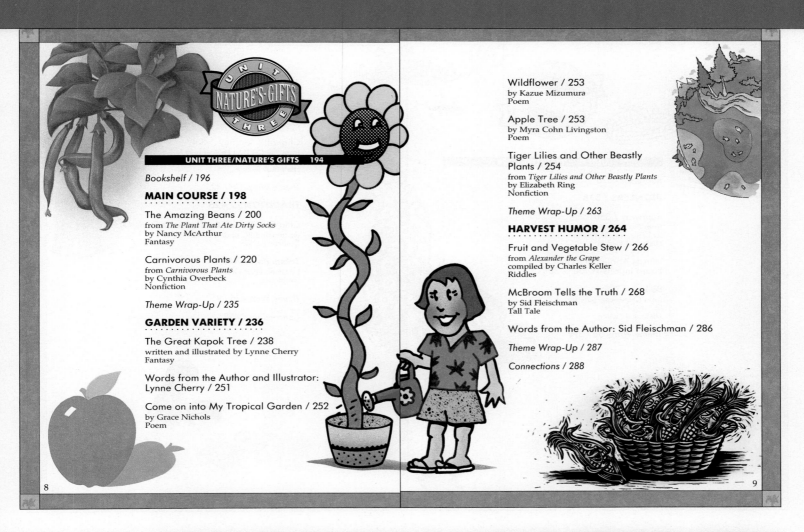

8

9

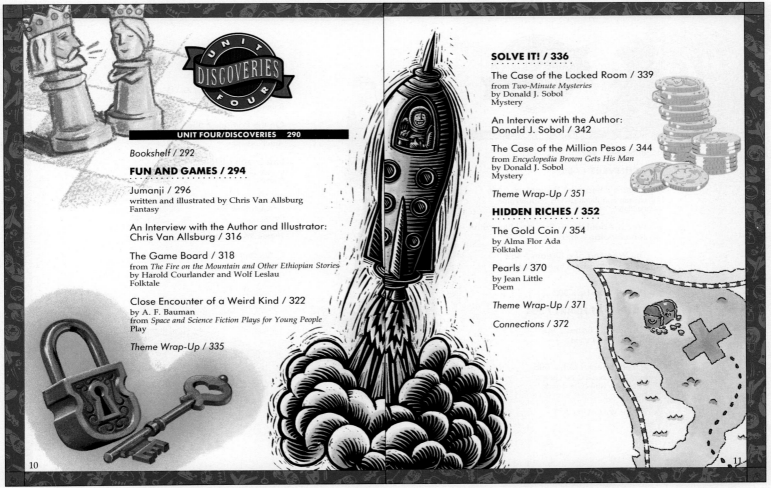

10

11

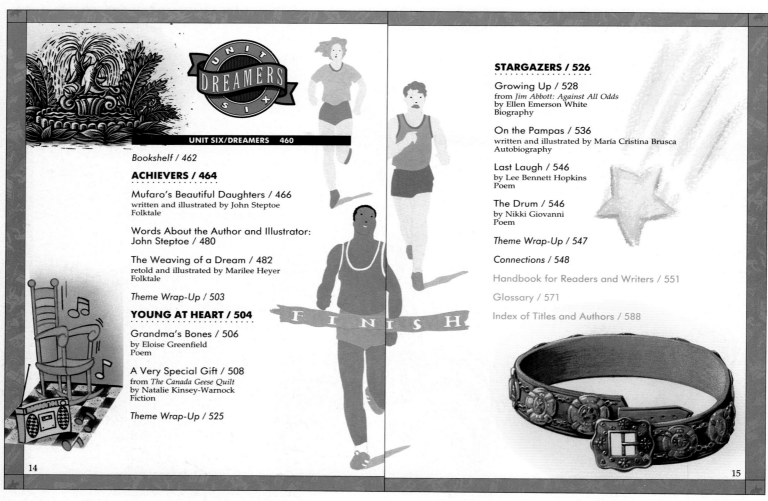

DISCOVERIES

UNIT FOUR

Planning Center

What's Ahead in "Discoveries"?

FUN AND GAMES: PAGES T514–T579   Invite your students to come join in the "Fun and Games" found in a fantasy, a folktale, and a play. From monkeys in the kitchen to aliens in the living room, the reading fun continues, even after the games are over.

SOLVE IT!: PAGES T580–T613   Challenge your students to "Solve It!" before Donald Sobol's detectives do. In these mystery stories, it will take critical thinking, not a magnifying glass, to close the cases.

HIDDEN RICHES: PAGES T614–T647   Reap a windfall of "Hidden Riches" when your students read this folktale and poem and learn that things may not always be what they seem.

Family Involvement

The *Family Involvement Activities* offer a variety of possibilities for extending each theme and expanding the unit focus. A Read-at-Home Story is also included for family members to read together.

Pacing

This unit is designed to take approximately five or six weeks to complete, depending on your students' needs.

Assessment and Evaluation

Title	Description	When and How It's Used
INFORMAL ASSESSMENT OPTIONS (Ongoing)		
Reading/Writing Portfolio	Contains samples of students' literacy development.	Collect samples of personal journals and writing throughout the unit. Hold periodic Portfolio Conferences.
Informal Assessment Notes	Appear throughout the *Teacher's Edition.*	Observe students' reading, writing, listening, and speaking behaviors. Keep Runnning Records of your observations.
Student Self-Assessment Notes	Appear throughout the *Teacher's Edition.*	Students monitor their use of reading and writing strategies.
Running Records	Ongoing assessment of students' reading, writing, listening, and speaking behaviors.	Record periodically to track students' progress.
FORMAL ASSESSMENT OPTIONS (End of Unit)		
Skills Assessment	Assesses mastery of strategies and skills taught in Learning Through Literature.	Administer at end of the unit.
Holistic Assessment	Evaluates students' ability to read and understand excerpts from literature.	Administer at end of the unit.
Integrated Performance Assessment	Assesses use of reading and writing strategies modeled and practiced in the classroom.	Administer at end of the unit.

HBJ Literature Cassette 2

Recordings of the following selections in "Discoveries" may be used for instruction or for students' listening enjoyment:

- "Jumanji"
- "The Gold Coin"

Audiovisual Materials and Software

The Best of Encyclopedia Brown by Donald Sobol. Random House. Students are invited to match wits with Encyclopedia Brown.   FILMSTRIP

The Dancing Granny and Other African Stories by Ashley Bryan. Caedmon. The author performs four African folktales.   AUDIOCASSETTE

Hidden Treasures. Mindscape Educational Software. Players attempt to uncover a hidden treasure in this program.   COMPUTER SOFTWARE

Jumanji by Chris Van Allsburg. Random House. A game comes startlingly to life in this story. FILMSTRIP/VIDEO

Knee-Knock Rise by Natalie Babbitt. Random House. In this suspense-filled fantasy, Egan discovers the mystery of the Megrimum's wail.   FILMSTRIP

Solve It! Sunburst, 1989. Students use logic and problem-solving techniques to solve six enticing mysteries.   COMPUTER SOFTWARE

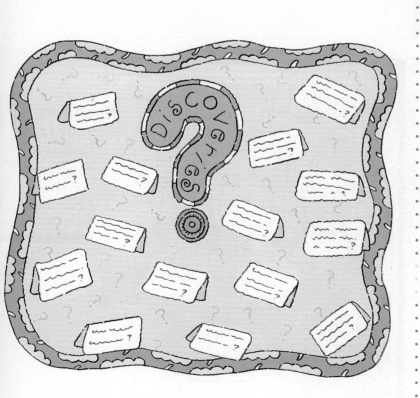

"Jason Caputo was on assignment in the Los Angeles Public Library. He smiled secretly to himself. To most observers, he was just an ordinary ten-year-old boy. . . . But to those in the know, he was Jace the Ace, junior photojournalist."

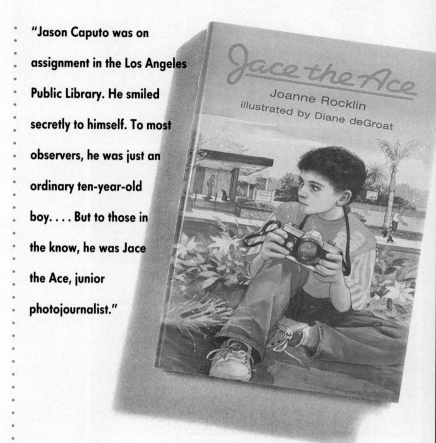

HBJ Treasury of Literature Library

Here is a sneak peek at some of the options you will find in the *HBJ Treasury of Literature Library Guide* for *Jace the Ace*.

- **Reading Cooperatively** in response groups
- **Reading Independently** during sustained silent reading periods
- **Directing the Reading** through questioning strategies
- **Reading Aloud** to encourage literature appreciation

Bulletin Board Idea

Draw a large question mark in the center of the bulletin board. Tell students that as they find puzzles, riddles, or brainteasers, they should copy them onto tent-shaped cards to post on the bulletin board. You may also wish to have students create cards with original riddles or puzzles based on books they have read independently. Each item posted should be in the form of the ones shown, so that other classmates can lift the front cover to *discover* the answer beneath.

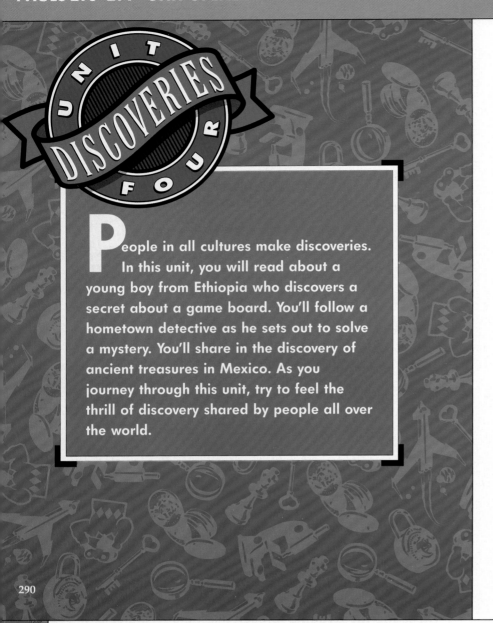

eople in all cultures make discoveries. In this unit, you will read about a young boy from Ethiopia who discovers a secret about a game board. You'll follow a hometown detective as he sets out to solve a mystery. You'll share in the discovery of ancient treasures in Mexico. As you journey through this unit, try to feel the thrill of discovery shared by people all over the world.

290

THEMES

FUN AND GAMES
296

SOLVE IT!
336

HIDDEN RICHES
352

Introducing "Discoveries"

Have students discuss what they think of when they hear the word *discoveries*. Ask them to read the unit introduction and preview the theme titles to help them set a purpose for reading the unit.

Ask students to discuss what they know about historic discoveries. Be sure they include discoveries made by people from a variety of cultures. Encourage students to speculate why discoveries are important to people from all cultures. CULTURAL AWARENESS

WRITER'S JOURNAL
pages 56–58:
Reading and writing about "Discoveries"

OOKSHELF

JACE THE ACE
BY JOANNE ROCKLIN

Ten-year-old Jason Caputo, who prefers to be called "Jace the Ace, junior photo-journalist," learns some valuable lessons as he solves the case of a "spy" named Sky.

HBJ LIBRARY BOOK

THE DISCOVERY OF THE AMERICAS
BY BETSY AND GIULIO MAESTRO

This nonfiction book tells how our part of the world was discovered and rediscovered by early explorers. AWARD-WINNING AUTHOR AND ILLUSTRATOR

WINDCATCHER
BY AVI

Tony does not look forward to spending the summer with his grandmother on the coast of Connecticut. But when he buys a small sailboat and learns about a sunken treasure, Tony's summer turns into an adventure. AWARD-WINNING AUTHOR

KNEE•KNOCK RISE
BY NATALIE BABBITT

Egan visits his relatives in the town of Instep and makes a discovery that the townspeople do not want to accept. NEWBERY HONOR, ALA NOTABLE BOOK

GRANDFATHER TANG'S STORY
BY ANN TOMPERT

Little Soo listens and watches as Grandfather Tang uses puzzles called tangrams to tell a story. She learns about a pair of foxes that make an important discovery. NOTABLE CHILDREN'S TRADE BOOK IN THE FIELD OF SOCIAL STUDIES

293

HBJ Library Book

Have students read the information about *Jace the Ace* and look at the cover illustration. Ask them to predict how they think Jace may solve the case by using a camera. Page T509 provides a preview of the lesson plans that can found in the *HBJ Treasury of Literature Library Guide*.

Read aloud
to students.

The Flying Saucer People

from *Einstein Anderson, Science Sleuth*
by Seymour Simon

Einstein had just come home from the beach when his mother phoned him from her office at the Sparta *Tribune*.

"I'm glad you're home, Adam," said Mrs. Anderson. "I have a favor to ask you."

"Sure, Mom," Einstein said. "What can I do you for?" Einstein liked to mix up his words. It was unfortunate, he felt, that nobody else liked it.

"Adam, there's someone visiting Sparta I want to interview for the newspaper. I'm going to invite him to the house for dinner this evening. And I'd like you to be around when I do the interview."

"Who's the person? And why do you want me to be around? Is there something wrong?"

"His name is Mr. Janus," Mrs. Anderson answered. "He's writing a book about something that happened to him. Or at least that he claims happened to him."

"What happened to him? What do you want me to do when he comes? Do you think he's not telling the truth? Is it something about science?" Einstein asked all the questions in a rush.

"Just hold on a minute and I'll tell you," his mother said with a laugh. "Janus says he was walking along a country road just outside of Sparta when he saw a flying saucer. The saucer landed and some little people with big heads came out and greeted him."

"Wow!" Einstein exclaimed. "A close encounter of the third kind. What else happened?"

"Janus says that the saucer people were able to talk to him in English with some kind of translation machine they carried. They asked him to go aboard their ship and took him to their base on the far side of the moon. They kept him there for a few days and then took him back and released him."

"That really sounds weird," Einstein said. "Do you believe his story?"

"That's why I'd like you to be around," Mrs. Anderson answered. "He sounds sincere, but he may just be trying to get publicity for his book. I'd like you to listen to what he has to say and then tell me in private whether he's made any scientific mistakes."

Einstein readily agreed. He loved reading science fiction stories, though he had his doubts about flying saucers.

Mr. Janus turned out to be a long, thin man with sharp features. His eyes were black and piercing. All through dinner he talked about his experiences with the saucer people. He said that they were about three feet tall with the general shape of humans. They had a head, two arms, and two legs. Their skin was a faint greenish color that seemed to glow. Their eyes were very round with no pupils, and their ears were pointed.

Einstein listened closely, but he could not make up his mind one way or another. If you believed in saucers, he thought, then there was nothing scientifically wrong in anything Mr. Janus was saying.

After dinner Dr. Anderson said that he and Dennis, Einstein's brother, would do the dishes. Dennis seemed to be about to protest, but Dr. Anderson gave him a look. Then Mrs. Anderson led Mr. Janus and Einstein.

SELECTION SUMMARY   Science whiz Adam Anderson, also known as "Einstein," tries to figure out if Mr. Janus was really taken to the moon by space creatures as he claims. After carefully listening to the details of the account, Einstein concludes that the whole story is fiction.

ABOUT THE AUTHOR   Seymour Simon, a former science teacher, has written many children's books with a science theme. What he really enjoys is "getting a letter from a child who tried out an experiment in one of my books."

Strategies for Listening

LISTENING/THINKING STRATEGY—NOTING DETAILS
Remind students that fictional writing often includes many facts. Explain that by focusing on the scientific details in this selection, they may be able to decide, along with the main character, whether or not an account of an abduction by aliens actually happened.

SET A PURPOSE FOR LISTENING   Remind students that the selections in this unit are about "Discoveries." Explain that in this selection a young science whiz tries to discover the truth. Tell them to listen for the scientific details in the story and to apply what they know.

into the den and shut the door.

"Would you continue with your story, Mr. Janus?" asked Mrs. Anderson. "You had just gotten to the part where the saucer people had given you a space suit and you were walking on the moon."

"The moon's surface was dusty and rocky," Mr. Janus said. "You know that there's no water or air on the moon. The temperature in the sunlight was over a hundred degrees Celsius. That's hot enough to boil water, if there was any. It's a good thing that the suit's air conditioning was working so well.

"The saucer people walked me over to a hill. When we got closer, I could hear a hammering going on behind the hill. It was not difficult climbing the hill, because of the moon's low gravity."

"Did you see what was going on behind the hill?" asked Mrs. Anderson.

"Yes," answered Mr. Janus. "When we got to the top of the hill, I could see that the saucer people were knocking down part of their base. They asked me to tell the people of the world their reasons for leaving. They had decided that the people on earth were not advanced enough to be welcomed into the Galaxy Federation of Intelligent Beings."

"That's too bad," Einstein said. But I can see why they felt that way, he thought. "Mom, would it be O.K. if I went outside to play now?"

"Would you excuse me for a second, Mr. Janus?" asked Mrs. Anderson. "I'll be back in a minute."

Einstein and Mrs. Anderson went outside the den. "Well, what do you think?" Mrs. Anderson asked. "Did Janus make any scientific errors?"

"As far as I can tell, just one," Einstein said. "But that error is enough of a whopper to make me think his whole story is fiction."

Can you solve the puzzle: What was the scientific error in the story of the saucer people?

"Was the error in his story that the temperature on the moon was hot enough to boil water?" Mrs. Anderson asked. "That seems wrong to me. I always thought the moon's surface was very cold."

"The moon's surface is either cold or hot," Einstein said. "Because the moon has no atmosphere, the surface temperatures are very extreme. In the shade, the temperature is lower than the coldest spot on earth. In the sun, the temperature is higher than the hottest spot here."

"Then what was the error, Adam?"

"The mistake that Janus made had to do with the lack of atmosphere on the moon," explained Einstein. "Mr. Janus said that he heard a hammering going on behind a hill. But sound must travel through air to be heard. How could Janus have heard the sound of hammering in a place that has no air?"

"Thanks, Adam. I knew I could count on you."

Responding to Literature

1. **Why do you think Mr. Janus was lying?** (Accept reasonable responses: to get publicity for his book.) CRITICAL: DRAWING CONCLUSIONS

2. **Why do you think some people believed Mr. Janus' story?** (Accept reasonable responses: There have been so many movies, articles, and books about encounters with aliens that they are beginning to seem real.) INFERENTIAL: DRAWING CONCLUSIONS

SPEAKING Have students form two groups. Ask one group to make up a mystery story that has a scientific fact as a clue. Have the other group try to solve the mystery. CREATIVE: ORAL COMPOSITION

Fun and Games

For pacing suggestions, see page T516.

THEME

FUN AND GAMES

Do you remember a time when you were bored and you couldn't find anything to do? The characters in the next three selections experience that same boredom. Then suddenly their ordinary days overflow with unexpected adventures.

CONTENTS

JUMANJI
written and illustrated by Chris Van Allsburg

AN INTERVIEW WITH THE
AUTHOR AND ILLUSTRATOR:
CHRIS VAN ALLSBURG

THE GAME BOARD
by Harold Courlander and Wolf Leslau

CLOSE ENCOUNTER
OF A WEIRD KIND
by A. F. Bauman

295

Discussing the Theme

Have students look at the photograph and read the information on Student Anthology pages 294–295. Then ask students to restate the theme focus in their own words. Encourage them to share ideas about what unexpected adventures might await the boy in the photograph. Ask students to speculate—based on selection titles—about what adventures might await the characters they will meet.

Reading/Writing Portfolio

Tell students to choose some of their writing responses for the selections in "Fun and Games" to save in their portfolios. Tell them also to add to their personal journals any thoughts and ideas about books they have read independently.

Managing the Literature-Based Classroom

Management Options

MAKE A TRANSITION As students move from one activity to another, occasionally have them do simple exercises such as these: (1) Have them close their eyes and concentrate on their breathing. Ask them to guess how long a minute is. Have students raise their hands when they think 60 seconds have passed. (2) Have students listen to the sounds around them and then write their responses in their personal journals or compile a class list. (3) Have them do neck exercises or toe flexes at their desks. (4) Invite students to think of other "desk exercises," and have a different student lead the exercises each day.

CREATE A GAME CENTER A game center can serve as a transition between activities and can be used to motivate students. Limit its use to free time, after completion of activities or after clean-up. Post rules for using the center. Bring in games and puzzles that can be completed in a brief amount of time. Encourage students to invent their own mazes, riddles, puzzles, and word games for classmates to work on.

PACING This theme has been designed to take about two weeks to complete, depending on your students' needs.

Meeting Individual Needs

STUDENTS AT RISK Have students complete the Vocabulary Strategies for "Jumanji" and for "Close Encounter of a Weird Kind" in small groups. Assign the same groups to read the selections cooperatively and help each other with Key Words and any other words group members find difficult.

GIFTED AND TALENTED As students complete writing activities such as the Writer's Workshop on Student Anthology page 335, invite them to explore a variety of options for publishing their writing. Encourage them to check the Publishing Options file for ideas. *Challenge Cards* provide additional activities to challenge students. Challenge notes throughout the lesson plans suggest additional activities to stimulate critical and creative thinking.

SPECIAL EDUCATION STUDENTS Before students with dyslexia read aloud "Close Encounter of a Weird Kind," have them place self-stick notes at the edge of the pages to mark the parts they will read. You might also have them use two different-colored notes on the interview to help them distinguish the interviewer's questions from Chris Van Allsburg's replies.

LIMITED ENGLISH PROFICIENT STUDENTS Before students read the selections, encourage them to discuss the concept of games and to play games in pairs with others who speak their first language. Ask them to share their thoughts in English with their classmates. Second-Language Support notes throughout the lesson plans offer strategies to help students acquiring English to understand the selections.

JUMANJI

CALDECOTT MEDAL
ALA NOTABLE BOOK
CHILDREN'S CHOICE

Written and Illustrated
by Chris Van Allsburg

JUMANJI

	TEACHING OUTLINE	Materials	Language Arts/ Integrated Curriculum	Meeting Individual Needs
Part 1 **Reading Literature** Pages T520–T532 	**Building Background** **Vocabulary Strategies** Key Words (Tested) **Strategic Reading** Preview and Predict Setting a Purpose **Options for Reading**	Transparency 30 Second-Language Support Manual Practice Book p. 79 Integrated Spelling p. 43 Integrated Spelling T.E. pp. 60–61 Student Anthology pp. 296–315 Response Card 3: Plot	**Spelling** Spelling Pretest Spelling-Vocabulary Connection	**Second-Language Support** Vocabulary T521 Strategic Reading T522, T527, T528 **Cooperative Reading** T523
Part 2 **Responding to Literature** Pages T533–T537 	**Story Follow-Up** Think It Over Write **Summarizing the Literature** **Appreciating Literature** **Critical Thinking Activities**	Writer's Journal p. 59 Practice Book pp. 80–81 Integrated Spelling p. 44 Integrated Spelling T.E. pp. 60–61 Literature Cassette 2 Language Handbook	**Vocabulary Workshop** Reviewing Key Words Extending Vocabulary Content-Area Words **Reading** Oral Rereading/Drama **Writing** A Fantasy A Paragraph **Spelling** Reviewing Spelling Words **Listening** Poems **Speaking** A Conversation	**Cooperative Learning** T534, T537
Part 3 **Learning Through Literature** Pages T538–T544 	**Introduce** Comprehension: Drawing Conclusions (Tested) **Review** Study Skills: Following Directions (Tested) Study Skills: Reference Sources (Tested)	Second-Language Support Manual Writer's Journal p. 60 Practice Book pp. 82–85	**Social Studies** Travel Guides Games **Science** Wild Animals Volcanoes **Math** Divide Numbers **Multicultural** Golden Cities	**Reteach** T539 **Challenge** T539, T540, T541 **Second-Language Support** Drawing Conclusions T539 **Cooperative Learning** T539, T540, T542, T543

KEY WORDS

stampede
volcano
erupts
lava
exhaustion
interrupted

Selection Summary

Peter and Judy play Jumanji, a board game, and are flabbergasted when the event in each square they land on becomes real. A lion, monkeys, rhinos, a monsoon, a lost guide, a dangerous python, and a volcanic eruption come to life in the house. Finally, Judy wins the game, and everything returns to normal.

Jumanji won the Caldecott Medal for its illustrations and was honored as one of the *School Library Journal* Best Books of the Year. It was also named one of the *New York Times* Best Illustrated Books, an ALA Notable Book, and a Children's Choice.

Family Involvement

Encourage family members to discuss with students how children's games have changed over the generations. You might suggest that family members of different ages list popular games from their childhood years and try playing some of them.

CHRIS VAN ALLSBURG

Chris Van Allsburg has won numerous awards for both the text and the illustrations in his books. He says it normally takes him four and one half months to produce a book. He usually writes the text first and then illustrates it. He prefers to write fantasies. As he says, "I like to create a world where not everything is possible, but where strange things may happen. I try not to use fantasy as a self-serving way to make an interesting story. . . . The demand I put on myself is that [fantasy] be logical. Once I create a fantastic premise, I apply that premise consistently."

ADDITIONAL READING

Another Book by Chris Van Allsburg

The Garden of Abdul Gasazi. Houghton Mifflin, 1979.   CHALLENGING

Other Books Designed for the Bored and Restless

Balloons: Building and Experimenting with Inflatable Toys by Bernie Zubrowski. William Morrow, 1952.   EASY

The Chocolate Touch by Patrick S. Catling. William Morrow, 1990.   EASY

The Shrinking of Treehorn by Florence P. Heide. Holiday House, 1971.   AVERAGE

Travel Tips from Harry: A Guide to Family Vacations in the Sun by Amy Hest. William Morrow, 1989.   AVERAGE

Part 1
Reading Literature

Building Background

Access prior knowledge and build vocabulary concepts.

Tell students that in the next story they will read, two children play a board game called Jumanji [jŏŏ·män′jē]. Have students brainstorm how a board game is played and what makes it fun.

Have students quickwrite lists.

Point out that in "Jumanji" the children play a jungle-adventure board game. Ask students to write short lists of words that describe what they would see, hear, or do in a jungle. Help students use their lists to develop a web about the dangers people might face on a jungle adventure.

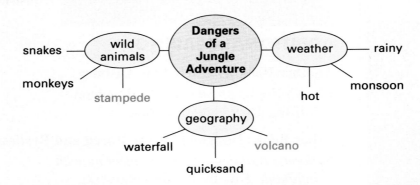

Vocabulary Strategies

Introduce Key Words and strategies.

Display Transparency 30 or the following story. Have students read the sentences silently, using context clues with phonetic and structural analysis to figure out each underlined word.

Transparency 30   Key Words

In the jungle, Jan and Bud are almost run over by a stampede of elephants. To escape, they climb a mountain, only to discover it is a volcano about to explode. A huge blast and flames come from the top of the volcano as it erupts.

Jan and Bud have to run from streams of hot lava. Overcome by exhaustion, the two friends fall asleep. However, their rest is interrupted by noisy, chattering monkeys.

CULTURAL AWARENESS

Students may be interested to know that the first board games were played nearly 4,500 years ago in Africa. The Asian board game of Go, which started over 3,000 years ago, is still popular today.

KEY WORDS

stampede
volcano
erupts
lava
exhaustion
interrupted

KEY WORDS DEFINED

stampede   sudden rushing away because of panic

volcano   mountain that may throw out hot rock

erupts   throws out hot rock

lava   very hot liquefied rock

exhaustion   state of being very tired

interrupted   stopped by breaking in

Check students' understanding.

Display or read aloud the following. Have students choose the word in each group that does not belong. Encourage them to explain why the word does not belong. The correct responses are underlined.   STRATEGY: SYNONYMS

• explodes	inactive	erupts
• <u>began</u>	interrupted	stopped
• volcano	mountain	valley
• exhaustion	<u>enjoyment</u>	tiredness
• liquid	solid	lava
• stampede	run	<u>walk</u>

Integrate spelling with vocabulary.

SPELLING-VOCABULARY CONNECTION *Integrated Spelling* page 43 reinforces spellings of the short *a*, short *i*, and short *o* sounds in the Key Word *stampede* and in other words. The spelling of the Key Word *volcano* is also included.

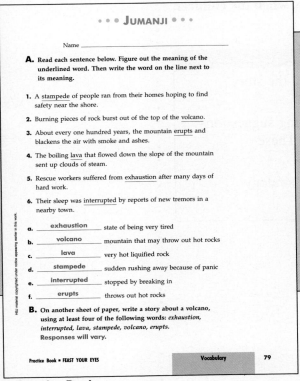

Practice Book

Practice Book

* * * JUMANJI * * *

Name _____

A. Read each sentence below. Figure out the meaning of the underlined word. Then write the word on the line next to its meaning.

1. A <u>stampede</u> of people ran from their homes hoping to find safety near the shore.

2. Burning pieces of rock burst out of the top of the <u>volcano</u>.

3. About every one hundred years, the mountain <u>erupts</u> and blackens the air with smoke and ashes.

4. The boiling <u>lava</u> that flowed down the slope of the mountain sent up clouds of steam.

5. Rescue workers suffered from <u>exhaustion</u> after many days of hard work.

6. Their sleep was <u>interrupted</u> by reports of new tremors in a nearby town.

a. _____exhaustion_____ state of being very tired

b. _____volcano_____ mountain that may throw out hot rocks

c. _____lava_____ very hot liquified rock

d. _____stampede_____ sudden rushing away because of panic

e. _____interrupted_____ stopped by breaking in

f. _____erupts_____ throws out hot rocks

B. On another sheet of paper, write a story about a volcano, using at least four of the following words: *exhaustion, interrupted, lava, stampede, volcano, erupts.*
Responses will vary.

Practice Book ■ FEAST YOUR EYES   Vocabulary   **79**

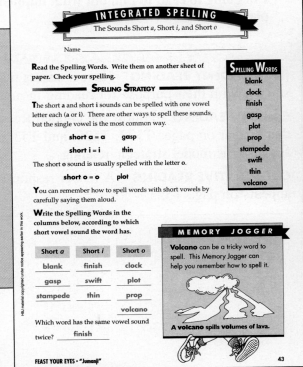

Integrated Spelling

INTEGRATED SPELLING
The Sounds Short *a*, Short *i*, and Short *o*

Name _____

Read the Spelling Words. Write them on another sheet of paper. Check your spelling.

SPELLING STRATEGY

The short a and short i sounds can be spelled with one vowel letter each (a or i). There are other ways to spell these sounds, but the single vowel is the most common way.

short a = a   gasp
short i = i   thin

The short o sound is usually spelled with the letter o.

short o = o   plot

You can remember how to spell words with short vowels by carefully saying them aloud.

Write the Spelling Words in the columns below, according to which short vowel sound the word has.

Short *a*	Short *i*	Short *o*
blank	finish	clock
gasp	swift	plot
stampede	thin	prop
		volcano

Which word has the same vowel sound twice? _____finish_____

SPELLING WORDS
blank
clock
finish
gasp
plot
prop
stampede
swift
thin
volcano

MEMORY JOGGER

Volcano can be a tricky word to spell. This Memory Jogger can help you remember how to spell it.

A volcano spills volumes of lava.

FEAST YOUR EYES • "Jumanji"   **43**

Strategic Reading

Preview and Predict

Help students preview the story.

Ask students to describe the steps involved in previewing a story. (read and think about the title, look at the illustrations, and read the introduction or the first few paragraphs) Have students preview "Jumanji," stopping on page 299 so they may still enjoy the surprise when the events that follow turn to fantasy.

Have students make predictions.

Ask students questions such as the following to help them predict what might happen in the story:

- **Why do you think the story is named after a game?**
- **Why might the game be fun for some but not for all?**
- **Think about the new vocabulary words. How do these words help you predict what might happen in the story?**

PERSONAL JOURNAL Have students add their predictions about the selection to their personal journals. Ask students to support their predictions.

Setting a Purpose

Have students set purposes.

Brainstorm with students what they want to find out when they read the story, based on their preview and what they already know. Remind students that setting a purpose for reading gives them a reason for reading, helps them focus on important ideas, and helps them understand what they read. Have students use their predictions to set a purpose for reading. Then invite them to share their purposes.

Model purpose-setting, if necessary.

If students have difficulty setting a purpose for reading, offer this suggestion:

> **I'm going to read to find out what happens when the children play the game.**

OPTIONS FOR READING

INDEPENDENT READING Have students read the story silently with their purpose for reading in mind.

GUIDED READING Follow the Guided Reading suggestions that appear on pages T523, T526, and T532. These suggestions model strategic reading.

COOPERATIVE READING A reader response strategy appears on page T523.

SECOND-LANGUAGE SUPPORT Explain to students that there are some English words that may look like words in their language but have a different meaning. These are called false cognates. For example, the English word *library* looks like the Spanish word *libraria*. However, *libraria* means bookstore, not library. Have students identify any false cognates while reading. (See *Second-Language Support Manual*.)

"Now remember," Mother said, "your father and I are bringing some guests by after the opera, so please keep the house neat."

"Quite so," added Father, tucking his scarf inside his coat.

Mother peered into the hall mirror and carefully pinned her hat in place, then knelt and kissed both children good-bye.

When the front door closed, Judy and Peter giggled with delight. They took all the toys out of their toy chest and made a terrible mess. But their laughter slowly turned to silence till finally Peter slouched into a chair.

"You know what?" he said. "I'm really bored."

Written and Illustrated by
CHRIS VAN ALLSBURG

297

Guided Reading

SET PURPOSE/PREDICT: PAGES 296–303 Have students read through page 303 to find out what happens when Judy and Peter start playing the game.

Cooperative Reading

READER RESPONSE STRATEGY: PAGES 296–303 Have each group of 3–5 students select a leader. Ask group members to read silently, and then encourage the leaders to use dialogue questions such as those below. (Response Card 3: Plot, on page R64, offers a wide variety of dialogue questions.)

- **What event surprises the children?**
- **What do you think they will do next?**

PAGES 304–315 After reading the story, the discussion leaders might ask:

- **Did the ending surprise you? Why or why not?**

"Me too," sighed Judy. "Why don't we g
outside and play?"

Peter agreed, so they set off across the st
to the park. It was cold for November. The
children could see their breath like steam. T
rolled in the leaves and when Judy tried to s
some leaves down Peter's sweater he jumpe
and ran behind a tree. When his sister caug
with him, he was kneeling at the foot of the
looking at a long thin box.

"What's that?" Judy asked.

"It's a game," said Peter, handing her th
box.

"'JUMANJI,'" Judy read from the box,
'A JUNGLE ADVENTURE GAME.'"

"Look," said Peter, pointing to a note
taped to the bottom of the box. In a childlik
handwriting were the words "Free game, fu
for some but not for all. P.S. Read instructi
carefully."

"Want to take it home?" Judy asked.

"Not really," said Peter. "I'm sure some
left it here because it's so boring."

"Oh, come on," protested Judy. "Let's g
a try. Race you home!" And off she ran wit
Peter at her heels.

Informal Assessment You can assess how
well a student is focusing on his or her purpose for
reading and, in doing so, help maintain that focus.
Whenever you think it appropriate after the student
has begun to read, ask questions such as these:

- What has happened in the story so far? Is that
  what you expected?
- Why did this happen? What do you think might
  happen next in the story because this happened?

Teaching Tip Explain to students that author
and illustrator Chris Van Allsburg includes a small
dog in most of his books. Tell students to look for
an illustration with a dog in it as they read the
story.

t home, the children spread the game out
 card table. It looked very much like the
s they already had. There was a board that
ded, revealing a path of colored squares.
squares had messages written on them. The
started in the deepest jungle and ended up
manji, a city of golden buildings and towers.
 began to shake the dice and play with the
 pieces that were in the box.
Put those down and listen," said Judy. "I'm
 to read the instructions: 'Jumanji, a young
le's jungle adventure especially designed for
ored and restless.

A. Player selects piece and places it in
est jungle. B. Player rolls dice and moves
 along path through the dangers of the
e. C. First player to reach Jumanji and yell
ity's name aloud is the winner.'"
s that all?" asked Peter, sounding
pointed.
No," said Judy, "there's one more
, and this is in capital letters: 'D. VERY
RTANT: ONCE A GAME OF JUMANJI IS
TED IT WILL NOT BE OVER UNTIL ONE
ER REACHES THE GOLDEN CITY.'"

**Expanding the Literature   Why do you
think the words for instruction D are written in
all-capital letters?** (Accept reasonable responses:
to show that it is a very important instruction; so
everyone will read those words.)   INFERENTIAL:
DRAWING CONCLUSIONS

**What clues does the author give on page 300
to help you predict that Jumanji will be an
exciting game?** (Accept reasonable responses:
It is designed for the bored and restless; it should
be played until someone reaches the Golden City.)
INFERENTIAL: MAKING PREDICTIONS

BALDWIN

"Oh, big deal," said Peter, who gave a b[...]
yawn.

"Here," said Judy, handing her brother t[...]
dice, "you go first."

Peter casually dropped the dice from his [...]
hand.

"Seven," said Judy.

Peter moved his piece to the seventh squa[...]

"'Lion attacks, move back two spaces,'" [...]
Judy.

"Gosh, how exciting," said Peter, in a ve[...]
unexcited voice. As he reached for his piece [...]
looked up at his sister. She had a look of
absolute horror on her face.

"Peter," she whispered, "turn around ve[...]
very slowly."

The boy turned in his chair. He couldn't [...]
believe his eyes. Lying on the piano was a li[...]
staring at Peter and licking his lips.

The lion roared so loud it knocked Peter [...]
off his chair. The big cat jumped to the floo[...]
Peter was up on his feet, running through th[...]
house with the lion a whisker's length behin[...]
He ran upstairs and dove under a bed. The [...]
tried to squeeze under, but got his head stuc[...]
Peter scrambled out, ran from the bedroom,[...]
slammed the door behind him. He stood in [...]
hall with Judy, gasping for breath.

"I don't think," said Peter in between ga[...]
of air, "that I want . . . to play . . . this gam[...]
anymore."

Guided Reading

**MONITOR COMPREHENSION: PAGES 296–303
What happens when the children start playing
the game?** (Peter lands on the square that reads
"Lion attacks." A lion appears.)   STRATEGIC
READING: RETURNING TO PURPOSE

**What hints do you have that Jumanji will not be
an ordinary game?** (The children find the game
in the park, they read the warning note on the
game box, and they learn that the game will not
end until a player reaches the Golden City.)
STRATEGIC READING: SUMMARIZING

SET PURPOSE/PREDICT: PAGES 304–315   Have
students predict what will happen next, based on
what they know about Jumanji. Have students read
the rest of the story to see if their predictions are
confirmed.

"But we have to," said Judy as she helped Peter back downstairs. "I'm sure that's what the instructions mean. That lion won't go away until one of us wins the game."

Peter stood next to the card table. "Can't we just call the zoo and have him taken away?" From upstairs came the sounds of growling and clawing at the bedroom door. "Or maybe we could wait till Father comes home."

"No one would come from the zoo because they wouldn't believe us," said Judy. "And you know how upset Mother would be if there was a lion in the bedroom. We started this game, and now we have to finish it."

Peter looked down at the game board. What if Judy rolled a seven? Then there'd be two lions. For an instant Peter thought he was going to cry. Then he sat firmly in his chair and said, "Let's play."

Judy picked up the dice, rolled an eight, and moved her piece. "'Monkeys steal food, miss one turn,'" she read. From the kitchen came the sounds of banging pots and falling jars. The children ran in to see a dozen monkeys tearing the room apart.

"Oh boy," said Peter, "this would upset Mother even more than the lion."

"Quick," said Judy, "back to the game."

305

Second-Language Support

Students may need help understanding the phrase *rolled a seven*. To explain what dice are, draw two cubes on the board, and add dots to the visible sides. Be sure that the number of dots on the two sides facing up equals a total of seven. Then pantomime throwing the dice onto a game board. Point out the sides that add up to seven, and explain how the number of dots that appear on the top of the dice indicates how many spaces to move.

MEETING INDIVIDUAL NEEDS

Peter took his turn. Thank heavens, he lan[ded] on a blank space. He rolled again. "'Monsoon season begins, lose one turn.'" Little raindrop[s] began to fall in the living room. Then a roll o[f] thunder shook the walls and scared the monke[ys] out of the kitchen. The rain began to fall in buckets as Judy took the dice.

"'Guide gets lost, lose one turn.'" The rain suddenly stopped. The children turned to see [a] man hunched over a map.

"Oh dear, I say, spot of bad luck now," h[e] mumbled. "Perhaps a left turn here then . . . [N]o . . . a right turn here . . . Yes, absolutely, I think, a right turn . . . or maybe . . ."

"Excuse me," said Judy, but the guide just ignored her.

". . . around here, then over . . . No, no . . . over here and around this . . . Yes, good . [. .] but then . . . Hm . . ."

Judy shrugged her shoulders and handed t[he] dice to Peter.

". . . four, five, six," he counted. "'Bitten [by] tsetse fly, contract sleeping sickness, lose one turn.'"

Judy heard a faint buzzing noise and watch[ed] a small insect land on Peter's nose. Peter lifted his hand to brush the bug away, but then stopped, gave a tremendous yawn, and fell so[und] asleep, his head on the table.

Expanding the Literature   **What has occurred so far to let you know that this story is a fantasy and not realistic fiction?** (The event in each square the children have landed on has become real.)   CRITICAL: DISTINGUISHING BETWEEN FANTASY AND REALITY

Second-Language Support
Some students may not understand the meaning of the word *guide* as it is used here. The meaning can be conveyed through pictures and pantomime. Point out that this guide is a humorous character— a guide's job is to show people where to go, but this guide is lost.

"Peter, Peter, wake up!" cried Judy. But it was no use. She grabbed the dice and moved to a blank. She rolled again and waited in amazement. "'Rhinoceros stampede, go back two spaces.'"

As fast as he had fallen asleep, Peter awoke. Together they listened to a rumble in the hallway. It grew louder and louder. Suddenly a herd of rhinos charged through the living room and into the dining room, crushing all the furniture in their path. Peter and Judy covered their ears as sounds of splintering wood and breaking china filled the house.

Peter gave the dice a quick tumble. "'Python sneaks into camp, go back one space.'"

Judy shrieked and jumped up on her chair.

"Over the fireplace," said Peter. Judy sat down again, nervously eyeing the eight-foot snake that was wrapping itself around the mantel clock. The guide looked up from his map, took one look at the snake, and moved to the far corner of the room, joining the monkeys on the couch.

Judy took her turn and landed on a blank space. Her brother took the dice and rolled a three.

"Oh, no," he moaned. "'Volcano erupts, go back three spaces.'" The room became warm and started to shake a little. Molten lava poured from the fireplace opening. It hit the water on the floor and the room filled with steam. Judy rolled the dice and moved ahead.

309

Cultural Awareness   Explain that the word *stampede* is taken from the Spanish word *estampada,* meaning "crash." Have students visualize a group of animals stampeding and decide why *estampada* was adopted into our language.

"'Discover shortcut, roll again.' Oh dear!" she cried. Judy saw the snake unwrapping itself from the clock.

"If you roll a twelve you can get out of the jungle," said Peter.

"Please, please," Judy begged as she shook the dice. The snake was wriggling its way to the floor. She dropped the dice from her hand. One six, then another. Judy grabbed her piece and slammed it to the board. "JUMANJI," she yelled, as loud as she could.

The steam in the room became thicker and thicker. Judy could not even see Peter across the table. Then, as if all the doors and windows had been opened, a cool breeze cleared the steam from the room. Everything was just as it had been before the game. No monkeys, no guide, no water, no broken furniture, no snake, no lion roaring upstairs, no rhinos. Without saying a word to each other, Peter and Judy threw the game into its box. They bolted out the door, ran across the street to the park, and dropped the game under a tree. Back home, they quickly put all their toys away. But both children were too excited to sit quietly, so Peter took out a picture puzzle. As they fit the pieces together, their excitement slowly turned to relief, and then exhaustion. With the puzzle half done Peter and Judy fell sound asleep on the sofa.

Expanding the Literature   What does the author do on page 310 to contribute to the feeling of suspense? (He adds the python while providing a possible escape from the game if Judy can reach Jumanji in time.)   CRITICAL: AUTHOR'S CRAFT/DETERMINING IMAGERY

Vocabulary Strategy   How can you use structural analysis and context clues to figure out the meaning of *shortcut*? (The two words that make up the compound word are *short* and *cut.* Using the meaning of *short,* "not long," the meaning of *cut,* "to make less," and the fact that Judy rolls again, you can see that *shortcut* must mean "a way to save time.")   STRATEGY: CONTEXT CLUES AND STRUCTURAL ANALYSIS

"Wake up, dears," Mother's voice called. Judy opened her eyes. Mother and Father had returned and their guests were arriving. Judy gave Peter a nudge to wake him. Yawning and stretching, they got to their feet.

Mother introduced them to some of the guests, then asked, "Did you have an exciting afternoon?"

"Oh yes," said Peter. "We had a flood, a stampede, a volcano, I got sleeping sickness, and—" Peter was <u>interrupted</u> by the adults' laughter.

"Well," said Mother, "I think you both got sleeping sickness. Why don't you go upstairs and put your pajamas on? Then you can finish your puzzle and have some dinner."

When Peter and Judy came back downstairs they found that Father had moved the puzzle to the den. While the children were working on it, one of the guests, Mrs. Budwing, brought in a tray of food.

"Such a hard puzzle," she said to the children. "Daniel and Walter are always starting puzzles and never finishing them." Daniel and Walter were Mrs. Budwing's sons. "They never read instructions either. Oh well," said Mrs. Budwing, turning to rejoin the guests, "I guess they'll learn."

Expanding the Literature   **What seem to be the rules Chris Van Allsburg has invented for Jumanji?** (1. The event in each square a player lands on becomes real. 2. The game will not end until someone wins. 3. When a player wins, all the things the game has created disappear.)
INFERENTIAL: UNDERSTANDING FANTASY

Both children answered, "I hope so," but they weren't looking at Mrs. Budwing. They were looking out the window. Two boys wer running through the park. It was Danny and Walter Budwing, and Danny had a long thin under his arm.

THINK IT OVER

1. Why was winning Jumanji so important?

2. Why didn't Peter want to take the Jumanji game h from the park?

3. Peter and Judy had different feelings at different po in the story. What were some of the different feelin they had?

4. What does it take to win a game of Jumanji?

WRITE

The message on the Jumanji game box read, "fun for s but not for all." Write a message telling what you thi about the game for the next person who finds it.

Guided Reading

MONITOR COMPREHENSION: PAGES 304–315
What happens as the children continue to play the game? (The events on each square become real until Judy wins. Then things return to normal.) **Is that what you predicted?** (Responses will vary.)
STRATEGIC READING: CONFIRMING PREDICTIONS

What do you think will happen to Danny and Walter Budwing? (Accept reasonable responses: They'll probably play the game and then not be able to end it until their parents return.)   CRITICAL: MAKING PREDICTIONS

Returning to the Predictions   Invite students to discuss the predictions that they made before reading and that they may have written in their personal journals. Encourage them to talk about how those predictions changed as they read the story.

Returning to the Purpose for Reading
Ask students to discuss what happened when the children played the game. (The event in each square they landed on became real. Everything that appeared during the game disappeared when the game was over.)

NOTE: Responses to the Think It Over questions and support for the Write activity appear on page T533.

Part 2
Responding to Literature

Think It Over

Encourage reader's response: student page 315.

1. **Why was winning Jumanji so important?** (The dangerous animals and events would not go away until the game was over.)   INFERENTIAL: SUMMARIZING

2. **Why didn't Peter want to take the Jumanji game home from the park?** (He thought it would be boring.)   LITERAL: NOTING IMPORTANT DETAILS

3. **Peter and Judy had different feelings at different points in the story. What were some of the different feelings they had?** (Accept reasonable responses: boredom; fear; relief.) INFERENTIAL: UNDERSTANDING CHARACTERS' FEELINGS

4. **What does it take to win a game of Jumanji?** (Accept reasonable responses: understanding and following directions; curiosity; bravery.)   CRITICAL: SYNTHESIZING

Write

Encourage writer's response: student page 315.

The message on the Jumanji game box read "fun for some but not for all." Write a message telling what you think about the game for the next person who finds it. Encourage students to think about their audiences as they write.   CREATIVE: WRITING A MESSAGE

Have students retell the story and write a summary.

Encourage students to summarize the story by recalling the major events. Have them identify the cause and effect in each link of the cause-and-effect chain below. Assist students in completing the links of the chain. (See *Practice Book* page 80 on T534.) Have students use their completed chains to write a brief summary statement.

(Peter and Judy are home alone. They go to the park and find a game.)	→	(Peter and Judy decide to play the game. They begin by reading the directions.)	→	(Peter lands on a square, and a lion appears in the house.)

STRATEGY CONFERENCE

Discuss with students how previewing and making predictions helped them understand, remember, and appreciate the story. Invite students to share other reading strategies, such as visualizing, that helped them understand what they read.

NOTE

An additional writing activity for this story appears on page T536.

INFORMAL ASSESSMENT

Having students order the **details** of a story in this way will help you informally assess how well they understood key relationships. Ask yourself: Did students grasp **time relationships**? Did students recognize the **causes of effects** and the **effects of causes**? Can students tell which details are more important than others?

Appreciating Literature

Have students share personal responses.

Have students work in small groups to discuss the story. Provide a general question such as the following to help the groups begin:

- **Did you share any of the feelings of the characters in the story? Explain your answer.**

PERSONAL JOURNAL Have students use their personal journals to write about ideas and feelings that are discussed in the groups. You may also refer them to their personal journals after they complete the activities below.

Critical Thinking Activities

Encourage both cooperative and individual responses.

RETELL THE STORY **How might the story have been different if Peter and Judy had never read the instructions?** Have students work in small groups to discuss how the story would have changed. Have groups make lists of possibilities and compare their lists until all ideas are exhausted. Then encourage students to retell the story, beginning by having one student state a sentence and then having each of the other students add a sentence to the previous one. CRITICAL: SPECULATING

MAKE A GAME **Create a new kind of game that Peter and Judy might want to play.** Have students work in groups to brainstorm what kind of game to make, what the board would look like, how someone would win, and what the name would be. Then have them write a list of rules and build the game. CREATIVE: INVENTING A GAME

STUDENT SELF-ASSESSMENT

Help students self-assess their listening by writing a list of good listening skills on the board. Have students nominate the best listeners from the discussion, giving reasons for their choices.

A good listener:

- pays attention to what others have to say
- adds ideas to what others have to say
- does not interrupt
- thinks about other people's ideas

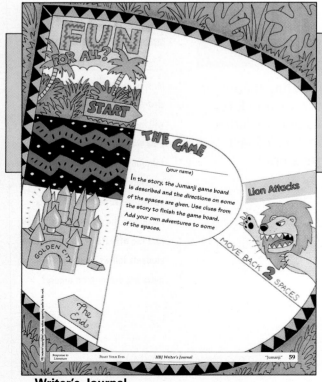

Writer's Journal

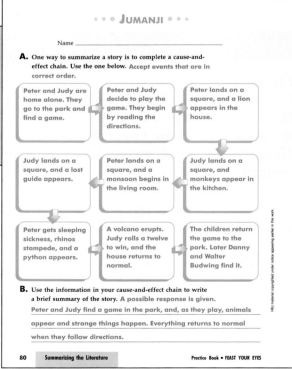

Practice Book

WRITER'S JOURNAL
page 59: Writing a personal response

PRACTICE BOOK
page 80: Summarizing the selection

VO·CAB·U·LAR·Y Workshop

Reviewing Key Words

Display the Key Words, and have students answer the following questions, orally or in writing:

1. *interrupted* **By what was Peter interrupted when he was explaining the adventure?** (the adults' laughter)

2. *volcano* **Why did the children become alarmed when Peter landed on the square that mentioned a volcano?** (The room became warm and shook; lava poured from the fireplace opening.)

3. *erupts* **Why did the room shake after Peter landed on the square that read "Volcano erupts"?** (When a volcano erupts, it explodes.)

4. *lava* **Why did the room become warm as lava poured out of the fireplace?** (Lava is very hot.)

5. *stampede* **How did Peter and Judy react when the rhinoceros stampede came rushing through the house?** (They covered their ears.) **Why did they react that way?** (because a herd of rhinos running through the house would be very noisy)

6. *exhaustion* **What did Peter and Judy do because they were overcome by exhaustion?** (They fell sound asleep.)

Extending Vocabulary

CONTENT-AREA WORDS Display a simple diagram of an erupting volcano similar to the one below, and have volunteers label it by using the vocabulary words *volcano, erupts,* and *lava.*

Have students add words they know that are associated with volcanoes. They may use their science textbooks or an encyclopedia as a resource for new words.

Guide students in naming categories under which they can place the words (such as *Parts, Causes,* and *Effects*) and then placing each word under the correct heading. Have students add additional categories and new science words to use in their writing.

PRACTICE BOOK
page 81: Writing content-area vocabulary

• • • JUMANJI • • •

Name _____

Peter gets bitten by a tsetse fly and contracts sleeping sickness. Read about this disease in the paragraphs below. Then draw a line under the best ending to each sentence that follows.

Sleeping sickness is a **serious disease** of tropical Africa. It is caused by a **protozoan** that can get into a person's body through a tsetse fly's bite. Once this single-celled animal is inside a person's body, it multiplies rapidly. The disease quickly spreads throughout the body, eventually reaching the brain.

In most cases, a complete **cure** is possible if the disease is treated before it reaches the brain. If left untreated, the disease will cause a **coma**, or loss of consciousness, and death.

1. Another word for *serious* is _____.
   certain   dangerous
   painless   slow

2. Another word for *disease* is _____.
   coma   measles
   illness   health

3. A protozoan is a _____.
   noisy creature   sneaky creature
   single-celled animal   dangerous insect

4. If a person is in a coma, he or she _____.
   can talk but can't walk   is unconscious
   can hear but not see   is cold

5. A cure is a _____.
   successful treatment   shot
   bath   bug spray

Practice Book • FEAST YOUR EYES   Content-Area Words   81

Practice Book

Integrated Language Arts

Oral Rereading/Drama

Ask students to describe how Judy and Peter felt before the lion appeared (bored) and how they felt afterward (very frightened). Then ask students to silently reread this section of the story (page 303, paragraph 2, to page 305, paragraph 4, when Peter says, "Let's play."). Model a few lines for students, using tone, pitch, and facial expression to communicate the feelings of the characters. Give students an opportunity to rehearse the scene, or another scene of their choosing, before they present it to classmates.   LISTENING/SPEAKING/READING

Writing About the Literature

WRITE A FANTASY   Have students work individually or in small groups to consider what might happen if the things in one of their favorite games came to life as they did in "Jumanji." Have students use the spaces on a game board to plan the events for their fantasy. WRITING

NOTE: An additional writing activity appears on page T533.

Reviewing Spelling Words

SPELLING WORDS: *blank, clock, finish, gasp, plot, prop, stampede, swift, thin, volcano*

Help students design a version of "Jumanji." Tape square pieces of paper to the floor to create the game board and label each space with instructions. Include spelling-related instructions such as "Spell This Word Correctly— Go Forward Four Steps." Decide on a starting point and a destination, and then have a student begin the game by throwing the dice and moving a marker. If a student lands on a spelling square, call out a word. The student advances if the word is spelled correctly. If not, the student retreats the same number of steps.   LISTENING/ SPEAKING/SPELLING

INTEGRATED SPELLING page 44: Spelling words with short vowel sounds

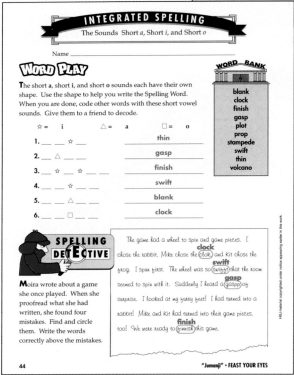

Integrated Spelling

Monkeys in the Kitchen

AVAILABLE ON PROJECT CARD

Ask students to create poems inspired by the Jumanji game. Tell them to feel free to use characters and events from the story or to make up new ones. You may want to read these lines as an example:

> Monkeys in the kitchen,
> Rhinos in the hall,
> A lion in the bedroom,
> And a snake against the wall.

Allow students time to rehearse their poems until they can recite them without prompts. Then have students present their poems in a poetry-reading session. LISTENING/READING/WRITING

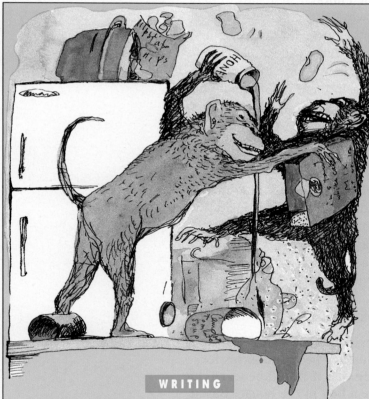

Was That a Roar I Heard?

AVAILABLE ON PROJECT CARD

COOPERATIVE LEARNING   Suppose that a group of neighbors complained about the strange noises coming from Judy and Peter's house. Ask students to imagine a telephone conversation between two neighbors. Have them create a character and brainstorm what their character might say and how he or she might react. Then ask students to work in groups to develop and act out the conversations. Tell them to make the conversations as funny as possible.   LISTENING/SPEAKING

WRITING

A Messy Good Time

Ask students to picture what a kitchen might look like after a dozen monkeys have finished playing in it. Display a sketch of a messy kitchen, similar to the one above. Have students copy the picture and draw a stick figure of themselves in the picture. Encourage them to fill in the large stains with words and phrases describing what they see upon entering the kitchen. Finally, have them write a paragraph describing such a scene. Display their pictures and paragraphs on a bulletin board.   WRITING

Part 3
Learning Through Literature

Drawing Conclusions

OBJECTIVE: *To use story information and real-life experiences to draw valid conclusions*

1	Focus

Discuss the importance of drawing conclusions.

Ask students how Peter feels when the children first start to play Jumanji and to tell why he feels this way. (He is bored because he and Judy have already played many games. He doesn't think the game will be fun.) Point out that the author does not actually tell the reader these things. Explain that being able to figure out things that are not directly stated will help them understand what they read.

2	Teach/Model

Teach how to draw valid conclusions.

Explain that authors do not always tell readers everything that happens in a story. Point out that readers must use information from the story plus their own experiences to figure out why story events occur and why characters behave as they do. Explain that when they do this, they are drawing a valid conclusion. Tell students that if there is insufficient evidence or personal knowledge, the conclusion is invalid. Model drawing conclusions beginning with the ninth paragraph on page 303.

> **I can figure out that Peter is terrified. He falls off his chair, runs through the house, dives under a bed, and gasps for breath. I also know from real life that it would be terrifying to turn around and suddenly see a lion in the house. Based on story evidence and my knowledge, I know this is a valid conclusion.**

Strategy: Use story information plus prior knowledge.

On the board, create a chart similar to the one below, having students provide the information for the first two boxes.

Clues from the Story (Peter ran through the house and dove under a bed. He gasped for breath.)	+	What I Know from Real Life (It would be very frightening to see a lion in your house.)	=	Conclusion Peter is terrified of the lion.

3 Practice/Apply

Have students apply the learning.

COOPERATIVE LEARNING Ask students to form pairs and to copy the chart outline onto a sheet of paper. Have partners skim the story, identify other conclusions they drew while reading, and add them to the chart.

4 Summarize

Informally assess the learning.

Have students take turns reading aloud the conclusion statements from the diagram and asking others to explain why each statement is a valid conclusion.

Have students summarize what they have learned. (Use story evidence plus prior knowledge to draw a valid conclusion.)

READER ←→ WRITER CONNECTION

Drawing Conclusions

▶ **Writers** tell readers some things and let them figure out other things for themselves. This is one way writers make stories fun to read.

▶ **Readers** have the interesting task of putting story information together with what they already know to figure out why story events happen and why characters behave in certain ways.

WRITE AN ADVENTURE STORY Have students write a story in which children are stranded on a deserted island. Remind students to add clues to the story so readers can draw conclusions.

RETEACH Follow the **visual, auditory,** and **kinesthetic/motor** models on page R47.

CHALLENGE Have students explain the conclusion Peter and Judy's parents drew at the end of the story when Peter described what had happened while they were gone. Ask students to tell why the parents drew this conclusion.

SECOND-LANGUAGE SUPPORT Students can demonstrate their understanding of the skill by answering this question: How did Peter and Judy feel when they finished playing Jumanji? Students can complete these sentence frames: Peter and Judy felt _____. I figured this out by _____. (See *Second-Language Support Manual.*)

WRITER'S JOURNAL page 60: Writing a story

PRACTICE BOOK page 82: Drawing conclusions

Writer's Journal

Practice Book

Following Directions

OBJECTIVE: *To interpret and follow directions*

Review

Review following directions.

Ask students what might happen if they did not follow the directions for building or baking something. Then have volunteers recall the guidelines for following oral or written directions. (carefully read or listen to all of the directions; check for key words such as *first* or *next;* follow each step of the directions in the order given; do exactly as the directions say)

Practice/Apply

Have students consider board-game instructions.

COOPERATIVE LEARNING Explain that one way to understand a set of directions is to ask questions about what is to be done. Have students form pairs to reread and discuss the instructions on page 300. Remind them to record their questions and responses.

Summarize

Informally assess the learning.

Have students read aloud their questions and responses about playing Jumanji. Then have them explain how questions help them remember the Jumanji instructions.

Have students summarize what they learned. (Follow oral or written directions exactly by listening carefully to each step and for key words. Pay attention to order.)

CHALLENGE Have students consider the instructions for another board game they are familiar with and write a paragraph telling what might happen if players did not read all the instructions or did not follow them in order.

PRACTICE BOOK
page 83: Following directions

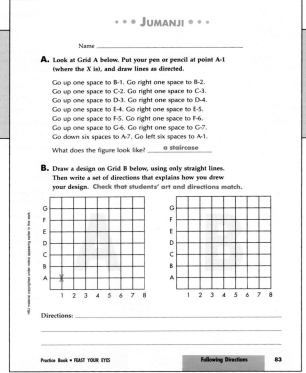

• • • JUMANJI • • •

Name _____

A. Look at Grid A below. Put your pen or pencil at point A-1 (where the X is), and draw lines as directed.

Go up one space to B-1. Go right one space to B-2.
Go up one space to C-2. Go right one space to C-3.
Go up one space to D-3. Go right one space to D-4.
Go up one space to E-4. Go right one space to E-5.
Go up one space to F-5. Go right one space to F-6.
Go up one space to G-6. Go right one space to G-7.
Go down six spaces to A-7. Go left six spaces to A-1.

What does the figure look like? ___a staircase___

B. Draw a design on Grid B below, using only straight lines. Then write a set of directions that explains how you drew your design. Check that students' art and directions match.

Directions: _____

Practice Book ▪ FEAST YOUR EYES   Following Directions   83

Practice Book

Reference Sources

OBJECTIVE: *To identify when to use an encyclopedia and a dictionary*

Review

Review the purpose of an encyclopedia and a dictionary.

Remind students that two useful reference sources are an encyclopedia and a dictionary. Have students describe each resource and explain how to use it. (An encyclopedia is a set of books, or volumes, containing information on different topics. A dictionary gives the meanings, spellings, and pronunciations of individual words. Both are arranged alphabetically with guide words at the top of each page to help locate information.)

Practice/Apply

Have students choose a reference source.

Have students tell whether they would use an encyclopedia or a dictionary to locate information on the following: inventors of games (E), how to spell *board* and *bored* (D), how to pronounce *tsetse fly* (D), locations of jungles (E).

Summarize

Informally assess the learning.

Have students discuss which resource they chose for each item. Have students summarize what they learned. (Use an encyclopedia to find information on a topic. Use a dictionary to find the meanings, spellings, and pronunciations of words.)

CHALLENGE Invite students to select a single-word topic they are interested in and locate an entry for it in an encyclopedia. Then have them look up their topic in a dictionary. Ask them to compare the information given in both sources.

PRACTICE BOOK
pages 84–85: Using reference sources

Practice Book

* * * JUMANJI * * *

Name _____

A. Read each question, and think about where you might find the answer. Then write *encyclopedia* or *dictionary* on the line.

1. What does the word *melody* mean? __dictionary__
2. What kind of a childhood did Abraham Lincoln have? __encyclopedia__
3. What happened during the Industrial Revolution? __encyclopedia__
4. What is the root word for *hypothermia*? __dictionary__
5. What are some synonyms for *good-looking*? __dictionary__
6. What was the birthplace of Martin Luther King, Jr.? __encyclopedia__
7. What is the difference in meaning between *forceful* and *pushy*? __dictionary__
8. What does the abbreviation *ibid.* mean? __dictionary__
9. What kinds of chemicals are used in developing photographs from negatives? __encyclopedia__
10. What is the history of the ballet? __encyclopedia__

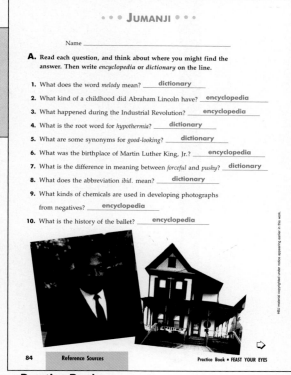

84   Reference Sources

Practice Book ▪ FEAST YOUR EYES

Practice Book

* * * JUMANJI * * *

Name _____

B. Read each entry. Where would you see such an entry—in an encyclopedia or in a dictionary? Write the answer on the line.

1. in·got [ing′gət] *n.* A mass of metal cast into the shape of a bar or block. __dictionary__
2. The original Luddites were followers of a legendary Ned Ludd. These 19th-century British laborers smashed textile-making machines that threatened their jobs. __encyclopedia__
3. India is a republic in southern Asia. Its largest city is Calcutta, and its capital is New Delhi. __encyclopedia__
4. hot air   *informal*   Empty, boastful talk. __dictionary__
5. ə = a in *above*, e in *sicken*, i in *possible*, o in *melon*, u in *circus* __dictionary__

C. In the left column are entry words. In the right column are guide words that might be found on the same page in a dictionary. Write the letter of the guide words on the line next to the corresponding entry word.

1. __f__ fortunate   a. gymnastics   gyve
2. __a__ gypsum   b. node   nondescript
3. __b__ nonchalant   c. forgetful   formulate
4. __e__ normal   d. gung ho   gymnastic
5. __d__ gutter   e. none   Norman
6. __c__ formalize   f. formulation   foster

Practice Book ▪ FEAST YOUR EYES   Reference Sources   85

Integrated **Curriculum**

SOCIAL STUDIES

Deserts, Cities, and Grasslands

AVAILABLE ON PROJECT CARD

CULTURAL AWARENESS   Point out that all the animals mentioned in the story make their home in Africa but that most of the African continent is not covered with jungle. Africa also contains large, modern cities; deserts; seacoasts; mountains; and grasslands. Have students find out about the many different peoples and places that are part of Africa. Suggest that they start by making a list of three questions about Africa for which they would like to find answers. A librarian or travel agent may be of help to students. After students gather information, have them make travel guides for people who are planning to visit specific regions in Africa.   READING/WRITING

MATH

A Lucky Throw

COOPERATIVE LEARNING   Tell students to imagine that the Jumanji game board has 48 spaces and that they are going to play using only one die. Have students form pairs, and ask them to calculate the number of times they would have to throw the die in order to reach the last space if the die indicated 2, 3, 4, and 5. Then have them tell which number, if consistently rolled on the die, would keep them from ever reaching the Golden City. LISTENING/SPEAKING

SCIENCE

Warning: Dangerous-Animal Crossing

USE REFERENCE SOURCES   Ask students how dangerous they think the animals that appeared in Judy and Peter's house were. Encourage them to go on their own fact-finding expeditions. Tell them to head straight for the school or classroom library and read about these animals. Students can then report back to share with classmates what they discovered.   LISTENING/SPEAKING/READING/WRITING

Integrated Curriculum

Volcano Erupts: Go Back Three Spaces

AVAILABLE ON PROJECT CARD

USE REFERENCE SOURCES Explain that volcanoes are a real danger faced by people in many parts of the world. Discuss fairly recent volcanic eruptions, such as the eruption of Mount St. Helens in the state of Washington and Kilauea on the island of Hawaii. Tell students that they can begin an imaginary journey to the "Ring of Fire" around the Pacific Ocean by finding out where some active volcanoes are located, how they were formed, and what happens when they erupt. Students may want to work together with friends to present a report to their classmates. To help their classmates understand what happens during a volcanic eruption, encourage them to show photographs from books and magazines or diagrams and drawings that they have made.   LISTENING/SPEAKING/READING/WRITING

Rapids Ahead: Lose One Turn

COOPERATIVE LEARNING   Have students work in groups to create an American version of the Jumanji game board. Let each group member select a wild animal or a natural disaster that is found in the United States. Then have the group assemble the selections into a new Jumanji-style game board for their classmates to view. READING/WRITING

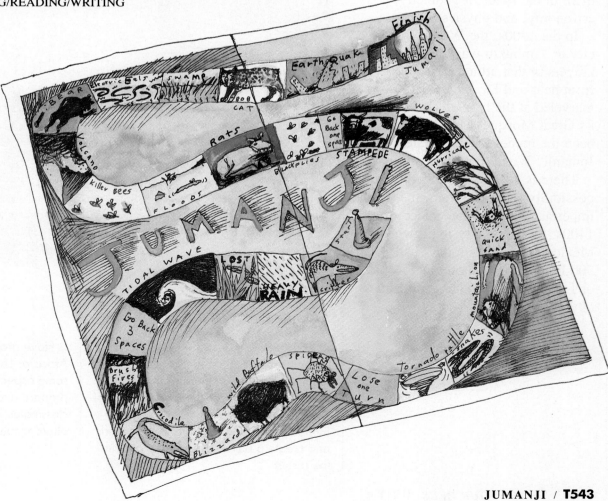

Glorious Cities of Old

READ ALOUD TO STUDENTS:

THE ANCIENT AFRICAN CITY OF ALEXANDRIA, IN EGYPT, MAY HAVE BEEN A CITY OF GOLDEN BUILDINGS AND TOWERS. In the second century B.C., this beautiful city was a model of intellectual progress. It had one of the greatest libraries the world had ever seen, copied from the fabulous libraries built in the literary age around 2040 B.C. in Kemet, Africa. With some 500,000 books written on papyrus, it drew researchers from all over the world. Great advances were made there in the fields of geometry, astronomy, and physics.

In the 1300s, the West African city of Timbuktu was the site of a university that attracted scholars from near and far. Travelers marveled at the high stone towers of its Great Mosque. Might this have been the model for the mysterious Jumanji? We do not know.

There is at least one other possibility—Tenochtitlán, the imperial capital of the Aztecs. In the 1400s, this great city, built where Mexico City stands today, had 300,000 people—more than Rome or London or any other European city at the time. ■

For hundreds of years Timbuktu was a trading center. Merchants traveled over land and along the Niger River to buy and sell salt, food, animals, leather goods, silk, and jewelry.

ACTIVITY CORNER

■ Ask students to imagine what the city of their dreams might be like. Encourage them to think about the ancient cities described here. Have them write a paragraph telling about that city. Students may wish to illustrate their work and create a bulletin board display with the results.

■ Have groups of students pick a city in Africa or Latin America and research some aspect of its past. They might then prepare an oral presentation for their classmates, with visual aids such as maps, photographs, and diagrams.

INTERVIEW

An Interview with the Author and Illustrator:
Chris Van Allsburg

Reading the Interview

Help students set a purpose for reading.

Have students recall what they remember about "Jumanji." Then ask students what kind of person might write and illustrate a fantasy story like "Jumanji." Tell students to imagine that they are going to interview the author and illustrator, Chris Van Allsburg. Have volunteers provide questions they might ask Van Allsburg. Write their questions on the board. Have students predict what Van Allsburg's answers to those questions might be.

Explain to students that they are going to read an interview with Van Allsburg. Suggest that they read the interview to see how closely the questions they would ask match the ones asked by interviewer Ilene Cooper and to find out how Van Allsburg answered those questions.

Responding to the Interview

Return to the purpose for reading.

Ask students which interview questions were similar to their own and whether Chris Van Allsburg answered those questions as they might have expected. Discuss what else they still would like to find out about him.

Encourage students to respond creatively.

You may wish to select one of the following activities for responding to the interview:

COOPERATIVE LEARNING: EXAMINING ART   Bring several of Chris Van Allsburg's books into the classroom. Have groups of students find pictures showing Fritz, the English bull terrier Van Allsburg includes in each of his books. Then arrange the books in order of when they were published and have students examine Van Allsburg's art to see how his style has changed over the years.   LISTENING/SPEAKING

WRITING A FANTASY   Have students reread Chris Van Allsburg's last answer. Ask them to write about an image in their own minds and to expand that image into a fantasy story.   READING/WRITING

PERSONAL JOURNAL: WRITING A PERSONAL RESPONSE
Encourage students to record in their personal journals their reactions to the interview. To get them started, you might suggest that they describe what kind of person Chris Van Allsburg is or speculate about how he might illustrate a well-known fairy tale.
WRITING

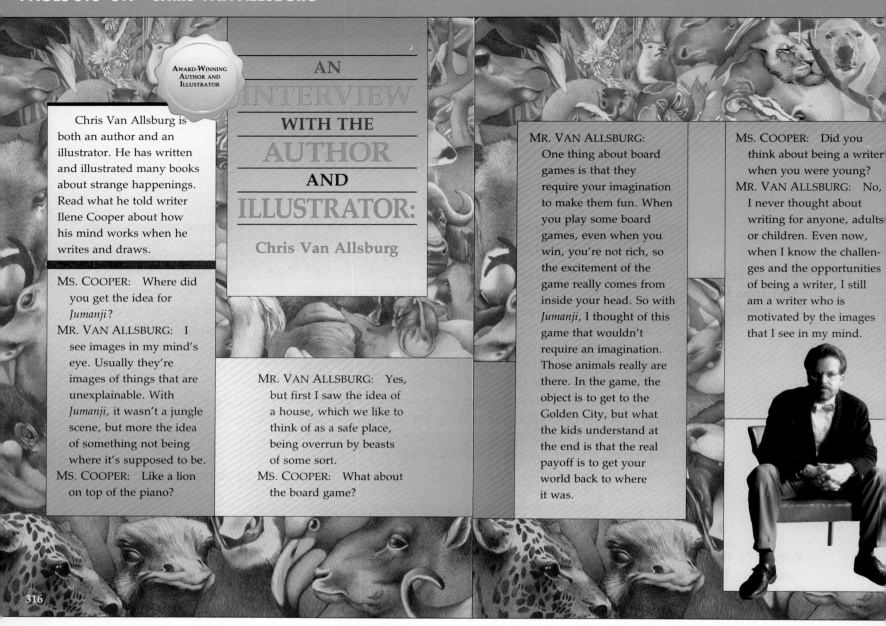

AWARD-WINNING
AUTHOR AND
ILLUSTRATOR

AN INTERVIEW WITH THE AUTHOR AND ILLUSTRATOR:

Chris Van Allsburg

Chris Van Allsburg is both an author and an illustrator. He has written and illustrated many books about strange happenings. Read what he told writer Ilene Cooper about how his mind works when he writes and draws.

MS. COOPER: Where did you get the idea for *Jumanji*?

MR. VAN ALLSBURG: I see images in my mind's eye. Usually they're images of things that are unexplainable. With *Jumanji*, it wasn't a jungle scene, but more the idea of something not being where it's supposed to be.

MS. COOPER: Like a lion on top of the piano?

MR. VAN ALLSBURG: Yes, but first I saw the idea of a house, which we like to think of as a safe place, being overrun by beasts of some sort.

MS. COOPER: What about the board game?

MR. VAN ALLSBURG: One thing about board games is that they require your imagination to make them fun. When you play some board games, even when you win, you're not rich, so the excitement of the game really comes from inside your head. So with *Jumanji*, I thought of this game that wouldn't require an imagination. Those animals really are there. In the game, the object is to get to the Golden City, but what the kids understand at the end is that the real payoff is to get your world back to where it was.

MS. COOPER: Did you think about being a writer when you were young?

MR. VAN ALLSBURG: No, I never thought about writing for anyone, adults or children. Even now, when I know the challenges and the opportunities of being a writer, I still am a writer who is motivated by the images that I see in my mind.

316

Expanding the Interview   Ilene Cooper uses the lion on top of the piano as an example of "something not being where it's supposed to be." What other examples from "Jumanji" could have been used to illustrate this? (Accept reasonable responses: the volcano in the living room.)   CRITICAL: AUTHOR'S CRAFT/IDENTIFYING WITH INCIDENTS

The Game Board

ABOUT THE AUTHORS   For over half a century, Harold Courlander has collected tales and music from dozens of cultures around the world. Courlander cowrote "The Game Board" and other Ethiopian tales with Wolf Leslau.

SELECTION SUMMARY   In this folktale from *The Fire on the Mountain and Other Ethiopian Stories,* a boy is coerced into trading his new gebeta game board for a knife and then is involved in several other trades. He eventually ends up with a game board like the one he had originally.

Building Background

Provide background and access prior knowledge about game boards.

Have students recall why Judy was eager to take the Jumanji game home from the park. (She and Peter were bored.) Explain that the folktale they are about to read is from the African nation of Ethiopia. Point out that in this folktale, a game board is used in different ways. Develop with students a word web like the one below that shows what a game board might be used for.

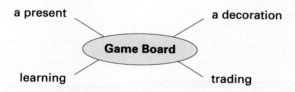

a present   a decoration

Game Board

learning   trading

Strategic Reading

Help students quickwrite predictions and set purposes.

Ask students to read the title and the first paragraph of the story. Have students predict how the game board might be used by the boy and other characters in the story. Students may write their predictions in their personal journals.

STUDENT-SET PURPOSE   Help students use their predictions to set a purpose for reading "The Game Board."

TEACHER-SET PURPOSE   If students have difficulty setting a purpose independently, offer this suggestion:

> **I'm going to read to find out how the game board is useful to some of the story characters.**

Have students read the folktale with their purposes for reading in mind.

CULTURAL AWARENESS

Point out that almost half of Ethiopia is surrounded by Somalia. In this area, people constantly trade with each other to get the necessities of life.

SECOND-LANGUAGE SUPPORT   Students will benefit from a thorough explanation of the function of a game board. You might ask students to discuss games with which they are familiar that involve boards. (See Second-Language Support Manual.)

THE GAME BOARD

AWARD-WINNING
AUTHOR

from *The Fire on the Mountain and Other Ethiopian Stories*
by Harold Courlander and Wolf Leslau
illustrated by Jaimie Bennett

From *The Fire on the Mountain and Other Ethiopian Stories* by Harold Courlander and Wolf Leslau. Copyright © 1950 by Holt, Rinehart and Winston; copyright © 1978 by Harold Courlander, Wolf Leslau, and Robert Kane. Reprinted by permission of Harold Courlander.

318

Once a man in the town of Nebri carved a beautiful gebeta[1] board for his son. He made it from the wood of an olive tree. When he was finished he showed his son how to play games upon it. The boy was very glad to have such a beautiful thing, and in the morning when he went out with the cattle to the valley where they grazed he took his gebeta board along. Everywhere he went he carried his board under his arm.

While he followed the cattle, he came upon a group of wandering Somalis with their camels, gathered around a small fire in a dry riverbed.

"Where in this country of yours can a man get wood?" the Somalis asked.

"Why, here is wood," the boy said. And he gave them the fine gebeta board, which they put into the fire.

As it went up in flames, the boy began to cry:

"Oh, now where is my fine gebeta board that my father has carved for me?"

"Do not make such turmoil," the Somalis said, and they gave him a fine new knife in place of the game board.

The boy took the knife and went away with his cattle. As he wandered he came to a place where a man was digging a well in the sand of the riverbed, so that his goats could drink.

"The ground is hard," the man said. "Lend me your knife to dig with."

The boy gave the man the knife, but the man dug so vigorously with it that it broke.

"Ah, what has become of my knife?" the boy wailed.

---

[1]gebeta [geh' beh · tah]: an Ethiopian version of a counting game played throughout Africa with beans or seeds on a carved board (actually two boards that fit together) having nine carved playing positions and a pocket at each end for winnings

---

Second-Language Support

Some students may not understand the meaning of *wandering* as it is used in the second paragraph. To aid their comprehension, pantomime the word *wandering* by moving around the room. Explain that *wandering* means "moving from place to place."

MEETING
INDIVIDUAL
NEEDS

Expanding the Literature   What is different about the way the boy and the Somali man think of the game board? (The boy thinks of the game as a special gift, but the Somali man sees it as a much-needed piece of firewood.)
INFERENTIAL: COMPARING AND CONTRASTING

"Quiet yourself," the man said. "Take this spear in its place." And he gave the boy a beautiful spear trimmed with silver and copper.

The boy went away with his cattle and his spear. He met a party of hunters. When they saw him one of them said:

"Lend me your spear, so that we may kill the lion we are trailing."

The boy gave him the spear, and the hunters went out and killed the lion. But in the hunt the shaft of the spear was splintered.

"See what you've done with my spear!" the boy cried.

"Don't carry on so," the hunter said. "Here is a horse for you in place of your spear."

The hunter gave him a horse with fine leather trappings, and he started back toward the village. On the way he came to where a group of workmen were repairing the highway. As they worked they caused a landslide, and the earth and rocks came down the mountain with a great roar. The horse became frightened and ran away.

"Where is my horse?" the boy cried. "You have made him run away!"

"Don't grieve," the workman said. "Here is an ax." And he gave the boy a common iron ax.

The boy took the ax and continued toward the village. He came to a woodcutter who said:

"Lend me your large ax for this tree. My ax is too small."

He loaned the woodcutter the ax, and the woodcutter chopped with it and broke it.

The boy cried, and the woodcutter said: "Never mind, here is a limb of a tree."

The boy took the limb upon his back and when he came near the village a woman said:

"Where did you find the wood? I need it for my fire."

The boy gave it to her, and she put it in the fire. As it went up in flames he said:

"Now where is my wood?"

"Here," the woman said, "here is a fine gebeta board."

He took the gebeta board under his arm and went home with the cattle. As he entered his house his father smiled and said:

"What is better than a gebeta game board to keep a small boy out of trouble?"

THINK IT OVER

1. *How did the boy end up with the same kind of object that he had when he left home?*

2. *Do you think that the gebeta board kept the young boy out of trouble? Explain your answer.*

WRITE

Think about something special that you own. Write sentences that tell what you would trade your possession for and why you would trade it.

321

Returning to the Predictions   Invite students to discuss the predictions that they made before reading the story and that they may have written in their personal journals. Encourage them to discuss whether those predictions changed as they read the story.

Returning to the Purposes for Reading Ask students to discuss how the game board is useful to the characters in the story. (It is used as a game and as firewood; and through trading it provides useful objects, such as a knife and an ax, for some of the characters.)

NOTE: Responses to the Think It Over questions and support for the Write activity appear on page T550.

Story Follow-Up

Think It Over

Encourage reader's response: student page 321.

1. **How did the boy end up with the same kind of object that he had when he left home?** (He traded the game board for a knife, the knife for a spear, the spear for a horse, the horse for an ax, the ax for some wood, and the wood for a gebeta board.)
INFERENTIAL: SUMMARIZING

2. **Do you think that the gebeta board kept the young boy out of trouble? Explain your answer.** (Accept reasonable responses: Yes; the boy was able to help a number of other people.) CRITICAL: MAKING JUDGMENTS

Write

Encourage writer's response: student page 321.

Think about something special that you own. Write sentences that tell what you would trade your possession for and why you would trade it. Encourage students to list reasons to support their decision. CREATIVE: WRITING A PERSONAL RESPONSE

Critical Thinking Activities

Encourage both cooperative and individual responses.

WRITE A NEW STORY ENDING Suppose the boy hadn't gotten a game board back. How might the story have ended? Remind students to consider the sequence of events. CREATIVE: EXPANDING STORY CONCEPTS

PROVIDE PERSONAL OPINIONS Several items were traded in the folktale. How useful might each item have been to the boy? Have small groups of students figure out the boy's best trade and his worst trade. CRITICAL: MAKING JUDGMENTS

INFORMAL ASSESSMENT

Critical thinking activities provide ample opportunities to note and assess important reading behaviors. Almost all **judgments, opinions,** and **conclusions** involve using story **details** to draw high-level **inferences.**

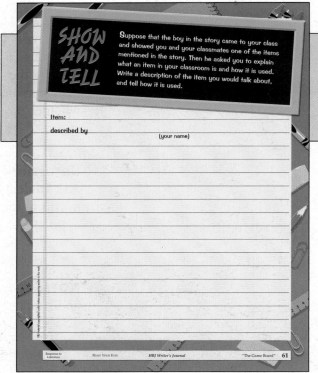

SHOW AND TELL

Suppose that the boy in the story came to your class and showed you and your classmates one of the items mentioned in the story. Then he asked you to explain what an item in your classroom is and how it is used. Write a description of the item you would talk about, and tell how it is used.

Item:

described by _____

(your name)

Response to Literature · FEAST YOUR EYES · HBJ Writer's Journal · "The Game Board" · 61

Writer's Journal

WRITER'S JOURNAL
page 61: Writing a creative response

CLOSE ENCOUNTER OF A WEIRD KIND

by A. F. Bauman • illustrated by Jeffrey Mangiat

from *Space and Science Fiction Plays for Young People*

CLOSE ENCOUNTER OF A WEIRD KIND

	TEACHING OUTLINE	Materials	Language Arts/ Integrated Curriculum	Meeting Individual Needs

Part **1** **Reading Literature**
 Pages T554–T563

	Building Background
	
	 Vocabulary Strategies
	 Key Words (Tested)
	
	 Strategic Reading
	 Preview and Predict
	 Setting a Purpose
	
	 Options for Reading
		Transparency 31
		 Second-Language
		  Support Manual
		 Practice Book p. 86
		 Integrated Spelling p. 45
		 Integrated Spelling T.E.
		  pp. 62–63
		 Student Anthology
		  pp. 322–334
		 Response Card 3: Plot
			Spelling
			 Spelling Pretest
			 Spelling-Vocabulary
			  Connection
				Second-Language Support
				 Vocabulary T555
				 Strategic Reading T556
				
				 Cooperative Reading
				  T557

Part **2** **Responding to Literature**
 Pages T564–T569

	Story Follow-Up
	 Think It Over
	 Write
	
	 Summarizing the Literature
	
	 Appreciating Literature
	
	 Critical Thinking Activities
		Writer's Journal p. 62
		 Practice Book pp. 87–88
		 Integrated Spelling p. 46
		 Integrated Spelling T.E.
		  pp. 62–63
		 Language Handbook
			Vocabulary Workshop
			 Reviewing Key Words
			 Extending Vocabulary
			  Acronyms
			
			 Reading
			 Oral Rereading/Drama
			
			 Writing
			 A Play
			 Movie Posters
			 Play Directions
			
			 Spelling
			 Reviewing Spelling
			  Words
			
			 Listening
			 Safety
			 Heating Methods
			
			 Speaking
			 Life on Leto
				Cooperative Learning
				 T565, T569

Part **3** **Learning Through Literature**
 Pages T570–T576

	Introduce
	 Decoding: Structural
	  Analysis (Tested)
	
	 Review
	 Literary Appreciation:
	  Story Elements
	  (Tested)
	 Literary Appreciation:
	  Play
		Transparency 32
		 Second-Language
		  Support Manual
		 Practice Book pp. 89–90
		 Writer's Journal p. 63
			Science
			 Space Vehicles
			 Planet Report
			 Scientific Puzzle
			
			 Art
			 Planetary Landscapes
			
			 Social Studies
			 Inventors and Inventions
			
			 Math
			 Estimating
			
			 Multicultural
			 Inventors
				Reteach
				 T571
				
				 Challenge
				 T571, T572, T573
				
				 Second-Language Support
				 Structural Analysis T571
				
				 Cooperative Learning
				 T571, T572, T574, T575

KEY WOR

UFO
triumphantly
monotones
ad lib
device
sheepishly
immersion heater

A.F. BAUMAN

Selection Summary

In this humorous science fiction play, three aliens from outer space visit the Wilson children. Theresa, Tom, and Jim are at home alone one evening while their parents go out. As the children play a game, they suddenly hear a loud boom and see blinking lights. They are astonished to discover that a flying saucer has landed in their backyard. Three space aliens from the planet Leto emerge and enter the house. The Letonians explain that their mission is to find a certain earthling invention that keeps "hot things hot" and "cold things cold." After presenting the Letonians with a bowl of ice and an immersion heater, both of which are rejected, Tom finally figures out that the Letonians are looking for a thermos bottle. He gives them one, and they depart happily. When Mr. and Mrs. Wilson return, they discount their children's story until they discover a spacesuit glove dropped by one of the Letonians.

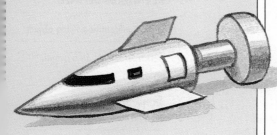

Family Involvement

Encourage family members to discuss science fiction stories they have enjoyed. You may want to suggest that favorite stories found in science fiction books be read to students.

Ann F. Bauman lives on a farm in Garnett, Kansas, where she enjoys gardening, fishing, and stargazing. Bauman recalls that she became interested in plays and science fiction as a child. "My mother was a fantastic storyteller, and my brother loved science fiction," she reports, adding that her love of drama is probably related to the time she spent listening to radio mystery shows when she was young.

Close Encounter of a Weird Kind was inspired by a conversation over lunch. One of Bauman's friends held up his thermos and asked her to guess what it contained. He pointed out that while the thermos kept his coffee hot, it also kept cold drinks cold. He wondered how the thermos knew what to do, and the idea for the play fell into place.

Ann Bauman has published several books and plays for children. In addition to writing, Bauman teaches at Johnson County Community College, where the students in her "Writing Literature for Children" class are sending their own literary efforts out for publication.

ADDITIONAL READING

Other Plays by A. F. Bauman

George and His Good Wife Elsie in *Plays, The Drama Publication for Children.* Plays, Inc., 1979.   AVERAGE

The Third Knot in *Children's Classics* edited by Janet L. Bolinske. Milliken Pub. Co., 1987.   EASY

Other Books About Discoveries

Across Town by Sara. Orchard, 1991.   EASY

Flatfoot Fox and the Case of the Missing Eye by Eth Clifford. Houghton, 1990.   EASY

Fourth Grade Rats by Jerry Spinelli. Scholastic, 1991.   AVERAGE

Outdoor Fun edited by Catherine Ripley. Joy, 1990.   AVERAGE

The True Story of the Three Little Pigs! as told to Jon Scieszka. Viking, 1989.   EASY

Part 1
Reading Literature

Building Background

Access prior knowledge and build vocabulary concepts.

Tell students that the next selection they will read is a play in which three children meet some visitors from outer space. Explain that fantasy stories about space travel and space creatures are called *science fiction*. Invite students to discuss science fiction books, movies, and TV programs with which they are familiar.

Encourage students to talk about characteristics of alien creatures in science fiction books and movies. Develop a web like the one below that shows some features of space creatures.

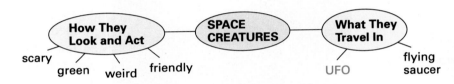

How They Look and Act — SPACE CREATURES — What They Travel In

scary   green   weird   friendly   UFO   flying saucer

KEY WORDS

UFO
triumphantly
monotones
ad lib
device
sheepishly
immersion heater

Vocabulary Strategies

Introduce Key Words and strategies.

Display Transparency 31 or the dialogue below. Have students read the sentences silently, using context clues with phonetic and structural analysis to decode each underlined word and to figure out its meaning.

Transparency 31   Key Words

Characters   IRA, *a human boy*; ZOGORF, *a space alien*; ROBONOID and ORBONOID, *two space robots*

IRA: Wow! A UFO! I've never seen an unidentified flying object!
ZOGORF: (*Triumphantly*): I'm so happy that we made it!
ROBONOID and ORBONOID: (*In monotones*): Observe-there-is-an-earthling-Greetings.
IRA: Hi! Hello! Um . . . how's it going? (*Continues to ad lib*) You speak English?
ZOGORF: (*Holds up a small box*): This device lets us understand all languages.
IRA: (*Sheepishly*): Oh. I should have known. How does it work?
ZOGORF: We heat the liquid in the box by putting this inside. (*Holds up an immersion heater*) Once the liquid is hot, we drink it. Then we understand all languages.

KEY WORDS DEFINED

UFO   unidentified flying object

triumphantly   in a proud, joyful way

monotones   words uttered in a single tone

ad lib   to make up on the spot

device   instrument or tool

sheepishly   awkwardly because of being shy or embarrassed

immersion heater   device that can be put into liquids to heat them

Check students' understanding.

Display the Key Words. Have student pairs create charts like the one below by adding related words or phrases in the second column. Have partners share their chart and discuss how the words in both columns are alike. Encourage students to add additional words or phrases to their chart.   STRATEGY: PRIOR KNOWLEDGE

Key Words	Related Words
device	appliance, tool, object
UFO	spaceship, flying saucer
sheepishly	shyly
ad lib	make up words as you speak
monotones	expressionless voice
immersion heater	gadget that heats the liquid around it
triumphantly	victoriously, happily

GLOSSARY   Encourage students to refer to the Glossary to confirm or to clarify their understanding of the new words.

Integrate spelling with vocabulary.

SPELLING-VOCABULARY CONNECTION   *Integrated Spelling* page 45 reinforces the spelling of abbreviations in the Key Word *UFO* and in other words. The spelling of the Key Word *ad lib* is also included.

SECOND-LANGUAGE SUPPORT   The words *triumphantly* and *sheepishly* may be pantomimed for students. Also, students will benefit from a brief discussion of space- and temperature-related terms (*space, planet, flying saucer, alien, earth; hot, cold, thermos*). (See *Second Language Support Manual.*)

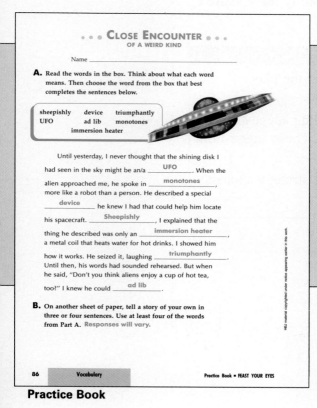

- - - **CLOSE ENCOUNTER** - - -
OF A WEIRD KIND

Name _____

A. Read the words in the box. Think about what each word means. Then choose the word from the box that best completes the sentences below.

> sheepishly   device   triumphantly
> UFO   ad lib   monotones
> immersion heater

Until yesterday, I never thought that the shining disk I had seen in the sky might be an/a ___UFO___ . When the alien approached me, he spoke in ___monotones___ , more like a robot than a person. He described a special ___device___ he knew I had that could help him locate his spacecraft. ___Sheepishly___ , I explained that the thing he described was only an ___immersion heater___ , a metal coil that heats water for hot drinks. I showed him how it works. He seized it, laughing ___triumphantly___ . Until then, his words had sounded rehearsed. But when he said, "Don't you think aliens enjoy a cup of hot tea, too?" I knew he could ___ad lib___ .

B. On another sheet of paper, tell a story of your own in three or four sentences. Use at least four of the words from Part A. **Responses will vary.**

86   Vocabulary

Practice Book • FEAST YOUR EYES

Practice Book

INTEGRATED SPELLING
Abbreviations

Name _____

Read the Spelling Words. Write them on another sheet of paper. Check your spelling.

SPELLING STRATEGY

An abbreviation is a short way to write a word. Most—though not all—abbreviations begin with a capital letter and end with a period. Other abbreviations are short ways of writing numbers or short ways to write popular words.

Ave. = Avenue   2nd = second

Dr. = Doctor   TV = television

Another kind of abbreviation is called an **acronym**. Acronyms are words made from the initials of several words.

UFO = Unidentified Flying Object

Write the abbreviations for the words below.

mister	Mr.
title of a married woman	Mrs.
television	TV
okay	OK
unidentified flying object	UFO
second	2nd
doctor	Dr.
avenue	Ave.
boulevard	Blvd.

FEAST YOUR EYES • "Close Encounter of a Weird Kind"   45

SPELLING WORDS
- ad lib
- Ave.
- Blvd.
- Dr.
- Mr.
- Mrs.
- OK
- 2nd
- TV
- UFO

MEMORY JOGGER

Ad lib means to make things up as you go along. This Memory Jogger will help you remember how to spell this term.

I **had** liberty to **ad lib**.

Integrated Spelling

PRACTICE BOOK
page 86: Reinforcing Key Words

INTEGRATED SPELLING
page 45: Writing and spelling abbreviations

NOTE: These pages may be completed now or after students have read the story.

Strategic Reading

Preview and Predict

Have students preview the literature.

Ask students what they can do to preview a play. (read the title, the cast of characters, the setting, and the stage directions that tell what is happening as the play opens) Have students preview the play and read through the first lines spoken by Mr. Wilson on page 323.

Have students make predictions.

Ask students questions such as the following to help them make predictions about what might happen in the play:

- **What might happen when the children are home alone?**
- **Why might creatures from another planet visit the Wilsons?**
- **Do you think the Letonians will be friendly? Why do you think this?**

PERSONAL JOURNAL Have students add their predictions about the play to their personal journals. Ask students to support their predictions.

Setting a Purpose

Have students set purposes.

Discuss with students what they want to find out as they read the play, based on their preview and on what they know about science fiction stories. Help them use their predictions to set a purpose for reading.

Model purpose-setting, if necessary.

If students have difficulty setting a purpose for reading, offer this suggestion:

I'm going to read to find out whether Mr. and Mrs. Wilson will believe that the Letonians really have visited their children.

> **OPTIONS FOR READING**
>
> **INDEPENDENT READING** Have students read the play silently with their purpose for reading in mind.
>
> **GUIDED READING** Follow the Guided Reading suggestions that appear on pages T557, T559, and T563. These suggestions model strategic reading.
>
> **COOPERATIVE READING** A reader response strategy appears on page T557.

by A. F. Bauman • illustrated by Jeffrey Mangiat
from *Space and Science Fiction Plays for Young People*

Characters

SON
LSON
WILSON } *twins, 12*
SON
SON, 9
ETONIANS, *creatures*
planet Leto

vening, the present.

SETTING: *Living room of the Wilson home. Exit to bedrooms is left; door to outside is center back, with windows on either side; exit to kitchen is right. A coffee table is in middle of room, with couch and chairs arranged around it. A board game is set up on coffee table. Magazines and an evening bag are on couch.*

AT RISE: TOM, THERESA, *and* JIM *are sitting around coffee table, playing the board game.*

JIM (*Moving his piece on the board game*): One, two, three! Hooray! I landed on Boardwalk. I'll buy it.

TOM: Sorry, Jim, you can't. You spent most of your money the last time around buying your third railroad.

THERESA: Yes, Jim. You've got to be careful how you use your money in this game.

JIM: Stop telling me how to spend my money, Theresa! (MR. *and* MRS. WILSON *enter right.*)

MRS. WILSON (*To* JIM *and* THERESA): Did I hear you two fighting again? I thought you all said you'd be good tonight.

TOM: We will, Mom. Don't worry.

MRS. WILSON: All right. I guess I'm a little uneasy about leaving you children here alone.

TOM (*Reassuringly*): Sure, Mom. We understand. But we really are old enough to take care of ourselves.

MR. WILSON (*To* MRS. WILSON): Yes, dear. Tom and Theresa can handle things much better than that last babysitter we had.

JIM: All she did was yell at me. She wouldn't let me play games or watch TV or anything. We just had to be quiet all evening while she talked to her boyfriend on the phone.

MR. WILSON (*Sternly, to* JIM): That's enough, Jim.

THERESA: We'll keep all the lights on, Mom, and all the doors and windows locked. Don't worry.

TOM: And we've got the fire department and police phone numbers right here. (TOM *holds up a small piece of paper.*) And the number of the place where you'll be.

323

Guided Reading

SET PURPOSE/PREDICT: PAGES 322–327 Have students read through page 327 to find out what weird things happen while the children are playing a game.

Cooperative Reading

READER RESPONSE STRATEGY: PAGES 322–325 Have each group of 3–5 students select a leader. Ask group members to read silently, and then encourage the leaders to use dialogue questions such as the one below. (Response Card 3: Plot, on page R64, offers a wide variety of dialogue questions.)

- **What problem do the children face in this section?**

PAGES 326–334 After reading, the discussion leaders might ask:

- **Did you guess what the Letonians wanted?**
- **Were there events in the play that surprised you?**

THERESA: Besides, you'll only be gone two or three hours.

MRS. WILSON (*To* THERESA): All right. But, Theresa, just one more thing—don't you tell Jim any ghost stories. You know what an imagination he has. Those stories of yours give him bad dreams for a week.

THERESA: O.K., Mom, I promise. Go ahead and have a good time.

TOM: Everything's cool. Enjoy yourselves.

MR. WILSON (*To* MRS. WILSON): Come on, dear, we'll be late. (*He picks up evening bag from couch and hands it to her.*)

MRS. WILSON (*To* MR. WILSON): I wouldn't be so worried if we lived in town. Out here the nearest house is two miles away.

MR. WILSON: Everything will be fine, honey. Come on, it's late. Let's go. (*They exit center.* TOM, THERESA, *and* JIM *go to window left, wave, then return to the game.*)

TOM: I think it was my turn. (*They* ad lib *playing game.*)

THERESA: Jim, isn't it about time you put your cat outside?

JIM: I almost forgot. Reginald's in the kitchen. I'll go let him out the back door. (JIM *exits.*)

TOM: Whose turn is it now?

THERESA: Jim's. We'll have to wait for him. (JIM *returns and sits.*)

TOM: It's your turn, Jim. Throw the dice. (*Suddenly, sound of a loud "boom" is heard, followed by a bright flash of light, seen through windows. Then a blinking light is seen through right window.* TOM, JIM, *and* THERESA *jump up, startled.*) What could that be?

324

JIM: Maybe it's a thunderstorm!

THERESA: No, Jim, the moon is bright, and the stars are out.

TOM: It's not a fire. That light keeps going on and off.

JIM (*Excitedly*): I don't smell any smoke.

TOM (*Trying to be calm*): It can't be burglars. They would sneak in quietly.

THERESA: It's O.K. We're safe. All the doors are locked.

JIM (*Sheepishly*): They *were* locked. But remember when I put out the cat?

THERESA: You left the back door unlocked! Oh, no!

TOM: But nobody is coming in, yet. (*Bravely*) I'm going over to the window to see what's making that light. (TOM *walks to window right and peers out.*) Look at that! A huge round thing as big as a fifty-foot-wide saucer.

THERESA: What? Let me see. (*She walks to window.* JIM *follows close behind.*) It does look like a saucer. And it's got a big flashing light on top!

JIM (*Looking out window*): Look—something's opening up on the bottom—it's a set of stairs unfolding down to the ground!

THERESA (*Watching*): And three weird creatures are climbing down!

TOM (*Trying to remain calm*): Well, gang, I guess we've got a UFO right in our own back yard.

THERESA: Those creatures are walking over to our back door! (TOM, JIM, *and* THERESA *run left, huddling close to one another. Sound of footsteps is heard from offstage.*)

JIM: They must be inside the house! What are we going to do?

Teaching Tip You might choose to have students present this selection as a radio play. Guide students in determining what to use for sound effects. Remind students that the audience can only hear a radio play, so they will need to identify the objects each child presents to the Letonians.

': There's nothing we can do. Just try to stop
[ta]king and be cool. (THREE LETONIANS *enter right,
[wal]king stiffly, wearing silvery costumes and green
[lizar]ds. They lift their visors, revealing green faces.
[TO]M, JIM, and THERESA jump back, frightened. LETO-
[NIA]NS speak in robot-like monotones.)

[?] LETONIAN: Do not be afraid.

[?] LETONIAN: We will not harm you.

[?] (Trying to be calm): Who are you?

[?] LETONIAN: We are from the planet Leto.

[THE]RESA (Scared): What do you want?

[?] LETONIAN: We are on a special mission. We have
[bee]n sent to bring something back from the earth to
[our] planet.

[?] LETONIAN: You earthlings have what we need.

[?] LETONIAN: On earth, you have something that
[will] keep cold things cold for a long time. The same
[dev]ice will keep hot things hot for a long time.

[?] LETONIAN: This is a strange but useful item. We
[can]not know how it can tell whether to keep things
[cold] or hot.

[?] LETONIAN: This is our assignment: To bring this
[inve]ntion back to Leto.

[?] LETONIAN: Can you help us?

[? (*H*]elpfully): I know what you need! I'll go get it!
[(He] runs, exits right.)

[THER]ESA: I wonder what he's going after?

[?:] I sure don't know. With his imagination, he
[could] think up just about anything. (JIM returns, carry-
[ing a] bowl of ice. He hands it to 2ND LETONIAN.)
[?:] Here's what you need!

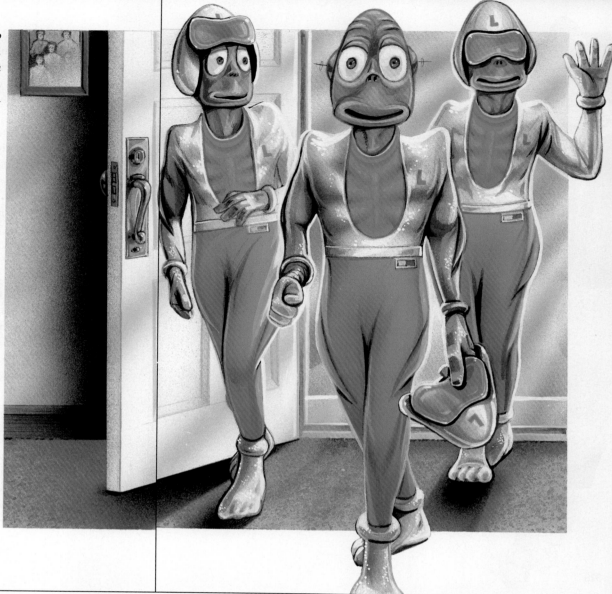

MONITOR COMPREHENSION: PAGES 322–327
**What weird things happen as the children play
a game?** (They hear a loud boom and see a UFO.
Letonians visit, looking for a special invention.)
STRATEGIC READING: RETURNING TO PURPOSE

**What events in the play create a feeling of
suspense?** (The children are home alone, with the
nearest house two miles away. A loud boom is
heard. Blinking lights appear. A door has been left
unlocked.) CRITICAL: SUMMARIZING

SET PURPOSE/PREDICT: PAGES 328–334 Ask
students to predict whether Mr. and Mrs. Wilson
will believe that Letonians have visited their
children. Have students read the rest of the play to
confirm their predictions.

2ND LETONIAN (*Looking in bowl*): We have ice on Leto. Thank you, but this is not what we need.

THERESA: Besides, Jim, ice certainly won't keep hot things hot.

JIM: Oh, now I know! Wait a second; I know just where it is! (JIM *exits right and quickly returns with an immersion heater.*) Mom uses this to heat up her coffee. (*Excited,* 1ST LETONIAN *takes off gloves, revealing green hands. He tries to stuff gloves into pocket, but one falls to floor and remains there, unnoticed.* 1ST LETONIAN *takes immersion heater from* JIM *and examines it.*)

2ND LETONIAN (*To* JIM): Will it keep hot things hot?

JIM: Sure. Mom can keep the coffee in her mug hot all day with that thing.

3RD LETONIAN (*To* JIM): And will it keep things cold?

JIM: No, it won't.

1ST LETONIAN: This is not what we want.

2ND LETONIAN: Our commander will be disappointed if we return from our trip without this invention.

3RD LETONIAN: We are told that it does not cost a lot of—of—of—what is it called?

THERESA: Money?

3RD LETONIAN: Yes, it does not cost a lot of money.

2ND LETONIAN: Our commander told us that almost every household in America has one.

TOM (*Wondering*): What could it be?

THERESA (*Thinking*): Beats me. Let's see—it keeps cold things cold for a long time.

328

1ST LETONIAN: And hot things hot for a long time.

TOM: And it doesn't cost a lot and most Americans have it in their homes.

JIM: At lunchtime, I always have a cold drink.

THERESA: And I always have a hot drink with my lunch.

TOM (*Triumphantly*): Hey, we've got what you need, Letonians! Wait right here. (TOM *runs off stage to kitchen carrying immersion heater, and comes back quickly with a thermos bottle.*) Here it is!

THERESA (*Excited*): Of course! A thermos! Nice going, Tom! Why didn't we think of that before?

JIM (*Also excited*): Yes, the same thing keeps hot things hot and cold things cold!

1ST LETONIAN (*Puzzled*): What is this great invention?

TOM: We call it a thermos bottle. (*Shows thermos to* THREE LETONIANS.) Here, let me show you how it works. You take the lid off, like this, see? Then you put in whatever you want to stay hot or cold.

THERESA: Then you make sure the lid is on tight. (*She takes thermos and lid from* TOM *and screws lid on thermos.*)

1ST LETONIAN: Will it keep cold things cold for a long time?

JIM (*Proudly*): Sure it will! My mom puts ice cubes in it in the morning when she fixes my cold drink. By lunchtime at school, the ice isn't even melted and my drink is icy cold.

2ND LETONIAN: Does this same invention keep hot things hot for a long time?

Expanding the Literature   What clues help you figure out what the Letonians want? (The device keeps hot things hot. It keeps cold things cold. It doesn't cost a lot of money. Almost every American household has one.)   METACOGNITIVE: DRAWING CONCLUSIONS

What happens that helps you predict that the Letonians might leave something behind by accident? (The first Letonian's glove falls to the floor and remains there unnoticed.)
METACOGNITIVE: MAKING PREDICTIONS

Cultural Awareness   Explain that the thermos, also known as a "vacuum bottle" or "Dewar Flask," was invented by British chemist Sir James Dewar in 1892.

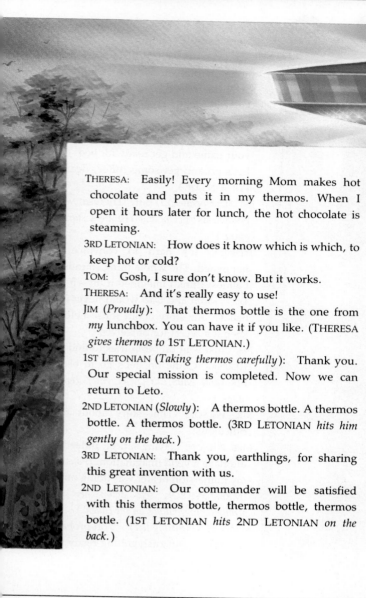

THERESA: Easily! Every morning Mom makes hot chocolate and puts it in my thermos. When I open it hours later for lunch, the hot chocolate is steaming.

3RD LETONIAN: How does it know which is which, to keep hot or cold?

TOM: Gosh, I sure don't know. But it works.

THERESA: And it's really easy to use!

JIM (*Proudly*): That thermos bottle is the one from *my* lunchbox. You can have it if you like. (THERESA *gives thermos to* 1ST LETONIAN.)

1ST LETONIAN (*Taking thermos carefully*): Thank you. Our special mission is completed. Now we can return to Leto.

2ND LETONIAN (*Slowly*): A thermos bottle. A thermos bottle. A thermos bottle. (3RD LETONIAN *hits him gently on the back.*)

3RD LETONIAN: Thank you, earthlings, for sharing this great invention with us.

2ND LETONIAN: Our commander will be satisfied with this thermos bottle, thermos bottle, thermos bottle. (1ST LETONIAN *hits* 2ND LETONIAN *on the back.*)

1ST LETONIAN: We do not need to write down the name of this invention. My co-captain (*Pointing to* 2ND LETONIAN) knows the name well.

3RD LETONIAN: We are very grateful for your help.

1ST LETONIAN: We must return to our planet now. Let us get back to our space vehicle.

JIM: O.K. I'll lock the door after you. (LETONIANS *and* JIM *walk off stage right.* THERESA *and* TOM *walk to window right, look out.*)

TOM: Look, Theresa. They're walking over to their spacecraft.

THERESA: And there they go up the steps. I can't see them any more.

TOM: The steps are folding back up into the spacecraft. (*There is another loud boom and flash of bright light. Flicker of light is seen, then fades and goes off.*)

JIM (*Walking quickly onstage from right*): Wow! What weird visitors!

THERESA: Boy, was I ever scared when they walked into the house.

TOM: Me, too. Maybe they were just as scared of us. But you could never tell by the way they talked.

331

Vocabulary Strategy   Point out the word *co-captain* on page 331, and ask students what prefix and base word they see. (*co-* and *captain*) Mention or have students suggest other words that begin with the prefix *co-*. (*co-worker, copilot, coeducational, cooperate*) Guide students to understand that the prefix *co-* often means "with another." Have students use this information and the sentence context to deduce what a *co-captain* is. (assistant commander of the spacecraft) STRATEGY: CONTEXT CLUES AND STRUCTURAL ANALYSIS

JIM (*Imitating* LETONIANS): Yes, we are scared of you, too, but we have a special mission.

THERESA: Wasn't that something? All they wanted was a thermos bottle.

JIM: Some special mission! I really liked the way they looked.

TOM: Just like space creatures in the movies. (MR. *and* MRS. WILSON *open center door and enter.*)

MR. WILSON (*Taking* MRS. WILSON's *coat*): How did it go, kids? Everything O.K.?

JIM (*Running up to* MR. *and* MRS. WILSON): Mom! Dad! A flying saucer landed in our back yard!

MRS. WILSON (*Humoring* JIM): Really, Jim?

JIM: Yes, Mom. Three space people from the planet Leto came inside our house!

MRS. WILSON (*Still humoring* JIM): My, what an adventure! Jimmy, you've got a big imagination. (TOM *sits and shakes his head.*)

THERESA: But he's right, Mother. They're called Letonians and they came here on a special mission. They talked funny and had green skin and silver suits and gloves and helmets!

MRS. WILSON: Now, Theresa, were you telling Jimmy scary stories again?

THERESA (*Exasperated*): No, Mother. It really happened.

MRS. WILSON: Theresa, you should write books. You're so good at thinking up stories that now even you are beginning to believe them. Anyway, I'm glad you had a nice evening.

MR. WILSON (*Looking around room*): It looks as if playing that game is about all you did while we

332

were gone. Everything's all right. The doors windows are still locked. (*To* MRS. WILSON) honey, I told you nothing would happen.

JIM (*Exasperated*): But it did! It really happe Honest! The Letonians were here, right in our living room.

MRS. WILSON: Yes, dear. Now you three put a your game and get ready for bed. (*To* MR. WILS Let's go and get some coffee, dear. (MR. *and* WILSON *exit.*)

JIM (*Exasperated*): But, Theresa, why won't believe us? (TOM *and* THERESA *start putting the* away.)

THERESA: It's hard to convince them it r happened. The whole thing sounds so unbeliev I almost think I imagined it myself.

TOM: Mom and Dad would never in a million believe our story about those Letonians. Let's keep it a secret for ourselves.

JIM: Just wait till Mom tries to find my thermos

THERESA: Come on, let's go to bed. (*They exit* MR. *and* MRS. WILSON *enter right, holding mugs.*)

MR. WILSON: That story about the spaceshi ridiculous!

MRS. WILSON: Flying saucer, indeed! Theresa al did have a vivid imagination. (*Pause*) I wonder my immersion heater was doing out on the cou (MRS. WILSON *sets down her mug and b straightening pillows on the couch.*)

MR. WILSON (*Sitting left*): You probably forgot t it away in your rush getting ready to go out.

Vocabulary Strategy   Have students identify the context clues that can help them figure out the meaning of the word *exasperated* on page 332. (Theresa's mother does not believe her and Theresa is feeling upset as she speaks, so *exasperated* must be another word for *frustrated* or must mean "out of patience.") Tell students that when a clue is not given in a sentence, they need to think about what is happening at that moment in the play.
STRATEGY: CONTEXT CLUES

MRS. WILSON (*Straightening magazines on coffee table*): But I wasn't in any rush. I had everything put away when we left.

MR. WILSON: O.K., dear, O.K. (*He drinks coffee.* MRS. WILSON *walks toward the chair on right where* 1ST LETONIAN *dropped his glove. With a quizzical look, she goes over and picks it up, holding it up for* MR. WILSON *to see.*)

MRS. WILSON: But where did this silver glove come from? I've never seen anything like it before! (*Musing*) I wonder if the children were telling the truth, after all? (*Quick curtain*)

THE END

THINK IT OVER

1. What does the title of this play mean?

2. What landed in the Wilsons' back yard?

3. Why did the Letonians visit Earth?

4. Do you think Mr. and Mrs. Wilson believed that the Letonians really visited their home? Why do you think as you do?

WRITE

Suppose you were traveling to another planet. Write a list of useful items you would take along. Include the reason you would take each thing.

For discussion of this page, please turn to T577.

THEME WRAP-UP

FUN AND GAMES

The characters in the selections you read had interesting days. Do you think Judy and Peter would have reacted differently from the way the Wilson children did if they had been visited by the Letonians? Tell why you think as you do.

Which adventure would you most like to have shared in? Support your choice with reasons.

WRITER'S WORKSHOP   Suppose the Letonians brought a weird game with them to exchange for the thermos. Make up a name, an object, and rules for the game. Then write a paragraph of information about the game. Include the steps of how to play. Share your paragraph with a group of classmates. You may wish to design a game board and play the game with your classmates.

335

Guided Reading

MONITOR COMPREHENSION: PAGES 328–334
Do Mr. and Mrs. Wilson believe that Letonians have visited their house? (only after they find an unusual silver glove) **Is this what you predicted would happen?** (Responses will vary.)
STRATEGIC READING: CONFIRMING PREDICTIONS

How do the children figure out the Letonians want a thermos? (They try things that might fit the description: ice, an immersion heater, a thermos.)   STRATEGIC READING: SUMMARIZING

Returning to the Predictions   Invite students to discuss the predictions that they made before they began reading and that they may have written in their personal journals. Encourage them to talk about how these predictions changed as they read the play.

Returning to the Purpose for Reading
Ask students what makes Mr. and Mrs. Wilson believe that the Letonians really have visited the children. (After the children go to bed, Mrs. Wilson finds a silver glove and begins to think that the children are telling the truth.)

NOTE: Responses to the Think It Over questions and support for the Write activity appear on page T564.

Part 2
Responding to Literature

Story Follow-Up

Think It Over

Encourage reader's response: student page 334.

1. **What does the title of this play mean?** (Accept reasonable responses: It means a meeting with weird creatures. It describes the meeting between the Letonians and the Wilsons.) INFERENTIAL: SUMMARIZING
2. **What landed in the Wilsons' back yard?** (a spaceship carrying creatures from the planet Leto) LITERAL: NOTING IMPORTANT DETAILS
3. **Why did the Letonians visit Earth?** (They were looking for a device that can keep hot things hot and cold things cold.) LITERAL: RECOGNIZING CAUSE-EFFECT
4. **Do you think Mr. and Mrs. Wilson believed that the Letonians really visited their home? Why do you think as you do?** (Accept reasonable responses: Yes, because they found the glove left by a Letonian; No, because the story was fantastic and because they acted as though they didn't believe the children.) CRITICAL: MAKING JUDGMENTS

Write

Encourage writer's response: student page 334.

Suppose you were traveling to another planet. Write a list of useful items you would take along. Include the reason you would take each thing. Encourage students to consider items that are practical. CREATIVE: WRITING A LIST

Summarizing the Literature

Have students retell the play and write a summary.

Guide students in summarizing the play by helping them begin the problem-solution map below. Have them finish it independently. (See *Practice Book* page 87 on T565.) Students may use their completed map to retell the story and to write a brief summary statement.

Problem: What is the problem?
(When the Wilson children are home alone, strange creatures land in the back yard.)

Solution: How do the children solve the problem?

Result: What happens after the Letonians leave?

STRATEGY CONFERENCE

Ask students what they found difficult about reading the selection. Together, brainstorm strategies, such as visualizing, that might have helped them better understand the play.

NOTE

An additional writing activity for this play appears on page T567.

Appreciating Literature

Have students share personal responses.

Have students work in small groups to discuss the play. Provide a general question such as the following to help the groups begin:

- **What is your favorite part of this play? Explain why.**

PERSONAL JOURNAL   Have students use their personal journals to write about ideas and feelings that are discussed in the groups. You may also refer them to their personal journals after they complete the activities below.

Critical Thinking Activities

Encourage both cooperative and individual responses.

GUESS RIDDLES   "Something that keeps cold things cold and hot things hot" is a kind of riddle—the answer is "a thermos." Suppose the Letonians had wanted something else besides a thermos. Make up a riddle for another household object. Have students write their riddle on paper, trade riddles with a classmate, and guess the answer.   CREATIVE: WRITING RIDDLES

PERFORM A SKIT   What might have happened if Mr. and Mrs. Wilson had returned home before the Letonians left? Have students form small groups and discuss how this might have changed the ending of the play. Suggest that each group present its idea by performing a brief skit.   CRITICAL: SPECULATING

STUDENT SELF-ASSESSMENT

Help students self-assess their participation in the discussion by using questions such as the following:

- Did I listen carefully to other students' ideas?
- Did I add ideas to help clarify the group's ideas?

Writer's Journal

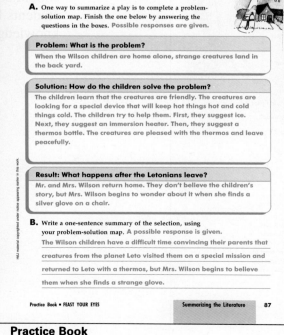

Practice Book

WRITER'S JOURNAL
page 62: Writing a personal response

PRACTICE BOOK
page 87: Summarizing the selection

VO·CAB·U·LAR·Y Workshop

Reviewing Key Words

Have students write the Key Words on individual index cards. Read aloud the following sentences, and ask students to hold up the card containing the word that completes each sentence.

1. *(sheepishly)* Because he is embarrassed, Jim answers _____.
2. *(triumphantly)* Tom speaks _____ after he figures out what the Letonians need.
3. *(device)* The thermos bottle is a good example of a simple but useful _____.
4. *(UFO)* The kind of _____ the Letonians travel in is a flying saucer.
5. *(immersion heater)* Another handy invention is the _____, which Mrs. Wilson uses to heat coffee.
6. *(monotones)* The Letonians speak in _____, which means each creature speaks in a flat tone of voice.
7. *(ad lib)* The stage directions say to _____ playing the game because it is a play.

PRACTICE BOOK
page 88: Identifying acronyms

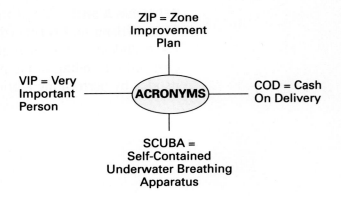

· · · CLOSE ENCOUNTER · · ·
OF A WEIRD KIND

Name _____

A. On each line provided, write the letter of the phrase that matches the abbreviation or acronym.

1. ___d___ AWOL   **a.** unidentified flying object
2. ___f___ NASA   **b.** disk operating system
3. ___b___ DOS   **c.** zone improvement plan
4. ___e___ RAM   **d.** absent without leave
5. ___c___ ZIP   **e.** random-access memory
6. ___a___ UFO   **f.** National Aeronautics and Space Administration

B. If the following were acronyms, what might they mean? Write a possible meaning on the line provided. Possible responses are given.

1. GLUB   Great League of Unusual Baby-sitters
2. DIRT   Dynamic, Industrious, Right Thinkers
3. STAR   Super Talented Athletes of Rochester
4. YSNOD   Youth Saying NO to Drugs
5. SMILE   Students Making Incredibly Laughable Errors

C. Imagine that you and a group of your friends think you see some UFOs and have a "close encounter" with some alien creatures. You want to start a club for people who claim to have had similar experiences. On another sheet of paper, design an advertisement inviting people to join this club. Make up an appropriate acronym for your club's name. Responses will vary.

88   Acronyms   Practice Book ▪ FEAST YOUR EYES

Practice Book

Extending Vocabulary

ACRONYMS Point out that the Key Word *UFO* is an abbreviation. The letters in *UFO* represent the first letters of each word in the phrase *unidentified flying object*. Explain that some abbreviations spell words or are used as words. These words are called *acronyms*. *OPEC* is an acronym. It stands for *Organization of Petroleum Exporting Countries*. Draw the beginning of a web on the board. Write the word *Acronyms* in the inner circle. Then have students complete the web with abbreviations or acronyms and the words they stand for. Discuss why such abbreviations might be useful in communication.

```
                 ZIP = Zone
                 Improvement
                    Plan
                       |
VIP = Very             |            COD = Cash
Important  ——— ( ACRONYMS ) ———    On Delivery
Person                 |
                       |
                 SCUBA =
                 Self-Contained
                 Underwater Breathing
                 Apparatus
```

Have each student make a clue card for an abbreviation or an acronym. Point out that one side of the card should contain the abbreviation or acronym and the other side should contain the words it represents. Then have students form teams and challenge one another's knowledge of abbreviations and acronyms.

READING

Oral Rereading/Drama

Have students form groups of six and perform the scene in which the Letonians first arrive (beginning on page 325 with Jim's line "Maybe it's a thunderstorm!" and ending on page 326 with Jim's line "I know what you need! I'll go get it!"). Encourage students to select another passage for dramatization, if they wish. Model how to read the dialogue and to follow the stage directions. Then have students begin by rereading the passage silently, paying particular attention to the stage directions. Encourage students to choose roles, and then give the actors an opportunity to rehearse the scene before presenting it.   LISTENING/SPEAKING/READING

WRITING

Writing About the Literature

WRITE A PLAY   Have students write their own play about weird or extraordinary events. To help students get started, have them form small groups and imagine that they are at a museum with family members when unusual events begin to happen. Encourage groups to brainstorm ideas for odd events that could occur, but tell them to make sure that some evidence of the event is left behind, as the Letonian's glove is in the play. Write the following diagram on the board to help groups generate ideas:

Event		Evidence
A dinosaur eats the exotic-plant exhibit.	→	Huge footprints remain in the exhibit hall.

Suggest that students refer to the format of the play they have just read as they write their play.   LISTENING/ SPEAKING/WRITING

NOTE: An additional writing activity appears on page T564.

SPELLING

Reviewing Spelling Words

SPELLING WORDS: *2nd, ad lib, Ave., Blvd., Dr., Mr., Mrs., O.K., TV, UFO*

Begin a master list of spelling words by writing down all the words from the spelling lesson and from the additional spelling words list. (See *Integrated Spelling Teacher's Edition.*) Add to this master list several other words that can be abbreviated. Then distribute the master list to groups of three to five students. Ask each group to write the correct abbreviation for each word. Encourage students to use the dictionary if they need help. READING/WRITING/SPELLING

INTEGRATED SPELLING page 46:
Writing abbreviations

INTEGRATED SPELLING
Abbreviations

Name _____

WORD PLAY

Abbreviations are usually made up of one or more letters already in the word. Write the missing letters for each word in the blanks below, and then write each abbreviation on the line.

1. **M** ISTE **R**   Mr.
2. **T** ELE **V** ISION   TV
3. **U** NIDENTIFIED   UFO
   F LYING
   O BJECT
4. **D** OCTO **R**   Dr.
5. **A** **V** ENUE   Ave.
6. **B** OU **L** E **V** AR **D**   Blvd.

SPELLING DETECTIVE

When they got back to the planet Leto, the three Letonians filed a report. As you read it, you will find six misspellings of abbreviations. Circle them and write the correctly spelled abbreviation above each mistake.

We landed in the backyard of the Wilson **Ave.** home at 31 Milton (Aven.) right off 5eton **Blvd.** (Boulvd.) (Letonian coordinates 36^, 47 Ọ, as stated). Three small earthlings were at **Mr.** **Mrs.** the Wilson home. (Mir) and (Msr) Wilson were out for the evening. I would say the trip was **OK** (O.J.) I only wish those earthlings wouldn't call **UFO** our spaceship a (UOF) After all, we know what it is. If they don't, that is their problem.

46

"Close Encounter of a Weird Kind" • FEAST YOUR EYES

Integrated Spelling

Now Appearing at a Theater Near You

AVAILABLE ON PROJECT CARD

Have students design posters for a movie version of "Close Encounter of a Weird Kind." Tell them to include phrases that describe the setting, the characters, and the actions. Display the posters on a blank wall or bulletin board, with a banner across the top that reads "Coming Attractions." WRITING

Strangers at the Door

Remind students that soon after Mr. and Mrs. Wilson leave the house, Theresa, Tom, and Jim have to deal with strangers coming onto their property and even through their unlocked back door. Luckily for the Wilson children, the Letonians mean them no harm. To help students get ready to deal with the approach of real-life strangers, suggest that students invite the school's safety officer or another law-enforcement officer into the classroom to discuss how to avoid letting strangers know they are at home with no parent or other adult on the premises. Before the officer visits, have students brainstorm and write down questions they want to ask. After the interview, have each student work with a partner to create a poster depicting a safety tip mentioned by the officer. If possible, display the posters where students from other classrooms can see them. LISTENING/ SPEAKING/WRITING

Life on Leto

Have pairs of students brainstorm ideas about Letonian culture. Suggest that they think about the customs, food, music, education, homes, recreation, sports, and transportation that might be part of life on the planet Leto. Suggest that partners take notes on their brainstorming session and then prepare a brief presentation for classmates. Have each pair present its version of Letonian culture. Encourage students to discuss the creativity of each version. LISTENING/ SPEAKING/WRITING

LISTENING

Heat Around the World

AVAILABLE ON PROJECT CARD

CULTURAL AWARENESS Point out that devices such as immersion heaters, gas stoves, and microwave ovens are common in the United States as well as in many other parts of the world. Explain that various cultures have different methods of heating their homes and cooking food. The following are examples:

- Many Irish people burn peat moss for heat. Peat moss is cut in chunks from peat bogs.
- In the volcanic regions of Japan, some people have built their homes next to vents in the earth from which hot steam rises. Each of these families keeps a cooking pot outside the house over the vent.

Invite students from various cultural backgrounds to describe the methods of heating homes and of cooking with which they are familiar. Some students may enjoy interviewing people or doing library research to learn more about this topic. LISTENING/SPEAKING/READING/ WRITING

WRITING

The Play's the Thing

COOPERATIVE LEARNING Have students work in groups to brainstorm directions for putting on a play. Explain to students that they should list steps that are necessary to perform any kind of play. Encourage members of each group to suggest ideas. Have students record their directions on a drama poster. Before students write their directions, review the imperative verb form with them. Point out that directions are written directly to the reader, so each sentence usually begins with a verb. LISTENING/ SPEAKING/WRITING

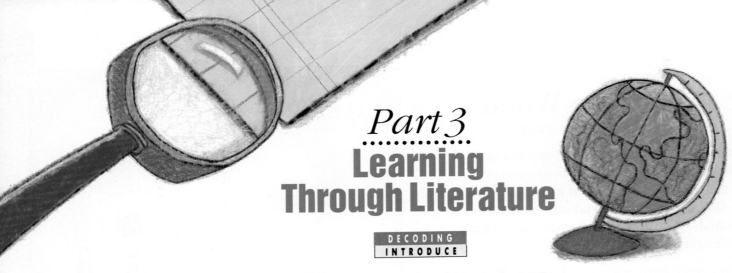

Part 3
Learning Through Literature

DECODING
INTRODUCE

Structural Analysis

OBJECTIVE: *To use base words, prefixes, and suffixes for independent decoding of words*

1   Focus

Explain the value of recognizing prefixes and suffixes.

Remind students that in "Close Encounter of a Weird Kind," the father is uneasy about leaving the children at home and that soon thereafter the Letonians walk stiffly into the house through the back door. Write *uneasy* and *stiffly* on the board, underlining the prefix *un-* and the suffix *-ly*. Explain that knowing how to recognize a word to which a beginning or an ending has been added will help students figure out many new words as they read.

2   Teach/Model

Teach how to decode words.

Tell students that *un-* is a *prefix*, a group of letters added to the beginning of a word, and that it can mean "not." Point out that adding a prefix to a word will change its meaning. Then explain that *-ly* is a *suffix*, a group of letters added to the end of a word, and that it can mean "in a certain way." Tell students that adding a suffix to a word can change the meaning and will change how the word is used.

Display Transparency 32, or write the following paragraph on the board. Then read the sentences aloud.

Transparency 32   Prefixes and Suffixes

Mom asked us not to <u>excite</u> the space aliens. She said they might be <u>excitable</u> after their long trip. Our mission seemed <u>impossible</u>, but we decided it was possible that they were friendly. We told them that they were in a dangerous location, and then we saw their spacecraft disappear.

Model the process.

When I read the word *excitable*, I see the base word *excite* and the suffix *-able*. Seeing these two word parts helps me pronounce *excitable*. I know that *-able* often means "likely to become." Knowing this and using context clues, I can figure out that *excitable* means "likely to become excited."

3 Practice/Apply

Have students determine word meanings.

COOPERATIVE LEARNING Ask students to work in pairs to identify each word with a prefix or a suffix in the remaining sentences. *(impossible, friendly, dangerous, disappear)* Have them make a chart with the following headings: *Word, Prefix, Base Word, Suffix, Word Meaning.* Tell students to use context clues or a dictionary to help them determine the meaning of each word.

4 Summarize

Informally assess the learning.

Check understanding of the lesson by having students compare their chart with those of their classmates. Ask students to explain how using word parts helped them pronounce each word and determine the word's meaning.

Ask students to summarize what they learned. (Recognizing prefixes, base words, and suffixes can help in determining pronunciations and meanings of unfamiliar words.)

MEETING INDIVIDUAL NEEDS

RETEACH Follow the **visual, auditory,** and **kinesthetic/motor** models on page R48.

CHALLENGE Have students write a story about aliens, using words with prefixes or suffixes that they locate in the play.

SECOND-LANGUAGE SUPPORT Help students identify the base word and the affixes in words such as *unlock, reappear, slowly, quietly,* and *player.* (See Second-Language Support Manual.)

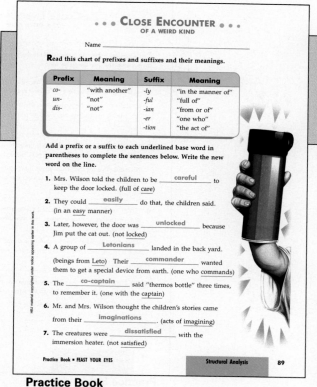

PRACTICE BOOK
page 89: Using structural analysis

Practice Book

Story Elements

OBJECTIVE: *To use setting, characters, and plot to gain meaning*

Review

Review how story elements work together.

Tell students that they can better understand and appreciate "Close Encounter of a Weird Kind" if they see how its characters, setting, and plot all work. Write the chart below on the board, and discuss how Jim's action was related to the setting and how the plot developed because of Jim's action.

Setting	Character's Action	Plot
Children are home alone.	Jim leaves a door unlocked.	The Letonians enter the house.

Practice/Apply

Have students apply the learning.

COOPERATIVE LEARNING Discuss how the play might change if it is set in a school cafeteria. Have student pairs create a new ending for the play.

Summarize

Informally assess the learning.

Discuss how the plot and the characters change when the play is put in a different setting.

Have students summarize the learning. (Characters' actions and setting help develop the plot.)

CHALLENGE Have students imagine that Jim had locked the door. Ask students to write and share a new ending for the play based on this different action.

PRACTICE BOOK
page 90: Analyzing story elements

··· CLOSE ENCOUNTER ···
OF A WEIRD KIND

Name _____

The sentences below are taken from the story. Read them, and then answer the questions that follow.

1. MRS. WILSON *(To MR. WILSON)*: I wouldn't be so worried if we lived in town. Out here the nearest house is two miles away.
   What does this tell the reader about the setting? <u>The place is a rural area, two miles from the nearest neighbor. It doesn't tell anything about the time.</u>

2. TOM *(Reassuringly)*: Sure, Mom. We understand. But we really are old enough to take care of ourselves.
   What does this tell the reader about Tom's character? <u>He feels confident about being alone in a house. He is also concerned about his mother's worries.</u>

3. THERESA: It's O.K. We're safe. All the doors are locked.
   JIM *(Sheepishly)*: They *were* locked. But remember when I put out the cat?
   What does this tell the reader about the characters? <u>Theresa thinks a lock on a door is enough to keep them safe; Jim is careless about safety measures.</u>

4. 1ST LETONIAN: We are on a special mission. We have been sent to bring something back from the earth to our planet.
   What does this tell the reader about the plot? <u>The plot concerns alien beings sent to earth to obtain something. It is a science-fiction story.</u>

90   Story Elements   Practice Book ■ FEAST YOUR EYES

Practice Book

Play

OBJECTIVE: *To identify the characteristics of a play*

Review

Discuss the characteristics of a play.

Remind students that "Close Encounter of a Weird Kind" is a play. Have students recall what a play is. (a story written to be acted) Tell students that a play has a list of characters and gives the reader directions on how to move and to speak the words.

Have students open their books to the first page of the play. Model identifying a play by recognizing its format:

When I look at "Close Encounter of a Weird Kind," I see that the characters are listed at the beginning of the story. That clue tells me that this is a play.

Practice/Apply

Have students apply the learning.

Have students provide other characteristics of a play. Ask volunteers to list these characteristics on the board.

Summarize

Informally assess the learning.

Review with students what they included in their list. Discuss how a play's format helps people act it out.

Have students summarize what they learned. (A play is written to be acted. Directions tell how to speak and to move.)

CHALLENGE Encourage students to select a short story with dialogue. Have students rewrite the story as a play. Remind them to put in parentheses the directions to the reader.

A NEW START

Imagine that your family has just adopted a child. Today the child will arrive at your home. Choose one part of the day, and write a scene in a play about it. Begin with a list of characters, including yourself. Have each character speak at least once.

CHARACTERS: _____ (include your name)

SETTING (time and place): _____

As the curtain rises, the characters are _____
_____ (What are they doing?)

☆ (character's name) _____

☆ (character's name) _____

☆ (character's name) _____

☆ (character's name) _____

Play   FEAST YOUR EYES   HBJ Writer's Journal   "Close Encounter of a Weird Kind"   63

Writer's Journal

WRITER'S JOURNAL
page 63:   Identifying the characteristics of a play

Integrated Curriculum

Space Traffic
AVAILABLE ON PROJECT CARD

COOPERATIVE LEARNING Ask students what they know about various kinds of space vehicles, such as rockets, satellites, space probes, and so on. Have pairs of students research some aspect of space travel and write a report based on their research. Encourage partners to create diagrams of the space vehicles they research. Then have partners share their findings. LISTENING/SPEAKING/READING/ WRITING

Lovely Leto

USE AN ENCYCLOPEDIA Encourage students to draw or to paint an illustration of the imaginary planet Leto. Suggest that they look in an encyclopedia for ideas. If possible, show students some paintings by Chesley Bonestell, the famous painter of planetary landscapes. You may also wish to have students write a description of Leto, modeled after encyclopedia descriptions of real planets. READING/WRITING

Planetary Profiles

USE REFERENCE SOURCES Display a map or a chart of the solar system, and discuss its features. Point out to students that ongoing space exploration is revealing new information about the nature of the solar system. Then have individuals or small groups select and research one of the planets in the solar system. They should write a report about the planet, explaining its basic features and including pictures and other graphic sources if possible. Students might enjoy presenting their report to classmates. LISTENING/SPEAKING/ READING/WRITING

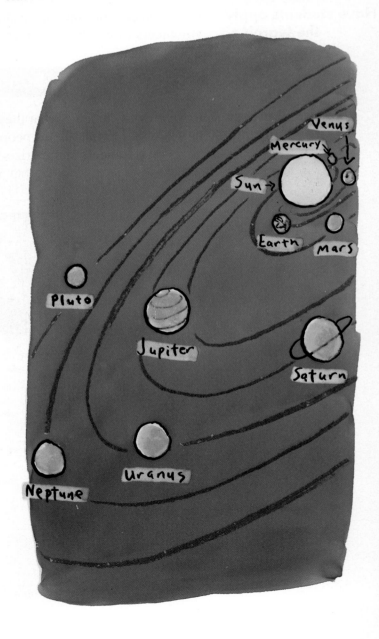

SOCIAL STUDIES

Tools, Toys, and Trinkets

CULTURAL AWARENESS   Point out that some inventions, such as the thermos and the immersion heater in the play, have interesting histories. Explain that inventions and inventors from all around the world have had a great impact on civilization. For example, Granville T. Woods made significant contributions to the development of America's railroads. Have students work in groups of three and brainstorm an invention to research. Possible topics include the automobile, telephone, telegraph, TV, radio, electric refrigerator, aluminum can, fork, and button. Groups should prepare an oral report on the history of their invention. Encourage students to include pictures or diagrams if possible.   LISTENING/SPEAKING/READING/WRITING

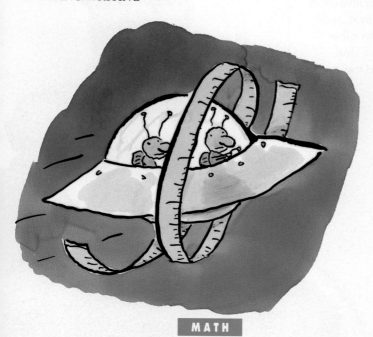

MATH

How Wide Is It?

AVAILABLE ON PROJECT CARD

COOPERATIVE LEARNING   Remind students that when Tom first sees the Letonian spacecraft, he says it is "as big as a fifty-foot-wide saucer." Tell students that Tom is making an *estimate,* or a *guess,* about the size of the saucer and that in order to find out how wide it really is, he would need to measure it. Have students work in small groups to estimate the height, width, and length of various objects in the classroom and then to measure those objects to see how accurate their estimates were. Encourage each group to create a chart showing their estimates and the actual measurements of the objects and to share their chart with classmates. Each group will need a tape measure or yardstick for this activity. LISTENING/SPEAKING/WRITING

SCIENCE

Why in the World?

"Close Encounter of a Weird Kind" includes many scientific puzzles, such as *How does a thermos work?* and *Why do ice cubes melt in warm weather?* Have students research one of these puzzles or another puzzle that they would like to solve. Have students take notes when researching. Ask volunteers to present their findings to classmates. Encourage students to compare their findings and to discuss why they agree or disagree with one another.   LISTENING/SPEAKING/READING/WRITING

Fire and Ice

READ ALOUD TO STUDENTS:

HOW LONG HAVE WE BEEN

ABLE TO KEEP "HOT THINGS

HOT AND COLD THINGS

COLD"? People have been using fire for heating and ice for cooling for thousands of years. Fire is still the most common way to cook and heat, but keeping things cold is another story.

In 1851, the first patent for a refrigeration machine went to Dr. John Gorrie. He was working on ways to keep rooms cool for his patients with malaria.

During the 1940s, African American Frederick Jones invented the first truck refrigeration system, revolutionizing the food industry. He studied refrigeration on his own at the public library and then set to work to solve the problem of food spoiling in unrefrigerated trucks. Jones's invention allowed frozen foods to be transported by truck throughout the United States. Later Jones designed refrigeration systems for the United States Army and Marines to keep food cold in the field.

Who put heating and cooling together and invented the thermos? This honor belongs to British chemist James Dewar, who created the first vacuum flask—or thermos—in 1892. ∎

ACTIVITY CORNER

▪ Available on Project Card
Invite groups of students to research other inventions such as the automatic lubricator for engines created by Elijah McCoy or the traffic light invented by Garrett Morgan. Have them explain how each invention changed the way we live.

▪ Have groups of students hold an "Invention Convention," where each group creates and displays an invention that would improve people's lives, such as a robot room cleaner. Invite other classes, parents, administrators, and community members to attend the convention.

*T*hink of how John Gorrie, Frederick Jones, and James Dewar have made life more comfortable.

Frederick M. Jones' Air Conditioning Unit patented July 12, 1949

THEME WRAP-UP

Fun and Games

Remind students that the selections in this theme told about characters who had some very unusual days. Guide students to recall that they read about a fantastic game, a gift, and a useful invention. Explain that the questions on page 335 will help them think further about the ideas presented in these selections.

Note that pages T578–T579 provide support for applying the writing process to the last question.

THEME WRAP-UP

FUN AND GAMES

The characters in the selections you read had interesting days. Do you think Judy and Peter would have reacted differently from the way the Wilson children did if they had been visited by the Letonians? Tell why you think as you do.

Which adventure would you most like to have shared in? Support your choice with reasons.

WRITER'S WORKSHOP Suppose the Letonians brought a weird game with them to exchange for the thermos. Make up a name, an object, and rules for the game. Then write a paragraph of information about the game. Include the steps of how to play. Share your paragraph with a group of classmates. You may wish to design a game board and play the game with your classmates.

335

Theme Wrap-Up

DISCUSSION QUESTIONS, PAGE 335

The characters in the selections you read had interesting days. Do you think Judy and Peter would have reacted differently from the way the Wilson children did if they had been visited by the Letonians? Tell why you think as you do. Have students think about what Judy and Peter are like and imagine them in a new situation. (Accept reasonable responses: No, because they were able to adjust to unusual situations, too.) CRITICAL: AUTHOR'S CRAFT/IDENTIFYING WITH CHARACTERS

Which adventure would you most like to have shared in? Support your choice with reasons. Suggest that students imagine themselves in each situation and think about what they would have done. (Responses will vary.) CRITICAL: EXPRESSING PERSONAL OPINIONS

WRITER'S WORKSHOP See pages T578–T579 for applying the writing process. **Suppose the Letonians brought a weird game with them to exchange for the thermos. Make up a name, an object, and rules for the game. Then write a paragraph of information about the game. Include the steps of how to play. Share your paragraph with a group of classmates. You may wish to design a game board and play the game with your classmates.** You may prefer to allow students to respond in their own way. WRITING PROCESS: A PARAGRAPH OF INFORMATION

Writer's Workshop

PARAGRAPH OF INFORMATION

For More Discussion & Practice:

LANGUAGE HANDBOOK

Discuss with students what their favorite board games are. Ask if they had any trouble reading or understanding the directions when they first played the game. Then invite them to describe how they might explain the game to a friend. Talk about what they would need to say to make their explanation clear so that their friend could easily understand and play the game. Suggest that students refer to the Handbook in the *Writer's Journal* as they write, revise, and proofread their paragraphs of information.

Prewriting

Before students begin to write, invite them to imagine what kind of games the Letonians may enjoy playing. Have students

- think about their audience and their purpose.
- use a chart to organize ideas for their game. Encourage students to include lists of materials needed and steps telling how to play. Remind students to put the steps in order. Their charts may resemble the following:

Game Name: Planet Hoppers			
Introduction	**Materials**	**Steps/Rules**	**Object**
board game: interplanetary race	board tokens for spaceships dice	1. Put tokens on *Start*. 2. Throw dice. 3. can move only if no one is in the spaceship	first to land on Leto

Encourage students to use their imaginations, but remind them to keep the game simple enough to be described in one paragraph.

Drafting

Invite students to write a draft of the paragraph of information. Remind them to

- write a topic sentence that identifies the game.
- refer to their prewriting chart to describe the rules and steps for playing.
- end with a statement explaining how to win the game.
- write freely without worrying about spelling, punctuation, or grammar.

COMPUTER CONNECTION   Students may want to use a computer during the revising stage so that they can easily modify and rearrange the details in their paragraphs.

Responding and Revising

Suggest that each student read his or her paragraph aloud to a partner. Offer the following tips for partners to discuss. Then have students revise their work.

- Are details included that do not relate to the game? If so, cut them.
- Does the paragraph clearly explain how to play the game? If not, use clear, exact words. (See the Language/Literature Link below.)
- Does the paragraph end with a sentence that tells how a player can win the game? If not, add or replace a sentence to explain this.

STUDENT SELF-ASSESSMENT OPTION   Students may use the Writing Self-Assessment Checklist in the *Portfolio Teacher's Guide*. Suggest that as they use the checklist, they focus on the organization of the paragraph and on the effective use of adjectives.

Proofreading

Offer these tips to help students proofread their work and make changes:

- Look for errors in capitalization and punctuation.
- Check to see that the first line of the paragraph is indented.
- Draw a line around any words that appear to be misspelled. Find out how to spell them correctly.

Publishing

If you wish, discuss with students options for publishing their paragraphs of information. Some students may want to explain their game and save their paragraphs in their reading/writing portfolios. Others may prefer to display their game and their paragraphs in a game corner.

LANGUAGE/LITERATURE LINK

Using Exact Words

Explain that when writing a paragraph of information, writers need to use exact words to present their facts so that readers can clearly picture and understand the subject. Discuss with students why the second of the two sentences below is more exact.

1. Someone can move something if no one is there.
2. A player can move a game piece to a space only if no game piece is already in the space.

Suggest to students that they check their work to make sure they have used exact words.

Speaking Option

SHOW AND TELL   The Writer's Workshop may be adapted for students to plan an oral presentation of the paragraph of information. Encourage students to follow the guidelines offered for Prewriting, Drafting, and Responding and Revising. Offer the following tips to help students give their presentations:

- Practice reading your paragraph so that you can present your information clearly.
- If you designed a game board, hold it up so that the audience can see it as you explain the rules.
- Make eye contact with the audience.

Invite each student to give his or her oral presentation to a small group of classmates.

For pacing suggestions, see page T582.

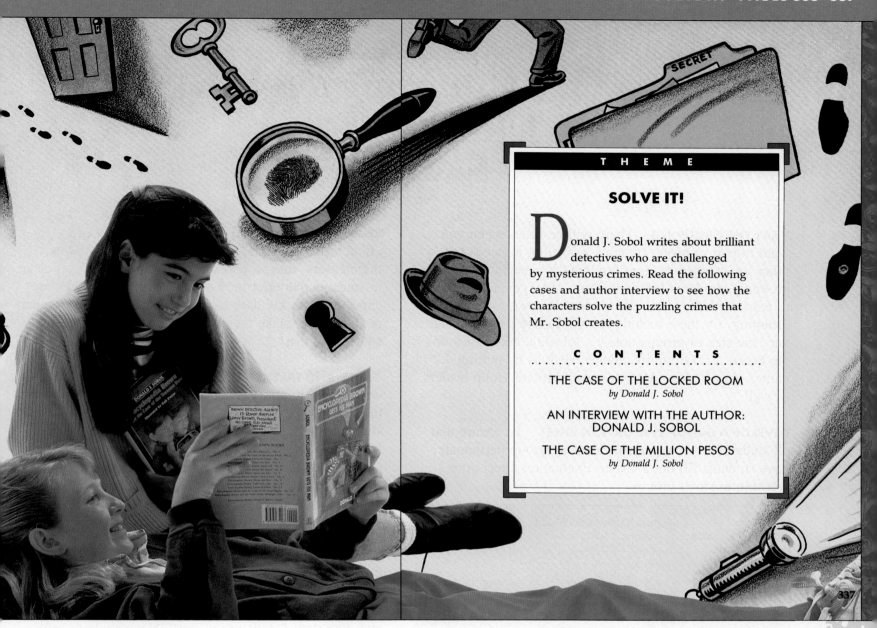

337

Discussing the Theme

Encourage students to look at the picture and read the theme focus on Student Anthology page 337. Ask students to share the titles of any mysteries they have read. Talk about what happens in a mystery story. Then discuss how a mystery is like a puzzle. Invite students to read the selection titles and speculate, based on the titles and the picture, what kind of puzzling crimes will be solved in this theme.

Reading/Writing Portfolio

Point out to students that they should keep their writing responses for the "Solve It!" selections in their portfolios. Remind them also to add to their personal journals any thoughts and ideas about books they have read independently.

Managing the Literature-Based Classroom

Management Options

VARY THE GROUPING   There will be times when you want to pair or group students according to needs but other times when random grouping is acceptable. When grouping choice is left to students, they generally choose to work with the same classmates. To ensure variation in grouping, try these techniques: (1) Rotate members and vary the size of groups; make a schedule and post it on the board. (2) Group by chance, such as by pulling names out of a hat. Also, be sure to rotate group leaders as well.

DEVELOP A GROUP EVALUATION SHEET   To ensure that all students in a cooperative learning group participate, have students fill out a Group Evaluation Sheet after working in small groups.

Group Evaluation Sheet

Student's Name _____

Date _____
Activity _____

1. Did I participate in group discussion?   yes ___ no ___
2. Did I listen to what other group members
   were saying?   yes ___ no ___
3. Did I keep to the topic?   yes ___ no ___
4. Did the group meet its goal?   yes ___ no ___
5. Did the members work together well?   yes ___ no ___
Positive Comments: _____

_____

PACING   This theme has been designed to take about two weeks to complete, depending on your students' needs.

Meeting Individual Needs

STUDENTS AT RISK   To help motivate alienated, uninterested students, refer them to a file of riddles, brainteasers, mazes, and short whodunits. Make it clear to students that after they use these materials, they are expected to tackle their assignments. During independent reading time, make these materials available for all students to use.

GIFTED AND TALENTED   Have students work together to write a two-minute mystery. Encourage students to first brainstorm story problems and solutions. Then have each student think up clues. Students may want to use their idea in the letter for the Writer's Workshop. *Challenge Cards* provide additional activities to challenge students. Challenge notes throughout the lesson plans suggest additional activities to stimulate critical and creative thinking.

SPECIAL EDUCATION STUDENTS   Students who have difficulty remembering details may find it hard to solve the mysteries in this theme. Encourage them to use graphic organizers to take notes about characters, events, and important details in the story. Have students refer back to these notes as they read the story and look for clues.

LIMITED ENGLISH PROFICIENT STUDENTS   Have students complete the Vocabulary Strategies and Vocabulary Workshop for "The Case of the Locked Room" and "The Case of the Million Pesos" in small groups. Include English-proficient students in the groups. Second-Language Support notes throughout the lesson plans offer strategies to help students acquiring English to understand the selections.

MYSTERY

The Case of the Locked Room

ABOUT THE AUTHOR   A master of mystery, Donald J. Sobol is the creator of the popular Encyclopedia Brown detective series. Among Sobol's many awards is the Edgar from the Mystery Writers of America.

SELECTION SUMMARY   The puzzle in this mystery is how Marty Scopes replaces ice cubes with ginger ale in a glass that has been locked in a safe in a locked room, without blind Archer Skeat hearing him. The solution is that the ice cubes are really frozen ginger ale, and they melt while Marty waits in the hall.

Building Background

Provide background and access prior knowledge about mysteries.

Point out that "The Case of the Locked Room" is a mystery. Invite students to explain what makes a story a mystery. (It has a puzzle or a crime that needs to be solved.) Then have students tell how they read a mystery differently from other stories. Develop a list of their suggestions, such as the one below.

Tips for Reading a Mystery

1. Look for clues to the solution as you read.
2. Think about what did not happen as well as what did happen.
3. Evaluate each detail, thinking about its possible importance.

Strategic Reading

Help students quickwrite predictions and set purposes.

Ask students to read the title and the first two paragraphs on page 339 and consider mystery stories they have read. Have them predict what kind of mystery might involve a locked room.

Ask students to write in their personal journals what they think will happen in the story. Remind them that they can change their predictions as they read.

STUDENT-SET PURPOSE   Help students use their predictions to set a purpose for reading "The Case of the Locked Room."

TEACHER-SET PURPOSE   If students have difficulty setting a purpose independently, offer this suggestion:

> **I'm going to read to find out how Marty tricks Archer out of ten thousand dollars.**

Have students read the mystery with their purposes for reading in mind.

TEACHING TIP

Point out that this selection is preceded by a quote from the author with additional author information. Have students read this information before beginning the mystery. Encourage students to discuss Sobol's purpose for reading.

SECOND-LANGUAGE SUPPORT   Discuss the meaning of *puzzle* and *mystery*. Talk about puzzles students have worked on. Relate the concept of a mystery to a puzzle made up of many separate pieces that fit together to make a picture. Explain that a mystery story is like a puzzle for the reader to put together. (See *Second-Language Support Manual*.)

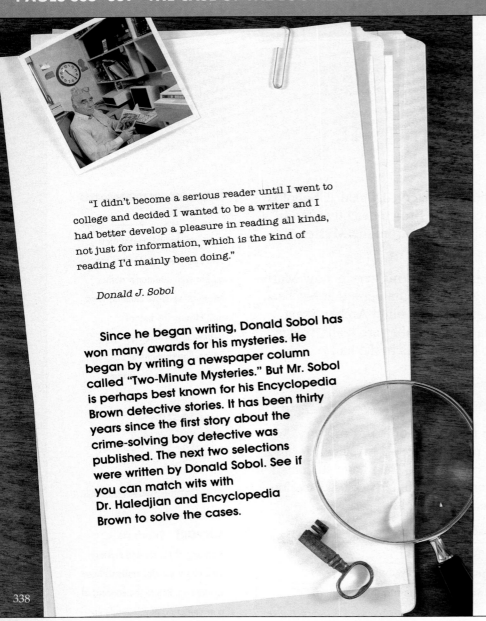

> "I didn't become a serious reader until I went to college and decided I wanted to be a writer and I had better develop a pleasure in reading all kinds, not just for information, which is the kind of reading I'd mainly been doing."

Donald J. Sobol

Since he began writing, Donald Sobol has won many awards for his mysteries. He began by writing a newspaper column called "Two-Minute Mysteries." But Mr. Sobol is perhaps best known for his Encyclopedia Brown detective stories. It has been thirty years since the first story about the crime-solving boy detective was published. The next two selections were written by Donald Sobol. See if you can match wits with Dr. Haledjian and Encyclopedia Brown to solve the cases.

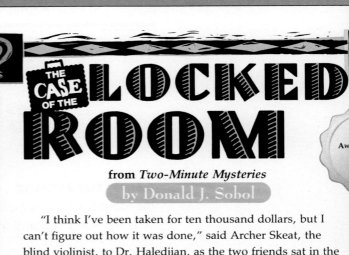

THE CASE OF THE LOCKED ROOM

from *Two-Minute Mysteries*

by Donald J. Sobol

"I think I've been taken for ten thousand dollars, but I can't figure out how it was done," said Archer Skeat, the blind violinist, to Dr. Haledjian, as the two friends sat in the musician's library.

"Last night Marty Scopes dropped by," continued Skeat. "Marty had a ginger ale—and we got to chatting about the locked room mysteries till I made this crazy ten-thousand-dollar bet.

"Marty then went to the bar over there, filled a glass with six cubes of ice and gave it to me. He took a bottle of ginger ale and left the room.

"I locked the door and the windows from the inside, felt to make sure that Marty's glass held only ice, and put it into the wall safe behind you. Then I turned off the lights and sat down to wait.

"The bet was that within an hour Marty could enter the dark locked room, open the locked safe, take out the glass, remove the ice, pour in half a glass of ginger ale, lock the safe, and leave the room, locking it behind him—all without my hearing him!

illustrated by Steven Meyers

Second-Language Support
Some students may have trouble understanding the phrase *I've been taken for ten thousand dollars*. Ask them what the word *taken* means to them. Then explain that the phrase is an expression that means "I've been fooled or tricked out of something."

Expanding the Literature   Why does Archer, who is blind, turn out the lights before sitting down to wait for Marty? (Marty is not blind. With the lights turned off, it will be more difficult for Marty to enter the room and find the safe without being heard.)   INFERENTIAL: DRAWING CONCLUSIONS

"When the alarm rang after an hour, I had heard nothing. Confidently, I unlocked the door. I kept Marty whistling in the hall when I crossed the room to the opposite wall and opened the safe. The glass was inside. By heavens, it was half filled with ginger ale and only ginger ale. I tasted it! How did he do it?"

"Undoubtedly by means of an insulated bag," replied Haledjian after a moment's thought. "There is nothing wrong with your hearing. But no man could have heard—"

Heard what?

Solution

Ice melting. Marty had brought with him frozen cubes of ginger ale. After setting up the bet, he had slipped the ginger ale cubes into the glass. While they melted in the glass inside the safe, Marty waited in the hall!

THINK IT OVER

1. Describe the mystery that Archer Skeat was trying to solve.

2. Why was it important that Marty keep whistling while Archer Skeat crossed the room to open the safe?

WRITE

Write a clue that would have helped Archer Skeat solve the mystery.

341

Returning to the Predictions   Review with students the predictions that they made before reading and that they may have written in their personal journals. Encourage them to talk about whether their predictions changed as they read the story.

Returning to the Purposes for Reading
Ask students how Marty tricked Archer out of ten thousand dollars. (Marty made a bet with Archer that he couldn't lose, probably because he had planned it beforehand.)

NOTE: Responses to the Think It Over questions and support for the Write activity appear on page T586.

Story Follow-Up

Think It Over

Encourage reader's response: student page 341.

1. **Describe the mystery that Archer Skeat was trying to solve.** (He could not figure out how Marty had entered a locked and dark room and replaced ice cubes with ginger ale in a glass locked in a safe without Archer's hearing him.)
   INFERENTIAL: SUMMARIZING

2. **Why was it important that Marty keep whistling while Archer Skeat crossed the room to open the safe?** (Archer could hear where Marty was if he whistled.)   INFERENTIAL: DRAWING CONCLUSIONS

Write

Encourage writer's response: student page 341.

Write a clue that would have helped Archer Skeat solve the mystery. Suggest that students list important story details. Then have them decide where in the story they might be able to most logically insert a clue.   CREATIVE: INVENTING NEW SCENES

Critical Thinking Activities

Encourage both cooperative and individual responses.

CREATE A PLAN OF ACTION   What detail was vital to the success of Marty's plan? What might he have done if this detail did not exist? Suggest that students work in small groups to brainstorm how Marty might have succeeded in fooling Archer if Archer were not blind.   CREATIVE: INVENTING NEW SCENES

DISCUSS PROS AND CONS   Do you think that Archer should pay the bet? Encourage students to discuss the pros and cons of this issue with a partner.   CRITICAL: MAKING JUDGMENTS

INFORMAL ASSESSMENT

Critical thinking activities provide ample opportunities to note and assess important reading behaviors. Almost all **judgments, opinions,** and **conclusions** involve using story **details** to draw high-level **inferences.**

Writer's Journal

WRITER'S JOURNAL
page 64:   Writing a personal response

An Interview with the Author:
Donald J. Sobol

Reading the Interview

Help students set a purpose for reading.

Point out to students that it takes a clever person to write a mystery story. Ask students what they feel they learned about the author of "The Case of the Locked Room," Donald J. Sobol, from reading the story and the quote and information on Student Anthology page 338.

Explain to students that they are going to read an interview with Donald Sobol. Ask students what questions they would ask Sobol if they could speak to him in person. Write their questions on the board. Then suggest that students read the interview to see whether their questions about Sobol are answered.

Responding to the Inverview

Return to the purpose for reading.

Have students tell whether any of their questions were answered and, if so, what Donald Sobol's responses were. Then encourage students to suggest additional questions they would like to ask the author.

Encourage students to respond creatively.

You may wish to select one of the following activities for responding to the interview:

COOPERATIVE LEARNING: WRITING A MYSTERY STORY
Remind students how Donald Sobol goes about writing a mystery story. Invite students to work in small groups and try Sobol's technique for writing a mystery story. Encourage them to think of the ending of the story first—who did what, how it was done, and so on. Then have students work together to write the story. Invite one member of each group to read the finished mystery aloud.   LISTENING/SPEAKING/READING/WRITING

PERSONAL JOURNAL: KEEPING YOUR KERNELS   Remind students that Donald Sobol says that he keeps files in which he saves all kinds of bits and pieces of information based upon everyday things that spark his interest. Invite students to keep a record of story "kernels" that spark their interest. Encourage them to be especially observant for five days and to jot down any events that could be the ideas for funny, interesting, or mysterious stories. At the end of the five days, invite students to share some of their "kernels."   LISTENING/SPEAKING/READING/WRITING

SECOND-LANGUAGE SUPPORT Explain to students that *gimmicks* in a story are tricks or things that are not easy to see. A gimmick in a mystery might be a clever, perhaps a surprise, solution to the story.

An Interview with the Author:

DONALD J. SOBOL

Donald J. Sobol works hard to write the mysteries that never seem to stump the amazing Encyclopedia Brown. In this interview, Mr. Sobol shares with writer Ilene Cooper some of the tricks of his trade and some good tips for future writers.

MS. COOPER: How do you write the Encyclopedia Brown books? I've read that you keep files where you store all kinds of interesting facts you might use in stories.

MR. SOBOL: That's correct, Ms. Cooper, I keep files. And what goes into my files are simply what I call gimmicks. I think I have forty categories in all. What happens in the construction of the mystery story for me is that I pull out a file and the heading is, let's say, "food," and I rifle through whatever notes I have in that file under "food" until something ignites, or sparks me. I use that as the solution. I do not start to write the

mystery until I already know how the story's going to end, who did it, how it was done, and so forth. The solution takes about two weeks. The rest of the writing takes about two days.

MS. COOPER: Where do you get these gimmicks, these kernels of ideas that you use?

MR. SOBOL: Everywhere. They come from my five senses, but mainly from what I see and what I read. We all know that reading is the other side of writing and if you don't read, you probably won't enjoy writing. For those who want to write, it's especially important, but even for those who don't want to pursue writing as a career, you're going to deprive yourself of an awful lot of pleasure down through the years if you don't read.

MS. COOPER: What advice do you have for young writers?

MR. SOBOL: I tell them to keep at it, keep reading, keep writing, and keep trying to find out what makes people and everything around you tick.

342

Expanding the Interview   Donald Sobol says that "reading is the other side of writing." What do you think he means? Do you agree with him? (Accept reasonable responses: Sobol feels that people who enjoy reading would most likely enjoy writing. He feels that readers are better able to be writers, since reading, like everyday life, adds to a person's experience.)
INFERENTIAL: DRAWING CONCLUSIONS

THE CASE OF THE MILLION PESOS

from *Encyclopedia Brown Gets His Man*

by Donald J. Sobol

THE CASE OF THE MILLION PESOS

	TEACHING OUTLINE	Materials	Language Arts/ Integrated Curriculum	Meeting Individual Needs

Part 1 Reading Literature
 Pages T592–T598

	Building Background
	
	 Vocabulary Strategies
	 Key Words (Tested)
	
	 Strategic Reading
	 Preview and Predict
	 Setting a Purpose
	
	 Options for Reading
		Transparency 33
		 Second-Language
		   Support Manual
		 Practice Book p. 91
		 Integrated Spelling p. 47
		 Integrated Spelling T.E.
		   pp. 64–65
		 Student Anthology
		   pp. 344–350
		 Response Card 8:
		   Written Conversation
			Spelling
			 Spelling Pretest
			 Spelling-Vocabulary
			   Connection
				Second-Language Support
				 Vocabulary T593
				 Strategic Reading T594,
				   T597
				
				 Cooperative Reading
				 T595

Part 2 Responding to Literature
 Pages T599–T603

	Story Follow-Up
	 Think It Over
	 Write
	
	 Summarizing the Literature
	
	 Appreciating Literature
	
	 Critical Thinking Activities
		Writer's Journal p. 65
		 Practice Book p. 92
		 Integrated Spelling p. 48
		 Integrated Spelling T.E.
		   pp. 64–65
		 Language Handbook
			Vocabulary Workshop
			 Reviewing Key Words
			 Extending Vocabulary
			   Content-Area Words
			
			 Reading
			 Oral Rereading/Readers
			   Theatre
			
			 Writing
			 A Story
			 Puns
			 Baseball Cards
			
			 Spelling
			 Reviewing Spelling
			   Words
			
			 Speaking
			 Radio Broadcast
			
			 Listening
			 Poems and Songs
				Cooperative Learning
				 T600, T603

				  KEY WO...
				 internation...
				 double
				 discouraged
				 fielded
				 innocent
				 framed
				 testify

Part 3 Learning Through Literature
 Pages T604–T610

	Introduce
	 Vocabulary: Multiple-
	   Meaning Words
	
	 Review
	 Comprehension:
	   Drawing Conclusions
	   (Tested)
	 Literary Appreciation:
	   Figurative Language
		Transparency 34
		 Second-Language
		   Support Manual
		 Practice Book
		   pp. 93–95
			Social Studies
			 Maps
			 Baseball Reports
			 Baseball History
			
			 Math
			 Estimating
			
			 Art
			 Making Money
			
			 Science
			 Classifying Fingerprints
			
			 Multicultural
			 Money
				Challenge
				 T605, T606, T607
				
				 Second-Language Support
				 Multiple-Meaning Words
				 T605
				
				 Cooperative Learning
				 T607, T608, T609

DONALD SOBOL

Selection Summary

Encyclopedia Brown solves a bank robbery in Mexico while sitting on second base in Idaville, talking to his friend Tim Gomez. Tim's Uncle Duffy, a famous Mexican baseball star, is in jail, accused of stealing one million pesos. Tim is convinced that Duffy was framed by his longtime rival, Pedro Morales. Morales told the police that he overheard an argument between Duffy and another man in which Duffy said he'd counted his share of the stolen pesos that afternoon and found one thousand pesos missing. Morales even produced a handful of the stolen pesos and claimed the bills had blown out of Duffy's open window during the argument. Encyclopedia proves Duffy's innocence by figuring out that it would take five days and nights—not one afternoon—to count half a million pesos.

Donald Sobol lives in Florida with his family, where he enjoys scuba diving, boating, fishing, and restoring antique cars. He became a full-time writer at age thirty; since then he has completed almost twenty *Encyclopedia Brown* books and various historical books, including *The First Book of Medieval Man* and *The Wright Brothers at Kitty Hawk*. His first *Encyclopedia Brown* book was rejected twenty-six times, but once he found a publisher, he quickly built up an enthusiastic audience. He says, "Readers constantly ask me if Encyclopedia Brown is a real boy. The answer is no. He is, perhaps, the boy I wanted to be—doing things I wanted to read about but could not find in any book when I was ten."

ADDITIONAL READING

Other Books by Donald J. Sobol

Encyclopedia Brown's Book of the Wacky Outdoors. William Morrow, 1987. AVERAGE

Encyclopedia Brown and the Case of the Disgusting Sneakers. William Morrow, 1990. AVERAGE

The Wright Brothers at Kitty Hawk. Scholastic, 1987. AVERAGE

Other Books About Mysteries and Numbers

How Much Is a Million? by David M. Schwartz. Lothrop, Lee & Shepard, 1985. EASY

Lost in the Amazon: A Miss Mallard Mystery by Robert Quackenbush. Pippin Press, 1990. AVERAGE

Sebastian (Super Sleuth) and the Mystery Patient by Mary Blount Christian. Macmillan, 1991. AVERAGE

Family Involvement

Encourage family members to discuss times when they were confronted by a mystery such as losing or misplacing something. Suggest that students ask family members how they went about trying to solve the mystery and whether the mystery was finally solved.

Part 1
Reading Literature

Building Background

Access prior knowledge and build vocabulary concepts.

Inform students that the next selection, "The Case of the Million Pesos," tells about a bank-robbery mystery set in Mexico and solved by super-sleuth Encyclopedia Brown. Ask students to recall the elements of a mystery story.

Explain that the money stolen in the story was in *pesos*, the unit of money used in Mexico. Work with students to write the currency names for the United States, Canada, and Mexico on a chart similar to the one below. Then find each country on a map.

Canada	Mexico	United States
Canadian dollar	peso	dollar

Vocabulary Strategies

Introduce Key Words and strategies.

Display Transparency 33, or write the following paragraphs on the board. Have students read the movie poster silently, using context clues with phonetic and structural analysis to decode and figure out the meanings of the underlined words. Help students with pronunciation if necessary.

Transparency 33   Key Words

DON'T MISS Crime on the Diamond

DON'T MISS *Crime on the Diamond*!

The catcher had played for baseball teams in many different countries. He was an <u>international</u> baseball star.

Whiff Williams hit a <u>double</u> and ran to second base. But second base was gone! The team manager, who wanted very much to win, became so <u>discouraged</u> that he quit. Without second base, any balls <u>fielded</u>, or caught, by the shortstop had to be thrown either to first or third base.

An <u>innocent</u> fan was arrested by the police but was let go because they could not prove he was guilty. They had accused him of stealing second base. The hot dog seller knew that the evidence was false and that the fan had been <u>framed</u>. Will he tell what he saw when he goes to court to <u>testify</u>?

CULTURAL AWARENESS

Students may be interested to know that the Mexican government issues pesos in both coins and bills. Have Mexican American students bring in Mexican currency to show to the other students. Encourage them to discuss the values of the coins and bills.

KEY WORDS

international
double
discouraged
fielded
innocent
framed
testify

KEY WORDS DEFINED

international   in more than one country

double   in baseball, a hit that enables a batter to get to second base

discouraged   feeling let down

fielded   caught or picked up a baseball and threw it to the right player

innocent   not guilty

framed   caused an innocent person to look guilty by presenting false evidence

testify   declare under oath in court

Guide students in completing a predict-o-gram.

Have students predict how the author will use the words in the story by thinking about whether each word might have to do with the *characters*, the *setting*, a *problem*, *characters' actions*, or a *resolution*. Guide them in using the Key Words to complete the predict-o-gram below. Have students discuss why they placed the words as they did. Also explain that they will come back to the predict-o-gram after reading and will discuss why these words are important in the story.

Model for students the placement of the first word.

STRATEGY: CLASSIFYING

Since *international* has to do with places, I predict that the author will use the word to describe the story setting.

Characters	Setting	Problem	Actions	Resolution
discouraged	international	framed	double fielded	innocent testify

Integrate spelling with vocabulary.

SPELLING-VOCABULARY CONNECTION *Integrated Spelling* page 47 reinforces spellings of the /f/ sound in the Key Words *fielded* and *testify*. The spelling of *discourage* is also included.

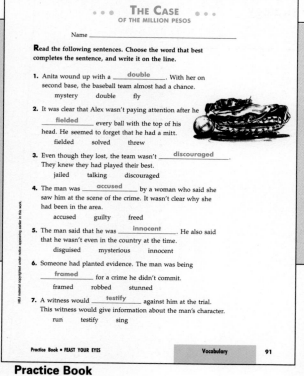

Practice Book

... **THE CASE** *...*
OF THE MILLION PESOS

Name _____

Read the following sentences. Choose the word that best completes the sentence, and write it on the line.

1. Anita wound up with a ___double___. With her on second base, the baseball team almost had a chance.
   mystery   double   fly

2. It was clear that Alex wasn't paying attention after he ___fielded___ every ball with the top of his head. He seemed to forget that he had a mitt.
   fielded   solved   threw

3. Even though they lost, the team wasn't ___discouraged___. They knew they had played their best.
   jailed   talking   discouraged

4. The man was ___accused___ by a woman who said she saw him at the scene of the crime. It wasn't clear why she had been in the area.
   accused   guilty   freed

5. The man said that he was ___innocent___. He also said that he wasn't even in the country at the time.
   disguised   mysterious   innocent

6. Someone had planted evidence. The man was being ___framed___ for a crime he didn't commit.
   framed   robbed   stunned

7. A witness would ___testify___ against him at the trial. This witness would give information about the man's character.
   run   testify   sing

Practice Book ■ FEAST YOUR EYES   Vocabulary   91

Integrated Spelling

INTEGRATED SPELLING
The Sound /f/

Name _____

Read the Spelling Words. Write them on another sheet of paper. Check your spelling.

SPELLING STRATEGY

The sound /f/ has several different spellings. Here are some examples:

/f/ = f	fake, testify
/f/ = gh	cough
/f/ = ph	photo, alphabet

Picturing ways to spell the sound /f/ in a word will help you remember how to spell the word. Use a dictionary if you're not sure which spelling is correct.

Which four Spelling Words spell the sound /f/ with the letter *f*?
fake   field
figure   testify

In which two Spelling Words is the sound /f/ spelled with the letters gh?
cough   laugh

In which three Spelling Words is the sound /f/ spelled with the letters ph?
alphabet   photo
graph

Which Spelling Word does not have the sound /f/? ___discourage___

FEAST YOUR EYES • "The Case of the Million Pesos"   47

SPELLING WORDS
alphabet
cough
discourage
fake
field
figure
graph
laugh
photo
testify

MEMORY JOGGER
Here is a Memory Jogger that will help you remember how to spell **discourage**.

Have **courage:**
I won't **discourage** you!

Strategic Reading

Preview and Predict

Guide students in previewing the mystery.

Remind students that thinking about the title and the first page of a story can help them preview a selection. Ask students to read the title and page 344.

Then ask students questions such as the following to help them make predictions about what might happen in the story:

- **What happened to the million pesos?**
- **Who could be the robber?**

PERSONAL JOURNAL Have students add their predictions about the story to their personal journals. Remind students to support their predictions.

Setting a Purpose

Have students set purposes.

Discuss with students what they want to find out when they read the story, based on their preview and what they already know. Have students use their predictions to set a purpose for reading.

Model purpose-setting, if necessary.

If students have difficulty setting a purpose, offer the following suggestion:

I want to read to find out what happened to the million pesos, and how Encyclopedia will solve the case.

OPTIONS FOR READING

INDEPENDENT READING Have students read the story silently with their purpose for reading in mind.

GUIDED READING Follow the Guided Reading suggestions that appear on pages T595 and T598. These suggestions model strategic reading.

COOPERATIVE READING A reader response strategy appears on page T595.

SECOND-LANGUAGE SUPPORT Ask students to share their predictions orally and write them on the board to provide a model of correct usage. You may also wish to have students quickwrite in their first language. (See Second-Language Support Manual.)

THE CASE OF THE MILLION PESOS

AWARD-WINNING
AUTHOR

from *Encyclopedia Brown Gets His Man*

by Donald J. Sobol

Encyclopedia solved mysteries at the dinner table. He solved mysteries in the garage. He solved mysteries at the scene of the crime.

There were no other places in Idaville, he thought, to solve mysteries.

He was wrong.

There was second base.

While sitting on second base, he solved a robbery that had taken place in a country a thousand miles away.

illustrated by Steven Meyers

Encyclopedia got his start as an international detective during an evening baseball game. His grounder slipped through Benny Breslin at short-stop. Encyclopedia wound up with a double.

Tim Gomez, the next batter, ended the inning by striking out. The game was immediately called on account of darkness. The score was 12 to 3.

Encyclopedia sat down on second base, discouraged. Benny Breslin flopped upon the grass beside him.

"We were going good," said Encyclopedia. "All we needed were nine runs to tie."

"I'm glad they stopped it," said Benny, a home-run hitter. "I've raced around the bases five times. My legs are falling off."

Sally walked over from first base. She looked troubled.

"What's bothering Tim Gomez?" she asked Encyclopedia. "He struck out six times in a row. Something is on his mind."

"Baseballs," said Benny. "He fielded every fly with the top of his head. He didn't catch one all game."

"Be quiet," whispered Encyclopedia, for Tim was passing near them.

"Sorry," Tim apologized. "I played like a cow on crutches."

"Forget it," said Encyclopedia.

"Aren't you feeling well?" asked Sally.

"I'm worried about my uncle, Duffy Gomez," said Tim. "He's in jail in Mexico City."

345

Guided Reading

SET PURPOSE/PREDICT: PAGES 344—350   Have students read through page 350 to find out what mystery Encyclopedia Brown has to solve.

Cooperative Reading

READER RESPONSE STRATEGY: PAGES 344—350 Have students work in pairs. Ask each student to read silently and then use the strategy described below to analyze the beginning of the story. (Response Card 8: Written Conversation, on page R69, gives complete directions for using the strategy.)

1. Each student writes a comment and a question.
2. Students pass their papers to their partners.
3. Each student writes down the answer to the question and adds a new question.
4. The papers are passed back, and each student answers the new question he or she receives.

PAGES 344—350   After reading, have students repeat steps 1–4. Encourage partners to discuss their completed papers.

Duffy Gomez, Mexico's greatest baseball player, in jail! Encyclopedia, Sally, and Benny were stunned by the news.

"What did he do?" asked Benny.

"The police say he robbed a bank," answered Tim. "But I don't believe it!"

"What does your uncle say?" asked Encyclopedia.

"He says he's <u>innocent</u>," replied Tim. "The police threw him in jail just the same. He's being <u>framed</u>!"

"By whom?" asked Sally.

"By a man named Pedro Morales. He's hated my uncle for years," said Tim. "Pedro was in love with my Aunt Molly. She turned him down to marry Uncle Duffy."

"So Pedro accused your uncle of robbing a bank," said Sally. "What a low way to get back!"

"Doesn't your uncle have an alibi?" asked Encyclopedia. "Can't he prove he was somewhere else when the bank was robbed?"

"He was at a movie. Nobody saw him, though," said Tim. "Uncle Duffy wears a fake beard when he goes out in public. If he didn't disguise himself, baseball fans would mob him."

"Being at a movie is a pretty weak alibi," said Encyclopedia regretfully. "Your uncle will have a hard time making a judge and jury believe him."

"The real robber is bound to be caught," said Sally. "Don't you worry, Tim."

"There isn't much time left," said Tim. "Uncle Duffy goes on trial next week. Pedro will <u>testify</u> against him."

Informal Assessment   Assessing whether students are fulfilling the established purpose for reading involves asking questions like the following:

- Is this what you expected to happen next?
- If so, what did you read earlier that helped you predict this? Which details helped you make your prediction?

This assessment will also encourage students to watch for and select details that fulfill their purpose for reading.

Sally glanced at Encyclopedia for help.

"Don't ask me," mumbled Encyclopedia.

"You *can't* say no," urged Sally. "Give it a try, Encyclopedia!"

"I can tell you everything about the case," said Tim eagerly. "I've read the newspaper stories my uncle sent from Mexico."

Encyclopedia considered the problem; namely, trying to solve a bank robbery in Mexico while sitting on second base in Idaville.

"You can't do Tim's uncle any harm," said Sally.

Encyclopedia couldn't argue with that. "You win," he said. "Tell me what you know, Tim."

"The National Bank of Mexico City was robbed last month by two masked men. They got away with a million pesos in one-peso bills," said Tim.

"That's about eighty thousand dollars," exclaimed Encyclopedia.

"Two weeks later," continued Tim, "Pedro Morales says he passed my uncle's house. It was late at night. There was a light in the living room. Pedro says he saw my uncle arguing with another man."

"Did Pedro overhear what was said?" asked Encyclopedia.

"Yes, the window was open," replied Tim. "Pedro claims my uncle said that he had counted the money again that afternoon. His share wasn't half the million pesos—it was a thousand pesos short."

"What happened next?" said Sally.

"According to Pedro," said Tim, "the other man got excited. He threw some money into my uncle's face and shouted, 'There's a thousand pesos. I never want to see your ugly face again!'"

"How did Pedro know they were talking about the stolen money?" asked Encyclopedia.

"Pedro says he didn't know—then," replied Tim. "Some of the one-peso bills the man threw at my uncle flew out the open window. Pedro picked them up. On a hunch, he brought them to the police. The numbers on the bills proved they were stolen from the bank."

"If Pedro had some of the stolen money," said Sally, "he must have had something to do with the robbery himself!"

"I agree," said Encyclopedia. "Pedro lied. His story just doesn't add up!"

WHAT WAS PEDRO'S LIE?

349

Second-Language Support

You may need to explain these idioms to students: *give it a try* ("please try"); *you win* ("I will do as you say"); and *got away with* ("escaped with"). Also explain that the phrase *a thousand pesos short* indicates that a thousand pesos were missing.

Solution

Pedro's mistake was in claiming that Tim's uncle said that he had "counted the money again that afternoon," and that "his share wasn't half the million pesos." Remember, the stolen money was in the form of one million one-peso bills. Tim's uncle could not have counted half a million bills, his share, in one afternoon. It would have taken him five days—counting day and night!

Think It Over

1. *How did Encyclopedia Brown help Tim Gomez?*
2. *Why was Uncle Duffy's alibi weak?*
3. *How did Encyclopedia know that Duffy Gomez was innocent?*
4. *Would you go to Encyclopedia Brown if you had a mystery to solve? Explain your answer.*

Write

Write a letter to Encyclopedia Brown telling him why you think he is or is not a good detective.

350

THEME WRAP-UP

SOLVE IT!

Think about the mysteries and detectives that Donald Sobol created. Do you think that solving mysteries is a tough job? Explain why you think as you do.

How are Dr. Haledjian and Encyclopedia Brown alike and how are they different? What characteristics that they share make them good detectives?

WRITER'S WORKSHOP Pretend that you are a mystery writer like Donald Sobol. Write a letter to Mr. Sobol, explaining an idea for another two-minute mystery that he might like to write about in one of his books. Remember to include a possible solution in the body of your letter.

For discussion of this page, please turn to T611.

Guided Reading

MONITOR COMPREHENSION: PAGES 344–350
What case must Encyclopedia Brown solve? (Tim Gomez's Uncle Duffy has been wrongfully accused of robbing a bank.) STRATEGIC READING: CONFIRMING PREDICTIONS

How did Pedro frame Uncle Duffy? (Pedro brought the police some stolen bills that he said had blown out of the window during an argument between Duffy and another man.) STRATEGIC READING: SUMMARIZING

Returning to the Predictions Invite students to discuss the predictions that they made before they began reading and that they may have written in their personal journals. Encourage them to talk about how those predictions changed as they read the story.

Returning to the Purpose for Reading
Ask students what happened to the million pesos and how Encyclopedia solved the case. (Pedro Morales took the money. Encyclopedia solved the mystery by figuring out that Pedro had lied.)

NOTE: Responses to the Think It Over questions and support for the Write activity appear on page T599.

Part 2
Responding to Literature

Story Follow-Up

Encourage reader's response: student page 350.

Think It Over

1. **How did Encyclopedia Brown help Tim Gomez?** (He helped Tim prove his Uncle Duffy's innocence.) INFERENTIAL: DRAWING CONCLUSIONS
2. **Why was Uncle Duffy's alibi weak?** (Nobody saw him go to the movie, because he was alone and in disguise.) LITERAL: NOTING IMPORTANT DETAILS
3. **How did Encyclopedia know that Duffy Gomez was innocent?** (He knew that Pedro had lied when he figured out that it was impossible to count half a million bills in one afternoon.) INFERENTIAL: SUMMARIZING
4. **Would you go to Encyclopedia Brown if you had a mystery to solve? Explain your answer.** (Responses will vary. Students should cite evidence about Encyclopedia Brown's abilities as a detective.) CRITICAL: MAKING JUDGMENTS

Write

Encourage writer's response: student page 350.

Write a letter to Encyclopedia Brown explaining why you think he is or is not a good detective. Encourage students to support their view. CRITICAL: MAKING JUDGMENTS

Summarizing the Literature

Have students retell the story and write a summary.

Ask students to imagine they are detectives and have them summarize the story by completing the Detective's Report below. Help students begin the report and have them finish it independently. (See *Practice Book* page 92 on T600.) Students may use their completed reports to write a brief summary statement and retell the story.

Detective's Report
Your Name: _____ Date: _____
Where did this crime take place? _____ (Mexico)
What was the crime? _____ (Someone stole one million pesos.)
Who were the suspects? **What** was the evidence against them?

Suspects	Evidence
1. (Duffy Gomez)	_____
2. (Pedro Morales)	_____
How was the case solved?	

STRATEGY CONFERENCE

Ask students how the reading strategies they chose for this story would have been different if the selection were nonfiction. Also discuss how their rate of reading might change for reading a nonfiction piece.

NOTE

An additional writing activity for this selection appears on page T602.

INFORMAL ASSESSMENT

Having students **summarize** in this way will help you informally assess how well they comprehended the **main idea** and **details** of the selection. It also will help you see how well they recognized the importance of particular details in contributing to this main idea.

Appreciating Literature

Have students share personal responses.

Have students work in small groups to discuss the story. Provide a general question such as the following to help the groups begin:

- **Would you change the ending of this story? Explain how your ending would be different.**

PERSONAL JOURNAL Have students use their personal journals to write about ideas and feelings that are discussed in the groups. You may also refer them to their personal journals after they complete the activities below.

Critical Thinking Activities

Encourage both cooperative and individual responses.

ROLE-PLAY A SCENE How do you think Pedro and Duffy will present their arguments in court? Imagine that Encyclopedia goes to Mexico City to serve as Duffy's lawyer. Act out a courtroom scene in which the story characters appear before a judge. Have different students play the roles of Duffy, Encyclopedia, Pedro, Pedro's lawyer, the judge, and other witnesses students think of. After the case has been argued, the judge should come to a decision. CREATIVE: PREDICTING OUTCOMES

WRITE DIRECTIONS Imagine you have half a million one-peso bills. What would be the quickest and easiest way to count them? You may use helpers if you wish. Have students work independently or in pairs to write down the steps they would follow to count half a million bills. CRITICAL: SOLVING PROBLEMS

STUDENT SELF-ASSESSMENT

Help students self-assess their participation in the discussion by using questions such as the following:

- Did I listen carefully to other students' ideas?
- Did I give reasons for my ideas and opinions?

Writer's Journal

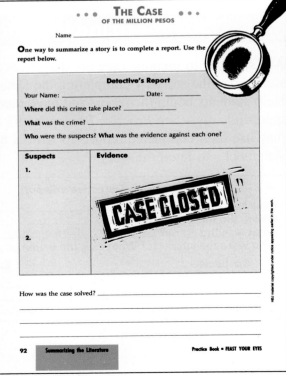

Practice Book

WRITER'S JOURNAL
page 65: Writing a personal response

PRACTICE BOOK
page 92: Summarizing the selection

VO·CAB·U·LAR·Y Workshop

Reviewing Key Words

Duplicate on the board the vocabulary predict-o-gram below that students completed before reading. Have students confirm or modify their initial predictions and tell, orally or in writing, how each word is important in the story. Possible responses are given below.

Characters	Setting	Problem	Actions	Resolution
discouraged	international	framed	double fielded	innocent testify

- *International* described Encyclopedia Brown's detective work after he had solved cases in the United States and Mexico. (setting)
- *Fielded* is a baseball word. When Tim fielded the ball poorly, everyone knew that he was upset. (actions)
- *Double* is another baseball term. Encyclopedia hit a double, but his team lost anyway. (actions)
- *Innocent* described Duffy Gomez at the end of the story. (resolution)
- *Discouraged* tells how some of the characters felt at one time or another. Encyclopedia was discouraged when his team didn't win, Tim was discouraged when his uncle was accused, and Duffy himself must have felt discouraged, too. (characters)
- Duffy had been *framed* by Pedro Morales. (problem)
- *Testify* is important because that's what Pedro was going to do in court to convince people that Duffy was guilty. (actions or resolution)

Extending Vocabulary

CONTENT-AREA VOCABULARY Have students recall that some of the words they read in "The Case of the Million Pesos" have to do with court cases. With students' input, draw on the board a web similar to the one below.

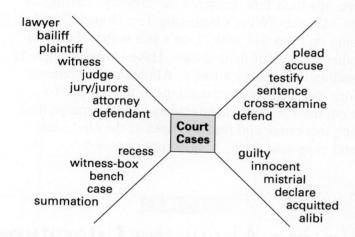

lawyer
bailiff
plaintiff
witness
judge
jury/jurors
attorney
defendant

Court Cases

plead
accuse
testify
sentence
cross-examine
defend

recess
witness-box
bench
case
summation

guilty
innocent
mistrial
declare
acquitted
alibi

Have students add to the web other words they know that have to do with court cases. If they have difficulty thinking of words, encourage them to use a thesaurus.

Suggest that students use some of the words in the web to write a summary of what might happen when Uncle Duffy's case goes to court.

Integrated Language Arts

READING

Oral Rereading/ Readers Theatre

Have students present a Readers Theatre rendition of the scene in which Tim describes the mystery, starting on page 345 with "What's bothering Tim Gomez?" and ending on page 347 with "Don't you worry, Tim," or another passage of their choice. Have students begin by rereading the passage silently. Allow them to rehearse before they present their readings to the others. To present their performance, readers should arrange their chairs in a circle and read the lines as the characters would have said them.   LISTENING/READING

WRITING

Writing About the Literature

WRITE A STORY   Ask students to imagine another mystery involving Encyclopedia, Tim, and Sally that takes place in Idaville. Have each student write a mystery story. Explain that Encyclopedia should be the character who figures out the solution to the mystery. To help students begin, have them develop a chart such as the one below. Explain that they can invent other characters in addition to the three from this story. Guide students as they brainstorm ideas about the characters, the problem, the events, and the solution. Invite students to read aloud their finished stories.   LISTENING/SPEAKING/ READING/WRITING

Setting	Characters	Problem	Events	Solution
Idaville	Encyclopedia, Tim, and Sally	Baseballs disappear during Little League games.	During a game, balls disappear one by one; Encyclopedia finds one with teeth marks.	Ump, the team mascot, has been taking balls.

NOTE: An additional writing activity appears on page T599.

SPELLING

Reviewing Spelling Words

SPELLING WORDS: *alphabet, cough, discourage, fake, field, figure, graph, laugh, photo, testify*

Make a collage of pictures of words that contain the /f/ sound. Display the collage, and place writing paper next to it. In an envelope, place the list of the words depicted in the collage. Have the students write as many of the words as they can find in the collage. Then have them check their list against the one in the envelope to see how they have done.   WRITING/SPELLING

INTEGRATED SPELLING   page 48: Writing words with the /f/ sound

INTEGRATED SPELLING
The Sound /f/

Name _____

WORD PLAY

Imagine that you and a friend have just solved a puzzling mystery. Write about the case for your fellow detectives, using the Spelling Words.

_____ Answers will vary. _____
_____
_____
_____

WORD BANK

alphabet
cough
discourage
fake
field
figure
graph
laugh
photo
testify

SPELLING DETECTIVE

Sandy and her brother Jack keep a crime notebook. When Sandy proofread this crime report, she found four misspellings. Help her fix the spelling errors by circling each misspelling. Then write the word correctly above the mistake.

Last night, Jack and I both heard a scream.
I got my camera and took a (poto) **photo** of the crime scene. Mama told us that her ring had been on top of the sink. Jack was looking everywhere. He said, "Don't (discurrage) **discourage** me!"

Then Jack pointed to the open window. I started to (laugg) **laugh**. On the windowsill were some paw prints. "Those prints will lead us to your ring. Why, this mystery was as simple as the (alfabet)! **alphabet**"

48   "The Case of the Million Pesos" • FEAST YOUR EYES

Integrated Spelling

It's a Grand Slam!

AVAILABLE ON PROJECT CARD

COOPERATIVE LEARNING   Encyclopedia and his friends play a baseball game in the first part of the story. Have students write a "radio broadcast" of Encyclopedia's game and record the program on a tape recorder. Two students can be the play-by-play announcers; others can provide "color" (background information and gossip about the players), sound effects, commercials, and so on. Encourage students to listen to real baseball broadcasts on local radio stations to help them get ideas.
LISTENING/SPEAKING/WRITING

Baseballs on My Mind

Have students recall that Benny Breslin uses two different meanings for the word *mind* in his joke about Tim Gomez's problems with fly balls. Tell them that this type of joking is sometimes called *punning*. Invite students to create puns using the following words from the story: *framed, bills,* and *fans,* as well as any other multiple-meaning words they think of. Brave punsters may wish to read their puns aloud to classmates.
LISTENING/READING/WRITING

I'll Trade You One Duffy for Two Tims

AVAILABLE ON PROJECT CARD

Have students make baseball cards for their favorite story characters. If possible, provide real baseball cards for students to use as models. Then ask volunteers to tell their own birth date and birthplace. As they do, write the dates and places on the board, calling attention to the use of capital letters and commas and the order of the information in each item. When students make up birth dates and birthplaces for the story characters, remind them to put the information in the correct order and to use capitals and commas where appropriate.

Suggest that students use whatever information is available in the story and invent the rest for the baseball cards they create. Have students read and compare one another's cards.   LISTENING/SPEAKING/READING/WRITING

Take Me Out to the Ball Game

Have interested students collect songs, poems, comedy routines such as "Who's on First?," anecdotes, and amazing statistics related to baseball. Invite them to share the materials they collect by singing, reciting, storytelling, or performing skits. Invite other students to listen in order to enjoy and appreciate the presentations.
LISTENING/SPEAKING/READING

Part 3
Learning Through Literature

Multiple-Meaning Words

OBJECTIVE: *To determine the meaning and pronunciations of homographs by applying contextual analysis*

1 Focus

Explain the value of using context clues.

Ask volunteers to give two meanings for the word *bat*. ("a flying mammal"; "a stick used to hit a baseball") Ask students which meaning they would expect to find used in "The Case of the Million Pesos" and why. Explain that using context clues will help readers determine the meaning of a multiple-meaning word.

2 Teach/Model

Teach the strategy.

Point out that a homograph, one kind of multiple-meaning word, has more than one meaning and often has different pronunciations. Explain that by using sentence context, students will know which meaning and which pronunciation are being used.

Display Transparency 34 or the definitions and sentences. Model using context clues to decide the meanings and pronunciations of the underlined homographs in the first group of sentences.

Transparency 34   Multiple-Meaning Words

1. **wound**: an injury caused by something cutting the skin
2. **wound**: wrapped or coiled
   A. The doctor covered the <u>wound</u> with a bandage.(1)
   B. Encyclopedia <u>wound</u> tape around his wrist before putting on his glove.(2)

3. **row**: to make a boat move by using oars
4. **row**: a group of things in a straight line
5. **row**: a quarrel
   C. The umpire and the manager disagreed, and they had quite a <u>row</u>.(5)
   D. Lori can <u>row</u> the boat across the lake.(3)
   E. Tim sat in the first <u>row</u> to watch the game.(4)

Have students apply the learning.

Have students read the remaining words and definitions and then use sentence context to figure out which homograph is being used in each sentence.

| 4 | Summarize |

Informally assess the learning.

Have students read aloud the sentences and point out the context clues that helped them determine which meaning is being used.

Have students summarize what they learned. (Two words can be spelled alike but have different meanings and pronunciations. Using sentence context can help readers figure out which meaning is being used.)

CHALLENGE Have students make a list of multiple-meaning words in other selections and the context clues that help them know the meaning that is being used.

SECOND-LANGUAGE SUPPORT Students can demonstrate their understanding of the skill by illustrating two meanings for the words *bat* and *row*. Have students then say a sentence describing each picture. (See *Second-Language Support Manual*.)

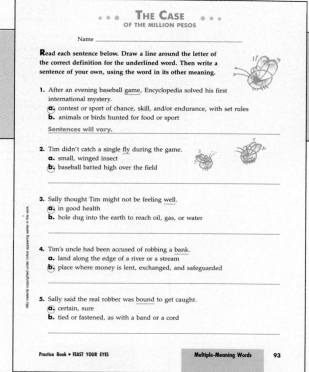

• • • **THE CASE**
OF THE MILLION PESOS

Name _____

Read each sentence below. Draw a line around the letter of the correct definition for the underlined word. Then write a sentence of your own, using the word in its other meaning.

1. After an evening baseball <u>game</u>, Encyclopedia solved his first international mystery.
   a. contest or sport of chance, skill, and/or endurance, with set rules
   b. animals or birds hunted for food or sport
   Sentences will vary.

2. Tim didn't catch a single <u>fly</u> during the game.
   a. small, winged insect
   b. baseball batted high over the field

3. Sally thought Tim might not be feeling <u>well</u>.
   a. in good health
   b. hole dug into the earth to reach oil, gas, or water

4. Tim's uncle had been accused of robbing a <u>bank</u>.
   a. land along the edge of a river or a stream
   b. place where money is lent, exchanged, and safeguarded

5. Sally said the real robber was <u>bound</u> to get caught.
   a. certain, sure
   b. tied or fastened, as with a band or a cord

Practice Book ▪ FEAST YOUR EYES   Multiple-Meaning Words   93

Practice Book

PRACTICE BOOK
page 93: Writing
multiple-meaning words

Drawing Conclusions

OBJECTIVE: *To draw conclusions using story evidence and real-life experiences*

Review

Strategy: Have students use story evidence plus prior knowledge.

Remind students that authors do not always tell everything that happens. Discuss how to draw conclusions. Then model the strategy using this diagram:

Story Information Encyclopedia says "Be quiet" when Benny tells how badly Tim has played.	+	**What I Know** People don't want to make friends feel bad.	=	**Conclusion** Tim is Encyclopedia's friend, and he cares about Tim's feelings.

Practice/Apply

Have students draw conclusions.

Have students write down one thing that the author did not tell the reader and then write the clues used to draw the conclusions.

Summarize

Informally assess the learning.

Ask students to read aloud their conclusions and tell what story clues and what information from real life they used to help them.

Have students summarize what they learned. (Draw conclusions by combining clues from the story with information from real life.)

CHALLENGE Have students write paragraphs in which they give clues but do not state what is actually happening. Have them exchange paragraphs with partners to draw conclusions about each other's work.

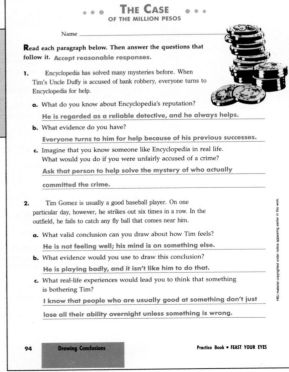

THE CASE
OF THE MILLION PESOS

Name _____

Read each paragraph below. Then answer the questions that follow it. *Accept reasonable responses.*

1. Encyclopedia has solved many mysteries before. When Tim's Uncle Duffy is accused of bank robbery, everyone turns to Encyclopedia for help.

    a. What do you know about Encyclopedia's reputation?
    He is regarded as a reliable detective, and he always helps.

    b. What evidence do you have?
    Everyone turns to him for help because of his previous successes.

    c. Imagine that you know someone like Encyclopedia in real life. What would you do if you were unfairly accused of a crime?
    Ask that person to help solve the mystery of who actually
    committed the crime.

2. Tim Gomez is usually a good baseball player. On one particular day, however, he strikes out six times in a row. In the outfield, he fails to catch any fly ball that comes near him.

    a. What valid conclusion can you draw about how Tim feels?
    He is not feeling well; his mind is on something else.

    b. What evidence would you use to draw this conclusion?
    He is playing badly, and it isn't like him to do that.

    c. What real-life experiences would lead you to think that something is bothering Tim?
    I know that people who are usually good at something don't just
    lose all their ability overnight unless something is wrong.

94   Drawing Conclusions   Practice Book • FEAST YOUR EYES

Practice Book

PRACTICE BOOK
page 94: Drawing conclusions

Figurative Language

OBJECTIVE: *To identify and interpret figurative language*

Review

Review figurative language.

Ask students what Benny really means when he says that his legs are "falling off." (His legs are tired.) Remind students that authors use figurative language to make their writing more colorful. Use the diagram below to model analyzing figurative language.

Example	Literal	Figurative Meaning
on his mind	"on top of his head"	"bothering him"

Practice/Apply

Analyze figurative language.

COOPERATIVE LEARNING   Suggest that students work in small groups to make a chart of other examples of figurative language from this or other selections students have read.

Summarize

Informally assess the learning.

To check students' understanding, ask them to share their charts and then use their examples in sentences.

Have students summarize what they learned. (Figurative language is an expression that does not mean exactly what it says.)

CHALLENGE   Challenge students to find additional places in the story where figurative language might be used. Suggest that they work individually or in groups to generate figurative language.

• • •   THE CASE   • • •
OF THE MILLION PESOS

Name _____

A. The underlined part of each sentence below is an example of figurative language. Rewrite each sentence, expressing the same idea without figurative language. Responses will vary.

1. My legs are falling off.

2. Something is on his mind.

3. I played like a cow on crutches.

4. Encyclopedia, Sally, and Benny were bowled over by the news.

5. The police threw him in jail just the same.

B. Use figurative language to complete each sentence.
Possible responses are given.

1. Benny ran the bases like a winning racehorse

2. It got so dark that even the stars closed their eyes

3. Encyclopedia was a bloodhound on a fresh trail

4. Pedro Morales was as low as a snake

Practice Book ■ FEAST YOUR EYES   Figurative Language   95

Practice Book

PRACTICE BOOK
page 95:   Using figurative language

Integrated **Curriculum**

North of the Border

USING MAPS The story says that Mexico was a thousand miles from Idaville. Have groups of students work with a map of the United States to determine which states Idaville might be in (which states have towns that are one thousand miles away from Mexico). Make sure the map students are working with has a distance scale. Students can also determine which states are farthest from Mexico and which ones are closest to it.
LISTENING/SPEAKING/READING

MATH

And-a-One-and-a-Two

AVAILABLE ON PROJECT CARD

COOPERATIVE LEARNING Encyclopedia figures that it would take five days and nights to count half a million pieces of paper money. Have pairs of students conduct an experiment to see whether it would really take that long. For example, students could find out how many pieces of paper a person can count in ten minutes. Then, with the aid of a calculator, they can use those results to predict how many pieces a person could count in an hour, in a day, and so on. Have partners summarize their findings in a paragraph or two, explaining their methods and conclusions. LISTENING/SPEAKING/WRITING

SOCIAL STUDIES

The National Pastime

COOPERATIVE LEARNING Have groups of students work together to research the history of baseball, from its beginnings in the colonial era to the present day. Individual students should concentrate on a specific question about baseball history, such as: Who were the greatest players? How have the rules changed over the years? When were the major leagues formed? After students finish their research and combine their information, they can present their findings to classmates and answer other students' questions. LISTENING/SPEAKING/READING/WRITING

The Big Leagues

AVAILABLE ON PROJECT CARD

CULTURAL AWARENESS   The story says that Duffy Gomez was Mexico's greatest baseball player. Have students find out which Mexican baseball teams he could have played for. Suggest that students use reference materials to make a list of teams in the two Mexican professional baseball leagues. Then have them locate the teams' hometowns on a map of Mexico. Students can present their findings in a brief report.   LISTENING/ SPEAKING/READING/WRITING

ART

Funny Money

CULTURAL AWARENESS   Have students find pictures or actual examples of different kinds of paper money, such as Canadian dollars, Mexican pesos, or German marks. Then have them design their own paper money for an imaginary country. The money should show the name of the country and the value; it might also have pictures, sayings, serial numbers, or whatever else students want to include.   READING/WRITING

SCIENCE

Who Did It?

COOPERATIVE LEARNING   Help students make a set of thumbprints for each class member by using a stamp pad and absorbent paper. Have interested students research the four major types of fingerprint patterns—*loop, whorl, arch,* and *accidental* (often a combination of the other three)—and report their findings. Then have students work in groups to classify the prints. They might create and display a graph that depicts the number of students with each type of print.   LISTENING/ SPEAKING/READING/WRITING

Money, Money, Money

READ ALOUD TO STUDENTS:

PEOPLE DID NOT ALWAYS USE

MONEY TO BUY WHAT THEY

NEEDED. Instead, they bartered, or exchanged what they had for what they needed. For example, a farmer might have traded several bags of flour for a blanket.

In time, people found it more convenient to have a standard form of money. The first coins, minted by a people living in what is today Turkey, were made of gold, silver, or a mixture of these two "precious metals." A variety of other objects have served as money throughout history. Two thousand years ago, salt, mined in the Sahara Desert in North Africa, was considered worth its weight. It was carried on camels for 1,000 miles to West Africa. Roman soldiers received part of their pay in salt, an important seasoning. Their word *salarium* ("money to buy salt"), is the root of our word *salary*. Native Americans used beads made from shells, called *wampum*, as money.

Paper money was probably first made in China, out of tree bark, or so Marco Polo reported in 1295. Today, paper money is at least partly backed by either gold or silver, which still are valued above all other forms of money.■

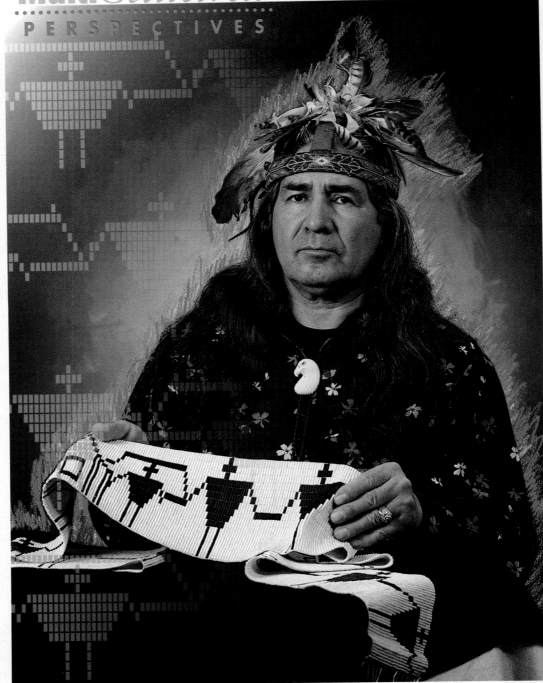

Wampum, a form of money used by Native Americans

ACTIVITY CORNER

■ **Available on Project Card**
Have small groups of students choose a country and research the forms, appearance, and value of the currency used. Then allow each group to prepare a presentation in which they share what they've learned, using visual aids. Encourage students to set aside a time each day for a one-week period when they will practice buying and selling items using a country's currency. The "currency of the week" should be alternated, allowing all countries to be included.

■ Encourage students to come up with their own form of exchange. Ask them to determine one object that is important to them and that might serve as a kind of money for young people. They might write a brief persuasive paragraph outlining their reasons for choosing that object.

Solve It!

Review with students that the characters in this theme's stories were able to solve some puzzling crimes through clever thinking. Help students recall that they read about a glass of ice that mysteriously turned to ginger ale while locked in a safe and about an accusation of a suspect in a bank robbery who was found to be innocent. Explain to students that the questions on page 351 will help them think further about these selections.

Note that pages T612–T613 provide support for applying the writing process to the last question.

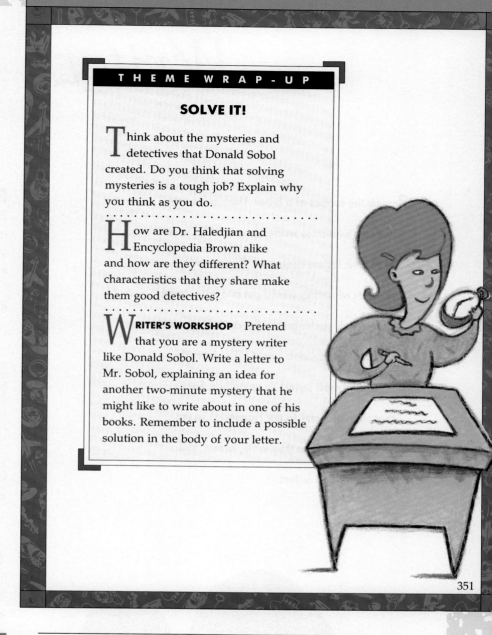

THEME WRAP-UP

SOLVE IT!

Think about the mysteries and detectives that Donald Sobol created. Do you think that solving mysteries is a tough job? Explain why you think as you do.

How are Dr. Haledjian and Encyclopedia Brown alike and how are they different? What characteristics that they share make them good detectives?

WRITER'S WORKSHOP   Pretend that you are a mystery writer like Donald Sobol. Write a letter to Mr. Sobol, explaining an idea for another two-minute mystery that he might like to write about in one of his books. Remember to include a possible solution in the body of your letter.

351

Theme Wrap-Up

DISCUSSION QUESTIONS, PAGE 351

Think about the mysteries and detectives that Donald Sobol created. Do you think that solving mysteries is a tough job? Explain why you think as you do. Ask students if they solved the mysteries before reading the solutions. (Accept reasonable responses: Yes, you have to think logically about every detail.)   CRITICAL: MAKING JUDGMENTS

How are Dr. Haledjian and Encyclopedia Brown alike and how are they different? What characteristics that they share make them good detectives? Suggest that students compare the detectives' ages and solution methods. (Accept reasonable responses: Both solve a crime by using logic. Dr. Haledjian is an adult, while Encyclopedia Brown is a young person.) INFERENTIAL: COMPARING AND CONTRASTING

WRITER'S WORKSHOP   See pages T612–T613 for suggestions for applying the writing process. **Pretend that you are a mystery writer like Donald Sobol. Write a letter to Mr. Sobol, explaining an idea for another two-minute mystery that he might like to write about in one of his books. Remember to include a possible solution in the body of your letter.** You may prefer to allow students to respond to the theme in their own way.   WRITING PROCESS: A LETTER TO THE AUTHOR

Writer's Workshop

LETTER TO THE AUTHOR

For More Discussion & Practice:

LANGUAGE HANDBOOK

Review the format of a letter. Then invite any students who have written to an author to tell what their letters contained. Discuss with students what they would put in a letter to an author. Ask students how the content of a letter that explains an idea would differ from the content of most letters to an author. Suggest that students refer to the Handbook in the *Writer's Journal* as they write, revise, and proofread their letters.

Prewriting

Before students write, encourage them to think about other mystery stories they have read or heard. Have students

- think about their mystery idea and their purpose for explaining it.
- use brainstorming lists to plan their idea. Suggest that they use their lists to explore different ways to solve the mystery. The lists may resemble the following:

Possible Beginnings	Possible Problems	Possible Complications	Possible Solutions
The coach's big trophy has been broken.	The trophy was on the floor in a tiny closet.	None of the team members could lift it.	A heavy object fell on it when someone slammed the closet door.

Suggest that students review their lists and select the simplest and most logical ideas for their letter.

Drafting

Invite students to write a draft of their letter to Donald Sobol. Point out that they should

- write the heading and the greeting.
- explain the purpose of the letter in the first sentence of the body.
- refer to their lists and explain their mystery idea in a logical order.
- write a closing.
- sign their names.
- write freely without worrying about spelling, punctuation, or grammar.

COMPUTER CONNECTION Students may want to use a computer during the revising stage so that they can easily add details to their paragraphs.

Responding and Revising

Suggest that students work in pairs to read their letters aloud and discuss their ideas. Offer the following tips. Then have students revise their work.

- Does the letter state the purpose for writing? If not, change the opening.
- Does the letter clearly and smoothly explain the mystery idea and its solution? If not, reorder sentences, combine ideas into new sentences, and add anything that is missing. (See the Language/Literature Link below.)
- Is the letter in the correct form? If not, add any parts that are missing.

STUDENT SELF-ASSESSMENT OPTION Students may use the Writing Self-Assessment Checklist in the *Portfolio Teacher's Guide*. Suggest that as they use the checklist, they focus on the format of the letter and the clear presentation of ideas.

Proofreading

Offer these tips to help students proofread their work and make changes:

- Check for punctuation errors, especially comma errors in the heading, the greeting, and the closing.
- Make sure that the first line of each paragraph is indented.
- Look for errors in grammar.

Publishing

If you wish, talk with students about different options for publishing their letters. Some may be interested in actually sending their letters to the author and saving a copy in their reading/writing portfolios. (Students may mail the letters in care of the publisher.) Students may also create a booklet of mystery ideas.

LANGUAGE/LITERATURE LINK

Combining Sentences with the Same Subject

Explain to students that successful mystery writers make their point without repeating ideas. A way to cut unnecessary words and avoid short, choppy sentences is to combine sentences that have the same subject. Subject words such as *he, she,* and *they* signal sentences that might be combined. Encourage students to check their writing and combine sentences that have the same subject.

Speaking Option

VOICE MAIL The Writer's Workshop may be adapted for students to plan an oral reading of the letter. Encourage students to follow the guidelines offered for Prewriting, Drafting, and Responding and Revising. Offer the following tips to help students deliver their oral readings:

- Rehearse reading your letter aloud so that you are familiar with the words and the organization.
- Practice reading your letter to a partner. Read slowly and clearly and not too softly or too loudly. Try to present your letter without looking at it.
- Work on expressing yourself so that your audience sees that you like what you have written.

Invite students to read their letters to a small group of classmates.

Hidden Riches

The Gold Coin

Pearls

from *Hey World, Here I Am!*

For pacing suggestions, see page T616.

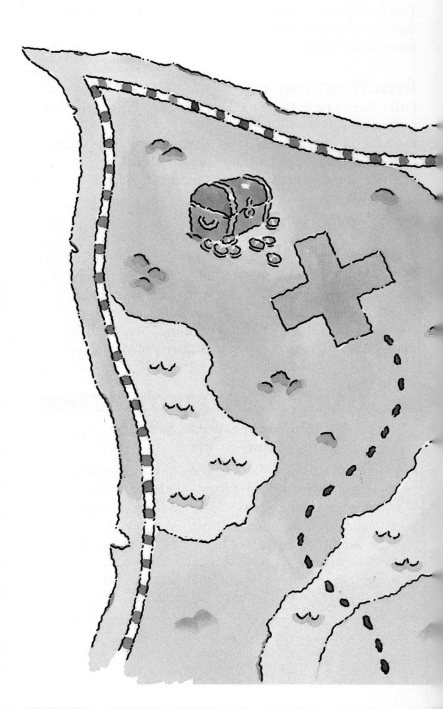

353

Discussing the Theme

Invite students to read the theme focus on Student Anthology page 353 and look at the illustration. Encourage students to suggest things that are more valuable than money or riches. (Accept reasonable responses: friendship, working toward a goal, helping others.) Discuss how these things might change a person's view of life. Then ask students to speculate what hidden riches might be found in the story and poem and how they might change those who discover them.

Reading/Writing Portfolio

Remind students that their writing responses for the selections in "Hidden Riches" should be kept in their portfolios. Remind them also to add to their personal journals any thoughts and ideas about books they have read independently.

Managing the Literature-Based Classroom

Management Options

PROMOTE STUDENT RESPONSIBILITY To ensure that activities run smoothly with a minimum of teacher direction, make students responsible whenever possible. Organize materials so students can find them and return them to the proper place. Post charts, lists, and instructions so students can refer to them independently. Use a check-out system for all books and materials. Assign jobs, such as keeping the Publishing Center stocked with materials or putting up artwork, to students on a rotating basis. Have students act as group leaders, answering questions, assisting other group members, and keeping the group on task.

PAIRED READING To give students a change of pace and build upon their experience with paired reading, you may want to try combining pairs of reading partners into groups of four or forming groups of three reading partners. Students may take turns reading aloud, as they do in paired reading. You may want to remind them to practice good listening manners in their discussions.

PACING This theme has been designed to take about two weeks to complete, depending on your students' needs.

Meeting Individual Needs

STUDENTS AT RISK Motivate alienated, uninterested students to show interest in a story by encouraging them to read it aloud in groups of five or six students. Stories with a great deal of dialogue, such as "The Gold Coin," are especially good for this activity. Each student can read one or two of the characters' parts, and one student can read as the narrator.

GIFTED AND TALENTED Encourage students to put on a puppet show of "The Gold Coin." Invite younger students or siblings to attend the performance. *Challenge Cards* provide additional activities to challenge students. Challenge notes throughout the lesson plans suggest additional activities to stimulate critical and creative thinking.

SPECIAL EDUCATION STUDENTS Encourage students to record important events as they read the story. Have students use these notes for Summarizing the Literature on page T631.

LIMITED ENGLISH PROFICIENT STUDENTS Assign students to work as buddies. Have pairs read "The Gold Coin" together and later work together to revise their paragraphs for the Writer's Workshop on Student Anthology page 371. Second-Language Support notes throughout the lesson plans offer strategies to help students acquiring English to understand the selections.

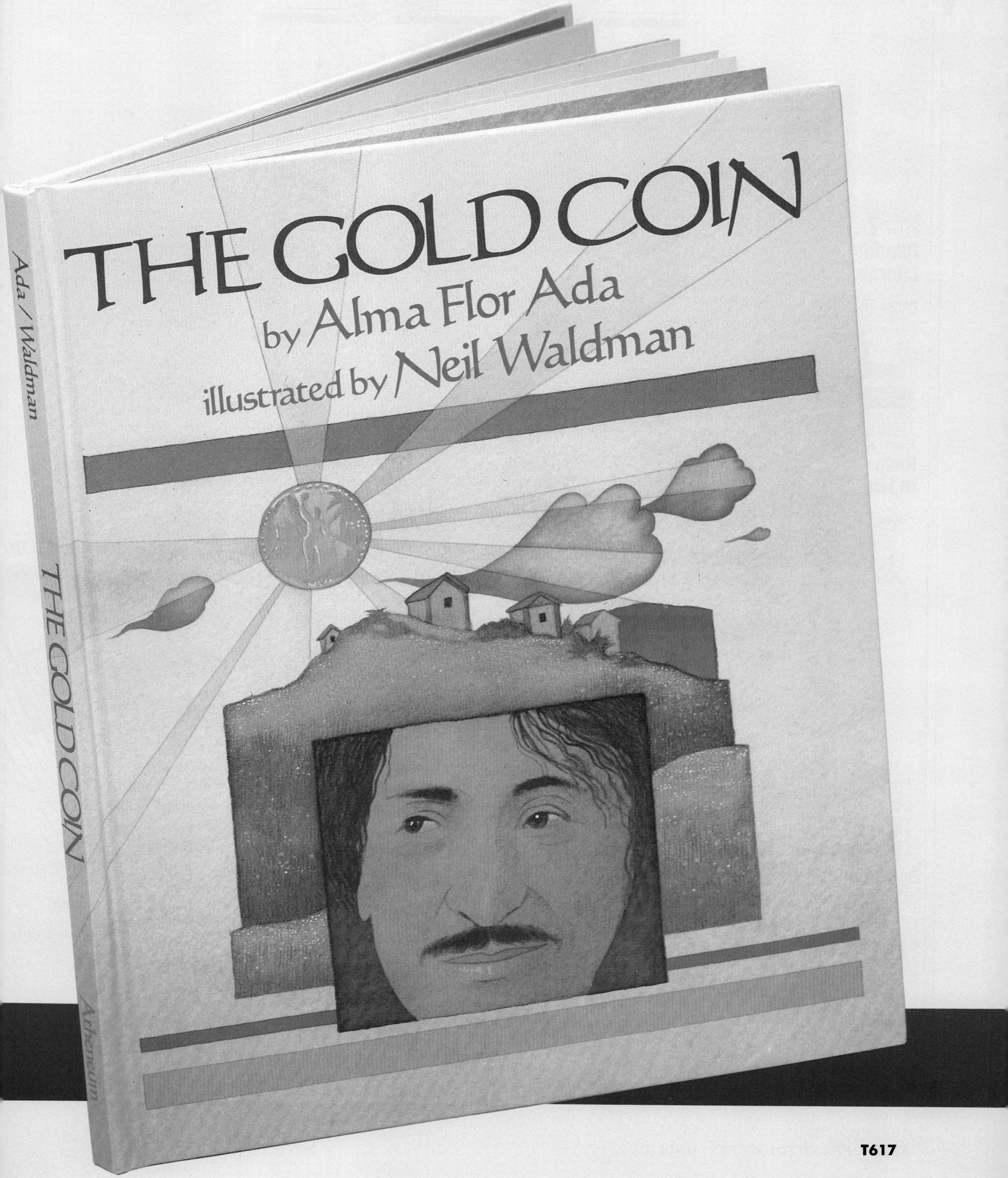
THE GOLD COIN
by Alma Flor Ada
illustrated by Neil Waldman
Ada / Waldman
THE GOLD COIN
Atheneum

LESSON PLANNER

THE GOLD COIN

	TEACHING OUTLINE	Materials	Language Arts/ Integrated Curriculum	Meeting Individual Needs

Part 1
Reading Literature
Pages T620–T630

	Building Background
	Vocabulary Strategies
	Key Words (Tested)
	Strategic Reading
	Preview and Predict
	Setting a Purpose
	Options for Reading
		Transparency 35
		Second-Language
		  Support Manual
		Practice Book p. 96
		Integrated Spelling
		  p. 49
		Integrated Spelling T.E.
		  pp. 66–67
		Student Anthology
		  pp. 354–369
		Response Card 1:
		  Characters
			Spelling
			Spelling Pretest
			Spelling-Vocabulary
			  Connection
				Second-Language Support
				Vocabulary T621
				Strategic Reading T622,
				  T625
				Cooperative Reading
				  T623

Part 2
Responding to Literature
Pages T631–T635

	Story Follow-Up
	Think It Over
	Write
	Summarizing the Literature
	Appreciating Literature
	Critical Thinking Activities
		Writer's Journal p. 66
		Practice Book p. 97
		Integrated Spelling
		  p. 50
		Integrated Spelling T.E.
		  pp. 66–67
		Literature Cassette 2
		Language Handbook
			Vocabulary Workshop
			Reviewing Key Words
			Extending Vocabulary
			  Names from Different
			  Languages
			Reading
			Oral Rereading/Drama
			Writing
			Fable
			Diary Entry
			Essay
			Spelling
			Reviewing Spelling Words
			Speaking
			Changing the Story
			Listening
			Crop Information
				Cooperative Learning
				T632, T635

Part 3
Learning Through Literature
Pages T636–T642

	Introduce
	Comprehension: Making
	  Generalizations
	Review
	Literary Appreciation:
	  Story Elements
	  (Tested)
	Decoding: Structural
	  Analysis (Tested)
		Second-Language
		  Support Manual
		Writer's Journal p. 67
		Practice Book
		  pp. 98–101
			Social Studies
			Mapmaking
			Distributing Funds
			Math
			Taking a Survey
			Science
			Learning About Herbs
			Art
			Making a Mosaic
			Multicultural
			People Who Care
				Challenge
				T637, T638, T639
				Second-Language Support
				Making Generalizations
				T637
				Cooperative Learning
				T637, T640

KEY WORDS

stunned
ransacked
urgently
shriveled
lumbered
herbs

Selection Summary

Juan is a pale and sickly thief who steals at night. One evening he overhears an old woman remark that she must be the richest woman in the world. Because she is holding a gold coin, Juan thinks she must have more gold hidden away. When the woman leaves, Juan ransacks her hut and finds nothing, so he begins a search that leads him from home to home where the woman, Doña Josefa, nurses the sick. At each home, Juan arrives just after Doña Josefa has left. While traveling, Juan regains his physical health and appreciation of kindness and beauty as he assists others with their work and receives help from them. Juan finally catches up with Doña Josefa at her hut. Juan learns that she has but one gold coin, which she had offered to each of her patients, but they all refused it. Just as she hands Juan the coin, saying that he must be in great need, a young girl whose mother is having a baby comes to find Doña Josefa. In a surprise ending, Juan offers to repair Doña Josefa's hut, and he gives her back the gold coin, saying that the new baby will need it more than he.

Family Involvement

Encourage family members to discuss with students ways in which they have helped their friends or relatives in times of need. If no such occasions have occurred, you might suggest that students learn how their families might be prepared to help.

ALMA FLOR ADA

Alma Flor Ada was born in Cuba in 1938, and now lives in San Mateo, California. She is the author of numerous textbooks, educational materials, and magazine articles in Spanish. *The Gold Coin* is her first book published in English. As she recalls, "My vocation as a writer started as a young child. . . . I made a firm commitment while in the fourth grade to devote my life to producing schoolbooks that would be fun—and since then I am having a lot of fun doing just that!"

ADDITIONAL READING

Other Books That Will Surprise

As: A Surfeit of Similes by Norton Juster. William Morrow, 1989.   AVERAGE

The Eleventh Hour by Graeme Base. Abrams, 1989.   AVERAGE

Flat Stanley by Jeff Brown. Harper, 1964. AVERAGE

Punching the Clock: Funny Action Idioms by Marvin Terban. Clarion, 1990. AVERAGE

Tuesday by David Wiesner. Clarion, 1991. EASY

Part 1
Reading Literature

Building Background

Access prior knowledge and build vocabulary concepts.

Tell students that the next story, "The Gold Coin," is about an old woman who helps her friends and neighbors. Begin a discussion about ways in which people help others. Ask students to make a web of ways in which people help others. Completed webs may look like the following:

Vocabulary Strategies

Introduce Key Words and strategies.

Display Transparency 35 or the following story. Invite students to read the sentences silently, using context clues with phonetic and structural analysis to decode and figure out the meanings of the underlined words. Then ask volunteers to read each sentence aloud. Help them with pronunciation if necessary.

Transparency 35   Key Words

One day, I came home from school and was <u>stunned</u> to find a <u>ransacked</u> apartment. Things had been pulled apart and thrown everywhere. I ran next door and <u>urgently</u> called the police. The officers arrived quickly, and we made a list of the things that had been stolen.

Then I noticed a few <u>shriveled</u> leaves lying on the floor in a corner of the kitchen where I keep some plants. Exhausted, I <u>lumbered</u> over to have a closer look. It seemed that the thief had even taken a flowerpot in which I had planted my favorite <u>herbs</u>, basil and mint.

CULTURAL AWARENESS

Students may be interested to know that gold has appealed to people of all cultures. Tell students that the search for a mythical place called *El Dorado* led the Spanish to settle Mexico, where this story takes place, and much of South America.

KEY WORDS

stunned
ransacked
urgently
shriveled
lumbered
herbs

KEY WORDS DEFINED

stunned shocked

ransacked searched thoroughly

urgently demanding quick action; demanding in a strong and serious way

shriveled curled up, withered, shrunk and wrinkled

lumbered moved along in a heavy, clumsy way

herbs plants whose leaves, stems, roots, flowers, and berries are used for medicines and seasonings

Check students' understanding.

Display the Key Words. Then read the following sentences aloud, repeating the underlined word or words. Have students write down a Key Word that means almost the same thing as the words you repeat.   STRATEGY: SYNONYMS

1. The cut flowers were <u>wrinkled and shrunken</u> from being out of water too long. *(shriveled)*
2. I was <u>shocked</u> when I opened the door and heard all my friends <u>shout</u>, "Happy birthday!" *(stunned)*
3. The poor family needed food supplies <u>immediately</u>. *(urgently)*
4. The bear in the zoo <u>walked heavily</u> over to the pail of food. *(lumbered)*
5. Mom flavored the salad with lots of <u>leaves and stems of certain plants</u>. *(herbs)*
6. We put things back where they belonged in the <u>thoroughly searched</u> house. *(ransacked)*

Integrate spelling with vocabulary.

SPELLING-VOCABULARY CONNECTION *Integrated Spelling* page 49 reinforces spellings of words that end in *-ed* or *-ing*, such as the Key Word *stunned* and other words. The spelling of the Key Word *herbs* is also included.

SECOND-LANGUAGE SUPPORT Point out that the Key Word *urgently* is an adverb, and that many adverbs end in *-ly*. Have students identify another adverb that ends in *-ly* in the story on Transparency 35. (quickly) Then ask them to change the following words into adverbs and use them in sentences: *rapid, slow, quiet, immediate.* (See Second-Language Support Manual.)

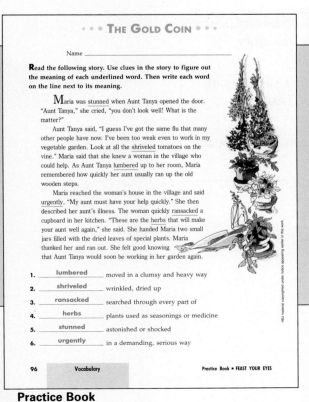

• • • THE GOLD COIN • • •

Name _____

Read the following story. Use clues in the story to figure out the meaning of each underlined word. Then write each word on the line next to its meaning.

Maria was <u>stunned</u> when Aunt Tanya opened the door. "Aunt Tanya," she cried, "you don't look well! What is the matter?"

Aunt Tanya said, "I guess I've got the same flu that many other people have now. I've been too weak even to work in my vegetable garden. Look at all the <u>shriveled</u> tomatoes on the vine." Maria said that she knew a woman in the village who could help. As Aunt Tanya <u>lumbered</u> up to her room, Maria remembered how quickly her aunt usually ran up the old wooden steps.

Maria reached the woman's house in the village and said <u>urgently</u>, "My aunt must have your help quickly." She then described her aunt's illness. The woman quickly <u>ransacked</u> a cupboard in her kitchen. "These are the <u>herbs</u> that will make your aunt well again," she said. She handed Maria two small jars filled with the dried leaves of special plants. Maria thanked her and ran out. She felt good knowing that Aunt Tanya would soon be working in her garden again.

1.	lumbered	moved in a clumsy and heavy way
2.	shriveled	wrinkled, dried up
3.	ransacked	searched through every part of
4.	herbs	plants used as seasonings or medicine
5.	stunned	astonished or shocked
6.	urgently	in a demanding, serious way

96   Vocabulary   Practice Book ▪ FEAST YOUR EYES

Practice Book

INTEGRATED SPELLING
Words with *-ed* and *-ing*

Name _____

Read the Spelling Words. Write them on another sheet of paper. Check your spelling.

SPELLING STRATEGY

To spell a word that ends in *-ed* or *-ing*, find the base word. If you want to add *-ed* or *-ing* to a verb, the base word will give you a clue about how to do this. With verbs that end with a short vowel and one consonant letter, double the final consonant before adding the *-ed* or *-ing*.

step + p + ing = stepping

stun + n + ed = stunned

Read the base words below. Then add *-ed* and *-ing*. Remember to double the final consonant.

	-ed	-ing
wrap	wrapped	wrapping
brim	brimmed	brimming
stun	stunned	stunning
step	stepped	stepping
mop	mopped	mopping
trim	trimmed	trimming
chop	chopped	chopping
shop	shopped	shopping
beg	begged	begging

SPELLING WORDS
begging
brimming
chopped
herb
mopped
shopping
stepping
stunned
trimmed
wrapped

MEMORY JOGGER

You'll be able to remember the **h** in the word **herb** if you remember this Memory Jogger.

Eat an **herb** to be **healthy**.

FEAST YOUR EYES • "The Gold Coin"   49

Integrated Spelling

• **PRACTICE BOOK**
• page 96: Reinforcing Key Words
•
• **INTEGRATED SPELLING**
• page 49: Writing and spelling words that end in *-ed* or *-ing*
•
• **NOTE:** These pages may be completed now or after students have read the story.

Preview and Predict

Help students preview the literature.

Review the steps involved in previewing a selection. (read and think about the title, look at the illustrations, and read the introduction and the first paragraphs) Encourage students to read the story title, look at the illustrations, and read the first three paragraphs.

Guide students in making predictions.

Ask students questions such as the following to help them make predictions about what might happen in the story:

- **Do you think Juan enjoys his way of life?**
- **What do you think the woman means when she says she must be the richest person in the world?**
- **Why might Juan be interested in the gold coin?**

PERSONAL JOURNAL Have students add their predictions about the selection to their personal journals. Ask students to support their predictions.

Setting a Purpose

Have students set purposes.

Discuss with students what they think they want to find out when they read the story, based on their preview and on what they already know. Have them use their predictions to set a purpose for reading.

Model purpose-setting, if necessary.

If students have difficulty setting a purpose for reading, offer this suggestion:

> **I'm going to read to find out what Juan will learn when he tries to get the gold coin.**

OPTIONS FOR READING

INDEPENDENT READING Have students read the story silently with their purpose for reading in mind.

GUIDED READING Follow the Guided Reading suggestions that appear on pages T623, T627, and T630. These suggestions model strategic reading.

COOPERATIVE READING A reader response strategy appears on page T623.

SECOND-LANGUAGE SUPPORT Have Spanish-speaking students teach the other students the correct pronunciation of the names of the characters in Spanish. (See Second-Language Support Manual.)

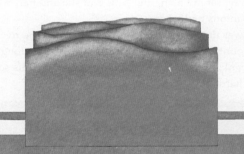

Juan had been a thief for many years. Because he did his stealing by night, his skin had become pale and sickly. Because he spent his time either hiding or sneaking about, his body had become shriveled and bent. And because he had neither friend nor relative to make him smile, his face was always twisted into an angry frown.

One night, drawn by a light shining through the trees, Juan came upon a hut. He crept up to the door and through a crack saw an old woman sitting at a plain, wooden table.

What was that shining in her hand? Juan wondered. He could not believe his eyes: It was a gold coin. Then he heard the woman say to herself, "I must be the richest person in the world."

355

Guided Reading

SET PURPOSE/PREDICT: PAGES 354–363   Have students read through page 363 to find out what begins to happen to Juan as he searches for the gold.

Cooperative Reading

READER RESPONSE STRATEGY: PAGES 354–357
Have each group of 3–5 students select a leader. Ask group members to read silently, and then encourage the leaders to use dialogue questions such as the one below. (Response Card 1: Characters, on page R62, offers a wide variety of dialogue questions.)

- **Which character do you trust, Juan or the old woman? Why?**

PAGES 358–369   After reading, the discussion leaders might ask:

- **Have you changed your mind about which character you would trust? Why or why not?**

Juan decided instantly that all the woman's gold must be his. He thought that the easiest thing to do was to watch until the woman left. Juan hid in the bushes and huddled under his poncho, waiting for the right moment to enter the hut.

Juan was half asleep when he heard knocking at the door and the sound of insistent voices. A few minutes later, he saw the woman, wrapped in a black cloak, leave the hut with two men at her side.

Here's my chance! Juan thought. And, forcing open a window, he climbed into the empty hut.

He looked about eagerly for the gold. He looked under the bed. It wasn't there. He looked in the cupboard. It wasn't there, either. Where could it be? Close to despair, Juan tore away some beams supporting the thatch roof.

Finally, he gave up. There was simply no gold in the hut.

All I can do, he thought, is to find the old woman and make her tell me where she's hidden it.

So he set out along the path that she and her two companions had taken.

It was daylight by the time Juan reached the river. The countryside had been deserted, but here, along the riverbank, were two huts. Nearby, a man and his son were hard at work, hoeing potatoes.

CULTURAL AWARENESS Students may not be familiar with the Spanish word *poncho*. Explain that a poncho is a type of cloak that is made from a large piece of cloth with a slit in the middle for the head to go through. If possible, show students a picture of a poncho, or draw a simple sketch on the board.

Informal Assessment You can informally assess your students' abilities to identify cause and effect and causal chains in stories that they read. On occasion, ask questions such as these:

- Why does this character do what he or she does?
- Are there any other reasons for the character's actions?
- What do you think will happen because this character does what he or she does and says what he or she says?

It had been a long, long time since Juan had spoken to another human being. Yet his desire to find the woman was so strong that he went up to the farmers and asked, in a hoarse, raspy voice, "Have you seen a short, gray-haired woman, wearing a black cloak?"

"Oh, you must be looking for Doña Josefa," the young boy said. "Yes, we've seen her. We went to fetch her this morning, because my grandfather had another attack of—"

"Where is she now?" Juan broke in.

"She is long gone," said the father with a smile. "Some people from across the river came looking for her, because someone in their family is sick."

"How can I get across the river?" Juan asked anxiously.

"Only by boat," the boy answered. "We'll row you across later, if you'd like." Then turning back to his work, he added, "But first we must finish digging up the potatoes."

The thief muttered, "Thanks." But he quickly grew impatient. He grabbed a hoe and began to help the pair of farmers. The sooner we finish, the sooner we'll get across the river, he thought. And the sooner I'll get to my gold!

It was dusk when they finally laid down their hoes. The soil had been turned, and the wicker baskets were brimming with potatoes.

"Now can you row me across?" Juan asked the father anxiously.

"Certainly," the man said. "But let's eat supper first."

Juan had forgotten the taste of a home-cooked meal and the pleasure that comes from sharing it with others. As he sopped up the last of the stew with a chunk of dark bread, memories of other meals came back to him from far away and long ago.

By the light of the moon, father and son guided their boat across the river.

"What a wonderful healer Doña Josefa is!" the boy told Juan. "All she had to do to make Abuelo better was give him a cup of her special tea."

"Yes, and not only that," his father added, "she brought him a gold coin."

Juan was stunned. It was one thing for Doña Josefa to go around helping people. But how could she go around handing out gold coins—*his gold coins*?

35

Second-Language Support

If you have Spanish-speaking students, they may want to explain the words *Doña* and *Don*. Alternatively, tell students that the terms *Doña* and *Don* are titles of respect that are used only before the first names of women and men.

When the threesome finally reached the other side of the river, they saw a young man sitting outside his hut.

"This fellow is looking for Doña Josefa," the father said, pointing to Juan.

"Oh, she left some time ago," the young man said.

"Where to?" Juan asked tensely.

"Over to the other side of the mountain," the young man replied, pointing to the vague outline of mountains in the night sky.

"How did she get there?" Juan asked, trying to hide his impatience.

"By horse," the young man answered. "They came on horseback to get her because someone had broken his leg."

"Well, then, I need a horse, too," Juan said urgently.

"Tomorrow," the young man replied softly. "Perhaps I can take you tomorrow, maybe the next day. First I must finish harvesting the corn."

So Juan spent the next day in the fields, bathed in sweat from sunup to sundown.

Yet each ear of corn that he picked seemed to bring him closer to his treasure. And later that evening, when he helped the young man husk several ears so they could boil them for supper, the yellow kernels glittered like gold coins.

360

CULTURAL AWARENESS   The Mexican constitution of 1917 redistributed about 50 percent of the nation's farmland from *haciendas*, large plantations owned by wealthy Spaniards, to *ejidos*, plots owned and worked by members of a community. A farmer may work a plot as an individual or as part of a group. Corn is the major farm crop in the southern part of the Central Plateau. Although modern machinery, such as a corn picker, is often used to harvest it, there are still many *ejidos* on which ancient farming procedures are employed.

While they were eating, Juan thought about Doña Josefa. Why, he wondered, would someone who said she was the world's richest woman spend her time taking care of every sick person for miles around?

The following day, the two set off at dawn. Juan could not recall when he last had noticed the beauty of the sunrise. He felt strangely moved by the sight of the mountains, barely lit by the faint rays of the morning sun.

As they neared the foothills, the young man said, "I'm not surprised you're looking for Doña Josefa. The whole countryside needs her. I went for her because my wife had been running a high fever. In no time at all, Doña Josefa had her on the road to recovery. And what's more, my friend, she brought her a gold coin!"

Juan groaned inwardly. To think that someone could hand out gold so freely! What a strange woman Doña Josefa is, Juan thought. Not only is she willing to help one person after another, but she doesn't mind traveling all over the countryside to do it!

"Well, my friend," said the young man finally, "this is where I must leave you. But you don't have far to walk. See that house over there? It belongs to the man who broke his leg."

The young man stretched out his hand to say good-bye. Juan stared at it for a moment. It had been a long, long time since the thief had shaken hands with anyone. Slowly, he pulled out a hand from under his poncho. When his companion grasped it firmly in his own, Juan felt suddenly warmed, as if by the rays of the sun.

But after he thanked the young man, Juan ran down the road. He was still eager to catch up with Doña Josefa. When he reached the house, a woman and a child were stepping down from a wagon.

"Have you seen Doña Josefa?" Juan asked.

"We've just taken her to Don Teodosio's," the woman said. "His wife is sick, you know—"

"How do I get there?" Juan broke in. "I've got to see her."

"It's too far to walk," the woman said amiably. "If you'd like, I'll take you there tomorrow. But first I must gather my squash and beans."

So Juan spent yet another long day in the fields. Working beneath the summer sun, Juan noticed that his skin had begun to tan. And although he had to stoop down to pick the squash, he found that he could now stretch his body. His back had begun to straighten, too.

363

Guided Reading

MONITOR COMPREHENSION: PAGES 354–363
What begins to happen to Juan as he searches for the gold? (His body begins to change—he gets tan, he can now stretch, and he can straighten his back.)   STRATEGIC READING: RETURNING TO PURPOSE/SUMMARIZING

Juan begins to wonder why Doña Josefa, who says she is the richest woman in the world, cares for sick people. Do you think Doña Josefa is rich? Explain your answer. (Accept reasonable responses: Yes; she is rich in things other than money.)   CRITICAL: SPECULATING

SET PURPOSE/PREDICT PAGES 364–369   Have students predict whether they think Juan will eventually catch up to Doña Josefa and steal her gold. Ask them to read the rest of the story to confirm their predictions.

Later, when the little girl took him by the hand to show him a family of rabbits burrowed under a fallen tree, Juan's face broke into a smile. It had been a long, long time since Juan had smiled.

Yet his thoughts kept coming back to the gold.

The following day, the wagon carrying Juan and the woman lumbered along a road lined with coffee fields.

The woman said, "I don't know what we would have done without Doña Josefa. I sent my daughter to our neighbor's house, who then brought Doña Josefa on horseback. She set my husband's leg and then showed me how to brew a special tea to lessen the pain."

Getting no reply, she went on. "And, as if that weren't enough, she brought him a gold coin. Can you imagine such a thing?"

Juan could only sigh. No doubt about it, he thought, Doña Josefa is someone special. But Juan didn't know whether to be happy that Doña Josefa had so much gold she could freely hand it out, or angry for her having already given so much of it away.

When they finally reached Don Teodosio's house, Doña Josefa was already gone. But here, too, there was work that needed to be done. . . .

364

Vocabulary Strategy   **How can you figure out the meaning of the word *burrowed* on page 364?** (When I read, I use context clues and visualize the scene described in the sentence. By doing this, I find out that the rabbits are under a fallen tree. The rabbits must have dug a hole in which to live in the ground under the tree. Therefore, *burrowed* must mean "living in a hole.")   STRATEGY: CONTEXT CLUES

Expanding the Literature   **How does the author bring Juan to the conclusion that Doña Josefa is special?** (Accept reasonable responses: Over and over again, Juan keeps missing Doña Josefa because she is on her way to help others. Someone who is always helping others is a special person.)   METACOGNITIVE: DRAWING CONCLUSIONS

Juan stayed to help with the coffee harvest. As he picked the red berries, he gazed up from time to time at the trees that grew, row upon row, along the hillsides. What a calm, peaceful place this is! he thought.

The next morning, Juan was up at daybreak. Bathed in the soft, dawn light, the mountains seemed to smile at him. When Don Teodosio offered him a lift on horseback, Juan found it difficult to have to say good-bye.

"What a good woman Doña Josefa is!" Don Teodosio said, as they rode down the hill toward the sugarcane fields. "The minute she heard about my wife being sick, she came with her special herbs. And as if that weren't enough, she brought my wife a gold coin!"

In the stifling heat, the kind that often signals the approach of a storm, Juan simply sighed and mopped his brow. The pair continued riding for several hours in silence.

Juan then realized he was back in familiar territory, for they were now on the stretch of road he had traveled only a week ago—though how much longer it now seemed to him. He jumped off Don Teodosio's horse and broke into a run.

This time the gold would not escape him! But he had to move quickly, so he could find shelter before the storm broke.

Out of breath, Juan finally reached Doña Josefa's

hut. She was standing by the door, shaking her head slowly as she surveyed the ransacked house.

"So I've caught up with you at last!" Juan shouted, startling the old woman. "Where's the gold?"

"The gold coin?" Doña Josefa said, surprised and looking at Juan intently. "Have you come for the gold coin? I've been trying hard to give it to someone who might need it," Doña Josefa said. "First to an old man who had just gotten over a bad attack. Then to a young woman who had been running a fever. Then to a man with a broken leg. And finally to Don Teodosio's wife. But none of them would take it. They all said, 'Keep it. There must be someone who needs it more.'"

Juan did not say a word.

"You must be the one who needs it," Doña Josefa said.

She took the coin out of her pocket and handed it to him. Juan stared at the coin, speechless.

At that moment a young girl appeared, her long braid bouncing as she ran. "Hurry, Doña Josefa, please!" she said breathlessly. "My mother is all alone, and the baby is due any minute."

"Of course, dear," Doña Josefa replied. But as she glanced up at the sky, she saw nothing but black clouds. The storm was nearly upon them. Doña Josefa sighed deeply.

367

Expanding the Literature   **Why do you think Juan has a hard time saying good-bye to Don Teodosio?** (Accept reasonable responses: Juan is beginning to enjoy farm life, the beauty of nature, and the kindness of others.)   INFERENTIAL: DRAWING CONCLUSIONS

How does the author's mention of an approaching storm add to the story? (Accept reasonable responses: It builds tension and hints that something is about to happen.)   CRITICAL: AUTHOR'S CRAFT/APPRECIATING IMAGERY

"But how can I leave now? Look at my house! I don't know what has happened to the roof. The storm will wash the whole place away!"

And there was a deep sadness in her voice.

Juan took in the child's frightened eyes, Doña Josefa's sad, distressed face, and the ransacked hut.

"Go ahead, Doña Josefa," he said. "Don't worry about your house. I'll see that the roof is back in shape, good as new."

The woman nodded gratefully, drew her cloak about her shoulders, and took the child by the hand. As she turned to leave, Juan held out his hand.

"Here, take this," he said, giving her the gold coin. "I'm sure the newborn will need it more than I."

THINK IT OVER

1. *In what way was Doña Josefa rich? Explain your answer.*
2. *How many gold coins did Doña Josefa have?*
3. *Describe the trouble Juan had in getting the gold coin.*
4. *What made Juan give back the gold coin?*

WRITE

Do you know someone who is like Doña Josefa? Write a poem telling how that person is special and how you feel about him or her.

Guided Reading

**MONITOR COMPREHENSION: PAGES 364–369
Does Juan eventually catch up to Doña Josefa and steal her gold?** (He catches up to her, but he doesn't steal her gold.) **Is this what you predicted would happen?** (Responses will vary.)
STRATEGIC READING: CONFIRMING PREDICTIONS/ SUMMARIZING

Why do you think Juan has a change of heart and volunteers to stay and repair the hut?
(Accept reasonable responses: He respects Doña Josefa for being a special person. He has learned to care about others.) INFERENTIAL: DETERMINING CHARACTERS' TRAITS/EMOTIONS

Returning to the Predictions Encourage students to discuss the predictions that they made before they began reading and that they may have written in their personal journals. Encourage them to talk about how those predictions changed as they read the story.

Returning to the Purpose for Reading
Ask students what Juan learns when he tries to get the gold coin. (He learns to do honest work, to appreciate the world around him, and to admire Doña Josefa.)

NOTE: Responses to Think It Over questions and support for the Write activity appear on page T631.

Part 2
Responding to Literature

Story Follow-Up

Think It Over

Encourage reader's response: student page 368.

1. **In what way was Doña Josefa rich? Explain your answer.** (Accept reasonable responses: She was rich because she gave to her friends, and they appreciated her for it.) CRITICAL: EXPRESSING PERSONAL OPINIONS

2. **How many gold coins did Doña Josefa have?** (one) LITERAL: NOTING IMPORTANT DETAILS

3. **Describe the trouble Juan had in getting the gold coin.** (He searched for Doña Josefa. At every home, he had to help the farm families before they could help him reach the next house.) INFERENTIAL: SUMMARIZING

4. **What made Juan give back the gold coin?** (Accept reasonable responses: After being with other people, Juan realized that others might need the gold more than he.) INFERENTIAL: DRAWING CONCLUSIONS

Write

Encourage writer's response: student page 368.

Do you know someone who is like Doña Josefa? Write a poem telling how that person is special and how you feel about him or her. Explain to students that their poems do not have to rhyme and can be any length. CREATIVE: WRITING A POEM

Summarizing the Literature

Have students retell the story and write a summary.

Encourage students to summarize the story by recalling key story elements. Guide students in beginning the story map below, and have them finish it independently. (See *Practice Book* page 97 on T632.) Students may use their completed story maps to retell the story and to write a brief summary statement.

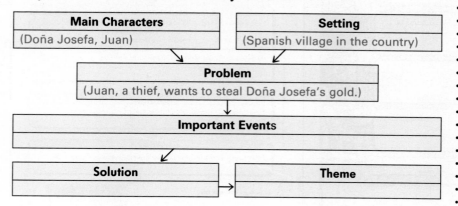

Main Characters		Setting
(Doña Josefa, Juan)		(Spanish village in the country)

Problem
(Juan, a thief, wants to steal Doña Josefa's gold.)

Important Events

Solution		Theme

STRATEGY CONFERENCE

Ask students what they found difficult about reading the story. Together, brainstorm strategies such as visualizing that might help them better understand the story.

NOTE

An additional writing activity for this selection appears on page T634.

Appreciating Literature

Have students share personal responses.

Have students work in small groups to discuss the story. Provide general questions such as the following to help the groups begin:

- **Do you feel there is a message for the reader in this work? What is it?**
- **Do you agree with it? Explain your answer.**

PERSONAL JOURNAL Have students use their personal journals to write about ideas and feelings that are discussed in the groups. You may refer them to their personal journals after they complete the activities below.

Critical Thinking Activities

Encourage both cooperative and individual responses.

DISCUSS OPINIONS Do you like the way the author has the main character learn new values? Explain why. Then discuss other ways the author could have accomplished the same thing. Encourage students to work in small groups to discuss their opinions and ideas. CRITICAL: MAKING JUDGMENTS

CREATE A SKIT How can you teach values? Work with your group to prepare a skit that teaches something you believe in strongly. After students have prepared skits, encourage them to present their skits to the other groups. CREATIVE: SOLVING PROBLEMS

STUDENT SELF-ASSESSMENT

Help students self-assess their listening skills by writing the following questions on the board:

- Was I able to visualize the speakers' ideas about this story?
- Were any of the ideas discussed similar to what I was thinking?

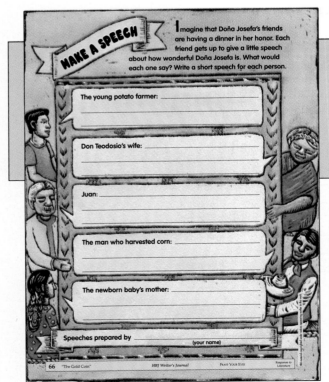

Writer's Journal

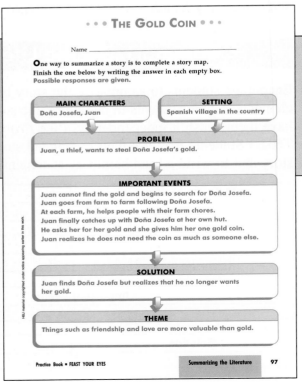

Practice Book

WRITER'S JOURNAL
page 66: Writing a personal response

PRACTICE BOOK
page 97: Summarizing the selection

VO·CAB·U·LAR·Y Workshop

Reviewing Key Words

Display the Key Words and have the students answer the following questions, orally or in writing:

1. *shriveled*   **If something is shriveled, how does it look?** (curled up, shrunken and wrinkled)
2. *stunned*   **Name a situation in which you would be stunned.** (Accept reasonable responses: if you found a lot of money.)
3. *urgently*   **If someone needs something urgently, when does she or he need it?** (immediately)
4. *lumbered*   **How would something move if it lumbered?** (slowly and heavily)
5. *herbs*   **What are herbs? How are they used?** (plants; they season food or can be made into medicines)
6. *ransacked*   **When might you find a ransacked room?** (Accept reasonable responses: after someone has searched very thoroughly for something.)

Extending Vocabulary

NAMES FROM DIFFERENT LANGUAGES   Remind students that the setting of "The Gold Coin" is a Spanish-speaking country. Ask volunteers to name the characters in the story and create a chart like the following on the board. Then assist students in thinking of possible English equivalents for each Spanish name.

Spanish Name	Possible English Name
Juan	John
Josefa	Josephine
Abuelo	Grandfather
Teodosio	Theodore

Next, distribute a strip of colored construction paper and crayons or paints to each student. Provide books that give names from other languages. Help students find equivalents of their own names in other languages. They may choose to learn the Spanish forms of their names or the equivalent, if any, in another language. Students who have non-English names may learn the English form of their names. Then invite students to use the art materials to make place cards with their names in another language.
CULTURAL AWARENESS

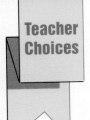

Teacher Choices

Integrated Language Arts

READING

Oral Rereading/ Drama

AVAILABLE ON PROJECT CARD

Ask students to work in small groups. Have group members choose one scene from the story and reread it silently. Then ask the groups to write additional dialogue and narration and to dramatize the scene. You may wish to have students make simple props and/or costumes. Allow groups time to rehearse, and then have them present their scenes for their classmates. LISTENING/ SPEAKING/READING/WRITING

WRITING

Writing About the Literature

WRITE A FABLE Explain that in "The Gold Coin" one of the characters learns an important lesson. Remind students that one kind of story in which a character learns a lesson is a fable. If necessary, review the meaning of *fable*: a brief story, usually with animal characters who possess human traits. Ask students to think of a lesson that could be taught in the form of a fable. Have them organize their ideas in a chart similar to the one below. Then have each student write a fable that presents a lesson. When the fables are finished, call on several volunteers to read their work to the others. LISTENING/READING/WRITING

FABLE CHART		
Lesson Learned	**Characters**	**Setting**
It is better to give than to receive.	animals or humans	a party

NOTE: An additional writing activity appears on page T631.

SPELLING

Reviewing Spelling Words

SPELLING WORDS: *begging, brimming, chopped, herb, mopped, shopping, stepping, stunned, trimmed, wrapped*

Encourage students to keep a notebook listing of words they find that fit the spelling pattern (doubling letters before adding *-ed, -ing*). Have them search for these words while they are reading, watching television, looking at billboards, etc. Encourage students to share their word list with classmates. Have them look up any unfamiliar words and read their definitions to classmates. LISTENING/READING/WRITING/SPELLING

> **INTEGRATED SPELLING**
>
> page 50: Writing words with *-ed* and *-ing* endings

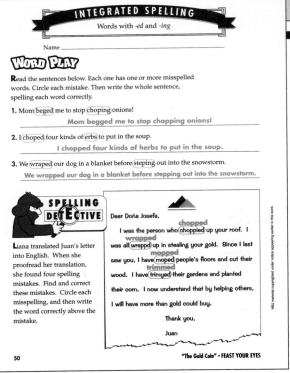

Integrated Spelling

SPEAKING

Just Suppose . . .

Remind students that Juan learned an important lesson from Doña Josefa without her ever realizing it. Point out that Juan gradually came to think differently about the way he lived as events led up to the end of the story. Ask students to think about what might have happened if Juan had met Doña Josefa earlier in the story. You may also wish to ask students whether they think Juan would have eventually changed as he did or if he might have remained a thief. Students should be prepared to support their thinking. Call on volunteers to share their ideas with classmates. LISTENING/SPEAKING

WRITING

In the Footsteps of a Thief

AVAILABLE ON PROJECT CARD

COOPERATIVE LEARNING Have students work in small groups. Ask them to imagine that they are Juan. Encourage them to think about why their attitude changes after several days of following Doña Josefa around the countryside. Then invite students to work together to write diary entries that span the time from when they first overhear Doña Josefa talking to herself through the offer to repair her hut. Remind students to record these events as Juan might have, using personal pronouns. Volunteers from each group may share their diary entries with classmates. LISTENING/SPEAKING/READING/WRITING

LISTENING

Crop Club

Invite a farmer from your community or a neighboring community and a representative from another country to discuss the crops that are grown in their areas. Ask speakers to focus on the farming techniques, machinery, and different uses for the crops. Encourage students to compare and contrast information about the different crops and to ask the speakers questions. LISTENING/SPEAKING

WRITING

Golden Touch

Remind students that Doña Josefa considered herself the richest woman in the world, yet she had only one gold coin. Ask students to speculate about what Doña Josefa meant by "rich." Then have them put their thoughts about the meaning of *rich* into the form of an essay of three or four paragraphs. To help them organize their ideas, you may wish to suggest that students make a map with the word "rich" at the center. Remind students to begin with a topic sentence and then add details and examples to support their ideas. You may want to have peers critique the essays. Some students may want to incorporate peers' suggestions into their work. Volunteers may share their work with classmates.
LISTENING/SPEAKING/READING/WRITING

Part 3
Learning Through Literature

Making Generalizations

OBJECTIVE: *To recognize and make generalizations*

1   Focus

Discuss how to recognize and make generalizations.

Tell students that when the farmer says to Juan, "I'm not surprised you're looking for Doña Josefa. The whole countryside needs her," he is making a *generalization*. Explain that a generalization is a general statement or idea reached as a conclusion by evaluating main ideas, details, and prior knowledge. The farmer is generalizing based on knowledge of times in the past when people had needed Doña Josefa's help.

2   Teach/Model

Teach how to make a generalization.

Explain to students that a generalization is a judgment or a conclusion. Point out that by evaluating what each character says about Doña Josefa, the reader can draw a conclusion, or make a generalization, about her. Then model making a generalization about Doña Josefa.

> **To make a generalization about Doña Josefa, I read what the characters say about her. A young boy says that Doña Josefa has healed his Abuelo by giving him a cup of her special tea. A young man mentions that she has helped his wife recover from an illness. A woman tells Juan that Doña Josefa has set her husband's broken leg. In all cases Doña Josefa brought the patient a gold coin. Based on what the characters say, I can generalize that Doña Josefa is a very generous woman who helps many people.**

Have students evaluate information.

Use a diagram to help students collect information about which they can make a generalization. Write *Generalization* and *Crops Grown in Mexico* on the board. Then work as a group to collect information from the selection and add it to the diagram.

(corn) — **Crops Grown in Mexico** — (potatoes)

(coffee)

Generalization: Many different crops are grown in Mexico.

Have students apply the learning.	**3** **Practice/Apply**

COOPERATIVE LEARNING Suggest that student pairs evaluate information about Juan. Remind them to evaluate Juan at the beginning of the story and at the end. Suggest that they complete a diagram about Juan. Then have students make a generalization about Juan.

Informally assess the learning.	**4** **Summarize**

Discuss the diagrams that students made about Juan. Encourage students to share and evaluate their generalizations.

Check understanding by having students summarize what they learned. (Generalizing is extending meaning by drawing a conclusion based on the selection's main ideas and details and on personal experience.)

READER ⬌ WRITER CONNECTION

Making Generalizations

▶ **Writers** make generalizations to lead readers to understand the point they are trying to make.
▶ **Readers** can make generalizations based on selection information and prior knowledge.

WRITE A DESCRIPTION Have students study pictures of birds in order to create a list of generalizations about birds. Then have students write a paragraph describing birds as if they were teaching a young child about birds.

CHALLENGE Have students write a paragraph on any subject. Then have them work in pairs, exchange papers, and make generalizations based upon each other's writing.

SECOND-LANGUAGE SUPPORT Students can demonstrate their understanding of generalizations by naming some of their favorite foods and then making a generalization about them. (See *Second-Language Support Manual*.)

Writer's Journal

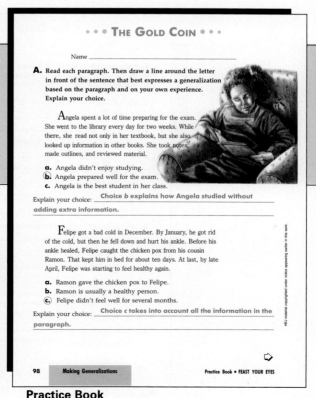

Practice Book

WRITER'S JOURNAL page 67: Writing a description

PRACTICE BOOK pages 98–99: Making generalizations

THE GOLD COIN / **T637**

Story Elements

OBJECTIVE: *To use setting, characters, and plot to gain meaning*

Review

Review how story elements work together.

Review the concepts of characters, setting, and plot. Tell students that they can better appreciate "The Gold Coin" by understanding how these elements work together in the story. Use the diagram below to model the story's development.

CHARACTER	SETTING	PLOT	
Juan, thief	Juan goes to . . .	What He Does	What He Learns
	Doña Josefa's hut	ransacks it	The gold is missing.

Practice/Apply

Have students analyze story elements.

Have students complete similar diagrams by analyzing what Juan does and what he learns in other instances.

Summarize

Informally assess the learning.

Using the completed diagrams, read the story elements that affect Juan at each place he visits. Discuss how the elements are related.

Ask students to summarize what they learned. (Story elements—characters, setting, and plot—work together to develop a story.)

CHALLENGE Have students think about how the plot might have changed if Juan hadn't helped anyone along the way or had just waited at the hut for Doña Josefa. Ask students to write a new plot and ending for the story.

PRACTICE BOOK
page 100: Using story elements

• • • THE GOLD COIN • • •

Name _____

Each sentence below is taken from the story. Read each one. On the line provided, write *character, setting,* or *plot* to tell which story element is demonstrated. Explain your answer.

1. Juan had been a thief for many years. ___*character—It tells something about Juan.*___

2. Juan decided instantly that all the woman's gold must be his. ___*character—It shows how greedy Juan is.*___

3. The countryside had been deserted, but here, along the riverbank, were two huts. ___*setting—It tells about the location where the story takes place.*___

4. But he quickly grew impatient. ___*character—It tells something about Juan.*___

5. Juan had forgotten the taste of a home-cooked meal and the pleasure that comes from sharing it with others. ___*character—It tells something about Juan.*___

6. By the light of the moon, father and son guided their boat across the river. ___*plot—It tells what happened.*___

7. "Over to the other side of the mountain," the young man replied, pointing to the vague outline of mountains in the night sky. ___*setting—It tells about where the story takes place.*___

8. So Juan spent the next day in the fields, bathed in sweat from sunup to sundown. ___*plot—It tells what happened.*___

100   Story Elements   Practice Book ▪ FEAST YOUR EYES

Practice Book

Structural Analysis

OBJECTIVE: *To use prefixes, Greek and Latin roots, and suffixes for independent decoding of words*

Review

Review using prefixes, roots, and suffixes.

Remind students that if a reader understands the pronunciations and meanings of prefixes, suffixes, and Greek or Latin roots, the meaning of the whole word will be easier to figure out. Display the following chart. Model identifying the prefix, the root, and the suffix, and the meaning of *predictable*.

Word	Prefix	Root	Suffix	Meaning
predictable	*pre-* ("before")	*dict* ("speak")	*-able* ("having qualities of")	"capable of telling about beforehand"

Practice/Apply

Have students apply the learning.

Have students add to the chart words with prefixes and/or suffixes and Greek or Latin roots from this or a previously read selection.

Summarize

Informally assess the learning.

Ask students to share their charts and explain how they determined pronunciations and meanings of the words.

Have students summarize the learning. (Prefixes, roots, and suffixes are clues to a word's pronunciation and meaning.)

CHALLENGE Have students examine dictionaries to find words that are related in meaning because of a common root. For example, students may find *grateful*, *gratify*, and *gratitude*.

PRACTICE BOOK
page 101: Using structural analysis

• • • THE GOLD COIN • • •

Name _____

A. Read the information in the chart. Using the definitions, answer each question below.

Prefix	Meaning	Suffix	Meaning
de-	"to remove"	-ly	"in the manner of"
im-	"not"	-less	"without"
		-er	"one who"; "more"

1. The Latin root *sperare* means "to hope." What do you think the English word *despair* means? _"without hope, to give up hope"_

2. The word *patient* means "calm and understanding." How would you describe someone who is not patient? _impatient_

3. The word *speech* means "the act of speaking." If someone could not speak for a time, what word would describe the person? _speechless_

4. The word *amiable* is from a Latin word meaning "friend." If someone acts amiably, how does he or she act? _in a friendly manner_

5. A farmer is one who farms. A teacher is one who teaches. What would you call one who heals? _a healer_

B. Use the base words below and the prefixes and suffixes in the chart to form words. Then write a sentence using each of the words you formed. Sentences will vary.

1. anxious _____

2. possible _____

Practice Book • FEAST YOUR EYES   Structural Analysis   101

Practice Book

Integrated **Curriculum**

SOCIAL STUDIES

Which Way Did He Go?

AVAILABLE ON PROJECT CARD

COOPERATIVE LEARNING   Remind students that Juan travels around the countryside and makes several stops before he finally finds Doña Josefa back at her own hut. Invite students to work in pairs and use story clues to create a map of Juan's travels. For example, one description indicates that there are mountains nearby. Encourage the pairs to make a rough draft of their maps first. Then provide them with small sheets of chart paper to elaborate on their ideas. Remind students to include a compass rose and a key to explain where various important events take place. When they are finished, have students explain what they have drawn.
LISTENING/SPEAKING/READING/WRITING

MATH

Money, Money, Money!

Invite students to take a survey by polling their classmates to find out how they earn or are given spending money. Encourage students to choose a way to record the information, such as tallying or recording information on a picture graph similar to the one below, or another type of graph. When the information has been recorded, have students take turns asking and answering questions based on their findings.   LISTENING/SPEAKING/ WRITING

Ways We Get Money

550
280
60
30

Chores   Allowance   Baby-sitting   Miscellaneous

SCIENCE

Take Your Medicine

CULTURAL AWARENESS   Remind students that Doña Josefa uses herbs to make medicines to treat her patients. Explain to students that Africans and North and South American Indians have known about the medicinal properties of certain plants for many hundreds of years. Provide students with books and reference sources, and have them find out more about herbs and how they are used. You may wish to suggest that students compile their findings into an herbal dictionary by pasting or drawing pictures of herbs and writing brief descriptions of the medicinal properties of each herb. When the book is finished, place it where students can refer to it.
READING/WRITING

SOCIAL STUDIES

If I Only Had . . .

Explain to students that in many cultures around the world, people dream about what they would do if they had a large sum of money. Invite students to imagine what they would do if they were suddenly given a lot of money. Have them express their ideas in a short story. When they have finished, invite students to share their stories.   LISTENING/SPEAKING/READING/WRITING

ART

Magnificent Mexico

AVAILABLE ON PROJECT CARD

CULTURAL AWARENESS   Have students research Mexico to find out about its famous statues, land formations, buildings, ruins, and so on. Then have each student make a mosaic of the item that they found most interesting. Remind students that a mosaic is a piece of art made of many small pieces of stone, paper, or other appropriate materials. Encourage students to share their mosaics with classmates and to explain why the subject of each mosaic is significant.   LISTENING/SPEAKING/ READING

The Healing Art

READ ALOUD TO STUDENTS:

MOTHER TERESA IS KNOWN ALL

OVER THE WORLD FOR HER

CARING, SENSITIVE WAYS.
Mother Teresa is an elderly Yugoslavian woman who has devoted her life to helping poor, sick, and orphaned children in the slums of Calcutta, India, and elsewhere.

Caring and compassion for people marked the life of Andrea Candalaria, who lived to be 113. During the battle of the Alamo, Candalaria was trapped inside the mission with the Texans who were fighting for their independence from Mexico. There was no possibility of getting the wounded men out, but Candalaria bravely nursed them all. Later, during a smallpox epidemic in Texas, Nurse Candalaria tirelessly cared for the sick without regard for her own safety.

African American Daniel Hale Williams was a skilled physician who performed the first successful open-heart surgery in 1893. But Williams also helped people in communities around the United States. He worked to build hospitals and schools to train medical personnel so that more African Americans could become doctors and nurses and health care services could be provided to more people. ■

ACTIVITY CORNER

■ Ask students to imagine they are Daniel Hale Williams on the day he was confronted with the patient dying from a stab wound. Have students write a journal entry in which they discuss their thoughts about whether or not to try open-heart surgery.

■ Have students write a newspaper article in which they report on a day in the life of Mother Teresa, Andrea Candalaria, or Daniel Hale Williams. Remind students to include in their article *what, when, where, who,* and *why.*

Mother Teresa and Daniel Hale Williams are some of the people who have devoted their lives to helping others.

POEM

Pearls

ABOUT THE POET   Jean Little wrote her first "book" when she was ten years old. At age twelve she began to write poems. Her father had a booklet of her poems printed privately when she was fifteen, and it was he who encouraged her to become a writer. Her first book, *Mine for Keeps,* won the Canadian Children's Book Award in 1961 and was an ALA Notable Book for 1962.

ABOUT THE POEM   "Pearls" is a poem in free verse with a surprise ending. It is contained in an anthology entitled *Hey World, Here I Am!* which was also an ALA Notable Book.

Reading the Poem

Help students set a purpose for reading.

Encourage students to think about some of the things that people consider treasures. Point out that Juan in "The Gold Coin" reconsidered what he most valued as treasure. Invite students to share the things they consider to be treasures. Suggest that they include both material and abstract items.

Have students read the poem's title. Ask them to predict whether they think the narrator considers pearls to be treasure. Read the poem aloud to model how to read free verse, and then invite students to read the poem aloud in unison.

Responding to the Poem

Return to the purpose for reading.

Ask students whether their predictions about what the narrator considers to be treasure were confirmed. Have volunteers point out any lines in the poem that caused them to change their predictions.

Encourage students to respond creatively.

You may wish to select one of the following activities for responding to the poem:

MAKING A BIRTHDAY DREAM   Recall with students that the narrator was given a string of pearls for her birthday. Ask them to think of something that they would like to receive on their next birthday. Provide students with a variety of art materials, such as paper, paints, and clay, and ask them to draw, paint, or sculpt a birthday dream. When students are finished, invite them to write a poem about their birthday dream in free verse or in rhyme. Invite students to read their poem aloud and to display their artwork.   LISTENING/READING/WRITING

FINDING OUT ABOUT PEARLS   Explain to students that natural pearls come from living things—oysters. Invite students to use reference sources to find out more about how pearls are made and how people obtain and use pearls. Encourage students to take notes and to put their findings into the form of a brief report. READING/WRITING

MEETING INDIVIDUAL NEEDS

SECOND-LANGUAGE SUPPORT   Share with students that a "string" of pearls is a necklace made up of pearls that are strung together like beads.

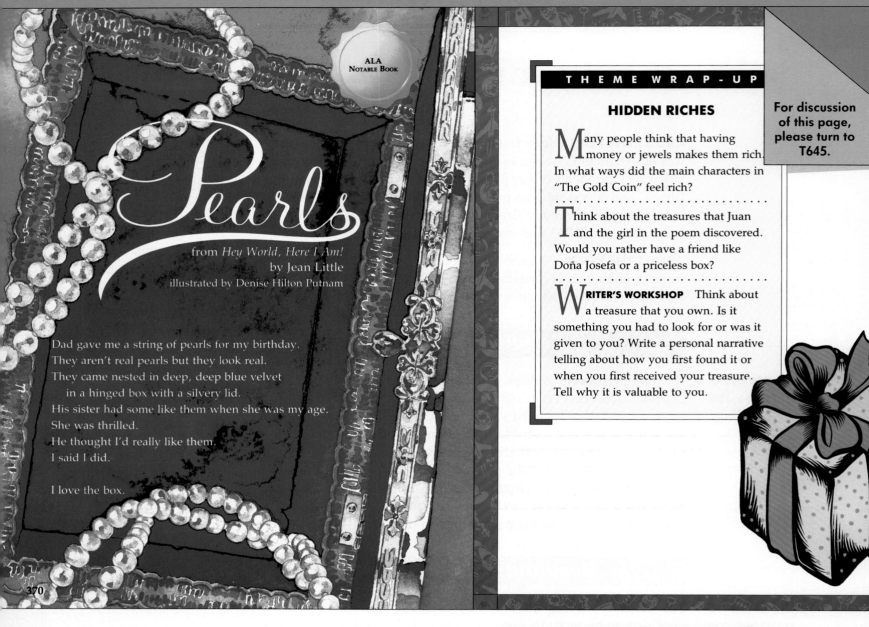

ALA
Notable Book

Pearls

from *Hey World, Here I Am!*
by Jean Little
illustrated by Denise Hilton Putnam

Dad gave me a string of pearls for my birthday.
They aren't real pearls but they look real.
They came nested in deep, deep blue velvet
    in a hinged box with a silvery lid.
His sister had some like them when she was my age.
She was thrilled.
He thought I'd really like them.
I said I did.

I love the box.

370

THEME WRAP-UP

HIDDEN RICHES

Many people think that having money or jewels makes them rich. In what ways did the main characters in "The Gold Coin" feel rich?

Think about the treasures that Juan and the girl in the poem discovered. Would you rather have a friend like Doña Josefa or a priceless box?

WRITER'S WORKSHOP Think about a treasure that you own. Is it something you had to look for or was it given to you? Write a personal narrative telling about how you first found it or when you first received your treasure. Tell why it is valuable to you.

For discussion of this page, please turn to T645.

Expanding the Poem How do you think the narrator feels about her birthday gift? How can you tell? (Accept reasonable responses: She prefers the box over the gift. She describes the box in vivid detail, and she says she loves the box. She seems to like the pearls only for her father's sake.)
INFERENTIAL: DRAWING CONCLUSIONS

A TREASURED GIFT

FOR MY CHILD

Suppose you are a parent and you have a special gift for your child. On this page, write the note that might be given with your gift. Then put yourself in the place of the child who receives the gift. Write a thank-you note for the gift on the next page.

Love,

68 "Pearls"   *HBJ Writer's Journal*   FEAST YOUR EYES   Response to Literature

WRITER'S JOURNAL pages 68–69: Writing a personal response

THEME WRAP-UP

Hidden Riches

Discuss how the story and poem in this theme focused on valuable treasures that have nothing to do with money. Remind students that they read about a man who discovers that the value of helping others is greater than any gold and about someone who finds a box more valuable than the pearls inside it. Explain to students that the questions on page 371 will help them think further about ideas from these selections.

Note that pages T646–T647 provide support for applying the writing process to the last question.

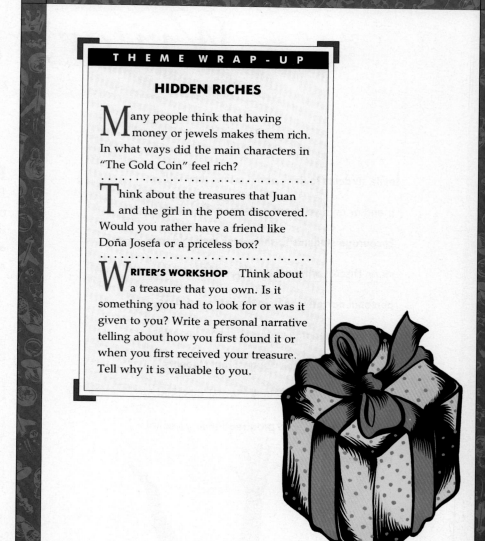

THEME WRAP-UP

HIDDEN RICHES

Many people think that having money or jewels makes them rich. In what ways did the main characters in "The Gold Coin" feel rich?

Think about the treasures that Juan and the girl in the poem discovered. Would you rather have a friend like Doña Josefa or a priceless box?

WRITER'S WORKSHOP   Think about a treasure that you own. Is it something you had to look for or was it given to you? Write a personal narrative telling about how you first found it or when you first received your treasure. Tell why it is valuable to you.

371

Theme Wrap-Up

DISCUSSION QUESTIONS, PAGE 371
Many people think that having money or jewels makes them rich. In what ways did the main characters in "The Gold Coin" feel rich?
Suggest that students review how the characters lived. (Accept reasonable responses: They felt rich in family, friends, and the beauty and bounty of the land around them.)   INFERENTIAL: DETERMINING CHARACTERS' EMOTIONS

Think about the treasures that Juan and the girl in the poem discovered. Would you rather have a friend like Doña Josefa or a priceless box?
Encourage students to think about what Doña Josefa did for the people and what they said about her as well as about how the girl in the poem felt about the gift. (Responses will vary.)   CRITICAL: EXPRESSING PERSONAL OPINIONS

WRITER'S WORKSHOP   See pages T646–T647 for suggestions for applying the writing process.
Think about a treasure that you own. Is it something you had to look for or was it given to you? Write a personal narrative telling about how you first found it or when you first received your treasure. Tell why it is valuable to you.
You may prefer to allow students to respond to the theme in their own way.   WRITING PROCESS: A PERSONAL NARRATIVE

Writer's Workshop

For More Discussion & Practice:

LANGUAGE HANDBOOK

Invite students to think about a time they told a friend or relative about an event in their lives. Encourage students to share how they told their story. Discuss what needs to be included in a personal narrative to help the listener picture what happened and understand how important it was to the narrator. Suggest that students refer to the Handbook in the *Writer's Journal* as they write, revise, and proofread their personal narratives.

Prewriting

Before students begin to write, tell them to close their eyes and recall when they first discovered or received their treasure. Invite students to

- think about their treasure and why it is important.
- use a story map to organize events that tell how they got their treasure. Suggest that they also include the feelings they had when they found or received the treasure. Story maps may resemble the following:

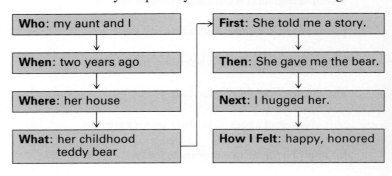

Who: my aunt and I	**First**: She told me a story.
When: two years ago	**Then**: She gave me the bear.
Where: her house	**Next**: I hugged her.
What: her childhood teddy bear	**How I Felt**: happy, honored

Suggest that students add to their story map as they remember more about the incident.

Drafting

Invite students to write a draft of the personal narrative. Point out that they should

- begin the narrative with a sentence that identifies their treasure.
- refer to their story map to describe how they found or were given their treasure.
- include an explanation of why the treasure is important to them and how they feel about it.
- write freely without worrying about spelling, punctuation, or grammar.

COMPUTER CONNECTION   Students may want to use a computer during the revising stage so that they can easily modify adjectives and descriptive phrases in their writing.

Responding and Revising

Invite students to exchange narratives with a partner, read each other's work silently, and discuss whether the narratives are complete. Offer the following tips. Then invite students to revise their work.

- Does the first sentence tell what the narrative is about? If not, revise or add information.
- Does the narrative present events in time order and give details about what people said, did, and felt? If not, cut or add details.
- Does the narrative vividly describe events? If not, replace dull words with vivid synonyms. (See the Language/Literature Link below.)

STUDENT SELF-ASSESSMENT OPTION   Students may use the Writing Self-Assessment Checklist in the *Portfolio Teacher's Guide*. Suggest that as they use the checklist they focus on the organization of the paragraph and the use of a variety of words.

Proofreading

Offer the following tips to help students proofread their work and make changes:

- Make sure that every sentence begins with a capital letter.
- Check for errors in grammar.
- Look for words that appear to be misspelled. Check them in a dictionary.

Publishing

You may wish to discuss with students options for publishing their personal narratives. Some students may wish to create a bulletin board display. Invite them to illustrate their narratives with pictures of themselves and of their treasures. Other students may share their narratives with family members and then save their work in their reading/writing portfolios.

LANGUAGE/LITERATURE LINK

Using a Thesaurus

Point out that successful writers use a variety of words in their personal narratives to keep their readers interested. A handy resource for words is a thesaurus, which lists groups of synonyms, or words with similar meanings. Invite students to look through "The Gold Coin" for examples of vivid words that keep the reader interested. Encourage students to check their work and use a thesaurus to replace dull words with more vivid ones.

Speaking Option

TELLING ABOUT A TREASURE   The Writer's Workshop may be adapted to allow students to give an oral reading of their personal narratives. Encourage students to follow the guidelines for Prewriting, Drafting, and Responding and Revising. Offer the following tips to help students read their personal narratives aloud:

- Practice reading your narrative aloud until you can read it smoothly and clearly.

- Speak slowly so that your audience can understand you.

- Use facial and voice expression to show your audience that you are interested in telling them about your subject.

Invite each student to read his or her personal narrative to an audience of classmates.

Connections

The Connections activities on Student Anthology pages 372–373 guide students to synthesize multicultural and content-area information with the unit theme. Before students begin the activities, ask them to review quickly the purpose-setting paragraph on page 290. Then have them identify their favorite selections from the unit and consider why each selection was included in this unit.

To prepare students for the Multicultural Connection, you might ask whether they have seen pictures of people wearing masks at a Mardi Gras celebration or in theatrical presentations.

Explain that the custom of wearing masks for ceremonies and theatrical presentations originated with the ancient civilizations of Greece, Africa, China, and Japan and with those of the North and South American Indians. Point out that masks are still used today in some classical theater presentations and in celebrations around the world.

CONNECTIONS

girl with festive

MULTICULTURAL CONNECTION

MEXICAN MASKS

Dr. Eduardo Matos Moctezuma of Mexico has directed many archaeological projects in order to learn more about the ancient people of his country. Dr. Moctezuma and other archaeologists around the world often are puzzled by what they find.

Many ancient Mexican masks have been discovered, but we can't be sure why these masks were made and worn. We know more about the Mexican masks of recent centuries. Generations of carvers handed down the art of maskmaking. Their striking masks were worn by dancers acting out folktales.

Mexican masks have made their way north. Today you might see the masks on the actors of a Mexican American theater group. Or you might see them displayed in a museum as the work of modern artists.

■ *With your classmates, choose a Mexican folktale or one from another culture. Then create masks for all the characters.*

SOCIAL STUDIES CONNECTION

MYSTERIES OF THE MAYA

Who were the mysterious people who created the early masks of Mexico? Read about one of the Mexican native groups, such as the Maya, the Aztecs, or the Toltecs. Use what you learn to create a bulletin board display. List some questions that archaeologists have answered and some they have not answered.

Mexican Indian cat mask

This chart might help you organize information.

Name of group	
A question	
Why this is a question	
What the answer is OR Why there is no answer	

ART CONNECTION

WHAT IS IT?

Archaeologists are often puzzled by the things they find. Puzzle your classmates in the same way by drawing a useful object that doesn't exist. Design the object so that its use makes sense once someone knows what it is. Challenge your classmates to tell what the object is for and to name it.

373

Multicultural Connection

MEXICAN MASKS   As students read about Mexican masks, remind them to look at the photographs and read the captions. Supply materials, such as poster board, scissors, markers, yarn, and hole punchers, with which students can make their own masks. Have groups of five or six students work together to choose a folktale and make masks.

Social Studies Connection

MYSTERIES OF THE MAYA   Encourage students to begin investigating Mayan civilization by imagining themselves as archaeologists on a dig and thinking about what they might uncover. Then have students "dig" into encyclopedias and social studies textbooks to find answers. Invite them to then complete the bulletin board activity.

Art Connection

WHAT IS IT?   Be sure that students understand the directions before they begin drawing their objects. Suggest that students look through mail-order catalogs if they are having difficulty thinking of something to draw.

Integrated Language Arts

Reviewing Vocabulary—Synonym Shuffle

- Write four Key Words from Unit 4 on the board. Have students name two synonyms for each. Refer to the following lists.

Key Word	Synonyms
1. exhaustion	1. tiredness, weakness
2. UFO	2. flying saucer, spacecraft
3. urgently	3. demandingly, immediately
4. device	4. machine, gadget

Write the following columns of words on the board, leaving a space for the first word in the second, third, and fourth boxes.

exhaustion spaceship tiredness weakness	(spaceship) UFO flying saucer immediately	(immediately) machine urgently demandingly	(machine) device gadget

Have students identify the three synonyms in the first box and tell which word does not belong. *(spaceship)* Ask a volunteer to "move" *spaceship* by crossing it out and writing it at the top of the second box. Have volunteers continue shuffling synonyms in this manner.

- Encourage students to work in groups to make Synonym Shuffles from the remaining Key Words or other interesting words encountered in this unit. Groups may exchange puzzles and compete to finish them.

Reviewing Spelling Words

Integrated Spelling page 51 provides a review of the Unit 4 spelling words. *Integrated Spelling* page 52 provides practice with frequently misspelled homophones.

Writing About "Discoveries"

You may wish to have students respond to the unit focus by writing a review or a letter asking for or giving advice to add to the magazines in their *Writer's Journals.* Provide them with copies of book, theater, or movie reviews and advice columns from magazines to use as examples. (See *Writer's Journal* pages 70–71.)

INTEGRATED SPELLING
pages 51–52: Reviewing unit words and homophones

WRITER'S JOURNAL
pages 70–71: Making Your Own Magazine

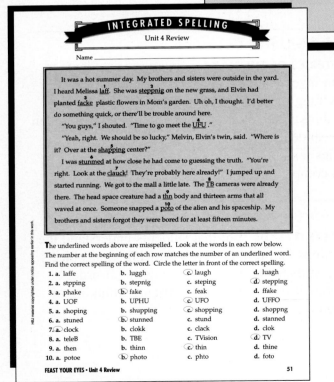

Integrated Spelling

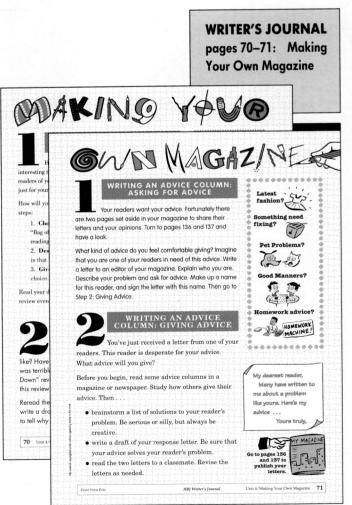

Writer's Journal

Assessment Options

Informal Assessment

See the suggestions below to informally assess students' progress in Unit 4.

INFORMAL ASSESSMENT NOTES AND CHECKLISTS

If you used the informal assessment notes in the lesson plans to evaluate students' reading and writing behaviors, you may now want to update your Running Records. You may also wish to have students complete the Self-Assessment Checklist in the *Portfolio Teacher's Guide.*

PORTFOLIO CONFERENCE

The Portfolio Conference provides you with an opportunity to learn about each student's

- interest in reading mysteries.
- general writing development.
- awareness of story elements, including plot, character, and setting.

Discuss the mystery stories that were read in Unit 4, focusing on whether the student liked them. Ask about similar stories the student has read.

Have the student select a favorite piece of writing from the portfolio. Perhaps the message he or she wrote for "Jumanji" or the clue to "The Case of the Locked Room" may be shared. Ask the student to comment on what he or she likes about the piece. Provide positive feedback and encouragement.

Formal Assessment

The formal assessment tools described below are available to meet your assessment needs.

SKILLS ASSESSMENT

The *Skills Assessment* for Unit 4 provides the teacher with feedback about students' mastery of the specific skills and strategies taught in Learning Through Literature. Skills tested in this unit are Story Elements, Following Directions, and Reference Sources. If students have difficulty, refer to pages R38, R40, R41, and R46 for visual, auditory, and kinesthetic/motor models that may be used to reteach skills tested in this unit.

HOLISTIC ASSESSMENT

The *Holistic Assessment* for Unit 4 may be used to assess a student's ability to understand passages written at the same level as the selections in the Student Anthology. If students have difficulty, refer them to the following sections in the Handbook for Readers and Writers: Active Reading Strategies, Reading Fiction, Reading Nonfiction, and Vocabulary Strategies.

INTEGRATED PERFORMANCE ASSESSMENT

The *Integrated Performance Assessment* for Unit 4 provides you with a profile of how well each student uses reading, writing, listening, and speaking strategies to read and respond to a piece of literature. Assessment results reflect how well students employ the strategies modeled and practiced in the classroom.

Break Time

Creative Problem-Solving

Here's a strategy that helps students discover their own problem-solving and decision-making skills. Point out to students that problems are generally ill-defined or "fuzzy" situations that require clarification and elaboration before solutions can be developed and tested. Present students with an actual school or classroom problem, and then have them apply the following steps:

1. *Fact-finding:* The first step in creative problem-solving requires students to collect information about the problem or topic. Students brainstorm a list of questions aimed at elaborating and defining details in the problem situation. The search for information may take students to field experts, media, and library reference materials.

2. *Problem-finding:* Using the new information, students attempt to synthesize facts to arrive at coherent, specific questions.

3. *Idea-finding:* Once the problem has been redefined, students brainstorm again, to create a list of possible solutions.

4. *Solution-finding:* Once students have generated possible solutions, they establish criteria by which they will evaluate and rank each potential solution.

5. *Acceptance-finding:* Finally, students formulate an action plan based on the solutions they selected.

Teacher as Problem-Solver

Problems in classroom management can disrupt a teacher's best-laid plans. Here's a ten-point list to help you evaluate your program and fine-tune your technique.

■ **Define the problem. Identify exactly what you want to change or improve.**

■ **Start out with the belief that solutions exist.**

■ **Solving a difficult problem takes time. Don't look for "quick fixes."**

■ **Remember that even the smallest change can have a powerful impact.**

■ **First, attack the problems you find most exasperating.**

■ **Analyze classroom procedures that continually cause problems.**

■ **Note students' reactions to different lesson formats or learning environments.**

■ **Remind yourself to remain calm.**

■ **Continue to question your own assumptions about learning.**

■ **Don't hesitate to rely on the expert advice of colleagues.**

EUREKA!

ANTI-GRAVITY RESEARCH

SCHWADRO

Reprinted by permission of H. L. Schwadron.

Never Trust a Calm Dog

Newton may have discovered the laws of motion and Einstein seems to have found some interesting things about space and time, but Tom Parker has really struck pay dirt with these useful generalizations (from *Never Trust a Calm Dog and Other Rules of Thumb*, HarperCollins, 1990):

1. People visiting theme parks are more likely to turn to the right.
2. The more buttons fastened on a person's shirt, the higher the I.Q.
3. Walking is faster than riding a bus if you are going less than a mile.
4. The distance from your elbow to your wrist equals the length of your foot.

UNIT FIVE

TRAVELERS

Planning Center

What's Ahead in "Travelers"?

PIONEERS: PAGES T660–T713 Invite your students to join the "Pioneers" in these selections of historical fiction and share the excitement of settling the Western frontier.

IMMIGRANTS: PAGES T714–T753 Your students can share in the adventures of the "Immigrants" in this story and poem as they journey to America.

TRADITIONS: PAGES T754–T811 Explore other cultures with your students in a fictional and a nonfictional selection. A dragon's dance and totem-pole carving will open their eyes to the "Traditions" of other cultures.

Family Involvement

The *Family Involvement Activities* offer a variety of possibilities for extending each theme and expanding the unit focus. A Read-at-Home Story is also included for family members to read together.

Pacing

This unit is designed to take approximately five or six weeks to complete, depending on your students' needs.

Assessment and Evaluation

Title	Description	When and How It's Used
INFORMAL ASSESSMENT OPTIONS (Ongoing)		
Reading/Writing Portfolio	Contains samples of students' literacy development.	Collect samples of personal journals and writing throughout the unit. Hold periodic Portfolio Conferences.
Informal Assessment Notes	Appear throughout the *Teacher's Edition*.	Observe students' reading, writing, listening, and speaking behaviors. Keep Running Records of your observations.
Student Self-Assessment Notes	Appear throughout the *Teacher's Edition*.	Students monitor their use of reading and writing strategies.
Running Records	Ongoing assessment of students' reading, writing, listening, and speaking behaviors.	Record periodically to track students' progress.
FORMAL ASSESSMENT OPTIONS (End of Unit)		
Skills Assessment	Assesses mastery of strategies and skills taught in Learning Through Literature.	Administer at end of the unit.
Holistic Assessment	Evaluates students' ability to read and understand excerpts from literature.	Administer at end of the unit.
Integrated Performance Assessment	Assesses use of reading and writing strategies modeled and practiced in the classroom.	Administer at end of the unit.

HBJ Literature Cassette 2

Recordings of the following selections in "Travelers" may be used for instruction or students' listening enjoyment:
- "Sailing"
- "Totem Pole"

Audiovisual Materials and Software

Eskimos: A Changing Culture. Phoenix/BFA, 1991. This shows how families of remote Nunivak Island have adapted to their environment and changing culture.   FILM/VIDEO

Jenny's Journey. Minnesota Educational Computing Corp. Students learn how to use a map, plan a route of travel, and take a drive through Lake City. COMPUTER SOFTWARE

Meet the Newbery Author: Laura Ingalls Wilder. Random House. A portrait of the author of the *Little House* books.   FILMSTRIP

Pecos Bill. SVS, 1989. Robin Williams narrates this rollicking tall tale of the legendary cowboy.   VIDEO

Regular Rolling Noah by George E. Lyon. American School Publishers, 1989. A boy's train trip from the hollows of Kentucky to the plains of Canada. FILMSTRIP

Sacajawea. FilmFair, 1990. The tale of the life of the Native American who guided Lewis and Clark is told in animation and eloquent narration.   FILM OR VIDEO

Watch the Stars Come Out by Riki Levinson. Reading Rainbow (Great Plains National Instructional Television Library). LeVar Burton hosts a show about immigrants. VIDEO

HBJ Treasury of Literature Library

Here is a sneak peek at some of the options you will find in the *HBJ Treasury of Literature Library Guide* for *Pueblo Storyteller*.
- **Reading Cooperatively** in response groups
- **Reading Independently** during sustained silent reading periods
- **Directing the Reading** through questioning strategies
- **Reading Aloud** to encourage literature appreciation

Bulletin Board Idea

Either draw or find large pictures of various kinds of travelers, including pioneers in covered wagons, immigrants traveling on a boat, passengers on a jet, a rider on horseback, passengers on a large cruise ship, a person hiking with a backpack, and so on. Draw students' attention to the bulletin board and invite them to identify the different modes of transportation and to share any travel experiences they have had. Then ask students to write on a card a paragraph telling how they like to travel. Post the cards on the bulletin board around the pictures.

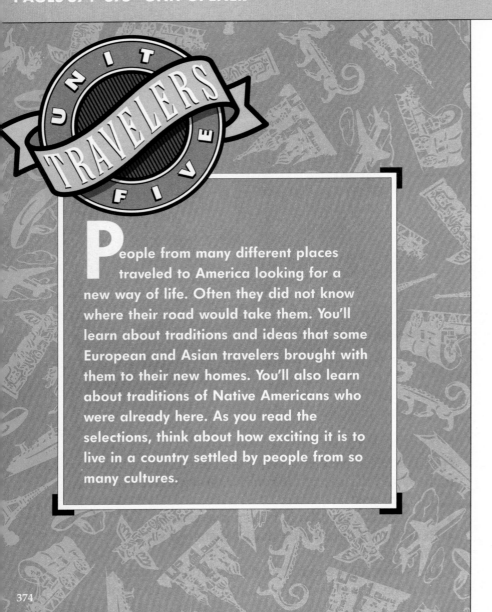

PIONEERS
378

IMMIGRANTS
400

TRADITIONS
426

eople from many different places traveled to America looking for a new way of life. Often they did not know where their road would take them. You'll learn about traditions and ideas that some European and Asian travelers brought with them to their new homes. You'll also learn about traditions of Native Americans who were already here. As you read the selections, think about how exciting it is to live in a country settled by people from so many cultures.

374

Introducing "Travelers"

Invite students to describe how they felt when they were *travelers*. Then have them read the unit introduction and preview the theme titles to help them set a purpose for reading the unit.

Ask students to discuss what they know about what overcrowded countries, such as Japan, are doing to handle travel problems. Encourage students to speculate how transportation methods of the future may change in countries around the world. CULTURAL AWARENESS

WRITER'S JOURNAL
pages 72–74:
Reading and writing about "Travelers"

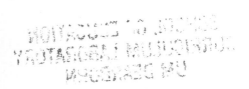

OOKSHELF

PUEBLO STORYTELLER
BY DIANE HOYT-GOLDSMITH

April, a ten-year-old Native American girl, learns many crafts and pueblo traditions from her storyteller grandparents. AWARD-WINNING AUTHOR

HBJ LIBRARY BOOK

MAKING A NEW HOME IN AMERICA
BY MAXINE B. ROSENBERG

This nonfiction book tells of five young people who have come to America from different countries. Their stories describe their feelings about America and about their homelands. AWARD-WINNING AUTHOR

ON THE BANKS OF PLUM CREEK
BY LAURA INGALLS WILDER

In the fourth book of Ms. Wilder's *Little House* series, Laura and her family move to Walnut Grove, Minnesota, and settle on the banks of Plum Creek. NEWBERY HONOR

THE CHICKENHOUSE HOUSE
BY ELLEN HOWARD

Until their new home is built, Alena's family must live in a chickenhouse. Alena finds that although the chickenhouse is cramped, it has its comforts. AWARD-WINNING AUTHOR

MEET KIRSTEN, AN AMERICAN GIRL
BY JANET SHAW

In 1854, Kirsten and her family leave their home in Sweden to come to America. This story tells of the hardships they face during their journeys to and across America.

377

HBJ Library Book

Invite students to share what they can tell about the book *Pueblo Storyteller* based on the cover illustration and the information provided. Page T655 provides a preview of the lesson plans that can be found in the *HBJ Treasury of Literature Library Guide*.

**Read aloud
to students.**

On the Way Home

The Diary of a Trip from South Dakota to Mansfield, Missouri, in 1894
by Laura Ingalls Wilder

August 20

Got a good start at 7:30 but the roads are awfully stony. Crops are poor. Everyone tells us they never get rain here when they need it. We went through Wall Street, it is nothing but a little country store. At noon we came to Mound City which is quite a city. We bought bread and an 8-cent pie and 2 cents worth of tomatoes. Tomatoes are 30 cents a bushel.

We stopped to eat dinner in the shade of a tree beside the road. Three emigrant wagons passed while we were eating. Two were going to Missouri and one coming back. This afternoon we saw three more, one going to Missouri, one coming back. Manly did not ask the other.

Water has been scarce all day and what little we found tasted so bad we could not get a good drink. It is clear and clean but it feels slick and tastes bitter, it spoils the taste of tea. The horses have to be very thirsty to take it.

Camped beside the road on the prairie. Bought a little hay and could get only a little water. Looks like rain.

August 21

It rained hard most of the night and was still pouring down when time came to get up. Manly put on his rubber coat, started the fire and put water on to heat, then fed our horses. By that time the rain was no more than a drizzle so I got out and made breakfast. We ate in the wagon, out of the wet.

Roads are muddy but sky is clear overhead. We went through Prescott, only a little station. Met a family of emigrants who have spent the last two months traveling in southwest Missouri. They do not like it at all down there. The man said, "Right there is the place to go if man wants to bury himself from the world and live on hoecake and clabber," and the woman agreed with him.

We passed another covered wagon stopped by the road, and those folks are on their way to Missouri. The whole country is just full of emigrants, going and coming. Fort Scott seemed to be crowded with them. We reached Fort Scott at 6 o'clock, and a man there said that 15 emigrant wagons went along that street yesterday.

SELECTION SUMMARY   When Laura Ingalls Wilder and her husband, Manly, journeyed in a wagon from South Dakota to Missouri in 1894, she recorded her impressions in a diary. Wilder tells of meeting other families and describes the changing countryside, the towns and cities along the way, and what life was like.

ABOUT THE AUTHOR   Laura Ingalls Wilder (1867–1957) is probably best known for her *Little House* books, a series of nine novels that capture the spirit of pioneer life in America. Most of the stories were based upon her experiences growing up in the Midwest. She tried to write the simple truth, her mind going "farther back and still farther, beyond ordinary remembrance."

Strategies for Listening

LISTENING/THINKING STRATEGY—MAKING INFERENCES
Tell students that listening to what a writer has to say and how it is expressed will help them make inferences, or conclude details, about the content.

SET A PURPOSE FOR LISTENING   Remind students that the selections in this unit are about "Travelers." Explain that this selection is a series of diary entries written during a family's journey from South Dakota to Missouri in 1894. Emphasize to students that paying attention to the writer's observations will help them realize what life was like a hundred years ago.

August 22

Exactly at 2:24 3/4 P.M. we crossed the line into Missouri. And the very first cornfield we saw beat even those Kansas cornfields.

We met 7 emigrant wagons leaving Missouri. One family had a red bird, a mockingbird, and a lot of canaries in cages hung under the canvas in the wagon with them. We had quite a chat and heard the mockingbird sing. We camped by a house in the woods.

August 23

Started out at 7:30. The country looks nice this morning. At 9:35 we came to Pedro, a little town on one side of the railroad tracks, and just across the tracks on the other side is the town of Liberal. A man in Pedro told us that one of the finest countries in the world will be around Mansfield.

In the late afternoon we went through Lamar, the nicest small city we have seen, 2,860 inhabitants. It is all so clean and fresh, all the streets set out to shade trees.

We camped among oak trees, not far from the camp of emigrants from Kentucky. Beautiful sturdy oak trees on both sides of the road.

August 24

On the road bright and early, 7:20. Weather cool and cloudy, looks like rain. Went through Canova in the morning. It is a little place. At noon we were going through Golden City, a nicer little place. The country looks good, but judging from weeds in the gardens and fields, the people are shiftless. This is a land of many springs and clear brooks. Some of the earth is yellow and some is red. The road is stony often.

Went through another little town, Lockwood, at 4 o'clock, and camped by a swift-running little creek of the clearest water. It is most delicious water to drink, cold, with a cool, snappy flavor.

Except in the towns, we have seen only one schoolhouse so far in Missouri.

We drove in the rain this afternoon, for the first time since we left Dakota. It was a good steady pouring rain, but we kept dry in the wagon and the rain stopped before camping time.

August 25

Left camp at 7:35. It rained again in the night and the road was muddy but after a few miles we came to country where it did not rain so the road was dry. The uplands are stony but there are good bottomland farms. Much timber is in sight, oaks, hickories, walnuts, and there are lots of wild crabapples, plums and thorn apples.

Well, we are in the Ozarks at last, just in the beginning of them, and they are beautiful. We passed along the foot of some hills and could look up their sides. The trees and rocks are lovely. Manly says we could almost live on the looks of them.

We stopped for dinner just before we came to the prettiest part, by the side of a swiftly running stream, Turnback River. We forded it, through the shallow water all rippling and sparkling.

There was another clear stream to cross before we came to Everton at 5 o'clock. Here we stopped to get the horses shod but there was not time to shoe them all today, so we camped by a creek in the edge of town for over Sunday.

Sunday, August 26

A day for writing, reading, sleeping. We let the children wade in the shallow creek, within our sight. I spent almost the whole time writing to the home folks about the country since Fort Scott and these hills and woods.

Responding to Literature

1. **How would you describe the author and the way she viewed her life?** (Accept reasonable responses: She was optimistic, and she made the best of her hardships.) INFERENTIAL: DETERMINING CHARACTER'S TRAITS

2. **Why do you think there was a bond among the travelers the Wilders met on the way?** (Accept reasonable responses: They were all strangers in new surroundings.) INFERENTIAL: DRAWING CONCLUSIONS

SPEAKING Ask volunteers to share their experiences in moving from one home to another. Encourage them to speculate on the differences in traveling between 1894 and the present. CREATIVE: ORAL COMPOSITION

Runaway

from *On the Banks of Plum Creek*

Words About the Author: Laura Ingalls Wilder

Sailing

from *Grasshopper Summer*

For pacing suggestions, see page T662.

THEME

PIONEERS

Imagine what it would have been like to live long ago in the wide, open spaces of the West. The characters in the following selections face challenges every day while settling the western frontier.

CONTENTS

RUNAWAY
by Laura Ingalls Wilder

**WORDS ABOUT THE AUTHOR:
LAURA INGALLS WILDER**

SAILING
by Ann Turner

379

Discussing the Theme

Invite students to look at the picture and read the theme focus on Student Anthology pages 378–379. Encourage them to think about what life might have been like in the early days of our country when pioneers were settling the West. Ask students to read the selection titles and speculate about what kinds of adventures the characters in the stories might have.

Reading/Writing Portfolio

Remind students to choose some of their writing responses for the selections in "Pioneers" to save in their portfolios. In addition, remind them to add to their personal journals any thoughts and ideas about books they have read independently.

Managing the Literature-Based Classroom

Management Options

DESIGNATE AN AUTHOR'S CHAIR   Put an "Author's Chair" in a designated spot when having students read their work or deliver oral presentations. Make the rules clear: When someone is in the chair, students must be courteous, quiet, and respectful and must treat the person as they would a published author. When guest speakers visit, have them use the Author's Chair also.

ASSESSING STUDENTS INFORMALLY   Consider assessment as an ongoing part of daily instruction. Observe students as they work in groups, and listen as they participate in discussions. Look for student strengths. Note what they have learned, how they have grown, what they know, and how they interact. Keep handy a stack of index cards, and record brief notes about significant student actions, behaviors, or achievements. Periodically, sort the cards by student. These notes can be used when scheduling groups or planning instruction, or during conferences.

PACING   This theme has been designed to take about two weeks to complete, depending on your students' needs.

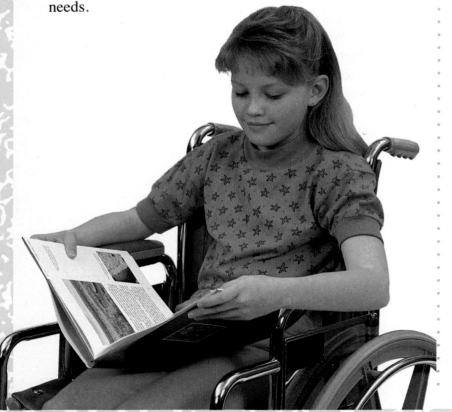

Meeting Individual Needs

STUDENTS AT RISK   To motivate students, you may want to record one episode of *Little House on the Prairie* from the TV series for students to view prior to or after reading "Runaway" and the feature on Laura Ingalls Wilder.

GIFTED AND TALENTED   Encourage students to compile a list of items a family would need to take in a covered wagon if they were going to travel westward to settle the new frontier. Enlist the help of a librarian to guide students in finding research materials. *Challenge Cards* provide additional activities to challenge students. Challenge notes throughout the lesson plans suggest additional activities to stimulate critical and creative thinking.

SPECIAL EDUCATION STUDENTS   To aid students in preparing an outline for the Writer's Workshop on Student Anthology page 399, suggest that they start by taking notes on index cards. Tell students to put one note on each card. Have students organize the cards by categories and label them. Encourage students to use these categories when writing their outlines.

LIMITED ENGLISH PROFICIENT STUDENTS   Before the oral rereading of the stories, have students read over their parts silently, making a list of words they may not know how to pronounce. Have students practice with English-proficient partners, who can help them pronounce the words. Second-Language Support notes throughout the lesson plans offer strategies to help students acquiring English to understand the selections.

NEWBERY HONOR

Runaway

from *On the Banks of Plum Creek*

by Laura Ingalls Wilder
illustrated by Garth Williams

LESSON PLANNER

RUNAWAY

	TEACHING OUTLINE	Materials	Language Arts/ Integrated Curriculum	Meeting Individual Needs
Part **1** **Reading Literature** Pages T666–T671 	**Building Background** **Vocabulary Strategies** Key Words (Tested) **Strategic Reading** Preview and Predict Setting a Purpose **Options for Reading**	Transparency 36 Second-Language Support Manual Practice Book p. 102 Integrated Spelling p. 53 Integrated Spelling T.E. pp. 72–73 Student Anthology pp. 380–385 Response Card 7: Responding Freely	**Spelling** Spelling Pretest Spelling-Vocabulary Connection	**Second-Language Support** Vocabulary T667 Strategic Reading T668 **Cooperative Reading** T669
Part **2** **Responding to Literature** Pages T672–T677 	**Story Follow-Up** Think It Over Write **Summarizing the Literature** **Appreciating Literature** **Critical Thinking Activities**	Writer's Journal p. 75 Practice Book p. 103 Integrated Spelling p. 54 Integrated Spelling T.E. pp. 72–73 Language Handbook	**Vocabulary Workshop** Reviewing Key Words Extending Vocabulary Specialized Vocabulary **Reading** Oral Rereading/Drama **Writing** Friendly Letter TV Script Diary Entry **Spelling** Reviewing Spelling Words **Speaking** Interviewing a Character Describing a Day Modern Objects **Listening** Historical Fiction	**Cooperative Learning** T673, T676
Part **3** **Learning Through Literature** Pages T678–T684 	**Introduce** Comprehension: Summarizing (Tested) **Review** Literary Appreciation: Historical Fiction **Maintain** Comprehension: Making Predictions (Tested)	Transparency 37 Second-Language Support Manual Writer's Journal pp. 76–77 Practice Book pp. 104–105	**Social Studies** Research Report Map and Atlas Study **Math** Word Problems **Science** Product Flavorings **Art** Diorama **Multicultural** Trailblazers in Medicine	**Reteach** T679 **Challenge** T679, T680, T681 **Second-Language Support** Summarizing T679 **Cooperative Learning** T679, T682, T683

KEY WORDS

dugout
yoked
attentive
contradicting

LAURA INGALLS WILDER

Popular with thousands of children since their publication in the 1930s and 1940s, the *Little House* books by Laura Ingalls Wilder tell the story of her life growing up on the American frontier. Born in Wisconsin in 1867, Laura lived in many places, including the Minnesota prairie dugout described in *On the Banks of Plum Creek*. She was 65 when her first book, *Little House in the Big Woods*, was published. "To my surprise the book made such a success and children all over the U.S. wrote to me begging for more stories," she said. "I began to think what a wonderful childhood I had had. How I had seen the whole frontier, the woods, the Indian country of the great plains, the frontier towns, the building of railroads in wild, unsettled country, homesteading and farmers coming in to take possession. I wanted children . . . to know what it is that made America as they know it." Seven more books followed.

In 1954, the American Library Association created and presented her the Laura Ingalls Wilder Medal, which is now given every five years to an outstanding author or illustrator of children's books.

ADDITIONAL READING

Other Books by Laura Ingalls Wilder

Farmer Boy. HarperCollins, 1933/1961.
CHALLENGING

Little House in the Big Woods.
HarperCollins, 1932/1959.   AVERAGE

Other Books About Pioneers

Cassie's Journey: Going West in the 1860s
by Brett Harvey. Holiday House, 1988.
AVERAGE

The Little House Cookbook: Frontier Foods from Laura Ingalls Wilder's Classic Stories by Barbara M. Walker.
HarperCollins, 1979.   CHALLENGING

The Tea Squall by Ariane Dewey.
Greenwillow, 1988.   AVERAGE

Part 1
Reading Literature

Building Background

Access prior knowledge and build vocabulary concepts.

Explain to students that the next story, "Runaway," is historical fiction about a family living on a midwestern farm in the 1870s. Review that historical fiction is a partially made-up story that takes place at a certain time in the past and is based on actual events or people.

Invite students to help you start a chart on the board that shows what they already know about life long ago on a prairie farm. (See *Practice Book* page 103 on T673.) Explain that they will complete the chart after they finish reading. The chart may resemble the following:

Prior knowledge about living on a prairie farm in the 1870s	What was learned about living on a prairie farm in the 1870s
1. travel by foot, horse, wagon 2. live far from towns 3. grow own food	

Vocabulary Strategies

Introduce Key Words and strategies.

Display Transparency 36, or write the following paragraph on the board. Have students read the paragraph silently. Encourage them to use context clues with phonetic and structural analysis to help them decode each underlined word and to figure out its meaning. Use the activity that follows to check understanding of the Key Words.

Transparency 36 Key Words

The family lived in a hillside dugout made of sod blocks. The wooden frame yoked the necks of the oxen together so that they could pull the wagon. The girls were attentive as their father showed them how to harness the oxen to the wagon. As usual, their brother was contradicting what their father was saying, so the girls did not know who was right.

CULTURAL AWARENESS

Explain that people all over the world live near or on land areas similar to the prairie mentioned in the story. Great grasslands of the world include the pampas of Argentina, the veld of South Africa, and the Canterbury Plains of New Zealand.

KEY WORDS

dugout
yoked
attentive
contradicting

KEY WORDS DEFINED

dugout rough shelter dug into the ground or a hillside and roofed with sod

yoked harnessed or fastened together with a wooden frame

attentive observant, watchful

contradicting disagreeing with, speaking against

Check students' understanding.

To check students' understanding of the Key Words, display or read aloud the following incomplete sentences. Have volunteers take turns completing the sentences.   STRATEGY: EXPLANATION

- A good time to be attentive is . . . .
- Oxen might be yoked when a farmer needs . . . .
- A dugout might be found . . . .
- If you are contradicting someone, you are probably . . . .

GLOSSARY   Encourage students to refer to the Glossary to confirm or to clarify their understanding of the new vocabulary.

Integrate spelling with vocabulary.

SPELLING-VOCABULARY CONNECTION   *Integrated Spelling* page 53 reinforces the spelling of compound words in the Key Word *dugout* and in other words. The spelling of the Key Word *yoke* is also included.

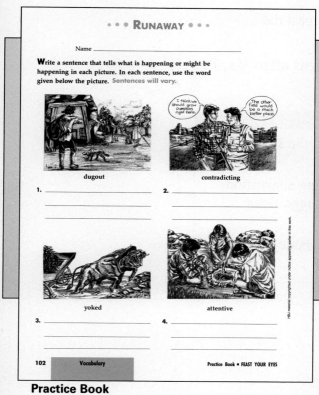

Practice Book

Integrated Spelling

Help students preview the literature.

Preview and Predict

Have students find "Runaway" in the Table of Contents. Ask them who wrote the story. You may wish to share the information about the author on page T665.

Ask students what they might do to preview the story. (read and think about the title, look at the illustrations, and read the introduction and the first few paragraphs) Encourage students to read the title and the introduction and to preview the first three paragraphs of the story.

Guide students in making predictions.

Ask students the following questions to help them predict what might happen in the story:

- **Who or what do you think the runaway is?**
- **What dangerous situation might happen?**
- **Why might the girls wish their parents would return?**

PERSONAL JOURNAL Have students add their predictions about the story to their personal journals. Ask students to support their predictions.

Setting a Purpose

Have students set purposes.

Brainstorm with students what they want to find out when they read the story, based on their preview and on what they already know about living on the American frontier in the 1870s. Remind students that setting a purpose for reading gives them a reason for reading, helps them stay focused on important events as they read, and helps them know what reading rate to choose. Encourage them to use their predictions to set a purpose for reading.

Model purpose-setting, if necessary.

If students have difficulty setting a purpose, suggest the following:

> **I'm going to read to find out what happens after Ma, Pa, and Carrie return home.**

OPTIONS FOR READING

INDEPENDENT READING Have students read the story silently with their purpose for reading in mind.

GUIDED READING Follow the Guided Reading suggestions that appear on pages T669 and T671. These suggestions model strategic reading.

COOPERATIVE READING A reader response strategy appears on page T669.

Runaway

from *On the Banks of Plum Creek*

by Laura Ingalls Wilder
illustrated by Garth Williams

When Pa, Ma, and little Carrie went into town for the day, Laura and Mary were left alone with Jack, their dog, to take care of everything. After lunch, the three were faced with a big problem. The cattle were tearing into the hay-stacks and eating all the hay. Jack and Laura and Mary finally were able to chase the cattle into the high prairie grasses away from the banks of Plum Creek.

ALL that long, quiet afternoon they stayed in the dugout. The cattle did not come back to the hay-stacks. Slowly the sun went down the western sky. Soon it would be time to meet the cattle at the big grey rock, and Laura and Mary wished that Pa and Ma would come home.

Again and again they went up the path to look for the wagon. At last they sat waiting with Jack on the grassy top of their house. The lower the sun went, the more attentive Jack's ears were. Often he and Laura stood up to look at the edge of the sky where the wagon had gone, though they could see it just as well when they were sitting down.

Finally Jack turned one ear that way, then the other. Then he looked up at Laura and a waggle went from his neck to his stubby tail. The wagon was coming!

381

Guided Reading

SET PURPOSE/PREDICT: PAGES 380–385
Encourage students to read through page 385 to find out how the characters feel at the end of the day.

Cooperative Reading

READER RESPONSE STRATEGY: PAGES 380–385
Have students work in pairs. Ask each pair to decide whether they will read silently or aloud and how frequently they will stop. At designated stopping points, each member of the pair should respond freely to what they have read so far. Have pairs continue the procedure until they reach the end of the story and then discuss it as a whole. (Response Card 7: Responding Freely, on page R68, gives complete directions for using the strategy.)

They all stood and watched till it came out of the prairie. When Laura saw the oxen, and Ma and Carrie on the wagon seat, she jumped up and down, swinging her sunbonnet and shouting, "They're coming! They're coming!"

"They're coming awful fast," Mary said.

Laura was still. She heard the wagon rattling loudly. Pete and Bright were coming very fast. They were running. They were running away.

The wagon came bumpity-banging and bouncing. Laura saw Ma down in a corner of the wagon box, hanging onto it and hugging Carrie. Pa came bounding in long jumps beside Bright, shouting and hitting at Bright with the goad.

He was trying to turn Bright back from the creek bank.

He could not do it. The big oxen galloped nearer and nearer the steep edge. Bright was pushing Pa off it. They were all going over. The wagon, Ma and Carrie, were going to fall down the bank, all the way down to the creek.

Pa shouted a terrible shout. He struck Bright's head with all his might, and Bright swerved. Laura ran screaming. Jack jumped at Bright's nose. Then the wagon, Ma, and Carrie flashed by. Bright crashed against the stable and suddenly everything was still.

Pa ran after the wagon and Laura ran behind him.

"Whoa, Bright! Whoa, Pete," Pa said. He held onto the wagon box and looked at Ma.

"We're all right, Charles," Ma said. Her face was grey and she was shaking all over.

Pete was trying to go on through the doorway into the stable, but he was yoked to Bright and Bright was headed against the stable wall. Pa lifted Ma and Carrie out of the wagon, and Ma said, "Don't cry, Carrie. See, we're all right."

Carrie's pink dress was torn down the front. She snuffled against Ma's neck and tried to stop crying as Ma told her.

"Oh, Caroline! I thought you were going over the bank," Pa said.

"I thought so, too, for a minute," Ma answered. "But I might have known you wouldn't let that happen."

"Pshaw!" said Pa. "It was good old Pete. He wasn't running away. Bright was, but Pete was only going along. He saw the stable and wanted his supper."

But Laura knew that Ma and Carrie would have fallen down into the creek with the wagon and oxen, if Pa had not run so fast and hit Bright so hard. She crowded against Ma's hoopskirt and hugged her tight and said, "Oh, Ma! Oh, Ma!" So did Mary.

382

Informal Assessment   You can informally assess your students' abilities to synthesize and to categorize by occasionally asking questions such as these:

- How would you categorize the main character?
- What characters in other stories you have read is she like?

"There, there," said Ma. "All's well that ends well. Now, girls, help bring in the packages while Pa puts up the oxen."

They carried all the little packages into the dugout. They met the cattle at the grey rock and put Spot into the stable, and Laura helped milk her while Mary helped Ma get supper.

At supper, they told how the cattle had got into the hay-stacks and how they had driven them away. Pa said they had done exactly the right thing. He said, "We knew we could depend on you to take care of everything. Didn't we, Caroline?"

They had completely forgotten that Pa always brought them presents from town, until after supper he pushed back his bench and looked as if he expected something. Then Laura jumped on his knee, and Mary sat on the other, and Laura bounced and asked, "What did you bring us, Pa? What? What?"

"Guess," Pa said.

They could not guess. But Laura felt something crackle in his jumper pocket and she pounced on it. She pulled out a paper bag, beautifully striped with tiny red and green stripes. And in the bag were two sticks of candy, one for Mary and one for Laura!

They were maple-sugar-coloured, and they were flat on one side.

Mary licked hers. But Laura bit her stick, and the outside of it came off, crumbly. The inside was hard and clear and dark brown. And it had a rich, brown, tangy taste. Pa said it was hoarhound candy.

After the dishes were done, Laura and Mary each took her stick of candy and they sat on Pa's knees,

outside the door in the cool dusk. Ma sat just inside the dugout, humming to Carrie in her arms.

The creek was talking to itself under the yellow willows. One by one the great stars swung low and seemed to quiver and flicker in the little wind.

Laura was snug in Pa's arm. His beard softly tickled her cheek and the delicious candy-taste melted on her tongue.

After a while she said, "Pa."

"What, little half-pint?" Pa's voice asked against her hair.

"I think I like wolves better than cattle," she said.

"Cattle are more useful, Laura," Pa said.

She thought about that a while. Then she said, "Anyway, I like wolves better."

She was not contradicting; she was only saying what she thought.

"Well, Laura, we're going to have a good team of horses before long," Pa said. She knew when that would be. It would be when they had a wheat crop.

THINK IT OVER

1. *What exciting event happened in this story?*
2. *Why do you think the oxen started running away?*
3. *What did Pa bring Laura and Mary from town?*

WRITE

Write a paragraph comparing and contrasting your life today with Laura's life more than 100 years ago. Tell how your lives are different and how they are the same.

385

Guided Reading

MONITOR COMPREHENSION: PAGES 380–385
How does Laura's family feel at the end of the day? (Everyone feels happy, contented, and thankful that no one is hurt.) STRATEGIC READING: CONFIRMING PREDICTIONS

Are the oxen stopped? How? (Yes. Pa shouts at Bright and forces him to swerve and to crash into the stable.) STRATEGIC READING: SUMMARIZING

Returning to the Predictions Invite students to discuss the predictions that they made before reading and that they may have written in their personal journals. Encourage them to talk about how those predictions changed as they read.

Returning to the Purpose for Reading
Discuss what happens after Ma, Pa, and Carrie get home. (After Pa stops the runaway, the family goes on with their day and evening. Pa gives the girls a special treat that he has bought in town.)

NOTE: Responses to Think It Over questions and support for the Write activity appear on page T672.

Part 2
Responding to Literature

Story Follow-Up

Think It Over

Encourage reader's response: student page 385.

1. **What exciting event happened in this story?** (The oxen ran away and nearly pulled the wagon with Ma and Carrie in it over the creek bank.) INFERENTIAL: SUMMARIZING
2. **Why do you think the oxen started running away?** (Accept reasonable responses: They may have seen something in the grass.) CRITICAL: SPECULATING
3. **What did Pa bring Laura and Mary from town?** (He brought each of them a stick of hoarhound candy.) LITERAL: NOTING IMPORTANT DETAILS

Write

Encourage writer's response: student page 385.

Write a paragraph comparing and contrasting your life today with Laura's life more than 100 years ago. Tell how your lives are different and how they are the same. Encourage students to think about what they do during a normal day and evening.
CREATIVE: WRITING A PARAGRAPH

Summarizing the Literature

Have students retell the story and write a summary.

Remind students of the chart they started before reading the story. Invite students to complete the chart independently, listing new information they learned while reading. (See *Practice Book* page 103 on T673.) Students may use the completed chart to help them tell about Laura and Mary's day and to write a brief summary statement.

Prior knowledge about living on a prairie farm in the 1870s	What was learned about living on a prairie farm in the 1870s
1. travel by foot, horse, wagon 2. live far from towns 3. grow own food 4. no television 5. depend on animals	1. (children had to do important chores) 2. (danger could happen at any time) 3. (treats were small and simple) 4. (people lived close to nature)

STRATEGY CONFERENCE

Discuss with students how previewing and making predictions helped them understand, remember, and appreciate the story. Invite students to share other reading strategies, such as summarizing, that helped them understand what they read.

NOTE

An additional writing activity for this story appears on page T675.

Appreciating Literature

Have students share personal responses.

Have students work in small groups to discuss the story. Provide a general question such as the following to help groups begin:

- **How does the author help the reader see, smell, hear, and feel the setting and the action in the story?**

PERSONAL JOURNAL   Have students use their personal journals to write about ideas and feelings that are discussed in the groups. You may also refer them to their personal journals after they complete the activities below.

Critical Thinking Activities

Encourage both cooperative and individual responses.

CREATE A CHART   Laura likes wolves better than cattle. Pa says cattle are more useful. Write what you think are each character's reasons. Then add your own reasons. Suggest that groups of students organize their ideas in a chart like the one below.   CRITICAL: MAKING JUDGMENTS

Cattle		Wolves	
Pa	**Laura**	**Laura**	**Pa**
pull wagons raise for food	get in hay run away	smart pretty	eat livestock fierce

MAKE A LIST   What details show that the story is historical fiction? How would these details change if the story took place today? Suggest that pairs of students list each historical item next to a modern-day counterpart.   CREATIVE: VISUALIZING

WRITER'S JOURNAL
page 75:   Writing a personal response

PRACTICE BOOK
page 103:   Summarizing the selection

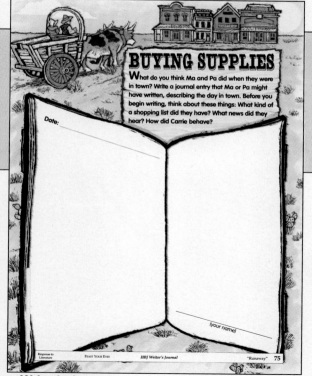

Writer's Journal

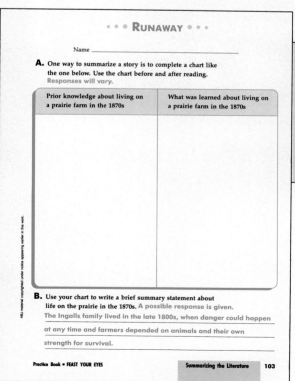

Practice Book

VO·CAB·U·LAR·Y Workshop

Reviewing Key Words

Display the Key Words. Have students answer the following questions orally or in writing:

1. *attentive* **How do you think Jack's ears looked when he was attentive?** (His ears were up.)

2. *dugout* **Why would a dugout be a good place to get out of the hot prairie sun?** (A dugout is dug into a hillside and often made of earth, which provides a cool shelter.)

3. *contradicting* **If Laura were contradicting what Pa said about cattle, what would she be doing?** (disagreeing with him)

4. *yoked* **If the oxen had not been yoked, what might have happened?** (They might have tried to run in opposite directions.)

Extending Vocabulary

SPECIALIZED VOCABULARY (SOCIAL STUDIES) Explain to students that in historical fiction they may often find words that name things special to the time in which the story takes place. Point out that a *sunbonnet* is a kind of hat that pioneer women wore to protect their faces from the strong prairie sun. Start the following chart on the board.

Clothes	Home	Food
sunbonnet hoopskirt	dugout	hoarhound candy

Encourage students to look through the story to find and suggest other special words that describe the historical period in which Laura lived. Next, invite students to add other words they think belong on the chart. Call on volunteers to describe each item. Then have students write the headings on a sheet of paper and write words describing items they believe are special to our time in history. Students might suggest words such as *jeans*, *condominiums*, and *pizza*.

Integrated Language Arts

READING

Oral Rereading/Drama

Invite small groups of students to select one of the following parts of the story to read aloud: waiting for the wagon, chasing and stopping the runaway, talking together after the oxen stop and getting ready for supper, having supper and the candy treat, or sitting outside after supper. Have groups decide who will read which sentences, and allow them time to rehearse. Remind students to use an appropriate reading rate and voice level to set the tone. For example, the runaway scene would be read somewhat faster and louder, with a sense of excitement. You may wish to demonstrate before groups begin rehearsing. Suggest that groups present their reading in story order.   LISTENING/SPEAKING/READING

WRITING

Writing About the Literature

WRITE A FRIENDLY LETTER   Review with students the parts and format of a friendly letter: heading, greeting, body, closing, and signature. Then invite students to imagine they are Laura writing a letter to a friend to tell about the runaway. Encourage students to think about what Laura has seen, done, and felt. Before students write, suggest that they use a web such as the one below to help them select which details to include.   LISTENING/SPEAKING/WRITING

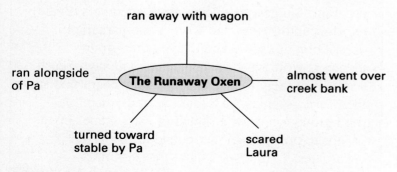

NOTE: An additional writing activity appears on page T672.

SPELLING

Reviewing Spelling Words

SPELLING WORDS: *afternoon, daylight, doorway, dugout, headache, inside, runaway, something, sunbonnet, yoke*

On a set of index cards, write nonsense compound words by miscombining the parts of real compound words. Show students each card. Ask them to break the nonsense word into its parts and to write each part. Afterward, have students write real compound words from the smaller words they have written. Have students share each compound word and discuss its meaning, looking up the word in the dictionary if necessary.
LISTENING/SPEAKING/READING/WRITING/SPELLING

INTEGRATED SPELLING page 54:
Writing compound words

INTEGRATED SPELLING
Compound Words

Name _____

WORD PLAY

Read the story below. The underlined words are scrambled compound words. Write each Spelling Word correctly.

    "What are you going to do this <u>afterbonnet</u>?" Jasper asked.
    "I am going to do <u>someout</u>," Demetria answered. "Would you like to play with me?"
    "I would," Jasper said, "but I have a terrible <u>headlight</u>. I think I should stay <u>inaway</u> while it is still <u>dayside</u>."
    "Come on," Demetria begged. "You can wear a <u>sunache</u>."

When you are done, make up your own silly story using scrambled compound Spelling Words. Trade with a friend, and write the words the correct way.

WORD BANK
afternoon
daylight
doorway
dugout
headache
inside
runaway
something
sunbonnet
yoke

SPELLING DETECTIVE

Phoebe noticed four misspellings in the diary she found. Find these and circle them. Then write each word correctly above the mistake.

We have spent the summer farming our new field. While we have long hours of delight, we have to grow all of our food for the winter. Father put a yoke on the oxen and hauled our crops back to the barn. This afternune I pulled out weeds. The sun was so hot and bright that it gave me a headake.

54

"Runaway" • FEAST YOUR EYES

Integrated Spelling

SPEAKING

Let's Talk

COOPERATIVE LEARNING Ask students to imagine that they have traveled back in time and have met Laura. Have them think of and write down questions they would ask her. Remind students to begin their questions with *Who, What, Where, When, Why,* or *How.* Invite students to work in pairs, taking turns reading their questions and playing the part of Laura to answer the questions as they think she would. LISTENING/SPEAKING/READING/WRITING

SPEAKING

Stepping into the Past

Invite students to imagine what it would be like to be a young person like Laura living on a prairie farm in a dugout home. Have them make some notes on what an average summer day would be like for them. Suggest that they think about what chores they would have, what they might do for fun, and what events might occur. Then encourage volunteers to describe their day to classmates. As a variation, students may wish to form pairs, to pretend they are siblings or best friends, and to role-play some of their day's activities. LISTENING/SPEAKING/WRITING

WRITING

Lights! Camera! Action!

AVAILABLE ON PROJECT CARD

COOPERATIVE LEARNING Ask students whether any of them have seen programs from the "Little House on the Prairie" television series (1974–1981). Point out that this series was based on the books written by Laura Ingalls Wilder. Have students work in groups. Invite them to imagine how they might turn the story "Runaway" into a television program. Suggest that some group members divide the story into scenes and write a one-paragraph description of each scene. Have other group members write what the characters will say in each scene. Tell them to also describe how characters say their lines, such as "in a loud, scared voice." A third group can draw a sketch of each scene. Invite groups to present their script and drawings to classmates. LISTENING/SPEAKING/ READING/WRITING

Gadgets and Gizmos?

AVAILABLE ON PROJECT CARD

Have students imagine what it would be like for someone from Laura's time and place to visit the present. Ask students to suggest things this person would know nothing about, such as cars, computers, televisions, telephones, elevators, cash registers, and so on. Write suggestions on the board, and have each student choose one. Give students time to write a list of what they would tell this person about how the item worked or how to use it. Then invite students to find a partner and to make a presentation to classmates. Direct one partner to play the visitor from the past while the other partner describes his or her object. Encourage the "visitor" to ask questions. Then have students reverse roles.   LISTENING/ SPEAKING/WRITING

Moments in History

Read aloud a passage from another historical fiction story. You may wish to select a story from the same time period as "Runaway," such as *Dakota Dugout* by Ann Turner. Encourage students to listen carefully for word clues that help them identify the story as historical fiction. List on the board the clues students suggest. Then discuss in what time period students think the story is set.   LISTENING/SPEAKING

Key to the Past

Explain to students that pioneer women often kept a diary of their daily life. Explain that a diary is personal writing usually not intended for others to read. Invite students to write a diary entry that Laura's mother might have made on the day of the runaway. Remind students to describe incidents from the mother's point of view and to include her thoughts and feelings about what happened.   WRITING

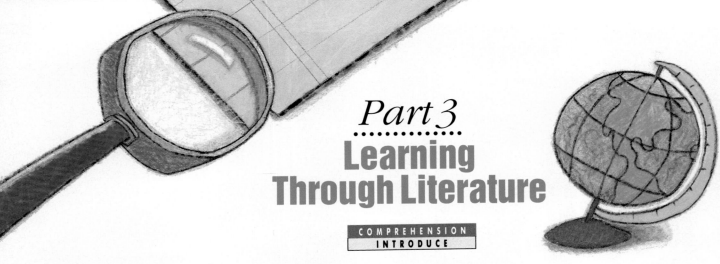

Part 3
Learning Through Literature

Summarizing

OBJECTIVE: *To develop global meaning through summarizing*

1 Focus

Discuss the importance of summarizing.

Point out to students that if someone asked what "Runaway" was about, they would summarize the story, or use their own words to combine, or synthesize, the important parts. Explain that knowing how to summarize a story will help them remember the most important parts.

2 Teach/Model

Teach and model how to summarize.

Explain that a story summary is short and tells only the important parts, and it includes a logical sequence of events. Remind students that the reader's opinion is not included. Model summarizing a passage from "Runaway."

> **To summarize the part about Pa's present, I decide what the main idea and the important details are. Pa always brings presents from town for the girls. This time he gives them something they've never had before—hoarhound candy. I summarize this part by saying, *Pa brings Mary and Laura a surprise present of hoarhound candy.***

Strategy: Use a story map to plan a summary.

Explain that a summary of a story can be made in three or four sentences. Point out that making a story map is one way to identify the important parts. Display Transparency 37 or the map below. Work with students to identify the important parts.

Transparency 37   Summarizing

Where/When Who/What	(prairie farm in the 1870s) (Laura and Mary wait for Ma, Pa, and Carrie to return.)
Problem Goal Events	(The oxen run away with the wagon.) (to stop them) (Pa hits and shouts at the oxen; the oxen almost go over the creek bank.)
Resolution	(The oxen turn just in time and head for the stable.)

3 — Practice/Apply

Have students write a summary.

COOPERATIVE LEARNING Suggest that students work in pairs to write a summary of "Runaway." Remind them to use the story map to assist them.

4 — Summarize

Informally assess the learning.

Have partners read their summary and discuss it. Identify any unimportant information or opinions they may have included. Have them revise their summary as necessary.

Ask students to summarize what they learned. (To summarize, readers combine, or synthesize, the important parts of a story in a logical order.)

READER ⟷ WRITER CONNECTION

Summarizing

▶ **Writers** use summarizing to help them decide what important parts they will include in their writing.

▶ **Readers** use summarizing to review and to remember important parts in stories they have read.

WRITE A SUMMARY Prepare a rambling set of directions on how to get to an art gallery. Have students write a summary of those directions.

RETEACH Follow the **visual, auditory,** and **kinesthetic/ motor** models on page R49.

CHALLENGE Have students summarize a short story they have recently read. Remind them to check their summary to make sure they have included only the important parts.

SECOND-LANGUAGE SUPPORT Students can demonstrate their understanding by orally summarizing what they do at school each day. If necessary, help them identify and delete opinions and unimportant details. Then help them note the important points. (See *Second-Language Support Manual.*)

Writer's Journal

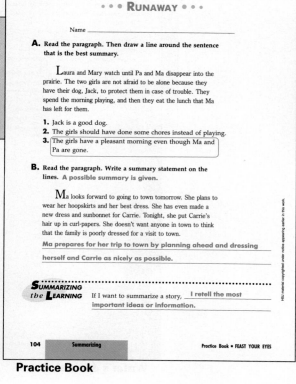

Practice Book

WRITER'S JOURNAL page 76: Writing a summary

PRACTICE BOOK page 104: Summarizing

Historical Fiction

OBJECTIVE: *To recognize the characteristics of historical fiction*

Review

Review the characteristics of historical fiction.

Review with students that, like "Runaway," all historical fiction is set in a certain time in history and is based on actual events. Use the chart below to model identifying historical and fictional elements of "Runaway."

Historical Fiction	
Historical Elements	**Fictional Elements**
characters based on real people setting	conversations some characters

Practice/Apply

Have students apply the learning.

Have students create their own chart describing the historical elements of "Runaway" and then add the fictional items.

Summarize

Informally assess the learning.

Discuss with students what they included on the chart and what helped them decide where to place each item.

Have students summarize what they learned. (Historical fiction contains both factual and fictional elements.)

CHALLENGE Encourage students to select a short example of historical fiction. Have them make a chart identifying historical and fictional details in the story. Ask them to identify the clues they used to decide in what time period the story is set.

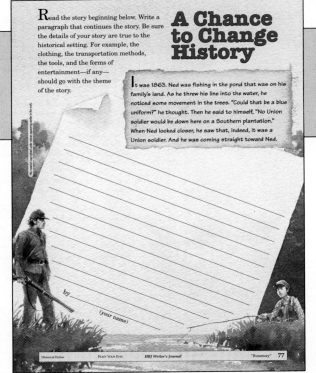

Read the story beginning below. Write a paragraph that continues the story. Be sure the details of your story are true to the historical setting. For example, the clothing, the transportation methods, the tools, and the forms of entertainment—if any—should go with the theme of the story.

A Chance to Change History

It was 1863. Ned was fishing in the pond that was on his family's land. As he threw his line into the water, he noticed some movement in the trees. "Could that be a blue uniform?" he thought. Then he said to himself, "No Union soldier would be down here on a Southern plantation." When Ned looked closer, he saw that, indeed, it was a Union soldier. And he was coming straight toward Ned.

by
_____
(your name)

Historical Fiction   FEAST YOUR EYES   *HBJ Writer's Journal*   "Runaway"   77

Writer's Journal

WRITER'S JOURNAL
page 77: Analyzing historical fiction

Making Predictions

OBJECTIVE: *To make predictions by using story evidence and prior knowledge*

Review

Review how to make predictions.

Discuss how to make a prediction. (use story evidence and what you already know; then decide what will happen next) Use the chart below to model making predictions:

What I Know	Prediction Questions
The wagon is going too fast.	Was this done on purpose? Is something wrong?
Pete and Bright are running away.	Will the oxen stop? Will the wagon go into the creek?

Practice/Apply

Have students make predictions.

Have students continue the chart, showing how, as they gather more evidence, they might adjust their prediction questions.

Summarize

Informally assess the learning.

Discuss with students what evidence they used to make their predictions.

Have students summarize what they learned. (To make predictions, use story evidence plus prior knowledge.)

CHALLENGE Have students choose a story and read up to a point when something is about to happen. Have them stop and write a prediction. Encourage them to read on to see whether their prediction is confirmed. Tell them to note any changes they have to make and to explain why.

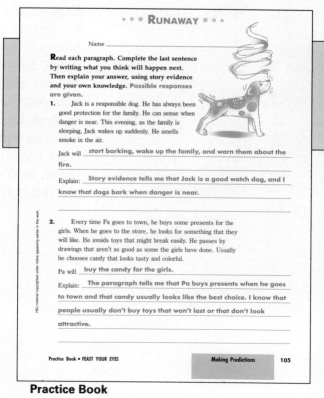

Practice Book

PRACTICE BOOK
page 105: Making predictions

Integrated
Curriculum

SOCIAL STUDIES

Animal Transport

CULTURAL AWARENESS   Review that Laura's family use oxen to pull their wagon and look forward to having a team of horses. Invite students to select another country and to use an encyclopedia or another reference source to research what types of animals are used for work in that country. For example, elephants are used in India, water buffalo in some Asian countries, camels in some parts of the Middle East, and llamas in South America. Have students write a research report and share their findings with classmates. Encourage them to display pictures of the animals.   LISTENING/SPEAKING/READING/WRITING

MATH

Pioneer Word Problems

AVAILABLE ON PROJECT CARD

COOPERATIVE LEARNING   Review with students some word problems in their math textbooks. Then invite students to work with a partner to make up two or three short, simple word problems based on "Runaway." Suggest that they first decide what operation they want to use: addition, subtraction, multiplication, or division. Then provide the following example: *There were 25 cows in the hay-stacks. Laura and Mary chased away 13 cows, but then 5 returned. How many cows were in the hay-stacks? (17)* When students have finished, encourage partners to exchange their problems with another pair of students and to try to solve them.   LISTENING/SPEAKING/ READING/WRITING

SCIENCE

Taste Survey

Explain to students that hoarhound, usually spelled *horehound,* is a type of mint plant from whose leaves a bitter extract is made and used to flavor candy and cough drops. Encourage students to accompany a parent or another adult family member to a store and to look at the ingredient labels on packages of cough drops. Ask students to report whether they find any cough drops flavored with hoarhound. Also have them write a list of other flavorings they see listed. Point out that some health food stores carry hoarhound candy.   LISTENING/ SPEAKING/READING/WRITING

ART

Prairie in a Box

AVAILABLE ON PROJECT CARD

COOPERATIVE LEARNING Review with students the pictures and descriptions of scenes in "Runaway." Invite students to work in small groups to make a diorama. Provide art materials for groups to create a diorama of a scene in the story. Students may select the dugout home, the stable, or the creek bank and the wagon. If possible, allow time for students to gather natural materials outside, such as twigs, bits of grass, and small rocks. Suggest that students bring from home a shoe box or a similar type of cardboard box in which to set the diorama. Display completed dioramas. LISTENING/SPEAKING

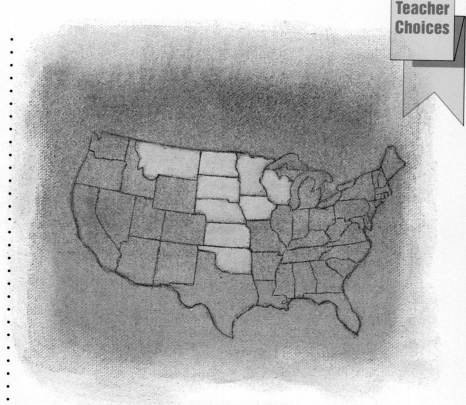

SOCIAL STUDIES

The Grand Prairie

USE A MAP AND AN ATLAS Explain to students that the American prairie was once a vast expanse of grass-covered land with few trees. Point out that little of the original prairie remains today because most of it has been turned into farmland. Provide physical maps of the United States. Help students study the maps to determine which states are "prairie states." Have students list the prairie states and a major city in each one and then use an atlas to find the date each prairie state joined the United States. READING/WRITING

Multi*Cultural*
P E R S P E C T I V E S

Trailblazers of a Different Kind

READ ALOUD TO STUDENTS:

NOT ALL TRAILBLAZERS CUT A

PATH THROUGH THE WIDE

PRAIRIE. Many have braved a wilderness of ignorance and prejudice to become pioneers of a different sort. These trailblazers are pioneers because they did something that no one had done before.

Dr. James Derham is a case in point. Born into slavery in 1762, Derham learned medicine from his owners, who were physicians. After he purchased his freedom, Dr. Derham became one of the most important physicians in New Orleans. His knowledge of medicine and his skills in dealing with disease impressed some of the best doctors of his time.

A century later, Dr. Florence Sabin pioneered the way for women research scientists. Born in Colorado in 1871, Dr. Sabin helped change the aim of medicine from curing to preventing disease. A brilliant student at Johns Hopkins, she built a model of a brain that is still used in schools worldwide. Dr. Flexner, head of the Rockefeller Institute, where Dr. Sabin later worked, called her "the greatest living woman scientist and one of the foremost scientists of all time." ■

Dr. Florence Sabin

ACTIVITY CORNER

■ **Available on Project Card**
Have interested students locate the names of other modern-day pioneers from various cultures. Remind them to consider contributions made by doctors as well as teachers, business people, and writers. Have students combine their information in a class book entitled "Pioneers of Today."

■ Invite students to create an award to be given in honor of Dr. Derham or Dr. Sabin, based on the person's life, work, and values. Students may wish to do additional research on their subjects before proceeding with their projects.

Working together, medical researchers have created vaccines and antibiotics to conquer many diseases.

ARTICLE

Words About the Author:
Laura Ingalls Wilder

Reading the Article

Help students set a purpose for reading.

Recall with students the selection "Runaway" and review the fact that the story is based on Laura Ingalls Wilder's real-life experiences. Ask students to think about possible reasons why an author might want to write about events from his or her own life.

Explain to students that they are going to read an article about Laura Ingalls Wilder. Suggest that students read to see whether there are any reasons given for why Wilder wrote about her actual experiences.

Responding to the Article

Return to the purpose for reading.

Ask students why Laura Ingalls Wilder chose to write about actual events in her life. Then ask students whether they agree with Laura Ingalls Wilder's reasons for writing about her childhood.

Encourage students to respond creatively.

You may wish to select one of the following activities for responding to the article:

RECORDING HISTORY Review the reasons Laura Ingalls Wilder had for writing her stories. Then invite students to imagine that they are older adults in the year 2060. Make a list with students of important events of the present they would like children in 2060 to know. The list might include efforts to improve the environment or changes in foreign governments. You may wish to provide recent newspapers and news magazines as references for ideas.   LISTENING/SPEAKING/READING

COOPERATIVE LEARNING: DISCOVERING THE LANDSCAPE
Remind students that the article mentions that the landscape of the prairie where the Wilder family settled was very different from that of the Wisconsin woods where Laura Ingalls Wilder was born. Invite students to work in pairs. Provide reference sources, and ask them to research what prairie regions looked like in the late 1800s, what kinds of wildlife were found there, and how a prairie environment differed from a wooded one. When they have completed their research, have partners report their findings to their classmates.   LISTENING/SPEAKING/READING/ WRITING

SECOND-LANGUAGE SUPPORT Explain to students that a *wagon train* was a group of several covered wagons that made the journey west together. Explain that pioneers felt that their trip west would be safer if many people traveled together. Generally, the wagons followed one behind the other, like the cars of a train.

WORDS ABOUT THE AUTHOR:

Laura Ingalls Wilder

AWARD-WINNING
AUTHOR

If the characters in "Runaway" seem real, it's because Laura Ingalls Wilder was writing about her own family. She wanted to write down her memories of growing up as a pioneer girl because she felt "they were stories that needed to be told." Even though Ms. Wilder's stories are set long ago, they appeal to young readers today.

Laura was born in a little log cabin in the big woods of Wisconsin in 1867. In *Little House in the Big Woods*, her first book, she wrote about her experiences growing up.

In her next book, *Little House on the Prairie*, which is also the title of a television series based on the family's experiences, Laura described the wagon-train trip that took the Ingalls family from Wisconsin to the Kansas prairie. The landscape of the prairie was very different from that of the Wisconsin woods. On the prairie, the sky seemed to go on forever. There weren't many other settlers, but there were Indians living on the land, which had once been their hunting ground.

When it appeared that the government was going to return the land to the Indians, the Ingalls family went back to Wisconsin, but Pa soon had an "itchy foot" and wanted to try the West again. This time, the family settled in Walnut Grove, Minnesota, which is the setting for "Runaway."

Hard times eventually forced the Ingalls family to move west again, to the Dakota Territory. By that time, Laura's older sister, Mary, had become blind from a fever, and there were still more troubles ahead. The frigid winter of 1880–1881 was so cold that people could barely stay warm and find enough food. The story of how the Ingallses managed to survive is told in Laura's book *The Long Winter*.

When she was 17, Laura was courted by a local farmer, Almanzo Wilder. They married in 1885. Laura described her early years of marriage in *The First Four Years*. She also wrote about Almanzo's childhood in *Farmer Boy*.

Laura didn't start writing until she was 65 years old. She wanted children to understand "more about the beginnings of things—what it is that made America." As you read Laura Ingalls Wilder's books, you feel like a pioneer child too because she wrote so vividly about an exciting period in history.

Expanding the Article   What do you think made Laura's father have an "itchy foot"?

(Accept reasonable responses: A strong desire to be a pioneer and live with his family out West, where life was unpredictable and exciting.)

INFERENTIAL: DETERMINING CHARACTERS' TRAITS

SAILING

from *Grasshopper Summer*

by Ann Turner

illustrated by Joel Spector

SAILING

	TEACHING OUTLINE	Materials	Language Arts/ Integrated Curriculum	Meeting Individual Needs
Part 1 **Reading Literature** Pages T690–T698 	**Building Background** **Vocabulary Strategies** Key Words (Tested) **Strategic Reading** Preview and Predict Setting a Purpose **Options for Reading**	Transparency 38 Second-Language Support Manual Practice Book p. 106 Integrated Spelling p. 55 Integrated Spelling T.E. pp. 74–75 Student Anthology pp. 388–398 Response Card 8: Written Conversation	**Spelling** Spelling Pretest Spelling-Vocabulary Connection	**Second-Language Support** Vocabulary T691 Strategic Reading T692, T695 **Cooperative Reading** T693
Part 2 **Responding to Literature** Pages T699–T703 	**Story Follow-Up** Think It Over Write **Summarizing the Literature** **Appreciating Literature** **Critical Thinking Activities**	Writer's Journal p. 78 Practice Book pp. 107–108 Integrated Spelling p. 56 Integrated Spelling T.E. pp. 74–75 Literature Cassette 2 Language Handbook	**Vocabulary Workshop** Reviewing Key Words Extending Vocabulary Alliteration **Reading** Readers Theatre **Writing** Informational Paragraph Friendly Letter **Spelling** Reviewing Spelling Words **Speaking** Presenting an Advertisement **Listening** A Description	**Cooperative Learning** T700, T703
Part 3 **Learning Through Literature** Pages T704–T710 	**Introduce** Comprehension: Paraphrasing (Tested) **Review** Study Skills: Graphic Aids (Tested)	Second-Language Support Manual Transparencies 39–40 Writer's Journal p. 79 Practice Book pp. 109–111	**Social Studies** Trail Foods Covered Wagons Railroad News **Music** Pioneer Songs **Science** Identifying Hawks **Math** Measuring a Claim **Multicultural** Railroad Workers	**Reteach** T705 **Challenge** T705, T706 **Second-Language Support** Paraphrasing T705 **Cooperative Learning** T705, T707, T709

KEY WORDS

territory
horizon
claim
file
scrunched
exploded
practical

ANN TURNER

Selection Summary

Sam White and his family leave Kentucky and travel long miles in a covered wagon to find a new home in the Dakota Territory. Sam tells of riding over miles of rolling, grass-covered hills that make him think of the sea. Along the way he wonders about living in a house dug into the side of a hill. He doesn't realize how much he enjoys the quiet prairie until they come to a town that seems noisy, crowded, dusty, and shabby. Sam doesn't feel right until they are rolling across the prairie once again. A night and a day later, they finally come to a stop. Sam, his brother, Billy, and Ma want to stay just where they are. Pa and Ma check the map and find the land is unclaimed. Billy and Pa search for water, while Sam secretly puts his mark on their piece of the Dakota Territory by digging a small hole, spitting into it, and mixing a small part of himself with the earth.

Family Involvement

Encourage family members to talk with students about their family history, including where the family lived before, how long ago they moved to this community, and how they traveled here. Suggest that they work together to write a brief family history and to illustrate it with photos or drawings and that they title it "Our Family."

Ann Turner's interest in what others may overlook started in her childhood. "Possibly because my liberal family was somewhat 'different' from the New Englanders of our town, I grew up being interested in different peoples and cultures," she says. "Living in the country and having an artist for a mother gave me a certain way of seeing, an eye for beauty and interest in what others might think ugly and dull. . . . I am concerned with the things that make each culture individual, and the traits that hold us together. In strange and beautiful ways we are the same, yet different. That is what I write of, and will probably continue writing of for a long, long time."

Many of Turner's books vividly portray the hard, lonely, and often exciting life that people lived on the western frontier in the 1800s. *Dakota Dugout, Third Girl from the Left,* and *Grasshopper Summer* all received numerous citations for their realistically accurate descriptions of life on the prairie.

ADDITIONAL READING

Other Books by Ann Turner

Dakota Dugout. Macmillan, 1985.   EASY

Heron Street. Harper, 1989.   EASY

Other Books About Pioneers

The Pony Express: Hoofbeats in the Wilderness by Joseph J. DiCerto. Franklin Watts, 1989.   AVERAGE

Where the Buffaloes Begin by Olaf Baker. Warne, 1981.   AVERAGE

Part 1
Reading Literature

Building Background

Access prior knowledge and build vocabulary concepts.

Point out to students that the next story, "Sailing," is from a book about a family who moves from Kentucky to the Dakota Territory by covered wagon in 1874. Have students think about what they would expect a story set in this time and place to include. Explain that recalling what they already know about traveling by covered wagon will help them better understand the story. Have students create a web including things they would expect to read in a story about traveling by covered wagon:

Vocabulary Strategies

Introduce Key Words and strategies.

Display Transparency 38 or the following story. Have students read the story silently. Encourage them to use context clues with phonetic and structural analysis to decode and to figure out the meanings of the underlined words. The activity may be used to check understanding of the Key Words.

Transparency 38   Key Words

Jack pointed to a spot of land on the map and said, "This is the <u>territory</u> we want." Pearl looked toward the <u>horizon</u>, where the sky met the flat land. "We can put in a <u>claim</u> to make the land ours. We'll <u>file</u> it at the courthouse in town so it's official," Jack added.
Pearl <u>scrunched</u> down behind the wagon seat. Then the water barrel <u>exploded</u>, and water drenched them. Pearl was upset, but Jack just said in a <u>practical</u> way, "We'll need to get more water before dinner."

CULTURAL AWARENESS

Students may be interested to learn that the name of the Dakota Territory is from the language of Native Americans who called themselves *dakhota*, meaning "friendly ones." The Dakota were Plains Indians.

KEY WORDS

territory
horizon
claim
file
scrunched
exploded
practical

KEY WORDS DEFINED

territory land, region

horizon line where earth and sky seem to meet

claim piece of public land a settler marks out for himself or herself

file to place among the records of a government office

scrunched squeezed

exploded violently burst out in all directions

practical having good sense

Check students' understanding.

On the board, draw a chart similar to the one below. Have students classify the Key Words according to the way they think the author will use them in "Sailing." Model the placement of the first word and the reason for its placement.   STRATEGY: CLASSIFYING

> The story is about a family traveling from Kentucky to the Dakota Territory in 1874. I know that Kentucky and North and South Dakota are states in the United States now. Since I know these states are places, the Dakota Territory must have been a place, too. So *territory* belongs in the first column.

Places in the Story	Actions in the Story	Descriptions of Story Characters
territory (horizon) (claim)	(file) (scrunched) (exploded)	(practical)

Discuss students' placement of words. A suggested placement for each word is shown above. Tell students that they will review their charts after they have read the story.

Integrate spelling with vocabulary.

SPELLING-VOCABULARY CONNECTION   *Integrated Spelling* page 55 reinforces the spellings of the /är/, /ôr/, or /âr/ sounds in the Key Word *territory* and in other words. The spelling of the Key Word *claim* is also included.

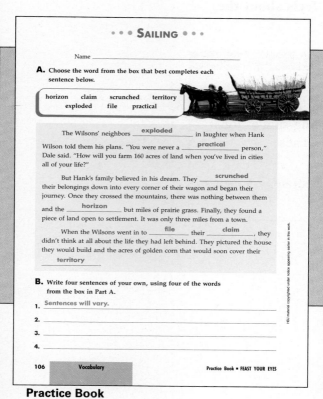

Practice Book

Integrated Spelling

PRACTICE BOOK page 106:   Reinforcing Key Words

INTEGRATED SPELLING page 55: Writing and spelling words with the /är/, /ôr/, or /âr/ sounds

NOTE: These pages may be completed now or after students have read the story.

Strategic Reading

Preview and Predict

Help students preview the literature.

Point out that the story "Sailing" is historical fiction. Explain that the characters, the actions, and the dialogue are fiction but that the time, the place, and the general events are based on fact.

Discuss the steps involved in previewing a story before reading. (thinking about the title, looking at the illustrations, reading the introduction and the first few paragraphs) Have students read the title and the introduction on pages 388 and 389 and preview page 389.

Have students make predictions.

Then ask questions such as the following to help students predict what might happen in the story:

- **Why is the family going to the Dakota Territory?**
- **What will they think of the Dakota Territory?**
- **How will they find a new home?**

PERSONAL JOURNAL Have students add their predictions about the story to their personal journals. Ask students to support their predictions.

Setting a Purpose

Have students set purposes.

Discuss with students what they want to find out when they read the story, based on their preview and on what they already know about traveling West in a covered wagon in 1874. Have students use their predictions to set a purpose for reading.

Model purpose-setting, if necessary.

If students have difficulty setting their own purpose, suggest the following:

> **I'm going to read to find out how Sam feels about the area where his family decides to settle.**

OPTIONS FOR READING

INDEPENDENT READING Have students read the story silently with their purpose for reading in mind.

GUIDED READING Follow the Guided Reading suggestions that appear on pages T693, T696, and T698. These suggestions model strategic reading.

COOPERATIVE READING A reader response strategy appears on page T693.

SECOND-LANGUAGE SUPPORT Display a map of the United States to show students the distance the Whites traveled from Kentucky to the Dakota Territory. Then have students work cooperatively to discuss what they think traveling in a covered wagon would be like. (See *Second-Language Support Manual.*)

SAILING

from *Grasshopper Summer*

by Ann Turner

illustrated by Joel Spector

from *Grasshopper Summer*

by Ann Turner

illustrated by Joel Spector

Sam White did not want to leave Kentucky, but his father was ready to look for their future in Dakota Territory. So, Ma, Pa, brother Billy, and Sam set out in a covered wagon, with their dog, Jake, on their journey to a new home.

THE LAND WAS CHANGING. The smaller hills and red rocks of the South were gone, and day by day, the land got more and more like a blanket—a brown-green, rumpled one. Grandma'd want to pull it neat and flat, but I liked it. Like the sea was supposed to be, and sometimes I felt we were on a boat sailing over an ocean.

We went over so many miles of grass, it all began to look the same. We got quieter the farther north we traveled. Sometimes the only sound I heard was the wind flapping our canvas top. Something about that wide blue sky, that endless grass, made us quiet. Like our voices were a fire we had to save.

389

Guided Reading

SET PURPOSE/PREDICT: PAGES 388–394   Have students read through page 394 to find out what Sam thinks about the prairie.

Cooperative Reading

READER RESPONSE STRATEGY: PAGES 388–398 Have students work in pairs. Ask each student to read silently and then use the strategy described below to analyze the beginning of the story. (Response Card 8: Written Conversation, on page R69, gives complete directions for using the strategy.)

1. Each student writes a comment and a question.
2. Students pass their papers to their partners.
3. Each student writes down the answer to the question and adds a new question.
4. The papers are passed back, and each student answers the new question he or she receives.

PAGES 388–398   Have students finish reading the story and repeat steps 1–4. Ask partners to discuss their completed papers.

After a few weeks of rolling over the new grass, Pa turned to us. "We're in Dakota Territory now. We got here!"

Billy said, "Looks just the same to me, Pa. Grass and grass and sky and wind."

Pa frowned.

"I like it, Pa," Billy hurried to say. "It's just it doesn't look any different."

Ma patted his arm and I silently agreed. I wondered if she was thinking about living in the ground, the way Pa said we would. Dig into a hill with the wind at our backs, he said. I wondered if it would feel like a grave instead of a house, but I didn't tell Billy that.

After another week, we came to the first town we'd seen in some time.

"What's that?" Billy asked.

You could hardly tell it was a town at first. There were just some bumpy bits on the horizon. Then, as the wagon rolled on, they became house roofs, then walls, and a dusty street snaked between them.

Pa stopped Ham and Duke outside the town, and Ma fidgeted with her hand-kerchief. She dabbed at her cheeks and hands, and pushed her straggly hair under the dusty bonnet.

"Walter, do I look all right?"

"You always look lovely, Ellen," Pa said.

She shook her head. "Bonnets are no use in this country—all that wind and sun." She "tcched." "You boys smooth down your hair and neaten up."

390

Billy stared at me and I stared at him. I straightened his dusty jacket and he brushed off my shoulders and we laughed. Used to be that I'd fuss at him and he'd fuss back. But ever since that time weeks ago when he was almost lost, I'd stopped picking at him quite so much.

Pa chirruped to the horses, and we went into town. There were five or six houses on either side, cows in back, and horses tied in front of the "Comfort Hotel." It was a skinny gray building like an old lady trying to pretty herself up. Faded pink curtains hung inside the windows, and the glass was smeary.

There were people all over the street, calling and talking to each other. "Harry!" someone shouted, and my ears hurt. "How's your boy? Alice doing well?" "Sure!" the other shouted back. Didn't they know you didn't need to shout on the prairie? That it was so quiet a whisper would do?

The only ones who were quiet were Indians. We'd seen a few on horseback when we traveled, but not many. Here an older man stood straight as a gun by the Comfort Hotel, and a younger one stood beside him. In the shadows crouched a woman. They didn't talk to each other, but the quiet around them seemed to join them up somehow, and we just looked noisy and silly compared to them.

Ma said, "Indians!"

"Hush," Pa said. "They have a right to be here, too. Just go about your business and don't fuss."

Expanding the Literature   Based on the description, what do you think the "Comfort Hotel" is like? (Accept reasonable responses: probably run-down, drab, not very comfortable.) CREATIVE: VISUALIZING

Why is the town such a shock to Sam? (Accept reasonable responses: After the extreme quiet of the prairie, the town seems too busy and noisy to Sam.)   INFERENTIAL: COMPARING AND CONTRASTING

"What's that, Pa?" Billy pointed to a long line of men outside a shabby building.

"That's probably the land claim office, Billy, and those men are waiting to file on their claims."

Pa stopped the horses by the general store and said, "You boys can come with us or stay here."

Billy jumped down and went in with Ma and Pa, but I stayed in the wagon. "Come on, Sam." He waved to me.

I shook my head, and couldn't explain to him that there were too many people and too many voices, and I just wasn't used to it. Made my neck itch, and I scrunched down to watch people while Ma and Pa bought supplies. Most folks looked like us, kind of tattered. Nobody was too neat—men had scrungy beards and blue denim overalls. Women were in calico with kids tugging at their hands. One yellow mutt with a sad tail lay in the street.

After a long, noisy time they came back, and Pa heaved a sack of flour into the wagon while Ma tucked a bag beside it.

"Glad I got that map, Ellen," Pa said. Even his voice sounded loud to me.

"Yes, Walter—I was glad to have a little conversation with the storekeeper. News!" Ma said.

"What news?" I asked. "I bet it's still the same. Storms. Woman has five babies. Horses run amok and little boy squashed. Tornadoes in the South and—"

"Railroads, Sam!" Billy broke in. "You forgot the railroads."

"Coming this way," Pa said. "It makes me think. . . ."

"Think what, Walter?" Ma hopped up onto the seat.

393

Second-Language Support

Students may need help understanding the term *general store.* Explain to students that in small towns long ago, and in some places today, one store would carry nearly everything the people in the area might want, including groceries, cloth and clothing, pots and pans, blankets, and farm tools. No one term could describe the variety of things the store offered, so people called it a *general* store. You may wish to ask students whether a similar type of store can be found in their neighborhood or in another country in which they have lived and what the store's name would be.

MEETING INDIVIDUAL NEEDS

Vocabulary Strategy
What clues can you use to figure out the meaning of the phrase *run amok* on page 393? (When I read the entire sentence, the context clue *little boy squashed* suggests that the horses had to be out of control enough to hurt someone. So *run amok* must mean "to act wildly enough to cause injury or damage.")

STRATEGY: CONTEXT CLUES

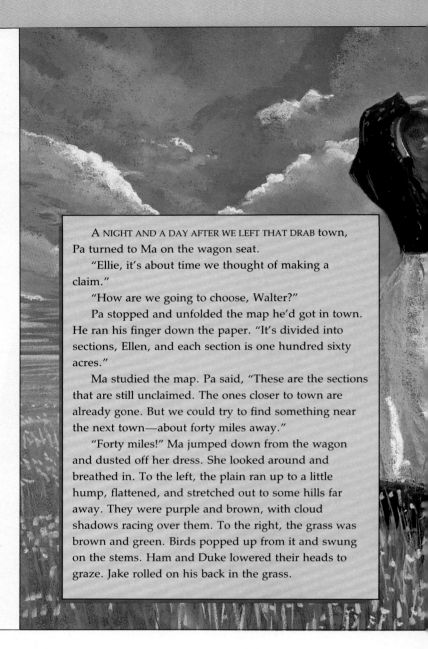

"Think that we may be getting near to stopping."

"It would be so wonderful to stop, just to sit for a while. Not to move," Ma sighed.

"The storekeeper drew me a rough map, Ellie, of the territory still open around here. Just in case."

Pa smiled at her, flicked the reins, and we set off down the street. I was so glad to be going again, to get out of that town and beyond all those voices and legs and arms. I didn't know if I wanted to stop moving or not.

"Sam, you should have seen the candy! And guns and knives and fishing poles!"

"Mmmph," was all I said to Billy.

I watched the prairie roll by, and it swept my mind clean—the cool wind and the sky so wide and high. Who wanted to look at candy?

Suddenly, Billy nudged me and pointed out the back. Two hawks dove after a pigeon. They screamed at that bird as it zigzagged and flew low.

"Come on, pigeon!" Billy called. "Fly faster!"

It whizzed to one side, raced to the other, gained height, dove, but the hawks stayed close behind. One of the hawks rose higher and higher, then screamed again. It sped down the sky and hit the pigeon so hard its feathers exploded into the air.

"Whooh! Hate to be that pigeon!" Billy sucked in a breath.

"Me, too." I looked through the back. There was no one out here on the prairie except us—us and those screaming hawks and the pigeon exploded into nothing. The wind blew the feathers away, it blew away the hawks' calls. I shivered and couldn't stop.

A NIGHT AND A DAY AFTER WE LEFT THAT DRAB town, Pa turned to Ma on the wagon seat.

"Ellie, it's about time we thought of making a claim."

"How are we going to choose, Walter?"

Pa stopped and unfolded the map he'd got in town. He ran his finger down the paper. "It's divided into sections, Ellen, and each section is one hundred sixty acres."

Ma studied the map. Pa said, "These are the sections that are still unclaimed. The ones closer to town are already gone. But we could try to find something near the next town—about forty miles away."

"Forty miles!" Ma jumped down from the wagon and dusted off her dress. She looked around and breathed in. To the left, the plain ran up to a little hump, flattened, and stretched out to some hills far away. They were purple and brown, with cloud shadows racing over them. To the right, the grass was brown and green. Birds popped up from it and swung on the stems. Ham and Duke lowered their heads to graze. Jake rolled on his back in the grass.

394

Guided Reading

MONITOR COMPREHENSION: PAGES 388–394
What does Sam think about the prairie? (Accept reasonable responses: He thinks that it all looks the same, that it looks like the ocean; he likes it.)
STRATEGIC READING: RETURNING TO PURPOSE

How do Ma, Pa, and Billy feel about the Dakota Territory? (Accept reasonable responses: Everyone is happy to be there; they want to settle down.)
STRATEGIC READING: SUMMARIZING

SET PURPOSE/PREDICT: PAGES 395–398   Have students predict where the White family will finally settle and why the Whites will choose that location. Encourage students to read to the end of the story to confirm their predictions.

"What's wrong with this?" Ma said.

"Here? But I thought you wanted
neighbors, to be closer to town. The last
one's more than a day away."

"I know. I know it's contrary of me,
but . . ." She walked back and forth,
taking deep breaths. Billy and I jumped
down beside her. The ground was springy
and soft, and I threw myself on it, rolling
and kicking my feet. Earth. Land that
didn't move under the wagon wheels.

Billy rolled beside me, and we rooted
and snorted like two spring pigs. Jake
bounced from my head to Billy's,
pretending to snap at us.

"Boys!" Ma reproved. But her mouth
twitched.

Pa laughed and jumped down beside
us. "If this doesn't beat all." He swung
Ma around until her bonnet fell off and
her hair streamed out behind.

"Walt! Put me down." He did, and
she looked like an Indian woman then,
with her brown face and hands and dark
hair. Grandma'd hate it. She'd want to
stuff Ma's hair under the bonnet and dab
cornstarch on her skin.

"Well, boys"—Pa kept his hand on
Ma's waist—"what do you think?"

We scrambled to our feet and Billy
said, "If there's water nearby, this looks
fine to me."

He sure was getting practical all of a
sudden. I hadn't even thought of water.

Pa pointed to some trees in the
distance. "Those are willows. Should
mean a creek over there."

"If this section's free," Ma said,
pinning up her hair. "*And* if no one
else wants it." She got the map from
the wagon, and she and Pa pored over
it, murmuring—"That track there—
meant to be a road—goes through the
middle of these four sections—
that pine there. . . ." I guess they were
figuring out landmarks. Billy and I lay
down in the grass and looked up at the
sky while they talked.

"You could fall into it," Billy said.

"Or swim around in it, like a blue sea."

"The air smells good!" He chewed on
some grass. "Clean, like laundry."

"Or potatoes baking."

"Mmm, I like it here." Billy rolled
onto his side. Pa yelled to us. "We're
clear, boys!" He ran over and pretended
to put his foot on each of our chests.
"We declare this to be Walter T.
White's—"

"And Ellen A. White's—" Ma put in.

"And Billy and Sam White's land,"
we all finished together.

Pa rubbed his chin. "Who'll come
with me to look for water?"

397

Teaching Tip Suggest that students close their
eyes while you read aloud portions of the text on
pages 395 and 396 that describe the land where the
Whites stop. Then talk about what the students
visualize.

Billy jumped up and they set off together, singing, while Ma pulled grass out of a circle to make a fire. "Sam, help me get dinner started." Of course Billy *would* get to go exploring while I had to help with supper.

"In a minute, Ma." I did something strange, then, something I never told anyone about, not even Billy. I went off behind the wagon, where no one could see me, and dug a tiny hole with my knife. The grass roots tangled up the dirt and it took a while. I sniffed the wet earth smell. Then I spat into the hole three times and mixed it in, tamping the grass hard on top.

"Samuel, you come here!" Ma's voice rose.

"Coming." I felt strange doing such a thing. But when I saw Pa and Billy running back toward the wagon, waving their hats and shouting, "We found water!" I knew why. I'd put a piece of myself into the earth. Samuel Theodore White, a Kentucky boy, had made his mark on Dakota Territory.

THINK IT OVER

1. *What was life like in 1874 for a family who traveled West?*

2. *What did the land look like in Dakota Territory?*

3. *Why didn't Sam want to go into the general store?*

4. *How did Sam feel about Dakota Territory? Tell how you know.*

WRITE

Would you like to have traveled to Dakota Territory with Sam and his family? Write a list of reasons that support your decision.

398

THEME WRAP-UP

PIONEERS

Life was difficult for pioneer families. Which of the hardships challenging the families you read about do you think was the most difficult to face? Tell why you think as you do.

In what ways was life on the Minnesota prairie like life in the Dakota territory?

WRITER'S WORKSHOP Choose another pioneer that you have heard about or read about. Remember that a pioneer is a person who settles in a new country or region. Read about and take notes on how that person lived and what he or she contributed to the settling of the frontier. Organize your notes into an outline. Then write a research report about the pioneer you chose and share your report with your classmates.

For discussion of this page, please turn to T711.

Guided Reading

MONITOR COMPREHENSION: PAGES 395–398
Where do Sam and his family finally settle?
(They find a grassy spot with trees and a stream that is about a night and a day's travel from the last town through which they passed.) **Is this what you predicted would happen?** (Responses will vary.) STRATEGIC READING: CONFIRMING PREDICTIONS

Why are the Whites happy with their choice of a place to build a new home? (Accept reasonable responses: The spot is pretty, there is water, the air is clean, the section seems to be unclaimed, and the distance from nearby towns seems to suit all of them.) STRATEGIC READING: SUMMARIZING

Returning to the Predictions Invite students to discuss the predictions that they made before reading and that they may have written in their personal journals. Encourage them to talk about how those predictions changed as they read the story.

Returning to the Purpose for Reading Discuss how Sam feels about the area where the Whites choose to settle. (Sam appreciates the peacefulness, the openness, and the quietness of the prairie in the Dakota Territory. He makes his mark on the property they choose and feels he is a part of the land.)

NOTE: Responses to the Think It Over questions and support for the Write activity appear on page T699.

Part 2
Responding to Literature

Story Follow-Up

Think It Over

Encourage reader's response: student page 398.

1. **What was life like in 1874 for a family who traveled West?** (Accept reasonable responses: Life wasn't easy; the trip was long and dusty; the family had to rely on itself for its needs and survival; the family had to create a new home for itself.)
   INFERENTIAL: DETERMINING MAIN IDEA

2. **What did the land look like in Dakota Territory?** (mostly rolling hills with brown and green grass, a few scattered trees and towns)   LITERAL: NOTING IMPORTANT DETAILS

3. **Why didn't Sam want to go into the general store?** (He may have felt that the inside of the store would be noisier and more crowded than the town and would make him feel even more closed in.)   INFERENTIAL: DRAWING CONCLUSIONS

4. **How did Sam feel about Dakota Territory? Tell how you know.** (The endless prairie and the wide-open sky made his mind feel clean and calm. However, at times he felt small and alone. In the town, he felt closed in and attacked by noise.)
   INFERENTIAL: DETERMINING CHARACTERS' EMOTIONS

Write

Encourage writer's response: student page 398.

Would you like to have traveled to Dakota Territory with Sam and his family? Write a list of reasons that support your decision. Encourage students to be specific about what they would have liked or not liked.   CREATIVE: WRITING A LIST

Summarizing the Literature

Have students retell the story and write a summary.

Encourage students to summarize the story by creating a character map about Sam. Guide students in beginning the map. Then have them complete it independently. (See *Practice Book* page 107 on T700.) Students may use their completed maps to retell the story and write a brief summary statement. Maps may resemble the following:

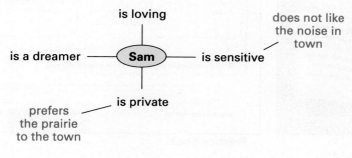

STRATEGY CONFERENCE

Ask students what they found difficult about reading the story. Together, brainstorm strategies such as visualizing that might have helped them better understand the story.

NOTE

An additional writing activity for this story appears on page T702.

INFORMAL ASSESSMENT

Having students summarize in this way will help you informally assess how well they comprehended the **theme** of the story. It also will help you see how well they recognized the importance of particular **details** in contributing to this theme.

Appreciating Literature

Have students share personal responses.

Have students work in small groups to discuss the story. Provide general questions such as the following to help the groups begin:

- **Why did the author choose to tell the story from Sam's point of view?**
- **How might the story have been different if told from another character's point of view?**

PERSONAL JOURNAL   Have students use their personal journals to write about ideas and feelings that are discussed in the groups. You may also refer them to their personal journals after they complete the activities below.

Critical Thinking Activities

Encourage both cooperative and individual responses.

LIST CHARACTERS' THOUGHTS   **What if the story included each character's thoughts about the town? Write what you think these thoughts would show.** Invite students to work in small groups to discuss their ideas. Suggest that they write the characters' names and list what each one would have thought of the town.   CRITICAL: AUTHOR'S CRAFT/IDENTIFYING WITH CHARACTERS

MAKE A LIST   **What do you think the Whites were able to carry with them in the covered wagon from Kentucky to the Dakota Territory? What would you take if you had traveled with them?** Have students work in pairs to make a list. Suggest that they think of supplies, household goods, and farm tools a family might need to start a new home. Remind students that the space was limited.   CREATIVE: VISUALIZING

WRITER'S JOURNAL
page 78: Writing a personal response

PRACTICE BOOK
page 107: Summarizing the selection

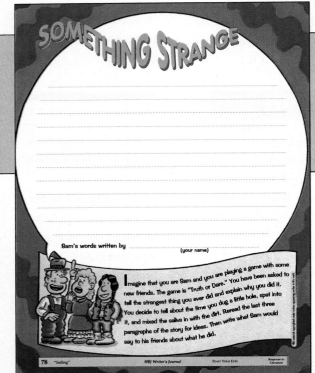

Writer's Journal

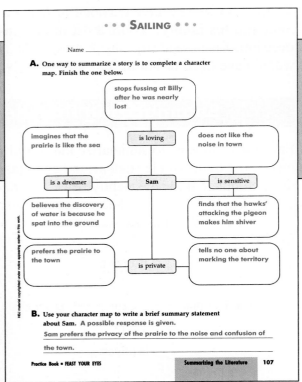

Practice Book

STUDENT SELF-ASSESSMENT

Help students self-assess their listening skills by writing the following questions on the board:

- Was I able to visualize the speakers' ideas about this story?
- Were any of the ideas discussed similar to what I was thinking?
- Which things that were discussed reminded me of other stories I know?

VO·CAB·U·LAR·Y Workshop

Reviewing Key Words

To review the Key Words, display the chart that students started before reading. Have students tell, orally or in writing, how each word is used in the story. Possible responses are given below.

Places in the Story	Actions in the Story	Descriptions of Story Characters
territory horizon claim	file scrunched exploded	practical

- Dakota Territory is where the Whites went. (place)
- While traveling on the prairie, they saw the town on the horizon. (place)
- The word *practical* tells what Sam thought Billy was when Billy remembered that water is important in choosing land. (characters)
- The Whites chose a *claim,* a piece of land, to settle. (place)
- The Whites *file,* or record, information about their claim in a government office. (action)
- Sam wanted to get away from the noise and the people in the town, so he *scrunched* down in the wagon. (action)
- Suddenly, dozens of pigeon feathers were sent out in all directions when the feathers *exploded* into the air. (action)

Extending Vocabulary

ALLITERATION   Read aloud the following phrases from "Sailing": *red rocks, bumpy bits.* Ask students what they notice about the sound of each phrase. (The words in each phrase begin with the same consonant, *r* or *b.*) Explain that the repetition of a consonant sound at the beginning of words is called *alliteration.* Point out that the author does this to create an effect and that sometimes the repetitive sounds occur at the ends of words, as in *endless grass.* Encourage students to find other examples of alliteration in the story, such as *many miles, long line, stood straight,* or *made his mark.*

   Invite students to add words to each phrase to extend the alliteration. (Accept reasonable responses: *many miles moving merrily, long line leaving the lake, stood straight and stared,* or *made his mark on my map.*) Then have students make up their own alliterative phrases or sentences. You may wish to suggest that students include their alliterations in a poem.

> **PRACTICE BOOK**
> page 108:   Using alliteration

• • • SAILING • • •

Name _____

A. Read the following pairs of phrases. In each pair, draw a line under the one that a poet might use to express an idea.

1. the wild wind	the playful wind
2. a lot of grass	grass going on and on
3. pretty pink petunia	pretty yellow tulip
4. a fearless fox	a noisy fox
5. a calico curtain	a plain curtain
6. a clean blue robe	a clean green gown
7. whisper or wail	whisper or yell
8. hawks rose to the sky	hawks rose higher
9. plenty of potatoes	brown potatoes
10. left his mark	made his mark

B. The items numbered below are mentioned in the story. Use each one in an alliterative phrase, such as *high hills.* Possible responses are given.

1. bonnet   beautiful blue bonnet
2. wagon   wobbly wagon
3. building   big building
4. prairie   peaceful prairie
5. horse   harmless horse
6. territory   terrific territory
7. pigeon   poor pigeon

108   Alliteration   Practice Book • FEAST YOUR EYES

Practice Book

Integrated
Language Arts

READING

Oral Rereading/ Readers Theatre

AVAILABLE ON PROJECT CARD

Invite groups of five students to each select a different section of "Sailing" to read aloud as a Readers Theatre. Have groups decide who will play which part. For the part of Sam, suggest that one group member play Sam the narrator, and another read Sam's dialogue. Students may also wish to take turns as the narrator. Encourage groups to use the author's descriptions of how the characters talk to help students decide how to pitch their voice or to position their body. You may wish to model using expression when reading dialogue. Have students review their part silently, and allow time to rehearse. When students are ready, have each group present its reading. Students may wish to arrange chairs to represent the covered wagon.   LISTENING/READING

WRITING

Writing About the Literature

WRITE AN INFORMATIONAL PARAGRAPH   Invite students to imagine that a newspaper in New York City has asked Sam to write a paragraph describing the Dakota Territory. Tell students to write the paragraph as if they were Sam and to include information that people who have never seen the territory might want to know. Suggest that students use a web, such as the one below, to organize the details they want to include.   LISTENING/ WRITING

NOTE: An additional writing activity appears on page T699.

SPELLING

Reviewing Spelling Words

SPELLING WORDS: *claim, cornstarch, dark, hardly, horseback, prepare, soar, stare, store, territory*

Have students find the spelling words in a dictionary. Then ask them to write the dictionary pronunciation for each word. Tell students to include all of the respelling symbols. Point out that in some words the same combination of letters produces different sounds. (For example, the letters *are* can make the /är/ and /âr/ sounds.) Then have students exchange papers, read the symbols, and write each word correctly.   READING/ SPELLING

> **INTEGRATED SPELLING** page 56: Writing and spelling words with the /är/, /ôr/, or /âr/ sounds

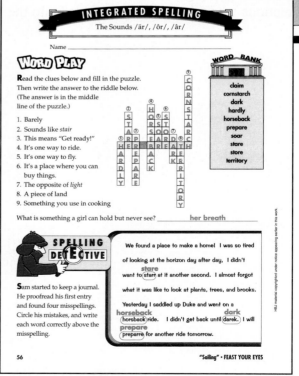

Integrated Spelling

News from the Prairie

Remind students that "Sailing" ends just as the Whites find the land they want for their new home. Invite students to imagine that a year has passed. Discuss the experiences Sam and his family might have had in that time. For example, they would have built a home, planted and harvested crops, and dealt with weather. Have students write a letter from Sam to his grandmother in Kentucky. Encourage students to describe some things that have happened and to report on how the family is doing. Review the parts of a friendly letter (heading, greeting, body, closing, and signature) before students begin. Call on volunteers to share their letters. LISTENING/SPEAKING/READING/WRITING

LISTENING

Making a Mark

Review with students how Sam makes his mark on the land his family chooses for their new home in the Dakota Territory. Ask students to think of special things they might do or they have ever done to welcome themselves to a new home. Examples might include walking around the inside of each room and saying hello, writing their name on a piece of paper and burying it in the yard or putting it in a secret spot in their new home, or positioning something from their old home, such as a picture, in the same kind of place in their new home. Have students work in pairs to develop a few ideas. Then ask partners to describe their procedures to the others. LISTENING/SPEAKING

SPEAKING

Advertising the Dakota Territory

AVAILABLE ON PROJECT CARD

COOPERATIVE LEARNING   Have students work in groups to create an advertisement. Invite them to brainstorm ideas about how they would advertise the Dakota Territory to encourage people to settle there. Then have them plan a poster advertising the unclaimed land still available. Suggest that some group members work on the text of the ad and others develop a picture to illustrate the ad. Encourage groups also to think of an attention-getting title or headline. Provide groups with poster board and art materials. Have each group present its ad to the others.   LISTENING/SPEAKING/WRITING

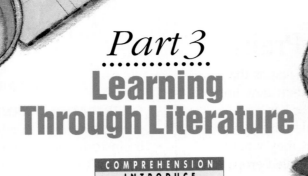

Part 3
Learning Through Literature

Paraphrasing

OBJECTIVE: *To develop global meaning through paraphrasing*

1   Focus

Discuss the importance of knowing how to paraphrase.

Ask students whether they have ever read a book and then told a friend or relative about it. Explain that knowing how to retell or to paraphrase a passage or a story in their own words will help them understand what they read.

2   Teach/Model

Teach how to paraphrase.

Explain that a paraphrase restates a story or a passage in a person's own words without changing its meaning. Point out that a paraphrase should include the main idea, but it should not include the reader's opinion of what the writer says. Model how to paraphrase the passage on page 390 where the Whites approach the town.

> **I reread the passage and think about the main idea. Then I retell in my own words what happens:** *At the thought of meeting other people, Ma worries about what she and her family must look like after weeks in the prairie sun and wind, so she tries to clean up.*

Help students paraphrase using a story frame.

Point out to students that a story frame can help them remember a story's events. Display Transparency 39 or write the partial story frame on the board. Have students work with you to complete the frame.

Transparency 39   Story Frame

The story ("Sailing") takes place (on the prairie in Dakota Territory). The characters are (Ma, Pa, Sam, and Billy White), who have moved from (Kentucky) in a (covered wagon) to find (a new home in Dakota Territory). The story is told by (Sam). After many weeks on the prairie, the family comes (to a small town). Sam (stays in the wagon) while the rest of the family goes (into the general store), because he does not like (all the people and the noise).

3 Practice/Apply

Have students complete the story frame.

COOPERATIVE LEARNING   Have students work with a partner to write the rest of the story frame. Remind them to continue presenting the story events in chronological order. Suggest that they complete the frame with these sentence beginnings: *Then,* *Finally,* and *The story ends when.*

4 Summarize

Informally assess the learning.

Call on pairs to use their story frame to paraphrase parts of "Sailing." Discuss whether their paraphrase retells the story logically without changing the meaning or leaving out important ideas.

Have students summarize what they learned. (Paraphrasing is restating the story or the passage in your own words without changing the meaning.)

READER ⬌ WRITER CONNECTION

Paraphrasing

▶ **Writers** use paraphrasing to help them determine the most effective way to express their ideas in writing.

▶ **Readers** use paraphrasing to remember what happens in a story and to make sure they understand what they have read.

WRITE A NEWS STORY   Have students rewrite a news story, paraphrasing it so it will fit into a five-second time slot on a news show.

RETEACH Follow the visual, auditory, and kinesthetic/motor models on page R50.

CHALLENGE Encourage students to write a paraphrase of a story they have recently read. Have them check to make sure they retold the story in order and expressed in their own words the important ideas.

SECOND-LANGUAGE SUPPORT Have students demonstrate their understanding by having them paraphrase the main events in a previously read story. Remind students to focus on the main character(s) and what happens at the beginning, the middle, and the ending of the story. (See *Second-Language Support Manual.*)

WRITER'S JOURNAL page 79: Writing a paraphrase

PRACTICE BOOK page 109: Paraphrasing

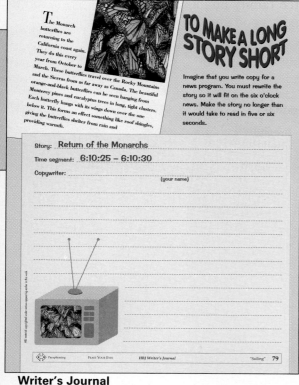

Writer's Journal

Practice Book

(Practice Book page content:)

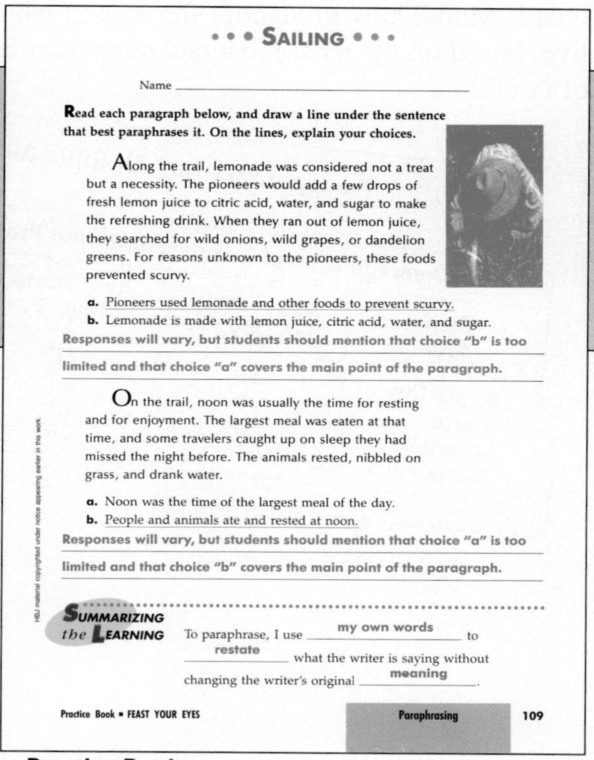

• • • SAILING • • •

Name _____

Read each paragraph below, and draw a line under the sentence that best paraphrases it. On the lines, explain your choices.

Along the trail, lemonade was considered not a treat but a necessity. The pioneers would add a few drops of fresh lemon juice to citric acid, water, and sugar to make the refreshing drink. When they ran out of lemon juice, they searched for wild onions, wild grapes, or dandelion greens. For reasons unknown to the pioneers, these foods prevented scurvy.

a. Pioneers used lemonade and other foods to prevent scurvy.
b. Lemonade is made with lemon juice, citric acid, water, and sugar.

Responses will vary, but students should mention that choice "b" is too limited and that choice "a" covers the main point of the paragraph.

On the trail, noon was usually the time for resting and for enjoyment. The largest meal was eaten at that time, and some travelers caught up on sleep they had missed the night before. The animals rested, nibbled on grass, and drank water.

a. Noon was the time of the largest meal of the day.
b. People and animals ate and rested at noon.

Responses will vary, but students should mention that choice "a" is too limited and that choice "b" covers the main point of the paragraph.

SUMMARIZING *the* **L**EARNING   To paraphrase, I use __my own words__ to __restate__ what the writer is saying without changing the writer's original __meaning__.

Practice Book • FEAST YOUR EYES   **Paraphrasing**   109

(Writer's Journal page content:)

The Monarch butterflies are returning to the California coast again. They do this every year from October to March. These butterflies travel over the Rocky Mountains and the Sierras from as far away as Canada. The beautiful orange-and-black butterflies can be seen hanging from Monterey pines and eucalyptus trees in long, tight clusters. Each butterfly hangs with its wings down over the one below it. This forms an effect something like roof shingles, giving the butterflies shelter from rain and providing warmth.

TO MAKE A LONG STORY SHORT

Imagine that you write copy for a news program. You must rewrite the story so it will fit on the six o'clock news. Make the story no longer than it would take to read in five or six seconds.

Story: __Return of the Monarchs__

Time segment: __6:10:25 – 6:10:30__

Copywriter: _____
                    (your name)

Graphic Aids

OBJECTIVE: *To understand how and when to use graphic aids*

Review

Review kinds and purposes of graphic aids.

Remind students that graphic aids are visual ways of showing information that might be difficult to describe in words. Review the features of the following graphic aids:

- Map: locational drawing that shows roads, rivers, towns, cities, places of interest, states, countries, or continents; includes coordinates for locating specific areas
- Table: drawing that organizes information in columns and rows

CHALLENGE Have students work in pairs to choose an article from the newspaper and create a graphic aid for it that would help the reader better understand the article.

Practice/Apply

Have students create graphic sources.

Point out that Sam and his family look at maps to note their direction of travel and the distance they cover on their journey. They also use the map they obtain in town to determine whether the land they want to settle is available. Have student pairs locate maps of the Dakota Territory (or of the Midwest, including present-day South Dakota) that show various natural landmarks such as mountains, lakes, rivers, and plains. Encourage students to create their own versions of the area where Sam's family travels between Kentucky and the Dakotas. Remind them to include a compass rose and a legend.

Then display Transparency 40 or draw the table on the board. Model how to identify the area in which the family might live, based on the most moderate temperatures and a good amount of rainfall.

Transparency 40   Graphic Aids

Average Annual Temperatures and Precipitation		
City/ Area	Avg. Temp. January, °F.	Avg. Temp. July, °F.	Precipitation Rain/Snow
Rapid City	24°	71°	18 in.
Pierre	16°	75°	14 in.
Mitchell	19°	79°	22 in.
Sioux Falls	16°	75°	26 in.

Model the thinking.

The table lists four areas that might be good for planting wheat. The Rapid City area has the mildest winter temperature, at 24°F, but the summer temperature of 71°F may not be warm enough for growing crops. Then I notice that the area with the next mildest winter temperature is Mitchell, with 19°F, and that its summer temperature is the highest of the four areas. Its average precipitation is also good. The Mitchell area is probably the best listed in the table for the family's purposes.

COOPERATIVE LEARNING   Have students work in groups to produce other tables of information that the Whites might find useful in their travels.

Summarize

Informally assess the learning.

Discuss with students how they collected information and organized their graphic aids. Invite students to share their graphic aids during the discussion.

Ask students to summarize what they learned. (Graphic aids are visual ways of showing a reader information that is difficult to understand. By following routes on maps and comparing entries in tables, I can draw conclusions that will be useful for my own purposes.)

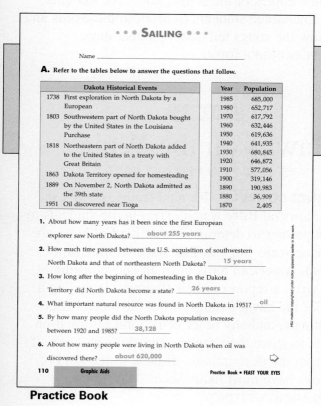

• • • SAILING • • •

Name _____

A. Refer to the tables below to answer the questions that follow.

Dakota Historical Events			Year	Population
1738	First exploration in North Dakota by a European		1985	685,000
			1980	652,717
1803	Southwestern part of North Dakota bought by the United States in the Louisiana Purchase		1970	617,792
			1960	632,446
			1950	619,636
1818	Northeastern part of North Dakota added to the United States in a treaty with Great Britain		1940	641,935
			1930	680,845
			1920	646,872
			1910	577,056
1863	Dakota Territory opened for homesteading		1900	319,146
1889	On November 2, North Dakota admitted as the 39th state		1890	190,983
			1880	36,909
1951	Oil discovered near Tioga		1870	2,405

1. About how many years has it been since the first European explorer saw North Dakota? ____about 255 years____

2. How much time passed between the U.S. acquisition of southwestern North Dakota and that of northeastern North Dakota? ____15 years____

3. How long after the beginning of homesteading in the Dakota Territory did North Dakota become a state? ____26 years____

4. What important natural resource was found in North Dakota in 1951? ____oil____

5. By how many people did the North Dakota population increase between 1920 and 1985? ____38,128____

6. About how many people were living in North Dakota when oil was discovered there? ____about 620,000____

110   Graphic Aids   Practice Book ■ FEAST YOUR EYES

Practice Book

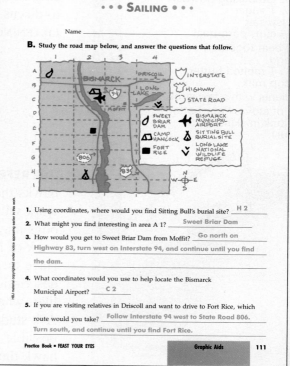

• • • SAILING • • •

Name _____

B. Study the road map below, and answer the questions that follow.

1. Using coordinates, where would you find Sitting Bull's burial site? ____H 2____

2. What might you find interesting in area A 1? ____Sweet Briar Dam____

3. How would you get to Sweet Briar Dam from Moffit? ____Go north on Highway 83, turn west on Interstate 94, and continue until you find the dam.____

4. What coordinates would you use to help locate the Bismarck Municipal Airport? ____C 2____

5. If you are visiting relatives in Driscoll and want to drive to Fort Rice, which route would you take? ____Follow Interstate 94 west to State Road 806. Turn south, and continue until you find Fort Rice.____

Practice Book ■ FEAST YOUR EYES   Graphic Aids   111

Practice Book

PRACTICE BOOK
pages 110–111: Using graphic aids

Integrated
Curriculum

SOCIAL STUDIES

Trail Cooking

Point out to students that the Whites have to cook their food over a campfire while on the trail to the Dakota Territory. Brainstorm with students what foods the Whites might have eaten. Explain that cornmeal was easily stored and that corn bread could be quickly fried in a skillet. If facilities permit, you may wish to demonstrate making corn bread in a skillet. Have students help you mix the batter. Otherwise, bring to class small squares of corn bread for students to sample. Explain that to make butter, many pioneers tied a covered pail of milk to the wagon. The moving wagon bounced the milk so much that balls of butter would form after a few hours. Have students make butter for their corn bread by helping them take turns using a hand-held mixer to whip a pint of cream until butter forms.   LISTENING

Simple Skillet Corn Bread

1. Mix together: ³/₄ cup flour
                 2 ¹/₂ tsp baking powder
                 1 ¹/₂ T sugar
                 ³/₄ tsp salt
                 1 ¹/₄ cups cornmeal
2. In a separate bowl beat together:
                 1 egg
                 2 ¹/₂ T melted butter
                 1 cup milk
3. Combine all ingredients with a few strokes.
4. Heat skillet on top of stove. Pour batter into the hot pan. Cook in skillet until done (about ¹/₂ hour).

MUSIC

Skip to My Lou

Explain that pioneers often eased the hardships of travel by playing the fiddle and by singing songs in the evening. If one is available, play a cassette or a record of some of the more popular songs, such as "Skip to My Lou," "Home, Sweet Home," "Shenandoah," "Buffalo Gals," "Ho! Westward Ho! " and "Sweet Betsy from Pike." Provide copies of the songs, and have students sing along. Encourage students to listen to the words and to discuss how the songs tell about pioneer days.
LISTENING/SPEAKING/READING

SCIENCE

Hawks on the Wing
AVAILABLE ON PROJECT CARD

USE REFERENCE SOURCES   Remind students about the hawks that Sam and Billy watch. Then invite students to work with a partner to determine what kind of hawk the boys may have seen. Suggest that students look in a book of North American birds or in an encyclopedia. Have them write a report on their findings, including a description of the hawk's range, what the hawk looks like, what it eats, and any other behavioral information. Ask students to share their reports and show pictures, if possible. From the descriptions, discuss which kind of hawk the boys have most likely seen.   LISTENING/
SPEAKING/READING/WRITING

Acres to Acres

Remind students that the Whites want to claim a section of land that measures 160 acres. Name a familiar place, such as the schoolyard or a park, that is about 1 acre in size. Have students try to imagine how big 160 acres is. Draw a square on the board to represent 1 square mile, or 640 acres. Help students determine how many sections of 160 acres there are in 1 square mile. (4 sections) Have students try to picture what buildings and streets in the neighborhood around their school would be included in a section 160 acres in size. (One way to figure this is to imagine a square that extends 1/2 mile north and 1/2 mile east of the school.) You may wish to draw the buildings and the streets in the square to help students picture this.
LISTENING/SPEAKING

Prairie Ships

USE REFERENCE SOURCES Remind students that Sam feels as though he is in a boat sailing over an ocean while he travels across the prairie. Have students work with a partner. Invite pairs to investigate why some covered wagons were called prairie schooners. Suggest that students trace a picture of a prairie schooner and then write a description of this type of wagon under the picture. Partners may also be interested in contrasting the hourly speed (mph) of a covered wagon with other forms of transportation to further appreciate the length of the Whites' journey. A possible resource is *If You Traveled West in a Covered Wagon* by Ellen Levine (Scholastic, 1986). LISTENING/SPEAKING/READING/WRITING

Railroad News

AVAILABLE ON PROJECT CARD

COOPERATIVE LEARNING Remind students that the White family is excited to hear that railroads will be coming to the Dakota Territory. Have students work in pairs to research railroads in the United States and to write a news release that describes the progress of the railroad. Have each pair prepare a map of the United States in the late 1800s and plot the railroad that would have gone through the Dakota Territory. Ask partners to share their news release and map with classmates.
LISTENING/SPEAKING/READING/WRITING

Working on the Railroad

READ ALOUD TO STUDENTS:

THE SETTLEMENT OF THE AMERICAN WEST WAS MADE POSSIBLE BY THE RAILROAD.

In 1869, a railway linking the west and east coasts was completed. The rails were laid mainly by immigrant laborers: Chinese, Irish, and Mexican. When they finished this difficult feat, the United States was on its way to having a world-class railway system. Yet there were still improvements to be made in safety and service.

In 1869, George Westinghouse received a patent on an automatic air brake. This made it possible for new, high-speed trains to run more safely. Later he invented the first practical railroad signaling systems.

In 1887, Granville Woods, a self-taught inventor, designed another safety improvement. His telegraph system allowed moving trains to communicate with each other and with the station. Woods's brilliant electrical inventions made him one of the leading scientists of the industrial age. ■

The inventions of Granville Woods and George Westinghouse helped make the railroad safe for travelers.

ACTIVITY CORNER

■ Have small groups of students locate in biographies and other reference sources additional information about George Westinghouse and Granville Woods. Encourage them to make a bulletin board display of the information they find along with pictures of their inventions.

■ The inventions of Granville Woods and George Westinghouse were significant scientific advances a hundred years ago. Invite students to imagine what inventions Woods and Westinghouse might produce if they were living now. Suggest that students write a short description of an imaginary invention of Woods and Westinghouse and illustrate it.

THEME WRAP-UP

Pioneers

Recall with students that the selections in this theme were about pioneer families and about a woman who actually was a pioneer. Help students recall the Wilder and White families and the fact that Laura Ingalls Wilder, the author of "Runaway," was a real person who was a pioneer. Tell students that the questions on page 399 will also help them recall and think about the ideas presented in the selections.

Note that pages T712–T713 provide support for applying the writing process to the last question.

THEME WRAP-UP

PIONEERS

Life was difficult for pioneer families. Which of the hardships challenging the families you read about do you think was the most difficult to face? Tell why you think as you do.

In what ways was life on the Minnesota prairie like life in the Dakota territory?

WRITER'S WORKSHOP   Choose another pioneer that you have heard about or read about. Remember that a pioneer is a person who settles in a new country or region. Read about and take notes on how that person lived and what he or she contributed to the settling of the frontier. Organize your notes into an outline. Then write a research report about the pioneer you chose and share your report with your classmates.

399

Theme Wrap-Up

DISCUSSION QUESTIONS, PAGE 399

Life was difficult for pioneer families. Which of the hardships challenging the families you read about do you think was the most difficult to face? Tell why you think as you do. Encourage students to recall the events in the stories. (Accept reasonable responses: keeping the wagon from going over the bank because it took strength, speed, and courage to stop the runaway oxen.) CRITICAL: MAKING JUDGMENTS

In what ways was life on the Minnesota prairie like life in the Dakota territory? Help students recall what life was like for the Wilder family and the White family before comparing the two families' experiences. (Accept reasonable responses: There were few people living nearby.) INFERENTIAL: MAKING COMPARISIONS

WRITER'S WORKSHOP   See pages T712–T713 for applying the writing process. **Choose another pioneer that you have heard about or read about. Remember that a pioneer is a person who settles in a new country or region. Read about and take notes on how that person lived and what he or she contributed to the settling of the frontier. Organize your notes into an outline. Then write a research report about the pioneer you chose and share your report with your classmates.** You may prefer to allow students to respond in their own way.   WRITING PROCESS: A RESEARCH REPORT

Writer's Workshop

For More Discussion & Practice:
LANGUAGE HANDBOOK

Encourage students to tell what a research report is. (a report that gives facts about something or someone) Then invite students to think about the elements that go into the writing of a successful research report, and list them on the board. (Accept reasonable responses: select an interesting topic, gather and organize information, classify the information into categories.) Suggest that students refer to the Handbook in the *Writer's Journal* as they write, revise, and proofread their research reports.

Prewriting

Before students begin to write, invite them to name pioneers they have read about, heard about, or seen television programs or movies about. Have students

- brainstorm subjects for the report.
- list ideas on a brainstorming chart such as the one below to organize their ideas and evaluate possible subjects.

Possible Subject: John Glenn		
When and Where Subject Lived	**Frontier Explored**	**Contributions**
Ohio	space	first person to circle Earth in a spaceship

Encourage students to list ideas for at least two different pioneers before deciding which one to research.

Drafting

Ask students to write a draft of the report. Remind them to

- use their brainstorming chart for ideas.
- do research and take notes.
- organize notes into an outline.
- write an opening paragraph that will attract a reader's attention.
- begin each paragraph with a topic sentence.
- follow each topic sentence with detail sentences that give facts from their research.
- write freely without worrying about spelling, punctuation, or grammar.

COMPUTER CONNECTION   Students may want to use a computer during the drafting stage so that they can easily organize their notes into an outline.

Responding and Revising

Suggest that students read over their report. Offer the following suggestions, and then have students revise their work.

- Is there too little or too much information? If so, add or cut information.
- Is the report well organized? If not, check it against the outline.
- Does the report have a good opening and closing? If not, rewrite to capture the reader's interest. (See the Language/Literature Link below.)

STUDENT SELF-ASSESSMENT OPTION   Students may use the Writing Self-Assessment Checklist in the *Portfolio Teacher's Guide*. Suggest that as they use the checklist, they focus on whether the beginning of their report captures the reader's interest.

Proofreading

Offer the following tips to assist students in proofreading their work and making changes:

- Check for errors in capitalization and punctuation.
- Be sure that the first lines of all paragraphs have been indented.
- Draw a line around any words that appear to be misspelled and find out how to spell them correctly.

Publishing

You may wish to offer suggestions about how students can publish their work. For instance, some students may wish to make covers from construction paper and turn their reports into books. Others may wish to read their reports aloud to family members and then save them in their reading/writing portfolios.

LANGUAGE/LITERATURE LINK

Capturing the Reader's Interest

Remind students that successful writers try to write so as to capture their reader's interest from the very first sentence. One way to do this is to get the reader to want to find out more about the subject. Explain that the beginning and ending paragraphs of a research report are particularly important. The beginning paragraph is the place to invite readers to continue reading to find out more. The ending paragraph sums up what was written, if possible, in an interesting way. Ask students to check their research reports to make sure they have captured their reader's interest.

Speaking Option

FEATURE NEWS INTERVIEW   You may prefer to adapt the Writer's Workshop to have students use their written reports as the basis for creating an oral news interview. Ask students to pretend that they are the person about whom they wrote the report. Have them follow the guidelines for Prewriting, Drafting, and Responding and Revising. Then offer the following speaking tips to help students deliver oral interviews:

- Read your report several times so that you are familiar with the pioneer's life.

- Make eye contact with the audience.

- Speak slowly, clearly, and loudly.

Invite students to identify themselves as the pioneer they wrote about. Have them answer interview questions as you role-play the interviewer. Ask each student questions such as the following:

- In what area did you explore or settle?

- What contributions do you feel you have made?

- Would you encourage others to be pioneers? Explain why or why not.

THEME

IMMIGRANTS

D id you ever wonder what it would be like to move to a new country or travel far, far away? The following poem and selection tell about the many problems some people face when they travel to faraway places.

CONTENTS
....

FAR, FAR WILL I GO
by Knud Rasmussen

CHANAH'S JOURNEY
by Evelyn Wilde Mayerson

401

Discussing the Theme

Call students' attention to the photograph on Student Anthology pages 400–401. Invite students to answer the question in the theme focus and share any travel experiences they may have had. Encourage students to read the selection titles and think about the kinds of travelers immigrants are. Ask them to speculate about the thoughts and feelings immigrants might have on their journeys.

Reading/Writing Portfolio

Remind students to place their writing responses for the selections in "Immigrants" in their portfolios. Suggest that they add to their personal journals any thoughts and ideas about books they have read independently.

Managing the Literature-Based Classroom

Management Options

PLANNING FOR PRESENTATIONS   When the whole class meets to listen to a presentation, either by a classroom visitor or a group of students, you may want to consider how to arrange the furniture to maximum advantage. For an informal feeling, the speaker or speakers may join the others in a circle. For some purposes, though, you may prefer to place chairs in a semicircle or several short rows so that the speaker faces the audience.

KEEP THE NOISE DOWN   Though conversation is a recommended and integral part of classroom curriculum, you can cut down on noise generated by various groups working on different activities at the same time by using these suggestions: Require that noisy activities be performed in only one area. Create a "quiet corner" in the room for independent reading and other quiet individual activities. Separate work areas with vision screens constructed from large cardboard cartons. To help groups work quietly in the Revising Center, have readers write their comments on self-stick notes instead of discussing them aloud.

PACING   This theme has been designed to take about two weeks to complete, depending on your students' needs.

Meeting Individual Needs

STUDENTS AT RISK   Encourage students to first read "Far, Far Will I Go" silently and then close their eyes to visualize the images as you read the poem aloud. Then invite students to "draw" the images in their minds. Have them compare "drawings" and discuss how readers use their imaginations to complete the pictures poets create.

GIFTED AND TALENTED   Encourage students to think critically by asking them the following questions: If you were immigrating to this country and could only bring the possessions you could fit in one suitcase, what would you bring? What would you leave behind? Have students write or draw their answers. *Challenge Cards* provide additional activities to challenge students. Challenge notes throughout the lesson plans suggest additional activities to stimulate critical and creative thinking.

SPECIAL EDUCATION STUDENTS   As students read the story, have them mark important details with colored self-stick notes. Using these notes, students can easily retrieve information from the story for summarizing.

LIMITED ENGLISH PROFICIENT STUDENTS   Before students create their charts for Building Background in "Chanah's Journey," have them share their own experiences of what it was like to immigrate to the United States. Suggest that students first share their recollections with other students who speak the same first language before sharing in their small groups. Second-Language Support notes throughout the lesson plans offer strategies to help students acquiring English to understand the selections.

POEM

Far, Far Will I Go

ABOUT THE POET Knud Rasmussen was a Danish explorer who brought back to his country a large collection of Inuit poetry from the Arctic.

ABOUT THE POEM "Far, Far Will I Go" is one poem in a volume of Inuit poetry entitled *Beyond the High Hills*. The book received an ALA Notable Book citation.

SECOND-LANGUAGE SUPPORT Explain to students that *yonder* is a word that means "a place that is at some distance but within sight." Ask students to share from their first languages any words or phrases that have similar meanings.

Reading the Poem

Help students set a purpose for reading.

Have students listen as you read aloud "Far, Far Will I Go." Explain that the poem describes a journey that an Inuit, or Eskimo, takes. Encourage students who have traveled from or to other countries to share their experiences. Suggest that students listen to see whether there are any similarities between the narrator's feelings about the journey and their own feelings about a trip they have taken.

Responding to the Poem

Return to the purpose for reading.

Encourage students to compare and contrast the journey described in the poem with a trip they have taken. Ask students to discuss any obstacles the narrator faces in achieving his goal. After the discussion, invite students to work in small groups to do a choral reading of the poem.

Encourage students to respond creatively.

You may wish to select one of the following activities for responding to the poem:

WRITING FREE VERSE Point out to students that "Far, Far Will I Go" is a poem without a rhyme scheme. Instead, the poet has chosen the words very carefully to tell a story that almost has the feeling of a song. Invite students to write their own free-verse poems that tell a story. Ask volunteers to share their work. LISTENING/READING/WRITING

COOPERATIVE LEARNING: PERFORMING A DRAMATIC INTERPRETATION Invite students to work in small groups to present a dramatic interpretation of the poem. Encourage them to decide how they want to depict the action in the poem, whether or not they would like to read the poem as they perform, and what props, if any, they want to make. Allow students time to assign roles and rehearse. When students are ready, invite them to perform their interpretations for their classmates. LISTENING/SPEAKING/READING

FAR, FAR WILL I GO

from *Beyond the High Hills* • by Knud Rasmussen
illustrated by Bryan Haynes

ALA
NOTABLE BOOK

Far, far will I go,
Far away beyond the high hills,
Where the birds live,
Far away over yonder, far away over yonder.

Two pieces of rock barred the way,
Two mighty rocks,
That opened and closed
Like a pair of jaws.
There was no way past,
One must go in between them
To reach the land beyond and away,
Beyond the high hills,
The birds' land.

Two land bears barred the way,
Two land bears fighting
And barring the way.
There was no road,
And yet I would gladly pass on and away
To the farther side of the high hills,
To the birds' land.

402

Expanding the Poem   How do you think rocks can "open and close"? (Responses will vary.)   INFERENTIAL: DRAWING CONCLUSIONS

With all the difficulties of the journey, do you think the narrator will be able to complete it? Explain your answer. (Accept reasonable responses: yes; the narrator appears to have the determination to go on, with no thought of turning back.)   CRITICAL: SPECULATING

FROM HERE TO THERE

Put yourself in the place of the speaker in the poem. Imagine that you are able to get past the pieces of rock and the bears that are in your way. Write a story in your journal about what happens next. Include some information about why you want to go "far away beyond the high hills." Also include what you plan to do when you get there.

_____'s Journal
(your name)

80   "Far, Far Will I Go"   *HBJ Writer's Journal*   FEAST YOUR EYES   Response to Literature

WRITER'S JOURNAL
page 80:
Writing a personal response

Chanah's Journey

from *The Cat Who Escaped from Steerage*

by Evelyn Wilde Mayerson   illustrated by Mike Dooling

CHANAH'S JOURNEY

	TEACHING OUTLINE	Materials	Language Arts/ Integrated Curriculum	Meeting Individual Needs
Part 1 Reading Literature Pages T722–T735 	**Building Background** **Vocabulary Strategies** Key Words (Tested) **Strategic Reading** Preview and Predict Setting a Purpose **Options for Reading**	Transparency 41 Second-Language Support Manual Practice Book p. 112 Integrated Spelling p. 57 Integrated Spelling T.E. pp. 76–77 Student Anthology pp. 404–424 Response Card 2: Setting	**Spelling** Spelling Pretest Spelling-Vocabulary Connection	**Second-Language Support** Vocabulary T723 Strategic Reading T724, T726 **Cooperative Reading** T725
Part 2 Responding to Literature Pages T736–T741 	**Story Follow-Up** Think It Over Write **Summarizing the Literature** **Appreciating Literature** **Critical Thinking Activities**	Writer's Journal p. 81 Practice Book p. 113 Integrated Spelling p. 58 Integrated Spelling T.E. pp. 76–77 Language Handbook	**Vocabulary Workshop** Reviewing Key Words Extending Vocabulary Proper Nouns **Reading** Oral Rereading/Readers Theatre **Writing** Personal Narrative Figurative Language Business Letter Story Continuations **Spelling** Reviewing Spelling Words **Listening** A Story Family Traditions **Speaking** Special Possessions	**Cooperative Learning** T737, T740
Part 3 Learning Through Literature Pages T742–T750 	**Introduce** Literary Appreciation: Characterization **Review** Study Skills: Graphic Aids (Tested) Comprehension: Paraphrasing/ Summarizing (Tested) Comprehension: Drawing Conclusions (Tested)	Second-Language Support Manual Transparencies 42, 43 Writer's Journal p. 82 Practice Book pp. 114–118	**Social Studies** Coming to America Travel Routes **Math** Graphs **Music/Dance** Birthdays **Science** Discussing Technology **Art** Fancy Names **Multicultural** Immigrants	**Challenge** T743, T745, T746, T747 **Second-Language Support** Characterization T743 **Cooperative Learning** T743, T745, T748

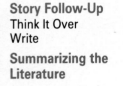

KEY WORDS

immigrants
steerage
greenhorn
inspection
dilemma
interpreter

Selection Summary

Chanah and her family have just traveled across the Atlantic Ocean in the steerage section of a large ship. They have left their home in Poland to come to America and begin a new life. The ship anchors near Ellis Island, where the immigrants must be processed before being allowed to stay. Chanah's cousin Yaacov is deaf, and the family fears that Yaacov's disability will cause him to be sent back to Poland. Chanah and her father, mother, brother, and grandmother successfully pass inspection. When the inspector discovers Yaacov's deafness, he is at the point of turning the boy back. Chanah intervenes and proves that Yaacov is indeed very bright. She demonstrates that he, like most immigrants, speaks a different language—in his case, one that uses hand signals rather than spoken words. Before the family begins their next journey, an acquaintance Chanah made on the third-class deck returns the little cat, Pitsel, that Chanah lost aboard ship. Chanah's mother allows her to keep Pitsel, and the family leaves for New Jersey, where they plan to run a farm.

Family Involvement

Suggest that family members discuss with students the countries from which their ancestors originally came and the modes of transportation they used to come to the United States or to travel in the United States.

EVELYN WILDE MAYERSON

Evelyn Wilde Mayerson has written several adult novels, including *No Enemy But Time, Sanjo,* and *Well and Truly.* She is also the author of the children's novel *Coydog.* Ms. Mayerson is currently a professor of English at the University of Miami. She has also taught psychiatry at several schools of medicine.

ADDITIONAL READING

Other Books About Immigrants

Ellis Island: New Hope in a New Land by William Jay Jacobs. Charles Scribner's Sons, 1990.   AVERAGE

The King of Prussia and a Peanut Butter Sandwich by Alice Fleming. Charles Scribner's Sons, 1988.   AVERAGE

Mr. Blue Jeans: A Story about Levi Strauss by Maryann N. Weidt. Carolrhoda, 1990. AVERAGE

A Portrait Of Me by Barbara Aiello and Jeffrey Shulman. 21st Century, 1989.   CHALLENGING

Part 1
Reading Literature

Building Background

Access prior knowledge and build vocabulary concepts.

Tell students that the next story, "Chanah's Journey," is about a young girl and her family who travel to America in the early 1900s to begin a new life. Encourage students to share what they know about the countries their ancestors came from and the modes of transportation they used to get here.

Ask students to think about the advantages and disadvantages of moving to America that immigrants might have considered before deciding to come here a hundred years ago. Invite students to work in groups to discuss and create a chart like the one below.

Advantages	Disadvantages
opportunities for jobs and education freedom to make choices opportunity to achieve a higher standard of living	speaking a different language traveling in steerage dilemma of leaving family making a dangerous journey

Vocabulary Strategies

Introduce Key Words and strategies.

Display Transparency 41, or write the following paragraph on the board. Invite students to read the sentences silently, using context clues with phonetic and structural analysis to decode the underlined words and to figure out their meanings.

Transparency 41 Key Words

When my grandmother was a young girl, she came to this country from Russia. She and many other immigrants boarded a ship and lived in its bottom section, called steerage. When the ship anchored in New York Harbor, my grandmother felt like a greenhorn, a newcomer unfamiliar with American customs.

In spite of the long, hard journey, Grandmother was healthy and fit, and she passed the inspection. But she was faced with a difficult decision, or dilemma. Should she tell the Russian interpreter that she didn't know how to speak English? She decided to tell the interpreter, and he said he would show her where she could get help.

Check students' understanding.

Display the Key Words, and have students write each word on an individual index card. Read aloud each of the following sentences, and have students hold up the card of the word that is described in the sentence. STRATEGY: DEFINITIONS

1. *(steerage)* The poorest passengers traveled in the most uncomfortable part of the ship.
2. *(immigrants)* The people getting off the ship were people coming to live in a new country.
3. *(inspection)* The officer gave them a quick examination to check their health.
4. *(interpreter)* The translator told the inspector what the immigrant was saying.
5. *(dilemma)* Matthew was faced with a difficult choice when he had to decide where to live.
6. *(greenhorn)* The newcomer felt like a person who had no experience with the local customs.

Integrate spelling with vocabulary.

SPELLING-VOCABULARY CONNECTION *Integrated Spelling* page 57 reinforces spellings of the /e/ and /u/ sounds in the Key Word *inspection* and in other words. The spelling of the Key Word *immigrants* is also included.

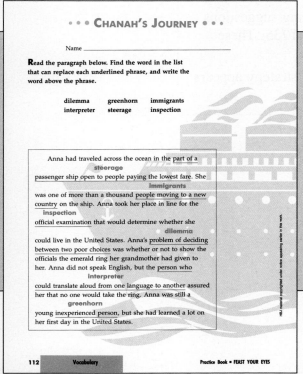

• • • CHANAH'S JOURNEY • • •

Name _____

Read the paragraph below. Find the word in the list that can replace each underlined phrase, and write the word above the phrase.

dilemma	greenhorn	immigrants
interpreter	steerage	inspection

Anna had traveled across the ocean in the part of a
steerage
passenger ship open to people paying the lowest fare. She
immigrants
was one of more than a thousand people moving to a new
country on the ship. Anna took her place in line for the
inspection
official examination that would determine whether she
dilemma
could live in the United States. Anna's problem of deciding
between two poor choices was whether or not to show the
officials the emerald ring her grandmother had given to
her. Anna did not speak English, but the person who
interpreter
could translate aloud from one language to another assured
her that no one would take the ring. Anna was still a
greenhorn
young inexperienced person, but she had learned a lot on
her first day in the United States.

112   Vocabulary   Practice Book • FEAST YOUR EYES

Practice Book

INTEGRATED SPELLING
The Sounds Short *e* and Short *u*

Name _____

Read the Spelling Words. Write them on another sheet of paper. Check your spelling.

——— SPELLING STRATEGY ———

The short *e* sound can be spelled with *e* or with *ea*. The short *u* sound can be spelled with *u* or with *o*.

short e = e	test	short u = u	pumpkin
short e = ea	breath	short u = o	among

To spell words with either sound, it will help to remember the different letters you can use. If you aren't sure how to spell the word, look it up in a dictionary.

Write each Spelling Word with the short *e* sound next to its spelling of that sound.

e   inspection   test
ea   breath   health

Write each Spelling Word with the short *u* sound next to its spelling of that sound.

u   gull   pumpkin   tug
o   among   money

Which Spelling Word doesn't have the short *e* or short *u* sound? **daylight**

SPELLING WORDS

among
breath
gull
health
immigrant
inspection
money
pumpkin
test
tug

MEMORY JOGGER

In **immigrant**, one **m** follows the other.

The word **immigrant** can be tricky for even the best spellers. This Memory Jogger will help you remember how to spell it.

FEAST YOUR EYES • "Chanah's Journey"   57

Integrated Spelling

Preview and Predict

Help students preview the literature.

Review the steps involved in previewing a story. (reading and thinking about the title, looking at the illustrations, and reading the introduction and the first paragraphs) Encourage students to look at the illustrations and to read the introduction on page 404.

Have students make predictions.

To help students make predictions about what might happen in the story, ask them questions such as these:

- **What might happen if Yaacov does not pass the inspection?**
- **Will Chanah find the cat? How?**

PERSONAL JOURNAL   Have students add their predictions about the story to their personal journals. Ask students to support their predictions.

Setting a Purpose

Have students set purposes.

Brainstorm with students what they want to find out as they read the story, based on their preview and on what they already know. Have students use their predictions to set a purpose for reading.

Model purpose-setting, if necessary.

If students have difficulty setting their own purpose, offer this suggestion:

> **I'm going to read to find out what Chanah and her family's first experiences in America will be like.**

OPTIONS FOR READING

INDEPENDENT READING   Have students read the story silently with their purpose for reading in mind.

GUIDED READING   Follow the Guided Reading suggestions that appear on pages T725, T729, T732, and T735. These suggestions model strategic reading.

COOPERATIVE READING   A reader response strategy appears on page T725.

SECOND-LANGUAGE SUPPORT   Call on students who have recently immigrated to America to describe the experience. Then, after students read the story, you may wish to have them compare immigration to America in the early 1900s to immigration today. (See *Second-Language Support Manual*.)

HANAH'S JOURNEY

from *The Cat Who Escaped from Steerage*   by Evelyn Wilde Mayerson   illustrated by Mike Dooling

Chanah and her family are crossing the Atlantic Ocean [to] a new life in America. Her [mother] Rifke and Yonkel, and her [brother] Benjamin, are traveling with [R]aizel, Yaacov, and Schmuel, [gran]dmother Tante Mima. [Chan]ah is sad because Pitsel, [who s]he found before they [left] has escaped from her [when C]hanah and Yaacov last [saw her on] the third-class deck, [and th]ey made friends with a [lady w]ith a feather in her hat. [If Pitse]h leaves the ship without [her sh]e will never see her again. [As the] ship nears land, the [girl w]onders if they will pass [inspectio]n because Yaacov is deaf. [An] officer who knows the [family ha]s written a note for the [inspector]s at Ellis Island.

AWARD-WINNING BOOK

THE NEXT MORNING they awoke to an awful din. Eager to find out what all the commotion was about, Chanah's family ran out on deck in an awkward cluster, banging into other people, even knocking over a cooking pot and a checkerboard. Each one holding the hand of another, they quickly saw that everything was veiled in an early-morning mist as dense as steam from a kettle.

Then something wondrous appeared. To their left, rising before them, stood a giant statue of a woman holding aloft a torch in one hand and clutching a book in the other. Rays like the spokes on a wheel poked from her head.

Tante Mima tried to cover Chanah's eyes. "Don't look," she said. "She's in her nightgown."

405

Guided Reading

SET PURPOSE/PREDICT: PAGES 404–413   Have students read through page 413 to find out what might happen to Yaacov when he goes before the inspector.

Cooperative Reading

READER RESPONSE STRATEGY: PAGES 404–408
Have each group of 3–5 students select a leader. Ask group members to read silently, and then encourage the leaders to use dialogue questions such as the one below. (Response Card 2: Setting, on page R63, offers a wide variety of dialogue questions.)

- **What does the setting tell you about Chanah's journey?**

PAGES 409–424   After reading, the discussion leaders might ask:

- **How does the setting change when Chanah and her family leave the ship?**

"If the Americans want to put the Statue of Liberty in a nightdress," said Yonkel, "it's their business."

Everyone in <u>steerage</u> began to shout at the same moment. Some began to cry. Parents picked up babies and small children and held them up to see the lady with the torch. Chanah felt as if the lady were looking right at her. She did not really believe it, but it was nice to pretend until Benjamin spoiled it by saying that she was only made of copper.

Things happened quickly after that. A booming gun salute was fired from an island to their right. Crewmen ran shouting among the passengers in the steerage hold with orders for all people to wear their tickets in plain sight, the men to fasten them to their caps, the women to their dresses. Then, carrying bills of lading in their trembling hands, the steerage passengers gathered on deck with their bundles, trunks, boxes, baskets, while the passengers on the upper decks threw down coins or waved to people waiting on the wharf.

"Don't pick up their pennies," warned Yonkel. "Soon we will be richer than rich."

"I," said Rifke, "will settle for a roof over my head and a floor that doesn't rock."

They were poked and shoved into a long line that led down the gangplank, where they were herded into waiting ferries. At this moment, Yaacov's mother thought she saw her husband, Shimson, waiting on the wharf. She began to wave to a man who waved back, but before she could be certain, she was rudely shoved along with everyone else into a ferry.

"Wave to your father, Schmuel," she shouted.

"Where?" asked Schmuel. "I don't see him."

406

Informal Assessment You can informally assess whether students are using vocabulary strategies as they read, which ones they tend to use, and how effectively they use them. To do this, ask the following questions:

- Are there any words in this story that are unfamiliar to you? Point out one.
- How did you figure out what this word meant? If that hadn't worked, what else could you have done?

Second-Language Support
Students may not be familiar with the Statue of Liberty. Explain that this statue is of a woman holding a book under one arm and lifting a torch high in her other hand. Explain that people traveling to the United States by ship pass the statue when they sail into New York Harbor. Tell students that the Statue of Liberty is a patriotic symbol of freedom. You may wish to check understanding by asking students how they think the immigrants on board Chanah's ship must feel when they finally see the Statue of Liberty.

"Why do you tell them that that man is Shimson," asked Rifke, "when you are not sure? When you cannot even see his face?"

"It will help to have something good to think about," replied Yaacov's mother, "while we wait in that place." She pointed in the direction of Ellis Island, to which they were headed.

Chanah paid attention to none of this. She was taking one last look at the ship that had been her home for the last two weeks. If there was any hope of ever seeing Pitsel again, it would be gone the minute she stepped foot on the ferry. Her deep sigh went unheard when passengers suddenly began to tug and shout as their baggage was torn from them and thrown into the ferry's lower deck. Most had not been separated from their possessions since they had left their homes, and having their personal belongings yanked from their hands was an unsettling experience.

For Chanah's family it was less so, mainly because they had so little of value. Whatever was important, like the silver cups, the brass candlesticks, and the gold coins, was carried on their persons.

Chanah wondered about the woman from third class. Did she have to go to Ellis Island? Did they tug the luggage from her hands, too?

"Where are we going now?" asked Tante Mima. "Are they sending us back already?"

"Not back, Mama," replied Yonkel. "Just to Ellis Island."

"What for?" asked Tante Mima.

"To look us over. To make sure that we're fit to enter." He said this softly, so that Yaacov's mother wouldn't have more to worry about than she already had.

THE FERRY RIDE to Ellis Island was brief, only fifteen minutes by Yonkel's pocket watch, the time it takes to pluck a chicken, pinfeathers and all. As Chanah and her family stepped on the dock, they were surrounded by guards who looked as if they did not know how to smile, all scowling and gesturing, shouting commands, pulling the immigrants into separate groups, then counting them and shoving them into line when they did not move quickly enough.

Chanah and her family were pushed into a red-brick building, where they climbed a staircase, lugging their bundles and their baskets one step at a time. At the top of the staircase they were stopped by a team of doctors in long gray coats who inspected their faces, hair, necks, and hands, with careful attention to their eyes, then listened to their hearts. Others did not pass inspection and were taken out of line, including the Russian family, who were all being detained to determine if they were carrying disease.

When the doctors finally waved them through, Chanah and her family stepped down another flight of stairs into a great hall. Yaacov, Schmuel, and Raizel were right behind them. The conclusion that none of them dared make was that the note from the ship's officer had somehow been lost.

The great hall below was divided into a maze of passageways for the immigrants to pass through, clearance lines bound by iron pipe railings with benches to sit on. There they waited to be called before an inspector who would ask them twenty-nine questions. Everything depended on the answers they gave. Even though they might be prepared, there was always the fear that the all-powerful officials would find cause to send one back. Parents could be separated from children, husbands from wives. Everyone had heard of someone who had had that experience.

Expanding the Literature   What happens when Chanah and her family arrive at Ellis Island? (First, they are pushed, carrying all their possessions, into a red-brick building. Next, at the top of a staircase, they are stopped by doctors who inspect them. Then, they go down the staircase into a great hall containing passageways, where an inspector asks them questions.)   INFERENTIAL: SUMMARIZING

Chanah's family moved along a few feet of bench space at a time in a string of human beads jerking forward one by one. After what seemed like forever, they were next.

The first question was directed to Yonkel. "Who paid for your fare?" the inspector asked through an <u>interpreter</u>.

Yonkel straightened his collarless jacket. "I did," he replied proudly.

"Do you have a job waiting for you?"

"Yes. In Woodbine, New Jersey. I go to work on a farm."

"Is anyone meeting you?"

"No."

This answer seemed to bother the inspector, who made a note on a piece of paper.

Yonkel was next asked if he and Rifke were married. Rifke, offended, jumped up. "Of course we are married," she shouted. "What do you think we are?"

"When and where?" demanded the inspector. Rifke gave him the date and the name of the village. She would have told him more, but Yonkel gave her a warning look and she sat down, her arms angrily crossed.

"How much money do you have?"

Yonkel wanted no unexpected whacks on the head from thieves in the night. "Five dollars in gold," he whispered.

"Show it to me," demanded the inspector.

This presented a problem. Should Yonkel show his coins, which he had kept so

410

carefully hidden, and risk losing them without money, they were considered charges. If the authorities decided tha was so, they would all have to wait in detention rooms from which hardly a was released except to be sent back to they came from.

Yonkel reluctantly took off his sho while the inspector and the interprete laughed. Then each family member w asked his or her name, after which a occurred. The inspector issued landin for all of them, including Tante Mima whose answers were not always on th mark, especially when they asked if s knew where she was and she replied she wasn't sure, but it was definitely the Taj Mahal.

"Thank you," said Yonkel, using u of his eleven English words.

Dragging their belongings, they pa through the maze of iron railings. The they waited on the other side behind mesh fence for Yaacov, Schmuel, and close enough to hear what the inspec saying to them.

Yaacov stood before the high benc his knickers and visored hat. When th inspector asked him his name, his mo stepped forward. "He has a sore throa she explained. "Not a sickness. Just h From calling geese. See, I have wrapp neck in flannel."

Teaching Tip Point out to students that Chanah and her family must learn to speak English when they begin life in America. Encourage students to share their ideas about how Chanah and her relatives can go about learning to speak English and why this is important.

"You've been on the ship for two weeks," said the inspector when the interpreter had relayed Raizel's answer. "As far as I know, there was not a goose among you." He laughed at his own joke.

Then things took a serious turn. The officials conferred. One stepped behind Yaacov and clapped his hands behind Yaacov's head. Chanah, who saw this coming, pointed from the fence and Yaacov turned.

"He seems to hear all right," said the interpreter.

"I'm not so sure," said the inspector. "He was slow in turning. Whisper your name, boy. Even with a sore throat, you can whisper."

"He wants your name," said the interpreter.

Yaacov drew an imaginary line down the center of his body, turned in one direction, then the other.

"What is he doing?" asked the inspector. "Is he having some kind of fit? If that's what he's doing, the interview is over."

Chanah broke from her family, ducked beneath the iron pipe, and ran to the high bench. "I know what he's doing."

The inspector leaned over his desk to peer at Chanah. "Who are you to him?" he asked.

"He's my cousin. He can talk," insisted Chanah. "He just talks with his hands. Tell him something else," she said to Yaacov.

Yaacov pointed to the inspector's pocket watch, made rippling hand motions, then a pinch of his thumb and forefinger.

"He's saying you have a drop of water inside your watchcase."

The inspector looked. Sure enough, there was a tiny drop of water under the case.

"At least we know his eyesight is good," he said.

Yonkel decided it was time to join the protest. "A different language," he shouted through the mesh. "Like all the different languages here. You need an interpreter, that's all."

Then the inspector lost his temper. "Get that little girl out of here!" he shouted. "Things are getting out of hand. Tell them to be quiet or we'll send them all back."

The inspector appeared to be troubled. He seemed to be thinking, You let in someone who's deaf, then you let in someone else who's blind. Where's it all going to end?

When the inspector shook his head, no one needed an interpreter to figure out that Yaacov would not be permitted to enter.

A great scream went up from Raizel, the kind that rattles from the throat and makes all within hearing feel their scalps crawl. Rifke began to wail, Yonkel to shout.

The interpreter, used to such scenes, explained, "The boy has to return. The mother and the other boy can stay, but this one has to go back to Poland."

Raizel began to shriek and tear at her dress, while every other mother and father in the waiting room pressed forward with their hands at their hearts, their throats, knowing that at any time, this could happen to them.

Yaacov's mother was in a painful dilemma. What to do? Her choice was simple, yet terrible: to return with Yaacov, and perhaps never see her husband, Shimson, again; worse, to let Yaacov return alone to live with distant relatives, perhaps never to see him again.

Guided Reading

MONITOR COMPREHENSION: PAGES 404–413
What could happen to Yaacov as he goes before the inspector? (Yaacov and his mother could be sent back to Poland, or he could be sent back alone.) STRATEGIC READING: RETURNING TO PURPOSE

What questions does the inspector ask Yonkel? (who paid for their fare, does Yonkel have a job in America, is anyone meeting them, is he married, how much money does he have) **Why do you think he asks these questions?** (Accept reasonable responses: He wants to be sure that the people who enter the country have a promising future.) STRATEGIC READING: SUMMARIZING

SET PURPOSE/PREDICT: PAGES 414–419 Have students read through page 419 to find out whom Chanah meets on the pier.

Chanah broke free from Benjamin's clutch, ducke[d] beneath the railing, and again approached the inspe[ctor's] bench. This time one of her black stockings had falle[n] her high-topped shoes, but she made no move to pi[ck] up. "He knows everything," she said. "He can tell y[ou] what you had for breakfast this morning and what y[ou] had for lunch. Ask him."

"The boy is entitled to an appeal," said the interp[reter] to the inspector. "You and I both know that can inc[lude] the testimony of either relatives or lawyers."

"We can't afford a lawyer," shouted Yonkel.

Suddenly weary, the inspector's shoulders sagge[d]. "All right," he said. "Tell him to tell me what I had [to] eat today."

Chanah asked Yaacov. Yaacov in turn made han[d] motions that Chanah interpreted.

"He said you had sausage and bread for lunch w[ith] coffee to drink, and eggs for breakfast."

"I'll be," said the inspector. "How did he do that[?]"

Chanah conferred with Yaacov. "He smells the sausage on your breath, and he sees the coffee on y[our] teeth, the bread crumbs on your beard, and the egg [on] your mustache."

The inspector cocked an eye. He reminded Chan[ah] of a rooster that used to strut in a neighbor's yard. [How] does he know that I didn't have the eggs for lunch?"

"Because the egg on your mustache is dry. If yo[u] had had it for lunch, the pieces would still be damp[."]

The two men looked at each other while the oth[ers] held their breath. Then the inspector winked at the interpreter. "I say we let in a kid with a sore throat[."] No translation was needed. The smiles told it all.

Vocabulary Strategy **How can you figure out the meaning of the word *conferred* used on page 415?** (I use context clues and read the sentences that appear before and after the word *conferred*. I see that Chanah is trying to help Yaacov and in doing so confers with him before answering the inspector's question. I decide that *conferred* means "talked to" or "consulted.")
STRATEGY: CONTEXT CLUES

Teaching Tip Point out to students that at the time this story takes place, the American Sign Language, currently used in the United States, had not yet been established. Many different methods were being developed and used by groups or individuals. Explain that Yaacov seems to have developed a sign language that those close to him understand.

When the inspector stamped a landing permit for Yaacov, Yaacov's mother grabbed his hand and kissed it.

"Oh, now," said the inspector, "don't be making me out to be some saint." Then he became all business. "Next," he shouted, "we haven't got all day," as another family with patient, hopeful eyes came forward, bringing their belongings on their backs and their children in their arms.

—◦⟫◦✦◦⟪◦—

Chanah's family's last stop before they took the return ferry was the money exchange booth. Yonkel decided to cash only one gold coin and save the other for emergencies, which, in a family, come along at a fearsome rate. Besides, he reasoned, paper money can tear, paper money can burn, paper money can go out of fashion if one's country loses a war. But a gold coin . . . you cannot even bite into a gold coin.

Yonkel made another choice, one that cost him some of his money. A boat was available to take them directly to New Jersey, but Yonkel wanted to be sure that his cousin Shimson's family were safely met. He would take the ferry with them to New York City. It would cost him extra. A few pennies, he thought. What did it matter? If he and his entire family, including Yaacov, could make it safely through the inspection at Ellis Island, earning money would be easier than slapping a potato pancake on a griddle.

THE FAMILY RAN from the shelter of the pier to the streets and back again, looking for Shimson. If the docks of New York City were a confusion, the streets beyond were more so, with horse-drawn carriages, cable cars whirring from overhead tracks, and once in a while, when one could take one's eyes from the tops of the tall buildings, a true wonder, a horseless carriage.

Yonkel decided that they were better off waiting under the shelter of the pier. Sooner or later, Shimson would find them. Yonkel led them to the exit ramp of the ferries, where they stood rooted like trees among a horde of immigrants heading for the crowded streets.

Some were vaguely familiar. Some they knew, like the German couple who stopped to say good-bye, the father carrying the chair carved with lions, the mother proudly holding their new baby with the red ribbon pinned to her swaddling shawl.

As the waiting grew tiresome, Chanah and her family sat on their bundles until Yaacov suddenly began flicking each side of his waist and pointing excitedly to someone in the crowd.

"Look," shouted Chanah. "Yaacov is making the fringe on his father's prayer shawl!" Then Shimson appeared, excusing himself as he pushed through the crowd, looking exactly like an American. Yonkel said it was his beard, which had been shaved off. Rifke said it was more likely his suit of clothes, made of first-class American material.

"Shimson!" shouted Raizel, who had not seen her husband in two years. "Papa," shouted Schmuel, who bolted clumsily on his fat, stubby legs. Yaacov ran smiling and silent, flicking his hands at his waist.

417

Expanding the Literature   What kind of person do you think Yonkel is? What event helps you learn more about his character?

(Accept reasonable responses: He is a thoughtful person who cares very much about his family. He spends additional money to take the ferry with Shimson's family to make sure that they are safely met in New York City.)   METACOGNITIVE: DETERMINING CHARACTERS' TRAITS

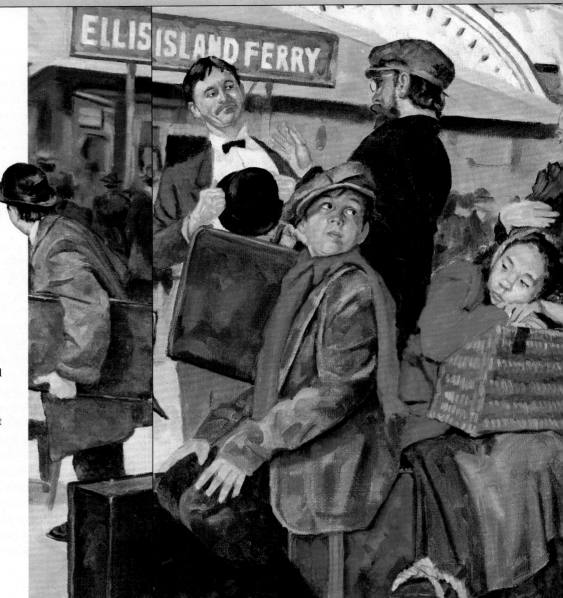

Shimson was all good news. He had a job in the garment industry, an excellent one. He was a pants presser. In fact, he had jobs lined up for every member of his family. Raizel would sew at home while he would take the boys, both of them, to the shop, where Schmuel would sweep and Yaacov would pull threads.

"Why can't I pull threads?" complained Schmuel. "Why isn't he the one to sweep?"

Shimson paid no attention to his older son and turned to Yonkel. "Stay in New York," he advised. "With all the family working, you will be able to put aside some money."

"I don't think so," replied Yonkel. "I have made up my mind to go to New Jersey."

Rifke whispered in his ear.

"Besides," added Yonkel, "my children will go to school."

"The girl, too?" asked Shimson, with some surprise.

Yonkel wanted to say, *Especially* the girl, especially after what she did this day for your son, but such comments would make Benjamin feel unworthy. Instead he said, "Why not the girl?"

While Shimson gathered his family's belongings, assigning to each a parcel to carry, Yaacov pulled his hat over one eye and looked over his shoulder.

Chanah turned and recognized the woman from third class standing alone in the throng, like a pebble in a stream only feet from where they stood. Chanah approached the woman timidly.

"There you are," said the woman with a great sigh. "I was getting ready to let it go."

418

Guided Reading

MONITOR COMPREHENSION: PAGES 414–419
Whom does Chanah meet on the pier? (the woman from third class whom she had met on the trip) STRATEGIC READING: RETURNING TO PURPOSE

Are Yaacov, his mother, and his brother reunited with his father? How do they find each other? (Yes; Yaacov spots his father coming toward them on the pier.) STRATEGIC READING: SUMMARIZING

SET PURPOSE/PREDICT: PAGES 420–424 Have students predict whether Chanah will be reunited with Pitsel and, if so, if she will be allowed to keep the cat. Ask students to read the rest of the story to see whether their predictions are confirmed.

"Let what go?" asked Chanah, wondering if she
[me]nt the feather.

"See for yourself." The woman handed Chanah her
[the] flower-printed hatbox. Scratching sounds could be
[hear]d coming from inside.

"Go on," said the woman. "Open it."

[C]hanah carefully lifted the lid of the hatbox. Inside
[was] a scrawny, tired-looking, unhappy cat. Chanah
[sat] down, tears shining in her eyes, picked up the
[crea]ture, and held her to her chest. "Pitsel. I thought I
[wou]ld never, never see you again," she crooned.

"And a fine mess it made of my hatbox," said the
[wom]an. "I can never use it again, I can tell you that."

[T]hen Yonkel came shouting through the crowd.

"[The]re you are! Didn't I tell you never to leave our side?
[Neve]r! Your mother is beside herself. Why would you
[give] us such a fright?"

[C]hanah wiped the tears that streamed down her
[face.] "Look, Papa," she said. "The lady kept her for me."

"What was I to do?" said the woman. "The creature
[follo]wed me to my cabin. It must have been the smoked
[fish] I had wrapped inside a napkin. Once it was inside,
[ther]e was the problem of getting rid of it. I didn't want
[anyo]ne to think it belonged to me. So I hid it in my
[hatb]ox, which, I might add, will never be the same."

"Thank you," said Chanah in English.

"What did she say?" asked the woman.

"[S]he spoke English," replied Yonkel. "And she
[than]ked you, as I do. Is anyone meeting you?" he asked.

"[M]y sister and her husband. They were supposed to
[be he]re two hours ago. I decided that as long as I was
[waiti]ng for them, I would watch to see if you came out."

Expanding the Literature   **Why do you
think Yonkel and Rifke are so worried about
Chanah when she strays away?** (Accept
reasonable responses: Since they are newcomers in
a very confusing and crowded foreign land, they
are very afraid that Chanah will get lost and not be
able to find her way back to them.)   INFERENTIAL:
DETERMINING CAUSE-EFFECT

"If they don't show up," he said, "you are welcome to come with us to New Jersey. We are going to a farm community where there is work for all who want it and plenty of room."

"Heaven forbid," she said. "I grew up on a farm. I have no intention of going back to one, especially in a place I never heard of. Besides, I will soon have my own apartment."

Just then a woman yelled, "There she is! Looking like a greenhorn!" and a couple broke from the crowd to wrap the woman from third class in a warm embrace. The man picked up her baggage and they led her away while the woman said, "You can't sleep on the couch. Stan's cousin is sleeping there. But we made a bed for you in the kitchen."

Rifke had been standing behind Yonkel's shoulder. "No one wants to go with us to New Jersey," she said. "Maybe they know something we don't." She forgot about New Jersey when she saw the cat. Cats carried typhus, ringworm, and heaven knows what else. They were even known to suck the breath from a sleeping baby. Rifke put her hands on her hips. "No cat," she said.

Then Benjamin did something he seldom did. He put in a good word. "Cats also kill mice, Mama," he said. "And there are a lot of mice in the country."

Raizel also intervened. "Rifke, if it wasn't for Chanah, I hate to think what would have happened today."

Tante Mima had the last word. "Let the child have her cat," she said, "so we can go and I can get off my feet."

Rifke, outnumbered, gave in. "All right," she said. "But not in the house." She turned to Yonkel. "We are going to have a house, aren't we?"

"There will be a house," replied Yonkel. He did not add, Maybe not today. Neither did he say, Maybe not tomorrow. All he said was, "In this country, everything is possible."

———❖———

With tears and promises to write and visit, Chanah and her family said good-bye to Shimson, Raizel, Schmuel, and Yaacov and boarded the ship for New Jersey.

Chanah stood at the railing, with the basket partially opened so Pitsel could feel the sea breeze on her face. The cat, who seemed to know that all was going reasonably well, poked her head out of the basket and sniffed the salt air.

Expanding the Literature   **How does Yonkel feel about living in America? How do you know?** (Accept reasonable responses: Yonkel likes his new country and is very positive about what his life will be like. When Yonkel says "In this country, everything is possible," it indicates that he thinks it's possible for good things to happen to the family while living in America.)
METACOGNITIVE: DRAWING CONCLUSIONS

That's some terrible-looking animal," said Rifke to
~kel.

I wouldn't worry," said Yonkel. "In New Jersey,
will not be able to tell her from an American cat.
~ my words."

~hen Tante Mima, too weary to stand, sat on her
age. "This is positively the last boat they'll ever get
~n again. I may be an old lady, but I can still put my
down."

~What does it mean, Bubbi," asked Chanah, "to put
foot down?"

~t means to be stubborn. It means to say yes or no
~mean it. Like what you did today for your cousin.
~put your foot down. And they listened." Tante
~a bent over to pull up Chanah's stocking. "Chanah,
~ah," she said, "what a little woman
~re going to be."

THINK IT OVER

~scribe Chanah's adventures as an immigrant arriving in a
~ country.

~w did Yaacov communicate?

~at did Chanah do to help Yaacov enter the United States?

~ you think it was difficult to travel to an unfamiliar country
~n immigrant? Explain why you think as you do.

WRITE

~e that you have a friend who is immigrating to the United
~ Write a letter to this friend that tells why his or her trip
~ worth the effort.

THEME WRAP-UP

IMMIGRANTS

Throughout history, people have traveled great distances for many reasons. What does America have to offer immigrants? Support your ideas with examples from the poem and selection you read.

. . . .

Look back at the poem and the selection. How was the Eskimo's journey like the trip that Chanah and her family made to America?

. . . .

WRITER'S WORKSHOP   Imagine that Chanah, Benjamin, Yaacov, and Schmuel are new students in your school and that they are nervous about being in a new school and in a new land. What could you say to convince them that they will grow to like America? Write one or more persuasive paragraphs telling them what a great land America is. Share your writing with your classmates.

For discussion of this page, please turn to T751.

425

Guided Reading

MONITOR COMPREHENSION: PAGES 420–424
Is Chanah reunited with Pitsel at the end of the story? (yes) **Is that what you predicted would happen?** (Responses will vary.) **Why do you think Chanah is allowed to keep the cat?** (Chanah has behaved so heroically in helping to convince the inspector to allow Yaacov to enter the country, her family wants to reward her.)
STRATEGIC READING: CONFIRMING PREDICTIONS

Why do you think Chanah says thank you in English? (Accept reasonable responses: She is in America now and wants to act like an American.)
INFERENTIAL: DRAWING CONCLUSIONS

Returning to the Predictions   Invite students to discuss the predictions that they made before they began reading and that they may have written in their personal journals. Encourage them to talk about how those predictions changed.

Returning to the Purpose for Reading
Ask students what Chanah and her family's first experiences in America are like. (They face uncomfortable conditions on Ellis Island and are asked personal questions there. They face crowded streets in an unfamiliar land whose language is not yet their language.)

NOTE: Responses to the Think It Over questions and support for the Write activity appear on page T736.

Part 2
Responding to Literature

Story Follow-Up

Encourage reader's response: student page 424.

Think It Over

1. **Describe Chanah's adventures as an immigrant arriving in a new country.** (Chanah finds and then loses a small cat, she helps Yaacov pass inspection, she gets her cat back.) INFERENTIAL: SUMMARIZING
2. **How did Yaacov communicate?** (by signaling with his hands) LITERAL: NOTING IMPORTANT DETAILS
3. **What did Chanah do to help Yaacov enter the United States?** (She convinced the inspector that Yaacov was like all immigrants—he just spoke a different language.) INFERENTIAL: DETERMINING MAIN IDEA
4. **Do you think it was difficult to travel to an unfamiliar country as an immigrant? Explain why you think as you do.** (Accept reasonable responses: Yes; because the journey was long and uncomfortable, and when the immigrants arrived, they could not speak English.) CRITICAL: MAKING JUDGMENTS

Write

Encourage writer's response: student page 424.

Imagine that you have a friend who is immigrating to the United States. Write a letter to this friend that tells why his or her trip will be worth the effort. Encourage students to explain the changes in technology that would make the journey easier today. CREATIVE: WRITING A LETTER

Summarizing the Literature

Have students retell the story and write a summary.

Encourage students to summarize the story by recalling key events. Guide students in beginning the story map below, and have them finish it independently. (See *Practice Book* page 113 on T737.) Students may use their completed maps to retell the story and write a brief summary statement.

Setting(s)	(Passenger ship, Ellis Island, New York City pier)
Characters	(Chanah, Rifke, Yonkel, Benjamin, Aunt Raizel, Tante Mima, the inspectors, Yaacov, Schmuel, Shimson, the woman from the third-class deck)
Main problem	(Chanah and her family are afraid that Yaacov will not pass inspection.)
Event 1	
Event 2	
Event 3	
Solution	

STRATEGY CONFERENCE

Discuss with students how previewing and making predictions helped them understand, remember, and appreciate the selection. Invite students to share other reading strategies, such as visualizing, that helped them understand what they read.

NOTE

An additional writing activity for this story appears on page T739.

Appreciating Literature

Have students share personal responses.

Have students work in small groups to discuss the story. To help groups begin, provide a general question such as the following:

- **What word or phrase would you use to describe each of the characters in this story? Why?**

PERSONAL JOURNAL Have students use their personal journals to write about ideas and feelings that are discussed in the groups. You may also refer them to their personal journals after they complete the activities below.

Critical Thinking Activities

Encourage both cooperative and individual responses.

LIST CHARACTER TRAITS Because of Chanah's actions, Yaacov is admitted into the United States. What kind of person is Chanah? Make a list of her character traits. Encourage students to work in small groups to list Chanah's personality traits.
CRITICAL: DETERMINING CHARACTERS' TRAITS

WRITE A PARAGRAPH At the end of the story, Chanah's grandmother says, "What a little woman you are going to be." Think about her statement. What kind of woman do you think Chanah will be? Write a paragraph explaining your ideas. Encourage students to work in pairs to develop their paragraphs.
CREATIVE: IMAGINING CHARACTERS IN THE FUTURE

STUDENT SELF-ASSESSMENT

Help students self-assess their participation in the discussion by using questions such as the following:

- Did I listen carefully to other students' ideas?
- Did I give reasons for my ideas and opinions?
- Did I add ideas to help clarify the group's ideas?

Write a Conversation

by _____
(your name)

The people on the ship see the Statue of Liberty in the morning. If they were to talk about the things they see and feel, what might they say? Write a conversation that the immigrant characters below might have.

Writer's Journal

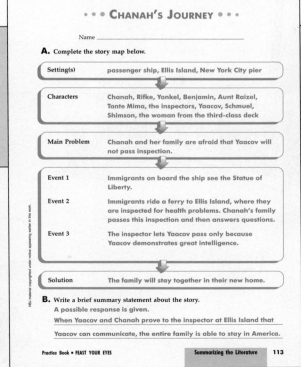

• • • CHANAH'S JOURNEY • • •

Name _____

A. Complete the story map below.

| Setting(s) | passenger ship, Ellis Island, New York City pier |

| Characters | Chanah, Rifke, Yonkel, Benjamin, Aunt Raizel, Tante Mima, the inspectors, Yaacov, Schmuel, Shimson, the woman from the third-class deck |

| Main Problem | Chanah and her family are afraid that Yaacov will not pass inspection. |

Event 1	Immigrants on board the ship see the Statue of Liberty.
Event 2	Immigrants ride a ferry to Ellis Island, where they are inspected for health problems. Chanah's family passes this inspection and then answers questions.
Event 3	The inspector lets Yaacov pass only because Yaacov demonstrates great intelligence.

| Solution | The family will stay together in their new home. |

B. Write a brief summary statement about the story.
A possible response is given.
When Yaacov and Chanah prove to the inspector at Ellis Island that Yaacov can communicate, the entire family is able to stay in America.

Practice Book • FEAST YOUR EYES   Summarizing the Literature   113

Practice Book

WRITER'S JOURNAL
page 81: Writing a personal response

PRACTICE BOOK
page 113: Summarizing the selection

VO·CAB·U·LAR·Y
Workshop

Reviewing Key Words

Display the Key Words and the following chart headings on the board. Then explain to students that they are to classify the Key Words according to the way the author uses them in "Chanah's Journey." Model for students the placement of the first word. (Possible responses are given.)

Setting	Characters	Problems
steerage	(greenhorn) (immigrants)	(inspection) (interpreter) (dilemma)

Students may enjoy adding headings for additional categories, such as *What Happens in the Story* and *How the Story Ends,* and classifying other words from the story.

Extending Vocabulary

PROPER NOUNS   Explain to students that because most of the characters in "Chanah's Journey" are from outside the United States, many of their names may seem unusual. Ask volunteers to name the characters in the story starting with Chanah's grandmother. Then draw the following family chart with labels on the board. Have students identify the appropriate place for each character's name to complete the chart. Give students the option of designing their own family chart.

grandmother
Tante Mima

wife   cousin   son   wife
(Raizel)   **Shimson** ◄───► **Yonkel**   (Rifke)

children   grand-children

(Schmuel) (Yaacov)   (Chanah) (Benjamin)

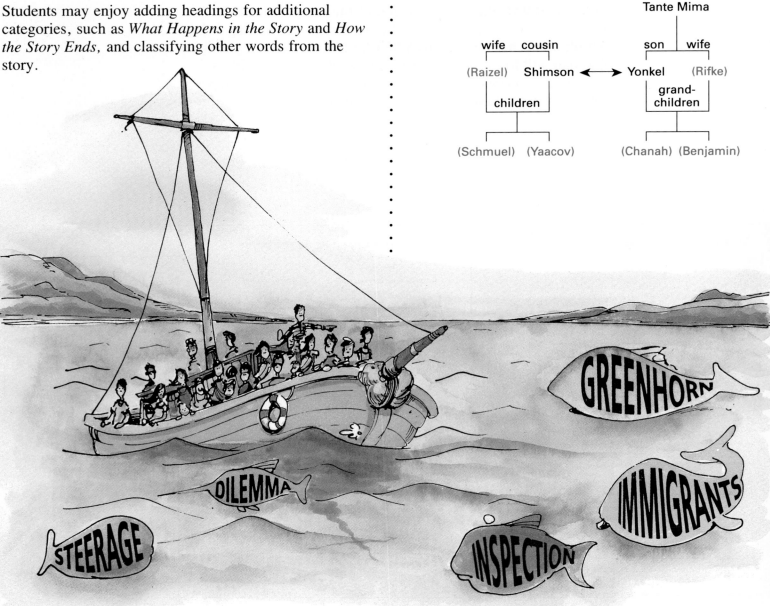

Integrated Language Arts

Oral Rereading/ Readers Theatre

Recall with students some of the more vivid scenes in the story, such as when Chanah's family sights the Statue of Liberty for the first time, when they are inspected on Ellis Island, or when they are standing on the pier in New York City. Ask students to work in small groups to select a passage they especially enjoyed. Have all group members reread the passage silently. Then invite them to choose parts and to read the passage aloud in the form of a Readers Theatre. Allow groups time to rehearse, and then have them present their scene for classmates.

LISTENING/SPEAKING/READING

Writing About the Literature

WRITE A PERSONAL NARRATIVE Recall with students that "Chanah's Journey" told the story of a very important trip that a young girl takes with her family. Ask students to think of trips that they have taken or to imagine a trip they would like to take. Then ask them to write two or three paragraphs that describe one of these trips and any significant events that occurred during it. Before they begin writing, have students picture the trip and write notes about where they went, who traveled with them, and what they and their companions said and felt. Have students organize these details in a chart like the one below. Encourage students to use the chart to help them visualize the trip once more as they write.

WRITING

Who Went on the Trip	
Where We Traveled	
What Happened	
What Was Said	

NOTE: An additional writing activity appears on page T736.

Reviewing Spelling Words

SPELLING WORDS: *among, breath, gull, health, immigrant, inspection, money, pumpkin, test, tug*

Conduct a spelling bee. First, brainstorm with students a list of words that have the /e/ or /u/ sound. Write the words on a master list visible only to you. Then have students form two teams. Clip one sheet of chart paper to the board for each team. Read a word to the first student in Team A, and ask that student to spell the word. If the speller answers correctly, Team A receives a point. If the speller answers incorrectly, the word remains on the list. The team with the most correctly spelled words wins.

LISTENING/SPEAKING/SPELLING

INTEGRATED SPELLING

page 58: Writing words with the /e/ and /u/ sounds

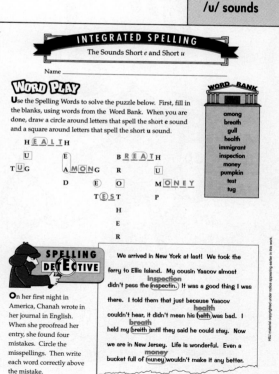

Integrated Spelling

WRITING
Figurative Language

At the end of the story, Chanah asks Tante Mima what "to put your foot down" means. As Chanah and her family learn English, they may find many phrases confusing at first. Have students brainstorm such phrases (for example: *raining cats and dogs)*, and list them on the board. Ask volunteers to explain the meaning of each phrase. Students may enjoy illustrating the literal and actual meaning of each phrase. The illustrations could then be compiled into a booklet.   LISTENING/SPEAKING/WRITING

LISTENING
Incredible Journeys

Read aloud a fairy tale, such as an episode from *The Wizard of Oz, Jack and the Beanstalk,* or *Hansel and Gretel,* in which the main character(s) takes a journey. After the story, encourage students to point out similarities and differences between the tale and "Chanah's Journey."   LISTENING/SPEAKING

WRITING
A Citizen's Letter

COOPERATIVE LEARNING   Recall with students how nervously Chanah and her family are anticipating the inspection by government officials before they can enter the United States. Explain to students that today if citizens of the United States want to make their government officials aware of their feelings, they are free to write letters to their government representatives. Explain that in this way, people can try to change laws or to create new ones. Invite small groups of students to work together to think about creating a new law. Ask them to designate one group member to act as secretary, taking notes about the group's ideas. Then review the format and parts of a business letter, and have group members work together to write a letter to a lawmaker. When the letters are finished, ask one member of each group to read the letter aloud.   LISTENING/SPEAKING/READING/WRITING

Coming to America

CULTURAL AWARENESS Hold a discussion about the possessions immigrants used to bring with them to America. Remind students that most immigrants traveled in steerage, where there was little room for people's belongings. Ask students to pretend they are living in another country about a hundred years ago and are about to embark on the long journey to America. Invite students to think about what they would want to take with them on their trip. Tell students to choose one item that is most important to them. Supply drawing paper and crayons or markers, and ask students to draw the object. When they are finished, invite students to display their pictures and to explain what the object is and why it is important to them. LISTENING/SPEAKING

Family Traditions

AVAILABLE ON PROJECT CARD

CULTURAL AWARENESS Remind students that immigrants bring with them many of the traditions and customs of the countries from which they come. Invite students to think about a tradition that is upheld in their own families, or have students learn about a custom that is practiced in a country from which they or their ancestors came. Have them work in small groups and take turns explaining the tradition or custom and directing the groups in a skit that demonstrates it. After all group members have had a turn being the director, have them decide which tradition or custom they would like to present to the others. Allow the groups time to rehearse, and, if possible, have them present their skits to another class. LISTENING/SPEAKING/READING

On and On

AVAILABLE ON PROJECT CARD

Recall with students that the story "Chanah's Journey" describes Chanah's trip to and arrival in America up to the point where the family leaves for New Jersey to begin a new life. Ask students to imagine what life might have been like for Chanah in New Jersey. Invite students to write a brief continuation of Chanah's story. Suggest that they speculate about how easy or difficult it might have been for Chanah to visit her cousins Raizel, Shimson, Schmuel, and Yaacov in New York City. Students may wish to illustrate their story ending. When they are finished, encourage several volunteers to share their work. LISTENING/READING/WRITING

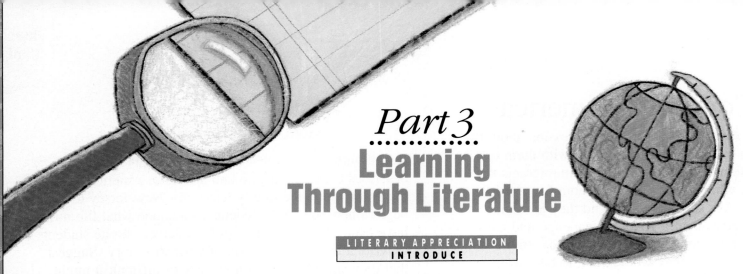

Characterization

OBJECTIVE: *To use direct and indirect characterization*

1   Focus

Discuss the value of understanding a character's traits.

Recall with students that in "Chanah's Journey" there are several characters. Point out that recognizing a character's traits will help them understand why the character behaves in certain ways.

2   Teach/Model

Teach the strategy.

Explain that a character's traits are the qualities by which the character can be identified. Point out that authors tell about a character's traits through the character's words, actions, and thoughts as well as through other characters' words and reactions.

Read aloud the third paragraph on page 408. Then model for students how to identify a character's traits.

> **First, I'll have to think about what the author says about the character. I can tell that even though everyone else is excited about leaving the ship, Chanah is sad to leave her cat, Pitsel. This tells me that Chanah is a kind and caring person.**

Have students identify characters' traits.

Display Transparency 42, or the following sentences from the story. Have students read the sentences, identify a trait, and tell how the trait was revealed.

> ### Transparency 42   Characterization
>
> 1. A great scream went up from Raizel, the kind that rattles from the throat and makes all within hearing feel their scalps crawl. (emotional, caring)
> 2. Chanah broke from her family, ducked beneath the iron pipe, and ran to the high bench. "I know what he's doing." (helpful, self-confident)
> 3. Yonkel decided that they were better off waiting under the shelter of the pier. (careful, responsible)

3 — Practice/Apply

Have students apply the learning.

COOPERATIVE LEARNING Have students refer to the story and identify another character trait for one of the characters by finding a sentence or paragraph that reveals the trait through the character's words, actions, or thoughts.

4 — Summarize

Informally assess the learning.

Have students discuss the character traits they found and give evidence to support their answers.

Check students' understanding of the lesson by asking them to summarize what they learned. (Character traits are the qualities that make characters special and perhaps different from other characters. Authors help us learn about characters through the character's words, actions, and thoughts.)

READER ⟷ WRITER CONNECTION

Characterization

▶ **Writers** can develop well-rounded and realistic characters by thinking about the traits each character has before writing about that character.

▶ **Readers** can better understand what they are reading and why characters behave in certain ways by recognizing the characters' traits.

WRITE A CHARACTER SKETCH Have students write a character sketch based on a picture of people watching a circus act.

CHALLENGE Have students write a one-paragraph character sketch about a character from a previous selection or about a character of their own invention.

SECOND-LANGUAGE SUPPORT Students can demonstrate their understanding of character traits by describing a character trait for the woman from the third-class deck. (See *Second-Language Support Manual.*)

Writer's Journal

WHAT A CHARACTER!

Imagine that you are a writer looking for an interesting character for your new book. Choose one of the people in this circus audience. Make up a name for the character. Describe the character in terms of personality, attitude, and habits.

Story character: _____
by _____
(your name)

DESCRIPTION:

82 "Chanah's Journey" HBJ Writer's Journal FEAST YOUR EYES Characterization

---

Practice Book

• • • CHANAH'S JOURNEY • • •

Name _____

Read each of the following passages from the story. Notice that each passage hints that the character or characters are angry, hopeful, frightened, or unhappy. Imagine that you are the author. Write a sentence that tells about the character's or characters' mood, feelings, or personality. Possible responses are given.

1. "She depended on me," was all Chanah could say. She didn't care if the Americans thought she had sense or not. __Chanah is not one to worry about what other people think of her.__

2. Tante Mima solved the problem by offering to carry the basket herself along with the two rock-hard loaves of bread in which the silver cups were safely tucked. __Tante Mima is always looking for ways to help others.__

3. Everyone in steerage began to shout at the same moment. Some began to cry. __Most of the people are so excited that they don't know whether to laugh or cry.__

4. "I," said Rifke, "will settle for a roof over my head and a floor that doesn't rock." __Rifke is a very practical person who doesn't want much more than is necessary for basic comfort.__

5. "It will help to have something good to think about," replied Yaacov's mother, "while we wait in that place." __She is afraid of what might happen.__

114 Characterization Practice Book ■ FEAST YOUR EYES

Practice Book

WRITER'S JOURNAL
page 82: Using characterization

PRACTICE BOOK
page 114: Identifying characterization

Graphic Aids

OBJECTIVE: *To interpret information on various graphic aids*

Review

Have students identify and use maps and tables.

Explain to students that if Chanah's family had a picture map of New York City, they might not have been so confused when they arrived. Display Transparency 43, or the following map:

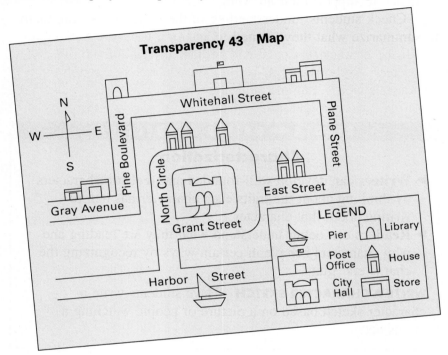

Transparency 43 Map

Ask students to imagine that Shimson sends Chanah's father the map and tells Yonkel to walk from the pier to meet him at the Whitehall Street post office. Encourage several volunteers to trace a route with their fingers. Have volunteers explain what a compass rose is and what it shows. Do the same for the legend. Then have students retrace their route by explaining in which directions Chanah's family must walk if they take that route to the post office.

Point out to students that ships were being used for travel thousands of years before Chanah and her family journeyed to America. Display the table below and model how to read for information.

Important Dates in Ship Development		
Date	**Location or People**	**Invention or Development**
3200 B.C.	Egyptians	sails
500 B.C.	Greeks	vessels with two masts
A.D. 1300	northern Europe	stern rudder
1807	American Robert Fulton	*Clermont,* first commercial steamboat

Have students use graphic sources.

COOPERATIVE LEARNING Have students work in groups and ask each other questions about Transparency 43. Ask students to create copies of the map and add coordinates. Then have them write questions about locating information using the coordinates. Suggest that students also research information to add to the table about ship development.

Summarize

Informally assess the learning.

Have groups exchange maps and questions and demonstrate how they knew answers to the questions. Then ask students to share their tables and the information they discovered.

Have students summarize what they learned. (Maps provide information about the relative shapes and sizes of areas and the relative distances between locations. Tables present information under column heads.)

MEETING INDIVIDUAL NEEDS

CHALLENGE Have students make a map that shows one route to follow from their home to the public library or to some other landmark.

• • • CHANAH'S JOURNEY • • •

Name _____

A. Refer to the table below to answer the questions that follow.

Who	When	Number
Irish	1840s and 1850s	$1\frac{1}{2}$ million
Germans	1840s to 1880s	4 million
Danes, Norwegians, and Swedes	1870s to 1900s	$1\frac{1}{2}$ million
Poles	1880s to 1920s	1 million
Austrians, Czechs, Hungarians, and Slovaks	1880s to 1920s	4 million
Italians	1880s to 1920s	$4\frac{1}{2}$ million
Mexicans	1910 to 1920s	700,000
	1950s to 1980s	2 million
Cubans	1960s to 1980s	800,000
Dominicans, Haitians, and Jamaicans	1970s and 1980s	400,000
Vietnamese	1970s and 1980s	400,000

1. Three different groups of immigrants came to the United States starting in the 1880s and continuing into the 1920s. Who were they? __Poles; Austrians, Czechs, Hungarians, and Slovaks; and Italians__

2. From which country did the largest number of immigrants come? __Italy__ How many came from that country? __about $4\frac{1}{2}$ million__

3. About how many immigrants came to the United States between 1840 and 1990? __about 20,800,000__

4. Which group came in two separate waves? __Mexicans__ How much time passed between waves? __about 30 years__

Practice Book ▪ FEAST YOUR EYES

Graphic Aids   115

Practice Book

• • • CHANAH'S JOURNEY • • •

Name _____

B. Study the following map. Then answer the questions that follow.

1. If Chanah wants to travel from New York City to Utica, New York, what directions would you give her? __Responses will vary.__

2. Which coordinates would you use to help Chanah locate Ogdensburg? __A 3__

3. What lake would you visit in the area with the coordinates A 4? __Lake Champlain__

4. What directions might you follow to travel from Albany to Hornellsville? __Responses will vary.__

5. Which coordinates would help you find the location of Lake Erie? __B 1 and C 1__

116   Graphic Aids

Practice Book ▪ FEAST YOUR EYES

Practice Book

PRACTICE BOOK
pages 115–116:
Using graphic aids

Paraphrasing/Summarizing

OBJECTIVE: *To develop global meaning through paraphrasing and summarizing*

Review

Review paraphrasing and summarizing.

Recall with students that they can paraphrase a selection by retelling it in their own words. Then explain that a summary is usually a brief restatement of a longer passage or selection. Display the following paraphrase and summary of page 406.

Paraphrase (paragraph 6, sentence 1) The many passengers were pushed from the ship to ferries.	**Summary** Everyone was excited as people began to prepare to leave the ship. Passengers waved to people on the wharf. Yaacov's mother thought she saw her husband and waved.

Practice/Apply

Have students apply the learning.

Have students write paraphrases and summaries of another section of the story.

Summarize

Informally assess the learning.

Tell students to exchange their papers with a partner and identify which part of the story is being paraphrased and summarized.

Have students summarize. (To paraphrase, retell a passage in your own words. To summarize, synthesize the important parts.)

PRACTICE BOOK
page 117:
Paraphrasing/
summarizing

• • • CHANAH'S JOURNEY • • •

Name _____

A. Read the following paragraphs. Then read the statements that follow. Put a check mark by the details you would include in a summary of the first two paragraphs.

One of the most exciting moments in crossing the ocean occurred when another ship came in sight. Soon that ship would come close enough to "speak." The captains of the two ships would then exchange the latest news.

When the ships reached port, each captain could report having seen the other ship safe and on course. This news was published right away in the newspaper. People back home would then know that the ship carrying their loved ones had been seen.

Upon arriving in America, some immigrants bought land that was already cleared. However, there was one advantage to buying land that was not cleared. A skilled woodcutter could cut trees down for 50 cents a day and then could build a home with the logs.

People who came from countries where wood was scarce were amazed by this news. In the old country, oak trees were used to make furniture for royalty. In the new country, oak was used for fence rails. This was only one of the things that convinced the settlers that they were coming to a country of great wealth.

_____ Ships crossing the ocean met to "speak."

✓ The captains would exchange news.

_____ The passengers might plan a party.

✓ People back home would be glad to hear that their loved ones had been seen.

B. On another sheet of paper, write a paraphrase of the third and fourth paragraphs. Responses will vary.

Practice Book • FEAST YOUR EYES   Paraphrasing/Summarizing   117

Practice Book

Drawing Conclusions

OBJECTIVE: *To draw conclusions by using information from a story and experiences from real life*

Review

Review drawing conclusions.

Recall with students that authors do not always state everything that happens. Review how to draw conclusions. (Use information from the story and what you already know from real life.) Use the chart below to model how to draw conclusions.

Story Information Yaacov is deaf and uses a kind of sign language.	+	Experiences Some deaf people talk with their hands.	=	Conclusion Yaacov cannot speak.

Practice/Apply

Have students draw conclusions.

Ask students to make their own chart of another conclusion that can be drawn from the story.

Summarize

Informally assess the learning.

Review the completed charts, and ask students to share prior knowledge or experiences that helped them draw the conclusion.

Have students summarize what they learned. (To draw a conclusion, use story evidence plus prior knowledge.)

CHALLENGE Have students write a paragraph that tells about something a character does, but not why she or he does it. Then have students exchange stories with a partner and draw conclusions about why their partner's character performs the action.

PRACTICE BOOK page 118: Drawing conclusions

• • • CHANAH'S JOURNEY • • •

Name _____

A. Read each sentence below. Put a check mark beside each conclusion you can draw.

1. Certain that Chanah had caught ringworm from the cat, Rifke's main interest was health, and she continued to comb kerosene through Chanah's scalp before braiding her hair.

   ✔ Kerosene was one treatment for ringworm.

   ___ Chanah doesn't care about her hair.

   ✔ Chanah's mother cares about her daughter.

   ✔ Chanah's hair is long enough to braid.

2. Chanah had seen grapes only once.

   ___ Chanah's family is too poor to buy grapes.

   ✔ Where Chanah comes from, grapes are scarce.

   ___ Chanah doesn't notice things around her.

   ___ Chanah never goes shopping with her mother.

3. The ferry ride to Ellis Island was brief, only fifteen minutes by Yonkel's pocket watch, the time it takes to pluck a chicken, pinfeathers and all.

   ___ Yonkel's watch doesn't keep good time.

   ✔ It takes fifteen minutes to pluck a chicken.

   ✔ The ferry went to Ellis Island.

   ✔ Yonkel has a pocket watch.

B. Look at the items you didn't mark. Why didn't you mark them? The passages say nothing about those items.

118   Drawing Conclusions   Practice Book ■ FEAST YOUR EYES

Practice Book

Integrated
Curriculum

SOCIAL STUDIES

Come to the U.S.A.!

USE AN ALMANAC Explain to students that the United States government keeps careful records of the number of people who immigrate to this country each year. Ask students to work in small groups to inquire into present-day immigration statistics. Encourage them to look in an almanac to find out from which countries people are coming, an approximate yearly figure for each country, and, if possible, some of the reasons why people are immigrating to the United States. When the groups have completed their research, have them present their findings. LISTENING/SPEAKING/READING/WRITING

MATH

Graph It!
AVAILABLE ON PROJECT CARD

COOPERATIVE LEARNING Point out to students that it is usually easier to look at and compare statistics when the information is placed in a graph. Ask students to work in small groups to put the statistics they found from the immigration activity just described into graph form. Explain that they may use picture graphs or circle graphs. Then ask questions such as these:

- **From which country did the most immigrants come last year?**
- **From which country did the fewest immigrants come last year?**

Students may enjoy graphing statistics about their classmates. Take a survey to find out from which countries students' ancestors came. Then have students put the figures into graph form and answer questions about the information. LISTENING/SPEAKING/WRITING

MUSIC/DANCE

Let's Celebrate!

CULTURAL AWARENESS Point out to students that our country has always been a nation of immigrants. Explain that although immigrants are not always able to bring many possessions with them, they do bring many customs and traditions. Tell students that the concept of birthday parties began many hundreds of years ago in Europe. Explain that various immigrant groups have brought special birthday or birthday-like customs with them to America. For example, Swedish people celebrate "Name Days," and many ethnic groups sing special birthday songs and perform customary dances. Have students work in small groups to learn about different ethnic customs surrounding birthday celebrations. If possible, ask students to learn how to sing special birthday songs and perform special dances. When their research is complete, have the groups take turns presenting their findings. Encourage them to play any music they found out about and to teach the whole group birthday songs and dances. LISTENING/SPEAKING/READING/WRITING

SCIENCE

High Tech

Explain to students that many of the ways families do things have changed since the time of their great-grandparents. Point out that in the late nineteenth and the early twentieth centuries, families were often large, and children in the family were needed to help with the family work. Invite students to brainstorm and list family activities and how they have changed over the last hundred years. To help students get started, ask them to think about how families do things today, such as how they travel, buy groceries, work, clean clothes, and so on. Then have students compare these to the ways families in Chanah's time might have done the same things. Compile students' suggestions into a chart under the headings *Family Ways Long Ago* and *Family Ways Today*. Then lead students in a discussion of how scientific technology has brought about these changes. LISTENING/SPEAKING

I'LL SHOW YOU HOW TO DO IT FASTER, BETTER, AND MORE EFFICIENTLY.

SOCIAL STUDIES

Trace Your Routes

Trace or copy a simple outline map of the world, and distribute a copy to each student. Assist students in labeling the continents and the United States. Ask students to lightly color the land areas brown and the water areas blue. Then ask them to recall the countries their ancestors came from. Ask students to put their pencils on the map in the approximate location of the country(ies) of their family's origin and to mark each point with an *X*. Have them point to the United States and mark the approximate location of their state. Then have them draw a dashed line that indicates a possible route their ancestors may have taken to reach the place where they live now.   LISTENING/SPEAKING

ART

Fancy Names
AVAILABLE ON PROJECT CARD

Distribute drawing paper and a variety of art materials. Invite students to use their surname as the basis for an elaborate design. Tell them that they may use any of the materials to turn their last name into a fancy composition. When they have finished, display their work on a bulletin board entitled "A Celebration of Me."   WRITING

Multi*Cultural*
PERSPECTIVES

Three Immigrants' Journeys

READ ALOUD TO STUDENTS:

MANY IMMIGRANTS HAVE HAD

TO OVERCOME OBSTACLES TO

MAKE A HOME AND ACHIEVE

SUCCESS IN THE UNITED

STATES. In 1847, when he was nineteen years old, Yung Wing made the long and difficult journey from China to study at Yale University. While at Yale, Yung Wing took American citizenship, and later married a native-born American woman. The first Chinese student to graduate from Yale, Yung Wing became a distinguished businessman.

More than 100 years later Ileana Ros-Lehtinan achieved a first. In 1989 she became the first Cuban American and the first Hispanic woman to be elected to Congress. Born in Havana, Cuba, in 1952, Congresswoman Ros-Lehtinan lives in Florida.

An even more recent immigrant, Eugene Trinh, came to the United States from Vietnam. Like Yung Wing, Trinh was educated at Yale University, receiving a Ph.D. in physics in 1978. Trinh went to work for NASA and was trained to be an astronaut to conduct experiments aboard Spacelab 3. ■

People such as Yung Wing, Ileana Ros-Lehtinan, and Eugene Trinh continue to enter the United States and embark on a new life.

ACTIVITY CORNER

■ **Available on Project Card**
Have students interview a relative or a friend who has immigrated to this country. Invite students to tape-record an oral history of the person's experiences as an immigrant and share the tape with their classmates.

■ Encourage students to create a class quilt, each student contributing a block that tells the story of how one of his or her relatives came to America. Students can use paper or fabric for their squares.

Immigrants

Remind students that the selections in this theme described journeys taken by immigrants. Guide them to recall that they read about a journey taken by a family who dreamed of becoming Americans. Explain to students that the questions on page 425 will encourage them to think further about the ideas expressed in the selections.

Note that pages T752–T753 provide support for applying the writing process to the last question.

THEME WRAP-UP

IMMIGRANTS

Throughout history, people have traveled great distances for many reasons. What does America have to offer immigrants? Support your ideas with examples from the poem and selection you read.

Look back at the poem and the selection. How was the Eskimo's journey like the trip that Chanah and her family made to America?

WRITER'S WORKSHOP Imagine that Chanah, Benjamin, Yaacov, and Schmuel are new students in your school and that they are nervous about being in a new school and in a new land. What could you say to convince them that they will grow to like America? Write one or more persuasive paragraphs telling them what a great land America is. Share your writing with your classmates.

425

Theme Wrap-Up

DISCUSSION QUESTIONS, PAGE 425
Throughout history, people have traveled great distances for many reasons. What does America have to offer immigrants? Support your ideas with examples from the poem and selection you read. Ask students what America offered Chanah's family. (Accept reasonable responses: freedom to choose where to live.)   CRITICAL: SYNTHESIZING

Look back at the poem and the selection. How was the Eskimo's journey like the trip that Chanah and her family made to America? Encourage students to think about both journeys before comparing them. (Accept reasonable responses: Neither the Eskimo nor Chanah's family were certain what lay ahead at their destination.)
INFERENTIAL: MAKING COMPARISONS

WRITER'S WORKSHOP   See pages T752–T753 for applying the writing process. **Imagine that Chanah, Benjamin, Yaacov, and Schmuel are new students in your school and that they are nervous about being in a new school and in a new land. What could you say to convince them that they will grow to like America? Write one or more persuasive paragraphs telling them what a great land America is. Share your writing with your classmates.** You may prefer to allow students to respond in their own way.
WRITING PROCESS: A PERSUASIVE PARAGRAPH

Writer's Workshop

For More Discussion & Practice:
LANGUAGE HANDBOOK

Encourage students to share times when they tried to convince someone of something. Ask students to think about how they accomplished this and what they said. Guide students to think about persuasion techniques that would be helpful when they want to write to convince someone of something. Suggest that students refer to the Handbook in the *Writer's Journal* as they write, revise, and proofread their persuasive paragraphs.

Prewriting

Before students write, encourage them to imagine what it would feel like to be a new student in a school in another country. Have students

- think about their audience and purpose for writing.
- make a list similar to the one below to help organize their ideas. Encourage students to list reasons why America is a great country in which to live. The lists might be similar to the following:

Why America Is a Great Country

1. People are free to communicate their ideas.
2. People choose their own leaders.
3. There are enormous amounts of goods and numbers of services available to people.

Tell students to add reasons to their list as they consider what they like about living in America.

Drafting

Ask students to write a draft of the persuasive paragraph. Remind them to

- write a topic sentence that tells how they feel.
- use the prewriting list for examples to support their opinions.
- write freely without worrying about spelling, punctuation, or grammar.

COMPUTER CONNECTION   Students may want to use a computer during the revising stage so that they can easily arrange the details in a logical order.

Responding and Revising

Ask students to read their persuasive paragraph to a partner and discuss how convincing the writing is. Offer the following suggestions; then encourage students to revise their work.

- Does your paragraph make your purpose clear? If not, add or cut information.
- Is the paragraph in an order that makes sense? If not, put details in a logical order.
- Have you used positive words and examples? If not, add them. (See the Language/Literature Link below.)

STUDENT SELF-ASSESSMENT OPTION   Students may use the Writing Self-Assessment Checklist in the *Portfolio Teacher's Guide*. Suggest that as they use the checklist, they focus on the use of examples to support their opinions.

Proofreading

Offer the following tips to help students proofread their work and make changes:

- Check for errors in capitalization.
- Be sure to add commas between words in a series.
- If words appear to be misspelled, draw a line around them and find out how to spell them correctly.

Publishing

You may wish to discuss various options for publishing students' persuasive paragraphs. Some may wish to read their work aloud to classmates and then save their work in the reading/writing portfolios. Others may enjoy making posters that express their opinions.

LANGUAGE/LITERATURE LINK

Using Examples

Remind students that successful writers support their opinions with facts. Explain that some facts are general; that is, they are true of many people or things. Other facts give examples. Explain that an example is a fact that is true either about one particular person or thing or about a small group. An example may be used to support a general fact. Suggest that students check their work to make sure that they have used general facts and examples to support their opinions.

Speaking Option

AD FOR AMERICA   The Writer's Workshop may be adapted to have students pretend to convince the story characters with an oral presentation, much like a commercial advertisement persuading people that America is a great place to live. Ask students to follow the guidelines for Prewriting, Drafting, and Responding and Revising. Then offer the following speaking tips to help students with their oral presentations:

- Practice reading what you wrote so that you do not have to read it word for word. Jot down notes to help you when speaking.
- Illustrate your presentation with pictures or other visual aids.
- Speak loudly and clearly. Try to sound convincing.
- Summarize what you want your audience to do or think.

Invite students to take turns delivering their oral presentations to small groups of classmates, acting as the story characters.

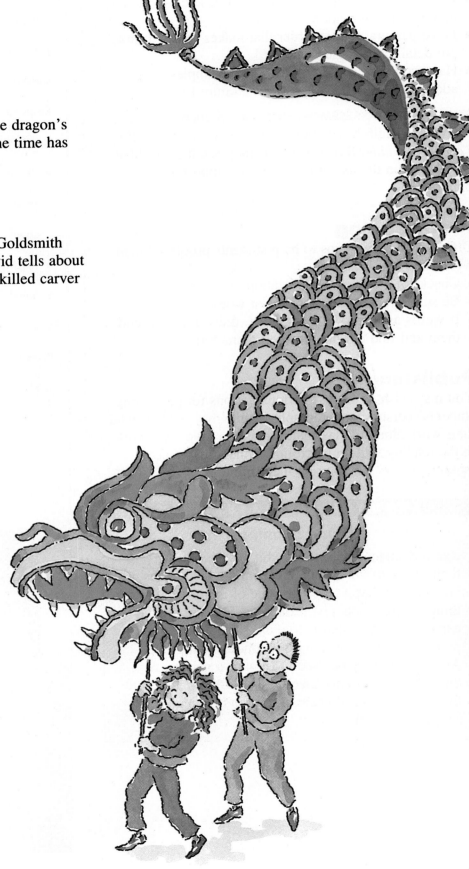

Chin Chiang and the Dragon's Dance

Totem Pole

For pacing suggestions, see page T756.

THEME

TRADITIONS

Traditions are important to many people. They are usually customs that began many years ago and have been passed down from one generation to another. The characters in the following selections find personal honor in their cultural traditions.

CONTENTS

CHIN CHIANG
AND THE DRAGON'S DANCE
written and illustrated by Ian Wallace

TOTEM POLE
by Diane Hoyt-Goldsmith

427

Discussing the Theme

Draw students' attention to the illustration on Student Anthology pages 426–427. Invite them to read the theme focus and speculate on why a theme entitled "Traditions" might have been included in a unit called "Travelers." Finally, ask students to think about the kinds of characters they might meet in the upcoming selections and how traditions play a significant role in their lives.

Reading/Writing Portfolio

Remind students to keep their writing responses for the selections in "Traditions" in their portfolios. Remind them also to add to their personal journals any thoughts and ideas about books they have read independently.

Managing the Literature-Based Classroom

Management Options

SCHEDULING ACTIVITIES   To make your classroom run smoothly, combine activities whenever possible. As students work on a writing activity, begin small-group activities, or meet with individual students for skill instruction or conferences. Incorporate content-area subjects like science and social studies with language arts. Direct students to centers or small-group activities during morning arrival time.

SIMPLIFY THE ENVIRONMENT   To make more room for various learning centers, activities, displays, and storage, look for ways to reorganize and simplify the classroom environment. You can cut down on clutter by eliminating seldom-used materials, equipment, extra desks, and other furniture. Only keep in the room what is being used. Take down displays regularly, and replace with current activity or theme material.

PACING   This theme has been designed to take about two weeks to complete, depending on your students' needs.

Meeting Individual Needs

STUDENTS AT RISK   Have students work in pairs to think up questions for the SQ3R Strategy. Then have the same pairs of students read "Totem Pole" together. Allow partners to work together to answer questions and summarize passages.

GIFTED AND TALENTED   Have students work in small groups to create a bulletin board display of changes in overseas travel over the past 100 years. Encourage students to illustrate the major forms of travel that have been developed and to include factual information for each. *Challenge Cards* provide additional activities to challenge students. Challenge notes throughout the lesson plans suggest additional activities to stimulate critical and creative thinking.

SPECIAL EDUCATION STUDENTS   If students have difficulty with note taking, have them (1) work on listing main ideas only, (2) work with students who work more quickly, or (3) use their own method of taking notes instead.

LIMITED ENGLISH PROFICIENT STUDENTS   Students with a limited English vocabulary may have difficulty selecting customs or traditions for the quickwrite activity. Group these students with others who speak the same first language. Encourage them to help each other think of appropriate words. Provide them with a dictionary and a thesaurus. Second-Language Support notes throughout the lesson plans offer strategies to help students acquiring English to understand the selections.

CHIN CHIANG
AND THE DRAGON'S DANCE

WRITTEN AND ILLUSTRATED BY

IAN WALLACE

CHIN CHIANG AND THE DRAGON'S DANCE

	TEACHING OUTLINE	Materials	Language Arts/ Integrated Curriculum	Meeting Individual Needs
Part 1 **Reading Literature** Pages T760–T768 	**Building Background** **Vocabulary Strategies** Key Words (Tested) **Strategic Reading** Preview and Predict Setting a Purpose **Options for Reading**	Transparency 44 Second-Language Support Manual Practice Book p. 119 Integrated Spelling p. 59 Integrated Spelling T.E. pp. 78–79 Student Anthology pp. 428–439 Response Card 3: Plot	**Spelling** Spelling Pretest Spelling-Vocabulary Connection	**Second-Language Support** Vocabulary T761 Strategic Reading T762, T767 **Cooperative Reading** T763
Part 2 **Responding to Literature** Pages T769–T773 	**Story Follow-Up** Think It Over Write **Summarizing the Literature** **Appreciating Literature** **Critical Thinking Activities**	Writer's Journal p. 83 Practice Book p. 120 Integrated Spelling p. 60 Integrated Spelling T.E. pp. 78–79 Language Handbook	**Vocabulary Workshop** Reviewing Key Words Extending Vocabulary Onomatopoeia **Reading** Oral Rereading/Drama **Writing** Personal Narrative A Letter **Spelling** Reviewing Spelling Words **Speaking** Teaching a Dance **Listening** A Story	**Cooperative Learning** T770, T772
Part 3 **Learning Through Literature** Pages T774–T780 	**Introduce** Study Skills: Note-Taking Strategies **Review** Comprehension: Paraphrasing/ Summarizing (Tested) **Maintain** Decoding: Structural Analysis (Tested)	Transparency 45 Second-Language Support Manual Practice Book pp. 121–124	**Social Studies** New Year Celebrations Around the World **Math** Using a Calendar **Art** Masks and Lanterns **Science/Social Studies** Amazing Invention **Physical Education** Dragon Game **Multicultural** The First Calendars	**Challenge** T775, T776, T777 **Second-Language Support** Note-Taking Strategies T775 **Cooperative Learning** T775, T779

KEY WORDS

splendid
prosperity
clamor
muffled
clumsy
balance

IAN WALLACE

Ian Wallace grew up in Niagara Falls, Ontario, when he was a boy and his grandparents them tales from long ago. Perhaps this him to say, "My love of story and come to me like a sky bolt out of a That singular love came in the age-old children since time immemorial, in the of home, from the resonant voice of grandparent."

Chin Chiang and the Dragon's one of several books for children illustrated by Wallace. It has won awards, including the International Books for Young People Honor Award for illustration and the Frances Howard-Gibbon Illustrator's from the Canadian Association of Literature for Best Illustrated Book.

Canada. He recalls times visited, bringing with is what inspired storytelling did not thunderous cloud. . . . way that it has for security and comfort a parent or a

Dance is written and many Board on List Amelia Award Children's

ADDITIONAL READING

Other Books by Ian Wallace
Bird Life with Rob Hume and Rick Morris. Usborne, 1984. CHALLENGING

Morgan the Magnificent. McElderry, 1987.   EASY

Other Books About Traditions
The President's Cabinet and How It Grew by Nancy Winslow Parker. HarperCollins, 1978, 1991.   AVERAGE

Pueblo Boy: Growing Up in Two Worlds by Marcia Keegan. Cobblehill, 1991. AVERAGE

The Remembering Box by Eth Clifford. Houghton, 1985.   AVERAGE

When I Was Young in the Mountains by Cynthia Rylant. E.P. Dutton, 1982. EASY

Part 1
Reading Literature

Building Background

Tell students that the next story, "Chin Chiang and the Dragon's Dance," is about a young boy who dreams of making his family proud of him by dancing the traditional dragon's dance. Discuss what it is that makes people feel proud of themselves.

Have students create a web by writing qualities they possess or would like to possess that inspire pride and respect. Students' webs may be similar to the following:

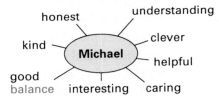

honest
understanding
kind
clever
Michael
helpful
good
balance   interesting   caring

Vocabulary Strategies

Introduce Key Words and strategies.

Display Transparency 44, or write the following story on the board. Invite students to read the story silently, using context clues with phonetic and structural analysis to decode and figure out the meanings of the underlined words.

Transparency 44   Key Words

The sun was shining, and it was a splendid day for our summer picnic. A small group of us planned to dance. The dance would tell about our good fortune and prosperity.

When my turn came to dance alone, I heard the clamor of loud voices from the audience. In a soft, muffled whisper, my best friend urged me not to be clumsy and fall.

Because I thought about every step, I stayed on my feet and did not lose my balance through the entire dance. My friends were very proud of me!

CULTURAL AWARENESS

Students may find it interesting that the first known dragon myth came from ancient Babylonia and spread from there to India, China, Greece, and Europe. Dragons later appeared in British legends about St. George and King Arthur.

KEY WORDS

splendid
prosperity
clamor
muffled
clumsy
balance

KEY WORDS DEFINED

splendid grand, magnificent, glorious

prosperity success, good fortune

clamor loud continuing noise, especially of voices

muffled softened (sound), made less loud or less clear

clumsy awkward in moving

balance steady condition or position

Check students' understanding.

Display the Key Words. Have pairs of students create charts similar to the one below. Tell them to write the Key Words in the first column and words or phrases that are related to the Key Words in the second column.   STRATEGY: PRIOR KNOWLEDGE

Key Words	Related Words
clumsy	not graceful
prosperity	success, good fortune
clamor	loud noise
balance	ability to do physical things without falling
muffled	not loud, hard to hear
splendid	magnificent, wonderful

Integrate spelling with vocabulary.

SPELLING-VOCABULARY CONNECTION *Integrated Spelling* page 59 reinforces spellings of syllable patterns in the Key Words *balance, clamor* and in other words. The spelling of the Key Word *splendid* is also included.

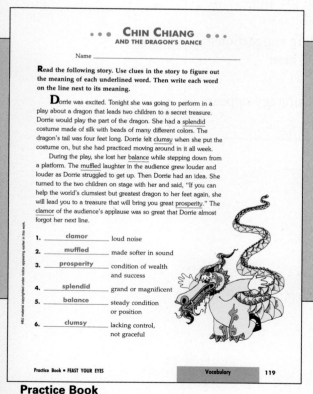

• • • CHIN CHIANG • • •
AND THE DRAGON'S DANCE

Name _____

Read the following story. Use clues in the story to figure out the meaning of each underlined word. Then write each word on the line next to its meaning.

Dorrie was excited. Tonight she was going to perform in a play about a dragon that leads two children to a secret treasure. Dorrie would play the part of the dragon. She had a splendid costume made of silk with beads of many different colors. The dragon's tail was four feet long. Dorrie felt clumsy when she put the costume on, but she had practiced moving around in it all week.

During the play, she lost her balance while stepping down from a platform. The muffled laughter in the audience grew louder and louder as Dorrie struggled to get up. Then Dorrie had an idea. She turned to the two children on stage with her and said, "If you can help the world's clumsiest but greatest dragon to her feet again, she will lead you to a treasure that will bring you great prosperity." The clamor of the audience's applause was so great that Dorrie almost forgot her next line.

1. _____clamor_____ — loud noise
2. _____muffled_____ — made softer in sound
3. _____prosperity_____ — condition of wealth and success
4. _____splendid_____ — grand or magnificent
5. _____balance_____ — steady condition or position
6. _____clumsy_____ — lacking control, not graceful

Practice Book • FEAST YOUR EYES   Vocabulary   119

Practice Book

INTEGRATED SPELLING
Syllable Patterns

Name _____

Read the Spelling Words. Write them on another sheet of paper. Check your spelling.

— SPELLING STRATEGY —

When a word has one consonant between two vowels, divide the word *before* the consonant if the first vowel sound is long: **ti-ny, mo-tel**.

When a word has one consonant between two vowels, divide the word *after* the consonant if the first vowel sound is short and the first syllable is accented: **nev-er, drag-on**.

Divide each Spelling Word into syllables.

balance	bal	ance
clamor	clam	or
dragon	drag	on
favor	fa	vor
motel	mo	tel
never	nev	er
parents	par	ents
tiny	ti	ny

SPELLING WORDS
balance
clamor
dragon
favor
motel
never
parents
splendid
tiny
tonight

Which Spelling Word divides between its two smaller words?

_____tonight_____

MEMORY JOGGER

The word **splendid** divides between two consonants: **splen-did**. Here is a Memory Jogger that will help you remember how to spell **splendid**.

Which **splendid** speller spelled *katydid?*
Speller **Len did!**

FEAST YOUR EYES • "Chin Chiang and the Dragon's Dance"   59

Integrated Spelling

Strategic Reading

Preview and Predict

Help students preview the literature.

Review the steps involved in previewing a story. (read and think about the title, look at the illustrations, and read the introduction and the first paragraphs) Encourage students to read the story title, look at the illustrations, and read the first page.

Guide students in making predictions.

Ask students questions such as the following to help them make predictions about what might happen in the story:

- **Do you think Chin Chiang will overcome his fear?**
- **Will Chin Chiang dance the dragon's dance?**
- **Do you think Chin Chiang will make his family proud?**

PERSONAL JOURNAL   Have students add their predictions about the story to their personal journals. Ask students to support their predictions.

Setting a Purpose

Have students set purposes.

Ask students to share what they think they might find out as they read the story, based on their preview and what they already know. Have students use their predictions to set a purpose for reading.

Model purpose-setting, if necessary.

If students have difficulty setting a purpose for reading, offer this suggestion:

> **I'm going to read to find out how Chin Chiang's grandfather feels about him at the end of the story.**

OPTIONS FOR READING

INDEPENDENT READING   Have students read the story silently with their purpose for reading in mind.

GUIDED READING   Follow the Guided Reading suggestions that appear on pages T763, T766, and T768. These suggestions model strategic reading.

COOPERATIVE READING   A reader response strategy appears on page T763.

SECOND-LANGUAGE SUPPORT   Ask Chinese-American students to discuss the customs surrounding the New Year's celebration. Have students from other countries describe how people in their native countries celebrate the new year. (See Second-Language Support Manual.)

CHIN CHIANG
ND THE DRAGON'S DANCE

W R I T T E N   A N D   I L L U S T R A T E D   B Y
I A N   W A L L A C E

AWARD-WINNING
ILLUSTRATOR

From the time Chin Chiang stood only as high as his grandfather's knees, he had dreamed of dancing the dragon's dance. Now the first day of the Year of the Dragon had arrived and his dream was to come true. Tonight he would dance with his grandfather. But instead of being excited, Chin Chiang was so scared he wanted to melt into his shoes. He knew he could never dance well enough to make Grandfather proud of him.

429

Guided Reading

SET PURPOSE/PREDICT: PAGES 428–434 Have students read through page 434 to find out whom Chin Chiang meets and how Chin Chiang thinks this person can help him.

Cooperative Reading

READER RESPONSE STRATEGY: PAGES 428–433 Have each group of 3–5 students select a leader. Ask group members to read silently, and then encourage the leaders to use dialogue questions such as those below. (Response Card 3: Plot, on page R64, offers a wide variety of dialogue questions.)

• **What is Chin Chiang's problem? How do you think it will be solved?**

PAGES 434–439 After reading the story, the discussion leaders might ask:

• **What is the solution to Chin Chiang's problem?**

He stopped sweeping the floor of his family's shop and looked into the street where his mother and father were busy with other shopkeepers, hanging up paper lanterns shaped like animals, fish and birds.

"It's time to practice our parts in the dragon's dance for the last time before the other dancers arrive, Chin Chiang. The afternoon is almost over," called Grandfather Wu from the bakeroom behind the shop.

"If I were a rabbit, I could run far away from here," Chin Chiang said to himself, "but then Mama, Papa and Grandfather really would be ashamed of me." So very slowly he walked into the bakeroom where Grandfather Wu stood waiting. He was wearing the splendid fierce dragon's head that he would put on again that night for the parade.

"Pick up the silk tail on the floor behind me," said his grandfather from inside the dragon's head, "and together we will be the most magnificent dragon that anyone has ever seen."

Chin Chiang did as he was asked, but as his grandfather started to dance, Chin Chiang did not move. "Grandfather can hide under the dragon's head," he whispered, "but if I trip or fall, I have nowhere to hide. Everyone will say, 'There goes clumsy Chin Chiang.'"

Grandfather Wu stopped dancing. "A dragon must have a tail as well as a head," he said gently.

Chin Chiang looked down at his shoes. "I can't dance the dragon's dance," he said.

"You have trained for a long time, Chin Chiang. Tonight, when you dance, you will bring tears of pride to your parents' eyes. Now come, join me and practice just as we have practiced before."

430

But when Chin Chiang tried to leap he tripped, stumbled and fell. Why had he ever thought he could dance the dragon's dance? Why had he ever wanted to? He was much too clumsy.

Informal Assessment   You can assess how well students focus on the purpose for reading and, in doing so, help maintain that focus. Whenever you think it appropriate after students have begun to read, ask questions such as these:

- What has happened in the story so far? Is this what you expected?
- Why did this happen? What do you think might happen next in the story because this happened?

Teaching Tip   Call students' attention to the illustrations in this selection, and discuss how they add to the mood of the story.

He jumped up and ran—away from his grandfather, out of the shop, into the market street. He stopped long enough to pick up a rabbit lantern, poke two holes for eyes and shove it over his head.

"Look, look. It's the dragon's tail!" called Mrs. Lau, dangling a speckled salmon for Chin Chiang to see. "Tonight, when you dance, the Great Dragon who lives in the clouds above the mountains will be honored, and next year he will fill our nets with beautiful fish like this."

Chin Chiang turned away.

"And he will grow oranges of a size and color never seen before," called Mr. Koo.

"What they say is true," added Mr. Sing. "The Great Dragon will bring prosperity and good fortune, if your dance pleases him."

But Chin Chiang remembered what one of the other dancers had once told him. If the dance was clumsy, the Great Dragon would be angry. Then he might toss the fruit from the trees and flood the valley. *It will all be my fault,* thought Chin Chiang. *Grandfather Wu will have to choose someone else to dance with him.* He waited to hear no more and raced across the market street.

"Our fish!" called Mrs. Lau.

"Our oranges!" called Mr. Koo.

Chin Chiang turned the corner.

"Our dance," called Grandfather Wu, from the doorway.

Looking out through the lantern, Chin Chiang hurried along the road by the sea to the public library, which he

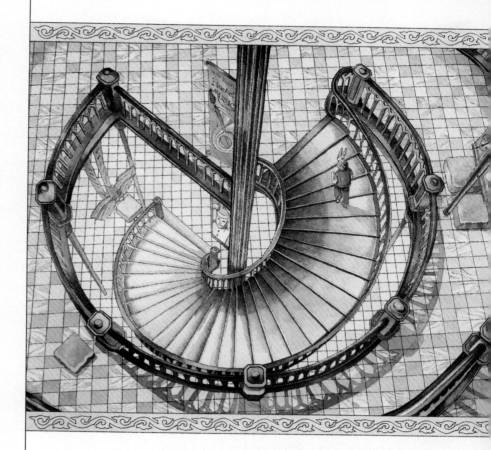

had visited many times when he wanted to be alone. He opened the door and ran up the stairs, round and round, higher and higher, up, up, up, to the door at the top that led out to the roof.

433

Vocabulary Strategy   How can you figure out the meaning of the word *dangling* on page 432? (By reading the paragraph in which the word appears, I can visualize what is happening in the story. A shopkeeper named Mrs. Lau is holding up a salmon for Chin Chiang to see. I know that when a fish is held up, it swings and sways in the air. *Dangling* must mean "swinging and swaying.")
STRATEGY: PRIOR KNOWLEDGE AND VISUALIZING

From his perch in the sky he could see the mountains rising above the sea and below him the animal lanterns, which would glow like tiny stars tonight. Chin Chiang felt happier than he had for many days.

"I never expected to meet a rabbit on top of this roof," called a strange voice.

Chin Chiang turned around quickly. A woman carrying a mop and pail was coming toward him.

"I'm not a rabbit," he said shyly. "I am Chin Chiang," and he pulled off the lantern.

"Oh, that is much better," she said. "Greetings, Chin Chiang. My name is Pu Yee. May I enjoy the view with you?" She didn't wait for a reply. "In a little while I'll be watching the New Year's parade from here. I used to dance the dragon's dance when I was young, but not any more. My feet are too old, and they are covered with corns."

"My grandfather dances the dragon's dance," said Chin Chiang, "and his corns are as old as yours."

Pu Yee laughed. "His old shoes may move his old bones, but my feet will never dance again."

A wonderful idea suddenly came to Chin Chiang. What if he had found someone to dance in his place? He would show Pu Yee his part in the dance right now. No one would see them if they tripped or fell. "You can help me practice what my grandfather taught me," he said.

"Oh, my creaky bones, what a funny sight that will be," said Pu Yee.

"You can dance," he told her. Cautiously Chin Chiang gave a little jump. Pu Yee jumped too. He shook slowly at first and she shook too. Next they leaped into the air, landed together and spun on their heels. Before long Pu Yee had forgotten her creaky bones. Then Chin Chiang stumbled and fell.

"Let's try again," said Pu Yee, picking him up.

While they danced, darkness had crept down slowly from the mountains to the city below. Then, from far off, Chin Chiang heard the lilting tune of pigeons with whistles tied to their tail feathers. They had been set free from their cages in the marketplace and were flying high above the buildings. Chin Chiang knew this meant that the New Year Festival had begun.

"We must go, Pu Yee. We're late," said Chin Chiang. "The pigeons are flying free."

"I'm not late," she replied. "I'm staying here."

But Chin Chiang pulled her by the hand, and they hurried down the stairs together—round and round, down, down, down, to the market street. The sound of firecrackers exploded in their ears while the eager crowd buzzed and hummed. Chin Chiang pushed his way forward, but Pu Yee pulled back. In the noise and confusion Chin Chiang let go of her hand, and suddenly he came face to face with the dragon whose head was wreathed in smoke.

434

Guided Reading

MONITOR COMPREHENSION: PAGES 428–434
Whom does Chin Chiang meet on the library roof? (a woman named Pu Yee) **How does Chin Chiang think Pu Yee might help him?** (He thinks Pu Yee might dance for him in the parade.)
STRATEGIC READING: RETURNING TO PURPOSE

Why does Chin Chiang run away? (He thinks he is too clumsy to dance the dragon's dance.)
INFERENTIAL: DETERMINING CAUSE-EFFECT

Why does Chin Chiang feel better sitting on the roof of the library? (Accept reasonable responses: He is alone in a favorite place.) STRATEGIC
READING: SUMMARIZING

SET PURPOSE/PREDICT: PAGES 435–439 Ask students to predict whether Pu Yee will help Chin Chiang solve his problem. Have students read the rest of the story to confirm their predictions.

"Where have you been, Chin Chiang? I have been sick with worry," called Grandfather Wu in a <u>muffled</u> voice. Chin Chiang did not reply. "Come now, take up the tail before the smoke disappears and everyone can see us."

Chin Chiang stood still, his feet frozen to the ground. The <u>clamor</u> of the street grew louder, stinging his ears. "I can't dance, Grandfather," he said.

Grandfather Wu turned away. "You can dance, Chin Chiang. Follow me."

"Look, look. Here comes the dragon!" called Mr. Sing. The crowd sent up a cheer that bounced off windows and doors and jumped into the sky.

Chin Chiang was trapped. Slowly he stooped and picked up the tail. Grandfather Wu shook the dragon's head fiercely until Chin Chiang started to kick up his heels to the beat of the thundering drum.

Then, suddenly, Chin Chiang stumbled, but instead of falling he did a quick step and recovered his <u>balance</u>. Excitedly, he leaped into the air, and again, and higher again. And as the dance went on, Chin Chiang's feet moved more surely, his steps grew firmer and his leaps more daring. Mrs. Lau and Mr. Koo cheered from their market shops while people poured out of their houses onto balconies and sidewalks, filling the streets. High in the sky flags of fire and falling moons burst into light. They sizzled and sparkled, rocketed straight up and whistled to the ground.

Just then Chin Chiang caught sight of a familiar face in the crowd. It was Pu Yee. Chin Chiang leaped to the sidewalk and pulled her into the street.

"I can't, Chin Chiang," she said, pulling away. "My bones. My corns. My knees."

437

Second-Language Support

Students may need help understanding the idiom *frozen to the ground*. Tell students to visualize an airplane with its wheels stuck in ice. Ask students whether the plane can take off, and have them discuss why or why not. Explain that this idiom means "unable to move."

"Pu Yee, yes, you can," Chin Chiang assured her. "Look at me!" Hesitantly she took hold of the tail and together they kicked up their heels just as they had on the rooftop, while the throngs of people cheered them on. Up one street and down another they danced, to the beat of the thundering drum.

All too soon the dragon lifted its head and shook its tail for the last time. The dance was over. Pu Yee hugged Chin Chiang close.

438

Grandfather Wu smiled inside the dragon's head. "Bring your new friend to our home for dinner, Chin Chiang," he said. Pu Yee and Chin Chiang hopped quickly over the doorstep and into the bakeshop.

The family exchanged gifts of fine teas in wooden boxes, new clothes and small red envelopes of Lucky Money. Then they sat together to share plates of meat dumplings and carp, bowls of steaming soup and trays of delicious pastries and cakes and fresh fruit.

"To Chin Chiang, the very best dragon's tail I have ever seen," said Grandfather Wu, raising his glass in a toast.

Chin Chiang's face glowed with pride. "To a prosperous Year of the Dragon," he said, raising his glass to his mama, papa, grandfather and his new friend Pu Yee.

THINK IT OVER

1. *How did Pu Yee and Chin Chiang help each other?*

2. *Why didn't Chin Chiang want to dance the dragon's dance?*

3. *When Chin Chiang ran away from the bakeshop, where did he go?*

4. *Do you think Chin Chiang should have run away from what he feared? Explain why you think as you do.*

WRITE

Write a news story that tells about Chin Chiang's dance.

Guided Reading

MONITOR COMPREHENSION: PAGES 435–439
How does Pu Yee help Chin Chiang solve his problem? (Accept reasonable responses: She helps give Chin Chiang confidence.)   STRATEGIC READING: CONFIRMING PREDICTIONS

What happens when Chin Chiang meets his grandfather? (Chin Chiang is trapped and must dance. He finds that he is not clumsy.) STRATEGIC READING: SUMMARIZING

Returning to the Predictions   Encourage students to discuss the predictions that they made before they began reading and that they may have written in their personal journals. Then ask them to explain how these predictions changed as they read the story.

Returning to the Purpose for Reading Ask students how Chin Chiang's grandfather feels about him at the end of the story. (His grandfather feels proud of Chin Chiang.)

NOTE: Responses to the Think It Over questions and support for the Write activity appear on page T769.

Part 2
Responding to Literature

Story Follow-Up

Think It Over

1. **How did Pu Yee and Chin Chiang help each other?** (Pu Yee helped give Chin Chiang self-confidence, and Chin Chiang helped Pu Yee enjoy dancing as she had when she was young.) INFERENTIAL: SUMMARIZING

2. **Why didn't Chin Chiang want to dance the dragon's dance?** (He was afraid that he would fall and disgrace himself. He thought if he didn't dance well, the Great Dragon would be angry.) INFERENTIAL: DETERMINING CAUSE-EFFECT

3. **When Chin Chiang ran away from the bakeshop, where did he go?** (the library) LITERAL: NOTING IMPORTANT DETAILS

4. **Do you think Chin Chiang should have run away from what he feared? Explain why you think as you do.** (Responses will vary.) CRITICAL: EXPRESSING PERSONAL OPINIONS

Encourage reader's response: student page 439.

Write

Encourage writer's response: student page 439.

Write a news story that tells about Chin Chiang's dance. Encourage students to answer the journalistic questions *who*, *what*, *when*, *where*, *why*, and *how* in their news story. CREATIVE: WRITING A NEWS STORY

Summarizing the Literature

Have students retell the story and write a summary.

Have students summarize the story by recalling key events and important details. Help students begin the story map below, and have them finish it independently. (See *Practice Book* page 120 on T770.) Students may use their completed map to retell the story and to write a brief summary statement.

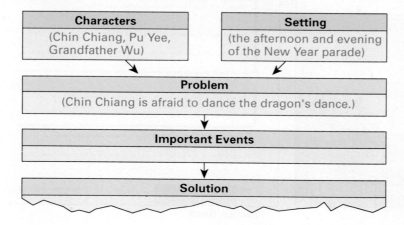

Characters	Setting
(Chin Chiang, Pu Yee, Grandfather Wu)	(the afternoon and evening of the New Year parade)

Problem
(Chin Chiang is afraid to dance the dragon's dance.)

Important Events

Solution

STRATEGY CONFERENCE

Have students in small groups hold strategy conferences, looking back at the story and discussing the strategies they used and where they applied them. Encourage group members to respect each other's use of reading strategies.

NOTE

An additional writing activity for this story appears on page T772.

INFORMAL ASSESSMENT

Having students summarize in this way will help you informally assess how well they comprehended the **main idea** of the story. It also will help you see how well they recognized the importance of particular **details** in contributing to this main idea.

Appreciating Literature

Have students share personal responses.

Have students work in small groups to discuss the story. Provide a general question such as the following to help groups begin:

- **Do any events, ideas, or actions in this story remind you of something that has happened to you? Explain your answer.**

PERSONAL JOURNAL Have students use their personal journals to write about ideas and feelings that are discussed in the groups. You may also refer them to their personal journals after they complete the activities below.

Critical Thinking Activities

Encourage both cooperative and individual responses.

DISCUSS IDEAS **Do you think that Grandfather Wu realizes that Chin Chiang is scared? Why do you think that?** Have students work in small groups to discuss their ideas. CRITICAL: SPECULATING

PRESENT A DRAMATIZATION **Imagine that Pu Yee and Chin Chiang did not meet. How do you think the story would have been different? Work with your group to dramatize a new story ending.** Have students work in small groups to discuss their ideas. Then ask group members to agree upon one possible story ending. Allow students time to create dialogue and to rehearse. When they are ready, have the groups present their dramatization to the others. CREATIVE: INVENTING NEW ENDINGS

STUDENT SELF-ASSESSMENT

Help students self-assess their participation in the discussion by using questions such as the following:

- Did I listen carefully to other students' ideas?
- Did I give reasons for my ideas and opinions?
- Did I add ideas to help clarify the group's ideas?

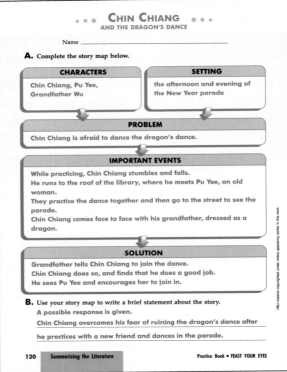

A NEW FRIEND

Put yourself in Pu Yee's place. You are in the bakeshop, celebrating the New Year with Chin Chiang and his family. Then Chin Chiang's grandfather asks, "How did you meet Chin Chiang? And why did you dance the dragon's dance with us?" What would you say?

I, _____ , met Chin Chiang
        (your name)

_____
_____
_____
_____
_____
_____
_____

Writer's Journal

CHIN CHIANG
AND THE DRAGON'S DANCE

Name _____

A. Complete the story map below.

CHARACTERS	SETTING
Chin Chiang, Pu Yee, Grandfather Wu	the afternoon and evening of the New Year parade

PROBLEM
Chin Chiang is afraid to dance the dragon's dance.

IMPORTANT EVENTS
While practicing, Chin Chiang stumbles and falls.
He runs to the roof of the library, where he meets Pu Yee, an old woman.
They practice the dance together and then go to the street to see the parade.
Chin Chiang comes face to face with his grandfather, dressed as a dragon.

SOLUTION
Grandfather tells Chin Chiang to join the dance.
Chin Chiang does so, and finds that he does a good job.
He sees Pu Yee and encourages her to join in.

B. Use your story map to write a brief statement about the story.
A possible response is given.
Chin Chiang overcomes his fear of ruining the dragon's dance after
he practices with a new friend and dances in the parade.

120 Summarizing the Literature   Practice Book ■ FEAST YOUR EYES

Practice Book

WRITER'S JOURNAL
page 83: Writing a personal response

PRACTICE BOOK
page 120: Summarizing the selection

VO·CAB·U·LAR·Y Workshop

Reviewing Key Words

Display the Key Words, and have students answer the following questions, orally or in writing:

1. *splendid*   Why might *splendid* be a good word to use to describe the dragon's head that Grandfather Wu wears in the dragon's dance? (The head is very large, probably beautifully painted, and quite a sight to see.)

2. *clumsy*   Why does Chin Chiang think that he is clumsy? (because he stumbles and falls)

3. *prosperity*   If people are experiencing a period of prosperity, what is happening? (Things are going well for them.)

4. *muffled*   How does Grandfather Wu's muffled voice sound? (not clear; soft and difficult to understand)

5. *clamor*   The people are making a clamor. What are they doing? (They are making a lot of noise.)

6. *balance*   How does Chin Chiang recover his balance? (by doing a quick step)

Extending Vocabulary

ONOMATOPOEIA   Read aloud the following passage from the story, emphasizing the italicized words:

> High in the sky flags of fire and falling moons burst into light. They *sizzled* and sparkled, rocketed straight up and *whistled* to the ground.

Then write the word *onomatopoeia* on the board. Explain to students that onomatopoeia is the use of words that sound like the thing or action they describe. Read the passage again slowly, and ask students which words are examples of onomatopoeia. Read the italicized words again in a manner that helps students gain an understanding of onomatopoeia.

Next, call on volunteers to suggest other onomatopoetic words from the story, as you list the words on the board. (*buzzed, hummed, muffled, thundering*) Then have students suggest other words to add to the list.

Splendid
Clumsy
Prosperity
muffled
clamor
balance

Language Arts

READING

Oral Rereading/ Drama

AVAILABLE ON PROJECT CARD

COOPERATIVE LEARNING   Encourage students to find their favorite part of the story and reread that part silently. Then have them work in small groups to read these favorite parts aloud. Have each group member choose a role to read, selecting group members to read the other roles as he or she reads the favorite part aloud. Next, ask each group to choose one of the scenes. Allow students time to rehearse, and then ask them to present their scene to the others.   LISTENING/SPEAKING/READING

WRITING

Writing About the Literature

WRITE A PERSONAL NARRATIVE   Remind students that "Chin Chiang and the Dragon's Dance" describes an important event in a young boy's life. Ask students to think of important events in which they have participated. Encourage students to make a list of several events, such as those in the chart below. Then have them select one event about which to write a personal narrative. Have students visualize the event and write notes about what they and other people said, did, and felt. Have students organize these details and use them to describe the event and their feelings.   WRITING

Important Events
1. running in a big race
2. dancing in a recital
3. playing the lead in a play

NOTE: An additional writing activity appears on page T769.

SPELLING

Reviewing Spelling Words

SPELLING WORDS: *balance, clamor, dragon, favor, motel, never, parents, splendid, tiny, tonight*

Brainstorm with students a list of as many words as possible that fit the spelling rule. You may want to refer to the additional spelling words list in the *Integrated Spelling Teacher's Edition.* Ask students to spell words for you as you write them on the board. Then have students use the listed words in sentences that tell how Chin Chiang might describe his experience to a friend. Write the sentences students suggest on chart paper. Have students take turns reading the sentences aloud.
LISTENING/SPEAKING/READING/SPELLING

> **INTEGRATED SPELLING**
> page 60:   Writing words with syllable patterns

INTEGRATED SPELLING
Syllable Patterns

Name _____

WORD PLAY

Start with the syllable in the first column, and read across the row until you find the syllable that will complete the word. Circle the number in the box. Then write the Spelling Word on the correct line.

	er	tel	ents	on	night	or	ny
to	7	3	2	6	①	5	4
ti	3	1	4	7	6	5	②
mo	4	③	1	5	7	6	2
drag	3	2	4	⑦	1	5	6
nev	⑤	4	3	2	6	1	7
par	1	7	⑥	3	2	4	5
clam	2	5	3	1	7	④	6

1. ___tonight___
2. ___tiny___
3. ___motel___
4. ___clamor___
5. ___never___
6. ___parents___
7. ___dragon___

SPELLING DETECTIVE

Chin Chiang wrote a letter to his cousin. When he proofread his letter, he found four misspellings. Find the errors and circle them. Then write each word correctly above the mistake.

Dear Cousin,
   Well, I did it, finally. (Tonight) I danced the (dragin) dance in the New Year's parade. I told you in my last letter that I thought I would (nevver) be able to do it. And I almost didn't. Guess what? I kept my (ballence) even though I was very nervous. Now I can't wait to dance next year.

60   *"Chin Chiang and the Dragon's Dance"* • **FEAST YOUR EYES**

Integrated Spelling

Dancing Feet

AVAILABLE ON PROJECT CARD

Remind students that Chin Chiang has spent a long time learning the dragon's dance from Grandfather Wu. Invite students to think of a dance they know. Ask them to review the steps of the dance in their mind and then write the steps in list form. Then have students take turns being the teacher and explaining to the group how the dance is done. Encourage them to use their list to help with their explanation.   LISTENING/SPEAKING/WRITING

A Friendly Letter

Ask students whether any of them have pen pals. Invite students to share their experiences with writing and receiving pen pal letters. Then discuss the format and the parts of a friendly letter, including the heading, the greeting, the body, the closing, and the signature. Invite students to imagine that Chin Chiang has a pen pal to whom he wants to write a letter describing how he spent New Year's evening. Ask students to imagine they are Chin Chiang and to write a friendly letter to a pen pal. When students have finished, encourage them to read their letters aloud.   LISTENING/SPEAKING/READING/WRITING

Dragon Tales

CULTURAL AWARENESS   Remind students that dragons are found in legends and tales from around the world. Select some of those tales and read them aloud. Encourage students to discuss how the dragons in the stories are similar to and different from one another and the Great Dragon mentioned in "Chin Chiang and the Dragon's Dance."   LISTENING/SPEAKING

Part 3
Learning Through Literature

Note-Taking Strategies

OBJECTIVE: *To develop note-taking strategies*

1	Focus

Point out the value of taking notes.

Remind students that in "Chin Chiang and the Dragon's Dance," one of Chin Chiang's favorite places is the library. Ask students why people usually go to a library. (to take out books, to read, to study, to do research) Explain that one way to organize information for a report or to study is to take notes.

2	Teach/Model

Teach a note-taking strategy.

Explain to students that one method of note taking is to write on index cards important ideas and related facts that may be used in writing a report or preparing for a test. Display Transparency 45, or write the following hints on the board, and discuss them with students.

Transparency 45   Note Taking

1. Write each main idea as a heading.
2. Write the most important facts and details in phrases under the heading, putting the author's ideas into your own words.
3. Write the title, the author's name, and the date of publication of your source.

Model how to take notes.

Using the hints, model how to take notes on "Chin Chiang and the Dragon's Dance" for a report on the Chinese New Year. Begin by writing on the board the main idea *People dance the dragon's dance* and the details *One person is the head, One person is the tail,* and *Dragon's head is wreathed in smoke.* Include the source at the bottom. Explain that completed cards can be sorted to create an outline to use when writing a report.

Work with students to take notes on another main idea from the story, such as *Chinese New Year is a huge celebration that takes place in the streets.*

Have students take notes with a partner.

COOPERATIVE LEARNING   Have students work in pairs to take notes from a reference book about the Chinese New Year celebration, a nonfiction selection they have already read, or a section of a social studies or science textbook.

| 4 | Summarize |

Informally assess the learning.

Ask student pairs to read their notes aloud. Have all students compare and contrast these notes with the notes they took from the story.

Check understanding by having students summarize what they learned. (One note-taking method includes writing the important details and the source on an index card. Notes should be written in phrases, and the author's ideas should be paraphrased.)

CHALLENGE   Have students take notes on a general topic of their choice. Then have them use their notes to write a short report.

SECOND-LANGUAGE SUPPORT   Students can demonstrate their understanding of note taking by writing three details from the ending of "Chin Chiang and the Dragon's Dance" that tell how Chin Chiang and his family end their celebration of the New Year. (See *Second-Language Support Manual*.)

PRACTICE BOOK
pages 121–122:
Taking notes

CHIN CHIANG
AND THE DRAGON'S DANCE

Name _____

Read the information in Passage 1 below. Then complete the note card on the next page. Do the same thing for Passage 2.

1.   The Chinese New Year has been celebrated for five thousand years. The Little New Year, a time of preparation, takes about a month. Food is prepared and homes are cleaned for the big celebration. Then the New Year is celebrated for five days. After that, preparations for the three-day Festival of Lanterns begin. These preparations take about ten days. When you add it all up, you can see that, altogether, the preparations and celebrations take about a month and a half. (*The Chinese New Year* by Cheng Hou-tien. Holt, Rinehart, and Winston, 1976.)

2.   Firecrackers were first used in China in the tenth century. They were discovered by accident, but the Chinese soon saw that they were perfect for celebrating weddings, victories, eclipses of the moon, and the New Year. The Chinese called these early fireworks "arrows of flying fire." (*Extraordinary Origins of Everyday Things* by Charles Panati. HarperCollins, 1987.)

Practice Book • FEAST YOUR EYES   Note-Taking Strategies   **121**

Practice Book

CHIN CHIANG
AND THE DRAGON'S DANCE

Name _____

Main Idea: _The Chinese New Year takes about six weeks to_ celebrate.

Details: five thousand years old
Little New Year, one month, preparation of food and house
New Year, five-day celebration
Festival of Lanterns, ten days of preparations, three-day celebration
Source: _The Chinese New Year_ by Cheng Hou-tien. Holt, Rinehart, and Winston, 1976.

Main Idea: _firecrackers discovered in China in the tenth century_

Details: wedding celebrations
victories
eclipses of the moon
New Year celebration
"arrows of flying fire"
Source: _Extraordinary Origins of Everyday Things_ by Charles Panati. HarperCollins, 1987.

122   Note-Taking Strategies   Practice Book • FEAST YOUR EYES

Practice Book

Paraphrasing/Summarizing

OBJECTIVE: *To develop global meaning through paraphrasing and summarizing*

Review

Review paraphrasing and summarizing.

Remind students that a summary combines, or synthesizes, important parts of a passage or a selection. Review that to paraphrase students restate the major ideas in their own words.

Practice/Apply

Have students paraphrase and summarize.

Have students paraphrase the first paragraph of the selection. Then have them write a summary of the story up to the point where Chin Chiang meets Pu Yee.

Summarize

Informally assess the learning.

Review students' paraphrases and summaries by asking volunteers to read their work aloud.

Ask students to summarize what they learned. (Paraphrasing is retelling in one's own words the main idea of a statement. A summary is a brief restatement that combines, or synthesizes, the essential ideas of a passage.)

CHALLENGE Have students paraphrase a section of their choice in "Chin Chiang and the Dragon's Dance." Then have them write a summary of what happens after Chin Chiang meets Pu Yee.

PRACTICE BOOK
page 123: Paraphrasing/summarizing

CHIN CHIANG
AND THE DRAGON'S DANCE

Name _____

A. Read each paragraph below, and write a summary of it.
Possible responses are given.

1. Long before European settlers arrived in America, the Iroquois Indians celebrated the New Year noisily. They would gather up clothes, furnishings, and wooden household goods. They also would gather up uneaten corn and other grains and toss everything into a great bonfire. This was to show that a new life—a new year—was starting and the old was over.

   Long before any Europeans came to America, the Iroquois Indians celebrated the New Year by tossing old things into a great bonfire.

2. In America, some colonists began to celebrate the New Year by following the example of the Iroquois Indians. In the seventeenth century, Dutch settlers in New York set off firecrackers and homemade bombs. They also fired shotguns into the air to celebrate. Because their possessions were few, they stopped short of a huge Iroquois-like bonfire.

   Dutch colonists in America celebrated the New Year as noisily as the Iroquois Indians did, but they didn't burn their old possessions.

B. Read each statement below. Then paraphrase it.

1. People once calculated time by observing the sun, the moon, and the stars.
   Response will vary.

2. The Chinese New Year begins at the second new moon after the beginning of winter, and each month begins with a new moon.

Practice Book • FEAST YOUR EYES   Paraphrasing/Summarizing   123

Practice Book

DECODING
MAINTAIN

Structural Analysis

OBJECTIVE: *To use prefixes and suffixes to decode words*

Review

Review decoding words with prefixes and suffixes.

Remind students that a prefix and a suffix change a word's meaning, and a suffix changes how a word is used. Point out that Grandfather Wu speaks gently to Chin Chiang. Display the following chart, and model decoding the first word.

Word	Prefix	Base Word	Suffix
gently		gentle (appear)	-ly
disappears	(dis-)		(-s)
movement		(move)	(-ment)
reopened	(re-)	(open)	(-ed)

Practice/Apply

Have students apply the learning.

Ask students to copy and complete the chart by writing the base words and the prefixes or suffixes in the appropriate columns.

Summarize

Informally assess the learning.

When students have finished, ask volunteers to read the words aloud and use them in sentences.

Have students summarize the learning. (Prefixes and suffixes change meanings of words. Suffixes change the way words are used.)

CHALLENGE Have students locate two words in this or a prior selection that contain prefixes and suffixes. Ask students to add the words to their chart and write each word in an original sentence.

PRACTICE BOOK
page 124: Using prefixes and suffixes

CHIN CHIANG
AND THE DRAGON'S DANCE

Name _____

Study the chart below. On the line in each sentence, write the correct form of the base word, which appears in parentheses.

Prefix	Meaning
re-	"again"
un-	"not"
pre-	"before"
dis-	"not"

Suffix	Meaning
-ment	"the act of"
-ful	"full of"
-ion	"state of"
-er	"one who"
-ly	"in the manner of"

1. At first, Chin Chiang is ____unsure____ of himself. (sure)

2. Chin Chiang's grandfather is ____hopeful____ that his grandson will again join in the dance. (hope)

3. Chin Chiang feels ____disloyal____ because he doesn't want to dance. (loyal)

4. Meeting Pu Yee is the best ____development____ that could have taken place. (develop)

5. When she was younger, Pu Yee was a ____dancer____ in the dragon's dance. (dance)

6. In the ____confusion____ of the moment, Chin Chiang comes face to face with the dragon. (confuse)

7. Chin Chiang is now ready to ____rejoin____ his grandfather for the dance. (join)

8. The family ____happily____ has a meal together. (happy)

9. Chin Chiang wishes the party could go on until the ____predawn____ hours. (dawn)

124   Structural Analysis   Practice Book • FEAST YOUR EYES

Practice Book

CHIN CHIANG AND THE DRAGON'S DANCE / T777

Teacher Choices

Integrated Curriculum

MATH

Check Your Calendar

CULTURAL AWARENESS   Explain to students that the Chinese New Year does not coincide with the New Year's Day celebration in the United States. Provide students with a calendar on which holidays are marked, and challenge them to find the Chinese New Year. (It is usually sometime in February.) Ask them to tell what the date is, and what day of the week it falls on.

Explain that there are twelve different Chinese years. For example, in "Chin Chiang and the Dragon's Dance," the new year is the Year of the Dragon. Provide students with reference resources, and ask them to find and list the names of the other Chinese years. Have them write what Chinese year each of the next twelve years will be. Some students may wish to work backward to discover the Chinese year of their birth and that of other family members.   LISTENING/READING/WRITING

SOCIAL STUDIES

New Year Celebrations Around the World

AVAILABLE ON PROJECT CARD

CULTURAL AWARENESS   Explain to students that people in many countries celebrate the beginning of the year. Invite students to work in small groups to research New Year celebrations around the world and to write a report on their findings. Ask each group to select a country, or assign a country to each group. Then provide encyclopedias and other reference resources. Suggest that group members research different aspects of the New Year celebration. For instance, one member might learn about special foods that are prepared, another might research music and dancing, another might find out about special events such as parades or pageants, and so on. Remind students to take clear notes about their topic. Group members may wish to hold a New Year Festival to share their findings. Students may want to decorate booths with illustrated posters and photographs that show the various aspects of each country's celebration. LISTENING/SPEAKING/READING/WRITING

ART

Animals, Animals

Remind students that Grandfather Wu wears a dragon mask and that Chin Chiang makes a rabbit lantern into a mask. Suggest that students create animal masks or lanterns. They may wish to review the story illustrations or other reference sources for ideas. Have students display or model their completed work and describe where they obtained their ideas.   LISTENING/SPEAKING/ READING

PHYSICAL EDUCATION

Chase the Dragon's Tail

AVAILABLE ON PROJECT CARD

Explain to students that Chinese children have played a game called "Chase the Dragon's Tail" for many hundreds of years, and the game is still played today. Invite students to play the game by forming a single line, one behind the other. The student at the beginning of the line is called the head. The player at the end of the line is called the tail. Ask students to put their hands on the shoulders of the person in front of them. The object of the game is for the head to catch the tail. The students in between do everything they can to prevent the head from catching the tail, but they must be careful not to break the line. As students play the game, the moving line of players actually looks like a twisting, turning dragon. The more players there are, the more fun the game is. When the head finally catches the tail, the head leaves the line and the tail moves to the front of the line to become the new head. The game is over when only two players are left.   LISTENING

SCIENCE/SOCIAL STUDIES

Amazing Invention

COOPERATIVE LEARNING   Explain to students that the compass may have been invented in China. If possible, display a compass, and explain what it is and what it does. Then provide a map of China, and have children use directional terms including *north, south, east,* and *west* to describe the locations of cities in China. LISTENING/SPEAKING

Keeping Track of Time

READ ALOUD TO STUDENTS:

THE STORY "CHIN CHIANG AND THE DRAGON'S DANCE" TAKES PLACE ON THE FIRST DAY OF THE YEAR OF THE DRAGON, CALCULATED ACCORDING TO THE CHINESE CALENDAR.

Calendars have been used for thousands of years to keep track of time. They are based on natural, repeating events, such as the seasons. In Africa, ancient Egyptians knew, for example, that the river flooded in the spring every year. So from spring flood to spring flood was one year-long cycle.

As early as 4000 B.C. the Egyptians were using a shadow stick, called a *merket,* to divide the day into hours. Based on that, they devised the first calendar with 365 days. Later in the ancient world, astronomers worked out sophisticated calendars based on complex calculations involving the sun, moon, planets, and stars.

The Mayans, a people of southern Mexico, observed the movements of the moon and Venus. By the year A.D. 800, they had created a calendar that was more accurate than the ones Europeans were using at the time. With knowledge came power. The astronomer-priest who could foretell such a terrifying event as a solar eclipse was a great leader indeed. ■

Ancient Mayan astronomers in Chichén Itzá and Egyptians in Africa calculated time by studying the movements of the moon, stars, and planets. The Mayan months are shown.

ACTIVITY CORNER

■ Have students work in small groups to find out more about the various types of calendars used in different parts of the world today. Suggest that each group choose a calendar and give an oral report on how it works, how it originated, and how it differs from the classroom calendar.

■ Organize a sky-watchers club to study the night sky. Students might learn to locate certain stars the same way ancient peoples did—by recognizing patterns, or constellations. They could then map the sky at certain times of the year to see how the star groups move across the sky. Students might do research to find out the stories that different cultures made up to explain the constellations. Invite students to share the stories they found in a storytelling session.

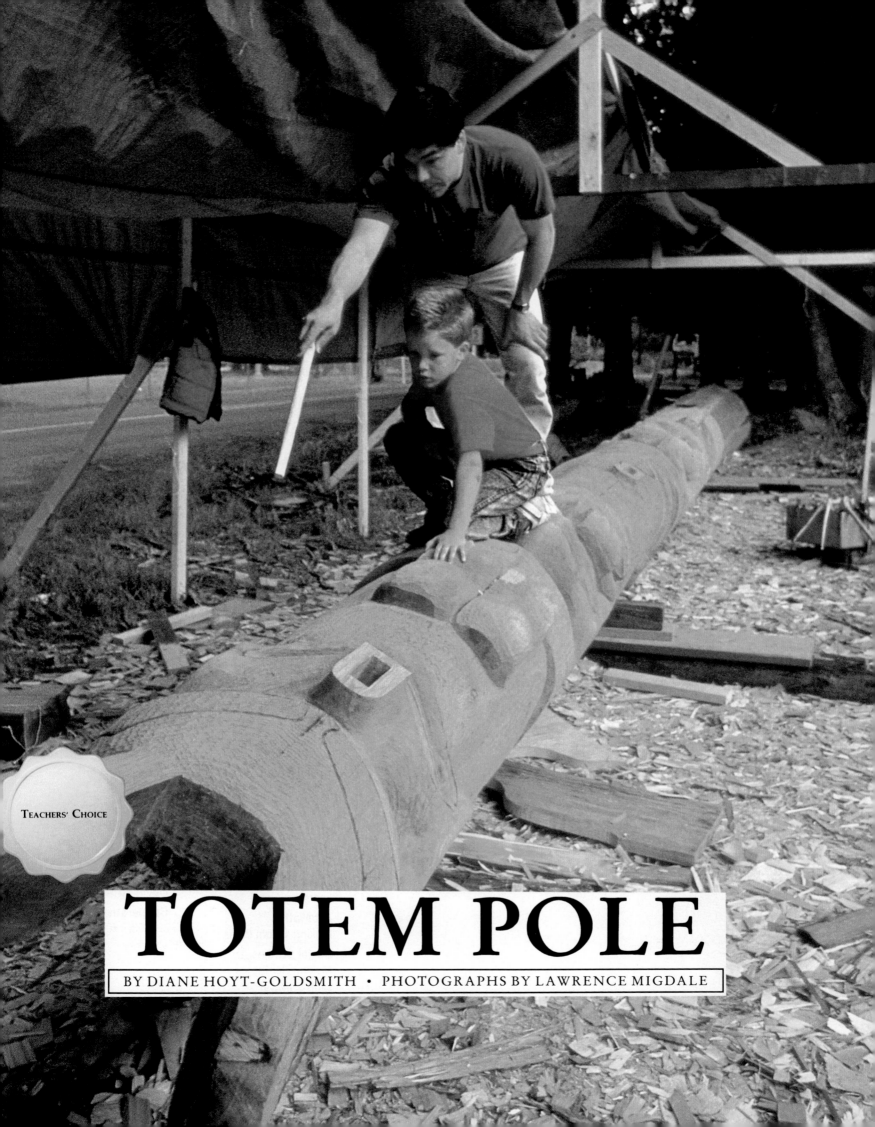

TOTEM POLE

BY DIANE HOYT-GOLDSMITH • PHOTOGRAPHS BY LAWRENCE MIGDALE

LESSON PLANNER

TOTEM POLE

	TEACHING OUTLINE	Materials	Language Arts/ Integrated Curriculum	Meeting Individual Needs
Part 1 **Reading Literature** Pages T784–T795 	**Building Background** **Vocabulary Strategies** Key Words (Tested) **Strategic Reading** Using the SQ3R Strategy Setting a Purpose **Options for Reading**	Transparency 46 Second-Language Support Manual Practice Book p. 125 Integrated Spelling p. 61 Integrated Spelling T.E. pp. 80–81 Student Anthology pp. 440–456 Response Card 7: Responding Freely	**Spelling** Spelling Pretest Spelling-Vocabulary Connection	**Second-Language Support** Vocabulary T785 Strategic Reading T786, T789 **Cooperative Reading** T787
Part 2 **Responding to Literature** Pages T796–T801 	**Story Follow-Up** Think It Over Write **Summarizing the Literature** **Appreciating Literature** **Critical Thinking Activities**	Writer's Journal p. 84 Practice Book p. 126 Integrated Spelling p. 62 Integrated Spelling T.E. pp. 80–81 Literature Cassette 2 Language Handbook	**Vocabulary Workshop** Reviewing Key Words Extending Vocabulary Native American Words **Reading** Oral Rereading/Drama Totem Poles **Writing** How-to Paragraph Invitation Business Letter **Spelling** Reviewing Words **Speaking** Planning a Ceremony Thank-You Speech **Listening** An Indian Legend	**Cooperative Learning** T797, T800  KEY WO reservatio clan traditions charcoal precious ceremony
Part 3 **Learning Through Literature** Pages T802–T808 	**Introduce** Comprehension: Fact and Opinion (Tested) Study Skills: Outlining	Transparencies 47, 48 Second-Language Support Manual Writer's Journal p. 85 Practice Book pp. 127–129	**Social Studies** Using a Map **Art** Body Painting **Science** Learning About Wood **Math** Learning About Scale **Art/Math** Making Totem Poles **Social Studies/Art** Making Heirlooms **Multicultural** Artists	**Reteach** T803 **Challenge** T803, T805 **Second-Language Support** Fact and Opinion T803 Outlining T805 **Cooperative Learning** T803, T805, T806, T807

Selection Summary

David is a member of the Tsimshian Indian tribe, one of many tribes of the Northwest Coast Indians. In "Totem Pole," David takes great pride in describing his father's work—carving and painting totem poles from wood. David takes the reader through each step in the making of a totem pole, from felling the tree to raising the completed pole. Throughout his narrative, David tells of the ways and traditions of his clan, including special clothing and ceremonies. The raising of the totem pole David's father has made is the focus of an important ceremony at which David and his father perform a dance of celebration.

Family Involvement

Suggest that family members discuss which Native American tribes once inhabited the land on which their community is built. Have students find out what names in their community or nearby are derived from Native American names or words.

DIANE HOYT-GOLDSMITH

Diane Hoyt-Goldsmith is especially interested in the art and traditions of the Pacific Northwest Coast Indians. She collects totem poles, ceremonial artifacts, masks, and bentwood boxes from a variety of Northwest Coast Indian tribes. She works as an art director for Square Moon Productions, a book-packaging company, and lives with her husband and two children in Orinda, California.

ADDITIONAL READING

Another Book by Diane Hoyt-Goldsmith

Hoang Anh: A Vietnamese American Boy. Holiday House, 1992.   CHALLENGING

Other Books About Traditions

The American Family Farm by Joan Anderson. Harcourt Brace Jovanovich, 1989.   CHALLENGING

Friendship Across Arctic Waters by Claire Rudolf Murphy. Lodestar Books, 1991. CHALLENGING

Penny in the Road by Katharine Wilson Precek. Macmillan, 1989.   AVERAGE

Pioneer Children of Appalachia by Joan Anderson. Clarion, 1986.

Part 1
Reading Literature

Building Background

Access prior knowledge and build vocabulary concepts.

Tell students that the next selection they will read is called "Totem Pole." Explain that making totem poles is one kind of special tradition practiced by some Native American tribes. Encourage students to share what they know about totem poles.

Remind students that many people follow customs and traditions that were established long ago and that many of these are still practiced today. Tell students that thinking about what they already know about traditions will help them better understand the selection.

Have students quickwrite a list.

Invite students to work in pairs to create and share a list of customs or traditions from their own background. The completed lists might include the following:

Traditions
1. songs, dances, and ceremonies
2. arts such as pottery, jewelry, and needlework
3. eating certain foods at special times

Vocabulary Strategies

Introduce Key Words and strategies.

Display Transparency 46 or the following story. Invite students to read the story silently, using context clues with phonetic and structural analysis to decode and figure out the meanings of the underlined words.

Transparency 46   Key Words

Our class visited land set aside by the government for the Navaho Indians, called a reservation. We saw one small group of families. This clan was practicing the ancient traditions, or ways, of the tribe.

One woman was drawing a picture with a piece of charcoal. The drawing was the design for a very valuable silver and turquoise pin. This precious pin would be worn in a special ceremony honoring the ancient ways of the Navaho people.

CULTURAL AWARENESS

Students may be interested to know that totem poles are carved from wood. People of many cultures have carved wood, stone, metal, bone, ivory, and other materials. A carving of a bison, found in a cave in France, dates from about 9000 B.C. It was carved from a reindeer antler.

KEY WORDS

- reservation
- clan
- traditions
- charcoal
- precious
- ceremony

KEY WORDS DEFINED

reservation   land set aside by the government for a special purpose

clan   group of related families

traditions   beliefs, customs, opinions, and stories handed down from parents to children

charcoal   form of carbon made by heating wood to a high degree in a closed container without air; used for fuel, as a filter, and for drawing

precious   having great value

ceremony   special act done on a special occasion

Check students' understanding.

Display a list of the Key Words and the chart below. Have students name the Key Words that have the same meanings as the synonyms and add them to the chart. STRATEGY: SYNONYMS

Synonyms	Key Words
celebration, wedding, banquet	(ceremony)
customs, rules, beliefs	(traditions)
related families	(clan)
special land	(reservation)
valuable, priceless, dear	(precious)
a form of carbon, a tool for drawing	(charcoal)

Integrate spelling with vocabulary.

SPELLING-VOCABULARY CONNECTION *Integrated Spelling* page 61 reinforces spellings of the long *i* and the long *o* sounds in the Key Word *charcoal* and in other words. The spelling of the Key Word *ceremony* is also included.

SECOND-LANGUAGE SUPPORT Ask students questions about the story on the Transparency 46 to reinforce meanings of the underlined words. For example: *What did the woman use to draw a picture?* (a piece of charcoal) (See *Second-Language Support Manual.*)

● ● ● TOTEM POLE ● ● ●

Name _____

Read each sentence below. Draw a line under the correct meaning of the word in dark print in each sentence.

1. Some Native Americans of the Northwest are not able to follow the **traditions** of their great-grandparents.
   a. customs or beliefs passed on from generation to generation
   b. political beliefs of a country
   c. ways of conducting scientific experiments

2. Native Americans who live on a **reservation** usually have a strong tribal identity.
   a. broad stretch of land covered with trees
   b. land set aside by the government for a special purpose
   c. abandoned park

3. When a chief erected a totem pole, a **ceremony** was held to honor the chief's ancestors.
   a. act performed on special occasions
   b. task or chore done every day
   c. contest to determine athletic skill

4. The artist used **charcoal** to draw the figures on the totem pole before carving them out.
   a. a carving tool
   b. a wedge-shaped piece of metal
   c. black substance made by burning wood

5. Sometimes the chief of a **clan** invited many people to an enormous feast.
   a. union of states or countries
   b. group of related families
   c. company that makes and sells a product

6. Native Americans of the Northwest considered copper a **precious** metal and often gave articles made of it as gifts.
   a. highly valued   **b.** ordinary   **c.** not worth much

Practice Book ■ FEAST YOUR EYES   Vocabulary   **125**

Practice Book

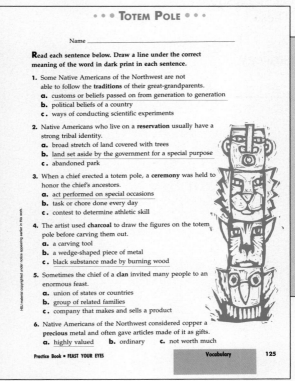

╾═══ INTEGRATED SPELLING ═══╾
The Sounds Long *i* and Long *o*

Name _____

Read the Spelling Words. Write them on another sheet of paper. Check your spelling.

━━ **SPELLING STRATEGY** ━━

There are many ways to spell the long *i* and long *o* sounds. Here are some examples of ways to spell these sounds:

long **i** = **i** library	long **o** = **oa** groan
long **i** = **igh** bright	long **o** = **ow** tomorrow
	long **o** = **o** ceremony

One way to remember how to spell these sounds is to think of other words in which the sound is spelled the same way. The dictionary will help you if you are not sure about a spelling.

Write the Spelling Words beside the correct spelling of the sounds long *i* and long *o* on the lines below.

long i = i	library	pint	
long i = igh	bright	high	
long o = oa	charcoal	coast	groan
long o = ow	shadow	tomorrow	
long o = o	ceremony		

SPELLING WORDS
bright
ceremony
charcoal
coast
groan
high
library
pint
shadow
tomorrow

━━━ **MEMORY JOGGER** ━━━

There is no *e* in **money** when it is in **ceremony**.

When you can't remember how to spell the word **ceremony**, this Memory Jogger will help you.

FEAST YOUR EYES • "Totem Pole"   **61**

Integrated Spelling

● **PRACTICE BOOK** page 125: Reinforcing Key Words

● **INTEGRATED SPELLING** page 61: Writing and spelling words with long *i* and long *o* sounds

● **NOTE:** These pages may be completed now or after students have read the selection.

Using the SQ3R Strategy

Help students preview the selection.

Remind students that one strategy for reading nonfiction is SQ3R. Write the following steps on the board: Survey, Question, Read, Recite, Review. Then invite students to survey the title, headings, photographs, and captions. Ask students to identify the topic. (carving a totem pole and raising it)

Have students make predictions.

Remind students that the next step involves turning the headings or captions into questions. Have students write questions based on their preview that they want to have answered as they read the selection. Their lists of questions are likely to include the following:

- **How is a totem pole carved?**
- **What do the carvings on a totem pole represent?**
- **How is a totem pole raised?**

Remind students that they will read to answer their questions.

Setting a Purpose

Have students set purposes.

Point out that the next step is to read the selection carefully, taking notes on their questions. Help students set a purpose based on the questions they formulated after surveying the selection. Explain that after reading they will recite or orally summarize what they have learned and then review what they have read.

OPTIONS FOR READING

INDEPENDENT READING Have students read the selection silently with their purpose for reading in mind.

GUIDED READING Follow the Guided Reading suggestions that appear on pages T787, T790, and T795. These suggestions model strategic reading.

COOPERATIVE READING A reader response strategy appears on page T787.

SECOND-LANGUAGE SUPPORT Read aloud the title, headings, and captions for students. Ask students to describe what they see in the pictures. (See *Second-Language Support Manual.*)

Teachers' Choice

TOTEM POLE

BY DIANE HOYT-GOLDSMITH • PHOTOGRAPHS BY LAWRENCE MIGDALE

 My name is David. I live in a small town called Kingston in Washington State. In the summer, I like to hunt for salmonberries and blackberries in the fields near our house.

My brother and I like to look out over Puget Sound, watching for the ferry from Seattle. Sometimes, we spot a pair of eagles flying high overhead. This makes us feel lucky because our family belongs to the Eagle Clan, which is our family group within the Tsimshian (*TSIM-shee-an*) tribe.

Our father is an Indian. He was brought up by his grandparents in Metlakatla (*MET-lah-CAT-lah*), on Annette Island in Alaska. He was raised in the old ways and traditions. He learned how to hunt, to fish, and to carve.

In our tribe, a person belongs to the same clan as his mother does. Our mother is not Indian. Her ancestors emigrated to the United States from Europe many generations ago. When I was two years old, she was adopted in a special ceremony by two members of the Eagle Clan in Metlakatla. This makes my brother and me members of the Eagle Clan too.

My father is an artist, a wood-carver. Ever since I was little, I have watched him take a piece of wood and carve a creature from it. Sometimes it is a wolf, sometimes a bear, and sometimes an eagle, the symbol and totem of our clan.

441

Guided Reading

SET PURPOSE/PREDICT: PAGES 440–446   Have students read through page 446 to find out what a totem pole is.

Cooperative Reading

READER RESPONSE STRATEGY: PAGES 440–456 Have students work in pairs. Ask each pair to decide whether they will read silently or aloud and how frequently they will stop. At designated stopping points, each member of the pair should respond freely to what they have read so far. Have pairs continue the procedure until they reach the end of the selection and then discuss it as a whole. (Response Card 7: Responding Freely, on page R68, gives complete directions for using the strategy.)

My father has a special cedar box. It is very important to him because it was made by my great-great-grandfather five generations ago. My father painted an eagle on the lid, and now he keeps his carving tools inside.

The box was first used to store food. When my father was a young boy, he was in charge of keeping the food box safe. When his family went out to hunt or fish, he carried the box from the boat up to the camp and stored it in a safe place. The foods his family had prepared for the journey were kept inside the box—the dried meat and fish, and the hardtack. These were the only foods the family would have to eat while they were camping.

My father says that even now, when he opens the box to take out a tool, he can smell the foods that were once stored inside. The faint scent brings him strong memories of the salt air, the hardtack, the fresh salmon, and even the smoke of the cooking fire where his family gathered. These memories are precious to him. The smells make the past come alive, he says.

When I open the box, all I can smell are the steel and leather tools inside. But the past comes alive for me when I hear the strike of the adze and hear my father tell his stories. He likes to tell me what it was like to grow up in Alaska.

One of my favorite stories is a Tsimshian tale called "The Legend of the Eagle and the Young Chief." Maybe I like it best because I belong to the Eagle Clan.

Informal Assessment   You can informally assess your students' abilities to identify important details in texts that they read. On occasion, ask questions like these about nonfiction selections:

- Suppose you wanted to remember some of the details in this article and had a few minutes to make notes. Which details and ideas would you write in your notes?
- Why did you pick those details or ideas?

When my father first began to teach me about the Tsimshian songs, dances, and legends, he made some special clothes for me to wear. These clothes are called "regalia." They are worn for certain ceremonies, dances, and celebrations.

Sometimes in the afternoons, I go to my father's workshop. I look inside the trunk that holds all the regalia he has made. I dress in my special clothes to practice the dances my father taught me.

The first thing my father made for me is a headdress out of leather and decorated with ermine skins. On the front, there is a small eagle's face carved from a piece of cedar wood and painted blue and brown. This is called a frontlet. The eagle is shown on all our regalia because the eagle is our family crest. My Indian name is Lap'aigh laskeeg *(lah-pah-AG-a-lah-SKEEK)*. It means "He Who Flies Like the Eagle" in the Tsimshian language.

My father made me an apron out of deerskin which is painted with an eagle design. I have leggings made of soft leather. They have a fringe with deer hooves hanging down. The hooves knock together as I dance and make a rattling sound as I move.

I also have a button blanket that I wear. On the back there is another large eagle design. It is outlined in hundreds of tiny white buttons. In the old days, the Tsimshian blankets were first woven from cedar bark and then decorated with rows of tiny white shells. But in the 1800s, when Europeans began to trade with the tribes along the coast, the Indians began to use bright red "trade cloth" for the blankets and machine-made buttons of mother-of-pearl for decoration.

Second-Language Support
Students may need help reading the phonetic respellings and pronouncing the Native American names. You may also wish to tell students that syllables that appear in capital letters in a phonetic respelling are stressed.

(Meeting Individual Needs)

Expanding the Literature   When David grows up, what items will make the past come alive for him? (Accept reasonable responses: The cedar box and its tools will remind him of his father's carving ability; the trunk of regalia will remind him of all the ceremonies he attended as a child.)   CRITICAL: SPECULATING

How do you think David feels about his family traditions? (Accept reasonable responses: He is proud of his heritage; he is pleased to take part in traditions and keep them alive.)   INFERENTIAL: DETERMINING CHARACTERS' EMOTIONS

CARVING THE POLE

My father is carving a totem pole for the Klallam (*KLAH-lum*) Indians who live on the Port Gamble Reservation near our home. Although my father belongs to a different tribe, the Tsimshian, he was asked to carve the pole because of his skill. It is common among the Northwest Coast Indians for one tribe to invite an artist from another tribe to carve a pole for them. The pole will be made from a single log, forty feet long. It will have animals and figures carved on it, important characters from Klallam myths and legends.

My father says that a totem pole is like a signboard. He tells me that it is a system for passing on legends and stories from one generation to another for people who have no written language. A totem pole is like a library for a tribe!

The first step in making a totem pole is to find a straight tree. It must be wide enough to make a strong pole. The best trees for a totem pole have few branches. Where a branch joins the trunk a knot forms, making the carving very difficult.

Nearly all totem poles are carved from cedar logs. Cedar trees grow very straight and are common in the evergreen forests along the coastline near our home. The wood of the cedar is soft and easy to carve. It does not rot and insects will not destroy it. A totem pole carved from a cedar log can last a hundred years or more.

After the right tree is found and cut down, all the branches are removed with an axe and the bark is stripped from the outside of the log. In the old days, the Indians had no saws or axes, so even cutting the tree down was a harder job than it is today. Back then, the carvers used a hammer and chisel to cut a wedge at the base of the tree. This weakened the tree, and in a strong wind storm, the tree would fall.

When the log is ready to be carved, my father makes a drawing of how the pole will look when it is finished. He draws the animals for the totem pole on a sheet of paper. He might begin by drawing each animal separately, but before he starts to carve he will draw a picture of how the completed pole will look.

Next he uses a stick of charcoal to make a drawing on the log itself. Then he stands up on the log to see how the figures and animals look. When he is satisfied with the drawing, he takes up his tools and begins to carve.

Guided Reading

MONITOR COMPREHENSION: PAGES 440–446

What is a totem pole? (A totem pole is a tall log that has been carved with animals and figures from myths and legends. It is like a library for the tribe.) STRATEGIC READING: RETURNING TO PURPOSE

How does David's father keep the traditions of his tribe and clan alive? (through teaching David stories, songs, and dances; by making clothes for David; by carving totem poles) STRATEGIC READING: SUMMARIZING

SET PURPOSE/PREDICT: PAGES 447–456 Ask students to read to find out what is done with a totem pole after the figures are carved and painted.

The totem pole for the Klallam tribe has six figures, one on top of the other. At the very top of the pole is the Thunderbird. He brings good luck to the Klallam village. The Klallam people believe the Thunderbird lives on the Olympic mountain range, across the water from their reservation, in the place where the mountains touch the sky. They say that when Thunderbird catches the great Killer Whale, you can hear thunder and see lightning in the sky.

Below Thunderbird is the figure who represents the Klallam people. The figure holds Killer Whale by the tail. Together, they tell the legend of a tribal member named Charlie who rode out to sea on the back of a Killer Whale.

The fourth animal on the pole is Bear, who provided the Indian people with many important things. His fur gave warmth and clothing. His meat gave food. His claws and teeth were used for trinkets and charms and to decorate clothing.

The next figure is Raven, who brought light to the Indian people by stealing the Sun from Darkness. Raven is the great trickster. Sometimes he does things that are good, but sometimes he does things that are bad.

The last figure on the pole is a Klallam Chief. The chief on the pole holds a "speaker stick," a symbol of his leadership and his important position in the tribe. In the Klallam culture, when a chief holds the speaker stick, all the people pay attention and listen to what he says.

Thunderbird

Klallam Figure

Killer Whale

Bear

Raven

Klallam Chief

copyright ©1989 David Boxley

449

Vocabulary Strategy   **How can you figure out the meaning of the word *trinkets* on page 449?** (I read the sentence and paragraph in which the word appears. *Trinkets* is contained in the sentence *His claws and teeth were used for trinkets and charms and to decorate clothing.* Trinkets must be like charms or other decorations.)
STRATEGY: CONTEXT CLUES

As my father carves the pole, he brings all of these characters to life. He works on the pole every day. He uses many tools: the adze, chisels, and handmade knives. He even uses a chain saw for the largest cuts!

This totem pole is special to me. I am finally old enough to help my father with the work. He lets me sweep away the wood shavings as he carves. I can also take care of the tools he uses—the adze, the saws, the handmade knives, and the chisels.

As I get older, I'll learn how to use my father's carving tools safely and to help him really carve a pole. But for now, I just practice on some bits of wood I find lying around. Like my father, I look for the animal shapes hidden inside the wood.

In the old days, it used to take a year to carve a totem pole. In those days, the blade of the adze was made of stone and was nearly as sharp as the steel blades my father uses today. Knives, for the carving of fine details, were made from beaver teeth or from large shells.

My father says that it is the artist's skill with the adze that makes a totem pole great. Each artist has his own way of carving. The strokes of the adze create a pattern in the wood, like small ripples across the wide water.

My father makes the work look easy. He cuts into the wood quickly, as if it were as soft as soap. I know carving is much harder than he makes it look. I know because I've tried it.

After all the figures and animals are carved into the log, I help my father paint the pole. We make the eyes dark. We paint the mouths red. Whale's back and dorsal fins are black. Raven and Thunderbird have wings with patterns of red and black. The colors my father shows me are taken from the old traditions of the Tsimshian people. From a distance, the pole will look powerful and strong.

Teaching Tip   Point out how the author helps the reader visualize the skillful carving of an artist by comparing the pattern in the wood to small ripples across the water and by describing cutting into the wood as if it were "as soft as soap."

Vocabulary Strategy   How can you tell what the word *dorsal* means on page 451? (The word *dorsal* is contained in a sentence about a whale: *Whale's back and dorsal fins are black.* Since the whale's back and dorsal fins are going to be painted black, the dorsal fin is probably also on the whale's back.)   STRATEGY: CONTEXT CLUES

Finally, after two months of hard work, my father puts away his tools and packs up his paintbrushes. The totem pole is finished.

RAISING THE POLE

The Klallam tribe decides to hold a special ceremony to raise the totem pole. It will follow the ancient traditions of the Northwest Coast Indian people. After the ceremony, there will be a feast like the potlatch of the old days. There will be many guests. There will be traditional songs and dances, and food prepared by the villagers. If this were a traditional potlatch, the Klallam would give money or gifts to every guest.

On the day of the ceremony, we arrive on the Klallam Reservation early. I look at the pole, lying on its back in the early morning light. Each figure on the pole is strong. Looking at the totem pole, I can hardly believe my father made it.

Soon the guests begin to arrive. Many are from the Klallam village. Others are from Seattle and the surrounding towns. Some people have even come from other states.

My father and I dress in our regalia. Although my little brother is too young to dance, he wears his button blanket and headdress for the occasion. Most of my family have come to celebrate the raising of the pole. My mother is here with my grandmother and grandfather. I know my father wishes that *his* grandfather could be here too. Although my great-grandfather is in Alaska, we know he is thinking about us today.

When all the guests have arrived, my father invites everyone to help carry the pole to the place where it will be raised. It weighs over three thousand pounds and it takes fifty strong men and women to carry it. Long pieces of wood are placed underneath the back of the pole. Standing two by two, the people lift the pole when my father gives the command. They carry it slowly down the road to the place where it will stand.

In the old days, every totem pole stood so it faced the water. This was because the visitors to a village would always arrive by canoe. But today, things are different. Since people come to the reservation by car, the pole is placed to face the road.

Expanding the Literature   Why do you think the Klallam tribe holds a special ceremony when the totem pole is raised?
(Accept reasonable responses: The raising of a totem pole is a special and traditional event; ceremonies are usually held for special events.)
INFERENTIAL: DETERMINING CAUSE-EFFECT

It used to be that a totem pole was raised in position by hand, with many people pulling it up with ropes. The modern way is to use a powerful truck with a crane attached. The crane slowly lifts the pole while a group of singers chant and dance.

As the pole is raised higher and higher, their voices grow louder and louder. It takes a number of tries to get the pole in the right position, but finally it is done. The pole stands straight, facing south toward the road that leads into the Klallam Reservation.

454

Expanding the Literature   In what ways has the Klallam tribe changed tradition? In what ways is it the same? (The totem pole is placed facing the road instead of facing the water because now people visit by road. It is still placed so people see it when they enter the reservation. Now the pole is raised by a truck with a crane instead of by people with ropes. The carvings on the pole are still traditional figures important in Klallam culture.)   INFERENTIAL: COMPARING AND CONTRASTING

Now it is time for my father and me to dance. Holding ceremonial wooden adzes, we begin to perform the Carver's Dance at the base of the totem pole. This dance was created by my father to show that the work on the pole is finished. We dance to show how proud we are.

THINK IT OVER

1. *What things has David learned from his father or his Indian tribe?*

2. *Why is the cedar box important to David's father?*

3. *Why is the totem pole important to the Northwest Coast Indians?*

WRITE

Write a journal entry telling about a tradition that your family practices. Explain why you would want to share this tradition with others.

THEME WRAP-UP

TRADITIONS

Cultural traditions are important to many people. In what ways does learning traditions enrich the lives of Chin Chiang and David?

How are the traditions of Chin Chiang's and David's families similar? In what ways are the traditions different?

WRITER'S WORKSHOP Choose a tradition that you and your family share. How is the celebration of this tradition similar to and different from the celebration that Chin Chiang or David took part in? Write one or more paragraphs that compare and contrast your family tradition with one of the traditions in the selections.

For discussion of this page, please turn to T809.

457

Guided Reading

MONITOR COMPREHENSION: PAGES 447–456
What is done with a totem pole after the figures are carved and painted? (Many people work together to raise the pole, and a ceremony is held.)
STRATEGIC READING: CONFIRMING PREDICTIONS

What are the steps in making a totem pole? (Find and cut a tree; remove its branches; draw a picture of how the pole will look; draw the pictures on the log; carve the pole; paint the pole.)
STRATEGIC READING: SUMMARIZING

How do you think the Klallam people feel after the totem pole is raised? (Proud that a great work of art greets visitors; proud that their legends and beliefs are displayed.) CRITICAL: AUTHOR'S CRAFT/IDENTIFYING WITH CHARACTERS

Returning to the Purpose for Reading
Ask students to tell what they learned from the selection. Have students recite their questions and answers, and remind them that in doing so they are completing the "Recite" step of the SQ3R strategy. They may want to review their favorite sections of the selection now or at a later time.

NOTE: Responses to the Think It Over questions and support for the Write activity appear on page T796.

Part 2
Responding to Literature

Story Follow-Up

Think It Over

Encourage reader's response: student page 456.

1. **What things has David learned from his father or his Indian tribe?** (He has learned customs and traditions, including stories, dances, songs, myths, and legends; and arts, such as how to carve and paint a totem pole and how to make regalia.)   LITERAL: NOTING IMPORTANT DETAILS
2. **Why is the cedar box important to David's father?** (Accept reasonable responses: It was made many years ago by his great-grandfather; it helps him to recall precious memories; it is the place where he stores his carving tools.)   LITERAL: RECOGNIZING CAUSE-EFFECT
3. **Why is the totem pole important to the Northwest Coast Indians?** (Accept reasonable responses: Its figures symbolize their heritage.)   INFERENTIAL: DETERMINING MAIN IDEA

Write

Encourage writer's response: student page 456.

Write a journal entry telling about a tradition that your family practices. Explain why you would want to share this tradition with others. Encourage students to include descriptive details.   CREATIVE: WRITING A JOURNAL ENTRY

Summarizing the Literature

Have students retell the selection and write a summary.

Encourage students to summarize the selection by recalling main ideas and details. Guide students in beginning the chart below, and have them complete it independently. (See *Practice Book* page 126 on T797.) Students may use their completed charts to write a brief summary statement.

Main Idea	Main Idea	Main Idea
(David's father shares Native American traditions with his son.)	(David's father is carving a totem pole for the Klallam tribe.)	(The pole is raised at a special ceremony.)
Detail	**Detail**	**Detail**
Detail	**Detail**	**Detail**

STRATEGY CONFERENCE

Have students hold strategy conferences in small groups, looking back at the selection and discussing the strategies they used and where they applied them. Encourage group members to respect each other's use of reading strategies.

NOTE

An additional writing activity for this selection appears on page T799.

Appreciating Literature

Have students share personal responses.

Have students work in small groups to discuss the selection. Provide a general question such as the following to help the groups begin:

- **How did the author's use of detailed descriptions help you visualize and better understand the selection?**

PERSONAL JOURNAL Have students use their personal journals to write about ideas and feelings that are discussed in the groups. You may also refer them to their personal journals after they complete the activities below.

Critical Thinking Activities

Encourage both cooperative and individual responses.

LIST SUGGESTIONS Do you think people should change and add to traditions, as the Klallam tribe did when they placed the totem pole by the road and as David's father did when he made up a dance? Or do you think traditions should stay the same? Have students work in small groups to discuss their ideas and to list suggestions. CRITICAL: MAKING JUDGMENTS

CULTURAL AWARENESS What could be included in a festival celebrating the culture of the Northwest Coast Indians? Have students work in small groups to plan a festival. Suggest that they draw up a schedule of events and a plan for displays. They may want to draw pictures of some of the exhibits. CREATIVE: PLANNING A FESTIVAL

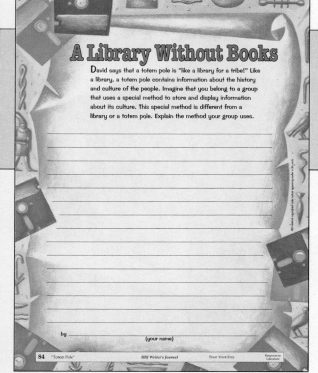

Writer's Journal

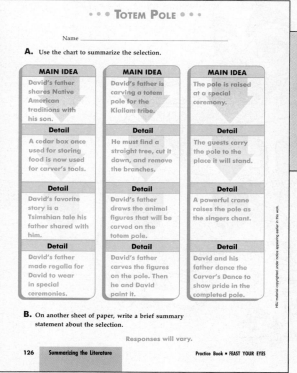

Practice Book

WRITER'S JOURNAL
page 84: Writing a personal response

PRACTICE BOOK
page 126: Summarizing the selection

VO·CAB·U·LAR·Y
Workshop

Reviewing Key Words

Display the Key Words and have students answer the following questions, orally or in writing:

1. *traditions*   **What traditions did David's father learn as he grew up?** (how to hunt, fish, and carve)

2. *ceremony*   **What special ceremony did the Klallam tribe have?** (a ceremony to raise the totem pole including a feast, songs, and dances)

3. *clan*   **What is the name of the clan to which David and his family belong?** (the Eagle Clan)

4. *precious*   **Why do you think traditions and customs are precious to the Klallam tribe?** (Accept reasonable responses: Traditions and customs are part of their heritage, which they want to preserve.)

5. *reservation*   **Is there an Indian reservation near your community? If so, what is its name?** (Responses will vary.)

6. *charcoal*   **Why do you think David's father used charcoal to make a sketch of the totem pole?** (Accept reasonable responses: Since he was sketching directly on the log, charcoal would make lines that show clearly.)

Extending Vocabulary

NATIVE AMERICAN NAMES AND CONCEPTS   Point out to students that because "Totem Pole" is a selection about Native American customs and traditions, there are many Native American names and concepts in the text. Ask students to find some of these words. List students' suggestions on the board in random order. (Words might include *totem, totem pole, reservation, Tsimshian, Metlakatla, Lap'aigh laskeeg, button blanket, Klallam, Thunderbird, potlatch, speaker stick.*) Then ask students to classify the words and make a chart with headings like the ones below.

Native American Names	Words for Things and Customs
Tsimshian Metlakatla Lap'aigh laskeeg Klallam	totem pole button blanket totem reservation speaker stick Thunderbird potlatch

Language Arts

READING
READING

Oral Rereading/Drama

Remind students that a potlatch is an Indian feast. Have students find and read silently the description of a potlatch on page 452, or have students choose another descriptive section. Model reading a few lines; then have students rehearse. Call on several volunteers to read the description aloud.   LISTENING/READING

WRITING

Writing About the Literature

WRITE A HOW-TO PARAGRAPH   Remind students that this selection describes the steps involved in making and raising a totem pole. Tell students that to explain in writing how to do something, the writer must be thoroughly familiar with all the steps in the process. Invite students to think of something they know how to make. Encourage them to imagine the steps they would follow to make this item. Have students begin by organizing their ideas into a sequence chart such as the one below. Then tell them to use the chart to write a paragraph that explains how to make the item.   WRITING

Making Muffins

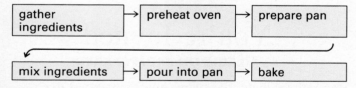

NOTE: An additional writing activity appears on page T796.

SPELLING

Reviewing Spelling Words

SPELLING WORDS: *bright, ceremony, charcoal, coast, groan, high, library, pint, shadow, tomorrow*

Make one flash card for each of the spellings of the long *o* and long *i* sounds taught in this lesson (*oa, ow, i,* and *igh*). Hold up one card at a time and ask students to list all the words they can think of with that sound and that spelling.

Have students form small groups. Ask each group to choose several words to write a poem. Ask groups to share their poems with classmates.   LISTENING/SPEAKING/READING/WRITING/SPELLING

> **INTEGRATED SPELLING** page 62: Writing words with the long o and long i sounds

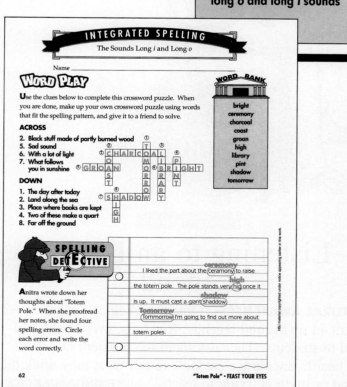

Integrated Spelling

Planning a Ceremony

COOPERATIVE LEARNING Remind students that the raising of a new totem pole is cause for the Klallam tribe to hold a special ceremony. Ask student pairs to imagine that they are holding a ceremony commemorating an important event. Allow them time to think about what kind of ceremony they want to have and what is being celebrated. Then invite the pairs to take turns telling the others about their plans. LISTENING/SPEAKING

Listening to an Indian Legend

CULTURAL AWARENESS Obtain a book of Native American myths and legends. Read one myth or legend aloud to students. Then ask them to comment on what they heard. Encourage students to tell what they think the legend or myth is trying to teach. LISTENING/SPEAKING

You're Invited

AVAILABLE ON PROJECT CARD

Remind students that many guests attended the ceremony for the raising of the totem pole. Explain that people usually receive invitations to a special event. Provide students with construction paper and crayons. Have them make an invitation inviting guests to a ceremony they have attended or would like to attend. Remind them to think of all of the information a guest will need and to include it inside the invitation. Encourage them to use markers to decorate the outside of the invitation in keeping with the kind of ceremony that is planned. Display the completed invitations around the classroom. WRITING

Writing a Business Letter
AVAILABLE ON PROJECT CARD

CULTURAL AWARENESS Remind students that one way to get current information about Pacific Northwest Coast Indians is to write a business letter to an expert or authority on the subject requesting the answers to specific questions or requesting information about a particular subject. Invite students to work in small groups. Have them discuss and agree upon additional information they would like to have. Review the format and parts of a business letter. Then ask each group to compose a business letter requesting information. When the letters are finished, have a representative from each group read the letter to the others.   LISTENING/SPEAKING/READING/WRITING

Thank You, Thank You, Thank You!

Ask students to imagine that the Klallam tribe wants to thank David and his father for making the totem pole and participating in the raising ceremony. Invite students to pretend that they are the chiefs of the Klallam tribe. Ask them to prepare notes for a speech thanking David and his father for their work. Allow time for students to rehearse their speeches. Then have them present them to the others.   LISTENING/SPEAKING/WRITING

Investigating the Past

CULTURAL AWARENESS Encourage students to recall the questions they wrote about the information they hoped to find in the selection. Ask them if all of their questions about totem poles were answered. Explain to students that they can learn more about totem poles by reading articles in encyclopedias or by locating books about totem poles and other Native American artifacts. Have students use these and other reference sources to learn three additional facts about totem poles. When their research is complete, invite students to share their findings with their classmates.   LISTENING/SPEAKING/READING/WRITING

TOTEM POLE / T801

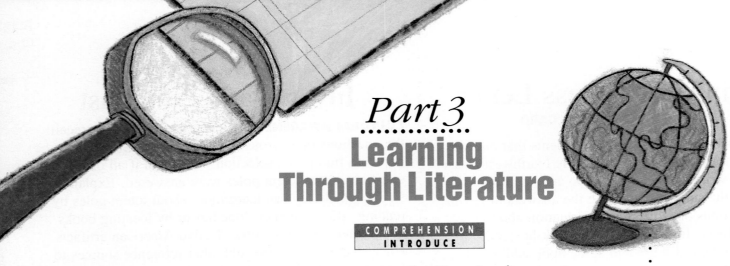

Part 3

Learning Through Literature

COMPREHENSION
INTRODUCE

Fact and Opinion

OBJECTIVE: *To distinguish between facts and opinions*

1	Focus

Discuss the importance of recognizing facts and opinions.

Explain to students that in "Totem Pole," David uses facts and opinions to make his story interesting. Point out that knowing how to tell the difference between facts and opinions helps readers learn what is true about a subject.

2	Teach/Model

Teach the difference between facts and opinions.

Explain that a fact is a statement based on direct evidence and can be supported and verified. Point out that an opinion is a statement of belief, judgment, or feeling that may be signaled by words such as *probably, perhaps, usually, often,* and *sometimes.*

Display Transparency 47 or the following sentences. Model how to tell whether the first sentence states a fact or an opinion.

> **Transparency 47   Fact and Opinion**
>
> 1. In our tribe, a person belongs to the same clan as his or her mother.
> 2. One of my favorite stories is a Tsimshian tale called "The Legend of the Eagle and the Young Chief."
> 3. The eagle is shown on all our regalia because the eagle is our family crest.
> 4. A totem pole is like a library for a tribe.
> 5. The Thunderbird brings good luck to the Klallam village.

I decide whether the sentence is based on evidence that can be checked, or whether it tells how the writer feels. It is possible to check whether people belong to the same clan as their mothers, so the sentence is a fact.

Discuss the second example.

Discuss with students how the second sentence is different from the first. (It describes David's feeling about a story and uses the adjective *favorite*. It states an opinion, not a fact.)

3 | Practice/Apply

Have students identify fact and opinion.

COOPERATIVE LEARNING Have students work in pairs to tell whether the remaining sentences are facts or opinions. (3, fact; 4, opinion; 5, opinion) Ask partners to take turns reading the sentences and giving reasons to support their responses.

4 | Summarize

Informally assess the learning.

Have students locate and write down two statements of fact and two of opinion from the selection. When they have finished, have students read the statements they found, tell whether they are facts or opinions, identify signal words, and give reasons to support their answers.

Have students summarize what they learned. (A fact is a statement that is based on direct evidence and can be supported and verified. An opinion is a statement of belief, judgment, or feeling. Signal words sometimes indicate whether a statement is fact or opinion.)

READER ⟷ WRITER CONNECTION

Fact and Opinion

▶ **Writers** may use facts to support opinions. Writers can include statements of both fact and opinion in their writing to persuade the reader to accept opinions as facts.

▶ **Readers** distinguish between statements of opinion and statements of fact to learn what is true about a subject.

WRITE A LETTER Have students write a letter about a picnic, inferring facts from a drawing and adding three opinions.

RETEACH Follow the visual, auditory, and kinesthetic/motor models on page R51.

CHALLENGE Have students write an informative paragraph in which they include two statements of fact and two statements of opinion.

SECOND-LANGUAGE SUPPORT Show students a picture and write several statements on the board relating to the picture. Then call on students to identify each statement as a fact or an opinion and to give reasons to support their answers. (See *Second-Language Support Manual.*)

WRITER'S JOURNAL page 85: Writing facts and opinions

PRACTICE BOOK page 127: Identifying facts and opinions

Writer's Journal

PICNIC IN THE PARK

Imagine that you were at the picnic pictured below. Write a letter to someone who wasn't there. In your letter, include at least three facts you can be sure of by looking at the picture. Also include at least three opinions you have about the picnic.

Dear _____ ,

Your friend,

_____
(your name)

Practice Book

• • • TOTEM POLE • • •

Name _____

On the line, write *fact* or *opinion* to describe each sentence below. Draw a line around words that signal an opinion.

1. Totem poles are found only in northwestern North America. ____fact____

2. European explorers first reported seeing totem poles in Alaska in the late 1700s. ____fact____

3. (I believe) totem poles are the (most beautiful) form of art ever found in northeastern North America. ____opinion____

4. Because no attempt is made to preserve them, totem poles last only about fifty or sixty years. ____fact____

5. (I think) totem poles are (beautiful) works of art that should be preserved. ____opinion____

6. Totem poles usually last for one lifetime. ____fact____

7. Totem-pole carvers are the (most talented) people in their tribe. ____opinion____

8. It requires a certain amount of skill to carve a totem pole. ____fact____

9. Twelve totem poles were displayed at the Chicago World's Fair in 1893. ____fact____

10. (I feel) that people who carve their own initials on totem poles should be arrested for vandalism. ____opinion____

SUMMARIZING the LEARNING I know that a statement is a fact if ____there is evidence to prove it____. I know that a statement is an opinion if ____it expresses a belief, a judgment, or a feeling____

Practice Book ▪ FEAST YOUR EYES | Fact and Opinion | **127**

Writer's Journal

Practice Book

TOTEM POLE / **T803**

Outlining

OBJECTIVE: *To develop an outline*

1 Focus

Discuss the importance of outlining.

Ask students to imagine that they read "Totem Pole" to write a report. Remind them that they want to organize the information so they can see the main ideas and important details at a glance. Tell students that one way to do this would be to write an outline.

2 Teach/Model

Teach outlining.

Explain to students that an outline is a framework for organizing information. Display Transparency 48 or the following outline. Read aloud the title and the parts of the outline, pointing out the form, the Roman and Arabic numbers, the letters, the capitalization, and the punctuation.

Transparency 48   Outline

Native American Life

I. Tribal Traditions
 A. Stories
 B. Songs
 C. Dance
 D. Regalia
  1. Headdress of leather and ermine
  2. Apron of deerskin
  3. Leather leggings
  4. Button blanket
II. Totem Poles
 A. (Carving the Pole)
  1.
  2.
 B. (Raising the Pole)
  1.
  2.

Model the thinking.

Model for students how to create an outline.

> The title of the outline is Native American Life. The selection I read has two main topics: tribal traditions and totem poles. On an outline the topics are preceded by Roman numerals. When I look in the selection for the main ideas that relate to the topic Tribal Traditions, I find Stories, Songs, Dance, and Regalia. I write the main ideas after capital letters to show the sequence. I look back in the selection and see that these are important details for Regalia: headdress, apron, leggings, and button blanket. I write the details in order after Arabic numbers.

Have students add to the outline.

Work with students to identify the main ideas that belong under the topic *Totem Poles*. Assist students in discovering that these are the headings in the selection. Ask volunteers to suggest details that could appear under Carving the Pole. (1. Find and cut down a straight tree; 2. Remove all branches; 3. Draw the finished pole; 4. Draw on the log; 5. Carve the figures; 6. Paint the pole.)

3 Practice/Apply

Have students complete the outline.

COOPERATIVE LEARNING   Have students work in pairs to outline the material that belongs under the main idea *Raising the Pole*.

4 Summarize

Informally assess the learning.

When the pairs have finished working, call on volunteers to write their outlines on the transparency or the board. Ask other students to identify topics, main ideas, and details. Then encourage pairs to compare their outlines to those on the board.

Check students' understanding of the lesson by asking them to summarize what they learned. (An outline is a way of organizing information. It shows how main ideas and details are related.)

CHALLENGE Have students outline a short chapter in a social studies or science textbook.

SECOND-LANGUAGE SUPPORT Students can demonstrate their understanding of outlining by identifying the title, topics, main ideas, and details on the outline on Transparency 48. (See *Second-Language Support Manual.*)

PRACTICE BOOK
pages 128–129:
Completing an outline

• • • TOTEM POLE • • •

Name _____

Read the paragraphs on this page. Then, on the next page, make an outline of the information they contain.

The Indians of the Northwest Coast made several kinds of totem poles. House pillars, probably the earliest type of totem pole ever made, were supports for heavy beams. Sometimes, carvings were made directly on the pillar. At other times, a false house pillar was constructed. Carvings were made on another piece of red cedar and then attached to the pillar. Removing this false front made it easy to save the carvings in case of flood, fire, or moving.

The memorial pole, honoring a chief who had died, was considered the most important kind of totem pole. The new chief would have the memorial pole carved and put up, but only after having ruled for a year.

The heraldic portal, or family pole, was placed in front of a home. A large opening near the pole's bottom allowed entrance to the home. Carvings on the pole told of the importance of the family living there.

The welcoming pole was used by people who lived on a waterfront. Usually found in pairs, these poles marked off land on the shore to show possession.

Finally, the shame pole was used to force payment of debts. The debtor's totem was carved upside down. When the story of the unpaid debt was shown in public, the debtor was usually shamed into paying right away.

128   Outlining   Practice Book ▪ FEAST YOUR EYES

Practice Book

• • • TOTEM POLE • • •

Name _____

Possible responses are given.

  I. **House Pillar or False House Pillar**
   A. Earliest type of totem made
   B. Used to support heavy beams in a building
   C. Carvings done either on pillar or on a false front
 II. **Memorial Pole**
   A. Honored a chief who had died
   B. Ordered by the new chief
III. **Heraldic Portal**
   A. Pole was placed in front of a home
   B. Large opening in pole's bottom for entrance to the home
   C. Carvings told importance of the family
 IV. **Welcoming Pole**
   A. Used on waterfronts
   B. Usually found in pairs
     1. Marked off land
     2. Showed possession
  V. **Shame Pole**
   A. Used to force payment of debt
   B. Debtor's totem carved upside down

Practice Book ▪ FEAST YOUR EYES   Outlining   129

Practice Book

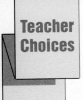

Integrated Curriculum

ART
Body Painting
AVAILABLE ON PROJECT CARD

COOPERATIVE LEARNING Explain to students that it was customary among many Native American groups to paint their bodies for important occasions and activities such as ceremonies, dances, hunts, and celebrations. Each person's body paint had a special meaning for the wearer. Invite students to work in pairs. Give each student a large piece of butcher paper. Then have them take turns tracing the outlines of each other's bodies on the butcher paper. Ask students to cut out their figures. Provide paints—especially black, blue, green, red, white, and yellow, which are traditional colors—and have students "paint their bodies." LISTENING/SPEAKING

SCIENCE
Knock on Wood

USE REFERENCE SOURCES Remind students that totem poles are made of the wood of the cedar tree because it is an easy wood to carve and because cedar tree trunks grow very straight. Have students do further research about different kinds of wood. Suggest that they find out which woods are the best for building such things as homes and furniture. In addition, students may be interested in learning about rare woods and what they look like. You may wish to have students take notes, put their notes in outline form, and then use their outlines to write brief reports. When they have finished their reports, have students share their findings with the others. LISTENING/SPEAKING/READING/WRITING

SOCIAL STUDIES
Where Are They?

CULTURAL AWARENESS Remind students that the selection "Totem Pole" gives information about tribes of the Pacific Northwest Coast Indians. Have students research to find out where those Indians live. Then, using a map of North America, encourage students to locate the areas in the United States and Canada where Pacific Northwest Coast Indians live and to share their information with classmates. LISTENING/SPEAKING/READING

MATH

Scaling the Heights

COOPERATIVE LEARNING   Remind students that the totem pole David's father made for the Klallam tribe was 40 feet tall. Help students gain an understanding of this height by asking them how many of a familiar, measurable object would have to be stacked on top of one another to equal a height of 40 feet. Have students work in pairs and use rulers to measure an object. Ask them to tell how many would have to be stacked up to equal 40 feet.   LISTENING/SPEAKING

ART/MATH

Making a Totem Pole

AVAILABLE ON PROJECT CARD

COOPERATIVE LEARNING   Explain to students that Northwest Coast Indians can carve totem poles because there are many forests in the region where they live. Invite pairs of students to work together to make a scale-model totem pole. Provide students with crayons, glue, drawing paper, and sheets of tag board or other lightweight cardboard. Have students decide before they begin how tall their totem pole will be and what measure would provide the best scale; for instance, $\frac{1}{2}$ inch for 1 foot. Instruct them to roll the cardboard and fasten it to form the log. Then have them cut six circles from the drawing paper and draw one totem on each circle. Have them glue the circles to the pole. Display the completed totem poles around the classroom. As each pole is added to the display, ask students to explain the significance of their totems.   LISTENING/SPEAKING

SOCIAL STUDIES/ART

My Grandmother Taught Me

CULTURAL AWARENESS   Remind students that the Northwest Coast Indians passed their traditions down from one generation to the next, creating a rich heritage. Explain to students that in many cultures around the world families, clans, and other social groups pass down traditions and customs. Some families have heirlooms—possessions that are passed from one generation to the next. Encourage students to share what they know about any special traditions, customs, or cultural heirlooms in their families. Then ask students to think about something that is special to them that they would like to pass down as an heirloom, tradition, or custom to future generations. Provide students with art materials and have them create a future family heirloom or draw the custom or tradition. When they have finished, encourage them to write a paragraph telling why their object, tradition, or custom is important enough to be passed on to future generations. Invite students to share their work with the rest of the group.   LISTENING/ SPEAKING/READING/WRITING

Art in Three Dimensions: Sculpture

READ ALOUD TO STUDENTS:

PEOPLE WHO CARVE TOTEM

POLES ARE WOOD SCULPTORS.
Sculptors work in a variety of different materials. (Mary) Edmonia Lewis (1845–after 1909), America's first African American woman artist, worked in stone. Lewis, whose mother was a Chippewa Indian and whose father was a freed black slave, is best known for her bust of Longfellow commissioned by the Harvard College Library in the late nineteenth century.

Japanese American sculptor Isamu Noguchi (1904–1988) won a major award in 1938 for a stainless-steel sculpture he created for New York's Rockefeller Center. He has also sculpted in marble and stone.

The whimsical wire sculptures of Alexander Calder (1898–1976) take the form one step further—to actual motion. He is celebrated for his colorful motor- or wind-driven mobiles. ■

ACTIVITY CORNER

■ Have pairs of students choose a sculptor, such as Meta Vaux Warrick Fuller, Auguste Rodin, or Julio González, and research the method the artist used to create his or her work. Students can share their findings and show pictures of the artists' works in oral reports.

■ Invite students to create their own sculptures in clay, soap, wood, plaster, papier-mâché, or wire. Students can hold a gallery show to display their finished work. You may wish to have each student explain why he or she used the particular material.

Edmonia Lewis, Isamu Noguchi, and Alexander Calder have been recognized for their fantastic sculptures.

Traditions

Recall with students that the selections in this theme were about two very different kinds of traditions. Guide them to remember Chin Chiang's great dilemma about dancing the dragon's dance in the New Year's parade and David's pride in his father's traditional skill. Explain to students that the questions on page 457 will also help them think about the ideas presented in the selections.

Note that pages T810–T811 provide support for applying the writing process to the last question.

THEME WRAP-UP

TRADITIONS

Cultural traditions are important to many people. In what ways does learning traditions enrich the lives of Chin Chiang and David?

. . . .

How are the traditions of Chin Chiang's and David's families similar? In what ways are the traditions different?

. . . .

WRITER'S WORKSHOP   Choose a tradition that you and your family share. How is the celebration of this tradition similar to and different from the celebration that Chin Chiang or David took part in? Write one or more paragraphs that compare and contrast your family tradition with one of the traditions in the selections.

457

Theme Wrap-Up

DISCUSSION QUESTIONS, PAGE 457
Cultural traditions are important to many people. In what ways does learning traditions enrich the lives of Chin Chiang and David? Guide students to recall each tradition and each character's feelings about his tradition. (Responses will vary.)   INFERENTIAL: SYNTHESIZING

How are the traditions of Chin Chiang's and David's families similar? In what ways are the traditions different? Have students clarify each tradition and then compare and contrast them. (Accept reasonable responses: Both families celebrate with costumes, dancing, and food. Chin Chiang celebrates the Year of the Dragon. David celebrates the raising of a totem pole.) INFERENTIAL: COMPARING AND CONTRASTING

WRITER'S WORKSHOP   See pages T810–T811 for suggestions for applying the writing process. **Choose a tradition that you and your family share. How is the celebration of this tradition similar to and different from the celebration that Chin Chiang or David took part in? Write one or more paragraphs that compare and contrast your family tradition with one of the traditions in the selections.** You may prefer to allow students to respond to the theme in their own way.   WRITING PROCESS: PARAGRAPH(S) OF COMPARISON AND CONTRAST

Writer's Workshop

PARAGRAPHS OF COMPARISON AND CONTRAST

For More Discussion & Practice:
LANGUAGE HANDBOOK

Ask students what it means to compare and contrast things. (tell how they are alike and different) Explain that when planning a paragraph of comparison and contrast, writers begin by evaluating the details they might use. They sort the details into three categories: things true only of one subject, things true only of the other subject, and things true of both subjects. Suggest that students refer to the Handbook in the *Writer's Journal* as they write, revise, and proofread their paragraphs of comparison and contrast.

Prewriting

Before students write, invite volunteers to share family traditions they participate in. Have students

- think about and list several family traditions and then select one.
- think about their audience and their purpose for writing.
- make a Venn diagram using the format below to show how their tradition and a tradition in one of the selections are similar and different.

Family Tradition Differences	Similarities	Selection Tradition Differences
1.	1.	1.
2.	2.	2.
3.	3.	3.

Encourage students to think about the steps, features, or details of their family tradition. Then have them think about which steps are similar to or different from those described in the selection they chose.

Drafting

Ask students to write a draft of the comparison and contrast paragraphs. Remind them to

- use their Venn diagram to help them organize similarities and differences.
- write a topic sentence that states what traditions are being compared.
- support the topic sentence with detail sentences that describe similarities and differences.
- write freely without worrying about spelling, punctuation, or grammar.

COMPUTER CONNECTION   Students may want to use a computer during the revising stage so that they can easily correct any punctuation or capitalization errors.

Responding and Revising

Ask students to read their paragraphs aloud to a partner. Have the pairs discuss whether the comparisons and contrasts are clearly expressed. Offer the following suggestions, and ask students to revise their work.

- Have you stated the comparison and the contrast? If not, add necessary information.
- Are the paragraphs organized correctly? If not, put them in the correct order.
- Have you used formal language? If not, rewrite, using formal language. (See the Language/Literature Link below.)

STUDENT SELF-ASSESSMENT OPTION Students may use the Writing Self-Assessment Checklist in the *Portfolio Teacher's Guide*. Suggest that as they use the checklist, they focus on the use of formal language and on correct punctuation and capitalization.

Proofreading

Make the following suggestions to help students proofread their work and make changes:

- Check for errors in capitalization and punctuation.
- Make sure that the first line of each paragraph is indented.
- Draw a line around any words that appear to be misspelled. Find out how to spell them correctly.

Publishing

Discuss with students alternatives for publishing their paragraphs of comparison and contrast. Some students may wish to compile their work into a class book of traditions or to simply save their work in their reading/writing portfolios. Others may prefer to make a split drawing that shows both traditions, one on each side of the page.

LANGUAGE/LITERATURE LINK

Using Formal and Informal Language

Explain to students that successful writers make sure that their language fits the type of writing they are doing. For most kinds of writing, they use formal language, which is the correct English found in books and articles. For friendly letters and story dialogue, writers may use informal language, which is the language of everyday speech. Ask students to check their work to make sure that they have used formal language.

Speaking Option

RADIO FEATURE STORY The Writer's Workshop may be adapted to have students share their comparison and contrast paragraphs by pretending that they are radio commentators. Have students follow the guidelines for Prewriting, Drafting, and Responding and Revising. Then offer the following speaking tips to help students pretend that they are giving a feature radio news report comparing traditions:

- Practice reading the paragraph until it sounds as though you are speaking to a radio audience.
- Speak expressively, especially when describing colorful features of each tradition.

Invite students to take turns sitting at a "feature news" desk to give their radio talks to classmates.

Connections

The Connections activities on Student Anthology pages 458–459 guide students to synthesize multicultural and content-area information with the unit theme. Before students begin the activities, ask them to review quickly the purpose-setting paragraph on page 374. Invite students to think about the selections in the unit and share their opinions about which ones they most enjoyed. Then ask them to think about why each selection was included in a unit entitled "Travelers."

To prepare students for the Multicultural Connection, ask them to consider how people in the United States travel and what kinds of transportation they use. Invite students to think about some of the advanced technology that has enabled people to travel more quickly and efficiently. Explain to students that modern technology is shared by many countries around the world. Point out that the Japanese have provided the world with many technological advances, including smaller, more fuel-efficient automobiles.

CONNECTIONS

MULTICULTURAL CONNECTION

RIDING JAPAN'S RAILS

In Japan, many travelers are whisked over the land so quickly that they seem to fly. They are riding in a "bullet train," which reaches speeds up to 135 miles (217 km) per hour.

The Japanese became worried about overcrowded roads, wasted fuel resources, and air pollution, so they made great improvements to their high-speed train system. In 1964, new rails were opened in Japan, and today more than a half million people use the trains each day.

side by side

■ *Find out how other countries, including the United States, are solving their transportation problems. Post pictures and facts on a bulletin board in a display titled "The Road to Tomorrow."*

SOCIAL STUDIES CONNECTION

ON THE MOVE

Find out more about how transportation methods have changed in the United States since 1750. Set up a classroom museum by displaying models and pictures.

You might use a chart like the one below to help you organize information.

Type of transportation		
Time period when used		
Rate of travel		
Advantages		
Disadvantages		

MUSIC CONNECTION

COMIN' ROUND THE MOUNTAIN

Travelers often sing traveling songs to make the time pass more quickly. You probably know many songs about sailing on the sea, riding on the road, and flying in the sky. Collect some traveling songs and sing them as a group. Talk about when and where the songs were first sung.

459

Multicultural Connection

RIDING JAPAN'S RAILS   Invite students to read the text and caption and look at the photographs and illustration. Help students find research materials, including books, news magazines, and encyclopedias. Have students work in groups to discover how various countries are attempting to solve their transportation problems. Encourage each group to choose a country. Invite students to write each fact they learn on a card and post it on the bulletin board along with pictures of different transportation vehicles.

Social Studies Connection

ON THE MOVE   Guide students in locating in encyclopedias information about transportation methods in the United States from 1750 to the present. Suggest that students use the chart to organize the information they find. Help students locate various art materials, including paper towel rolls, cardboard, scissors, and glue, that they will need to make models of old-fashioned forms of transportation.

Music Connection

COMIN' ROUND THE MOUNTAIN   Assist students in finding traveling songs. Suggest that they check the school or public library for songbooks that contain collections of traditional songs. Encourage students to bring to school recordings of traveling music to share with classmates.

Integrated Language Arts

Reviewing Vocabulary—Memory Match

- Write ten Key Words on the board, and ask students to work with a partner to define each word. Then have pairs write each of the words on an index card and the definitions on another set of index cards.
- Invite the two students to mix the word cards and definition cards separately and spread them face down in two groups on a table. Have them take turns turning over one card from each group. If the Key Word matches the definition, the student keeps the cards and takes another turn. If the cards don't match, the student returns each card to its group, placing each face down, and play passes to the other player. The person with more cards when all cards have been taken wins.
- Invite students to play Memory Match in different pairs or in small groups.

Reviewing Spelling Words

Integrated Spelling page 63 provides a review of the Unit 5 spelling words. *Integrated Spelling* page 64 provides practice with commonly confused homophones.

Writing About "Travelers"

You may wish to have students respond to the unit focus by writing poetry and consumer reports to add to the magazines in their *Writer's Journals*. Provide them with copies of poetry and consumer reports from magazines to use as examples. (See *Writer's Journal* pages 86–87.)

INTEGRATED SPELLING

pages 63–64: Reviewing unit words and commonly confused homophones

WRITER'S JOURNAL

pages 86–87: Making Your Own Magazine

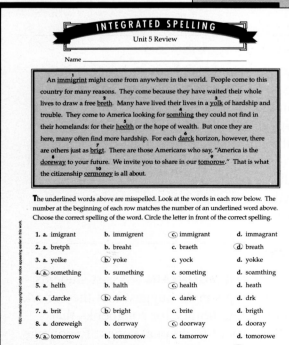

Integrated Spelling

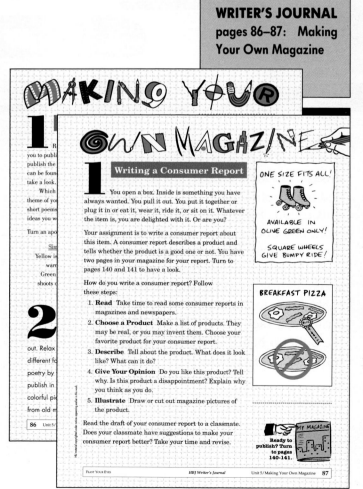

Writer's Journal

Assessment Options

Informal Assessment

See the suggestions below to informally assess students' progress in Unit 5.

INFORMAL ASSESSMENT NOTES AND CHECKLISTS

If you used the informal assessment notes in the lesson plans to evaluate students' reading and writing behaviors, you may now want to update your Running Records. You may also wish to have students complete the Self-Assessment Checklist in the *Portfolio Teacher's Guide*.

PORTFOLIO CONFERENCE

The Portfolio Conference provides you with an opportunity to learn about each student's

- interest in reading historical fiction.
- general writing development.
- knowledge of study skills such as using maps and other graphic aids to help in the comprehension of historical fiction.

Discuss the historical fiction selections in Unit 5. Encourage the student to choose a favorite and describe why he or she especially likes it. Discuss the student's feelings about reading historical fiction.

Invite the student to choose a piece of writing from the portfolio, such as the paragraph comparing Laura Ingalls Wilder's life to his or her life today or the news story describing Chin Chiang's dance. Encourage the student to tell what he or she likes about the piece, and offer positive feedback and encouragement.

Formal Assessment

The formal assessment tools described below are available to meet your assessment needs.

SKILLS ASSESSMENT

The *Skills Assessment* for Unit 5 provides the teacher with feedback about students' mastery of the specific skills and strategies taught in Learning Through Literature. Skills tested in this unit are Graphic Aids, Drawing Conclusions, Summarizing, and Paraphrasing. If students have difficulty, refer to pages R45, R47, R49, and R50 for visual, auditory, and kinesthetic/motor models that may be used to reteach skills tested in this unit.

HOLISTIC ASSESSMENT

The *Holistic Assessment* for Unit 5 may be used to assess a student's ability to understand passages written at the same level as the selections in the Student Anthology. If students have difficulty, refer them to the following sections in the Handbook for Readers and Writers: Active Reading Strategies, Reading Fiction, Reading Nonfiction, and Vocabulary Strategies.

INTEGRATED PERFORMANCE ASSESSMENT

The *Integrated Performance Assessment* for Unit 5 provides you with a profile of how well each student uses reading, writing, listening, and speaking strategies to read and respond to a piece of literature. Assessment results reflect how well students employ the strategies modeled and practiced in the classroom.

Break Time

The New Immigrants

Over a half-million immigrants enter the United States each year. Tens of thousands of these make their way into public schools from California to Florida. Coming mainly from South America and Asia, some arrive with money, an education, and possessions. Many more are fleeing war, hunger, and poverty in their native lands and arrive with little more than the clothes they are wearing.

Psychologists warn that in addition to facing cultural differences and lack of school skills, many of today's immigrant children also carry frightening memories of violence and atrocities.

Unfortunately, the new immigrants are arriving at a time when many forms of public assistance are being curtailed. According to the National Educational Association, federal funding for education has declined 21.5 percent, bilingual education has been cut 38 percent, and aid for disadvantaged children has been cut 20 percent.

With other social services already overburdened, much of the responsibility for these new arrivals falls to teachers. For this reason, educators need to familiarize themselves with the needs of immigrant children—particularly such needs as compassion and acceptance, true hallmarks of education.

TOUR THE USA WITHOUT LEAVING HOME

Give students a chance to let their imaginations roam in this plan-a-trip adventure. Have students form groups, and ask each group to brainstorm a list of destinations for an imaginary road trip.

Groups may wish to write to one of the state tourism agencies for travel guides, highway maps, and other information. Students may wish to plan an itinerary, including historic sites, national parks, museums, and festivals. Other planning activities can include making schedules, calculating expenses, forming a budget, and planning travel routes.

Students may also wish to create their own postcards based on their research. These could be completed and "mailed" to a classroom bulletin board.

THE FAR SIDE   By GARY LARSON

©Chronicle Features, 1984 Larson 5-22

"For heaven's sake, Elroy! . . NOW look where the earth is! . . Move over and let me drive!"

The Far Side cartoon by Gary Larson. Reprinted by permission of Chronicle Features, San Francisco, CA.

Aboard the Good Ship *Mayflower*

How aware are your students of what life was actually like aboard the *Mayflower*? Here are some activities to help students gain appreciation for the extraordinary feat of crossing the ocean in 1620.

1. The voyage of the *Mayflower* lasted many months. Have students form groups, and ask each group to compose a list of items they would have taken with them.

2. Conditions aboard the *Mayflower* were cramped. Focus students' attention on the space problem by marking off the dimensions of the ship (90 x 26 feet) on the school grounds. Invite 102 people (the number aboard ship) to stand inside the area. Have students discuss how this made them feel.

3. Have students create a mural depicting the voyage of the *Mayflower*. Remind them that the mural should tell a story.

4. Finally, ask students to keep a logbook in which they record fictitious events.

UNIT SIX

DREAMERS

Planning Center

What's Ahead in "Dreamers"?

ACHIEVERS: PAGES T824–T887 Cheer along with your students as they read these folktales about "Achievers" who gain unexpected rewards.

YOUNG AT HEART: PAGES T888–T923 Encourage your students to read this poem and fictional story about two "Young at Heart" grandmothers who will likely capture their hearts.

STARGAZERS: PAGES T924–T977 Invite your students to reach for the stars with these "Stargazers" in a biography, an autobiography, and poems and to discover what it takes to realize a dream.

Family Involvement

The *Family Involvement Activities* offer a variety of possibilities for extending each theme and expanding the unit focus. A Read-at-Home Story is also included for family members to read together.

Pacing

This unit is designed to take approximately five or six weeks to complete, depending on your students' needs.

Assessment and Evaluation

Title	Description	When and How It's Used
INFORMAL ASSESSMENT OPTIONS (Ongoing)		
Reading/Writing Portfolio	Contains samples of students' literacy development.	Collect samples of personal journals and writing throughout the unit. Hold periodic Portfolio Conferences.
Informal Assessment Notes	Appear throughout the *Teacher's Edition*.	Observe students' reading, writing, listening, and speaking behaviors. Keep Runnning Records of your observations.
Student Self-Assessment Notes	Appear throughout the *Teacher's Edition*.	Students monitor their use of reading and writing strategies.
Running Records	Ongoing assessment of students' reading, writing, listening, and speaking behaviors.	Record periodically to track students' progress.
FORMAL ASSESSMENT OPTIONS (End of Unit)		
Skills Assessment	Assesses mastery of strategies and skills taught in Learning Through Literature.	Administer at end of the unit.
Holistic Assessment	Evaluates students' ability to read and understand excerpts from literature.	Administer at end of the unit.
Integrated Performance Assessment	Assesses use of reading and writing strategies modeled and practiced in the classroom.	Administer at end of the unit.

HBJ Literature Cassette 2

Recordings of the following selections in "Dreamers" may be used for instruction or for students' listening enjoyment.
- "The Weaving of a Dream"
- "Grandma's Bones"

Audiovisual Materials and Software

A Conversation with Lee Bennett Hopkins. Tim Podell Productions, 1991. The poet discusses the fine art of appreciating poetry.   VIDEO

Helen Keller: Voice and Vision in the Soul. Aims Media. The life of the woman who triumphed over deafness and blindness is portrayed.   INTERACTIVE VIDEODISC

Mufaro's Beautiful Daughters by John Steptoe. Weston Woods, 1990. The king decides to take a wife, and two sisters are unknowingly tested in this African folktale.   FILM/FILMSTRIP/VIDEO

Nikki Giovanni. Pied Piper, 1979. The poet shows how colors, sounds, and rhythms can be turned into poetry.   FILMSTRIP

A Picture Book of Martin Luther King, Jr., by David Adler. Live Oak Media, 1990. The book about this famous dreamer is adapted for viewers.   VIDEO

The Reason I Like Chocolate and Other Children's Poems by Nikki Giovanni. Folkways/Scholastic. The poet reads her work, including "the drum."   AUDIOCASSETTE

"Jon wondered . . . . Matt just about said he shouldn't try carving because he was blind. How would Carver act toward him? Jon knew that somehow he'd find a way to meet him. He'd ask Carver to teach him, too. Maybe, just maybe, Carver would agree."

HBJ Treasury of Literature Library

Here is a sneak peek at some of the options you will find in the *HBJ Treasury of Literature Library Guide* for *Carver*.
- **Reading Cooperatively** in response groups
- **Reading Independently** during sustained silent reading periods
- **Directing the Reading** through questioning strategies
- **Reading Aloud** to encourage literature appreciation

Bulletin Board Idea

Invite students to share some of the things that they dream about becoming or doing. Provide a variety of art materials, and encourage students to select one or two of their dreams and draw or paint a picture or make a mural or poster that describes their dreams. Distribute sheets of paper to each student. Have them cut the paper in the shape of clouds and write two or three sentences that tell about their dreams. Post students' artwork and writing on the bulletin board, under the title *Dreams*. Invite students to take turns telling classmates about their dreams.

... i'm gonna beat
out my own rhythm
Nikki Giovanni

Everyone has a dream and a rhythm, a way of making that dream come true. Dr. Martin Luther King, Jr., had one of the most important dreams of our times. Do you dream of growing up to be like him or like another adult whom you admire? Or do you dream of winning a prize or leading a team to victory? As you read the selections in this unit, think about your own dream. You may find someone who shares it.

460

THEMES

ACHIEVERS
464

YOUNG AT HEART
504

STARGAZERS
526

Introducing "Dreamers"

Ask students to tell what the word *dreamers* means to them. Invite students to share times when someone else has called them a dreamer. Encourage them to read the unit introduction and theme titles. Ask them to speculate about how characters who are "Achievers," those who are "Young at Heart," and those who are "Stargazers" might all be dreamers.

Invite students to share what they know about dreamers from the past and from the present. Discuss with students what goals these dreamers set and whether they achieved their goals. Ask students to tell how achieving certain dreams benefits people around the world. CULTURAL AWARENESS

WRITER'S JOURNAL
pages 88–90:
Reading and writing about "Dreamers"

OOKSHELF

CARVER
BY RUTH YAFFE RADIN

Jon, blind since he was two years old, wants to carve wood just as his father used to. With the help of an old sculptor, Jon sees that it is possible to achieve his dreams in spite of his handicap. AWARD-WINNING AUTHOR

HBJ LIBRARY BOOK

GO FISH
BY MARY STOLZ

Thomas is tired of resting his broken ankle. Then Grandfather suggests that the two of them go fishing. During their time together, Thomas learns to appreciate Grandfather's wisdom. AWARD-WINNING AUTHOR

WHAT ARE YOU FIGURING NOW? A STORY ABOUT BENJAMIN BANNEKER
BY JERI FERRIS

Benjamin Banneker had many talents and was always eager to try new things. His biography tells of his wonderful accomplishments.

THE RING AND THE WINDOW SEAT
BY AMY HEST

When she was a little girl, Great-Aunt Stella learned a valuable lesson. She tells Annie the story of how she discovered what is important in life. AWARD-WINNING AUTHOR

YEH-SHEN: A CINDERELLA STORY FROM CHINA
BY AI-LING LOUIE

With the help of her fish friend, Yeh-Shen becomes a queen. This Asian tale is a retelling of the familiar Cinderella story. ALA NOTABLE BOOK, CHILDREN'S CHOICE, SLJ BEST BOOKS OF THE YEAR

463

HBJ Library Book

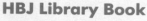

Invite students to read the information about *Carver* and look at the cover illustration. Ask students to imagine being blind and trying to carve a piece of wood. Discuss with students how they think Jon achieves his dream of carving. Page T819 provides a preview of the lesson plans that can be found in the *HBJ Treasury of Literature Library Guide*.

Read aloud to students.

The Wooden Horse

from *Spanish-American Folktales*
by Teresa Pijoan de Van Etten

Pablo helped Grandfather cut the soft pine wood into rectangles. Some of the wooden rectangles were very small—as small as your smallest finger. The smaller pieces were cut by Grandfather, carefully, with a hand ax. The larger wooden squares were cut by Pablo with a long ax. Pablo and his grandfather lived high on a hill that looked out over the village.

Grandfather sat down on an old tree trunk. "Pablo, I cannot carry all of this today. Would you take the cut wood to our roadside stand, cover it, and come back to eat? Then we can go back down to the road with our arms free."

Pablo agreed. Grandfather was ninety years old; his ripeness of age had taken his youthful energy. Pablo was fourteen years old, and was taller and stronger than Grandfather this summer. Pablo wrapped the cut wood in a burlap sack. He went down the path to the roadside stand.

Some of Grandfather's carving tools were already there. His sign banged back and forth in the morning breeze. It read "Benjamin Ortega, woodcarver."

Grandfather carved beautiful little animals, such as birds, beavers, squirrels, and cats. These small animals he pegged to branches of wood which were pegged into a tall round base that looked like a tree. Tourists would come and buy Grandfather's carvings.

Pablo thought Grandfather wouldn't mind his being a little late. He jumped the low wooden fence that ran along the ditch and hurried to a path that led to an old gray barn.

There were some other boys there. They were clicking their tongues trying to get señor Ortiz's new colt to gallop in the field. Pablo did not go to them.

He turned to look at the black stallion the Ortizes were selling. The horse was called *Relámpago*—which means "lightning."

Pablo wanted that horse, for he was sure he could win any rodeo prize or go anywhere in the world on Relámpago.

Grandfather had said no. They could barely afford to live themselves, never mind to own a fine, fat, well-bred stallion such as Relámpago.

SELECTION SUMMARY Fourteen-year-old Pablo desperately wants a certain black stallion. Although Grandfather says they cannot afford such a luxury, Pablo refuses to give up his dream. He is even willing to sacrifice the wooden horse his father had carved. Inevitably, the stallion is not to be his, but Pablo learns to appreciate his own wooden horse.

ABOUT THE AUTHOR Teresa Pijoan de Van Etten grew up on an Indian reservation. There she learned how the power of a story brings "life to the night fires" and that "everyone has the power of imagination and creativity." Today she is a professional storyteller as well as a writer.

Strategies for Listening

LISTENING/THINKING STRATEGY—VISUALIZING Tell students that they can better understand a story as they listen by creating a mental picture of what is happening. Explain that focusing on what the characters see, hear, and do will help them visualize the story.

SET A PURPOSE FOR LISTENING Remind students that the selections in this unit are about "Dreamers." Explain that this selection is a folktale. Point out that folktales often have an implied moral or lesson. In "The Wooden Horse" a boy dreams about owning a black stallion. Ask students to pay attention to what he does when he learns that he cannot have what he wants.

Relámpago stamped his feet in the stall. His mighty black head swung back and forth, desperate for the freedom to gallop. Pablo wanted to run to the gate, climb on the sleek black back, and ride off into a better world.

Instead, Pablo ran home. He heard Grandfather in the kitchen cooking breakfast. Pablo went to his little cot in the corner of the room and pulled out a bundle of cloth. He carefully unwrapped it. There in his hand he held a large oval shape of pine. The wood was smooth and dark from years of work. Pablo gently stroked it.

His father had started to carve a horse out of this oval of pine when Pablo was just a baby. His father had been killed in the Vietnam war. His mother had saved the barely-begun horse, and sometimes when Pablo was frightened, she let Pablo sleep with it—that is, she did until she died from pneumonia.

Pablo rubbed the wood with his fingers. He could finish this piece. His carving was good, for he had learned a great deal from watching his grandfather.

Grandfather did not know about the horse. Pablo decided that today he would work on it. Someday it would be finished. Someday very soon he would sell it for a real horse.

Pablo wrapped the wooden horse in its cloth and hid it in his shirt. Grandfather called to him, "Pablo, where are you? Breakfast is ready." Pablo hurried to the kitchen to eat.

Once the dishes were washed and the food stored and Grandfather had finished with his morning duties, they went on their way to the roadside stand. Pablo let Grandfather lean on him as they walked down the steep hill to the road.

People were waiting when they arrived at the stand.

Pablo watched as Grandfather talked with the people.

Grandfather was busy, and Pablo was preoccupied with the thought of the black stallion.

The bundle in his shirt was ready for carving. Pablo sat down under a tree behind the roadside stand. Grandfather was so busy that he would not notice his grandson's work behind him.

Pablo pulled his bundle out of his shirt and began to whittle on it. Every now and then people would come around him and watch. Pablo kept working. He steadied his hand and worked on the arch over the horse's eye, and then on the careful shape of each eye. The sweat from Pablo's brow dripped down his cheek. He lifted his head to watch Grandfather.

Grandfather was too busy to notice Pablo, and so Pablo continued. He worked until the sun was on the horizon and it was time to help Grandfather close the roadside stand.

They packed up their work and started for home. Grandfather did not cross the road right away, but walked along the ditch path by the low wooden fence.

They heard a truck's motor roar nearby. Pablo saw a large horse trailer pull away from the Ortiz's barn. It drove by the boy and his grandfather and turned onto the main highway. Relámpago was stamping his hooves and snorting in the back of the big silver horse trailer as it drove out of sight.

Pablo gasped when he saw this. His lip quivered as the horse was driven away. Pablo quickly looked down, for he didn't want his grandfather to know of his feelings.

Grandfather said nothing, and kept walking home. They laid down the carving tools, the cut wood, and the money box. Grandfather put his hand on Pablo's shoulder, and with his other hand he pulled the bundle out from Pablo's shirt.

"Pablo, you have one of the finest horses in all of Chimayo right here."

Pablo smiled. He would carve more horses, perhaps even one as fine as Relámpago.

Responding to Literature

1. **What do you think the black stallion represented to Pablo?** (Accept reasonable responses: hope and the freedom to go anywhere.) CRITICAL: DRAWING CONCLUSIONS

2. **Did Pablo think his grandfather realized how much he wanted Relámpago?** (Accept reasonable responses: not at first, but when Grandfather told him that his wooden horse was one of the finest, he knew Grandfather understood.) INFERENTIAL: DRAWING CONCLUSIONS

SPEAKING Ask volunteers to tell what they think would have happened if Pablo had been able to buy Relámpago. CREATIVE: ORAL COMPOSITION

Achievers

Mufaro's Beautiful Daughters

Words About the Author and Illustrator: John Steptoe

The Weaving of a Dream

For pacing suggestions, see page T826.

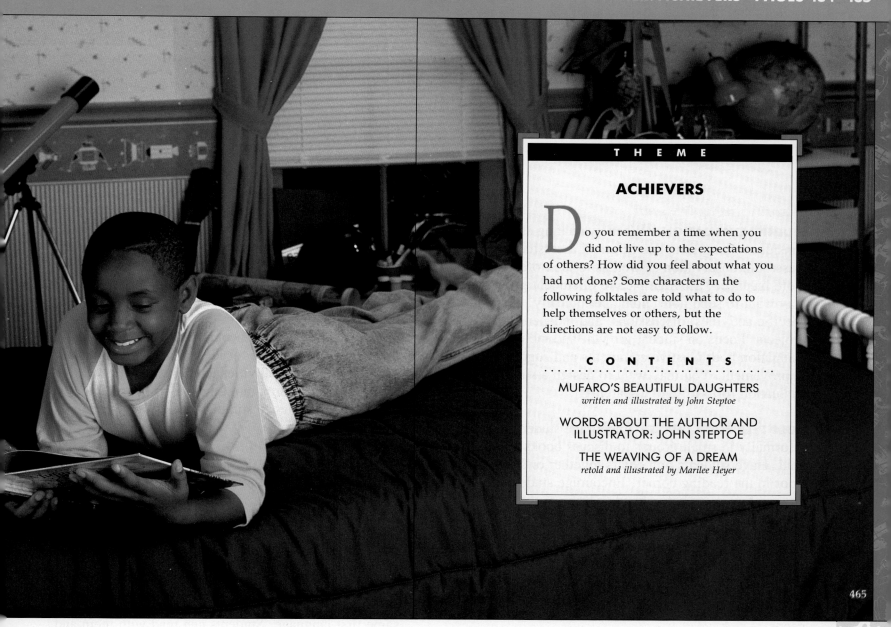

THEME

ACHIEVERS

Do you remember a time when you did not live up to the expectations of others? How did you feel about what you had not done? Some characters in the following folktales are told what to do to help themselves or others, but the directions are not easy to follow.

CONTENTS

MUFARO'S BEAUTIFUL DAUGHTERS
written and illustrated by John Steptoe

WORDS ABOUT THE AUTHOR AND ILLUSTRATOR: JOHN STEPTOE

THE WEAVING OF A DREAM
retold and illustrated by Marilee Heyer

465

Discussing the Theme

Invite students to look at the photograph on Student Anthology page 464 and to read the theme focus on page 465. Encourage students to think about times when they did not live up to the wishes of others, and invite them to share their experiences. Then ask students to read the selection titles and speculate how the characters in the selections might be achievers.

Reading/Writing Portfolio

Remind students to keep their writing responses for the selections in "Achievers" in their portfolios. Remind them also to add to their personal journals any thoughts or ideas about books they have read independently.

Managing the Literature-Based Classroom

Management Options

STUDENT EVALUATION   When evaluating students, consider writing samples, informal assessment, and classroom observation as well as tests in order to get a more balanced, accurate picture of student growth. You may want to send notes home periodically. Mention specific activities, discussions, and independent or group projects. Focus on student growth, and include in your evaluation both positive comments and suggestions for improvement. You may want to design a simple evaluation form to send to parents.

HOLD PEER BOOK CHATS   Encourage students to meet informally in small groups to discuss books they have read. Have students pull chairs together or sit on the floor in the reading corner. Encourage students to jot down a few notes beforehand to bring to the discussion. You may want to schedule peer book chats while you work on skills from Learning Through Literature with other students.

PACING   This theme has been designed to take about two weeks to complete, depending on your students' needs.

Meeting Individual Needs

STUDENTS AT RISK   To promote students' interest in folktales, play recordings by storytellers or invite a local storyteller to visit the class.

GIFTED AND TALENTED   Suggest that students explore other publishing options for the Write activity at the end of each selection. Encourage them to check the Publishing Options file for ideas. *Challenge Cards* provide additional activities to challenge students. Challenge notes throughout the lesson plans suggest additional activities to stimulate critical and creative thinking.

SPECIAL EDUCATION STUDENTS   Students may have difficulty remembering important vocabulary or frequently used words. Have them write these words and brief definitions on index cards or in an alphabetized journal, which they can refer to when needed.

LIMITED ENGLISH PROFICIENT STUDENTS   Raise students' self-esteem by having them work as buddies with younger students in your school or in their homes who speak the same first language. Students can read with them and help them complete assignments. Second-Language Support notes throughout the lesson plans offer strategies to help students acquiring English to understand the selections.

MUFARO'S BEAUTIFUL DAUGHTERS

	TEACHING OUTLINE	Materials	Language Arts/ Integrated Curriculum	Meeting Individual Needs
Part 1 **Reading Literature** Pages T830–T839 	**Building Background** **Vocabulary Strategies** Key Words (Tested) **Strategic Reading** Preview and Predict Setting a Purpose **Options for Reading**	Transparency 49 Second-Language Support Manual Practice Book p. 130 Integrated Spelling p. 65 Integrated Spelling T.E. pp. 86–87 Student Anthology pp. 466–479 Response Card 7: Responding Freely	**Spelling** Spelling Pretest Spelling-Vocabulary Connection	**Second-Language Support** Vocabulary T831 Strategic Reading T832, T835 **Cooperative Reading** T833
Part 2 **Responding to Literature** Pages T840–T845 	**Story Follow-Up** Think It Over Write **Summarizing the Literature** **Appreciating Literature** **Critical Thinking Activities**	Writer's Journal p. 91 Practice Book pp. 131–132 Integrated Spelling p. 66 Integrated Spelling T.E. pp. 86–87 Language Handbook	**Vocabulary Workshop** Reviewing Key Words Extending Vocabulary Adjectives **Reading** Oral Rereading **Writing** A Letter Journal Entries Want Ads **Spelling** Reviewing Spelling Words **Speaking** Dramatizing Vocally Presenting Ideas Using Puppets **Listening** Folktales	**Cooperative Learning** T841, T844
Part 3 **Learning Through Literature** Pages T846–T852 	**Introduce** Comprehension: Comparing and Contrasting (Tested) **Review** Decoding: Structural Analysis (Tested) **Maintain** Comprehension: Cause and Effect (Tested)	Second-Language Support Manual Writer's Journal p. 92 Practice Book pp. 133–135	**Social Studies** Mapmaking Comparing Folktales Exploring African Culture **Science** Sprouting Potatoes **Math** Estimating Distance **Art** Cloth Patterns **Multicultural** Women Rulers	**Reteach** T847 **Challenge** T847, T848, T849 **Second-Language Support** Comparing/Contrasting T847 **Cooperative Learning** T847, T850, T851

KEY WORDS

considerate
temper
praise
acknowledges
advise
bountiful
silhouetted

Selection Summary

This African folktale is about Mufaro [mōō • fär'ō] and his two beautiful daughters, Nyasha [nē • ä'sha] and Manyara [män • yär'ä]. Nyasha is kind and gentle, but Manyara is bad-tempered and jealous. One day Nyasha finds in her garden a small snake, which she befriends and calls Nyoka (nē • yō'kä). When a messenger arrives to announce that the king is looking for a wife, Mufaro and his daughters prepare to journey to the city. Eager to arrive there first, Manyara sneaks away in the night. On her journey, she encounters a small boy, an old woman, and a man. Manyara is unkind to each of them. The next morning, Nyasha also encounters the boy and the old woman, but she treats them with respect. When Nyasha arrives in the city, she sees Manyara rushing out of the king's chamber after being frightened by his appearance. Nyasha goes into the king's chamber and finds Nyoka, who transforms himself into the king. He tells her that he was the boy and the old woman, and that he is aware of her kindness. They are married, and Manyara becomes a servant in Nyasha's household.

Family Involvement

Encourage family members to talk with students about times when they have shown kindness to one another. You might suggest that each family member write a short note to someone else in the family, thanking him or her for the kindness that he or she has shown.

JOHN STEPTOE

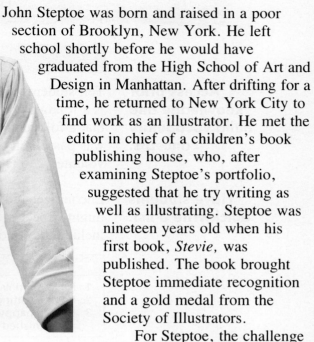

John Steptoe was born and raised in a poor section of Brooklyn, New York. He left school shortly before he would have graduated from the High School of Art and Design in Manhattan. After drifting for a time, he returned to New York City to find work as an illustrator. He met the editor in chief of a children's book publishing house, who, after examining Steptoe's portfolio, suggested that he try writing as well as illustrating. Steptoe was nineteen years old when his first book, *Stevie*, was published. The book brought Steptoe immediate recognition and a gold medal from the Society of Illustrators.

For Steptoe, the challenge to create children's books is fueled by a special concern for his readers. He explains, "Black children, all children, need good books. Good books are more than a luxury; they are a necessary part of a child's development and it's all of our jobs to see that we all get them."

ADDITIONAL READING

Other Books About Achievers

The Little Lame Prince by Rosemary Wells. Dial Books, 1990.   AVERAGE

My Sister, My Science Report by Margaret Bechard. Viking, 1990.   AVERAGE

Nothing's Fair in Fifth Grade by Barthe DeClements. Viking, 1981.   AVERAGE

The Present by Michael Emberley. Little, Brown, 1991.   AVERAGE

The Talking Eggs by Robert D. San Souci. Dial Books, 1989.   EASY

Part 1
Reading Literature

Building Background

Access prior knowledge and build vocabulary concepts.

Tell students that the next story, "Mufaro's Beautiful Daughters," is a folktale about the relationship between two sisters. Review that a folktale is a story that originally was not written down but was passed on orally from one storyteller to another. Call on volunteers to tell about folktales they have read or heard.

Have students quickwrite a list.

Encourage students to create and share a list of features they might expect to find in a folktale. The completed list might include the following:

Folktales
1. Have animals or objects acting like people
2. Have a setting in the country from which the story came
3. Have a happy ending, in which the good are rewarded and the bad are punished

Vocabulary Strategies

Introduce Key Words and strategies.

Display Transparency 49 or the following story. Have students use context clues with phonetic and structural analysis to decode and figure out the meanings of the underlined words. Ask volunteers to read each sentence aloud.

Transparency 49   Key Words

Sara is a <u>considerate</u> person who usually thinks of others before herself. Her sister Megan is usually in a bad <u>temper</u>, so she is often angry at others. People <u>praise</u> Sara for her kindness. She <u>acknowledges</u> their words with a smile and a "thank you." Their mother tries to <u>advise</u> Megan to say kind words, but Megan doesn't want to listen. Both sisters enjoy growing flowers and vegetables, but Sara's garden is more <u>bountiful</u>. Perhaps her plants produce more because of her kindness.

One night as Megan and Sara were talking, their mother saw them <u>silhouetted</u> against the window. She thought how alike they looked, yet she could see from the way Megan was standing that she was upset again.

CULTURAL AWARENESS

Students may be interested to learn that some familiar fairy tales are based on folktales. "Little Red Riding Hood" was an old folktale first published in France in 1697. "The Three Bears" first appeared in print in England between 1834 and 1847.

KEY WORDS

considerate
temper
praise
acknowledges
advise
bountiful
silhouetted

KEY WORDS DEFINED

considerate   thoughtful

temper   mood

praise   to express approval of

acknowledges   notices or recognizes

advise   to give advice or an opinion to

bountiful   plentiful, more than enough

silhouetted   outlined against a light background

Display the chart below. Have students read the Key Word and suggest words that are synonyms for it or words that are related to it. Then have students explain why they think their suggested words should be added to the second column.   STRATEGIES: SYNONYMS/PRIOR KNOWLEDGE

Key Words	Related Words
temper	(mood, sad, happy)
praise	(to express approval, think well of)
bountiful	(plentiful, more than enough)
considerate	(thoughtful, kind, sensitive)
silhouetted	(outlined against a light background, shadowy)
advise	(to give advice, to give an opinion)
acknowledges	(notices, recognizes)

GLOSSARY   Encourage students to refer to the Glossary to confirm or clarify their understanding of the new vocabulary.

**Integrate spelling
with vocabulary.**

SPELLING-VOCABULARY CONNECTION   *Integrated Spelling* page 65 reinforces spellings of suffixes in the Key Word *bountiful* and in other words. The spelling of the Key Word *temper* is also included.

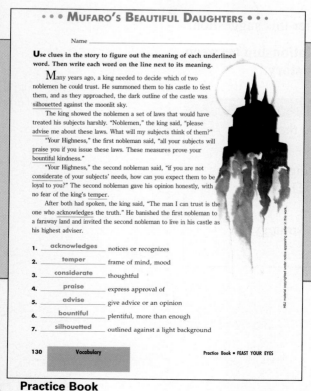

• • • MUFARO'S BEAUTIFUL DAUGHTERS • • •

Name _____

Use clues in the story to figure out the meaning of each underlined word. Then write each word on the line next to its meaning.

Many years ago, a king needed to decide which of two noblemen he could trust. He summoned them to his castle to test them, and as they approached, the dark outline of the castle was silhouetted against the moonlit sky.

The king showed the noblemen a set of laws that would have treated his subjects harshly. "Noblemen," the king said, "please advise me about these laws. What will my subjects think of them?"

"Your Highness," the first nobleman said, "all your subjects will praise you if you issue these laws. These measures prove your bountiful kindness."

"Your Highness," the second nobleman said, "if you are not considerate of your subjects' needs, how can you expect them to be loyal to you?" The second nobleman gave his opinion honestly, with no fear of the king's temper.

After both had spoken, the king said, "The man I can trust is the one who acknowledges the truth." He banished the first nobleman to a faraway land and invited the second nobleman to live in his castle as his highest adviser.

1. __acknowledges__ notices or recognizes
2. __temper__ frame of mind, mood
3. __considerate__ thoughtful
4. __praise__ express approval of
5. __advise__ give advice or an opinion
6. __bountiful__ plentiful, more than enough
7. __silhouetted__ outlined against a light background

130   Vocabulary   Practice Book • FEAST YOUR EYES

Practice Book

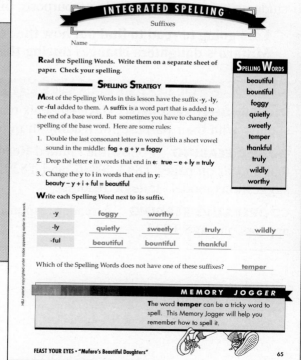

INTEGRATED SPELLING
Suffixes

Name _____

Read the Spelling Words. Write them on a separate sheet of paper. Check your spelling.

SPELLING STRATEGY

Most of the Spelling Words in this lesson have the suffix -y, -ly, or -ful added to them. A **suffix** is a word part that is added to the end of a base word. But sometimes you have to change the spelling of the base word. Here are some rules:

1. Double the last consonant letter in words with a short vowel sound in the middle: fog + g + y = foggy
2. Drop the letter e in words that end in e: true – e + ly = truly
3. Change the y to i in words that end in y: beauty – y + i + ful = beautiful

Write each Spelling Word next to its suffix.

-y	foggy	worthy		
-ly	quietly	sweetly	truly	wildly
-ful	beautiful	bountiful	thankful	

Which of the Spelling Words does not have one of these suffixes? __temper__

SPELLING WORDS
beautiful
bountiful
foggy
quietly
sweetly
temper
thankful
truly
wildly
worthy

MEMORY JOGGER

The word **temper** can be a tricky word to spell. This Memory Jogger will help you remember how to spell it.

FEAST YOUR EYES • "Mufaro's Beautiful Daughters"   65

Integrated Spelling

Strategic Reading

Preview and Predict

Help students preview the literature.

Have students locate "Mufaro's Beautiful Daughters" in the Table of Contents, and point out that the story was written and illustrated by John Steptoe. You may want to share with them the information about the author on page T829. Ask students who have read other stories by Steptoe to share what they recall.

Remind students that in addition to reading the title, looking at the illustrations, and reading the introductory paragraphs, they can use what they know about an author to make predictions about what they are going to read. Have students read the title and the first four paragraphs of the story.

Have students make predictions.

Ask students questions such as the following to help them make predictions about what might happen in the story:

- **What might happen to Manyara and Nyasha if good is rewarded and bad is punished in the story?**
- **What happy ending do you think the story might have?**

PERSONAL JOURNAL   Have students add their predictions about the selection to their personal journal. Ask students to support their predictions.

Setting a Purpose

Have students set purposes.

Discuss with students what they learned from previewing the story and what they know about folktales. Call on volunteers to explain the benefits of setting a purpose for reading. (It helps readers focus on important events and helps them adjust their reading rate.) Have students use their predictions to set a purpose for reading.

Model purpose-setting, if necessary.

If students have difficulty setting a purpose, offer this suggestion:

I am going to read to find out how the relationship between Mufaro's daughters changes during this story.

OPTIONS FOR READING

INDEPENDENT READING   Have students read the story silently with their purpose for reading in mind.

GUIDED READING   Follow the Guided Reading suggestions that appear on pages T833, T836, and T839. These suggestions model strategic reading.

COOPERATIVE READING   A reader response strategy appears on page T833.

SECOND-LANGUAGE SUPPORT   Have students use the illustrations to preview the story and make predictions. Ask them to determine where and when the story takes place and what kind of story they think it is. (See Second-Language Support Manual.)

JOHN STEPTOE

Mufaro's Beautiful Daughters

AN AFRICAN TALE

CALDECOTT
HONOR
ALA NOTABLE
BOOK
BOSTON GLOBE-
HORN BOOK
AWARD

A LONG TIME AGO, in a certain place in Africa, a small village lay across a river and half a day's journey from a city where a great king lived. A man named Mufaro lived in this village with his two daughters, who were called Manyara and Nyasha. Everyone agreed that Manyara and Nyasha were very beautiful. Manyara was almost always in a bad temper. She teased her sister whenever their father's back was turned, and she had been heard to say, "Someday, Nyasha, I will be a queen, and you will be a servant in my household."

"If that should come to pass," Nyasha responded, "I will be pleased to serve you. But why do you say such things? You are clever and strong and beautiful. Why are you so unhappy?"

467

Guided Reading

SET PURPOSE/PREDICT: PAGES 466–472   Have students read through page 472 to find out what Manyara does to try to become queen and whom she meets.

Cooperative Reading

READER RESPONSE STRATEGY: PAGES 466–479 Have students work in pairs. Ask each pair to decide whether they will read silently or aloud and how frequently they will stop. At designated stopping points, each member of the pair should respond freely to what they have read so far. Have pairs continue the procedure until they reach the end of the story and then discuss it as a whole. (Response Card 7: Responding Freely, on page R68, gives complete directions for using the strategy.)

"Because everyone talks about how kind *you* are, and they praise everything you do," Manyara replied. "I'm certain that Father loves you best. But when I am a queen, everyone will know that your silly kindness is only weakness."

Nyasha was sad that Manyara felt this way, but she ignored her sister's words and went about her chores. Nyasha kept a small plot of land, on which she grew millet, sunflowers, yams, and vegetables. She always sang as she worked, and some said it was her singing that made her crops more bountiful than anyone else's.

One day, Nyasha noticed a small garden snake resting beneath a yam vine. "Good day, little Nyoka," she called to him. "You are welcome here. You will keep away any creatures who might spoil

my vegetables." She bent forward, gave the little snake a loving pat on the head, and then returned to her work.

From that day on, Nyoka was always at Nyasha's side when she tended her garden. It was said that she sang all the more sweetly when he was there.

Mufaro knew nothing of how Manyara treated Nyasha. Nyasha was too considerate of her father's feelings to complain, and Manyara was always careful to behave herself when Mufaro was around.

Expanding the Literature **What do you learn about Nyasha from the way she treats Nyoka?** (She is kind and gentle.) INFERENTIAL: DETERMINING CHARACTERS' TRAITS

What clues does the author give that the snake might be important in the story? (Nyasha pats him; he is always at her side; she sings more sweetly when he is around.) INFERENTIAL: MAKING PREDICTIONS

468

Early one morning, a messenger from the city arrived. The Great King wanted a wife. "The Most Worthy and Beautiful Daughters in the Land are invited to appear before the King, and he will choose one to become Queen!" the messenger proclaimed.

Mufaro called Manyara and Nyasha to him. "It would be a great honor to have one of you chosen," he said. "Prepare yourselves to journey to the city. I will call together all our friends to make a wedding party. We will leave tomorrow as the sun rises."

"But, my father," Manyara said sweetly, "it would be painful for either of us to leave you, even to be wife to the king. I know Nyasha would grieve to death if she were parted from you. I am strong. Send me to the city, and let poor Nyasha be happy here with you."

Mufaro beamed with pride. "The king has asked for the most worthy and the most beautiful. No, Manyara, I cannot send you alone. Only a king can choose between two such worthy daughters. Both of you must go!"

That night, when everyone was asleep, Manyara stole quietly out of the village. She had never been in the forest at night before, and she was frightened, but her greed to be the first to appear before the king drove her on. In her hurry, she almost stumbled over a small boy who suddenly appeared, standing in the path.

"Please," said the boy. "I am hungry. Will you give me something to eat?"

"I have brought only enough for myself," Manyara replied.

"But, please!" said the boy. "I am so *very* hungry."

"Out of my way, boy! Tomorrow I will become your queen. How dare you stand in my path?"

Second-Language Support

Students may need help understanding the word *stole* as it is used here. Remind students that many words in English have multiple meanings. Explain that *stole* can mean "took something without permission" or "moved quietly without being noticed." Ask volunteers to pantomime how they think Manyara stole out of the village.

Teaching Tip

Point out the author's use of capital letters in the words *The Great King* on page 470. Explain that the capital letters show the reader that the words are important and are considered a title. Have students locate another example on this page. *(The Most Worthy and Beautiful Daughters in the Land)*

After traveling for what seemed to be a great distance, Manyara came to a small clearing. There, silhouetted against the moonlight, was an old woman seated on a large stone.

The old woman spoke. "I will give you some advice, Manyara. Soon after you pass the place where two paths cross, you will see a grove of trees. They will laugh at you. You must not laugh in return. Later, you will meet a man with his head under his arm. You must be polite to him."

"How do you know my name? How dare you advise your future queen? Stand aside, you ugly old woman!" Manyara scolded, and then rushed on her way without looking back.

472

Just as the old woman had foretold, Manyara came to a grove of trees, and they did indeed seem to be laughing at her.

"I must be calm," Manyara thought. "I will *not* be frightened." She looked up at the trees and laughed out loud. "I laugh at you, trees!" she shouted, and she hurried on.

It was not yet dawn when Manyara heard the sound of rushing water. "The river must be up ahead," she thought. "The great city is just on the other side."

But there, on the rise, she saw a man with his head tucked under his arm. Manyara ran past him without speaking. "A queen acknowledges only those who please her," she said to herself. "I will be queen. I will be queen," she chanted, as she hurried on toward the city.

Guided Reading

MONITOR COMPREHENSION: PAGES 466–472
What does Manyara do to try to become queen?
(First, Manyara tries to trick her father into deciding that only she will appear before the king. Then she leaves at night ahead of the others so she might be the first to meet him.) STRATEGIC READING: RETURNING TO PURPOSE

Why do Nyasha and Manyara plan to journey to the city? (The king has invited the daughters of the land to appear before him, and he will choose one of them to become queen.) STRATEGIC READING: SUMMARIZING

SET PURPOSE/PREDICT: PAGES 473–479 Have students predict whether Manyara will get her wish and become queen. Have students read the rest of the story to confirm their predictions.

...asha woke at the first light of dawn. As she put on ...est garments, she thought how her life might be ...d forever beyond this day. "I'd much prefer to live ... she admitted to herself. "I'd hate to leave this ... and never see my father or sing to little Nyoka ...

...r thoughts were interrupted by loud shouts and a ...tion from the wedding party assembled outside. ...ra was missing! Everyone bustled about, searching ...lling for her. When they found her footprints on ...th that led to the city, they decided to go on as ...d.

... the wedding party moved through the forest, ...y plumed birds darted about in the cool green ...s beneath the trees. Though anxious about her ...Nyasha was soon filled with excitement about all ...as to see.

They were deep in the forest when she saw the small boy standing by the side of the path.

"You must be hungry," she said, and handed him a yam she had brought for her lunch. The boy smiled and disappeared as quietly as he had come.

Later, as they were approaching the place where the two paths crossed, the old woman appeared and silently pointed the way to the city. Nyasha thanked her and gave her a small pouch filled with sunflower seeds.

The sun was high in the sky when the party came to the grove of towering trees. Their uppermost branches seemed to bow down to Nyasha as she passed beneath them.

At last, someone announced that they were near their destination.

475

Vocabulary Strategy   How can you figure out the meaning of the word *garments* on page 474? (When I read, I use context clues and also visualize the events being described. By doing this, I realize that it is early in the morning and that Nyasha is getting ready to go to the city to meet the king. When she is putting on her "finest garments," she must be putting on her best clothes. *Garments* must mean "clothes.")   STRATEGY: CONTEXT CLUES

Nyasha ran ahead and topped the rise before the others could catch up with her. She stood transfixed at her first sight of the city. "Oh, my father," she called. "A great spirit must stand guard here! Just look at what lies before us. I never in all my life dreamed there could be anything so beautiful!"

Arm in arm, Nyasha and her father descended the hill, crossed the river, and approached the city gate. Just as they entered through the great doors, the air was rent by piercing cries, and Manyara ran wildly out of a chamber at the center of the enclosure. When she saw Nyasha, she fell upon her, sobbing.

"Do not go to the king, my sister. Oh, please, Father, do not let her go!" she cried hysterically. "There's a great monster there, a snake with five heads! He said that he knew all my faults and that I displeased him. He would have swallowed me alive if I had not run. Oh, my sister, please do not go inside that place."

It frightened Nyasha to see her sister so upset. But, leaving her father to comfort Manyara, she bravely made her way to the chamber and opened the door.

On the seat of the great chief's stool lay the little garden snake. Nyasha laughed with relief and joy.

"My little friend!" she exclaimed. "It's such a pleasure to see you, but why are you here?"

"I am the king," Nyoka replied.

And there, before Nyasha's eyes, the garden snake changed shape.

Expanding the Literature   Why is Manyara's concern for her sister unusual? (She is usually selfish and mean, but here she wants to protect Nyasha.)   INFERENTIAL: DRAWING CONCLUSIONS

What clues in the illustrations help you determine the time and setting of this folktale? (Accept reasonable responses: The exotic plants reflect a rain forest or jungle setting; the rich clothing reflects an African setting; the unusual castle reflects a time long ago.)   CRITICAL: AUTHOR'S CRAFT/APPRECIATING ART

"I am the king. I am also the hungry boy with whom you shared a yam in the forest and the old woman to whom you made a gift of sunflower seeds. But you know me best as Nyoka. Because I have been all of these, I know you to be the Most Worthy and Most Beautiful Daughter in the Land. It would make me very happy if you would be my wife."

And so it was that, a long time ago, Nyasha agreed to be married. The king's mother and sisters took Nyasha to their house, and the wedding preparations began. The best weavers in the land laid out their finest cloth for her wedding garments. Villagers from all around were invited to the celebration, and a great feast was held. Nyasha prepared the bread for the wedding feast from millet that had been brought from her village.

Mufaro proclaimed to all who would hear him that he was the happiest father in all the land, for he was blessed with two beautiful and worthy daughters—Nyasha, the queen; and Manyara, a servant in the queen's household.

THINK IT OVER

1. *Do you think Mufaro's daughters were beautiful? Explain your answer.*

2. *Why was Manyara unhappy?*

3. *How did the king know to choose Nyasha for his queen?*

4. *When you are courteous or kind to others, do you expect a reward? Explain your answer.*

WRITE

Write a short folktale, using a classic tale like "Cinderella" as a model. Use your town or city for the setting.

479

MONITOR COMPREHENSION: PAGES 473–479
Does Manyara get her wish and become queen? (no) **Is that what you predicted would happen?** (Responses will vary.)   STRATEGIC READING: CONFIRMING PREDICTIONS

How does Nyasha react to each of the unusual characters she meets while traveling to see the king? (She gives food to the boy; she is polite to the old woman. She is brave when she expects to confront a monster.)   STRATEGIC READING: SUMMARIZING

Returning to the Predictions   Invite students to discuss the predictions that they made before they began reading and that they may have written in their personal journals. Ask them to talk about how those predictions changed as they read the story.

Returning to the Purpose for Reading
Ask students how the relationship between the two daughters has changed by the end of the story. (Manyara wanted to become queen and make Nyasha her servant. Manyara always thought of herself first until she was terrified by the monster and feared for Nyasha's safety. At the end of the story, Manyara is a servant in Nyasha's house.)

NOTE: Responses to the Think It Over questions and support for the Write activity appear on page T840.

Part 2
Responding to Literature

Story Follow-Up

Think it Over

Encourage reader's response: student page 479.

1. **Do you think Mufaro's daughters were beautiful? Explain your answer.** (Accept reasonable responses: Both daughters were beautiful in appearance; Nyasha's kindness added to her beauty.) CRITICAL: MAKING JUDGMENTS

2. **Why was Manyara unhappy?** (She was jealous of her sister. She thought her father loved Nyasha more.) INFERENTIAL: DETERMINING CHARACTERS' TRAITS

3. **How did the king know to choose Nyasha for his queen?** (In disguises, he had observed Nyasha's kindness and gentleness.) LITERAL: RECOGNIZING CAUSE-EFFECT

4. **When you are courteous or kind to others, do you expect a reward? Explain your answer.** (Accept reasonable responses: No, people can be kind without expecting rewards.) CRITICAL: EXPRESSING PERSONAL OPINIONS

Write

Encourage writer's response: student page 479.

Write a short folktale, using a classic tale like "Cinderella" as a model. Use your town or city for the setting. Remind students to include information that tells what their story characters are like. CREATIVE: INVENTING A FOLKTALE

Summarizing the Literature

Have students retell the story and write a summary.

Encourage students to summarize the story by recalling key story elements. Guide students in beginning the story frame below, and have them complete it independently. (See *Practice Book* page 131 on T841.) Students may use their completed story frames to retell the story and to write a brief summary statement.

> This story takes place (long ago, in Africa.)

> First we meet two sisters, (Nyasha and Manyara.)

> Nyasha is (beautiful and kind.)

> Manyara is (beautiful and mean.)

> One day the king announces (that he will choose a queen.)

STRATEGY CONFERENCE

Discuss with students how previewing and making predictions helped them understand, remember, and appreciate the selection. Invite students to share other reading strategies, such as visualizing, that helped them understand what they read.

NOTE

An additional writing activity for this selection appears on page T843.

Appreciating Literature

Have students share personal responses.

Have students work in small groups to discuss the story. Provide a general question such as the following to help the groups begin:

- **Would you change the ending of this story in any way? Explain how you would change it and why.**

PERSONAL JOURNAL   Have students use their personal journals to write about ideas and feelings that are discussed in the groups. You may also refer them to their personal journals after they complete the activities below.

Critical Thinking Activities

Encourage both cooperative and individual responses.

DISCUSS IDEAS   Do you think Manyara gets what she deserves? Explain your answer. Have students work in groups to discuss their ideas.   CRITICAL: MAKING JUDGMENTS

WRITE A STORY   Do you think Manyara might act differently in the future? Explain your opinions. Have students work in small groups to develop ideas for a sequel to this story in which Manyara demonstrates what her attitude might be like after working as a servant in Nyasha's house. Help students begin their sequels by asking questions such as these:

- **What problems might arise after Nyasha is queen?**
- **How might the problems affect Manyara?**

After students have discussed these story elements, have them write their sequels.   CREATIVE: INVENTING NEW SCENES

The KING'S CHOICE

When the king chooses Nyasha to be the queen, he probably makes a speech to the people. He would want to explain what it is about Nyasha that makes her the most beautiful and most worthy daughter in the land. If you were in the king's place, what would you say?

My People,

I, _____ (your name), thank you.

Response to Literature   FEAST YOUR EYES   HBJ Writer's Journal   "Mufaro's Beautiful Daughters"   91

Writer's Journal

• • • MUFARO'S BEAUTIFUL DAUGHTERS • • •

Name _____

Finish the story frame below by completing each sentence. Possible responses are given.

This story takes place **long ago, in Africa.**
First we meet two sisters, **Nyasha and Manyara.**
Nyasha is **beautiful and kind.**
Manyara is **beautiful and mean.**
One day the king announces **that he will choose a queen.**
After that, Manyara leaves **in the middle of the night to try to reach the king ahead of Nyasha.**
Along the way, Manyara is unkind to **everyone she meets.**
On her journey, Nyasha treats everyone she meets with **respect and kindness.**
At the gate of the city Manyara is terrified because **a monster greets her and tells her he knows all her faults.**
Nyasha goes to face the monster and finds **the snake that has kept her company in the garden is the king, and he wants to marry her.**
Manyara becomes **a servant in the royal household.**

Write a brief summary statement about the story. A possible response is given.
The king marries Nyasha because of her kindness to others, but Manyara becomes a servant in Nyasha's household because of her meanness to others.

Practice Book ■ FEAST YOUR EYES   Summarizing the Literature   131

Practice Book

Reviewing Key Words

Display the Key Words, and have students answer the following questions, orally or in writing:

1. *temper* **Which daughter is always in a bad temper?** (Manyara)
2. *praise* **Which daughter earns praise for her kindness?** (Nyasha)
3. *advise* **Which daughter becomes angry when someone tries to advise her about traveling to the city?** (Manyara)
4. *considerate* **Which daughter is too considerate of her father's feelings to complain?** (Nyasha)
5. *silhouetted* **Which daughter is the first to see an old woman silhouetted in the moonlight?** (Manyara)
6. *bountiful* **Which daughter is known for her rich, bountiful crops?** (Nyasha)
7. *acknowledges* **Which daughter claims that a queen speaks to or acknowledges only those who please her?** (Manyara)

Extending Vocabulary

ADJECTIVES Point out that the author uses the words *beautiful, kind,* and *greedy* to describe Mufaro's daughters. Remind students that words used to describe are called *adjectives*. On the board, draw a web similar to the following, and model where to place each adjective.

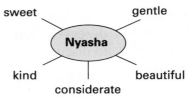

Have students search the story for other examples or think of their own adjectives to describe Nyasha. Next, remind students that authors often reveal information about characters by telling what a character thinks or does. Encourage students to think of a situation that might demonstrate each adjective they suggest. Invite volunteers to act out their situation and behavior as the others guess which adjective is being presented.

PRACTICE BOOK
page 132: Writing adjectives

••• MUFARO'S BEAUTIFUL DAUGHTERS •••

Name _____

A. On each line, write an adjective that could be added to the sentence. **Possible responses are given.**

1. One day, Nyasha noticed a small garden snake resting beneath a ___twisting___ yam vine.
2. Nyoka spent many days in the ___colorful___ garden while Nyasha tended it.
3. The Great King chose a ___young___ messenger to spread a message throughout the kingdom.
4. The Great King wanted a ___worthy___ wife.
5. A ___starving___ boy asked Manyara for some food.
6. "Tomorrow I will become your ___honored___ queen."

B. Write a sentence about each of the following characters and objects. Use at least three adjectives in each sentence, and circle them. **Sentences will vary. Possible adjectives are given.**

1. Mufaro: ___proud, loving, kind___
2. Nyoka: ___friendly, quiet, smart___
3. yams: ___sweet, orange, tasty___

132　Adjectives　Practice Book ▪ FEAST YOUR EYES

Practice Book

T842 / *FEAST YOUR EYES,* UNIT 6

Integrated Language Arts

READING

Oral Rereading/ Storytelling

Remind students that folktales like the one they just read were originally stories that were not written down but were passed on orally from storyteller to storyteller. Have students reread the story silently and then try telling it in their own words. Encourage students to add their own special touches to the story by adding or taking away descriptions, events, and characters. After students rehearse, invite them to present the story to others or to tape-record their presentation for a listening-center library. LISTENING/SPEAKING/READING

WRITING

Writing About the Literature

WRITE A LETTER Review with students Nyasha's daily activities when she lived in the village. Ask students to brainstorm what Nyasha's daily activities in the city might be. Have students write a letter from Nyasha to her father, telling about her new daily activities as queen. Suggest that students use a time line such as the following to list daily activities in the order in which they will happen. READING/WRITING

Nyasha's Daily Activities

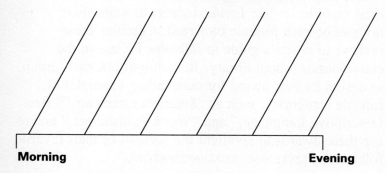

Morning   Evening

NOTE: An additional writing activity appears on page T840.

SPELLING

Reviewing Spelling Words

SPELLING WORDS: *beautiful, bountiful, foggy, quietly, sweetly, temper, thankful, truly, wildly, worthy*

Make word cards for each of the base words in the spelling list. As you hold up each card ask students to add one of the suffixes *-ly, -y, -ful* to the word, writing the new word next to the base word. Finally, have students describe the strategies they used to add each suffix to the word. LISTENING/SPEAKING/READING/ WRITING/SPELLING

INTEGRATED SPELLING page 66: Writing words with suffixes

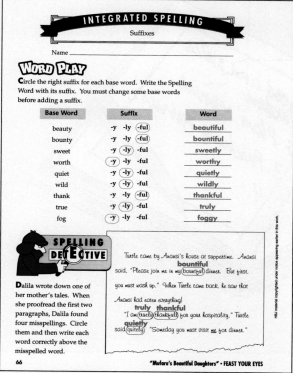

Integrated Spelling

SPEAKING

It's How You Say It!

Ask students to think about the differences between the personalities of Nyasha and Manyara. Point out that actors and actresses often rely on the tone of their voice to convey a message about their character's personality. Have students reread the story to locate passages in which the main characters are speaking. Encourage them to rehearse saying these words in the tone of voice they think the story character might have used. Then ask volunteers to read their favorite passages to the others.
LISTENING/SPEAKING/READING

WRITING

Details! Details!

AVAILABLE ON PROJECT CARD

COOPERATIVE LEARNING   Have students work in small groups to consider how Manyara might complete a series of journal entries for the first few months after she has become a servant in her sister's household. Suggest that students consider Manyara's thoughts regarding herself, her sister, her life in the royal household, and her father, and any other ideas that might reflect changes in Manyara's character. Each student in a group can write one day's journal entry. Have groups share their completed journals.
LISTENING/SPEAKING/WRITING/READING

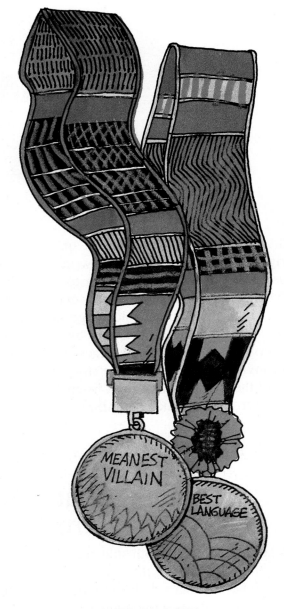

LISTENING

Tops in Tales

COOPERATIVE LEARNING   Have students form small groups to share their favorite folktales. Group members should take turns reading to the group one or more of their favorite stories. Invite students to write short reviews of each folktale they read. Combine these reviews to create a guide to folktales for use in the classroom or school library. In addition, ask each group to design its own award for outstanding examples of folktale categories, such as "Smartest Character," "Best Descriptive Language," and "Worst Punishment," and to use these awards to spotlight the reviews of their favorite folktales.   LISTENING/READING/WRITING

WRITING

Queen Wanted— Apply Within

Remind students that when the king was ready to marry, he sent his messenger throughout the kingdom to advertise his intentions. Suggest that the king's campaign might have been more efficient if he had used the want ads in the local newspaper instead. Ask students to write a humorous advertisement for the king. Have students begin by brainstorming a list of queenly qualifications. Provide examples of want ads for students to use as models, pointing out that such advertisements are usually brief. Have students assemble their completed advertisements on a want-ads page. SPEAKING/READING/WRITING

SPEAKING

Beauty Is . . .

Remind students that Mufaro considered both of his daughters beautiful. Encourage students to discuss their ideas about what makes a person beautiful. Then have them write lists of their ideas. Suggest that they begin with the following sentence stem: *You can tell a beautiful person by. . . .* Have students select their best idea and illustrate it on a large sheet of paper. Invite volunteers to share their completed work with the others and to explain why they selected this idea.

LISTENING/SPEAKING/WRITING

SPEAKING

Puppet Theater
AVAILABLE ON PROJECT CARD

CULTURAL AWARENESS Invite students to re-create the story of "Mufaro's Beautiful Daughters" using stick puppets that they make themselves. Have students research the region of southern Africa where the story originated, Zimbabwe, so that their scenery and props will look authentic. Students may wish to rewrite the folktale as a play and rehearse their performance before presenting it to the others. LISTENING/SPEAKING/READING/WRITING

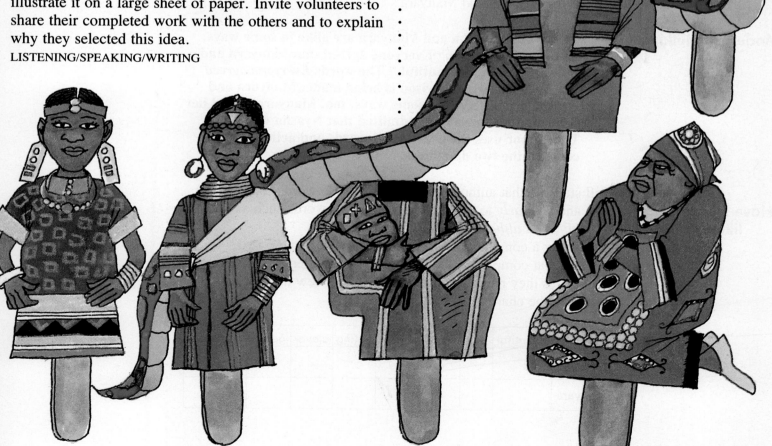

MUFARO'S BEAUTIFUL DAUGHTERS / **T845**

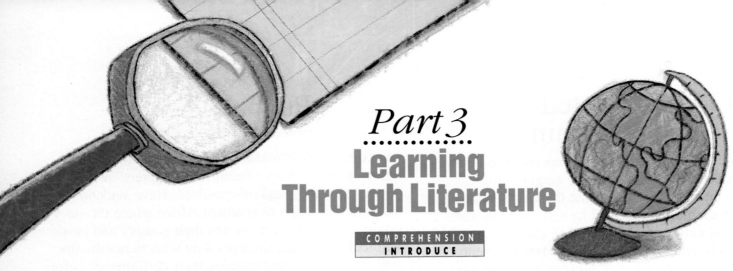

Part 3
Learning Through Literature

COMPREHENSION
INTRODUCE

Comparing and Contrasting
OBJECTIVE: *To determine likenesses and differences*

1	Focus

Discuss the value of comparing and contrasting.

Have students recall the opening of the story in which the author describes the characters of Nyasha and Manyara. Point out that being able to identify ways in which characters are alike and different will help students understand what they read.

2	Teach/Model

Teach the strategy.

Explain to students that as readers, they need to be aware of what things are being compared and contrasted and to think about how those things are alike or different. Model comparing and contrasting Nyasha and Manyara:

Model the thinking.

> **I know that Nyasha and Manyara are alike in some ways. As the author states, "Everyone agreed that Manyara and Nyasha were very beautiful." The words *Everyone agreed* are clues that a comparison is being made. Manyara and Nyasha are different in some ways, too. Manyara teased her sister in a mean way but admitted that Nyasha was kind. The author uses the characters' words and actions to contrast the two daughters.**

Strategy: Have students find likenesses and differences.

Tell students that authors will sometimes use words such as *also, too,* and *similarly* to signal comparison and words such as *but, yet, still,* and *although* to signal contrast.

Draw a comparison-and-contrast matrix on the board. Explain that completing the chart will help students compare and contrast as they read. Work as a group to review the story and to complete the chart.

	beautiful	kind	mean	greedy	young	clever	gentle	dishonest
Nyasha	✓	✓			✓	✓	✓	
Manyara	✓		✓	✓	✓	✓		✓

Have students apply the learning.

COOPERATIVE LEARNING Suggest that students work in pairs and use the comparison-and-contrast matrix to complete the Venn diagram that follows:

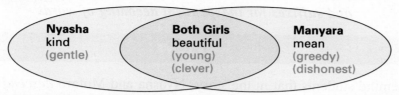

Nyasha
kind
(gentle)

Both Girls
beautiful
(young)
(clever)

Manyara
mean
(greedy)
(dishonest)

4 Summarize

Informally assess the learning.

Have students use their Venn diagram to compose sentences comparing and contrasting the characters of Nyasha and Manyara.

Have students summarize what they have learned. (To compare and contrast, think about how two or more people or things are alike or different. Some words signal comparison and contrast.)

READER ⟷ WRITER CONNECTION

Comparing and Contrasting

▶ **Writers** include dialogue and action, as well as signal words, to help readers compare and contrast.

▶ **Readers** decide how characters in a story are alike and different so they can better understand the characters.

WRITE PARAGRAPHS Have students analyze a series of photographs and write a paragraph of comparison and a paragraph of contrast.

MEETING INDIVIDUAL NEEDS

RETEACH Follow the **visual, auditory,** and **kinesthetic/motor** models on page R52.

CHALLENGE Have students choose two characters from other folktales they know and list ways the characters are alike and different. Then have students use their lists to write a paragraph comparing and contrasting the characters.

SECOND-LANGUAGE SUPPORT Students can demonstrate their understanding by composing sentences using these words that signal likenesses: *similarly, also, and, too*; and these words that signal differences: *although, but, unlike, yet.* (See Second-Language Support Manual.)

WRITER'S JOURNAL page 92: Writing comparisons and contrasts

PRACTICE BOOK page 133: Comparing and contrasting

Only one of the pictures in rows 2 and 3 matches the one in row 1. Which picture is it? Write two paragraphs. In the first, tell which details are different in some pictures. In the second, tell which details are the same in the matching pair.

3. MATCH THE MOUNTAIN CLIMBERS

by _____
(your name)

92 "Mufaro's Beautiful Daughters"   HBJ Writer's Journal   FEAST YOUR EYES   Comparing and Contrasting

Writer's Journal

• • • MUFARO'S BEAUTIFUL DAUGHTERS • • •

Name _____

Read the paragraph below. Draw a line around the word that gives a clue that two elements are being compared. Underline each word or phrase that gives a clue that two elements are being contrasted. Then answer the questions that follow.

Manyara was a beautiful young woman, and her sister Nyasha was beautiful, (too.) Their personalities, however, were quite different from each other. Manyara was almost always in a bad mood. Her sister, on the other hand, was usually in a good mood. Manyara was always mean to her sister, but Nyasha was always kind.

1. What is alike about the two sisters? _Both of them are beautiful._

2. What is different about them? _Manyara is usually in a bad mood, whereas Nyasha is usually in a good mood. Manyara is mean to her sister, but Nyasha is kind._

SUMMARIZING *the* **L**EARNING

1. As I read, I compare in order to identify how two things are _alike_. Sometimes a writer uses a signal word or phrase, such as _similarly, also, too, in the same way_, to show a comparison.

2. When I read, I contrast in order to identify how two things are _different_. Sometimes a writer uses a signal word or phrase, such as _but, yet, still, although, however, on the other hand_, to show a contrast.

Practice Book ▪ FEAST YOUR EYES   Comparing and Contrasting   **133**

Practice Book

Structural Analysis

OBJECTIVE: *To use Greek and Latin roots, prefixes, and suffixes for independent decoding of words*

Review

Review how to recognize prefixes, suffixes, and roots.

Remind students that in the story, Nyasha and Mufaro *descend* the hill. Display the diagram below, and model how to figure out the pronunciation and meaning of the word *descend*.

Prefix/Suffix *de-* "down"		Latin Root *scandere* "to climb"		Meaning *descend* "to climb down"
	+		+	

Practice/Apply

Have students apply the learning.

Ask volunteers to determine the pronunciations and meanings of each of the following words and add them to the diagram: *vision* (*visus*, "see," + *-ion*, "act of or result of") *disappear* (*dis-*, "not," + *apparēre*, "to show oneself")

Summarize

Informally assess the learning.

Discuss with students their diagrams and how they determined the pronunciations and meanings for the words.

Have students summarize. (Prefixes, suffixes, and roots can help you figure out the pronunciations and meanings of words.)

CHALLENGE Encourage students to work in pairs to search this story or previously read stories for words with prefixes, suffixes, or roots. Ask students to identify the word parts and to determine the meanings and pronunciations. Suggest that students then check a dictionary.

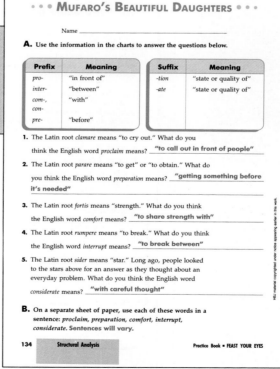

PRACTICE BOOK
page 134: Using prefixes, suffixes, and roots

Practice Book

* * * MUFARO'S BEAUTIFUL DAUGHTERS * * *

Name _____

A. Use the information in the charts to answer the questions below.

Prefix	Meaning
pro-	"in front of"
inter-	"between"
com-, con-	"with"
pre-	"before"

Suffix	Meaning
-tion	"state or quality of"
-ate	"state or quality of"

1. The Latin root *clamare* means "to cry out." What do you think the English word *proclaim* means? "to call out in front of people"

2. The Latin root *parare* means "to get" or "to obtain." What do you think the English word *preparation* means? "getting something before it's needed"

3. The Latin root *fortis* means "strength." What do you think the English word *comfort* means? "to share strength with"

4. The Latin root *rumpere* means "to break." What do you think the English word *interrupt* means? "to break between"

5. The Latin root *sider* means "star." Long ago, people looked to the stars above for an answer as they thought about an everyday problem. What do you think the English word *considerate* means? "with careful thought"

B. On a separate sheet of paper, use each of these words in a sentence: *proclaim, preparation, comfort, interrupt, considerate.* Sentences will vary.

134   Structural Analysis   Practice Book ▪ FEAST YOUR EYES

Cause and Effect

OBJECTIVE: *To determine cause-and-effect relationships*

Review

Have students identify effects with multiple causes.

Remind students that sometimes authors tell about events that happen, or *effects,* that are the result of several reasons, or *causes*. Ask students how to identify cause-and-effect relationships. Using the following diagram, model how to identify several causes and one effect.

Cause		Effect
Everyone talks about how kind Nyasha is.	↘	Manyara is jealous of Nyasha.
People praise Nyasha.	→	
Manyara thinks her father loves Nyasha more.	↗	

Practice/Apply

Have students apply the learning.

Have students use other story information to complete cause-and-effect diagrams. Ask them to share their ideas.

Summarize

Informally assess the learning.

Using the completed diagrams, ask questions such as: "What caused _____ ?" or "What happened when _____?"

Have students summarize what they learned. (An effect can have multiple causes.)

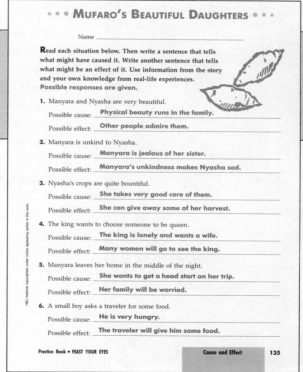

Practice Book

PRACTICE BOOK
page 135: Determining cause-effect relationships

Integrated Curriculum

SOCIAL STUDIES

Happy Trails

Encourage students to visualize information from the story so they can create an illustrated map of the area in which this story takes place. Have them label important landmarks in Mufaro's village and identify the route that might be taken to the king's city. Encourage students to share their completed maps and to explain any symbols they used.
LISTENING/SPEAKING/READING/WRITING

SCIENCE

How Does Your Garden Grow?

COOPERATIVE LEARNING   Have students recall that in the story, Nyasha grows yams in her small garden. Invite pairs of students to grow their yams or white potatoes in a window garden at school. Sprout the vegetable by suspending it with toothpicks from the mouth of a jar of water so that the tip of the vegetable just touches the water. Have partners observe their vegetables daily as roots and leaves begin to appear. Encourage students to research and write about other methods of sprouting vegetables and to present a set of directions to the others.
LISTENING/SPEAKING/READING/WRITING

SOCIAL STUDIES

Not Just Another Cinderella Story!

AVAILABLE ON PROJECT CARD

CULTURAL AWARENESS   Tell students that the story they just read is a folktale from an African country now known as Zimbabwe. Help students locate Zimbabwe on a world map. Remind students that different countries may have similar folktales. Have groups of students research folktales from other countries to find examples of stories in which two brothers, two sisters, or a brother and a sister are the main characters. Have students locate on the world map the country where their tale originated. Invite groups to read their stories aloud or to dramatize them for the others.   LISTENING/SPEAKING/READING

MATH

Are We There Yet?

COOPERATIVE LEARNING Have students work in small groups to discuss how they might use story clues to estimate the distance from Mufaro's village to the king's city. Have groups share their ideas. Then show students that they can base their estimate on the amount of time they think Mufaro and Nyasha spent walking and the time it takes to walk a mile. Then have students estimate the distance by multiplying the number of hours they think the journey took by an average rate of four miles per hour. Invite volunteers to share their estimate and their reasons with the others. LISTENING/SPEAKING/READING

ART

Dream Weavers

AVAILABLE ON PROJECT CARD

CULTURAL AWARENESS Remind students that at the end of the story, the "best weavers in the land laid out their finest cloth" for Nyasha's wedding garments. Have students ask the librarian to help them research the patterns used by the various craftspeople who live in the sub-Saharan region of Africa, and have them draw pictures of these patterns. Then have students use the patterns to design their own weaving. Some students may wish to try weaving on a cardboard loom. Invite volunteers to give directions for making and using a cardboard loom. LISTENING/SPEAKING/READING

SOCIAL STUDIES

Our African Heritage

CULTURAL AWARENESS Remind students that this folktale came to the United States as part of the African culture. Encourage students to explore foods, customs, expressions, and other aspects of our culture that can trace their roots back to African cultures. After students have completed their research, invite them to share their information in a report. LISTENING/SPEAKING/READING/WRITING

Hail to the Chief!

READ ALOUD TO STUDENTS:

WOMEN HAVE A LONG AND CELEBRATED HISTORY AS

RULERS. The first great woman ruler was Queen Hatshepsut of Egypt, who reigned in that African kingdom from 1503 to 1483 B.C. She sent large trading missions to foreign lands, and had magnificent temples constructed at home.

Thousands of years later, in the late nineteenth century, Queen Liliuokalani (lee-LEE-oo-oh-kah-LAH-nee) of Hawaii fought to prevent American sugar planters from seizing control of the island's lucrative sugar plantations. Another strong leader was Golda Meir. In 1973, Israeli premier Golda Meir (1898–1978) led her country to victory in the Yom Kippur War.

In 1979, Margaret Thatcher (1925–) became the first female prime minister of Great Britain. During her eleven-year tenure in office, she fought to reverse her country's economic decline. ■

Queen Hatshepsut, Golda Meir, Queen Liliuokalani, and Margaret Thatcher have led their countries to greatness.

ACTIVITY CORNER

■ Have students work in groups to locate information about other famous women rulers, such as Queen Elizabeth I of England and Indira Gandhi of India. Have students use their research to write a brief biography highlighting the important events in their subject's life.

■ Hold monthly elections for class officers. Have students campaign on specific platforms, debate the issues, run the election, and then hold office. To give everyone a chance to serve, each student should hold office only once. You may wish to have students discuss the leadership qualities necessary for various positions in student government.

Words About the Author and Illustrator:
John Steptoe

Reading the Article

Help students set a purpose for reading.

Remind students that John Steptoe both wrote and illustrated "Mufaro's Beautiful Daughters." Encourage them to share what they especially liked about the illustrations and the story. Then discuss with students what they think Steptoe had to know in order to write the story and draw the pictures. Point out that they are going to read an article about John Steptoe. Suggest that students read to find out more about Steptoe's approach to his art and writing.

Responding to the Article

Return to the purpose for reading.

Invite students to explain what they learned about John Steptoe's art and writing from the article. Ask them whether they were surprised to find out how long Steptoe spent writing and illustrating "Mufaro's Beautiful Daughters."

Encourage students to share other things they learned that they found especially interesting. Ask them to tell whether they believe Steptoe achieved in "Mufaro's Beautiful Daughters" his goal of encouraging children to take pride in themselves and to seek opportunities.

Encourage students to respond creatively.

You may wish to select one of the following activities for responding to the article:

DRAWING A PICTURE Discuss with students the colors and the style of painting John Steptoe used in his illustrations. Provide students with art materials, such as paper, paints, and brushes, and invite them to draw a scene to accompany a story they have written. Suggest that they try to use a style similar to Steptoe's. Encourage them to write a caption for their picture to describe the part of the story the picture illustrates.
LISTENING/SPEAKING/WRITING

PERSONAL JOURNAL: WRITING ABOUT DREAMS Invite students to describe in their personal journals a dream they have for their future. Suggest that their dream might involve a career, places they would like to visit or live in, or a great achievement they hope to accomplish. After students have finished writing, you may wish to call on volunteers to share one of their dreams.
LISTENING/SPEAKING/WRITING

CULTURAL AWARENESS

Point out to students that the Cinderella story has been retold in many different ways by various peoples around the world. Some other stories with the "Cinderella theme" include the Chinese tale *Yeh-Shen*, retold by Ai-Ling Louie (Philomel, 1982) and the African American folktale *The Talking Eggs* by Robert San Souci (Dial Books, 1989).

TEACHING TIP

You may wish to let students know that the majority of people in the country of Zimbabwe belong to either the Shona or the Ndebele group. Both groups have a rich oral tradition of storytelling and poetry.

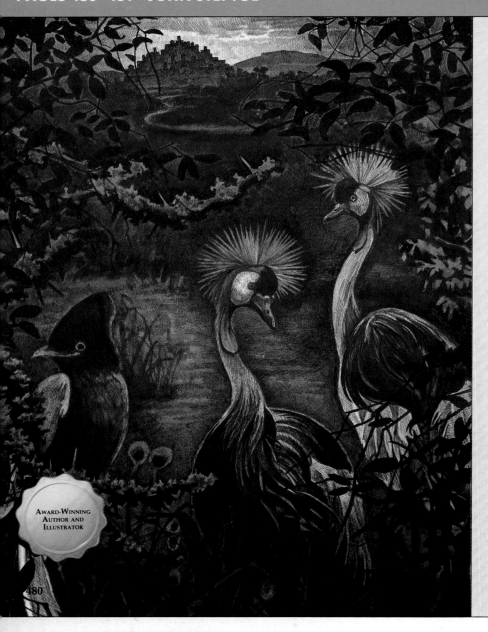

AWARD-WINNING
AUTHOR AND
ILLUSTRATOR

480

Which did you enjoy more about *Mufaro's Beautiful Daughters*—the story or the illustrations? John Steptoe spent more than two and a half years writing and illustrating this book. He worked at writing stories that African American children could relate to and that would encourage them to follow their dreams. The Cinderella theme came to Steptoe's mind, and he found that almost every culture has its own version of the classic tale. *Mufaro's Beautiful Daughters* was based on an African Cinderella tale. The story and the art were inspired by the people living near Zimbabwe in southern Africa.

John Steptoe was already an award-winning author and artist before *Mufaro's Beautiful Daughters* was published. He began drawing as a child and attended the High School of Art and Design in New York City for three years. Steptoe wrote his first book, *Stevie*, at the age of sixteen.

John Steptoe illustrated not only his own books but also stories written by other authors, including *Mother Crocodile*, another African tale. He received many awards for both his illustrations and his writing. Steptoe died in 1989.

John Steptoe believed that there were many young people like himself who wanted to accomplish something important in their lives. It was Steptoe's hope that he could help encourage children to seek opportunities, take pride in themselves, and achieve their dreams.

Expanding the Article   How do you think John Steptoe's attitude about himself affected the kind of characters he created? (Accept reasonable responses: He created young characters much like himself who have real problems and real dreams.)   INFERENTIAL: DRAWING CONCLUSIONS

THE WEAVING OF A DREAM

MARILEE HEYER

LESSON PLANNER

THE WEAVING OF A DREAM

Part 1
Reading Literature
Pages T858–T871

Part 2
Responding to Literature
Pages T872–T877

Part 3
Learning Through Literature
Pages T878–T884

TEACHING OUTLINE	Materials	Language Arts/ Integrated Curriculum	Meeting Individual Needs
Building Background **Vocabulary Strategies** Key Words (Tested) **Strategic Reading** Preview and Predict Setting a Purpose **Options for Reading**	Transparency 50 Second-Language Support Manual Practice Book p. 136 Integrated Spelling p. 67 Integrated Spelling T.E. pp. 88–89 Student Anthology pp. 482–502 Response Card 1: Characters	**Spelling** Spelling Pretest Spelling-Vocabulary Connection	**Second-Language Support** Vocabulary T859 Strategic Reading T860, T866, T869 **Cooperative Reading** T861
Story Follow-Up Think It Over Write **Summarizing the Literature** **Appreciating Literature** **Critical Thinking Activities**	Writer's Journal p. 93 Practice Book pp. 137–138 Integrated Spelling p. 68 Integrated Spelling T.E. pp. 88–89 Literature Cassette 2 Language Handbook	**Vocabulary Workshop** Reviewing Key Words Extending Vocabulary Time-Order/Setting Clue Words **Reading** Oral Rereading Folktale Encyclopedia **Writing** Descriptive Paragraph Catalog Entries Fortune Cookies Describing a Dream **Spelling** Reviewing Spelling Words **Speaking** Listing Tasks Demonstrating Weaving **Listening** Performing a Radio Play	**Cooperative Learning** T873, T876
Introduce Literary Appreciation: Imagery **Review** Comprehension: Comparing/Contrasting (Tested) **Maintain** Study Skills: Following Directions (Tested)	Transparency 51 Second-Language Support Manual Writer's Journal p. 94 Practice Book pp. 139–140	**Social Studies** Map of China **Math** Story Problems **Art** Chinese Designs Chinese Calligraphy **Science** Origin of Fibers **Music** Chinese Music **Multicultural** Artists	**Challenge** T879, T880, T881 **Second-Language Support** Imagery T879 **Cooperative Learning** T879, T882

KEY W...
brocades
shuttle
loom
design
embroidered
squandering

Selection Summary

This Chinese folktale tells of an old widow who supports herself and her three sons—Leme, Letuie, and Leje—with money she earns from selling her beautiful weavings. One day the widow trades her fabrics for a painting of a beautiful palace in which she wishes she could live. The youngest son suggests she make a weaving of the painting, because her weavings are so lifelike that it will be almost like living in the palace. While her family is admiring the completed brocade, the fabric is swept off by a great wind. In turn, the two older sons go after it, but when a fortune-teller informs them of the frightening obstacles they must face to retrieve the cloth from the fairies who have stolen it, they each decide instead to take a box of gold she offers. Finally, the youngest son, Leje, sets off to recover the brocade. He braves the obstacles and brings home the brocade, which turns into a real palace. In the end, everyone is happy except the two older brothers, who, having squandered all their money, turn up at the palace gates as beggars.

Family Involvement

Encourage family members to discuss with students how they can work together as a family unit to solve any problems they may face.

MARILEE HEYER

Marilee Heyer worked extensively as a commercial illustrator before turning her attention to children's literature. Both her books, *The Weaving of a Dream* and *The Forbidden Door*, have earned her praise for their richly detailed illustrations. The author and illustrator lives in California.

ADDITIONAL READING

Other Books About Achievers

Love You, Soldier by Amy Hest. Four Winds Press, 1991.   AVERAGE

People Who Make a Difference by Brent Ashabranner. Cobblehill, 1989.
   CHALLENGING

The Sailor Who Captured the Sea: A Story of the Book of Kells by Deborah Nourse Lattimore. HarperCollins, 1991.   AVERAGE

The Secret Language of the SB by Elizabeth Scarboro. Viking, 1990.   AVERAGE

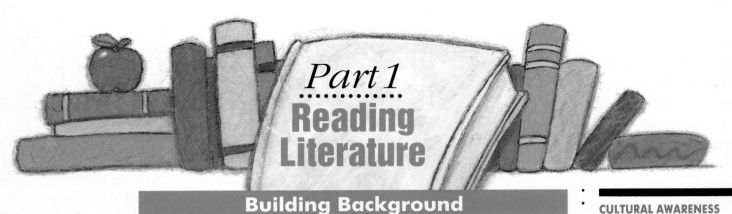

Part 1
Reading Literature

Building Background

Access prior knowledge and build vocabulary concepts.

Tell students that the next story is a folktale about an old woman who weaves a very special cloth. Have students discuss what they know about weaving by naming various uses for woven cloth, by describing designs they've seen, and by explaining some of the steps that weavers follow to create their cloth. Then work with the group to develop a web related to weaving. The completed web might include the following ideas:

Uses
clothing
wall hangings
decoration

Weaving

Equipment
loom
shuttle
thread
wool

Process
pass threads over
and under one another

Vocabulary Strategies

Introduce Key Words and strategies.

Display Transparency 50, or write the story on the board. Have students use context clues with phonetic and structural analysis to decode and figure out the meanings of the underlined words. Ask volunteers to read each sentence aloud.

Transparency 50   Key Words

Brocades are heavy fabrics that have interesting patterns woven into them. A shuttle is used in weaving the way a needle is used in sewing. Both tools carry the threads.

My first weaving was done on a very simple loom. I just wrapped the threads around an old picture frame. First, I drew on paper the design I wanted to weave, and then I wove the pattern I had drawn. I copied a beautiful embroidered cloth with pictures of red, white, and blue flowers sewn into it.

I would rather spend my free time weaving something useful than squandering it watching television.

CULTURAL AWARENESS

Students may be interested to learn that the oldest known loom for weaving cloth was discovered in Africa at Badari, Egypt. It is believed that the loom was used more than 6000 years ago.

KEY WORDS

brocades
shuttle
loom
design
embroidered
squandering

KEY WORDS DEFINED

brocades heavy fabrics with designs woven into them

shuttle weaving tool used to add threads to fabric

loom frame to hold cloth while it is being woven

design pattern or picture

embroidered decorated with sewn-on designs

squandering wasting

**Check students'
understanding.**

1. *shuttle* **If you had a shuttle in your hand, what would
   you probably be doing?** (weaving)   STRATEGY: PRIOR
   KNOWLEDGE
2. *loom* **Which word names the device that holds cloth
   while it is being woven?** *(loom)*   STRATEGY: DEFINITION
3. *brocades* **Where would you go to buy brocades?**
   (a fabric store)   STRATEGY: PRIOR KNOWLEDGE
4. *embroidered* **What would you need to make an
   embroidered shirt?** (a needle, some colored threads, a
   shirt)   STRATEGY: DESCRIPTION
5. *design* **Would you create a design for cloth before or
   after you have woven it?** (before)   STRATEGY: PRIOR
   KNOWLEDGE
6. *squandering* **Which word means about the same as
   wasting?** *(squandering)*   STRATEGY: DEFINITION

**Integrate spelling
with vocabulary.**

SPELLING-VOCABULARY CONNECTION   *Integrated Spelling*
page 67 reinforces spellings of the sounds /oi/ and /ou/ in the Key
Word *embroidered* and in other words. The spelling of the Key
Word *loom* is also included.

• • • THE WEAVING OF A DREAM • • •

Name _____

A. Read each sentence below. Figure out the meaning of the
underlined word. Then write the word next to its meaning.

The costumes that Jenelle saw were made of beautiful
<u>brocades</u>.

Although Jenelle knew little about weaving, she decided to
buy a <u>loom</u> and weave a blanket.

Her aunt accused her of <u>squandering</u> her money foolishly.

Jenelle added row after row of yarn with the <u>shuttle</u>.

She sketched a <u>design</u> of blue and gold flowers before
weaving the pattern.

Jenelle was proud of herself when her aunt opened the box
containing the blanket and an <u>embroidered</u> pillowcase.

1. ___design___ pattern or picture
2. ___embroidered___ decorated with sewn-on designs
3. ___loom___ frame on which thread or yarn is woven into cloth
4. ___squandering___ wasting
5. ___shuttle___ weaving tool used to carry yarn back and forth
6. ___brocades___ heavy cloths with designs woven into them

B. Use three of the underlined words in Part A in sentences of your own.

1. Sentences will vary. _____
2. _____
3. _____

136   Vocabulary   Practice Book ▪ FEAST YOUR EYES

Practice Book

INTEGRATED SPELLING
The Sounds /oi/ and /ou/

Name _____

Read the Spelling Words. Write them on a separate sheet of
paper. Check your spelling.

SPELLING STRATEGY

The sounds /oi/ and /ou/ can be spelled in different ways.
Knowing the different letters that spell these sounds will help
you remember how to spell words in which they occur.

The sound /oi/ can be spelled with the letters oi and oy:

   /oi/ = oi   choice   /oi/ = oy   royal

The sound /ou/ can be spelled with the letters ou and ow:

   /ou/ = ou   proud   /ou/ = ow   flower

Write each Spelling Word in the correct column below.
Then circle the letters that make the sound.

/oi/	/ou/
choice	allow
destroy	flower
embroider	mountain
joyful	proud
royal	

SPELLING WORDS

allow
choice
destroy
embroider
flower
joyful
loom
mountain
proud
royal

MEMORY JOGGER

This Memory Jogger will help you
spell the word **loom**.

The **loom** is in the **room**.

Which Spelling Word has neither the /oi/
nor the /ou/ sound? ___loom___

FEAST YOUR EYES • "The Weaving of a Dream"   67

Integrated Spelling

PRACTICE BOOK
page 136:   Reinforcing
Key Words

**INTEGRATED
SPELLING**
page 67: Writing words
with the /oi/ and /ou/
sounds

NOTE: These pages
may be completed now
or after students have
read the story.

Strategic Reading

Preview and Predict

Help students preview.

Review the strategy for previewing. (reading and thinking about the title, looking at the illustrations, and reading the opening paragraphs) Then guide students in previewing through page 485.

Have students make predictions.

Ask students questions such as the following to help them make predictions about what might happen in the story:

- **What might happen because the widow bought the painting instead of rice?**
- **What might the old widow's dream be?**
- **Who will help make her dream come true?**

PERSONAL JOURNAL Have students add their predictions about the selection to their personal journals. Ask students to support their predictions.

Setting a Purpose

Have students set purposes.

Discuss with students what they want to find out when they read the story, based on their preview and what they know from their own experiences.

Model purpose-setting, if necessary.

If students have difficulty, suggest this purpose-setting question:

I'm going to read to find out how the old widow might weave a dream come true.

OPTIONS FOR READING

INDEPENDENT READING Have students read the story silently with their purpose for reading in mind.

GUIDED READING Follow the Guided Reading suggestions that appear on pages T861, T865, and T871. These suggestions model strategic reading.

COOPERATIVE READING A reader response strategy appears on page T861.

SECOND-LANGUAGE SUPPORT Explain to students that when the context is not enough to identify the meaning of a word, they may need to look it up in their dictionaries. Ask them to mark each word they look up with a small dot. Encourage students to learn the words and add them to their vocabulary notebooks. (See *Second-Language Support Manual.*)

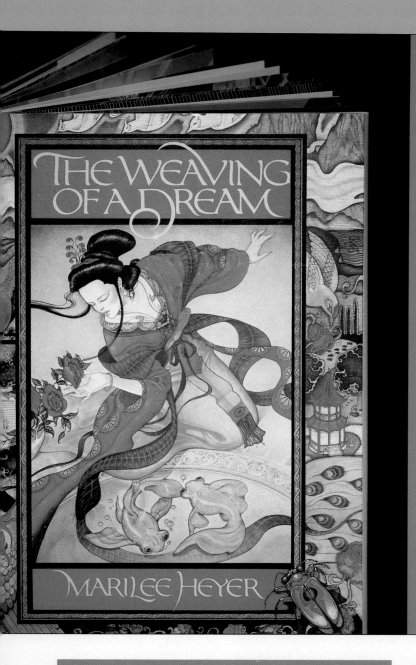

Long ago, in a land far to the east, there lived an old widow who had three sons. The eldest was Leme, the second was Letuie, and the youngest was Leje. They lived in a small cottage in a mist-filled valley at the foot of a high mountain.

Guided Reading

SET PURPOSE/PREDICT: PAGES 482–491   Have students read through page 491 to find out what happens to the old widow and the cloth she weaves.

Cooperative Reading

READER RESPONSE STRATEGY: PAGES 482–487
Have each group of 3–5 students select a leader. Ask group members to read silently, and then encourage the leaders to use dialogue questions such as the one below. (Response Card 1: Characters, on page R62, offers a wide variety of dialogue questions.)

- **How are Leme, Letuie, and Leje alike? How are they different?**

PAGES 488–502   After reading, the discussion leaders might ask:

- **Did any of the characters change during the story? If so, when did you notice the change?**

Everyone for hundreds of miles around knew the old widow, for she had a special gift. She could weave beautiful brocades that seemed to come alive under her fingers. The flowers, plants, birds, and animals she wove almost moved with the breeze. Her weaving was in constant demand at the marketplace in the village nearby. It was used to make dresses and jackets, curtains and coverlets. With the money she earned, the old widow supported her family, although the boys helped by chopping wood and selling it.

One day, while she was at the market selling some new weavings, she saw a most wondrous painting hanging in a stall nearby. It showed a large palace surrounded by beautiful flower gardens. There were vegetable gardens, too, fruit trees, pastures where cattle grazed, lovely birds, and even a fish pond. A river ran in front of the palace, and the whole painting was warmed by a great red sun. Everything she had always dreamed of was in the painting. She gazed at every detail, and her heart filled with happiness.

Although she knew she should not, she traded her brocades for the painting. I should be buying rice for my sons, she thought, but she could not help herself.

Three times on the way home she stopped to unroll the painting and gaze at it. "If only we could live in that palace," she whispered to herself.

When she got home she showed the painting to her sons and told them of her dream.

484

Informal Assessment Assessing whether students are fulfilling the established purpose for reading involves asking questions like the following:

- Is this what you expected to happen next?
- If not, what did you predict would happen? What did you read earlier that led you to believe that?

This assessment will also encourage students to watch for and select details that fulfill their purpose for reading.

Expanding the Literature Why is the old widow's special talent so important to her family? (Accept reasonable responses: Not only is her weaving a source of pride, it supports the family.) INFERENTIAL: DETERMINING MAIN IDEA

What do you think of the old widow's decision to buy the painting? Explain your opinion. (Responses will vary.) CRITICAL: EXPRESSING PERSONAL OPINIONS

"It's lovely, Mother," said Leme and Letuie. "But where is the rice you went to buy?" They didn't understand her desire to live in the picture palace.

"It's a silly dream, Old Mother," they said.

She turned to Leje, her youngest son, with a sadness in her eyes he had never seen before.

"Leje, I know that *you* will understand. I feel I must live in this lovely place or I will die," she sighed.

"Don't be sad, Mother. I will think of something."

As he comforted her an idea came to him.

"Why don't you do a weaving of the painting? Your weavings are so lifelike that, as you work on it every day, it will be almost like living there."

"You are right, Leje," she said with a smile. "It is the closest I will ever come to this lovely place."

She set to work by candlelight that very evening.

Once she started weaving she didn't stop. For days and months she worked, her shuttle flashing through the threads.

Leme and Letuie became very upset with their mother. One evening they even pulled her hands away from the loom.

"You are no longer making brocades to sell, Old Mother. Now we must all live on the money we make chopping wood, and we are tired of working so hard."

Leje ran to stop them.

"Let Mother be. She must weave the beautiful palace, or die of grief. I will chop all the wood."

From then on, Leje chopped day and night, cutting wood to sell for food.

The old widow continued to weave every hour, on and on, never stopping. At night she worked by candlelight. The smoke burned her eyes and made them red and sore, but she didn't stop. After one year, tears began to drop from her eyes onto the threads, and they became part of the river and fish pond she was weaving. After two years, blood dripped from her eyes onto her hand. Down her hand onto the shuttle it ran, and the drops of blood were woven into the splendid red sun and glowing flowers.

On and on she worked. At last, during the third year, she was finished. What a beautiful brocade it was, the most magnificent ever seen. Mother and sons stared at it in wonder. Even Leme and Letuie couldn't take their eyes from it. The garden, the flowers, the beautiful palace, songbirds of every kind, luscious fruits and vegetables ready to pick, all in the most perfect detail. Behind the palace were pastures for the fat sheep and cattle, and fields of maize and rice. The river sparkled in front, and the marvelous sun warmed every thread.

"Oh, Mother, how proud we are of your wonderful work!" whispered her sons.

The old widow stretched her tired back and rubbed her bloodshot eyes. A smile creased her wrinkled cheeks and slowly grew into a joyous laugh.

Vocabulary Strategy   Discuss with students how they can figure out the meaning of the word *luscious* on page 487. Remind them that by using context clues and trying to form a mental picture of the scene, they will know that *luscious* describes the fruits and vegetables that are ready to be picked in the garden. Explain that if those things are ripe, *luscious* must mean "juicy and delicious."

488

Teaching Tip Help students identify the things
pictured in the brocade—a palace, songbirds,
fruits, vegetables, sheep, cattle, maize (corn), and
rice. Ask students to name other things they see.

Suddenly, a great wind blew the hut door open with a crash! It raced through the room, knocking everything over. Then taking the wondrous brocade with it, it blew out the window and up into the sky to the east.

They all ran after it, screaming and waving their arms, but the brocade was gone. Vanished! When the boys turned, they saw their mother lying unconscious on the doorstep.

They carried her inside and laid her on the bed. Slowly she opened her eyes.

"Please, Leme, my oldest son," she said. "Go east, follow the wind, and bring my brocade back to me. It means more to me than my life."

Leme nodded, put on his sandals, took a few supplies, and headed east. Within a month's time he came to a mountain. When he reached the very top he saw a strange house made all of stone, with a stone horse standing by the door. The horse's mouth was open, as if it were trying to eat some of the red berries that were growing at its feet. On the front doorstep sat a white-haired old crone.

"And where are you headed, young man?" she croaked in a little-used voice.

"I'm going east," said Leme, "where the wind has carried off a beautiful brocade my mother spent three years weaving."

"Ah, that brocade," cackled the fortune-teller, for that is what she was. "The fairies of Sun Mountain sent the wind to bring it to them. They wish to copy its beautiful design. You may never find it. The way is very difficult."

"Please tell me how to get there," pleaded Leme.

"First, you must knock out your two front teeth and put them into the mouth of my stone horse. Then it will be able to move and eat the berries it has wanted for so long. When it has eaten ten berries, it will let you on its back and will carry you to Sun Mountain, but on the way you must first pass over Flame Mountain, which is constantly on fire. When the horse goes through the flames, you must not cry out, even if the pain is unbearable. Keep your cries to yourself, or you will immediately be burned to ashes.

"Next, you will come to the Sea of Ice. When you go through the ice, you must not cry out, though your whole body will become numb with cold. If you do cry out, you will sink to the bottom of the sea. If you pass through these places as I have told you, you then will see Sun Mountain and will be given your mother's fine brocade to carry home."

Leme ran his tongue over his front teeth. He thought of the burning fire and freezing ice, and he grew very pale.

The old fortune-teller saw his face and laughed. "You will not be able to endure it, young man, and after all, you need not. I will give you a box of gold; go home and live happily."

From inside the house she brought the box. Leme took it quickly and turned toward home. He had gone about a mile before he realized how much better it would be if he spent all the gold on himself instead of sharing it with his family. So, instead of going home, he headed south toward the big city.

Waiting for Leme's return, the old widow grew thinner and thinner. After two months she could wait no longer.

Guided Reading

MONITOR COMPREHENSION: PAGES 482—491
What happens to the old widow and the brocade she has woven? (The fairies send the wind to steal the brocade, and the old widow grows weak.)
STRATEGIC READING: RETURNING TO PURPOSE

What effect does the old widow's desire have on the lives of the people in her family? (Instead of the old widow taking care of her sons, they have to take care of her. Then, when the brocade is stolen, one son has to leave home to try to find it.)
INFERENTIAL: DETERMINING CAUSE-EFFECT/ SUMMARIZING

SET PURPOSE/PREDICT: PAGES 492—502   Have students predict what will happen next. Have students read the rest of the story to confirm their predictions.

"Letuie, you must go east and find my brocade. It means my life," she told her middle son.

Letuie agreed. He put on his sandals, took some supplies, and headed east. Within a month's time he was standing at the door of the stone house, listening to the old fortune-teller tell him he must knock out his teeth and go silently through fire and ice. Letuie also grew very pale. He, too, received a box of gold and went to the big city with it instead of returning home.

Again, the old widow waited. She grew as thin as a piece of old firewood. Every day she spent lying in her bed, staring at the door, waiting for Letuie's return. Every day when he didn't come, she wept. Her old tired eyes finally went blind from weeping.

Leje could stand it no longer.

"Old Mother, please let me go look for the brocade. Perhaps Leme and Letuie have been injured. I will search for them, too. I will ask the neighbors to care for you while I'm gone."

After thinking for a long time the old widow agreed, but she hated to let Leje leave, for she loved her youngest son the best.

Leje put on his sandals and took some supplies. He threw back his shoulders and proudly started on his mission to the east. In half the time it had taken his brothers, he reached the top of the mountain. Again there was the old fortune-teller with her stone horse. She repeated the instructions a third time and watched Leje's face closely. It didn't grow pale as his brothers' had, and when she offered him the gold that his brothers had accepted, he refused it.

Second-Language Support

Students may need help understanding the phrase *He threw back his shoulders*. Tell students that this sentence describes how the character was standing. Model the posture and ask students to suggest words they could use to describe a person standing with his or her shoulders thrown back. *(confident, proud, determined)* Have students reread the passage to find other clues that tell what kind of person Leje is.

"I must bring back the brocade for my mother or she will surely die."

Immediately he picked up a stone, knocked out his front two teeth, and fed them to the stone horse. After the horse had eaten the ten berries, Leje jumped on its back, and clinging to its mane, kicked the horse with his heels. High into the air the wonderful horse jumped, and away they flew, as fast as the wind they were following.

For three days and three nights they flew across the sky. At last they reached Flame Mountain. Into the fire they dashed without a pause. The red flames hissed around Leje and stabbed at his skin, but he didn't cry out. With teeth clenched tight, he endured the pain, and in half a day's time he came out of the flames and stood on the shore of the Sea of Ice. Again, without hesitation, he sped on. Steam rose from his burning-hot body as it hit the ice-cold water. He felt his legs and arms grow numb and bleed from the sharp edges of the ice, but he uttered no sound. In half a day's time he came out of the Sea of Ice, and before him, glowing in golden light, shone beautiful Sun Mountain. The warmth of it soothed his body and eased his pain.

The loveliest palace he had ever seen stood on the top of the mountain, and from its windows came the sound of women's voices singing and laughing.

Up the mountain the stone horse flew, and soon they stood before the palace door. There two very strange creatures, unlike anything Leje had ever seen before, stood guard, but not even they could stop him now. Down from the horse he jumped, and straight through the door he marched. The creatures didn't blink, nor did he.

Vocabulary Strategy   How can you figure out the meaning of the word *clenched* on page 494? (When I read, I use context clues. By doing this, I figure out that Leje is in pain but does not cry out or scream. *With teeth clenched tight* must mean that his mouth is "closed very tightly.") STRATEGY: CONTEXT CLUES

Expanding the Literature   To what might the author be comparing the flames of Flame Mountain and the ice in the Sea of Ice? (knives or swords with stabbing, sharp edges)   CRITICAL: AUTHOR'S CRAFT/DETERMINING IMAGERY

What do Leje's actions tell you about him? (He is very determined, unstoppable, fearless; he never hesitates.)   INFERENTIAL: DETERMINING CHARACTERS' TRAITS

In front of him was a great hall filled with beautiful fairies, all weaving as fast as they could. In the very center of the hall, for them to copy, hung his mother's brocade.

Startled by the sight of Leje, the fairies stopped their weaving and sat as still as stones.

"Don't be afraid," he told them. "I have only come for my mother's brocade."

At the thought of losing the brocade, some of the fairies began to cry, but one fairy stood and said, "Very well, you may have the brocade in the morning. Just allow us one more night of weaving so that we can finish. You may stay here with us and rest for the night."

Leje agreed, and the fairies sent one of the creatures to prepare for him a most delicious dinner, after which Leje fell into a deep sleep.

When the sun set and the light in the hall began to grow dim, one fairy hung a shining pearl that filled the hall with light. They continued weaving through the night.

One beautiful fairy, dressed all in red, finished her weaving first. She had always been the finest and the quickest of the weavers, but when she held her weaving next to the old woman's, hers looked very poor by comparison, for the colors were not as bright nor the stitches so fine.

Expanding the Literature   How does the author show that the old widow's brocade is truly remarkable? (Even the best weaver among the fairies cannot weave as well.)   CRITICAL: AUTHOR'S CRAFT/APPRECIATING IMAGERY

This brocade is so perfect, the fairy thought. Instead of trying to copy it, I wish I could become a part of it.

So while the other fairies worked on, the red fairy started to weave into the old widow's brocade a picture of herself sitting by the fish pond.

Late in the night Leje woke with a start.

Suppose the fairies will not give me the brocade in the morning, he thought. My poor mother has been ill so long. What will become of her?

As he looked around he saw that all the fairies had fallen asleep over their looms. There stood his mother's brocade, more lovely than ever by the light of the pearl. Quickly, Leje took down the brocade and ran to his waiting horse. Away into the moonlight they flew.

In three days and three nights they stood before the fortune-teller's house.

"Well done, my son," said the old woman. She took his teeth from the stone horse's mouth and put them back into Leje's mouth as if they had never been gone. The horse immediately froze into his old position.

"Quickly, my son, you must return home, for your mother is dying." From behind her back the old woman pulled a fine pair of embroidered boots and set them on the ground.

"Put these on; they will speed your way."

Hardly had Leje put the boots on than he was standing on his own doorstep. Inside, he saw his dear mother, now grown thinner than a splinter. At that very moment her heart was beating its last.

Second-Language Support

Students may need help understanding the word *start* as it is used on page 498. Point out to students that words in English often have more than one meaning. Explain that *start* can mean "the beginning" or "a sudden movement, made when someone is surprised." Ask students to decide which meaning makes the most sense in this sentence. Call on volunteers to explain their ideas.

MEETING INDIVIDUAL NEEDS

Expanding the Literature   Why might Leje doubt that the fairies will return the brocade?

(They had stolen it once; they begin to cry when he tells them he wants to take it back.)

INFERENTIAL: DETERMINING CAUSE-EFFECT

On page 493 the author compares the old widow to a piece of firewood, and then on page 498 to a splinter. How do these comparisons help you visualize the old widow? (Accept reasonable responses: These comparisons give the idea that the old widow has become more and more frail.)

CRITICAL: AUTHOR'S CRAFT/APPRECIATING IMAGERY

"No, Mother, don't die," cried Leje, running to her bedside. He pulled the brocade from his shirt and spread it over her. The warmth of its gleaming sun soothed her and pulled her back to life. She felt the delicate threads with her fingertips. Her eyes began to clear and her sight returned. She sat up in bed and gazed at the wonderful brocade that had taken three years from her and almost cost her her life.

"Oh, my most faithful son," she said, "help me take the brocade out of this dark hut into the sunlight, where we can see it better."

Outside they lovingly spread the brocade on the ground. Suddenly a soft, sweet-smelling breeze swept through the valley. It gently drew the brocade off the ground and spread it over the yard. Larger and larger and longer and wider it grew. Over the fence and over the house it spread, covering everything with its silken threads. The shabby hut disappeared, and in its place the brocade itself took on the very shape and form of the beautiful palace. Before their eyes the brocade was coming to life. The gardens, the fruit trees, the pasture—all became real. The colorful birds began to sing, the cattle grazed on the rich pasture grass, and there, sitting by the fish pond, was the red fairy, as bright as the sun overhead.

The old widow was greatly astonished, for she knew she had not woven a fairy into her brocade. But she welcomed her and brought her to live with them in the beautiful palace. She asked all her neighbors to live with them too, for there was more than enough room and they had all been kind to her while Leje was away. Leje and the red fairy were married, and so the weaving of the dream was completed.

Expanding the Literature   How can you tell that the old widow's brocade has special powers? (When Leje places it on his dying mother, the warmth from the brocade's sun brings her back to life. Outside, the brocade grows and grows as it comes to life.)   CRITICAL: DISTINGUISHING BETWEEN FANTASY AND REALITY

What do you think might have made the brocade become real? (Accept reasonable responses: Perhaps it was the old widow and Leje's faithfulness that made the dream come true.)   INFERENTIAL: SPECULATING

One day as Leje, the fairy, and his mother sat in the garden making toys for the new baby that would be coming soon, two beggars crept up and stared at them through the garden fence. They were Leme and Letuie. They had gone to the big city and lost all their gold, squandering it on themselves. Now they had nothing left. When they saw the happy scene before them, they thought of the terrible thing they had done. They were filled with grief and remorse, and they turned silently, picked up their begging sticks, and crept away.

THINK IT OVER

1. *Why did the widow suffer as much as she did?*

2. *How did the widow's sons feel about the brocade while she was weaving it?*

3. *Why did the fairies of Sun Mountain take the widow's beautiful brocade?*

4. *Why was it difficult for the widow's sons to find the brocade?*

5. *Do you believe that dreams can come true? Explain why you think as you do.*

WRITE

Write a paragraph describing a beautiful painting or piece of art that you have admired.

THEME WRAP-UP

ACHIEVERS

You read about characters who wanted to help others and, in doing so, they helped themselves. In what ways are Nyasha and Leje alike? Give examples of behavior that reveal what each is like.

. . . .

How do you think Manyara and Leje's brothers would have acted differently if the stories were set in modern times? Explain why you think as you do.

. . . .

WRITER'S WORKSHOP Suppose Nyasha's father and Leje's mother entered them in a contest for selecting the child who did the most good. Write a paragraph to persuade the judge to choose one of the children as the winner. Use convincing facts and examples from the selections.

For discussion of this page, please turn to T885.

503

Guided Reading

MONITOR COMPREHENSION: PAGES 492–502
Does the old widow ever get her brocade back? (yes) **Is that what you predicted would happen?** (Responses will vary.) STRATEGIC READING: CONFIRMING PREDICTIONS

How is goodness rewarded and evil punished in this story? (Accept reasonable responses: The old widow's dedication is rewarded by the return of her brocade; Leje's dedication to his mother is rewarded when her health returns; both are rewarded when the brocade comes to life; the older brothers become beggars because of their selfishness.) STRATEGIC READING: SUMMARIZING

Returning to the Predictions   Invite students to discuss the predictions that they made before they began reading and that they may have written in their personal journals. Encourage them to talk about how those predictions changed.

Returning to the Purpose for Reading
Ask students how the old widow could weave a dream come true. (The old widow dreamed of living in a beautiful palace and wove a picture of her dream. Her labor and her son's love helped make a dream come true.)

NOTE: Responses to the Think It Over questions and support for the Write activity appear on page T872.

Part 2
Responding to Literature

Story Follow-Up

Think It Over

Encourage reader's response: student page 502.

1. **Why did the widow suffer as much as she did?** (Accept reasonable responses: She was so devoted to her dream that when it was taken away, she began to lose hope.) INFERENTIAL: DRAWING CONCLUSIONS

2. **How did the widow's sons feel about the brocade while she was weaving it?** (Letuie and Leme were angry with her because she stopped weaving cloth to sell. Leje was sympathetic.) LITERAL: RECOGNIZING CHARACTERS' EMOTIONS

3. **Why did the fairies of Sun Mountain take the widow's beautiful brocade?** (They wanted to copy its beautiful design.) LITERAL: DETERMINING CAUSE-EFFECT

4. **Why was it difficult for the widow's sons to find the brocade?** (The brocade was in the palace of the fairies on Sun Mountain.) INFERENTIAL: DRAWING CONCLUSIONS

5. **Do you believe that dreams can come true? Explain why you think as you do.** (Responses will vary.) CRITICAL: EXPRESSING PERSONAL OPINIONS

Write

Encourage writer's response: student page 502.

Write a paragraph describing a beautiful painting or piece of art that you have admired. Encourage students to include details. CREATIVE: WRITING A DESCRIPTION

Summarizing the Literature

Have students retell the story and write a summary.

Encourage students to summarize the story by recalling key story events and arranging them on a time line to show the order in which they happened. Guide students in beginning the time line below, and have them finish it independently. (See *Practice Book* page 137 on T873.) Students may use their completed time lines to retell the story and to write a brief summary statement.

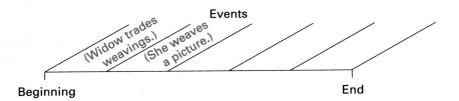

Events

(Widow trades weavings.)
(She weaves a picture.)

Beginning   End

STRATEGY CONFERENCE

Discuss with students how previewing and making predictions helped them understand, remember, and appreciate the selection. Invite students to share other reading strategies, such as summarizing, that helped them understand what they read.

NOTE

An additional writing activity for this selection appears on page T875.

INFORMAL ASSESSMENT

Having students order the **details** of a selection in this way will help you informally assess how well they understood key relationships. Ask yourself: Did students grasp **time relationships?** Did students recognize the **causes** of **effects** and the effects of causes? Can students tell which details are more important than others?

Appreciating Literature

Have students share personal responses.

Have students work in small groups to discuss the story. Provide a general question such as the following to help the groups begin:

- **If you could be any character in this story, who would you be? Explain why.**

PERSONAL JOURNAL   Have students use their personal journals to write about ideas and feelings that are discussed in the groups. You may also refer them to their personal journals after they complete the activities below.

Critical Thinking Activities

Encourage both cooperative and individual responses.

WRITE A SCENE   **Imagine that the three brothers set off after the brocade together. How might the story have been different?** Have students work in small groups to discuss their ideas and write a new scene.   CREATIVE: EXTENDING STORY CONCEPTS

DEVELOP A LIST   **Think about the characteristics of a folktale. How does this story fit your idea of what a folktale is like? Write a list of the story elements that make this story a good example of a folktale.** Have pairs of students work together to develop their lists.   CRITICAL: AUTHOR'S CRAFT/IDENTIFYING GENRE

Writer's Journal

· · · **THE WEAVING OF A DREAM** · · ·

Name _____

A. Finish the time line below by filling in the events of the story. Possible responses are given.

Time Line	
Beginning	A widow trades some weavings for a painting of a palace.
Event 1	She weaves a picture of the painting, and it takes three years.
Event 2	A wind sweeps the brocade away.
Event 3	The widow becomes sickened by her loss.
Event 4	The two older sons, one by one, go after the brocade.
Event 5	A fortune-teller tells each of them about the obstacles they must face to get the brocade back.
Event 6	Frightened by the dangers, the two sons take the box of gold she offers instead of retrieving the brocade.
Event 7	The third son, Leje, overcomes the obstacles, gets the brocade, and brings it back home.
Event 8	The brocade turns real. The red fairy, who has woven herself into the brocade, comes to life and marries Leje.
End	Everyone but the two older sons lives happily. They have spent all their money and end up as beggars.

B. On a separate sheet of paper, write a brief summary statement about the story. Responses will vary.

Practice Book • FEAST YOUR EYES   Summarizing the Literature   **137**

Practice Book

WRITER'S JOURNAL
page 93: Writing a personal response

PRACTICE BOOK
page 137: Summarizing the selection

VO·CAB·U·LAR·Y
Workshop

Reviewing Key Words

Display the chart below. Point to each Key Word and the example of a related word or phrase, one at a time. Have students read the Key Word and suggest words that are synonyms for it or words that are related to it. Then have students explain why they think their suggested words should be added to the second column.

Key Words	Related Words
design	pattern (picture, decoration)
brocades	heavy fabrics (woven designs, beautiful)
shuttle	tool (weaving)
loom	frame (holds cloth)
embroidered	decorated (sewn-on designs)
squandering	wasting (foolish, silly)

Extending Vocabulary

TIME-ORDER AND SETTING CLUE WORDS   Point out that the author uses special words to describe the time order and setting in which story events occur. On the board, draw a chart similar to the one below. Then have students skim the story to find examples of time-order and setting clue words the author used, and write them in the appropriate column. Students may wish to extend the lists with their own ideas or words and phrases they recall from other stories.

Have students work in pairs and use the list of time-order and setting clue words to write diary entries Leje might have written during his adventure.

Time Order	Setting

• • • THE WEAVING OF A DREAM • • •

Name _____

Read each pair of sentences below. Rewrite them, adding time-order words to make the sequence of events clear. You will need to reorder some sentences and combine other sentences.

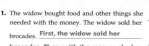

1. The widow bought food and other things she needed with the money. The widow sold her brocades. First, the widow sold her brocades. Then, with the money, she bought food and other things she needed.

2. The widow bought the painting. The widow showed the painting to her sons. After the widow bought the painting, she showed it to her sons.

3. A strong breeze blew the weaving away. The widow became ill from grief. The widow became ill from grief after a strong breeze blew the weaving away.

4. The fortune-teller gave Leme a box of gold. Leme went to the big city to live. After the fortune-teller gave Leme a box of gold, he went to the big city to live.

5. Letuie grew very pale. The fortune-teller told Letuie he must knock out his teeth and go silently through fire and ice. The fortune-teller told Letuie that he must knock out his teeth and go silently through fire and ice. Following that, Letuie grew very pale.

138   Time-Order and Setting Clue Words   Practice Book • FEAST YOUR EYES

Practice Book

Integrated Language Arts

READING

Oral Rereading/ Descriptive Paragraphs

Have students skim the story, looking for passages that are especially descriptive, such as the painting, the fortune-teller's instructions, Leje's journey. Ask students to reread silently, rehearse, and then to read aloud the portion they found most descriptive.   LISTENING/ SPEAKING/READING

WRITING

Writing About the Literature

WRITE A DESCRIPTIVE PARAGRAPH   Review with students the elements of a descriptive paragraph. (It has a topic sentence, gives details that appeal to the senses, groups details that belong together, and paints a vivid word picture.) Then have students look through books, magazines, and brochures to choose a photo or illustration of a "dream place." Ask students to write a paragraph describing the photo or illustration they select. Before they write, have students create a chart, such as the one below, to help them organize the details of their description.   LISTENING/WRITING

Climate	Who Lives There	Plants/Animals	Buildings
summer all year long	native people	palm trees, parrots, tropical fish	grass huts, wooden houses

NOTE: An additional writing activity appears on page T872.

SPELLING

Reviewing Spelling Words

SPELLING WORDS: *allow, choice, destroy, embroider, flower, joyful, loom, mountain, proud, royal*

Have each student work with a partner. Display the spelling words and ask students to create a mnemonic device (a sentence, a short poem, or a riddle) that will help them remember how to spell each word. For ideas, students can look through the Memory Joggers given in the lessons. Have students share their memory joggers with classmates.   LISTENING/SPEAKING/WRITING/ SPELLING

INTEGRATED SPELLING
page 68:   Writing words with the /oi/ and /ou/ sounds

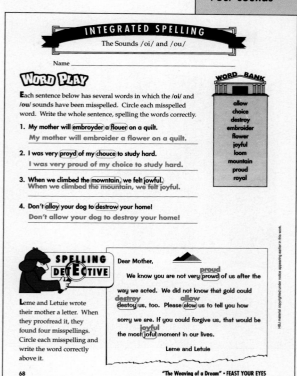

Integrated Spelling

Labors of Love

Remind students that the fortune-teller warned each of the three brothers about the challenges he would face if he pursued the stolen brocade. Have students brainstorm about other folktales they know in which the characters had to undertake difficult or heroic tasks to achieve their reward. Then ask students to create their own lists of heroic tasks, challenges, and problems based on school activities. Have volunteers share and explain their lists. LISTENING/SPEAKING/WRITING

WRITING

A Cottage Industry

COOPERATIVE LEARNING Discuss with students that even though her fame as a weaver was known for hundreds of miles, the old widow had to travel to market to sell her work. Point out that it would have been much more efficient for her to have asked her sons to develop a sales catalog for her weavings. Have students work in small groups to examine different catalogs, noting the language and formats used. Then ask each group to write a catalog the widow's sons might have created. Have students illustrate their catalogs with colorful brocades. LISTENING/SPEAKING/WRITING

Merry Widow Weaving Co.

SPEAKING

The Ins and Outs of Weaving

CULTURAL AWARENESS Have students research various craft books to find ideas for simple weaving projects. Encourage them to note special weaving techniques of various cultures. Then tell students to summarize, orally or in writing, the directions for beginning and completing a project they select. Suggest that students actually try to follow the directions to weave the projects they choose. Ask volunteers to share their completed work with the others and explain how it was made. LISTENING/ SPEAKING/READING/WRITING

READING

The Stuff Dreams Are Made Of

AVAILABLE ON PROJECT CARD

COOPERATIVE LEARNING Tell students they are going to work in groups to create a mini-encyclopedia about folktales. Have students brainstorm within this broad topic a list of subject areas that might be useful as separate encyclopedia entries. A few examples include creatures, places, prizes, obstacles, good characters and evildoers, as well as specific folktale titles. Assign each member of the group the task of collecting information and writing a specific encyclopedia entry. Suggest that students begin their search with examples contained in "The Weaving of a Dream," and encourage them to review other folktales they have enjoyed. Have students combine their completed entries to construct a class encyclopedia. Encourage students to refer to the encyclopedia when the topic *folktales* arises. LISTENING/SPEAKING/READING/WRITING

Dream a Dream

Have students write a personal dream about a goal they have, and ask them to list at least three things they could do to make the dream come true. After students have completed their lists, suggest that they exchange with a partner and ask partners to note any suggestions they would add to the person's personal dream-plan.
LISTENING/SPEAKING/READING/WRITING

LISTENING

Radio Play

AVAILABLE ON PROJECT CARD

Have students form groups and retell "The Weaving of a Dream" by performing it as a radio play. Remind students to decide which sections should have sound effects and to gather the materials they will need. Encourage actors to be separated from the audience by a curtain as they tell the story. After students have had an opportunity to rehearse, encourage them to present their radio play to their classmates.   LISTENING/SPEAKING/ READING

WRITING

Go for the Gold

Remind students that the fortune-teller could tell at a glance which of the sons would face the tasks and who would succeed. Have students write fortune cookies she might have prepared for each of the story characters. Encourage students to share their ideas with the others.
LISTENING/SPEAKING/WRITING

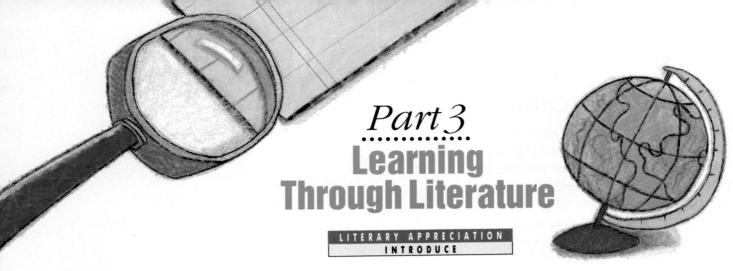

Part 3
Learning Through Literature

Imagery

OBJECTIVE: *To appreciate authors' use of words and phrases to form an image*

1	Focus

Discuss the importance of descriptive phrases.

Have volunteers tell what the brocade in "The Weaving of a Dream" looks like. Discuss with students how the author uses special words and phrases to describe different places, things, and events in the story. Explain that recognizing descriptive phrases will help them form mental pictures as they read.

2	Teach/Model

Teach how authors create images.

Explain that authors use vivid language to describe people, places, things, and ideas in stories in order to help readers create mental images. Then model understanding imagery with the first paragraph on page 490.

> **When I read the passage in which the wind takes the widow's brocade, I use my imagination to picture the wind in the room. The author describes the wind by saying it races through the room, it knocks everything over, and it takes the brocade. When I form an image of the wind in my mind, the wind seems like a strong, powerful person.**

Have students recognize imagery.

Display Transparency 51 or a chart similar to the one shown. Explain that authors often create imagery by using language that appeals to the readers' senses of touch, taste, smell, hearing, and sight. Ask students to recall Leje's journey to reclaim the brocade, and to identify one example of imagery and tell what senses it appeals to.

Transparency 51 Sensory Words					
Image	Touch	Taste	Smell	Hearing	Sight
red flames hissed					

3   Practice/Apply

Have students apply the learning.

COOPERATIVE LEARNING Suggest that students work in pairs to find other examples of imagery in the story and add these to the chart. For each example, have them identify what is being described and to what senses the description appeals.

4   Summarize

Informally assess the learning.

Have students use their charts to discuss the examples of imagery they found. Have them describe the mental pictures the imagery helped them create.

Check understanding of the lesson by having students summarize what they have learned. (By providing descriptions with vivid language, authors appeal to the senses and help readers create mental images as they read. Imagery can make an author's descriptions more lifelike.)

READER ⬌ WRITER CONNECTION

Imagery

▶ **Writers** include imagery to make their descriptions more lifelike.

▶ **Readers** use imagery to form mental pictures as they read.

WRITE A DESCRIPTION Have students imagine that they have just arrived at home after a day at the amusement park, and they want to describe their day to a friend who has been blind since birth. Tell students to take notes of the images they remember, using sensory details.

CHALLENGE Have students choose examples from their chart and create their own imagery by using words that appeal to different senses than those used by the author.

SECOND-LANGUAGE SUPPORT Students can demonstrate their understanding by illustrating an example of imagery they select from the story. Drawings should reflect the image the author is trying to present. (See *Second-Language Support Manual.*)

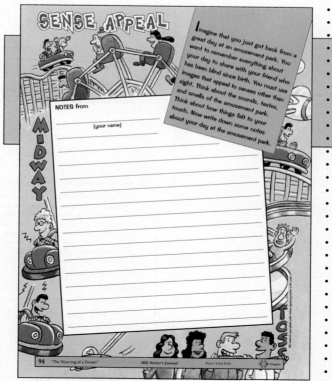

Writer's Journal

WRITER'S JOURNAL
page 94: Writing a description

Comparing and Contrasting

OBJECTIVE: *To determine likenesses and differences*

Review

Review comparing and contrasting.

Remind students that authors may show how things are alike, different, or both. On the board draw a Venn diagram like the one below.

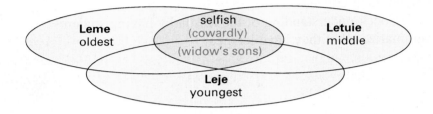

Practice/Apply

Have students apply the learning.

Have students copy the Venn diagram and add other information to compare and contrast the old widow's sons.

Summarize

Informally assess the learning.

Using students' completed diagrams, ask questions such as "How are the three sons alike?" and "How are they different?"

Have students summarize what they have learned. (Think about how people or things are alike and different.)

PRACTICE BOOK
page 139: Comparing and contrasting

• • • THE WEAVING OF A DREAM • • •

Name _____

A. Read the paragraph below. Then answer the question.

Leme, Letuie, and Leje were the three sons of an old widow. They had all been born in the small cottage in which they still lived. All of them were still dependent on their mother for support. Each son helped out by chopping wood and selling it.

What are five things that the three boys have in common? They are brothers. They were all born in the same cottage, in which they still live. They depend on their mother for support. They chop wood. They sell wood.

B. Read the paragraph below. Then answer the question.

Leme and Letuie didn't understand why their mother had bought a painting instead of food. Leje, on the other hand, understood perfectly. While their mother worked on the weaving, Leme and Letuie complained that they had to work too hard chopping wood. Leje, however, didn't mind working hard so his mother could work on her brocade. Although Leme and Letuie were afraid of the hardships described by the fortune-teller, Leje was brave.

What are three ways in which Leje is different from his two brothers? Leje understands his mother's desire to weave the painting into a brocade; his brothers don't. Leje doesn't mind working harder so his mother can work on the brocade; his brothers do mind. Leje is brave in the face of danger; his brothers aren't.

Practice Book • FEAST YOUR EYES   Comparing and Contrasting   139

Practice Book

Following Directions

OBJECTIVE: *To follow written and oral directions*

Review

Review following directions.

Have students recall how to follow directions. (First, read all of the directions. Look for words that signal the order in which things happen, such as *first, next,* and *then.*) Use the list below to model following directions to Sun Mountain.

1. First, you must knock out your teeth.
2. Then, you must pass over Flame Mountain.
3. Next, you must go through the Sea of Ice.
4. Then, you will see Sun Mountain.

Practice/Apply

Have students write directions.

Have students locate one set of directions in a previously read selection and make a similar list.

Summarize

Informally assess the learning.

Have students share their lists, naming the selection in which they found the directions. Ask them to point out signal words.

Have students summarize what they have learned. (Follow directions in order. Look for or include signal words to make the order clear.)

CHALLENGE Encourage students to create an illustrated map showing the route Leje follows to get to the fairies' palace on Sun Mountain. Remind students to verify the order in which Leje completes each step of his journey by rereading those passages from the story.

PRACTICE BOOK
page 140:   Following directions

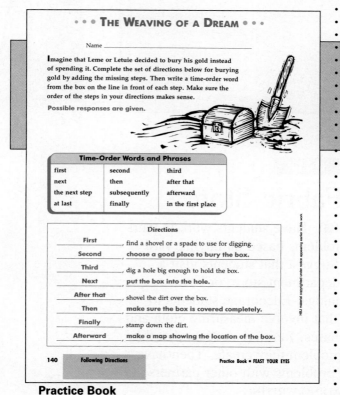

Practice Book

Integrated
Curriculum

Map of China

AVAILABLE ON PROJECT CARD

CULTURAL AWARENESS Encourage groups of students to work together to create an illustrated map of China. Ask them to collect photographs of Chinese landmarks, such as the Great Wall, the Forbidden City, or the Yangtze River, and have them place these on the map. Some students may wish to add their own drawings and illustrations to the map. Have students identify and locate the capital and other important cities in modern China. Encourage students to share their completed maps by explaining the significance of the illustrations and symbols they chose. LISTENING/SPEAKING/ READING/WRITING

In the Land of the Dragon

USE REFERENCE SOURCES Have students research art books to find examples of Chinese decorative art. Encourage students to find examples of Chinese clothes, porcelain, and woodwork. Have them discuss the different images (dragons, fish, birds, willows) that are used in the examples they find. Ask students to trace or sketch their favorite images. Students may wish to have their own art show to display their work. Or, students may wish to use the designs they find to decorate T-shirts they bring from home. LISTENING/SPEAKING/ READING

In the Fabric Store

COOPERATIVE LEARNING Have students work in pairs to develop math story problems based on buying yard goods in a fabric store. Suggest that students visit a neighborhood fabric or department store, or have available appropriate catalogs. Encourage students to develop math problems that involve measuring cloth and making change for purchases. Remind students that they must solve every story problem they create. Then have students exchange math problems with other partners. LISTENING/SPEAKING/READING/WRITING

Born to Weave

CULTURAL AWARENESS   Have students work in groups to research and report on the origin of different materials used around the world in weaving. Suggest that the research teams divide the tasks into three categories: animal sources, plant sources, and synthetic sources. Have students combine the information they find and share their completed reports.   LISTENING/SPEAKING/ READING/WRITING

MUSIC
Sounds of Another Land

CULTURAL AWARENESS   Have students listen to examples of music played on Chinese musical instruments. Then tell students to visualize the impressions they get from listening to a particular selection. Have students write a descriptive paragraph about the music. Encourage them to describe what the music makes them think of and how the music makes them feel. Call on volunteers to share their completed paragraphs with the others.   LISTENING/SPEAKING/ READING/WRITING

ART
The Writing on the Wall
AVAILABLE ON PROJECT CARD

CULTURAL AWARENESS   Have students research and trace examples of the symbols used in traditional Chinese calligraphy. Tell students to identify the meaning for each symbol they trace. Encourage students to practice drawing symbols, and suggest that they collect Chinese characters that stand for some aspect of their own personality. Have students share their completed drawings. LISTENING/SPEAKING/READING

Multi*Cultural*
PERSPECTIVES

Langston Hughes was a great writer.

Marian Anderson was known as one of the world's most popular singers.

People are drawn to the color and the content of this mural by Mexican artist Diego Rivera.

Powerful Works of Art

READ ALOUD TO STUDENTS:

POWERFUL WORKS OF ART CAN

DRAW US INTO THE WORLD

THE ARTISTS HAVE CREATED.
Artist Diego Rivera drew on the strength of the Mexican people and their Indian heritage in his work. His murals appear on the walls of libraries, schools, and government buildings in Mexico and the United States. Some are so huge and colorful that they invite the viewer to walk right into the past.

African American Langston Hughes was a master of many forms of writing, including poems, novels, and plays. In the works he wrote for children and adults he often commented on social issues in a humorous way. Hughes received many awards and honors for writings that told of the happiness and sadness in the lives of ordinary people, and his works have been translated into many languages.

The voice of Marian Anderson was rich and full of emotion. Concert crowds were entranced by the beauty and range of her vocal performance. One of the world's most popular singers, in 1955 she became the first African American to sing at the Metropolitan Opera House in New York City. ■

ACTIVITY CORNER

■ **Available on Project Card**
Encourage students to work together to create a mural that expresses their multicultural heritage in a colorful, inviting way. They might include scenes of Native American villages, colonial life, settlers on the Great Plains or in California, African Americans on their own farms, newly arrived Asian and Hispanic immigrants, as well as scientific advances and aspects of sports and popular culture. You may wish to have the mural divided into sections and have a group of students responsible for completing each section.

■ Invite students to write a poem or a story based on something important that happened in their lives. Encourage them to use descriptive words to paint scenes that might draw the reader in.

Achievers

Remind students that the selections in this theme were folktales in which some fantastic things happened. Help students recall the sisters, Nyasha and Manyara, and each one's personality traits. Then encourage students to consider the brothers in the story "The Weaving of a Dream." Ask them to think about other folktales and fairy tales that are similar in plot. Explain that the questions on page 503 will help them think further about ideas from these selections.

Note that pages T886–T887 provide support for applying the writing process to the last question.

THEME WRAP-UP

ACHIEVERS

You read about characters who wanted to help others and, in doing so, they helped themselves. In what ways are Nyasha and Leje alike? Give examples of behavior that reveal what each is like.

How do you think Manyara and Leje's brothers would have acted differently if the stories were set in modern times? Explain why you think as you do.

WRITER'S WORKSHOP Suppose Nyasha's father and Leje's mother entered them in a contest for selecting the child who did the most good. Write a paragraph to persuade the judge to choose one of the children as the winner. Use convincing facts and examples from the selections.

503

Theme Wrap-Up

DISCUSSION QUESTIONS, PAGE 503
You read about characters who wanted to help others and, in doing so, they helped themselves. In what ways are Nyasha and Leje alike? Give examples of behavior that reveal what each is like. Responses should reflect that both characters possess positive personality traits. (Accept reasonable responses: Both act in unselfish, caring ways.)   INFERENTIAL: DETERMINING CHARACTERS' TRAITS

How do you think Manyara and Leje's brothers would have acted differently if the stories were set in modern times? Explain why you think as you do. Encourage students to describe each setting before thinking about how the characters would act in modern times. (Accept reasonable responses: They might use modern technology.)   CRITICAL: AUTHOR'S CRAFT/IDENTIFYING WITH CHARACTERS

WRITER'S WORKSHOP   See pages T886–T887 for suggestions for applying the writing process. **Suppose Nyasha's father and Leje's mother entered them in a contest for selecting the child who did the most good. Write a paragraph to persuade the judge to choose one of the children as the winner. Use convincing facts and examples from the selections.** You may prefer to allow students to respond to the theme in their own way.   WRITING PROCESS: A PERSUASIVE PARAGRAPH

Writer's Workshop

For More Discussion & Practice:

LANGUAGE HANDBOOK

Ask students to review how they could convince someone to believe something. (Accept reasonable responses: provide strong reasons and facts to explain why the person should believe it.) Encourage them to share instances when they tried to convince someone of something and whether they were successful. Remind students that they would use persuasion techniques if they wanted to convince people. Suggest that students refer to the Handbook in the *Writer's Journal* as they write, revise, and proofread their persuasive paragraphs.

Prewriting

Before students write, have them discuss what qualities represent "goodness" in a person. Have students

- brainstorm personality traits of Nyasha and Leje.
- think about their audience and purpose.
- compare the actions showing the goodness of each character by making lists such as the one below. Students should use the lists to help them decide who is the "better" person.

Nyasha
1. was kind and considerate to her father.
2. was kind to her sister even when her sister was unkind to her.
3. showed kindness and compassion to all creatures.

Encourage students to add to their list as they recall more details from the stories.

Drafting

Ask students to write a draft of the persuasive paragraph. Remind them to

- refer to their lists for ideas.
- write a topic sentence.
- give facts that support their opinion.
- support facts with examples.
- write legibly and freely without worrying about spelling, punctuation, or grammar.

COMPUTER CONNECTION Students may want to use a computer during the revising stage in order to easily add facts and examples to support their opinions.

Responding and Revising

Suggest that students read their persuasive paragraph to a partner to evaluate the overall effectiveness of the draft. Offer the following suggestions, and then have students revise their work.

- Are all statements in an order that makes sense? If not, put them in logical order.
- Are the statements convincing? If not, add strong words and examples.
- Are all opinions supported with facts? If not, add facts.
- Can any sentences be combined? If so, combine them. (See the Language/Literature Link below.)

STUDENT SELF-ASSESSMENT OPTION Students may use the Writing Self-Assessment Checklist in the *Portfolio Teacher's Guide*. Suggest that as they use the checklist, they focus on combining sentences and on the use of commas.

Proofreading

Offer the following tips to assist students in proofreading their work and making changes:

- Check for errors in capitalization and punctuation.
- Be sure the first line of the paragraph is indented.
- Draw a line around any words that seem to be misspelled, and find out how to spell them correctly.

Publishing

You may wish to offer suggestions about how students can publish their work. For instance, some students may wish to read their persuasive paragraphs aloud and then save them in their reading/writing portfolios. Others may wish to make posters on which to display their writing.

LANGUAGE/LITERATURE LINK

Combining Sentences with the Same Predicate

Remind students that successful writers make their points quickly and clearly. They don't waste time repeating words. Explain to students that if two sentences have the same predicate, they can be joined by combining the subjects using the word *and*. Encourage students to check their work to see if any sentences that contain the same predicate can be combined.

Speaking Option

MOCK TRIAL The Writer's Workshop may be adapted to let students use their persuasive paragraphs as the basis for a mock trial. Invite students to pretend that they are attorneys attempting to defend their choice of Nyasha or Leje. Have them follow the guidelines for Prewriting, Drafting, and Responding and Revising. Offer these tips to help students deliver their arguments:

- Use your paragraph to point out examples of the character's positive actions.
- Practice saying what you want to tell the jury.
- Make eye contact and use good voice expression.
- Speak slowly, clearly, and loudly.

Invite classmates to act as the jury while pairs of attorneys, one arguing for Nyasha and the other for Leje, defend their choices.

Young at Heart

Grandma's Bones
from *Nathaniel Talking*

T891   A POEM by Eloise Greenfield
Listen as a young-at-heart grandma "plays her bones."

A Very Special Gift
from *The Canada Geese Quilt*

T893   REALISTIC FICTION by Natalie Kinsey-Warnock
Ariel is making a special gift for her new baby brother or sister. Little does she know that the gift will forge a strong bond between her and her grandmother.

For pacing suggestions, see page T890.

THEME

YOUNG AT HEART

Think about a time when a grandparent or another relative helped you solve a problem or shared your secrets. The grandmothers and grandchildren in the following poem and selection have fun together and help each other through difficult times.

CONTENTS

GRANDMA'S BONES
by Eloise Greenfield

A VERY SPECIAL GIFT
by Natalie Kinsey-Warnock

505

Discussing the Theme

Call attention to the illustration and the theme focus on Student Anthology pages 504–505. Invite students to think about and share anecdotes about their grandparents. Encourage students to read the titles of the poem and the story and to speculate about the ways grandparents and children might interact in these selections.

Reading/Writing Portfolio

Remind students to place their writing responses for the selections in "Young at Heart" in their portfolios. Remind them also to add to their personal journals any thoughts and ideas about books they have read independently.

Managing the Literature-Based Classroom

Management Options

SETTING UP AN EXHIBIT The theme "Young at Heart" is suitable for sparking interest in having the whole class participate in setting up a classroom exhibit. Discuss with students questions such as the following: How and where can we make space for the exhibit? What kinds of items should be included? How should these items be displayed? Who will be responsible for the setting up and taking down? Consolidate suggestions into a plan of action.

SCHEDULING TEACHER TIME Try these techniques for students who wish to schedule time to meet with you:
(1) Have students sign up on a list posted near your desk;
(2) Have students take a number;
(3) Have a stock of "memo" forms for students to communicate a purpose and request a time for meeting.

PACING This theme has been designed to take about two weeks to complete, depending on your students' needs.

Meeting Individual Needs

STUDENTS AT RISK To reduce boredom and behavior problems, play music, use audiovisual materials, and give demonstrations. You may want to set up a puppet-show area with a stage and encourage students to put on a theatrical presentation.

GIFTED AND TALENTED Have students interview classmates about their grandmothers and summarize their findings in a report to their classmates. Encourage students to work together to decide what questions they will ask their classmates. *Challenge Cards* provide additional activities to challenge students. Challenge notes throughout the lesson plans suggest additional activities to stimulate critical and creative thinking.

SPECIAL EDUCATION STUDENTS As students read "A Very Special Gift," have them look for words that give clues to the changing seasons. Tell students to write the names of the seasons, starting with *Spring,* on a sheet of paper and then jot down notes about the story under the proper headings. Encourage students to use these notes in discussions.

LIMITED ENGLISH PROFICIENT STUDENTS Students may need additional practice after the skill lesson on Referents in Learning Through Literature. Have students whose first language is English work as tutors, offering sentences for students to complete with the correct referent. Second-Language Support notes throughout the lesson plans offer strategies to help those students acquiring English to understand the selections.

Grandma's Bones

ABOUT THE POET   Commenting on young people and their elders, award-winning poet and writer Eloise Greenfield says, "I want to give children an appreciation for the contributions of their elders." She explains that older family members give children "valuable assistance in growing up" by offering practical guidance, moral support, and wisdom.

ABOUT THE POEM   "Grandma's Bones," as well as the other poems in *Nathaniel Talking,* is written from the point of view of a nine-year-old boy. It is a free-verse poem in three stanzas about Nathaniel and his grandmother. *Nathaniel Talking* was named an ALA Notable Book and a Coretta Scott King Honor Book.

Reading the Poem

Help students set a purpose for reading.

Ask students to name some music that is popular today and to demonstrate some dances they like to do. Explain that when their grandparents were young, the music was performed by big bands with many instruments, and a fast, energetic dance called the jitterbug was popular.

Ask students to predict how differences, such as tastes in music and dance, might affect the relationship between a nine-year-old boy and his grandmother. Suggest that students read to find out whether their predictions hold true for Nathaniel's relationship with his grandmother.

Responding to the Poem

Return to the purpose for reading.

Ask students whether their predictions about Nathaniel's relationship with his grandmother were confirmed. Encourage them to point out examples of the respect he has for her. Read the poem aloud to students. Then invite them to read it aloud with you.

Encourage students to respond creatively.

You may wish to select one of the following activities for responding to the poem:

COOPERATIVE LEARNING: RESEARCHING DANCE AND MUSIC
Have groups of students find out about the jitterbug and big-band music and report back to the group. Suggest that students begin their investigation by talking with older family members or friends.   LISTENING/SPEAKING/READING/WRITING

PERSONAL JOURNAL: WRITING A POEM   Have students write free-verse poetry to tell about an older relative or friend whom they love and respect. Suggest that they focus on what they have learned or might learn from this person.   WRITING

GRANDMA'S *Bones*

from *Nathaniel Talking* ·by Eloise Greenfield
illustrated by Jan Spivey Gilchrist

Grandma grew up
in the nineteen-forties
she can still do the jitterbug
a dance they used to do
to the music of Duke Ellington,
Benny Carter, Count Basie
and such

she can spin a yo-yo
much better than I
and sometimes she puts
two sticks called bones
between the knuckles
of one hand and goes

clack clack clackety
clackety clack
clackety clackety clackety
clack clack
uh clackety clack
uh clackety clack
clack clack clackety
clackety clack!

506

Expanding the Poem   What might Nathaniel learn from his grandmother? (Accept reasonable responses: how to spin a yo-yo better; more about the Jazz Age or his cultural heritage.)   CRITICAL: DRAWING CONCLUSIONS

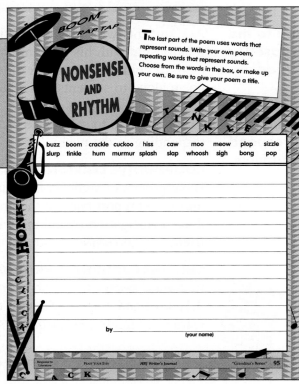

BOOM **RAP TAP**

NONSENSE AND RHYTHM

TINKLE

The last part of the poem uses words that represent sounds. Write your own poem, repeating words that represent sounds. Choose from the words in the box, or make up your own. Be sure to give your poem a title.

| buzz | boom | crackle | cuckoo | hiss | caw | moo | meow | plop | sizzle |
| slurp | tinkle | hum | murmur | splash | slap | whoosh | sigh | bong | pop |

by_____
(your name)

Response to Literature   Feast Your Eyes   HBJ Writer's Journal   "Grandma's Bones"   95

WRITER'S JOURNAL
page 95:
Writing a creative response

A VERY SPECIAL GIFT

from *The Canada Geese Quilt*

by Natalie Kinsey-Warnock

illustrated by Donna Diamond

ALA NOTABLE BOOK

A VERY SPECIAL GIFT

	TEACHING OUTLINE	Materials	Language Arts/ Integrated Curriculum	Meeting Individual Needs
Part 1 **Reading Literature** Pages T896–T907 	**Building Background** **Vocabulary Strategies** Key Words (Tested) **Strategic Reading** Preview and Predict Setting a Purpose **Options for Reading**	Transparency 52 Second-Language Support Manual Practice Book p. 141 Integrated Spelling p. 69 Integrated Spelling T.E. pp. 90–91 Student Anthology pp. 508–524 Response Card 4: Theme/Mood	**Spelling** Spelling Pretest Spelling-Vocabulary Connection	**Second-Language Support** Vocabulary T897 Strategic Reading T898, T900, T903, T904 **Cooperative Reading** T899
Part 2 **Responding to Literature** Pages T908–T913 	**Story Follow-Up** Think It Over Write **Summarizing the Literature** **Appreciating Literature** **Critical Thinking Activities**	Writer's Journal p. 96 Practice Book pp. 142–143 Integrated Spelling p. 70 Integrated Spelling T.E. pp. 90–91 Language Handbook	**Vocabulary Workshop** Reviewing Key Words Extending Vocabulary Classifying/Categorizing **Reading** Oral Rereading/Drama **Writing** Personal Narrative Flowers Poster **Spelling** Reviewing Spelling Words **Speaking** Designing a Family Quilt Designing a Farm Outdoor Things **Listening** Repeating Ideas	**Cooperative Learning** T909, T910, T911, T912
Part 3 **Learning Through Literature** Pages T914–T920 	**Introduce** Comprehension: Referents **Maintain** Comprehension: Paraphrasing/ Summarizing (Tested) Comprehension: Main Idea and Details (Tested)	Transparency 53 Second-Language Support Manual Practice Book pp. 144–146	**Math** Estimating Mileage **Social Studies** Researching Quilts Using Clues to Location Traditions **Art** Making a Quilt Pattern Creating a Collage **Science** Migration Report **Multicultural** Achievers	**Challenge** T915, T916, T917 **Second-Language Support** Referents T915 **Cooperative Learning** T915, T916, T918, T919

KEY WORDS
- crystalline
- migrating
- relief
- frail
- burden
- therapy
- appliquéd

NATALIE KINSEY-WARNOCK

In addition to being a writer, Natalie Kinsey-Warnock is an instructor of cross-country skiing and a painter. *The Canada Geese Quilt* is her first book. It reveals her love of the northeast Vermont landscape, where she grew up. She currently lives with her husband in Vermont.

DONNA DIAMOND

When Donna Diamond was sixteen, she decided that she wanted to illustrate children's books, but she was unsure about all that was involved in being an artist. Today, she travels to schools around the country, explaining to students how books are made from an illustrator's point of view. During her talks, she and the students illustrate a story together. She explains that art does not just materialize, but that there is a process and sometimes that process can be quite exciting.

ADDITIONAL READING

Another Book by Natalie Kinsey-Warnock
The Wild Horses of Sweetbriar. Cobblehill, 1990.   EASY

Other Books About Gifts
And the Winner Is . . . by Stephen Roos. Atheneum, 1989.   AVERAGE
Eight Hands Round: A Patchwork Alphabet by Ann Whitford Paul. HarperCollins, 1991.   AVERAGE
The House on Walenska Street by Charlotte Herman. E. P. Dutton, 1990.   AVERAGE
Sachiko Means Happiness by Kimiko Sakai. Childrens Press, 1990.   EASY

Part 1
Reading Literature

Building Background

Access prior knowledge and build vocabulary concepts.

Read aloud the title of the story and briefly discuss with students what might make a gift very special. Have students write some phrases to describe how they felt about a special gift they gave or received. You might have students organize their phrases in a word web like the one below.

proud   surprised

hard work — **Gift** — important

thoughtful   delighted

Vocabulary Strategies

Introduce Key Words and strategies.

Display Transparency 52 or the following story. Have students read the story silently, using context clues with phonetic and structural analysis to decode and figure out the meanings of the underlined words. Have volunteers read the sentences aloud, providing help with pronunciation if necessary. The activity that follows may be used to check understanding of the Key Words.

Transparency 52   Key Words

Josie stopped sewing and breathed in the clear, <u>crystalline</u> air. Up in the sky <u>migrating</u> geese honked their way south.

What a <u>relief</u> it was to be up and about again! She had been <u>frail</u> and unable to do much since her accident. She felt like a <u>burden</u> to others. But now the exercises she did in <u>therapy</u> had made her hand strong enough to sew again. She had even <u>appliquéd</u> the rose on the scarf she was making for Mother.

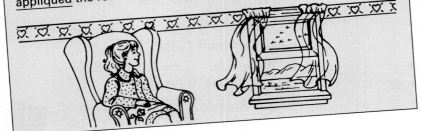

KEY WORDS

crystalline
migrating
relief
frail
burden
therapy
appliquéd

KEY WORDS DEFINED

crystalline transparent

migrating moving from one climate to another with the change of seasons

relief lessening of or freeing from something, as pain

frail weak

burden something difficult to carry or take care of

therapy exercises meant to correct disability

appliquéd trimmed with a cutout decoration

Check students' understanding.

Read aloud the words and phrases below. Have students pick out the word or phrase in each row that does not belong. Encourage them to explain why the word or phrase does not belong. The correct responses are underlined.   STRATEGY: CLASSIFYING

• therapy	bed rest	<u>exercises</u>
• relief	freedom from a responsibility	<u>stress</u>
• <u>settling</u>	moving	migrating
• trimmed with stars	<u>stuffed with cotton</u>	appliquéd
• delicate	frail	<u>strong</u>
• crystalline	pure	<u>stale</u>
• <u>a happy child</u>	a burden	a heavy load

Integrate spelling with vocabulary.

SPELLING-VOCABULARY CONNECTION *Integrated Spelling* page 69 reinforces spellings of words with the /ûr/ sound in the Key Word *burden* and in other words. The spelling of the Key Word *appliquéd* is also included.

SECOND-LANGUAGE SUPPORT Provide students with additional background information about the tradition and process of making a quilt. (See *Second-Language Support Manual.*)

Practice Book

• • • A VERY SPECIAL GIFT • • •

Name _____

A. Complete each sentence by choosing a word from the box and writing it on the line.

relief	appliquéd	burden
migrating	crystalline	frail	therapy

1. Months after her accident, Diane still looked thin and __frail__.

2. Diane's family listened with __relief__ when the doctor told them that Diane would recover completely.

3. Although Diane didn't always enjoy __therapy__, she knew that each hour of exercise made her feel stronger.

4. Diane's younger sister spent a lot of time with Diane and never made her feel that she was a __burden__.

5. Diane decided to make a quilt __appliquéd__ with cutouts of her sister's favorite toys.

6. Diane enjoyed walking in the woods behind her house, breathing the fresh, __crystalline__ air.

7. She watched the __migrating__ geese fly southward.

B. Choose two of the words from the box in Part A and use them in sentences of your own.

1. Sentences will vary. _____

_____

2. _____

Practice Book ■ FEAST YOUR EYES   Vocabulary   141

Integrated Spelling

INTEGRATED SPELLING
The Sound /ûr/

Name _____

Read the Spelling Words. Write them on a separate sheet of paper. Check your spelling.

SPELLING STRATEGY

The letters **er**, **ir**, or **ur** can all spell the /ûr/ sound. Here are some examples of words with this sound:

/ûr/ = **er**   herself   /ûr/ = **ir**   shirt

/ûr/ = **ur**   nurse

You can remember how to spell a word with the /ûr/ sound if you think of other words with the same spelling of this sound.

Write nine of the Spelling Words under their spellings of the /ûr/ sound.

er	ir	ur
deserve	birth	burden
germ	first	nurse
herself	shirt	turn

Which Spelling Word does not have the /ûr/ sound? __appliquéd__

SPELLING WORDS

appliquéd
birth
burden
deserve
first
germ
herself
nurse
shirt
turn

MEMORY JOGGER

What are the **q** and the **u** doing?
They are turning **applied** into **appliquéd**.

This Memory Jogger will help you remember how to spell the word **appliquéd**.

FEAST YOUR EYES • "A Very Special Gift"   69

PRACTICE BOOK
page 141:   Reinforcing Key Words

INTEGRATED SPELLING
page 69:   Writing and spelling words with the /ûr/ sound

NOTE: These pages may be completed now or after students have read the story.

Preview and Predict

Help students preview the literature.

Ask volunteers to tell how readers can get an idea of what a story will be about. (by reading and thinking about the title and the introduction and looking at the illustrations) Have students read the title and the introduction on page 509 and look at the illustration on page 508.

Have students make predictions.

Ask questions such as these to help students consider what might happen in the story:

- **What do you think the gift for the baby will be?**
- **How do you think Ariel will decide what gift to make?**

PERSONAL JOURNAL Have students add their predictions about the story to their personal journals. Ask students to support their predictions.

Setting a Purpose

Have students set purposes.

Brainstorm with students what they want to find out when they read the story, based on their preview and on what they know from their own experience. Have students use their predictions to set a purpose for reading.

Model purpose-setting, if necessary.

If students have difficulty setting a purpose for reading, offer this suggestion:

I'm going to read to find out what makes Ariel's gift for the baby so special.

> ### OPTIONS FOR READING
>
> **INDEPENDENT READING** Have students read the story silently with their purpose for reading in mind.
>
> **GUIDED READING** Follow the Guided Reading suggestions that appear on pages T899, T901, T905, and T907. These suggestions model strategic reading.
>
> **COOPERATIVE READING** A reader response strategy appears on page T899.

SECOND-LANGUAGE SUPPORT Encourage students to use picture clues to help with vocabulary and comprehension as they read. The illustrations in the story can help them visualize the events as they unfold. (See Second-Language Support Manual.)

ALA NOTABLE BOOK

A VERY SPECIAL GIFT

from *The Canada Geese Quilt*

by Natalie Kinsey-Warnock
illustrated by Donna Diamond

When Ariel's parents announced that they were having a new baby, Ariel was confused. She went out to her favorite tree to think about it, and her grandma followed her. They walked to the hayloft and discussed all the babies that Grandma had welcomed into her family and the wonderful friendships and memories that Grandma shared with them.

Ariel began to look forward to the arrival of the new baby. She wanted to make a very special gift for her new brother or sister, but she could not decide what the gift would be.

509

Guided Reading

SET PURPOSE/PREDICT: PAGES 508–513   Have students read through page 513 to find out whether Ariel and Grandma will make a gift together.

Cooperative Reading

READER RESPONSE STRATEGY: PAGES 509–512 Have each group of 3–5 students select a leader. Ask group members to read silently, and then encourage the leaders to use dialogue questions such as those below. (Response Card 4: Theme/Mood, on page R65, offers a wide variety of dialogue questions.)

- **How does Grandma feel about Ariel's talent?**
- **How does Ariel feel before she talks to Grandma? How does Ariel feel after she talks to Grandma?**

PAGES 513–524   After reading, discussion leaders might ask:

- **What events made you feel sad, happy, or worried as you read the rest of the story?**

Over the next few weeks, everyone's thoughts were on the baby. Papa whispered to Ariel that he was making a butternut cradle and asked if she wanted to help him build it. She said yes, but kept thinking about what she could do special for the baby. She could help Papa, but the cradle would still be his present, his idea.

Nothing I do will be good enough, she thought.

She went to talk to Grandma. She felt even closer to Grandma after their talk in the hayloft.

"I know what you mean," said Grandma. "I've been wondering what I could make, too."

"You?" Ariel asked, surprised. "You can make just about anything."

"Well," said Grandma, "I wanted to make a very special quilt for the baby. But I've only made quilts from patterns my mother taught me, handed down to her by her mother. I wish this quilt could be one that nobody's ever seen before. I hoped you'd draw it."

Ariel searched Grandma's face for hints of teasing, but saw none.

"Really?" she asked. "You think I could do it?"

Grandma stroked Ariel's hair.

"I know you could. You have so much talent. And it would mean so much to everyone."

"But, Grandma, don't you see?" Ariel cried. "It's the same thing as Papa's cradle. Even if I draw the design, you'll be the one making the quilt, so it'll be your present, not mine."

"Ariel," Grandma said, "I can sew, but I can't draw. I've always wished I could but I can't. But you can design a picture that's never been made into a quilt before."

510

Ariel had never thought of it like that. Her eyes sparkled.

Later, when Grandma went to the kitchen to start supper, she found Ariel sitting at the table, surrounded by crumpled paper.

"Looks like things aren't going so well," Grandma said.

"They're terrible," Ariel answered. "I don't know whether it's going to be a girl or boy, so I don't know what to draw."

Grandma sat thinking.

"This is going to be a special quilt because of you," she said, "so I think you should have the design show what's special to you. Why don't you think of it that way?"

Ariel worked on the drawing every afternoon when she got home from school. The geese were still migrating north, so she took her sketchbook to the wild apple tree and watched as the geese flew over. Out here, in the raw openness, she could feel what was important to her and the design came easily.

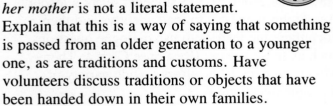

Second-Language Support
Students may need help understanding that the phrase *handed down to her by her mother* is not a literal statement. Explain that this is a way of saying that something is passed from an older generation to a younger one, as are traditions and customs. Have volunteers discuss traditions or objects that have been handed down in their own families.

She took the rolled drawing to Grandma's room.

"I got it done, Grandma," she said softly. She unrolled it on the bed.

On the paper, three Canada geese flew over a stand of cattails and an apple tree just in bloom. The shape of Miles Hill rose behind the tree.

Grandma didn't say anything, and Ariel said, "You don't like it, do you?"

Grandma hugged her.

"Ariel, it's wonderful," she said. "I was just a little scared. I'm not sure I'll be able to make the quilt as beautiful as that drawing deserves. Come, help me decide on the colors."

———————————

Spring came with a rush of wildflowers and soft rain. Papa was busy in the fields. Ariel planted the garden for her mother who found bending difficult. Ariel would hate the weeding later, but she did enjoy the planting: opening the brightly colored packets and pushing the seeds into the warm tilled earth.

In the evenings, Ariel helped Grandma cut out the pieces of cloth and watched as Grandma sewed them together. The quilt began to take on a life of its own, as if the geese really were rising from the cloth.

School let out in June and haying began. The most Papa would let Mama do was drive the horses ("Really, Austin," she would say, "I'm not helpless."), so Ariel worked on the wagon while Papa tossed the hay up to her. She stomped the hay down with her feet as he had shown her, so that the load held together for the bumpy ride back to the barn.

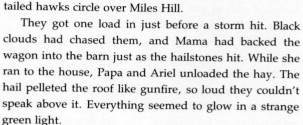

It was hot, tiring work. Ariel rushed to keep pace with her father. Sweat trickled down her back, and chaff stuck to her face and arms. Just when it seemed that the itch of the chaff would drive her crazy, they'd have a load and be riding back to the barn, a slight breeze cooling her skin. Then she could relax for a few minutes and watch red-tailed hawks circle over Miles Hill.

They got one load in just before a storm hit. Black clouds had chased them, and Mama had backed the wagon into the barn just as the hailstones hit. While she ran to the house, Papa and Ariel unloaded the hay. The hail pelted the roof like gunfire, so loud they couldn't speak above it. Everything seemed to glow in a strange green light.

Suddenly, Mama was standing in the doorway, her face unnaturally pale against the dark sky. There were red blotches on her arms where the hailstones had hit. Papa was beside her in an instant.

"Austin," she said, "it's Mother," and they both sprinted toward the house.

Ariel followed them, no longer aware of the storm. She'd heard the fear in Mama's voice; something was terribly wrong.

She stood on the porch, afraid to go into the house. The wind whipped at her clothes, and lightning tore jagged streaks through the sky. She shivered even though she wasn't cold.

Papa drove the car right up to the steps. He ran back into the house and, in a few minutes, he and Mama came back out, carrying Grandma. Grandma's eyes were closed, her face gray. Ariel shrank back against the porch railing. Papa lay Grandma in the back seat of the car.

513

Guided Reading

MONITOR COMPREHENSION: PAGES 508–513
Do Ariel and Grandma make a gift together?
(They begin to make a quilt together.)   STRATEGIC READING: RETURNING TO PURPOSE

How does Ariel decide what to draw for the quilt? (Grandma suggests that Ariel choose what is important to her, so Ariel works on the drawing outside.)   STRATEGIC READING: SUMMARIZING

What happens to make Ariel feel afraid?
(Grandma's eyes are closed and her face is gray.)
INFERENTIAL: DETERMINING CAUSE-EFFECT

SET PURPOSE/PREDICT: PAGES 514–520   Have students predict what will happen to Grandma, Ariel, and the quilting project. Have them read to the end of page 520 to find out whether Grandma gets better.

Mama ducked back onto the porch and gripped Ariel's arms.

"Ariel, we have to get Grandma to the doctor. I'm counting on you to take care of yourself. Just go inside and stay there."

"Is Grandma going to die?" Ariel asked. Her voice sounded cracked and wavering.

Her mother was trying hard not to cry.

"I don't know, honey," she said. Her mouth trembled. She climbed into the back seat, cradling Grandma's head in her lap. Ariel watched the car go down the driveway and disappear over the hill. She was alone.

She wandered from room to room. Her footsteps echoed on the pine floors. The old house seemed to be holding its breath, waiting for someone to fill its emptiness.

Ariel took the Iris quilt from Mama's cedar chest. She wrapped it around herself and sat in the rocker. The picture of Grandma as she was carried to the car played over and over in her mind. She imagined Papa and Mama coming home, both of them crying and she'd know Grandma was dead without them telling her.

Papa didn't get home until dusk. Ariel met him at the door and he gathered her up in his arms.

"Where's Mama?" Ariel asked, afraid to ask about Grandma.

"She's staying at the hospital," he said. "Grandma's very sick, and Mama doesn't want to leave her."

"I'm scared, Papa," said Ariel.

"So am I," he said, "but worrying won't help. We need to keep busy."

514

Vocabulary Strategy   Ask students how to figure out the meaning of *cradling* on page 514. (When I read, I use context clues and visualize the entire scene. By doing this, I find out that Mama has Grandma's head in her lap. *Cradling* must mean "holding something carefully as in a cradle.")   STRATEGY: CONTEXT CLUES

The days blurred together. Ariel felt numb, as if her body belonged to someone else. Mama stayed with Grandma. Meals were a strange mixture of leftovers and the few things Papa could cook. Papa and Ariel did the milking, forked hay down for the cows, curried and fed the horses, collected eggs, and tried to keep the house tidy. Papa did his best to keep Ariel's spirits up, but nothing loosened the fear that gripped her heart.

Ariel had a dream. In it, Grandma was at the cookstove, making pancakes. There was a rolled-up quilt on the table behind her. The quilt unfolded and geese began to fly out, their dark bodies filling the kitchen. Grandma raised her arms in front of her face and pushed through their beating wings. Ariel called after her, but Grandma kept walking into the darkness of their wings until she disappeared.

Ariel sat up in bed, her heart thudding. The eastern sky was just beginning to lighten.

The smell of pancakes drifted up the stairs. Ariel was out of bed in an instant, running barefoot down the stairs.

Grandma? she thought.

Mama and Papa stood by the stove, talking softly as Mama flipped the pancakes. Mama turned and saw Ariel.

"Mother's out of the woods now," she declared, brushing back tendrils of hair. She had stayed at the hospital four days, but to Ariel it seemed like months since Mama had been home. Mama had grown thinner, but that only emphasized the growing roundness of the baby. Papa hugged her.

"Claire," he said, "you've got to get some rest. You've run yourself ragged. It's not good for the baby."

Mama was too tired to protest.

"I do need some sleep," she admitted. She handed the spatula to Papa, and walked to the bedroom. Ariel followed at a distance. She watched as Mama lay down.

Mama turned over in bed, and saw her standing in the doorway. She held out her arms and Ariel rushed into them.

"I'm sorry I've been gone so much," Mama said, stroking Ariel's hair.

"When is Grandma coming home?" Ariel asked.

"Not for a long time, honey," Mama said. "She's been very sick. And even when she does come home, she'll be different."

"What do you mean, Mama?"

"Grandma had a stroke. She can't walk very well and it's hard for her to pronounce words. She's going to need all of us to help her." Mama sounded so tired. Ariel had a dozen questions to ask, but Mama was already drifting off to sleep.

⬧━━━━◆━━━━⬧

Grandma came home in August. Ariel was afraid of her. The frail, drooped-face woman in the bedroom couldn't be Grandma. Grandma had pink cheeks and busy hands; the woman in the bedroom was gray and shriveled.

Mama had said not to tire Grandma. Ariel told herself that that was the only reason she wasn't visiting with Grandma, but she knew it was more than that. She didn't like to look at Grandma. She didn't know what to say, or how to act. Ariel spent more and more time outside, helping Papa with his work. When she did come inside, if she didn't look at that closed door, she could almost forget how everything had changed.

517

Second-Language Support

Students may need help understanding the phrases *out of the woods* and *run yourself ragged*. To help students understand these phrases, reword each sentence using simple, literal language.

MEETING INDIVIDUAL NEEDS

It was almost a <u>relief</u> to start school. Then Ariel didn't need to make so many excuses. With school, chores, and homework, there just wasn't any time to visit with Grandma.

Then one evening, Mama came out of Grandma's bedroom, sat down heavily in the rocker and covered her face with her hands. Papa had just come in from doing the milking and saw her.

"What's wrong, Claire?" he asked. "Is it the baby?"

She shook her head.

"Oh, Austin," she said. "Mother's given up. I thought she'd get her strength back being home. She had <u>therapy</u> at the hospital, and the doctor said she was able to walk with a cane now. He thought she would do better at home, but she feels she's a <u>burden</u>, and she isn't even trying to get better. I just don't think I can take it anymore, watching her lie there like that."

Ariel hadn't realized before that this was as hard on Mama as it was on her. And even harder on Grandma. Grandma was lying in that room, feeling that the family would be better off without her.

If it was me who was sick, thought Ariel, Grandma would do everything she could to help me.

When she got home from school the next afternoon, she took a deep breath and walked into Grandma's room. She leaned against the door wondering what she would say.

Grandma looked pale and still, nothing like the determined, energetic woman Ariel remembered.

518

Second-Language Support

Students may need help understanding what Mama means when she says, "I just don't think I can take it anymore. . . ." Explain that seeing Grandma just lie in bed day after day, not trying to walk or talk, has tired Mama. She cannot bear it any longer. Help students understand how the characters feel at this point in the story by guiding students in completing these sentence frames:

- Mama feels <u>(tired/sad/disappointed)</u>.
- Grandma feels <u>(hopeless/sad)</u>.
- Ariel feels <u>(angry/alone/sorry)</u>.

"We had a test at school today," Ariel said, hesitantly, "and I got an A. We've been studying mythology. You'd read me all those stories before, anyway, remember? And I told the teacher the legend about the stars being the sun's children. She liked it."

Grandma hadn't moved or said a word. Ariel felt very uncomfortable. She knew she was rambling on to fill the silence. She sighed.

"Well, I'll see you tomorrow, Grandma," she said.

Mama met her in the hall. She hugged Ariel.

"Thank you for visiting with Grandma," Mama said. "I know it's not easy."

"Mama, I felt like I might as well be talking to an empty bed."

"I know, honey," said Mama. "But we've just got to keep on trying. Something will break through that wall she's put up."

Ariel began bringing things from her walks: an apple from her special tree, a bunch of ripe wild grapes she'd picked from the fencerow. One afternoon, she walked over to the bed, her hands cupped.

"Grandma, look!" She opened her hands; an orange monarch butterfly rested lightly on them. "I was walking home through the pasture and hundreds of butterflies flew up. Papa says they're migrating. Oh, Grandma, they were so beautiful! They filled the air." And for the first time, Ariel saw a flicker of interest in Grandma's eyes.

She's listening! Ariel thought, excitedly.

"They're still in the pasture," she said. "Let's go out and see them."

Grandma shook her head. Ariel leaned closer.

"Please, Grandma. Why have you given up? We need you. Please don't give up," she pleaded, and saw tears in Grandma's eyes.

It was a short walk. Grandma held Ariel's arm and took slow, halting steps, but there was color in her cheeks where there had been none before.

They stopped to pick chicory and Queen Anne's lace. Grandma cradled the wildflowers lovingly and looked out over the valley. The hillsides were beginning to change color. The late afternoon sun slanted across the fields. Grandma breathed the fall air deeply. For the first time since she'd been home, she looked happy.

Grandma began to talk. Her tongue moved clumsily over the words, but Ariel heard and understood them.

"I forgot life is so good," Grandma said.

When they got back to the house, Ariel lifted the quilt from its drawer and laid it in Grandma's lap.

"Now we can finish the quilt together," Ariel said.

Grandma held up her crooked hand.

"It won't be as good as if you sewed it," Ariel admitted, "but you can teach me."

Grandma gave her a questioning look.

"I know," Ariel said, laughing, "I hate to sew. And don't expect me to do it again. But this is a special occasion. Besides, you've done most of the work."

Before her stroke, Grandma had appliquéd all of the design, added a border of deep blue cloth, and started the quilting. In the past, Grandma's quick, sure fingers would have flown through the rest. Now it was up to Ariel.

Guided Reading

MONITOR COMPREHENSION: PAGES 514–520
Does Grandma get better? (She does not seem to get better.)   STRATEGIC READING: RETURNING TO PURPOSE

How does Ariel react after Grandma goes to the hospital and after she comes home? (Ariel is very worried while Grandma is away. When Grandma returns home, Ariel is afraid to go near her, so she avoids spending time with Grandma.)
STRATEGIC READING: SUMMARIZING

SET PURPOSE/PREDICT: PAGES 521–524   Have students think about the last two paragraphs on page 520 and predict whether Ariel will be able to help Grandma. Have students read the rest of the story to see whether Ariel's plan for helping Grandma works.

Papa was filling the barn with the summer's harvest, and Mama was so busy these days with canning and preserving the food from the garden and orchard that it was easy for Ariel to slip into Grandma's room to work on the quilt without getting questioned.

The quilting seemed agonizingly slow. Ariel made a lot of mistakes. She had to pull out stitches, and she pricked her fingers. Worst of all was sitting inside when the weather outside was so inviting.

As if to tease her, the days were especially lovely, the last warm days before the cold months of winter. The hills blazed with the scarlet and orange of maples, and the yellow of popples and birches. Apples and butternuts hung heavily from the trees along the fencerow, almost begging to be picked.

One afternoon, as Ariel walked home from school, one of the first great wedges of geese honked southward. Ariel watched them and her heart thrilled to their ancient song. She wished she was with them, sailing high and free on the wind. But Grandma was waiting.

Grandma's room seemed dark and airless compared to the deep ocean of sky and crystalline air. Ariel sat sulkily in her chair and picked up the quilt. She thought she could still hear the geese calling. She tugged at the knot in the thread until it broke, then threw the quilt to the floor.

"Oh, I'm so sick of sewing!" she cried. "A stupid quilt for a stupid baby. I'm never going to sew again. I hate it."

She jumped up and ran for the door.

"Ariel, wait," Grandma called.

Ariel spun around and before she could stop them, the words spilled out, "I want to be outside. I hate that quilt and I hate you!"

522

She froze in horror.

To her amazement, Grandma chuckled.

"Good for you," Grandma said in a slow, deliberate voice that was a result of her stroke. "Ever since I got home, you and your folks have been tiptoeing around here like you were on eggshells, afraid to say or do anything that might upset me. You're the first person to get mad, and I'm glad of it."

"But, Grandma, I didn't mean to say such a horrible thing. You must hate me."

"Oh, fiddlesticks, and I know you don't hate me. You're mad because I got sick and it made you scared. I get mad, too, because I can't do some of the things I used to."

Ariel ran to give Grandma a hug.

Expanding the Literature   How does the author's description of the seasons and months help you understand the story? (It helps you know how much time has passed.)

METACOGNITIVE: DETERMINING SEQUENCE

Why does Grandma laugh when Ariel throws down the quilt and says she hates Grandma? (She knows that Ariel doesn't really hate her: Ariel is just frustrated with her sewing. Grandma is also glad that someone has finally gotten angry instead of tiptoeing around.)   INFERENTIAL: DRAWING CONCLUSIONS

"I really love you, Grandma. And I think it's a beautiful quilt."

"But we'll both be glad when it's done, won't we?" Grandma said with a twinkle in her eye. "Run along and enjoy the afternoon. The quilt will still be here tomorrow."

After that, whenever Ariel got frustrated, she reminded herself of the battle Grandma faced. Grandma struggled with words, and with legs and hands that could no longer be trusted.

When the quilt was finally finished, Ariel was almost afraid to touch it. She'd never seen so beautiful a quilt.

THINK IT OVER

1. *How did Ariel and Grandma help each other?*

2. *Why couldn't Ariel decide what to make for the new baby?*

3. *Why do you think Grandma gave up after her stroke?*

4. *Do you think that the quilt in this story was important? Explain why you think as you do.*

WRITE

If you were Ariel, how would you have tried to help Grandma? Write a get-well message explaining why it's important to keep trying.

For discussion of this page, please turn to T921.

THEME WRAP-UP

YOUNG AT HEART

We can learn a lot from our grandparents and other older adults. Think about why the grandmothers you read about are important to their families. What do they contribute to the lives of their children and grandchildren?

What special qualities do the grandmothers in the poem and selection share?

WRITER'S WORKSHOP   Ask a grandparent or another older relative about what life was like when he or she was your age. Gather information about the time period when that person was young and the place where he or she lived. Write a report about that person's early life. You may want to include photographs with your report. Share your report with the person you wrote about.

525

Guided Reading

MONITOR COMPREHENSION: PAGES 521–524
Does Ariel's plan for helping Grandma work?
(yes) **Is that what you predicted would happen?**
(Responses will vary.)   STRATEGIC READING: CONFIRMING PREDICTIONS

What finally makes Grandma want to help herself? (Ariel helps Grandma remember how good life is.)   INFERENTIAL: DETERMINING CAUSE-EFFECT

What happens to the quilting project? (Ariel finishes the quilt with Grandma's direction.)
STRATEGIC READING: SUMMARIZING

Returning to the Predictions   Invite
students to discuss the predictions that they made before they began reading and that they may have written in their personal journals. Encourage them to talk about how those predictions changed.

Returning to the Purpose for Reading
Ask students to tell in their own words what made the quilt a very special gift. (It was created and sewn with love, thoughtfulness, and originality. It was also put together with great effort, because Ariel learned to do something she did not like.)

NOTE: Responses to the Think It Over questions and support for the Write activity appear on page T908.

Part 2
Responding to Literature

Story Follow-Up

Think It Over

Encourage reader's response: student page 524.

1. **How did Ariel and Grandma help each other?** (Ariel gave Grandma a reason to help herself get well. Grandma gave Ariel the confidence and support she needed to believe in herself.)   CRITICAL: SUMMARIZING

2. **Why couldn't Ariel decide what to make for the new baby?** (Nothing she thought of was *all* hers.)   INFERENTIAL: DETERMINING CAUSE-EFFECT

3. **Why do you think Grandma gave up after her stroke?** (Recovering from a stroke takes great effort, and Grandma had lost the will to make that effort.)   INFERENTIAL: DRAWING CONCLUSIONS

4. **Do you think that the quilt in this story was important? Explain why you think as you do.** (Responses will vary.)   CRITICAL: EXPRESSING PERSONAL OPINIONS

Write

Encourage writer's response: student page 524.

If you were Ariel, how would you have tried to help Grandma? Write a get-well message explaining why it's important to keep trying. Encourage students to decorate their cards.   CREATIVE: WRITING GET-WELL MESSAGES

Summarizing the Literature

Have students retell the story and write a summary.

Have students summarize the story by recalling key events and writing them in the chart below. Guide them in beginning the chart and have them finish it independently. (See *Practice Book* page 142 on T909.) Students may use their completed charts to retell the story and to write a brief summary statement.

	Before the Stroke	Right After the Stroke	At the End of the Story
Grandma	(Grandma is active, happy, and busy. She has the idea for making a quilt for the baby.)		
Ariel	(Ariel is close to Grandma. They talk together often.)		

STRATEGY CONFERENCE

Ask students what they found difficult about reading the story. Together, brainstorm strategies such as visualizing that might have helped them better understand the story.

NOTE

An additional writing activity for this selection appears on page T911.

INFORMAL ASSESSMENT

Having students **summarize** in this way will help you informally assess how well they comprehended the author's purpose. It will also help you see how well they recognized the way the author developed characters in this story.

Appreciating Literature

Have students share personal responses.

Have students work in small groups to discuss the story. Provide a general question such as the following to help the groups begin:

- **Does anyone in this story remind you of someone you know? Explain how.**

PERSONAL JOURNAL   Have students use their personal journals to write about ideas and feelings that are discussed in the groups. You may also refer them to their personal journals after they complete the activity below.

Critical Thinking Activities

Encourage both cooperative and individual responses.

MAKE A CHART   How is Ariel's daily life similar to or different from your own? Have students work in groups to make a chart comparing and contrasting their lives with Ariel's. Remind them to include the chores people do on a farm and the jobs they are responsible for.   CRITICAL: COMPARING AND CONTRASTING

DESIGN A PATTERN   Ariel's quilt design was special because it was her favorite scene. What scene would you choose for a quilt? Have students design a pattern for a quilt they might make. Encourage students to show their designs and explain why they are meaningful.   CREATIVE: EXPRESSING PERSONAL OPINIONS

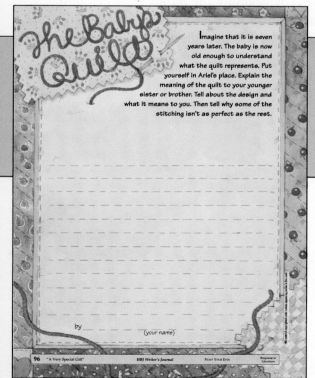

Writer's Journal

Imagine that it is seven years later. The baby is now old enough to understand what the quilt represents. Put yourself in Ariel's place. Explain the meaning of the quilt to your younger sister or brother. Tell about the design and what it means to you. Then tell why some of the stitching isn't as perfect as the rest.

by _____
(your name)

96   "A Very Special Gift"   HBJ Writer's Journal   FEAST YOUR EYES   Response to Literature

Writer's Journal

Practice Book

● ● ● A VERY SPECIAL GIFT ● ● ●

Name _____

A. One way to summarize a story is to write the key events on a chart. Finish the chart below. **Possible responses are given.**

	Before the Stroke	Right After the Stroke	At the End of the Story
Grandma	Grandma is active, happy, and busy. She has the idea for making a quilt for the baby.	She is frail, gray, and shriveled. She seems to have given up.	She is trying to walk. She has begun to talk. She still has trouble with her hands.
Ariel	Ariel is close to Grandma. They talk together often.	She is afraid, angry, and frustrated.	She has finished the quilt and has helped Grandma get better.
The Quilt	Ariel draws the design for the quilt. Grandma sews the quilt.	No one works on the quilt.	Ariel finishes the quilt with Grandma's help.

B. Write a one-sentence summary of the selection based on the information in your chart. **A possible response is given.**

When Ariel's grandmother suffers a stroke, it takes her a while before she wants to do things like finish the quilt she and Ariel started.

142   **Summarizing the Literature**   Practice Book ● FEAST YOUR EYES

Practice Book

VO·CAB·U·LAR·Y Workshop

Reviewing Key Words

Display the Key Words and have students answer the following questions, orally or in writing:

1. *crystalline*   **Compare the crystalline air outside with the air in Grandma's room.** (outside—clear and fresh; Grandma's room—stale)
2. *migrating*   **Which two types of animals in the story were described as migrating?** (Canada geese and monarch butterflies)
3. *relief*   **Why was it a relief for Ariel when school started?** (It was an excuse to avoid Grandma.)
4. *frail*   **Why was Grandma frail after her stroke?** (Her stroke had physically weakened her.)
5. *burden*   **Why did Grandma feel like a burden?** (She had to depend on family members.)
6. *therapy*   **What did Grandma learn to do in therapy?** (walk with a cane)
7. *appliquéd*   **What did Grandma do when she appliquéd Ariel's design on the quilt?** (sewed it on)

PRACTICE BOOK
page 143:   Classifying nouns

• • • A VERY SPECIAL GIFT • • •

Name _____

A. Fill in the web below with the names of vegetables and fruits that fit in the categories. Possible responses are given.

- Things we eat
  - Grow on plants
    - fruits — tomatoes, grapes
    - roots — carrots, potatoes
  - Grow on trees
    - apples
    - oranges

B. In the box below are words that describe types of weather. Classify or organize them into two groups in a web.
Possible responses are given.

snow   fog   rain   sleet

- Types of Weather
  - frozen — snow, sleet
  - non-frozen — rain, fog

Practice Book ■ FEAST YOUR EYES   Classifying/Categorizing   143

Practice Book

Extending Vocabulary

CLASSIFYING/CATEGORIZING   Explain that scientists classify, or categorize, living things into certain groups, such as *fauna* (animals) or *flora* (plants). Tell students that these categories can be divided into smaller categories, including *types of animals* or *types of plants*. Draw on the board a word map like the one below and guide students in adding story words.

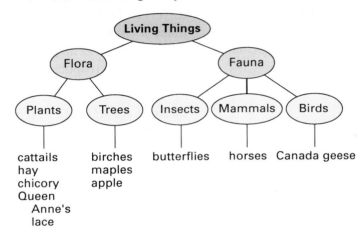

Living Things
- Flora
  - Plants — cattails, hay, chicory, Queen Anne's lace
  - Trees — birches, maples, apple
- Fauna
  - Insects — butterflies
  - Mammals — horses
  - Birds — Canada geese

COOPERATIVE LEARNING   Have students form pairs and create similar webs. Ask students to add more subcategories (*reptiles, amphibians*) or to reorganize the categories (by dividing the *plants* category into *vegetables* and *flowers,* for instance). Have students compare their webs and explain the addition of any new categories.

Language Arts

READING

Oral Rereading/Drama

COOPERATIVE LEARNING Have small groups of students choose the parts of Ariel, Grandma, and the narrator and reread the passage on pages 520–521 in which Ariel walks to the pasture with Grandma. Or, have them select another passage in which an important event occurs. Remind them to first reread the passage silently. Show students how to blend the narrator's lines with the dialogue by reading aloud a few lines of narration, with volunteers reading the dialogue. Encourage groups to rehearse together and then present their readings.
LISTENING/READING

WRITING

Writing About the Literature

WRITE A PERSONAL NARRATIVE Have students recall the phrases they wrote about giving or receiving a special gift and the web they completed before reading. Tell students that they will use those phrases to develop a story. Explain that a *personal narrative* is a story about a personal experience told from the first-person point of view by the author. If necessary, remind students that in a story told in the first person, the author refers to himself or herself as "I." To help students plan their stories, display the following chart and suggest that students use it to organize their ideas. WRITING

The Gift:	
Who gave it:	Who received it:
Important events:	Why it was special:

NOTE: An additional writing activity appears on page T908.

SPELLING

Reviewing Spelling Words

SPELLING WORDS: *appliquéd, birth, burden, deserve, first, germ, herself, nurse, shirt, turn*

Auction off spelling words to students. Write each word on a separate card. Then on a separate card, misspell each word, interchanging various spellings of the /ûr/ sound. Distribute approximately 50 tokens to each student.

Hold up one card at a time and have students bid on each word, with the card going to the highest bidder. The object is to acquire only correctly spelled words. When all the cards are gone, award 3 points for each correctly spelled word and subtract 5 points for each misspelled word. LISTENING/SPEAKING/SPELLING

INTEGRATED SPELLING page 70:
Writing words with the /ûr/ sound

INTEGRATED SPELLING
The Sound /ûr/

Name _____

WORD PLAY

Unscramble the Spelling Words and write each one on the line. Then find all the circled letters. Unscramble those letters to find out the answer to the riddle.

WORD BANK
appliquéd
birth
burden
deserve
first
germ
herself
nurse
shirt
turn

1. RESVEED — DESERVE
2. FLERESH — HERSELF
3. QUAPELIDP — APPLIQUED
4. STIRF — FIRST
5. RIBTH — BIRTH
6. SNURE — NURSE
7. RNTU — TURN
8. TRISH — SHIRT
9. MERG — GERM

Q. What clams up when you ask it for favors?
A. A SELFISH S H E L L F I S H !

SPELLING DETECTIVE

Cristal liked reading "A Very Special Gift" very much. She decided to write about her own experience. When she proofread what she had written, she found five mistakes. Circle each one, and then write the word correctly above the mistake.

My older brother Roberto was my favorite. Ever
birth
since my berth we were best friends. I was so sad
first
when he got sick. At furst I didn't know what to do.

One afternoon, I sat with him and held his hand. I was
turn   **nurse**
happy to take my trun to help him. Often, I helped nirse

Roberto. When he died, I missed him a lot. He was
burden
never a buredn. It makes me happy to know we had

some time together.

70   "A Very Special Gift" • FEAST YOUR EYES

Integrated Spelling

WRITING

A Year of Flowers

AVAILABLE ON PROJECT CARD

COOPERATIVE LEARNING   Recall with students that Ariel and Grandma picked Queen Anne's lace and chicory. Have students work in small groups to design and create flower calendars they can give as gifts to friends and family. Suggest that for each month, students choose a flower and research it to include a description and a drawing of it. You may want to supply students with calendars of the upcoming year for use as reference. Before students write the descriptions, review the use of descriptive adjectives. Discuss using specific, vivid adjectives (for example, *velvety* instead of *soft*) and guide students in creating a vivid description of one flower, such as a rose.   LISTENING/READING/WRITING

SPEAKING

A Family Quilt

CULTURAL AWARENESS   Have students talk with family members and discuss what designs they might include in a family quilt. Some designs might include special symbols, words, drawings of pets, scenes from vacations or trips, or anything else important to the family. Discuss symbols with students. Point out that a symbol is an object that stands for an idea. For example, to many Americans the bald eagle symbolizes freedom. Ask students from different countries to share information about symbols that are important to them. Encourage students to decide on a family symbol to incorporate into their quilts. Have students draw the quilt or write a description of it and then share their quilt design with classmates.   LISTENING/SPEAKING/WRITING

SPEAKING

Build Your Own Farm

AVAILABLE ON PROJECT CARD

COOPERATIVE LEARNING   Remind students that the family in "A Very Special Gift" lived on a farm. Have students work in small groups to design a farm they would like to live on. Students might draw a map, a diagram, or a mural of the farm. Encourage them to include and label various parts of the farm (farmhouse, fields, barn, pond, roads, and so on). Tell students to be as specific as possible by identifying what crops they would grow, what machines they would use, and what animals they would keep.   LISTENING/SPEAKING/WRITING

A Giant Basket of Baby Gifts

Have students form a circle. Ask each student to think of a present he or she could put in a giant gift basket for a new baby. Choose one student to start the game by saying: "I'll contribute a [red stroller]." The next student in the circle picks up the game by repeating the first student's gift and adding another. ("I'll contribute a [red stroller] and a [wind-up dog].") Continue around the circle, adding items until each student has had a chance to contribute.   LISTENING/SPEAKING

SPEAKING

And This One Is From . . .

Encourage students to bring in and share things they have collected on walks or hikes. These might include rocks, fossils, or pressed flowers. Have them share their collection with classmates, explaining where each item was found, what it is, and why it is special.   LISTENING/ SPEAKING

WRITING

Change It! Move It!

Have students think about the problems Grandma and other people who have suffered strokes have with moving around and talking. Suggest that students each think of one thing in their home, school, or community that could be changed to make the lives of people with disabilities easier. Have students create campaign posters for their choices, being sure to include the reasons for those choices. When students have finished, have them take turns presenting and discussing their work.
LISTENING/SPEAKING/WRITING

Part 3
Learning Through Literature

Referents

OBJECTIVE: *To identify referents and the words they replace*

1	Focus

Explain the importance of recognizing referents.

Explain to students that sometimes when authors are telling about characters or things, they use words, such as *he, she, others,* and *it* to refer to the characters and things. Point out that recognizing when authors use words to stand for or refer to other words will help them understand what they read.

2	Teach/Model

Model recognizing pronoun referents.

Display Transparency 53 or these sentences. Read the first group of sentences aloud and model the thinking.

Transparency 53   Referents

"But we'll be glad when it's done, won't we?" Grandma said with a twinkle in her eye. "Run along and enjoy the afternoon. The quilt will still be here tomorrow."
    After that, whenever Ariel got frustrated, she reminded herself of the battle Grandma faced.

> **As I read the first paragraph, I come to the pronoun referent *we*. I know that writers use pronouns, such as *he, her,* and *we,* to avoid repeating people's names. I can figure out that *we* refers to Grandma and Ariel, because Grandma is talking to Ariel.**

Guide students in identifying the person or item the remaining pronouns in the first paragraph refer to. (the quilt, Grandma)

Help students recognize other referents.

Display the following headings and explain that referents can substitute for any of the following: *person, object, action, place, numbers, idea.* Use the second paragraph on Transparency 53 to model other kinds of referents.

> **When I read the word *that*, I know it is replacing something written before it. I reread the paragraph and realize that the word *that* refers to the action that's mentioned in the first paragraph.**

Guide students in identifying the words that the referents *she* and *herself* replace.

CHALLENGE Have students select a paragraph from the story and rewrite it, replacing referents with the word or words they take the place of. Then have students trade paragraphs with a partner and figure out how to insert referents to make the paragraph more interesting to read.

SUPPORT Students can demonstrate their understanding by using referents to complete sentence frames such as these: Ariel liked geese; she liked drawing [them] . (See *Second-Language Support Manual.*)

3	Practice/Apply

Have students apply the learning.

COOPERATIVE LEARNING Have students work in pairs to locate sections of the story that contain referents and to identify the word or words each referent refers to.

4	Summarize

Informally assess the learning.

Have students read the passages they selected, name the referents, tell what each referent refers to, and explain how they decided.

Have students summarize what they learned. (Referents are pronouns or words that stand for, or rename, other words in writing.)

• • • A VERY SPECIAL GIFT • • •

Name _____

A. Read each pair of sentences below. Then rewrite the second sentence, using referents instead of the underlined words or phrases.
Possible responses are given.

1. In the fall the apples in the orchard will be ripe. Ariel will go to the orchard and collect apples for Grandma. _____ Ariel will go there and collect several for Grandma.

2. Ariel hopes Grandma will make apple pies. Grandma makes apple pies better than anyone else that Ariel knows. _____ She makes them better than anyone else that Ariel knows.

3. Ariel will sit on the porch and draw a picture of the orchard for Grandma. Ariel plans to give the picture to Grandma for Grandma's birthday. _____ She plans to give the picture to Grandma for her birthday.

B. Write one possible referent for each word or phrase below.
Possible responses are given.

1. Papa, Mama, Ariel, and Grandma: _____ they, them, themselves
2. Ariel: _____ she, her, herself
3. the baby: _____ he, she, him, her, herself, himself
4. Ariel's plan: _____ it, that
5. the doctor: _____ he, she, him, her, herself, himself
6. the stroke: _____ it, itself
7. the migrating birds: _____ they, them, themselves, several

144   Referents   Practice Book • FEAST YOUR EYES

Practice Book

PRACTICE BOOK
page 144: Using referents

Paraphrasing/Summarizing

OBJECTIVE: *To develop global meaning through paraphrasing and summarizing*

Review

Have students review paraphrasing/ summarizing.

Ask students to describe what they do when they paraphrase or summarize a story or an article. (Retell a passage briefly in one's own words; combine, or synthesize, the most important parts.) Remind students that both strategies help them remember what they read. Model the strategies by paraphrasing and summarizing page 510.

Practice/Apply

Have students paraphrase/ summarize.

COOPERATIVE LEARNING Have students work in small groups and choose one section of the story to paraphrase and one section to summarize.

Summarize

Informally assess the learning.

Have students read aloud their paraphrases and summaries and explain why they decided to include some events but not others.

Have students summarize what they learned. (Paraphrasing is putting things into one's own words; summarizing combines, or synthesizes, main parts of a selection.)

MEETING INDIVIDUAL NEEDS

CHALLENGE Have students write a brief summary of the entire story. Challenge them to keep the summary as short as possible while still including the most important ideas.

PRACTICE BOOK
page 145:
Paraphrasing/
Summarizing

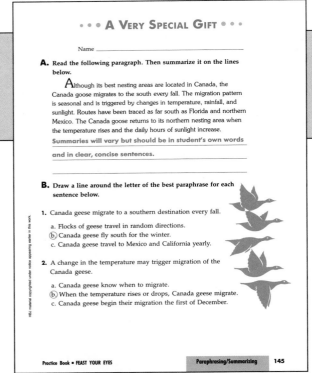

Practice Book

Main Idea and Details

OBJECTIVE: *To identify main ideas and supporting details*

Review

Review identifying main idea and details.

Recall with students that locating the main idea and supporting details helps them understand an author's most important points. Read aloud the beginning of the story, stopping after the line ". . . so it'll be your present, not mine" on page 510. Lead students to realize that the main idea is "Ariel wanted to give the baby a gift that would really be from her." The details about helping Papa and helping Grandma support the main idea.

Practice/Apply

Have students apply the learning.

Have students choose a passage from the story, figure out the main idea, and identify two supporting details.

Summarize

Informally assess the learning.

Have students share their passage and explain how they determined the main idea and supporting details.

Have students summarize what they learned. (The main idea is the author's most important point. Supporting details tell important information about the main idea.)

CHALLENGE Have students choose the character of either Ariel or Grandma and write a paragraph about the character in which the main idea is unstated. Encourage students to trade paragraphs and to decide what the main idea is by focusing on the details.

PRACTICE BOOK
page 146: Identifying main idea and details

---

* * * **A VERY SPECIAL GIFT** * * *

Name _____

Read each paragraph below. Then write its main idea and any three details.

Quilting is a very old art. Some ancient statues, dating back 3,000 years, show people wearing quilted clothing. Quilted clothing, especially the thick military jackets worn under armor, was used from the sixteenth century. In the eighteenth century, stylish women in Europe enjoyed the warmth of quilted silk petticoats and quilted coverlets.

Main idea: ___Quilting is a very old art.___

Detail 1: ___Accept any three details from the paragraph.___

Detail 2: _____

Detail 3: _____

A patchwork quilt is easy to make. Basically, you need only two skills. You need to be able to baste two pieces of fabric together, and you need to be able to sew a seam securely and straight. You may do your sewing by machine or by hand. Many people claim that hand-sewing gives the quilter a great sense of pride in fine needlework, but others find this process too slow.

Main idea: ___A patchwork quilt is easy to make.___

Detail 1: ___Accept any three details from the paragraph.___

Detail 2: _____

Detail 3: _____

146 Main Idea and Details   Practice Book ■ FEAST YOUR EYES

Practice Book

Integrated Curriculum

MATH

They Fly *How* Many Miles?

COOPERATIVE LEARNING   Encourage students to work in groups to find out more about the migrating habits of Canada geese and monarch butterflies by looking in encyclopedias and nature magazines. Have them then use a map of the Western Hemisphere that has a mileage scale to estimate the number of miles these creatures cover on their migrations. Suggest that they estimate both one-way and round-trip figures for the animals' migratory expeditions.   LISTENING/SPEAKING/READING

ART

A Very Special Classroom Quilt

COOPERATIVE LEARNING   Involve students in a quilt-making activity. Have each student draw and color his or her favorite landscape or design. Assemble the drawings in a large rectangle, trim the edges with brightly colored construction paper, and display the "quilt" on the wall. Have a quilt-sharing time in which each student gets to explain what is special about his or her particular design.   LISTENING/SPEAKING

SOCIAL STUDIES

Log Cabin, Wedding Ring, Nine Patch?

USE REFERENCE SOURCES   Remind students that Ariel and Grandma made a special quilt. Explain that quilt making was essential for people in the past. Encourage interested students to research quilt making. They may want to narrow the topic to one aspect of quilting, such as patterns, countries of origin, or quilting bees. Have students give oral reports of their findings.   LISTENING/SPEAKING/READING/WRITING

SOCIAL STUDIES

Be a Geography Detective

COOPERATIVE LEARNING   Tell students they can be geography detectives and figure out where Ariel and her family might live. Have students work in small groups and use the migration routes of the Canada geese and the monarch butterfly along with the references to summer weather and the type of crop the family farms to identify the states or provinces in which Ariel's family might live. Have students tell how they determined the location.   LISTENING/SPEAKING/READING

SCIENCE

Learning About Migration

AVAILABLE ON PROJECT CARD

USE REFERENCE SOURCES   Encourage students to research and report on the mysterious process of migration. Explain that many types of birds, fish, insects, and mammals migrate yearly, looking for more favorable weather and food. Suggest that the report include these topics: the types of migration, the reasons for migration, what triggers migration, and how migration is accomplished. Have students prepare a written report that they present orally to classmates. LISTENING/SPEAKING/READING/WRITING

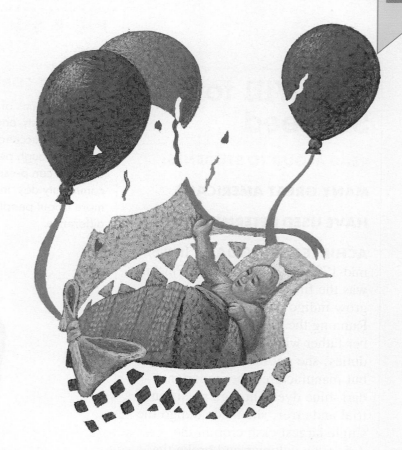

SOCIAL STUDIES

Welcome to the World!

CULTURAL AWARENESS   Tell students that every culture has its own way of welcoming a new baby into the world; for example, Americans give gifts and the Chinese give the baby a "red egg" party when it is one month old. Encourage students to ask family members about customs in their own cultural heritage. Have them report their findings to classmates.   LISTENING/SPEAKING

ART

A Collage of Beautiful Things

AVAILABLE ON PROJECT CARD

Remind students that when Ariel showed Grandma the butterflies and the meadow, Grandma recalled how good life was. Have students think of the things they consider most beautiful and create a collage that represents their beautiful things. Students might include objects from nature, "found" items, or pictures cut from magazines for their collages. Encourage students to share their collage and explain why they included what they did. LISTENING/SPEAKING

PERSPECTIVES

The Will to Succeed

READ ALOUD TO STUDENTS:

MANY GREAT AMERICANS

HAVE USED DETERMINATION TO

ACHIEVE THEIR GOALS. In the mid-1700s, Elizabeth Lucas Pinckney was the first person to successfully grow indigo plants in South Carolina. Running the colonial plantation for her father who was absent on military duties, she not only grew the crop but manufactured the important dark-blue dye. Through persistent trial and error, she made indigo the single largest cash crop in the American colonies and broke the hold the French had had on the dye.

Two centuries later, African American Charles Richard Drew overcame poverty and prejudice to become a surgeon. As the creator of the blood banks for England and the United States during World War II, Dr. Drew saved the lives of millions of people. He standardized the procedures for collecting and processing blood in order to avoid contamination and developed techniques for processing and storing liquid plasma. Then he refined the technique so that dried plasma could be used. Drew's pioneering work in blood chemistry paved the way for safe blood transfusions on the battlefield and under other emergencies. After the war, as Surgical Consultant to the U.S. Army's European theater of operation, he helped improve the quality of the hospitals in occupied Europe. ■

ACTIVITY CORNER

■ Have groups of students research other scientists, engineers, or doctors who have succeeded in improving society through persistence and genius. Students can present their findings in a community day, inviting visitors to learn more about people who have made a difference.

■ Ask students to think of people they know who have the very special gift of determination. Have students tape-record interviews of those people and present their recordings to classmates in the form of a radio talk show.

Dr. Charles Drew was a brilliant scientist and a dedicated teacher.

Young at Heart

Remind students that the selections in this theme described children interacting with their grandmothers. Guide students to recall the poem about Nathaniel's grandma and the story about Ariel and her grandma. Invite students to think about what the children learned from their grandmothers as well as what they might have taught their grandmothers. Explain to students that the questions on page 525 will encourage them to think more about the ideas presented in the selections.

Note that pages T922-T923 provide support for applying the writing process to the last question.

THEME WRAP-UP

YOUNG AT HEART

We can learn a lot from our grandparents and other older adults. Think about why the grandmothers you read about are important to their families. What do they contribute to the lives of their children and grandchildren?

What special qualities do the grandmothers in the poem and selection share?

WRITER'S WORKSHOP   Ask a grandparent or another older relative about what life was like when he or she was your age. Gather information about the time period when that person was young and the place where he or she lived. Write a report about that person's early life. You may want to include photographs with your report. Share your report with the person you wrote about.

525

Theme Wrap-Up

DISCUSSION QUESTIONS, PAGE 525

We can learn a lot from our grandparents and other older adults. Think about why the grandmothers you read about are important to their families. What do they contribute to the lives of their children and grandchildren? Encourage students to think about the role each grandmother plays in her family. (Accept reasonable responses: Nathaniel's grandmother teaches him about the music of the forties; Ariel's grandmother teaches her to sew a quilt.)
CRITICAL: MAKING JUDGMENTS

What special qualities do the grandmothers in the poem and selection share? Encourage students to think about each grandmother and then compare them. (Accept reasonable responses: Both seem wise.)   INFERENTIAL: MAKING COMPARISONS

WRITER'S WORKSHOP   See pages T922–T923 for applying the writing process. **Ask a grandparent or another older relative about what life was like when he or she was your age. Gather information about the time period when that person was young and the place where he or she lived. Write a report about that person's early life. You may want to include photographs with your report. Share your report with the person you wrote about.** You may prefer to allow students to respond to the theme in their own way.   WRITING PROCESS: A BIOGRAPHICAL REPORT

Writer's Workshop

For More Discussion & Practice:

LANGUAGE HANDBOOK

Encourage students to tell what a biographical report is. (a report that gives information about someone) Ask students what elements would go into the writing of a biographical report, and list them on the board. (Accept reasonable responses: select a candidate about whom to write; gather and organize information; classify the information into categories.) Suggest that students refer to the Handbook in the *Writer's Journal* as they write, revise, and proofread their biographical reports.

Prewriting

Before students write, invite them to tell classmates the person they have chosen to write about. Have students
- think about their audience and purpose for writing.
- make a list similar to the one below to help organize their ideas. Encourage students to list topics relevant to the person's life that might be included in the report. Then have students research each topic and put the information into the form of an outline.

(Person's Name)
1. Place of birth
2. What was happening in the country when the person was young?
3. What special memories or stories can the person tell about his or her youth?

Remind students to revise their outlines as they gather information from different sources.

Drafting

Ask students to write a draft of the biographical report. Remind them to
- use their outline for ideas.
- begin each paragraph with a topic sentence.
- include detail sentences that tell facts.
- write freely without worrying about spelling, punctuation, or grammar.

COMPUTER CONNECTION   Students may want to use a computer during the drafting stage to enable them to develop their ideas and organize their information in the form of an outline.

Responding and Revising

Ask students to read over their biographical report. Offer the following suggestions, and encourage students to revise their work.

- Is the report in an order that makes sense? If not, put facts in a logical order.
- Have you written an interesting opening and closing? If not, rewrite.
- Are there short, choppy sentences? If possible, combine them. (See the Language/Literature Link below.)

STUDENT SELF-ASSESSMENT OPTION   Students may use the Writing Self-Assessment Checklist in the *Portfolio Teacher's Guide*. Suggest that as they use the checklist, they focus on combining short sentences and using punctuation correctly.

Proofreading

Offer the following tips to help students proofread their work and make changes:

- Check for errors in capitalization and punctuation.
- Check to see that the first line of each paragraph is indented.
- If words appear to be misspelled, draw a line around them and find out how to spell them correctly.

Publishing

Talk with students about various options for publishing their biographical reports. Some may wish to design a cover and include photographs or illustrations with their biography. Encourage students, if possible, to share their finished report with the person whom they wrote about. Students may wish to simply share their reports with a small group of classmates before saving them in their reading/writing portfolios.

LANGUAGE/LITERATURE LINK

Combining Two Sentences

Remind students that successful writers want their sentences to sound smooth as well as to make sense. They know that one longer sentence sounds better than two short, choppy sentences. Point out the following sentences as ones that can be combined using *and: Thunder sounded. Lightning split the sky.* Suggest that students check their work for any short sentences that can be combined into one longer sentence.

Speaking Option

HOSTING A TV SHOW   The Writer's Workshop may be adapted to allow students to role-play a talk-show host of a program called "Biography." Ask students to follow the guidelines for Prewriting, Drafting, and Responding and Revising. Then offer the following speaking tips to help students with their program:

- Practice reading what you wrote so that you don't have to read it word for word. Jot down notes to help you when speaking.
- Illustrate your talk with pictures or other visual aids.
- Speak loudly and clearly.
- End the program in an interesting way.

Invite students to take turns pretending to be the talk-show host of a program about the person they interviewed and wrote about.

Stargazers

Growing Up

from *Jim Abbott: Against All Odds*

On the Pampas

from *Surprises*

Last Laugh

from *Surprises*

The Drum

For pacing suggestions, see page T926.

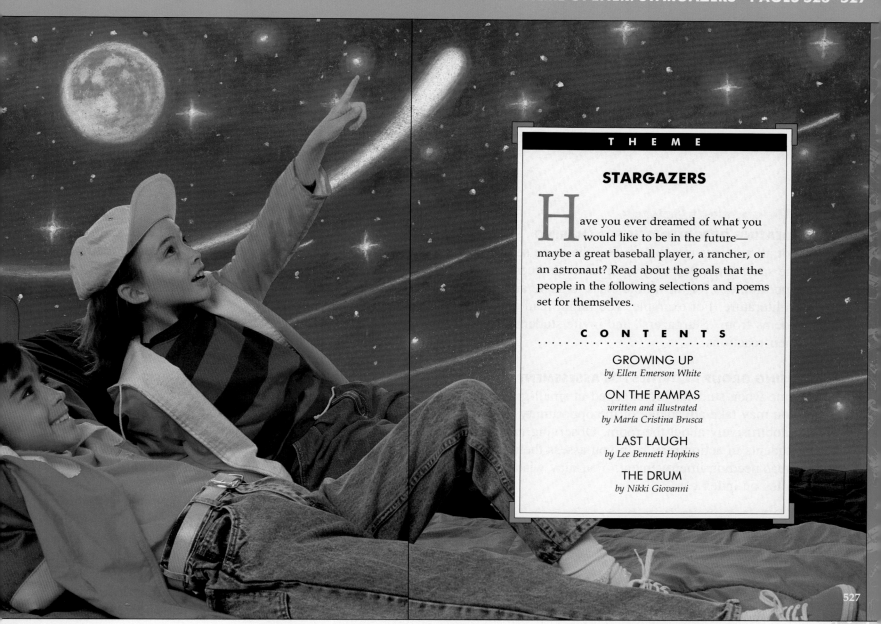

527

Discussing the Theme

Draw students' attention to the picture on Student Anthology page 526. Invite them to read the theme focus and selection titles on the next page and think about how a baseball player, a rancher, and an astronaut might be considered "Stargazers."

Reading/Writing Portfolio

Remind students to keep their writing responses for the selections in "Stargazers" in their portfolios. Remind them also to add to their personal journals any thoughts and ideas about books they read independently.

Managing the Literature-Based Classroom

Management Options

CREATING OPPORTUNITIES FOR SHARING Though not all students may be reading the same selection at the same time, you may wish to create occasional opportunities for the whole class to share an experience in literature. For example, you might read one of the poems from "Stargazers" and invite students to discuss their reactions.

USING GROUP ACTIVITIES FOR ASSESSMENT During a time when students are engaged in small-group activities, you may take advantage of the opportunity to circulate unobtrusively about the room. Observing individual students in action may help you assess their strengths and areas needing improvement. You may wish to jot brief notes on index cards.

PACING This theme has been designed to take about two weeks to complete, depending on your students' needs.

Meeting Individual Needs

STUDENTS AT RISK Students often become impatient with routine and respond to fast-paced instruction and quick gratification. To maintain interest, offer students short, lively versions of regular or extension activities.

GIFTED AND TALENTED Have students prepare brief addresses they can share with their classmates or with the school during morning announcements. These can be quotes or reports about the achievements of famous people. Tell students to keep their addresses to one minute in length. *Challenge Cards* provide additional activities to challenge students. Challenge notes throughout the lesson plans suggest additional activities to stimulate critical and creative thinking.

SPECIAL EDUCATION STUDENTS For students who are easily distracted, occasionally tape-record instructions for activities or comprehension questions. Allow students to work independently in a corner of the room, using tape recorders with headsets. Have them read along silently as they listen to the directions. This will reduce demands on teacher time and keep students on task.

LIMITED ENGLISH PROFICIENT STUDENTS Encourage any Spanish-speaking students to offer the correct pronunciation of Spanish terms as well as names of people and places in "On the Pampas." Second-Language Support notes throughout the lesson plans offer strategies to help those students acquiring English to understand the selections.

GROWING UP

from *Jim Abbott: Against All Odds* • by Ellen Emerson White • illustrated by Doug Suma

TEACHING OUTLINE	Materials	Language Arts/ Integrated Curriculum	Meeting Individual Needs
Part 1 Reading Literature Pages T930–T936 	**Building Background** **Vocabulary Strategies** Key Words (Tested) **Strategic Reading** Preview and Predict Setting a Purpose **Options for Reading**	Transparency 54 Second-Language Support Manual Practice Book p. 147 Integrated Spelling p. 71 Integrated Spelling T.E. pp. 92–93 Student Anthology pp. 528–535	**Spelling** Spelling Pretest Spelling-Vocabulary Connection	**Second-Language Support** Vocabulary T931 Strategic Reading T932, T935 **Cooperative Reading** T933
Part 2 Responding to Literature Pages T937–T941 	**Story Follow-Up** Think It Over Write **Summarizing the Literature** **Appreciating Literature** **Critical Thinking Activities**	Writer's Journal p. 97 Practice Book pp. 148–149 Integrated Spelling p. 72 Integrated Spelling T.E. pp. 92–93 Language Handbook	**Vocabulary Workshop** Reviewing Key Words Extending Vocabulary Classifying **Reading** Oral Rereading Athletes **Writing** Character Sketch Descriptions Compiling a Glossary **Spelling** Reviewing Spelling Words **Speaking** A Sportscast **Listening** A Poem	**Cooperative Learning** T938, T941
Part 3 Learning Through Literature Pages T942–T948 	**Introduce** Literary Appreciation: Biography and Autobiography **Review** Comprehension: Fact and Opinion (Tested) Study Skills: Reference Sources (Tested)	Second-Language Support Manual Writer's Journal pp. 98–99 Practice Book pp. 150–151	**Music** Writing Songs **Social Studies** Researching Sports International Sports **Math** Writing Math Problems **Science** An Experiment **Art** Making Sports Posters **Multicultural** Achievements of the Physically Challenged	**Challenge** T943, T944, T945 **Second-Language Support** Biography/Autobiography T943 **Cooperative Learning** T943, T946, T947

KEY WORDS

artificial
mound
rookie
leagues
technique
concentrate
competitive
eventful

ELLEN EMERSON WHITE

In addition to writing *Jim Abbott: Against All Odds*, Ellen Emerson White has written four books for young adults. She wrote her first novel, *Friends for Life*, when she was eighteen, and it was published three years later. While attending college, she wrote almost one book a year. However, she didn't know she wanted to be a writer when she was growing up. "I wanted to be in the FBI. I wanted to pitch for the Red Sox. I wanted to be a lawyer. I came [to college] as a lawyer . . . That lasted about a week and a half. Then I was a drama major for another week and a half. And finally I was an English major," she states.

ADDITIONAL READING

Other Books About Growing Up

Child of the Silent Night by Edith Fisher Hunter. Houghton Mifflin, 1963. CHALLENGING

The Hundred Dresses by Eleanor Estes. Harcourt Brace Jovanovich, 1944/1971. AVERAGE

Jobs for Kids: The Guide to Having Fun and Making Money by Carol Barkin and Elizabeth James. Lothrop, Lee and Shepard, 1990. AVERAGE

Max Malone Makes a Million by Charlotte Herman. Henry Holt, 1991. AVERAGE

True Stories about Abraham Lincoln by Ruth Belov Gross. Lothrop, Lee and Shepard, 1973/1990. AVERAGE

Part 1
Reading Literature

Building Background

Access prior knowledge and build vocabulary concepts.

Tell students that the next selection is a biography about a baseball player. Have students discuss what they know about baseball by describing its rules and by sharing the names of favorite teams and players. Remind students that recalling what they already know about a topic will help them focus on the kind of information that will be in a selection. Record what students know about baseball in a chart similar to this:

Baseball			
Teams	**Players**	**Positions**	**Rules**
major and	rookie	shortstop	
minor leagues		pitcher	

Vocabulary Strategies

Introduce Key Words and strategies.

Display Transparency 54 or the following conversation. Have students read the sentences silently, using context clues with phonetic and structural analysis to decode and figure out the meanings of the underlined words.

Transparency 54   Key Words

PAULA: That grass is so green. Is it real?
ASHLEY: No, it's <u>artificial</u> grass.
PAULA: What's that raised place?
ASHLEY: The pitcher stands on that <u>mound</u>.
PAULA: He looks nervous.
ASHLEY: He's a <u>rookie</u>. This is his first year playing on a big-league team. He was in the minor <u>leagues</u> before. Watch how he throws. What a great pitching <u>technique</u> he has!
PAULA: He looks like he is thinking hard. He must have to <u>concentrate</u> to do a good job.
ASHLEY: Both teams are trying hard to win. They are very <u>competitive</u>. We're sure to see lots of action. Your first baseball game will be an <u>eventful</u> one.

KEY WORDS

artificial
mound
rookie
leagues
technique
concentrate
competitive
eventful

KEY WORDS DEFINED

artificial not natural

mound slightly raised ground from which a baseball pitcher pitches

rookie first-year player in a professional sport; beginner

leagues groups of athletic teams

technique way or method of doing something

concentrate to focus one's entire attention

competitive wanting to win

eventful full of activities

Check students' understanding.

Read aloud the following incomplete sentences. Have volunteers take turns completing the sentences.   STRATEGY: EXPLANATION

- A good technique for passing a soccer ball is . . .
- Something you must concentrate on to do well is . . .
- One eventful day you've spent involved . . .
- Something that is artificial is . . .
- A rookie who plays in an important football game is probably . . .
- When a pitcher stands on a mound he is . . .
- Two major leagues in the United States are . . .
- Because the players were very competitive, they . . .

Integrate spelling with vocabulary.

SPELLING-VOCABULARY CONNECTION *Integrated Spelling* page 71 reinforces the spellings of words with three syllables such as in the Key Words *concentrate* and *eventful* and in other words. The spelling of the Key Word *rookie* is also included.

• • • GROWING UP • • •

Name _____

Read each sentence below. Draw a line under the correct meaning of the word in dark print in each sentence.

1. From the first day Hector held a baseball bat, he was a **competitive** player who tried to hit harder than anyone else.
   quick to argue   cooperative   <u>trying hard to win</u>

2. One of the **leagues** for young players asked Hector to join.
   coaches   <u>groups of sports teams</u>   fan clubs

3. Hector made an effort to **concentrate** on every move made by other players in order to improve his skill.
   <u>pay close attention</u>   relax   ask questions of others

4. He always faced the pitcher on the **mound** with confidence.
   home plate   third base   <u>raised ground on which pitcher stands</u>

5. Hector practiced the **technique** of taking a full swing to hit the ball.
   <u>method</u>   problem   sport

6. The most **eventful** day in Hector's life was the day he moved to another city to begin his career as a professional player.
   <u>full of important activities</u>   ordinary   stormy

7. Even though the grass in the field was **artificial** instead of real, Hector knew he would play well in his new surroundings.
   very long   colorful   <u>not natural</u>

8. Hundreds of fans stood up and cheered when the **rookie** hit his first home run as a professional player.
   <u>beginner</u>   manager   experienced player

Practice Book ▪ FEAST YOUR EYES   **Vocabulary**   **147**

Practice Book

INTEGRATED SPELLING
Three-Syllable Words

Name _____

Read the Spelling Words. Write them on a separate sheet of paper. Check your spelling.

━━━ SPELLING STRATEGY ━━━

One way to remember how to spell long words is to divide them into syllables.

manager   man ag er   important   im por tant

Nine of the Spelling Words have been divided into syllables below. Read the syllables. Then write the Spelling Words.

at	ten	tion	attention
pro	tec	tion	protection
e	vent	ful	eventful
im	por	tant	important
con	cen	trate	concentrate
pos	si	ble	possible
ex	cel	lent	excellent
va	ca	tion	vacation
man	ag	er	manager

SPELLING WORDS
attention
concentrate
eventful
excellent
important
manager
possible
protection
rookie
vacation

MEMORY JOGGER

Give a **cookie** to the **rookie**.   This Memory Jogger will help you remember how to spell the word **rookie**.

FEAST YOUR EYES ▪ "Growing Up"   71

Integrated Spelling

Preview and Predict

Help students preview the selection.

Using the Table of Contents, have students locate the first page of "Growing Up." Point out that an account of a person's life told by another person is known as a *biography*. Ask students what they can do to preview a biography. (read and think about the title, look at the illustrations, and read the introduction or the first few paragraphs) Have students read the title and the first three paragraphs and preview the illustrations.

Have students make predictions.

Identify the book title *Jim Abbott: Against All Odds* and discuss the title. Explain that *against all odds* refers to something that happened although there was little chance of it happening. Then ask students questions such as these to help them make predictions about the selection:

- **How did Jim Abbott become a professional baseball player?**
- **What special challenges does he face?**
- **Why is his life interesting?**

PERSONAL JOURNAL   Have students add their predictions about the selection to their personal journals. Ask students to support their predictions.

Setting a Purpose

Have students set purposes.

Ask students to write questions about Jim Abbott they think the selection might answer. Have several volunteers read their questions aloud. Have each student select the question in which he or she is most interested. Tell students that their self-selected question will become their purpose for reading.

Model purpose-setting, if necessary.

If students have difficulty setting a purpose, offer this suggestion:

> **One thing I want to find out when I read is what did Jim Abbott accomplish despite the odds against him.**

OPTIONS FOR READING

INDEPENDENT READING   Have students read the selection silently with their purpose for reading in mind.

GUIDED READING   Follow the Guided Reading suggestions that appear on pages T933, T934, and T936. These suggestions model strategic reading.

COOPERATIVE READING   A reader response strategy appears on page T933.

SECOND-LANGUAGE SUPPORT   Students may benefit from the Guided Reading activities and the additional guidance under the Student Anthology pages. (See Second-Language Support Manual.)

GROWING
UP

Angels
25

AWARD-WINNING
AUTHOR

n Abbott: Against All Odds • by Ellen Emerson White • illustrated by Doug Suma

It is a clear summer night at famous Fenway Park in Boston, and a rookie has come to town. He is tall, and strong, and young.

The California Angels, his team, is in a hot pennant race and tonight they need a win from their rookie pitcher. But he is facing the Boston Red Sox, the best hitting team in the American League.

The old green stadium is overflowing with die-hard Red Sox fans as the rookie takes the mound. *Noisy* die-hard Red Sox fans. But the rookie knows that he has to ignore the crowd—that he has to concentrate on tonight's game.

The rookie has an easy first two innings, but then, the Red Sox load the bases in the third. There are two outs, and the cleanup hitter, Mike Greenwell, strides to the plate. The crowd claps and cheers, begging their slugger to get a big hit.

The rookie takes a deep breath. The hitter waits, his bat up and ready. And the rookie strikes him out with his best fastball.

As the game goes on, the rookie strikes out more Red Sox hitters. Star first baseman Nick Esasky. Future Hall-of-Famer Dwight Evans. Rising star Ellis Burks. In the end, the rookie strikes out seven batters. He gives up four harmless hits and, most importantly, no runs.

When the rookie gets the final out of the game, giving his team a 4–0 victory, he starts to walk off the mound. All over Fenway Park, the Red Sox fans stand and applaud, cheering the rookie off the field. Their team may have lost, but they know that they have seen someone very special. That *this* is a pitcher.

This is Jim Abbott.

529

Guided Reading

SET PURPOSE/PREDICT: PAGES 528–531 Have students read through page 531 to find out what physical challenge Jim Abbott faces and what part his parents played.

Cooperative Reading

READER RESPONSE STRATEGY: PAGES 528–531 Have pairs of students share the questions they would like to find the answers to as they read. Then have them read the story silently, pausing periodically to discuss what they have learned with their partner.

READER RESPONSE STRATEGY: PAGES 532–535 After reading the selection, have partners discuss it by asking one another questions such as these:

- **Did you find the answer to your question? What was it?**
- **What did you like best about the selection?**

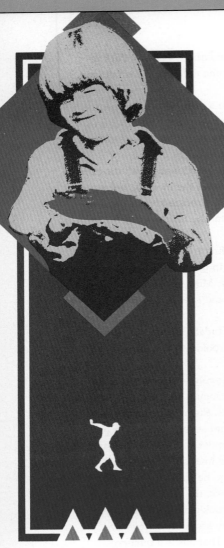

James Anthony Abbott was born on September 19, 1967, and has already led an eventful life. While attending the University of Michigan, he pitched his team to two Big Ten championships and was selected to the All-America team. Then, while playing in the Pan-American Games, he helped Team USA win the silver medal. Later, as a pitcher for the 1988 Olympic team, Jim was on the mound when the United States won the gold medal. Finally, Jim was picked by the California Angels in the major league baseball draft, becoming only the fifteenth player in the history of the draft to go straight to the big leagues without ever spending a day in the minors.

What makes all of this even more remarkable is that Jim Abbott has only one hand.

Born with a normal left arm, Jim has a right arm that is normal, too—except that it stops at the wrist. But from the time he was a small child, no one ever told Jim that he was handicapped, and he never acted that way. In fact, Jim was always about as far from handicapped as it was possible to be.

Jim was born and grew up in Flint, Michigan. His parents, Mike and Kathy Abbott, married very young and had to work hard to make ends meet. Jim's father is now a sales manager, and his mother is an attorney. She works for a law firm that focuses on educational issues. Education was always very important to the Abbotts.

"My parents always stressed school," Jim says now. "They wanted me to do well. They always said that I thought of sports first, but they made me think not just about baseball, but about getting good grades."

When Jim first went to school, a doctor fitted him with an artificial right hand, which had metal hooks on the end that he could clamp together to pick things up. But Jim never liked this fake, mechanical hand. By the time he was six, he had stopped wearing it completely.

Jim's parents always told him that he could do anything he wanted to do. They knew that their son loved sports. They hoped that Jim would play soccer—one of the few sports where he wouldn't need two hands—but right from the very beginning, Jim loved baseball. So, Jim's parents bought him a baseball glove. As it turned out, Jim's brother Chad was the one who liked soccer.

Guided Reading

MONITOR COMPREHENSION: PAGES 528–531
What challenge does Jim Abbott face? (He was born with only one hand.) **How did his parents help him?** (They told him he could do anything he wanted to do; they supported him.)   STRATEGIC READING: RETURNING TO PURPOSE

How do you know that Jim Abbott did not let having only one hand discourage him from doing what he loved? (He never acted as if he was disabled; he learned to do things with one hand; he became a championship pitcher.)
STRATEGIC READING: SUMMARIZING

SET PURPOSE/PREDICT: PAGES 532–535   Discuss with students whether their purpose-setting question was answered and what questions, if any, they still have about Jim Abbott. Then ask students what quality they think Jim Abbott has that helped him become a professional athlete. Have them read the rest of the selection to find out how he achieved this goal.

Now that he had a baseball glove, Jim had to learn how to throw—and catch—with the same hand. With his father's help, Jim developed what is now known as his famous glove switch. What he does is very complicated, but *looks* very easy. In fact, people often watch him play without even noticing that he is doing it all with just one hand.

As Jim throws the ball, he bends his right arm up in front of him and balances his glove on the end of it. Then, after he releases the ball, he slides his left hand into his glove. By the time the ball is batted or thrown back at him, he is ready to catch it. To watch Jim, it seems so easy. But, as is true for every great athlete, he practiced for many hours to perfect this.

Jim would practice this glove switch by playing catch with his father and by throwing a ball against the side of his house and catching it as it bounced off. He would move closer and closer to the house, throwing the ball harder and harder, and getting better and faster with the glove switch. Today, he is able to pitch the ball and get the glove onto his hand before the ball even gets to home plate.

After Jim catches the ball, he moves his glove up under his right arm, pulls his left hand out, and grabs the ball to throw it—all in one quick motion. And he almost never makes an error.

The very first game Jim pitched in Little League was a no-hitter. His team, Lydia Simon Real Estate, scored so many runs that the game was stopped after only five innings. Word quickly got around that there was a pitcher in Flint, Michigan, who was better with one hand than most other pitchers were with two. For the first time, Jim was interviewed by reporters. He has had

to deal with almost constant attention from reporters ever since.

Jim went on to pitch for Flint Central High School. He already had a very good fastball, but very few people believed that he would be able to field his position against more difficult competition. One high school team tested his fielding during his freshman year by having eight batters in a row bunt. The first hitter *did* get to first base safely, but Jim threw the next seven out. After that, teams didn't bunt against Jim very often.

"He was a tough kid, very competitive," Bob Holec, Jim's high school baseball coach, said. "You don't see too many like him. He was just a great kid. He was also very successful socially and academically. He had a lot of friends."

By the time Jim was a senior, he was pitching and playing first base. He also spent some time in the outfield and even played shortstop briefly. He pitched four no-hitters that year and had an incredible 179 strikeouts in only eighty innings. That averages out to *more* than 2 strikeouts per inning. Over the length of the season, he gave up fewer than two hits a game.

Second-Language Support

Students may need help understanding unfamiliar sports-related words such as *bunt*, *no-hitters*, and *strikeouts*. Explain these terms, using simple, literal language as well as pantomime, gestures, and diagrams as appropriate.

Jim was also a very good hitter. He would hold the bat in his left hand, bracing the handle against his right wrist. Using this technique, he batted .427 his senior year, with seven home runs and thirty-six RBIs.[1] He hit more home runs than anyone else on his team that year.

But there was more to Jim than just baseball. He was the top scorer in his school's intramural basketball league, and he played two years of varsity football. He was a punter, averaging thirty-seven-and-a-half yards per punt his senior year, and he was one of the team's quarterbacks.

Baseball coach Bob Holec is also one of the high school's football coaches. "I'll never forget this one game," he said, recalling one of the best punts Jim ever made. "Jim got a bad snap that went over his head, and he jumped up, snagged it with his one hand, and got the punt off. There were plenty of *oohs* and *aahs* from the crowd on *that* one." In fact, the whole time he played football, Jim never dropped a snap.

Then, late in the football season, when the starting quarterback became ineligible, Jim took over. He helped the Flint Central team get to the state play-offs, where they lost in the semifinals to the team that eventually won the state championship.

"He took a beating in that semifinal game," Coach Holec said, "but he still managed to get off four touchdown passes. He really came into his own at the end of the football season. You wish you had more like him."

---

[1]RBIs: runs batted in, runners in baseball that are driven to home plate by the batters

534

Jim's various athletic exploits resulted in more press attention than ever, and Coach Holec was particularly impressed by the way Jim handled the reporters.

"He's a very humble person," Coach Holec explained. "There was never any jealousy from his teammates. A lot of kids would get big-headed from all of the attention, but Jim never did. He always praised his teammates, never himself." Then Coach Holec paused. "I would give him the finest compliment of all—if I had a son, I'd like him to be like Jim Abbott."

THINK IT OVER

1. *Why is Jim Abbott an extraordinary athlete?*

2. *What position in baseball does Jim Abbott play?*

3. *Is playing baseball Jim Abbott's only great accomplishment? Explain your answer.*

4. *Would you like to play on a team with Jim Abbott? Explain your answer.*

WRITE

Write a letter to Jim Abbott explaining what you would like to do when you grow up.

Guided Reading

MONITOR COMPREHENSION: PAGES 532–535
Jim Abbott is a great athlete. What qualities does he display? (He is humble; he doesn't brag; he gives his teammates credit by praising them; he is determined, persistent, and hardworking.)
STRATEGIC READING: CONFIRMING PREDICTIONS

What else shows that Jim Abbott has a lot of determination and a great love for sports? (He learned to play basketball and became the top scorer in his school's intramural league; he played varsity football in high school and never dropped a snap.)   STRATEGIC READING: SUMMARIZING

Returning to the Predictions   Ask students to recall the predictions that they made before reading the selection and that they may have written in their personal journals. Have them tell how these predictions changed as they read the selection.

Returning to the Purpose for Reading
Have volunteers share their purposes for reading and tell whether their questions were answered in the selection.

NOTE: Responses to the Think It Over questions and support for the Write activity appear on page T937.

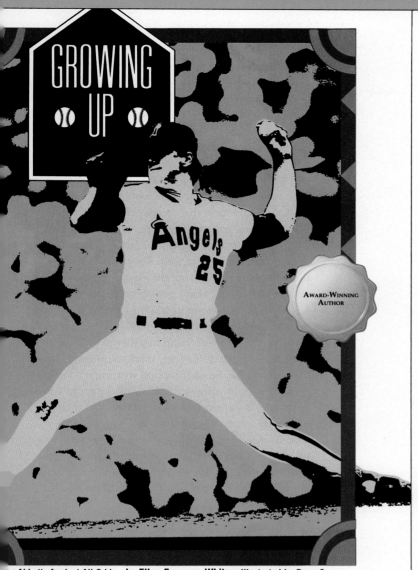

GROWING
UP

AWARD-WINNING
AUTHOR

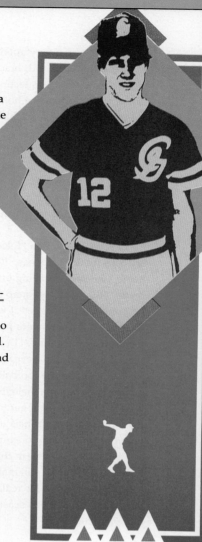

MEETING INDIVIDUAL NEEDS

Part 2
Responding to Literature

Story Follow-Up

Think It Over

Encourage reader's response: student page 535.

1. **Why is Jim Abbott an extraordinary athlete?** (Even though he has only one hand, he has excelled in baseball, football, and basketball.) CRITICAL: SUMMARIZING

2. **What position in baseball does Jim Abbott play?** (pitcher) LITERAL: NOTING IMPORTANT DETAILS

3. **Is playing baseball Jim Abbott's only great accomplishment? Explain your answer.** (No. He has shown that a missing hand is not a handicap; he has remained a humble person in spite of getting a lot of attention; he has also become very good at other sports.) CRITICAL: MAKING JUDGMENTS

4. **Would you like to play on a team with Jim Abbott? Explain your answer.** (Responses will vary.) CRITICAL: EXPRESSING PERSONAL OPINIONS

Write

Encourage writer's response: student page 535.

Write a letter to Jim Abbott explaining what you would like to do when you grow up. Encourage students to include information about the skills and interests they have now. CREATIVE: WRITING A LETTER

Summarizing the Literature

Have students retell the selection and write a summary.

Encourage students to summarize the selection by recalling important events in Jim Abbott's life in chronological order. Guide them in beginning the ladder graph below. Remind students that the author did not describe the events of Jim's life in order, so they will need to think about the order in which the events happened when they fill in the graph. Have students complete the graph independently. (See *Practice Book* page 148 on T938.) Students may use their graphs to write a brief summary statement.

The Life of Jim Abbott

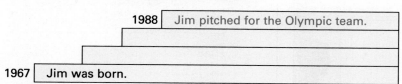

1988	Jim pitched for the Olympic team.
1967	Jim was born.

NOTE

An additional writing activity for this selection appears on page T940.

INFORMAL ASSESSMENT

Asking students to reorganize the information in a selection gives information about how well students have understood the selection. It will show whether students recognize important **details**, can record them accurately, and understand the **main ideas**.

Appreciating Literature

Have students share personal responses.

Have students work in small groups to discuss the story. Provide general questions such as the following to help the groups begin:

- **What quality of Jim Abbott strikes you as a good characteristic to develop within yourself over the years? Why?**

PERSONAL JOURNAL Have students use their personal journals to write about ideas and feelings that are discussed in the groups. You may also refer them to their personal journals after they complete the activities below.

Critical Thinking Activities

Encourage both cooperative and individual responses.

SHARE IDEAS **Think about Jim Abbott's love of baseball. What do you think are the rewards of playing on sports teams?** Have students work in small groups to share and discuss their ideas.   CRITICAL: EXPRESSING PERSONAL OPINIONS

WRITE INTERVIEW QUESTIONS **Imagine that you are a reporter conducting an interview. What three questions would you ask Jim Abbott?** Have students write their questions. Then invite volunteers to play the part of Jim Abbott and attempt to answer the questions.   CREATIVE: EXPANDING STORY CONCEPTS

STUDENT SELF-ASSESSMENT

Help students self-assess their listening during discussions by using questions such as the following:

- Did I try to see in my mind the things that others were talking about?
- Were the things that someone else talked about just like the things that I was thinking about?

Writer's Journal

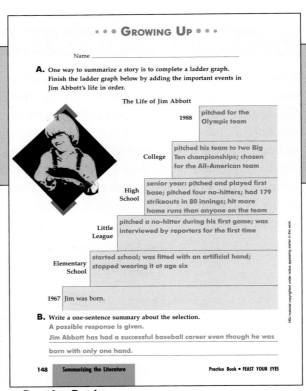

Practice Book

WRITER'S JOURNAL
page 97: Writing a personal response

PRACTICE BOOK
page 148: Summarizing the selection

VO·CAB·U·LAR·Y Workshop

Reviewing Key Words

Write each Key Word on an index card. Play a game of charades by having students form two teams. Distribute 4 cards to Team A and 4 cards to Team B. Have a student from Team A choose a card and pantomime the action of the word on the card. If Team B guesses the word, they score a point and take a turn. If not, Team A scores a point and continues with the next word. The team with the most points wins.

Extending Vocabulary

CLASSIFYING Explain that only people who know something about baseball or football would understand these sports terms: *takes the mound, shortstop, punter,* and *snaps.* Point out that each sport has its own special group of words. On the board draw a classification chart like the one below:

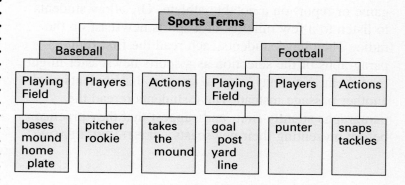

Discuss the reasons for organizing the words according to the categories shown. Then have students skim the selection and draw on their own experiences to suggest other terms. Add their suggestions to the chart.

Have students use at least five words from either of the two main categories to write a paragraph describing an exciting moment in a baseball or football game.

PRACTICE BOOK

page 149: Classifying words

• • • GROWING UP • • •

Name _____

A. Six sports are listed in the box below. On the lines below the box, describe three ways of classifying the sports. Possible responses are given.

| baseball | golf | basketball |
| surfing | gymnastics | mountain climbing |

1. played indoors or outdoors
2. played by teams or individuals
3. played with balls or without balls

B. Football is played on a football field. Where do people participate in the sports listed below? Write your answers on the lines.

1. golf _golf course_
2. basketball _basketball court_
3. surfing _ocean_
4. swimming _pool, lake, etc._
5. tennis _tennis court_
6. fishing _river, pond, etc._

C. Write the sports from Part B in the chart below to show how you classified them by place. Possible responses are given.

Land	Water
golf	surfing
basketball	swimming
tennis	fishing

Practice Book ▪ FEAST YOUR EYES   Classifying   149

Practice Book

Integrated Language Arts

Oral Rereading/Sports News Broadcast

If possible, record a sports news broadcast or feature in which the announcers summarize the highlights of a game or report on a notable athlete. Or, allow students to listen to a few minutes of a sports newscast on the radio. Then have students each read the first four paragraphs of the selection as a sports newscaster might read them. You may want to suggest that students read another passage instead. Have students reread the paragraphs silently first, and suggest that they practice before presenting their newscasts.   LISTENING/READING

Writing About the Literature

WRITE A CHARACTER SKETCH   Have students write a character sketch of someone they know and admire. Encourage them to interview the person, if possible. Suggest that students consider persons such as big sisters and brothers, coaches, teachers, and grandparents. Guide them in developing a chart like the one below to organize the information they gather.   LISTENING/SPEAKING/ WRITING

Character Traits	Words and Actions Showing These Traits
hardworking	spends two hours a day practicing
kind to others	volunteers in children's music program
talented	won all-city contest

NOTE: An additional writing activity appears on page T937.

Reviewing Spelling Words

SPELLING WORDS: *attention, concentrate, eventful, excellent, important, manager, possible, protection, rookie, vacation*

Have students form teams. Then brainstorm a list of 20 three-syllable words. Make individual flashcards for each syllable of the words. Write a number from 1–20 on the back of each card. Pin the cards on a bulletin board with the numbers face up. Have teams take turns turning over three cards at a time. When all three syllables of a word are found in one turn, remove the cards from the board. The team with the most three-syllable words wins. READING/SPELLING

> **INTEGRATED SPELLING** page 72: Writing words with three syllables

INTEGRATED SPELLING
Three-Syllable Words

Name _____

WORD PLAY

Write the Spelling Word for the first clue below. Notice that some blanks have arrows under them. If there is an arrow, write that letter again on the blank directly beneath it. Use the clues and the letters to write the other Spelling Words.

WORD BANK
attention
concentrate
excellent
important
manager
protection
rookie
vacation

1. A time of rest or freedom   V A C A T I O N
2. Keeping something safe   P R O T E C T I O N
3. Outstanding   E X C E L L E N T
4. Thought or care   A T T E N T I O N
5. Of great value   I M P O R T A N T
6. Person who directs or controls   M A N A G E R
7. To think hard   C O N C E N T R A T E
8. New person on a team   R O O K I E

SPELLING DETECTIVE

Philippa wrote a report about her favorite sport. When she proofread what she had written, she found six misspellings. Circle each one. Write the word correctly above it.

If you ever watch a game of baseball in Japan,
possible
it is (posible) you will think it is another sport. The
manager   **important**
(manger) is the most (importent) person. The
rookie
players, from the lowest (rookie) to the most
excellent
(excelent) player, do everything the manager tells
them. Players must give the game their entire
attention
(atention). They practice for hours!

72   "Growing Up" • FEAST YOUR EYES

Integrated Spelling

All-Time Greats!

CULTURAL AWARENESS Help students locate books or short selections about admirable athletes such as Jim Abbott and Roberto Clemente. After they have read about the athletes, ask each student to present a short speech telling why that person is outstanding. Students might enjoy working together to create a "Hall of Fame" bulletin board display. LISTENING/SPEAKING/READING/ WRITING

The Crowd Held Its Breath . . .

Encourage students to bring in and post action sports photographs from magazines and newspapers. Then ask each student to choose one and to write a brief, vivid description of what is happening in it. Remind them to use strong action verbs and colorful sports terms. If necessary, review how to use adverbs and adjectives in sentences. Suggest that students post their descriptions, together with the photographs, on a bulletin board. WRITING

And Now, Fans, the Bases Are Loaded . . .
AVAILABLE ON PROJECT CARD

COOPERATIVE LEARNING Discuss how a sportscaster gives a detailed, play-by-play description of a game. Encourage pairs of students to create a dialogue for two sportscasters in which they describe several minutes of a thrilling event. Tell them that they may choose an event described in the selection or one in which one of them participated. Have the pairs tape their sportscast and then play it for the others. LISTENING/SPEAKING

Grand Slams and Singles
AVAILABLE ON PROJECT CARD

COOPERATIVE LEARNING Have students work in small groups to create a glossary of terms used in baseball or another sport of their choice. Encourage them to interview sports fans to collect terms and definitions. Have them write each word or term on a separate note card for ease in alphabetizing and organizing. Suggest that the groups combine their efforts to create a master sports glossary. Remind students to use the Glossary in the Student Anthology as a model. LISTENING/WRITING

There Is No Joy in Mudville

Locate a copy of Ernest Lawrence Thayer's classic poem "Casey at the Bat." Begin by reading the poem aloud as students listen. Point out the rhythm and rhyme of the poem, and emphasize these elements as you read aloud. Then have students form groups to prepare a choral reading of the poem. You may want to have large groups read the whole poem or small groups read sections of the poem. LISTENING/READING

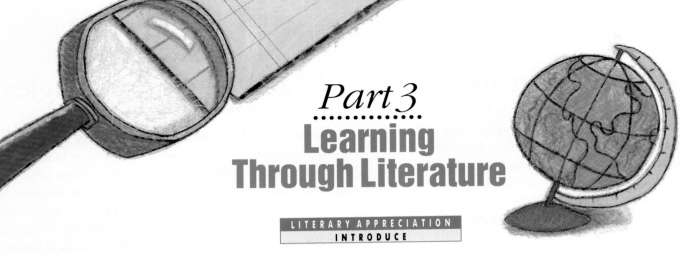

Part 3
Learning Through Literature

Biography/Autobiography

OBJECTIVE: *To recognize biography and autobiography*

1   Focus

Discuss how to identify a biography and an autobiography.

Ask students how they know "Growing Up" is a nonfiction selection. (It tells about a real person.) Explain that a work of nonfiction that tells about the life of a real person is either a biography or an autobiography. Tell students that reading biographies and autobiographies can help readers learn about people of interest to them.

2   Teach/Model

Teach the characteristics of each genre.

Explain that an *autobiography* is a person's account of his or her own life, and a *biography* is an account of a person's life as told by another person. Point out that biographies as well as autobiographies generally focus on a person's whole life, and usually begin with where and when the person was born. Then model recognizing the characteristics of a biography.

> **When I started reading "Growing Up," I thought that it was nonfiction because it mentioned real major league baseball teams and players. I thought it might be about exciting moments in baseball or about the traits that make a great pitcher. When I started to read about Jim Abbott's life, I realized I was reading a biography. I knew it wasn't an autobiography because it is not written by Jim Abbott himself; the author is Ellen Emerson White.**

Point out that because an autobiography is an account of a person's own life, it is written using first-person pronouns, such as *I, me, we.* Tell students that when someone writes a biography about someone else, third-person pronouns *(he, she, they)* are used.

Have students apply the learning.

COOPERATIVE LEARNING   Have students work in pairs to reword the second paragraph on page 531 as if Jim Abbott were writing an autobiography. Then have students rewrite the third paragraph on page 531 as if someone other than Jim were giving that information in a biography.

4 | **Summarize**

Informally assess the learning.

Have groups read aloud their paragraphs and explain how to tell the difference between a biography and an autobiography.

Have students summarize what they learned. (An autobiography is a person's account of his or her own life; a biography is an account of a person's life as told by someone else.)

READER ⟷ WRITER CONNECTION

Biography and Autobiography

▶ **Writers** tell about their own lives in autobiographies and tell about the lives of others in biographies.

▶ **Readers** pay attention to the information in biographies and autobiographies to learn about people.

WRITE PARAGRAPHS   Have students write a paragraph in the style of a biography and a paragraph in the style of an autobiography.

MEETING INDIVIDUAL NEEDS

CHALLENGE   Have each student write one paragraph about a favorite book character in the form of a biography and one paragraph about the same character in the form of an autobiography.

SECOND-LANGUAGE SUPPORT   Students can demonstrate their understanding by telling about their favorite cartoon character from the character's point of view and from the cartoonist's perspective. Guide them in the appropriate use of the personal pronoun *I* and the third-person pronouns *he* and *she*. (See *Second-Language Support Manual*.)

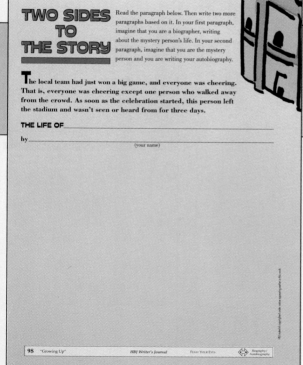

Writer's Journal

Writer's Journal

WRITER'S JOURNAL pages 98–99:   Writing biographical and autobiographical paragraphs

Fact and Opinion

OBJECTIVE: *To distinguish between fact and opinion*

Review

Review facts and opinions.

Ask students to describe the difference between facts and opinions. (Facts are statements that can be proved. Opinions are statements of belief or feeling.) Model the thinking.

> **I know the sentence "In the end, the rookie strikes out seven batters" is a fact because it contains information that can be checked: the game statistics. When I read that Jim Abbott is "someone very special," I may agree that Jim is special, but this is an opinion, not a fact.**

Practice/Apply

Have students distinguish between fact and opinion.

Have students locate two facts and two opinions in "Growing Up." Tell students that authors may try to persuade readers to agree with their point of view. Remind students to look for words that signal opinions such as *I think* and *I believe*.

Summarize

Informally assess the learning.

Have students read aloud their facts and opinions and explain why they classified each as they did.

Have students summarize what they learned. (Facts can be proved. Opinions are statements of belief.)

CHALLENGE Have students work in groups to create a scrambled list of statements that are facts and opinions about sports. Have the groups exchange lists and classify one another's statements under the headings *fact* and *opinion*.

PRACTICE BOOK
page 150: Writing facts and opinions

• • • GROWING UP • • •

Name _____

Read each sentence below, and draw a line under *fact* or *opinion* to tell which it states. If the sentence states a fact, write an opinion about it. If it states an opinion, write one fact that might support that opinion. Possible responses are given.

1. Jim Abbott was born without a right hand.
   fact   opinion
   Jim Abbott's love for baseball is what pushed him to succeed.

2. Jim was wise to focus on good grades as well as on baseball.
   fact   opinion
   Jim's parents helped to guide him by always stressing school.

3. Before age six, Jim stopped using his artificial hand.
   fact   opinion
   I believe he found it awkward.

4. The first game Jim pitched was a no-hitter.
   fact   opinion
   It was obvious that he would be a great pitcher.

5. Jim Abbott was the best quarterback at Flint High.
   fact   opinion
   No other quarterback at Flint High had better statistics than J. Abbott.

6. Jim Abbott pitched for the 1988 Olympic team.
   fact   opinion
   Jim Abbott was the best Olympic pitcher of all time.

7. Jim Abbott's mother is an excellent attorney.
   fact   opinion
   She has won many cases for her law firm's clients.

150   Fact and Opinion   Practice Book ■ FEAST YOUR EYES

Practice Book

Reference Sources

OBJECTIVE: *To use the dictionary and the encyclopedia to locate information*

Review

Review use of the dictionary and the encyclopedia.

Ask students how a dictionary and an encyclopedia are useful. (Dictionaries list words, their pronunciations, parts of speech, and definitions. Encyclopedias provide important information about major topics.) Remind students that an encyclopedia has an index to help users locate articles about topics that may not have separate entries.

Practice/Apply

Have students use the dictionary and the encyclopedia.

Ask students to find out what they can about baseball by looking in both a dictionary and an encyclopedia. Remind them to use the index of the encyclopedia.

Summarize

Informally assess the learning.

Have students compare the information they found in the two sources. Discuss when someone might choose each source.

Have students summarize the learning. (A dictionary helps you pronounce, define, and apply new words. An encyclopedia provides information about topics.)

CHALLENGE Have students use both a dictionary and an encyclopedia to find information about the roles of the different players on a football team.

PRACTICE BOOK
page 151: Using reference sources

• • • GROWING UP • • •

Name _____

A. Read each question below. After it, write *dictionary* or *encyclopedia* to tell where you would find the information.

1. What is the correct pronunciation of *stadium*? ___dictionary___
2. How old is Fenway Park in Boston? ___encyclopedia___
3. What is the major industry in Flint, Michigan? ___encyclopedia___
4. What does *artificial* mean? ___dictionary___
5. Who invented the first artificial limb, and when was it first used? ___encyclopedia___
6. How has the design of baseball bats changed over the years? ___encyclopedia___
7. Who are some of the most famous players in baseball history? ___encyclopedia___

B. Choose one of the topics below. Use a dictionary and an encyclopedia to research the topic. Then write about what you find in each reference source. **Responses will vary.**

baseball	football	tennis
soccer	basketball	volleyball

Dictionary entry: _____

_____

Encyclopedia entry: _____

_____

Practice Book ■ FEAST YOUR EYES   Reference Sources   151

Practice Book

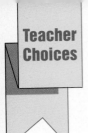

Integrated Curriculum

One, Two, Three Strikes You're Out!

Teach students the words and the tune to "Take Me Out to the Ball Game," and have students sing it together. Students may enjoy looking for other songs about outdoor activities, or writing new sports-related lyrics for familiar songs. For example, "Mary Had a Little Lamb" might become "Mary Had a Baseball Bat."
LISTENING/READING/WRITING

It Started With a Stick and a Rock

AVAILABLE ON PROJECT CARD

CULTURAL AWARENESS Remind students that many sports enjoyed in America originated in other countries. Have students research the origins of baseball and other sports. Encourage students to brainstorm a list of team sports. Then have students form groups, and have each group select one sport. Suggest that groups find the answers to questions such as these: *Who started the game? Where did it start? How did it spread? How has it changed over time?* Have students present their findings orally. LISTENING/SPEAKING/READING/WRITING

Big League/Little League

COOPERATIVE LEARNING Remind students that although baseball is played by both Little League and professional players, the sizes of the diamonds and the distances from the pitcher's mound to the plate are different. Have small groups of students research and list the distances and the sizes of the diamonds for Little League and big-league baseball. Then have students make up math problems involving the numbers they find, such as this: *How much farther does a big-league player have to run than a Little League player in circling the bases after hitting a home run?* Encourage students to exchange problems and find the solutions. READING/WRITING

The Harder You Throw . . .

Have students conduct experiments on the playing field to discover how increasing the force with which an object is thrown increases the velocity, which in turn increases the distance it travels. Suggest that students take turns throwing a ball slowly, throwing it quickly, and hitting it with a bat. Invite comments on the speed and force with which the ball is propelled, and have students measure the distance it travels. Ask students to record their observations and summarize the results.
LISTENING/SPEAKING/WRITING

ART

Scooping Up the Pelota with the Cesta

COOPERATIVE LEARNING Remind students that special terms are often used to describe the clothing and equipment used in various sports. Have students form groups, and assign each group a different specialty sport, such as ice hockey, jai alai, polo, or bobsledding. Ask each group to research its sport and to create a poster showing a player in the appropriate sportswear next to any special equipment required for the sport. Also suggest that the groups draw and label places where the sport is played (court, field, course, rink, and so on). Encourage bilingual students to contribute labels in other languages, as well. Give the groups an opportunity to display and describe their posters. LISTENING/SPEAKING/READING/WRITING

SOCIAL STUDIES

Sports World
AVAILABLE ON PROJECT CARD

CULTURAL AWARENESS Have students name sports, games, and leisure activities commonly enjoyed by people in their community. Then invite students from different cultural backgrounds to describe what people do for fun and exercise in the lands where their ancestors lived. Use a map of the world and self-sticking notes to label various activities enjoyed in different parts of the world. You might begin by posting the activities below on the map. LISTENING/SPEAKING

Scandinavia—cross-country skiing
England—walking, soccer (called *football*)
China—mah-jongg, t'ai chi ch'uan
Mexico—jai alai, baseball

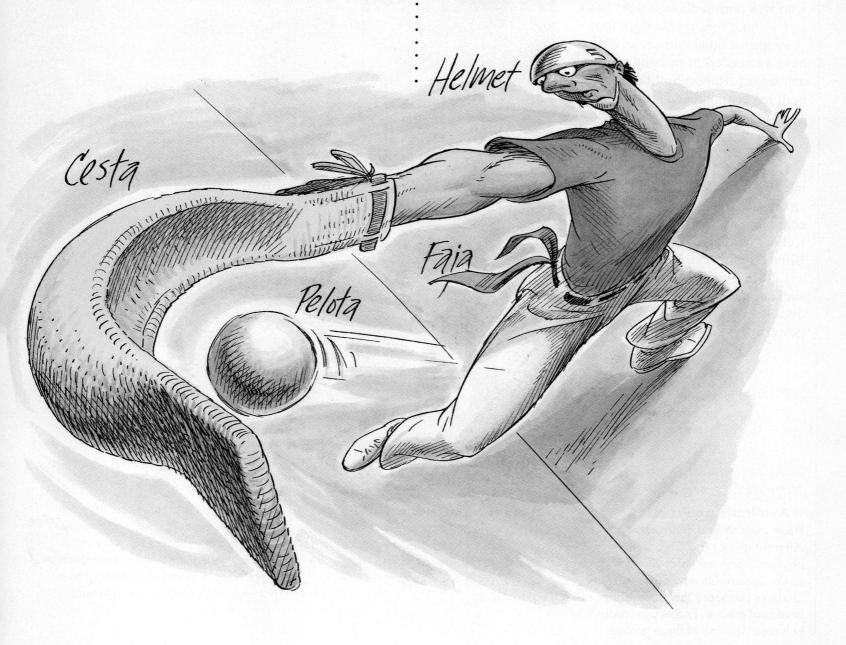

Amazing Achievements

READ ALOUD TO STUDENTS:

IN 1970, THE NEW ORLEANS

SAINTS SCORED AN EXCITING

UPSET VICTORY OVER DETROIT.
The crucial points came in the final moments of the game—a record-setting field goal by Tom Dempsey, who was born without a right hand and without toes on his right foot.

People in other careers as well have succeeded in meeting physical challenges. Robert Smithdas lost both his hearing and sight when in 1930 at age five he was stricken with meningitis. Nonetheless, Smithdas earned his Master's degree at New York University, becoming the first deaf-blind person to earn an advanced degree. He directs community relations for the Helen Keller National Center for Deaf-Blind Youths and Adults.

Eunice Fiorito, blind since age sixteen, has helped unite 36 million disabled Americans to give them a powerful voice in American life. ◼

Tom Dempsey, Jim Abbott, and Robert Smithdas have proven that being physically challenged is not a handicap.

ACTIVITY CORNER

◼ **Available on Project Card**
Have students find information about different groups that support the physically or mentally challenged, such as the Special Olympics Committee. Students can share their information in brief oral reports. Encourage students to volunteer for one of these groups.

◼ Have students research Braille and American Sign Language (the second most popular language in America) and explain to classmates how to read a few Braille words and sign some useful phrases.

◼ Have students pretend that they are scientists, engineers, or designers who create tools or devices for disabled people. Have them write a description or make a scale model of what they have just invented or would like to invent.

ON THE PAMPAS

María Cristina Brusca

ON THE PAMPAS

TEACHING OUTLINE	Materials	Language Arts/ Integrated Curriculum	Meeting Individual Needs
Part 1 **Reading Literature** Pages T952–T959 	**Building Background** **Vocabulary Strategies** Key Words (Tested) **Strategic Reading** Using the K-W-L Strategy Setting a Purpose **Options for Reading**	Transparency 55 Second-Language Support Manual Practice Book p. 152 Integrated Spelling p. 73 Integrated Spelling T.E. pp. 94–95 Student Anthology pp. 536–545 Response Card 7: Responding Freely	**Spelling** Spelling Pretest Spelling-Vocabulary Connection	**Second-Language Support** Vocabulary T953 Strategic Reading T954 **Cooperative Reading** T955
Part 2 **Responding to Literature** Pages T960–T965 	**Story Follow-Up** Think It Over Write **Summarizing the Literature** **Appreciating Literature** **Critical Thinking Activities**	Writer's Journal p. 100 Practice Book p. 153 Integrated Spelling p. 74 Integrated Spelling T.E. pp. 94–95 Language Handbook	**Vocabulary Workshop** Reviewing Key Words Extending Vocabulary Spanish Words **Reading** Oral Rereading/Drama **Writing** A Description A Postcard An Autobiographical Essay Keeping a Diary **Spelling** Reviewing Spelling Words **Listening** Poetry **Speaking** Planning a Fiesta Giving Directions	**Cooperative Learning** T961, T963, T964, T965
Part 3 **Learning Through Literature** Pages T966–T972 	**Review** Comprehension: Fact and Opinion (Tested) Comprehension: Comparing and Contrasting (Tested) **Maintain** Study Skills: Graphic Aids (Tested)	Practice Book pp. 154–157	**Social Studies** Tea Ceremonies **Art** Designing a Belt **Science** The Ñandú **Math** Determining Area **Music/Dance** Argentine Music and Dances **Multicultural** Saving Lives	**Challenge** T967, T968, T969 **Cooperative Learning** T966, T968, T969, T971

KEY WORDS

gauchos
lasso
brand
hooves
manes
siesta

Selection Summary
María Cristina Brusca, the author and narrator, relates the story of one special summer she spent on her grandparents' estancia [eh·STAHN·sēē·ah], a large ranch, on the pampas [POM·pas] of Argentina.

During that summer, María Cristina and her cousin Susanita took care of the horses and cattle, had adventures, and learned to do all the other things gauchos [GOU·chōz] do. At the end of the summer, María Cristina received the gift she had yearned to have—a real gaucho belt, decorated with silver coins. Her grandparents told her that the next summer she would also have her own horse, which is something every gaucho needs. María Cristina left, knowing she would have the whole winter to think of a name for her horse and to look forward to the next summer.

Family Involvement
Suggest that family members discuss special things they like to do over the summer months. Encourage students to share with the rest of the group special times they have spent with their families during the summer.

MARÍA CRISTINA BRUSCA

While María Cristina Brusca grew up in the Argentine city of Buenos Aires, some of her most special memories are of the times she spent on her grandparents' estancia on the pampas. She still visits her cousin Susanita, who now lives in Buenos Aires. Brusca lives in Kingston, New York, but she and her family often gather at La Carlota for reunions.

ADDITIONAL READING
Other Books About Stargazers
Follow the Dream: The Story of Christopher Columbus by Peter Sis. Knopf, 1991. AVERAGE

Hannah by Gloria Whelan. Knopf, 1991. AVERAGE

Make-Believe Ball Player by Alfred Slote. Lippincott, 1989. AVERAGE

Women in Space: Reaching the Last Frontier by Carole S. Briggs. Lerner Publications, 1988. CHALLENGING

A Young Painter: The Life and Paintings of Wang Yani—China's Extraordinary Young Artist by Zheng Zhensun and Alice Lowe. New China/Scholastic, 1991. CHALLENGING

Part 1
Reading Literature

Building Background

Access prior knowledge and build vocabulary concepts.

Explain that "On the Pampas" is about a young girl who visits her grandparents' ranch on the pampas, or grasslands, of Argentina. Refer students to *Practice Book* page 153 on T961, or draw on the board a K-W-L chart like the one below and have students copy it onto a sheet of paper. Guide students in completing the first column with what they know about ranches around the world.

What I Know	What I Want to Know	What I Learned
Some ranches are large.		

Vocabulary Strategies

Introduce Key Words and strategies.

Display Transparency 55 or write the following story on the board. Invite students to read the story silently, using context clues with phonetic and structural analysis to decode and figure out the meanings of the underlined words. Then read the story with students. The web may be used to check students' understanding of the Key Words.

Transparency 55   Key Words

My family visited a large ranch in South America where cowhands, or <u>gauchos</u>, looked after a huge herd of cattle. They used a looped rope called a <u>lasso</u> to catch the cattle so they could put the ranch's mark or <u>brand</u> on them.

I heard the sound of galloping horses' <u>hooves</u> and saw the horses' <u>manes</u>, the hair along their necks, flying as cowhands on horseback chased the cattle. After a busy morning, I enjoyed the gauchos' custom of taking an afternoon nap called a <u>siesta</u>!

KEY WORDS

gauchos
lasso
brand
hooves
manes
siesta

KEY WORDS DEFINED

gauchos   cowhands of the South American pampas

lasso   long rope with a loop at the end

brand   mark made on an animal by burning the hide with a hot iron

hooves   hard, horny coverings on the feet of animals such as horses and cattle

manes   long, heavy hair on horses' necks

siesta   afternoon nap

Check students' understanding.

Display the Key Words. Ask students to develop a web, such as one of the following, using as many Key Words as possible. Encourage them to explain why they placed the words where they did. At this point, students may not understand how the word *siesta* connects with people. Suggest that after they have read the selection, they will see how this word fits in with the others.
STRATEGY: CLASSIFYING

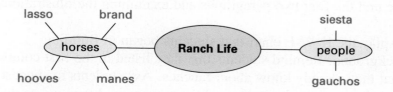

lasso   brand   siesta

(horses) —— (Ranch Life) —— (people)

hooves   manes   gauchos

Integrate spelling with vocabulary.

SPELLING-VOCABULARY CONNECTION *Integrated Spelling* page 73 reinforces spelling of consonant digraphs in the Key Word *gauchos* and in other words. The spelling of the Key Word *lasso* is also included.

SECOND-LANGUAGE SUPPORT Have some students pantomime or draw a picture to depict each Key Word, and have other students guess the Key Word. (See *Second-Language Support Manual*.)

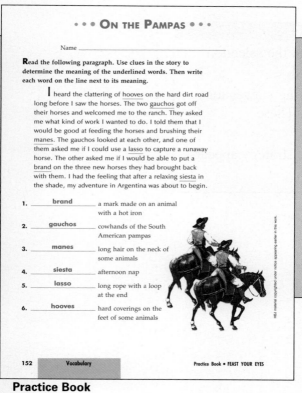

• • • ON THE PAMPAS • • •

Name _____

Read the following paragraph. Use clues in the story to determine the meaning of the underlined words. Then write each word on the line next to its meaning.

I heard the clattering of hooves on the hard dirt road long before I saw the horses. The two gauchos got off their horses and welcomed me to the ranch. They asked me what kind of work I wanted to do. I told them that I would be good at feeding the horses and brushing their manes. The gauchos looked at each other, and one of them asked me if I could use a lasso to capture a runaway horse. The other asked me if I would be able to put a brand on the three new horses they had brought back with them. I had the feeling that after a relaxing siesta in the shade, my adventure in Argentina was about to begin.

1. brand — a mark made on an animal with a hot iron

2. gauchos — cowhands of the South American pampas

3. manes — long hair on the neck of some animals

4. siesta — afternoon nap

5. lasso — long rope with a loop at the end

6. hooves — hard coverings on the feet of some animals

152   Vocabulary   Practice Book • FEAST YOUR EYES

Practice Book

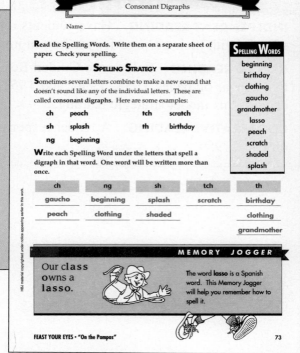

INTEGRATED SPELLING
Consonant Digraphs

Name _____

Read the Spelling Words. Write them on a separate sheet of paper. Check your spelling.

———— SPELLING STRATEGY ————

Sometimes several letters combine to make a new sound that doesn't sound like any of the individual letters. These are called **consonant digraphs**. Here are some examples:

ch	peach	tch	scratch
sh	splash	th	birthday
ng	beginning		

Write each Spelling Word under the letters that spell a digraph in that word. One word will be written more than once.

ch	ng	sh	tch	th
gaucho	beginning	splash	scratch	birthday
peach	clothing	shaded		clothing
				grandmother

SPELLING WORDS
beginning
birthday
clothing
gaucho
grandmother
lasso
peach
scratch
shaded
splash

MEMORY JOGGER

Our class owns a lasso.

The word **lasso** is a Spanish word. This Memory Jogger will help you remember how to spell it.

FEAST YOUR EYES • "On the Pampas"   73

Integrated Spelling

PRACTICE BOOK
page 152: Reinforcing Key Words

INTEGRATED SPELLING
page 73: Writing and spelling words with consonant digraphs

NOTE: These pages may be completed now or after students have read the selection.

Strategic Reading

Using the K-W-L Strategy

Help students preview the literature.

Tell students that the next selection, "On the Pampas," is an autobiography. Remind students that an autobiography includes factual information about the author, so the selection is also nonfiction. Have students preview the selection by reading the title and the first two paragraphs and examining the illustrations.

Have students make predictions.

Display the K-W-L chart that students began in Building Background. Remind students that they listed in the first column what they already know about ranches. Ask students to suggest what they would like to learn about ranches in Argentina as they read the selection. Have them add questions about what they would like to find out to the second column of their K-W-L chart. (See *Practice Book* page 153 on T961.)

What I Know	What I Want to Know	What I Learned
Some ranches are large.	What is an estancia?	

Tell students that after they have read the selection, they will add the information that they have learned to the third column.

Setting a Purpose

Have students set purposes.

Remind students that setting a purpose for reading helps them focus on the important ideas and therefore better understand what is read. Have students use the questions from the second column of their chart to set a purpose for reading. Then have students read the selection to try to find the answers to their questions. Students may wish to add other questions to the chart as they read.

> **OPTIONS FOR READING**
>
> **INDEPENDENT READING**   Have students read the selection silently with their purpose for reading in mind.
>
> **GUIDED READING**   Follow the Guided Reading suggestions that appear on pages T955, T956, and T959. These suggestions model strategic reading.
>
> **COOPERATIVE READING**   A reader response strategy appears on page T955.

SECOND-LANGUAGE SUPPORT   Have Spanish-speaking students work as peer tutors with other students to help them discover the meanings of the Spanish words in the selection. They may also be able to help with the pronunciation of Spanish words and names. (See *Second-Language Support Manual*.)

ON THE PAMPAS

María Cristina Brusca

AWARD-WINNING
ILLUSTRATOR

I grew up in Argentina, in South America. I lived with my family in the big city of Buenos Aires, but we spent our summers in the country, at my grandparents' *estancia*. One summer my parents and brother stayed in the city, so I went without them.

My grandmother met me at the station in Buenos Aires, and we had breakfast as we rode through miles and miles of the flattest land in the world—the pampas. All around us, as far as we could see, were fences, windmills, and millions of cattle grazing.

537

Guided Reading

SET PURPOSE/PREDICT: PAGES 536–539   Have students read through page 539 to find out what María Cristina's goal was while she was at her grandparents' ranch.

Cooperative Reading

READER RESPONSE STRATEGY: PAGES 536–545
Have students work in pairs. Ask each pair to decide whether they will read silently or aloud and how frequently they will stop. At designated stopping points, each member of the pair should respond freely to what they have read so far. Have pairs continue the procedure until they reach the end of the selection and then discuss it as a whole. (Response Card 7: Responding Freely, on page R68, gives complete directions for using the strategy.)

Our station, San Enrique, was at the end of the line, where the train tracks stopped. My grandfather was there to meet us in his pickup truck and take us the five miles to the estancia.

The ranch was called La Carlota, and the gates were made of iron bars from a fort that had been on that very spot a hundred years before. As we drove up to the gates, we were greeted by a cloud of dust and a thundering of hooves—it was my cousin Susanita, on her horse.

Susanita lived at the estancia all year round. She knew everything about horses, cows, and all the other animals that live on the pampas. Even though she was three years younger than me, she had her own horse, La Baya. Susanita was so tiny, she had to shimmy up La Baya's leg to get on her back. But she rode so well that the gauchos called her La Gauchita—"The Little Gaucho."

I didn't have a horse of my own, but old Salguero, the ranch foreman, brought me Pampita, a sweet-tempered mare, to ride. She wasn't very fast, but she certainly was my friend.

Susanita and I did everything together that summer. She was the one who showed me how to take care of the horses. We would brush their coats, trim their hooves, and braid their manes and tails.

Susanita was always ready for an adventure, no matter how scary. She used to swim in the creek holding on to La Baya's mane. At first I was afraid to follow her, but when she finally convinced me, it was a lot of fun.

I wanted to learn all the things a gaucho has to know. I wanted to ride out on the pampas every day, as Salguero did, and to wear a belt like his, with silver coins from all over the world and a buckle with my initials on

it. Salguero said I'd have to begin at the beginning, and he spent hours showing Susanita and me how to use the lasso.

It was going to take a while for me to become a gaucho. The first time I lassoed a calf, it dragged me halfway across the corral. But Salguero told me that even he had been dragged plenty of times, so I kept trying, until I got pretty good at it.

538

Guided Reading

**MONITOR COMPREHENSION: PAGES 536–539
What was María Cristina's goal for the summer at the ranch?** (to do the things a gaucho does)
STRATEGIC READING: RETURNING TO PURPOSE

What was La Carlota like? (a large cattle ranch on which lived horses, cattle, and gauchos and on which María Cristina's grandparents and her cousin Susanita also lived) STRATEGIC READING: SUMMARIZING

SET PURPOSE/PREDICT: PAGES 540–545 Have students predict whether María Cristina will achieve her goal of becoming a gaucho. Have them read the rest of the selection to confirm their predictions.

Whenever the gauchos were working with the cattle, Susanita was there, and before long I was too. Sometimes the herd had to be rounded up and moved from one pasture to another. I loved galloping behind hundreds of cattle, yelling to make them run. I never got to yell like that in the city!

One day we separated the calves from the cows, to vaccinate them and brand them with "the scissors," La Carlota's mark. That was more difficult—and more exciting, too. I tried to do what Salguero told me to, but sometimes I got lost in the middle of that sea of cattle.

At noon, everybody would sit down around one big table and eat together. I was always hungry. Grandma, Susanita's mother, and Maria the cook had been working hard all morning too. They would make soup, salad, and lamb stew or pot roast, or my favorite, *carbonada,* a thick stew made of corn and peaches.

After lunch the grown-ups took a *siesta,* but not us. We liked to stay outdoors. Some afternoons, when it was too hot to do anything else, we rode out to a eucalyptus grove that was nice and cool, and stayed there until it got dark, reading comic books or cowboy stories.

Other times we would gallop for two hours to the general store and buy ourselves an orange soda. Then, while we drank it, we'd look at all the saddles and bridles we planned to have when we were grown up and rich. Sometimes the storekeeper would take down a wonderful gaucho belt like Salguero's, and we would admire the silver coins and wonder where each one came from.

One day we rode far away from the house, to a field where Susanita thought we might find *ñandú* eggs. They

are so huge, you can bake a whole cake with just one of them. After riding around all afternoon, we found a nest, well hidden in the tall grass, with about twenty pale-yellow eggs as big as coconuts.

Salguero had warned us to watch out for the ñandú, and he was right! The father ñandú, who protects the nest, saw us taking an egg. He was furious and chased us out of the field.

541

Teaching Tip   Inform students that many cake recipes require three or more eggs in contrast to using a single ñandú egg for a cake, as mentioned on page 541.

The next day we used the ñandú egg to bake a birthday cake for my grandmother. We snuck into the kitchen while she was taking her siesta, so it would be a surprise. The cake had three layers, and in between them we put whipped cream and peaches from the trees on the ranch.

We had a wonderful party for my grandmother's birthday. The gauchos started the fire for the *asado* early in the evening, and soon the smell of the slowly cooking meat filled the air.

There was music, and dancing, too. We stayed up almost all night, and I learned to dance the *zamba,* taking little steps and hops, and twirling my handkerchief.

Most evenings were much quieter. There was just the hum of the generator that made electricity for the house. We liked to go out to the *mate* house, where the gauchos spent their evenings.

We listened to them tell stories and tall tales while they sat around the fire, passing the gourd and sipping mate through the silver straw. We didn't like the hot, bitter tea, but we loved being frightened by their spooky stories.

The summer was drawing to a close, and soon I would be returning to Buenos Aires. The night before I was to leave, Salguero showed me how to find the Southern Cross. The generator had been turned off, and there was only the soft sound of the peepers. We could see the horses sleeping far off in the field.

The next morning, my last at the estancia, Susanita and I got up before dawn. Pampita and the other horses were still out in the field. Salguero handed me his own horse's reins. He told me he thought I was ready to bring

in the horses by myself. I wasn't sure I could do it, but Susanita encouraged me to try.

I remembered what I'd seen Salguero do. I tried to get the leading mare, with her bell, to go toward the corral, and the others would follow her. It wasn't easy. The foals were frisky and kept running away. But I stayed behind them until finally the little herd was all together, trotting in front of me.

542

Vocabulary Strategy   **How can you figure out the meaning of the Spanish word *asado* [ah · SAH · dōh] on page 542?** (I can read the sentence and the paragraph in which the word is contained and figure out the word from context clues. The word *asado* is contained in the sentence *The gauchos started the fire for the* asado *early in the evening, and soon the smell of the slowly cooking meat filled the air.* If the smell of slowly cooking meat soon filled the air, *asado* must have something to do with meat.)   STRATEGY: CONTEXT CLUES

"And," she added, "there's something else every gaucho needs. Next summer, when you come back, you'll have your very own horse waiting for you!" She pointed to the leading mare's foal, the friskiest and most beautiful of them all.

Before I could say a word, the foal pranced over to me, tossing his head. I would have the whole winter to decide what to name him, and to look forward to my next summer on the pampas.

I was so busy trying to keep the foals from running off that I didn't notice the whole household waiting in the corral with Salguero. Everyone cheered as I rode in, and before I knew it, my grandfather was helping me off the horse. "You've become quite a gaucho this summer," he said. My grandmother held out a wonderful gaucho belt like Salguero's, with silver coins from around the world—and my initials on the buckle!

THINK IT OVER

1. *Describe what life was like at La Carlota.*

2. *What object did Salguero have that María Cristina, the girl who tells the story, hoped to have someday?*

3. *How might María Cristina's summer have been different if her parents and brother had gone with her to the estancia?*

4. *Would you like to visit Susanita and her family for a whole summer? Explain your answer.*

WRITE

Pretend that you are María Cristina and you have returned home to Buenos Aires. Write a friendly letter to Susanita at La Carlota, thanking her for showing you how to be a gaucho.

545

Guided Reading

MONITOR COMPREHENSION: PAGES 540–545
How did María Cristina achieve her goal? (At the end of the selection, Salguero told her to bring in the horses. She remembered what Salguero did and got the herd to the corral. Everyone cheered as she rode in.)   STRATEGIC READING: CONFIRMING PREDICTIONS/ SUMMARIZING

How do you think María Cristina felt at the end of the selection? (Accept reasonable responses: happy to hear the cheering, thrilled with the gift of the gaucho belt, delighted that she would be getting a horse of her own.)   CRITICAL: AUTHOR'S CRAFT/IDENTIFYING WITH CHARACTERS

Returning to the Purpose for Reading
Ask students to share the questions they wrote on their K-W-L charts before reading and the answers that they found during reading.

NOTE: Responses to the Think It Over questions and support for the Write activity appear on page T960.

Part 2
Responding to Literature

Story Follow-Up

Think It Over

Encourage reader's response: student page 545.

1. **Describe what life was like at La Carlota.** (Each day María Cristina rode a horse, helped the gauchos with their chores, worked with the cattle and horses, ate delicious foods, and had adventures with her cousin Susanita.)   INFERENTIAL: SUMMARIZING

2. **What object did Salguero have that María Cristina, the girl who tells the story, hoped to have someday?** (a gaucho belt with silver coins from around the world)   LITERAL: NOTING IMPORTANT DETAILS

3. **How might María Cristina's summer have been different if her parents and brother had gone with her to the estancia?** (Accept reasonable responses: She may not have spent as much time with Susanita and might not have become interested in learning how to be a gaucho.)   CRITICAL: SPECULATING

4. **Would you like to visit Susanita and her family for a whole summer? Explain your answer.** (Responses will vary.)   CRITICAL: EXPRESSING PERSONAL OPINIONS

Write

Encourage writer's response: student page 545.

Pretend that you are María Cristina and you have returned home to Buenos Aires. Write a friendly letter to Susanita at La Carlota, thanking her for showing you how to be a gaucho. Encourage students to include details from the selection.   CREATIVE: WRITING A LETTER

Summarizing the Literature

Have students complete the K-W-L chart.

Encourage students to summarize the selection by recalling facts they learned from their reading. Guide students as they complete the third column of their K-W-L chart, or suggest they complete it in pairs. (See *Practice Book* page 153 on T961.) Students may use their completed chart to help them retell the selection and to write a brief summary statement.

What I Know	What I Want to Know	What I Learned
Some ranches are large.	What is an estancia?	An estancia is a large ranch.

NOTE

An additional writing activity for this selection appears on page T963.

STRATEGY CONFERENCE

Discuss with students how using the K-W-L strategy helped them understand, remember, and appreciate the selection. Invite students to share other reading strategies, such as self-questioning, that helped them understand the selection.

Appreciating Literature

Have students share personal responses.

Have students work in small groups to discuss the selection. Provide a general question such as the following to help the groups begin:

- **What information in this selection did you think was the most interesting? Explain why you think as you do.**

PERSONAL JOURNAL   Have students use their personal journals to write about ideas and feelings that are discussed in the groups. You may also refer them to their personal journals after they complete the activities below.

Critical Thinking Activities

Encourage both cooperative and individual responses.

DISCUSS IDEAS   In what ways do you think María Cristina's stay at the estancia might have been different if Susanita did not live there? Have students discuss their ideas with a partner.   CRITICAL: SPECULATING

WRITE A NEW ENDING   What problem might María Cristina have had with the new foal when she returned to La Carlota the next summer? How might she have solved it? Have students work in pairs to write a new ending for the selection. When students have finished, have them share their work with other students.   CREATIVE: SOLVING PROBLEMS

SUMMER REPORT CARD

Student Maria Cristina Brusca

Teacher _____
(your name)

The author learned all about being a gaucho from Salguero, the author's teacher on the pampas. Imagine that you are Salguero and you are filling out a report card for each month of the summer. Write in the grades. Add a comment for each item, to explain the reasons for the final grade.

	June	July	Aug.	Comments
Riding horses				
Brushing horses				
Trimming horses' hooves				
Braiding manes and tails				
Using the lasso				
Rounding up cattle				
Bringing in the horses				
Finding ñandú eggs				
Dancing the zamba				

100 "On the Pampas"   HBJ Writer's Journal   FEAST YOUR EYES

Writer's Journal

• • • ON THE PAMPAS • • •

Name _____

A. One way to summarize a nonfiction selection is to complete a K-W-L chart. Use the one below before, during, and after you read.

K	W	L
What I Know	*What I Want to Know*	*What I Learned*
Responses will vary.		

B. Write a one-sentence summary about the selection.
A possible response is given.
Maria Cristina spent summers on her grandparents' estancia, where she learned all the things a gaucho had to know to work on a ranch.

Practice Book ■ FEAST YOUR EYES   Summarizing the Literature   **153**

Practice Book

VO·CAB·U·LAR·Y Workshop

Reviewing Key Words

List the Key Words on the board, and have each student draw three pictures in which two of the Key Words are illustrated.

Invite volunteers to describe each picture, using at least two vocabulary words.

mane
hooves

gaucho
siesta

Extending Vocabulary

SPANISH WORDS Point out that since "On the Pampas" is set in Argentina, the selection includes many Spanish words. Have students look through the selection and locate the Spanish words. Explain that some of the words appear in italic type. List on the board the Spanish words students find. (Words might include *estancia, pampas, gaucho, carbonada* [KAR · bō · nah · dah], *siesta, asado, zamba* [ZAM · bah], *corral, mate* [MAH · tay].) Ask students to define each word, using context clues from the selection. Write the definitions next to each word, making a chart such as the one below:

Spanish Word	Definition
estancia	large ranch
pampas	vast, treeless grasslands
gaucho	cowhand
carbonada	thick stew made of corn and peaches
siesta	afternoon nap
asado	slowly cooked meat
zamba	a dance
corral	pen where horses and cattle are held
mate	hot, bitter tea

Next, provide students with chart paper, paints, crayons, and a variety of other art materials. Invite students to work in small groups to make a mural of an estancia. Encourage students to include drawings that illustrate as many Spanish words from the chart as possible.

lasso
hooves

Integrated Language Arts

READING

Oral Rereading/ Drama

COOPERATIVE LEARNING Invite students to describe their favorite part of the selection. Have each student locate that part in the text and reread it silently. Then form groups and have students take turns reading their favorite part aloud. Next, ask students to dramatize each group member's favorite part of the selection in the form of a Readers Theatre. Model how to read or create a dialogue and how to develop lines for a narrator to speak. Allow groups time for rehearsal and then have them present their readings to classmates. LISTENING/ SPEAKING/READING

WRITING

Writing About the Literature

WRITE A DESCRIPTION Explain to students that when María Cristina wrote about the pampas, she included many details that appealed to the senses and helped the reader visualize what was happening. Have students review the selection for examples of things that appeal to the senses of sight, smell, taste, touch, and hearing.

Next, ask students to think about a special trip they have taken or would like to take. Encourage them to develop a chart such as the one below to organize their thoughts. Then have students use the information from the chart to write a description of their trip. Suggest that they give their description an appropriate title. When they have finished, invite students to take turns reading their description aloud. LISTENING/SPEAKING/READING/ WRITING

A Week at a Dude Ranch		
What I Did	**Whom I Went With**	**Using My Senses**
went to a dude ranch	dad and brother	saw cowhands heard animals touched horses tasted new foods

NOTE: An additional writing activity appears on page T960.

SPELLING

Reviewing Spelling Words

SPELLING WORDS: *beginning, birthday, clothing, gaucho, grandmother, lasso, ocean, peach, scratch, splash*

Tell students that many English words come from Spanish (for example: *lasso, alligator,* and *canyon*). Ask students to suggest words they think might be Spanish in origin. Then assign the words to several groups and ask each group to explore the etymology, or history, of the words. Suggest that students use dictionaries. Have the groups share their findings and ask students to identify the words with consonant digraphs. LISTENING/SPEAKING/ READING/SPELLING

> **INTEGRATED SPELLING**
> page 74: Writing and spelling words with consonant digraphs

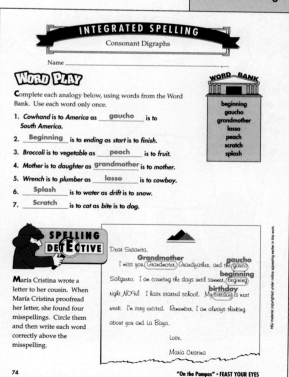

Integrated Spelling

Imagination Vacation

Have students write a postcard message telling what they are seeing and doing on an imaginary trip. Remind students that there is only a small space in which to write on a postcard, so the message must be brief. Have students use real postcards, if possible, or make postcards out of light cardboard or oaktag. When students have finished, invite them to read their postcard messages aloud. If students are interested, suggest that they also design an illustration for the front of the postcard.
LISTENING/SPEAKING/READING/WRITING

Poet's Corner

Have students locate poetry anthologies. Encourage them to search for poems about ranches, the Old West, horses, or any topic related to the selection. Ask volunteers to read several of the poems aloud. Then encourage students to comment on the imagery in the poems and to tell how they think the poetry is similar to or different from María Cristina's description of life at La Carlota.
LISTENING/SPEAKING/READING

Fiesta!

AVAILABLE ON PROJECT CARD

COOPERATIVE LEARNING   Explain to students that *fiesta* is a Spanish word that means "party." Ask students to imagine that their class is going to have a fiesta. Invite students to work in small groups to research the kinds of activities that are customary at a fiesta. When the groups have finished their research, assign each group a role in planning a fiesta that includes such things as costumes, traditions such as breaking a piñata, and authentic foods.
LISTENING/SPEAKING/READING

WRITING

I Always Wanted to . . .

Remind students that "On the Pampas" is an autobiographical selection. Explain that María Cristina wrote about a time in her life when she wanted to learn how to be a gaucho. Invite students to write autobiographical accounts of something they want to learn. Before they begin writing, encourage students to organize their ideas by using a graphic organizer such as a semantic web, a chart, or a list. When students have finished, have several volunteers read their work to classmates.   LISTENING/READING/WRITING

SPEAKING

Teacher, Teacher
AVAILABLE ON PROJECT CARD

COOPERATIVE LEARNING   Remind students that María Cristina learned to be a gaucho by watching and listening to other gauchos. Invite students to work with a partner. Ask them to take turns explaining to each other how to do something such as playing a simple game like "Tic-Tac-Toe" or "Hangman." When the partners have each had a turn being the "teacher," have them form larger groups and demonstrate what they taught. LISTENING/SPEAKING

WRITING

Dear Diary

Explain to students that writers often find ideas for stories in their own journals or diaries. If necessary, describe the kinds of things people usually record in diaries. Then invite students to create a fourth grade character and write diary entries from the character's point of view. Have students write about significant things that might happen over the period of one week. Ask them to begin a new page for each day, and help them bind the pages together when they are finished.   WRITING

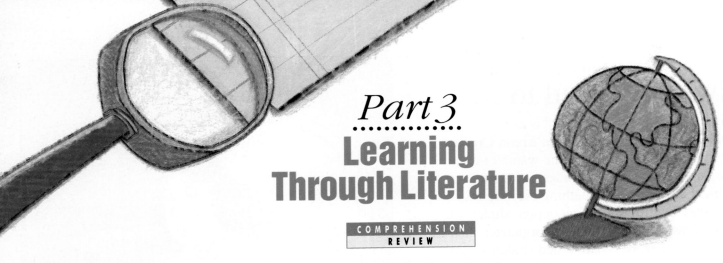

Part 3
Learning Through Literature

Fact and Opinion

OBJECTIVE: *To distinguish between fact and opinion*

Review

Review the difference between fact and opinion.

Remind students that because this selection is an autobiography, there are many statements of fact. Explain that they will also find opinions, since the author wrote about her summer vacation. Discuss how students can determine whether a statement is a fact or an opinion. (A fact is a statement that can be proven. An opinion tells how the author feels about something.)

Use the chart below to model distinguishing fact from opinion.

Statement	Fact	Opinion	Explanation
I grew up in Argentina, in South America.	✓		I can check to find out if this is true.

Practice/Apply

Have students find facts and opinions.

COOPERATIVE LEARNING Ask students to work in pairs and use the selection to locate two statements of fact and two statements of opinion. Then have students create charts of their statements. Tell students to add two of their own statements to the charts.

Summarize

Informally assess the learning.

Have students share their charts by reading aloud statements, identifying the facts or opinions, and explaining their answers. Ask student pairs to work together to create one chart.

Have students summarize what they learned. (Determine a fact by deciding whether a statement can be proven. Determine an opinion by deciding whether an author's feelings are included.)

CHALLENGE Have students write a descriptive paragraph in which they include two statements of fact and two statements of opinion.

• • • ON THE PAMPAS • • •

Name _____

A. Read the following paragraph. Decide which sentences in it are facts and which are opinions. Then write the number of each sentence in the appropriate place on the chart.

(1) Buenos Aires is a very interesting city. (2) It is the capital of Argentina. (3) Argentina is the second-largest country in South America, after Brazil. (4) Buenos Aires is located in eastern Argentina, near Uruguay. (5) It is Argentina's chief port and cultural center. (6) If you live in Argentina and you don't live in Buenos Aires, you should move. (7) If you live in, for example, Santiago, you really should consider moving to Buenos Aires. (8) There are many more interesting things to do and see in Buenos Aires than in any other city in Argentina.

Facts	Opinions
2, 3, 4, 5	1, 6, 7, 8

B. On the line before each sentence, write *F* if the statement is a fact or *O* if the statement is an opinion.

F _____ 1. Susanita lived at the estancia year-round.

O _____ 2. It's better to live on a ranch than in a city.

F _____ 3. Susanita had her own horse.

O _____ 4. The horse María finally got was better than Susanita's.

O _____ 5. Swimming in the creek on a horse was great fun.

F _____ 6. Carbonada is a thick stew made of corn and peaches.

F _____ 7. A ñandú egg is so big that it supplies all the egg needed for a whole cake.

154   Fact and Opinion   Practice Book • FEAST YOUR EYES

Practice Book

PRACTICE BOOK
page 154:
Distinguishing between fact and opinion

Comparing and Contrasting

OBJECTIVE: *To determine likenesses and differences*

Review

Strategy: Have students find likenesses and differences.

Ask students to recall how to compare and contrast important story details. (by looking at how two things are alike and how they are different) Use the diagram to model comparing and contrasting María Cristina and Susanita.

CHALLENGE Have students make a diagram and compare and contrast life in a big city such as Buenos Aires with life in the country, such as at La Carlota.

Practice/Apply

Have students apply the learning.

COOPERATIVE LEARNING Have students work in pairs to make a diagram that compares their summer with María Cristina's.

Summarize

Informally assess the learning.

Using the completed diagram, have students discuss how each detail helps the reader visualize the story setting.

Have students summarize what they learned. (Compare and contrast story details to understand likenesses and differences.)

• • • ON THE PAMPAS • • •

Name _____

A. Read each of the sentences below. On the line, write what is being compared.

1. Students in Argentina usually get the summer off, as do students in the United States. <u>summer schedule for students in Argentina and for students in the United States</u>

2. Grandma, like María, had been working hard all morning cooking lunch. <u>Grandma's and María's activities</u>

3. The oil fields in Argentina produce almost all the country's oil, and they provide natural gas, too. <u>Argentina's oil and natural gas sources</u>

B. Read each of the sentences below. On the line, write what is being contrasted.

1. Pampita wasn't a very fast horse, but Salguero's horse was quick. <u>Pampita's and Salguero's horse's speed</u>

2. Susanita was always ready for an adventure. María, however, was sometimes afraid. <u>Susanita's and María's taste for adventure</u>

3. On one hand, the grown-ups wanted a siesta after lunch. On the other hand, Susanita and María wanted to do things. <u>the girls' and the grown-ups' activities after lunch</u>

Practice Book ■ FEAST YOUR EYES   Comparing and Contrasting   155

Practice Book

PRACTICE BOOK
page 155: Comparing and contrasting

Graphic Aids

OBJECTIVE: *To interpret information on maps*

Review

Have students analyze a map.

Remind students that a map is one kind of graphic aid. Review that a map helps them see what a region of the earth looks like. Ask students what features on a map help them locate information. (coordinates, legend, compass rose)

Practice/Apply

Have students use a map.

COOPERATIVE LEARNING   Have students work in groups to locate a map of Argentina. Tell them to find the map legend and the compass rose, and to explain to each other what information these features give.

Summarize

Informally assess the learning.

Have students draw a map that shows where the school library is located. Tell them to include a legend.
    Have students summarize the learning. (Maps are drawings that show what a region of the earth looks like.)

CHALLENGE   Have students make a map that shows where their classroom is located within their school. Display the maps.

PRACTICE BOOK
pages 156–157:
Using graphic aids

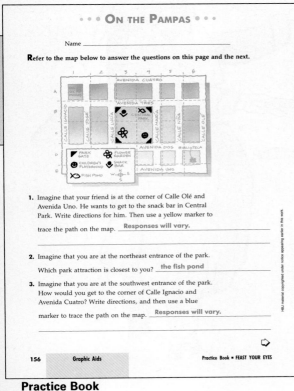

• • • ON THE PAMPAS • • •

Name _____

Refer to the map below to answer the questions on this page and the next.

1. Imagine that your friend is at the corner of Calle Olé and Avenida Uno. He wants to get to the snack bar in Central Park. Write directions for him. Then use a yellow marker to trace the path on the map. _Responses will vary._

2. Imagine that you are at the northeast entrance of the park. Which park attraction is closest to you? _the fish pond_

3. Imagine that you are at the southwest entrance of the park. How would you get to the corner of Calle Ignacio and Avenida Cuatro? Write directions, and then use a blue marker to trace the path on the map. _Responses will vary._

156   Graphic Aids   Practice Book ▪ FEAST YOUR EYES

Practice Book

• • • ON THE PAMPAS • • •

Name _____

4. Imagine that you are at the park. You want to meet a friend at the corner of Avenida Dos and Calle Lucía. Which park gate would be best to use? _the southwest gate, or the one near the flower garden_

5. Suppose your friend is at the corner of Calle José and Avenida Tres. She wants to meet you at the corner of Calle Niña and Avenida Dos. Write the directions you would give. Then use a green marker to trace the path on the map. _Responses will vary._

6. Imagine that you are at the biblioteca, or library. You want to go to the Big Six Movies. Write directions, and then use a pink marker to trace the path on the map. _Responses will vary._

7. What is the northeastern-most point on this map? Describe it below, and put a red X on the map. _northeast corner of Avenida Cuatro and Calle Olé_

8. What building can you locate using the coordinates D6? _biblioteca_

9. Make up your own question based on this map, and write the answer to your question. _Responses will vary._

Practice Book ▪ FEAST YOUR EYES   Graphic Aids   157

Practice Book

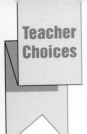

Integrated Curriculum

Tea for Two

CULTURAL AWARENESS   Tell students that in Argentina, at any time of the day or night, people drink mate, which is a kind of tea. Have students research tea ceremonies in various cultures. You may wish to tell them that Japan, China, and Great Britain are some of the countries that have tea-drinking rituals or customs. Have students work in small groups, and assign a specific country to each group. Encourage students to take notes. When they are finished, have groups present their findings to the others.   LISTENING/SPEAKING/READING/WRITING

Belt It

AVAILABLE ON PROJECT CARD

Remind students that María Cristina admired Salguero's beautiful belt with the silver coins. Explain to students that for special occasions gauchos usually wear wide leather belts that have silver coins worked into them. Provide students with art materials and have them design their own coin belts. When students have finished, invite them to share their work and to explain the meaning of their design. Then display their work on a bulletin board or around the classroom.   LISTENING/SPEAKING

Everybody, Tango!

AVAILABLE ON PROJECT CARD

CULTURAL AWARENESS Remind students that María Cristina mentioned a dance called the *zamba*. Explain to students that some people call Argentina the home of the tango, which is another popular dance. Invite students to work in small groups to research the music and dances of Argentina and to report their findings. If possible, have them locate and share pictures of dancers in costume as well as recordings of the dance music. LISTENING/ SPEAKING/READING/WRITING

SCIENCE

Bury Your Head in the Sand

USE REFERENCE SOURCES Remind students that María Cristina and Susanita found a ñandú egg and used it in a cake they made for their grandmother's birthday. Explain to students that a ñandú, also known as a rhea [rē · 'ə], is a very large bird similar to the ostrich. Have students research the ñandú. Ask them to find out where the bird can be found, what it eats, and if it has any special habits. When students have finished, have them share their findings with classmates. Then have students compare and contrast what they know about the ñandú with what they know about the ostrich. LISTENING/ SPEAKING/READING/WRITING

MATH

Lots of Land

COOPERATIVE LEARNING Remind students that an estancia is a very large ranch with many acres of land on the flat, grassy pampas. Review with students how to figure out area. Then pose the following math problem:

If La Carlota were rectangular in shape, and were 30 miles long and 15 miles wide, what would the area of the ranch be? (450 square miles)

Invite students to work in pairs to make up their own word problems involving area. Then have them exchange papers with another pair, and solve each other's problems. LISTENING/SPEAKING/READING/WRITING

Inventive Medicine

READ ALOUD TO STUDENTS:

THE GAUCHOS VACCINATED

CALVES TO PREVENT THEM

FROM CATCHING DISEASES.

Vaccination is an important medical discovery that has saved millions of animal and human lives. A vaccination is an injection of dead or weakened disease organisms into a healthy body to cause immunity.

A forerunner of vaccination was inoculation, which uses live organisms. A black slave named Onesimus had been inoculated against smallpox—a dreaded disease—in Africa. In 1721, during an epidemic of smallpox in America, Onesimus described the inoculation procedure to a physician. Convinced, the physician tried this procedure on his own son, and it worked. The news spread through the colonies and beyond. Eventually it led to the first vaccine for smallpox.

Another terrible disease subdued by vaccine was yellow fever. In the late 1800s, outbreaks of this disease killed thousands of Americans. A Cuban doctor, Carlos Finlay, believed that the disease was passed to humans by mosquito bites. When his theory was proved true by Dr. Walter Reed in 1900, development began on a vaccine to control yellow fever. ■

ACTIVITY CORNER

■ Have student groups find out about diseases for which there is no proven cure as yet. Encourage them to find out about the ongoing medical research and the possibility of cure in the future.

■ Tell students to imagine that they were reporters in the room when Onesimus was describing the inoculation procedure to a physician. Have them write a news article describing the scene and tell about the feelings that must have resulted from the successful inoculation of the physician's son.

Research by Finlay and Reed led to the development of a vaccine to control yellow fever.

POEMS

Last Laugh/The Drum

ABOUT THE POETS   Lee Bennett Hopkins is inspired by children, who he feels are natural poets. Hopkins has written or edited books about poetry for teachers and librarians, as well as novels and anthologies for young people. Nikki Giovanni has written several volumes of poetry for adults and children. She holds many honorary degrees.

ABOUT THE POEMS   "Last Laugh" is from *Surprises*, selected as an ALA Notable Book and one of the SLJ Best Books of the Year in 1984. "The drum" is contained in a collection entitled *Spin a Soft Black Song*, which was a *New York Times* Outstanding Book of the Year. Many of the poems in this collection express a child's view of the black experience.

Reading the Poems

Help students set a purpose for reading.

Recall with students the previous selection, "On the Pampas." Remind them that María Cristina's goal was to become a gaucho. Encourage students to share any experiences they have had in achieving a goal.

Ask students to determine what kind of attitude both narrators of the poems feel is needed in order to achieve one's goals. Then read "Last Laugh" and "the drum" to the students.

Responding to the Poems

Return to the purpose for reading.

Open a discussion in which you ask students to describe the attitude both narrators have about achieving long-term goals. Ask students to comment on how such an attitude might help each narrator reach her goal. Then invite several volunteers to read the poems aloud in a way that might express the narrators' attitude.

Encourage students to respond creatively.

You may wish to select one of the following activities for responding to the poems:

CONDUCTING AN INTERVIEW   Invite students to interview an older friend or family member who is pursuing a career of interest. Encourage students to formulate a list of questions about how the person became interested in the career and what steps were necessary to achieve his or her goals. Ask students to take notes during the interview and to use them to write a feature news story about the person.   LISTENING/SPEAKING/WRITING

PERSONAL JOURNAL: WRITING A POEM   Invite students to write a poem in free verse or in rhyme that describes how they plan to achieve one or some of their long-term goals. Encourage them to illustrate their work and to share it with their classmates.   LISTENING/READING/WRITING

TEACHING TIP

Point out to students that the rules of capitalization and punctuation have been relaxed in "the drum." Explain that writing a poem in this way is called "using poetic license."

SECOND-LANGUAGE SUPPORT   Share with students that in 1969, astronauts from the United States landed on the moon. The moon landing was broadcast live, so that as the astronauts were on the moon, their images were seen worldwide on TV.

ALA
NOTABLE BOOK
SLJ BEST BOOKS
OF THE YEAR

LAST LAUGH
by Lee Bennett Hopkins · from *Surprises*

They all laughed when I told them
I wanted to be

A woman in space
Floating so free.

But they won't laugh at me
When they finally see
My feet up on Mars
And my face on TV.

THE DRUM
by Nikki Giovanni

daddy says the world is
a drum tight and hard

and i told him

i'm gonna beat
out my own rhythm

AWARD-WINNING
AUTHOR

546

THEME WRAP-UP

STARGAZERS

The selections and poems that you read told about people who had confidence in being able to reach their goals. Which character do you think showed the most determination? Share your reasons for thinking as you do.

· ·

Think about the qualities that Jim Abbott and María Cristina share. How do their qualities make them special?

· ·

WRITER'S WORKSHOP Would you rather meet Jim Abbott, María Cristina, or one of the speakers of the poems? Choose two of the characters, and write one or more paragraphs that compare and contrast how each one reaches for the stars in his or her own way. Make a diagram to list the information you gather.

For discussion of this page, please turn to T975.

Expanding the Poems Explain to students that a metaphor is an indirect comparison of two unlike things, in which one thing is said to be the other. **To what is the drum being compared in the poem "the drum"?** (the world) INFERENTIAL: UNDERSTANDING FIGURATIVE LANGUAGE

The "daddy" in Nikki Giovanni's poem sees the world as "a drum tight and hard." Suppose the father's child asked him, "Daddy, why do you say that?" What do you think he would answer? Do you think he would tell his child about any experiences that had caused him to feel that way? Use the space above to write the father's answer to his child's question.

Why Do You Say That?

Imagine that you are the speaker in the poem. Explain to the "daddy" what you mean when you say, "i'm gonna beat / out my own rhythm." Write your answer in the space below.

by _____
(your name)

Response to Literature · FEAST YOUR EYES · *HBJ Writer's Journal* · "The Drum" **101**

WRITER'S JOURNAL
page 101:
Writing a personal response

THEME WRAP-UP

Stargazers

Remind students that the selections in this theme were about characters who were determined to achieve their goals. Guide students to recall the goals of Jim Abbott and María Cristina Brusca, as well as those of the speakers in the two poems. Ask students to speculate about whether they think the speakers in the poems will achieve their goals. Explain to students that the questions on page 547 will help them think further about the ideas presented in the selections.

Note that pages T976–T977 provide support for applying the writing process to the last question.

THEME WRAP-UP

STARGAZERS

The selections and poems that you read told about people who had confidence in being able to reach their goals. Which character do you think showed the most determination? Share your reasons for thinking as you do.

Think about the qualities that Jim Abbott and María Cristina share. How do their qualities make them special?

WRITER'S WORKSHOP   Would you rather meet Jim Abbott, María Cristina, or one of the speakers of the poems? Choose two of the characters, and write one or more paragraphs that compare and contrast how each one reaches for the stars in his or her own way. Make a diagram to list the information you gather.

547

Theme Wrap-Up

DISCUSSION QUESTIONS, PAGE 547

The selections and poems that you read told about people who had confidence in being able to reach their goals. Which character do you think showed the most determination? Share your reasons for thinking as you do. Encourage students to first identify how each character showed determination. (Responses will vary.)
CRITICAL: EXPRESSING PERSONAL OPINIONS

Think about the qualities that Jim Abbott and María Cristina share. How do their qualities make them special? Have students look at each character separately to determine what qualities make that person special. (Accept reasonable responses: It takes an exceptional person to be able to overcome obstacles and achieve his or her goals.)
CRITICAL: DETERMINING CHARACTERS' TRAITS

WRITER'S WORKSHOP   See pages T976–T977 for suggestions for applying the writing process.
Would you rather meet Jim Abbott, María Cristina, or one of the speakers of the poems? Choose two of the characters, and write one or more paragraphs that compare and contrast how each one reaches for the stars in his or her own way. Make a diagram to list the information you gather. You may prefer to allow students to respond to the theme in their own way.   WRITING PROCESS: PARAGRAPHS OF COMPARISON AND CONTRAST

Writer's Workshop

For More Discussion & Practice:

LANGUAGE HANDBOOK

Review with students what it means to compare and contrast things. (tell how things are alike and how they are different) Ask students how writers sort the details in paragraphs of comparison and contrast. (into three categories: things true only of one subject, things true only of the other subject, and things true of both.) Suggest that students refer to the Handbook in the *Writer's Journal* as they write, revise, and proofread their paragraphs of comparison and contrast.

Prewriting

Before students write, review with them that the characters they read about in this theme are "stargazers"—they all set goals and strived to reach those goals. Have students

- think about the characters in this theme.
- think about their audience and their purpose for writing.
- make a Venn diagram using the format below that shows how two characters were similar and different in their goals.

Character 1	Similarities	Character 2
1.	1.	1.
2.	2.	2.
3.	3.	3.

Encourage students to add details to their diagram as they think about how the characters went about accomplishing their goals. Then have them think about the ways in which the approaches were similar and the ways in which they were different.

Drafting

Ask students to write a draft of the comparison and contrast paragraphs. Remind them to

- use their Venn diagram to help them organize similarities and differences.
- write a topic sentence that identifies the characters and the goals that are being compared and contrasted.
- write detail sentences that describe similarities and differences to support the topic sentence.

COMPUTER CONNECTION   Students may want to use a computer during the revising stage in order to easily replace dull words with words that vividly describe the characters.

Responding and Revising

Ask students to read their paragraphs aloud to a partner. Have the pairs discuss whether the comparisons and contrasts are clearly expressed. Offer the following suggestions, and ask students to revise their work.

- Have you identified the characters and goals being compared and contrasted? If not, point them out in the first sentence.
- Are the paragraphs organized correctly? If not, put the paragraphs in correct order.
- Did you use strong describing words to paint a clear picture? If not, add describing words to dull sentences. (See the Language/Literature Link below.)

STUDENT SELF-ASSESSMENT OPTION   Students may use the Writing Self-Assessment Checklist in the *Portfolio Teacher's Guide.* Suggest that as they use the checklist, they focus on the use of vivid describing words to give the reader a clear picture.

Proofreading

Make the following suggestions to help students proofread their work and make changes:

- Check for errors in capitalization and punctuation.
- Check to be sure that the first line of each paragraph is indented.
- Draw a line around words that appear to be misspelled. Find out how to spell them correctly.

Publishing

Discuss with students alternatives for publishing their paragraphs of comparison and contrast. Some students may wish to compile their work into a book entitled *Reach for the Stars.* Others may prefer to make a split drawing, showing on each side one character after having achieved his or her goal. Have students save their drawings and paragraphs in their reading/writing portfolios.

LANGUAGE/LITERATURE LINK

Adding Describing Words to Sentences

Explain to students that successful writers choose the right describing words to create clear, strong pictures. Remind students that they can use a thesaurus to help them replace dull words with vivid words. Have students look through the stories in this theme to find examples of vivid describing words. Encourage students to check their work to make sure that they have used exact describing words and created clear, strong pictures.

Speaking Option

ORAL PRESENTATION   The Writer's Workshop may be adapted to have students share their comparison and contrast paragraphs through oral presentations. Have students follow the guidelines for Prewriting, Drafting, and Responding and Revising. Then offer the following speaking tips to help students give their oral presentations:

- Practice reading the paragraphs until you can read them smoothly.
- Maintain eye contact with the audience, and speak loudly.
- Speak expressively, especially when describing how each character achieved his or her goals.

Invite students to give their oral presentations to a group of classmates. You may wish to have students group their chairs together to simulate an audience.

Connections

The Connections activities on Student Anthology pages 548–549 guide students to synthesize multicultural and content-area information with the unit theme. Before students begin the activities, ask them to review quickly the purpose-setting paragraph on page 460. Encourage students to talk about the selections in the unit and to share their opinions about which one they most enjoyed. Then ask them to share whether any of the characters in this unit shared their personal dream.

To prepare students for the Multicultural

Connection, you might ask them to consider some famous Americans of the past and present who have had important dreams. Encourage students to name Americans from all walks of life and tell about their dreams and how these dreams were realized.

Explain to students that anyone can be a dreamer—regardless of age, gender, or ethnic background. If necessary, introduce Dr. Martin Luther King, Jr., as a famous African American who had an important dream.

CONNECTIONS

MULTICULTURAL CONNECTION

DREAM OF A BETTER WORLD

"I have a dream," said Martin Luther King, Jr., while standing in front of the Lincoln Memorial in 1963. Thousands of people listened to his historical speech.

King's dream was to live in a nation with equal rights and freedom for all—no matter what color one's skin is. King did more than just dream. He spent his life fighting for what he believed in. Thanks to King's hard work and the example he set, the dream is being achieved.

■ *Many other African Americans, such as Rosa Parks and Thurgood Marshall, have taken part in the equal rights struggle. Find out more about the history of this struggle in America. Create a collage showing what you learned.*

SOCIAL STUDIES CONNECTION

AMERICAN DREAMERS

There have been many great dreamers like Martin Luther King, Jr., whose work has made our nation a better place. Read about other leaders, such as doctors, scientists, and soldiers, who improved the lives of others. Use what you learn to create a class bulletin board gallery of great Americans.

You can use a web like the one shown to help you organize your ideas.

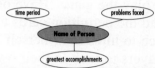

ART CONNECTION

YOUR OWN DREAM

What is your own dream for a better world? With a small group, make a mural that shows some changes that you would like to see. Together, write a poem that tells how people can make a dream come true. Share your mural and poem with the rest of your classmates.

549

Multicultural Connection

DREAM OF A BETTER WORLD   Invite students to read the feature. Then provide students with research materials such as encyclopedias and books about the lives of famous African Americans. Have them work in groups to learn more about Martin Luther King, Jr., and others who contributed to the struggle for equal rights. Suggest that each group select two or three people about whom to learn. Provide art materials, such as mural paper, old magazines, scissors, and paints, for students to use in creating their collages.

Social Studies Connection

AMERICAN DREAMERS   Guide students in thinking about leaders in various fields who are or were dreamers. Provide resources, including biographies of scientists and world leaders, and have students read about a person of their choice. Suggest that they put their findings into a web such as the one shown on page 549. You may also wish to have students present their findings on a bulletin board entitled "A Gallery of Great Americans."

Art Connection

YOUR OWN DREAM   Encourage students to think about how they would change the world to make it a better place. Then have them work in groups to make a mural that depicts some of the changes they would make. When they have finished, have them collaborate on a poem that tells how people can make dreams come true.

Integrated Language Arts

Reviewing Vocabulary—Go Fish

- Write ten Key Words on the board, and ask students to work with a partner to define each word. Then have pairs write each Key Word on an index card and the definitions on another set of index cards.
- Invite partners to play the game. Have one student mix the word cards and the definition cards together and give ten cards each to himself or herself and the partner. Invite players to look in their own hands for word cards and definition cards that match and then place them face down in a pile. Next, have one student select a card from the other's hand and try to match it with the corresponding word or definition card in his or her hand. Invite students to continue until all the cards have been matched. Finally, have students look at the pairs each has collected and review the meaning of each Key Word.

Reviewing Spelling Words

Integrated Spelling page 75 provides a review of the Unit 6 spelling words. *Integrated Spelling* page 76 provides practice with frequently misspelled abbreviations.

Writing About "Dreamers"

You may wish to have students respond to the unit focus by writing an advertisement to add to the magazines in their *Writer's Journals*. Provide them with copies of new-product ads and classified ads from magazines to use as examples. (See *Writer's Journal* pages 102–103.)

INTEGRATED SPELLING

pages 75–76: Reviewing unit words and abbreviations

WRITER'S JOURNAL

pages 102–103: Making Your Own Magazine

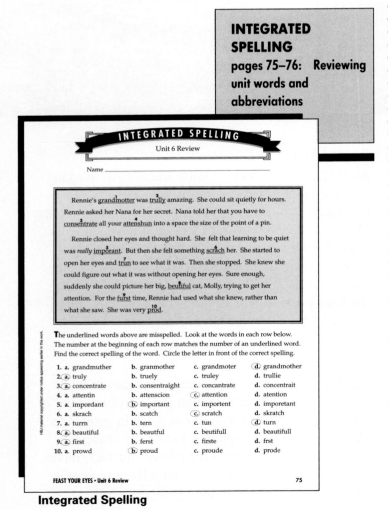

Integrated Spelling

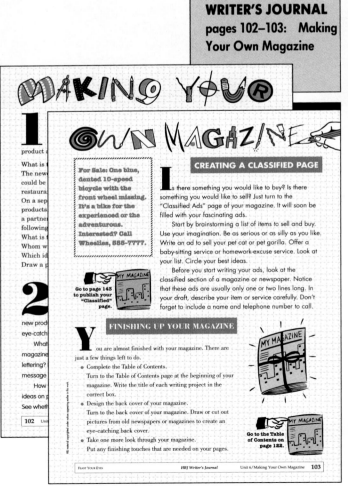

Writer's Journal

Assessment Options

Informal Assessment

See the suggestions below to informally assess students' progress in Unit 6.

INFORMAL ASSESSMENT NOTES AND CHECKLISTS

If you used the informal assessment notes in the lesson plans to evaluate students' reading and writing behaviors, you may now want to update your Running Records. You may also wish to have students complete the Self-Assessment Checklist in the *Portfolio Teacher's Guide*.

PORTFOLIO CONFERENCE

The *Portfolio Conference* provides you with an opportunity to learn about each student's

- interest in reading folktales and biographies.
- general writing development.
- knowledge of comparison and contrast to aid in the comprehension of two or more selections of the same genre.

Discuss the variety of selections in Unit 6. Encourage the student to choose a favorite and describe why he or she especially likes it. Discuss the student's feelings about reading folktales and biographies.

Invite the student to choose a piece of writing from the portfolio that he or she especially likes, such as the paragraph describing a beautiful painting or piece of art or the letter to Jim Abbott. Encourage the student to tell what he or she likes about the piece. Offer positive feedback and encouragement.

Formal Assessment

The formal assessment tools described below are available to meet your assessment needs.

SKILLS ASSESSMENT

The *Skills Assessment* for Unit 6 provides the teacher with feedback about students' mastery of the specific skills and strategies taught in Learning Through Literature. Skills tested in this unit are Comparing and Contrasting, Fact and Opinion, and Structural Analysis. If students have difficulty, refer to pages R44, R48, R51, and R52 for visual, auditory, and kinesthetic/motor models that may be used to reteach skills tested in this unit.

HOLISTIC ASSESSMENT

The *Holistic Assessment* for Unit 6 may be used to assess a student's ability to understand passages written at the same level as the selections in the Student Anthology. If students have difficulty, refer them to the following sections in the Handbook for Readers and Writers: Active Reading Strategies, Reading Fiction, Reading Nonfiction, and Vocabulary Strategies.

INTEGRATED PERFORMANCE ASSESSMENT

The *Integrated Performance Assessment* for Unit 6 provides you with a profile of how well each student uses reading, writing, listening, and speaking strategies to read and respond to a piece of literature. Assessment results reflect how well students employ the strategies modeled and practiced in the classroom.

reak ime

Taking the Lead in Leadership

Experts suggest that when it comes to transforming pipe dreams into reality, the critical factor is often the ability to use communication skills to work out solutions with others. The following communications tips, modeled after those of the corporate world, can help you become a more effective leader.

1. Use nonthreatening language. If you use positive words, chances are that people will *hear* what you're saying instead of focusing on the *way* you're saying it.

2. Encourage ideas and opinions from others.

3. Limit the use of jargon. Professional terms can get in the way of effective communication.

4. Be assertive. When asking for something, use direct language. Avoid qualifiers such as "just" and "sort of" and "if you have the time."

5. Create "win/win" situations. Keep calm and look for areas of agreement.

6. Remember the important role of nonverbal communication. The more professional you look, the more likely people will respond to you as a professional.

7. Remember that you are part of a system. Your contributions and ideas need to mesh with those of others in order for the entire school community to benefit.

FLY ME TO THE MOON

Though astronauts have walked on the moon, it still retains much of its fascination and mystery. You can use the moon as a focus for classroom activities such as these:

■ Talk about the "seas" on the moon's surface. Ask students to look up the names of the seas, choose a favorite, and write a legend about how the sea got its name.

■ Point out that other planets' moons have names, but the Earth's moon has always been just "the moon." Have students research other moons and then think of a name for Earth's moon.

■ Invite students to collect scientific facts about the moon. (Accept reasonable responses: Temperatures can range from −250°F to 215°F.) Ask students to figure out what might be inviting about these facts. (Accept reasonable responses: You could boil water without a stove.) Encourage students to create travel brochures for moon travel.

Drawing by Modell. © 1984 by The New Yorker Magazine, Inc. Reprinted by permission of *The New Yorker*.

Dreamers and Doers

What separates dreamers from doers is often a difference in self-esteem. Here are some suggestions to help students recognize their special talents.

1. People Recipes—Have students use recipe words ("a cup of humor") to describe their unique characteristics.

2. Brag Board—Set up a bulletin board where students can celebrate their own accomplishments. Make sure every student is included.

3. Student of the Day—Each day, post the silhouette of a different student. Give clues about the student's special traits, and ask classmates to guess his or her identity.

Handbook for Readers and Writers

CONTENTS

Handbook for Readers and Writers

The lessons on pages R3–R12 are designed to help students understand and apply the strategies outlined in the Handbook for Readers and Writers. Developing active reading strategies and related strategies for speaking, listening, writing, and researching will benefit students across all areas of the curriculum.

You will notice throughout the Handbook a focus on metacognition, encouraging students to think about what they are doing, to think about purpose, to think about process, and to think about thinking, so they will grow not only as readers and writers but also as thinkers.

HANDBOOK
FOR
READERS AND WRITERS

Using the Handbook

Have students preview the Table of Contents on page 551. Point out the organizational pattern of the Handbook—reading, speaking and listening, writing, and research. Remind students that as well as introducing them to and reminding them of concepts and strategies, the Handbook is a helpful reference tool to use at any time. Specific references to the Handbook are made in lessons in this *Teacher's Edition*.

ACTIVE READING STRATEGIES

A strategy is a specific plan for doing something successfully. Here are several strategies to use before, during, and after reading.

Lee knows that using reading strategies improves her understanding of what she is reading. Strategies also help her use her reading time more wisely.

Before reading, Lee

✓ **previews** what she is about to read. She reads the titles and the subtitles, looks at the pictures, and reads any captions. She may even read the first paragraph or two.

✓ **thinks about the topic** of the selection. She recalls what she already knows about the topic and anything she has heard or read about it.

✓ **predicts** what the selection will be about. She thinks about the clues she found while previewing the selection. Then she makes a guess about what she will learn from her reading.

✓ **sets a purpose** for reading. She decides whether she is reading to find out what happens, to learn information, or to study for a test.

✓ **chooses a reading rate.** She thinks about her purpose as she decides how quickly to read. If her purpose is to study for a test, she will read more slowly and carefully. She may even reread certain parts and take notes as she reads. She knows she can adjust her reading rate as she goes along.

During reading, Lee

✓ **remembers her predictions.** From time to time, she compares what she predicted to what she is reading. If she finds her predictions are not confirmed, she changes them.

✓ **relates what she is reading to what she knows,** to experiences she has had, or to other reading she has done. Sometimes she thinks of feelings she has had that are like those of a character she is reading about.

✓ **rereads** a paragraph or two when she realizes she didn't quite understand what she read the first time. Sometimes she rereads in order to figure out the meaning of an unfamiliar word.

After reading, Lee

✓ **reviews her purpose for reading and her predictions.** She compares her predictions to what she read. She may decide that she did not learn what she expected to. She may need to read something else to answer some questions she still has.

✓ **summarizes** the information she learned. She lists the main points that were new to her that she wants to remember.

552

Active Reading Strategies

Exploring the Strategies Read aloud the introductory information on page 552. Then have students silently read about active reading strategies. To help students think about the strategies in terms of their own experience, you may want to ask how they may already have applied a particular strategy in their reading or how they could apply it. Encourage them to offer specific ideas about how each strategy can help them. Ask volunteers to restate what they have read.

Following Up You may want to use these suggestions with all or some of your students.

- Choose a short story and have small groups of students discuss how they would apply each strategy in reading it.
- Encourage students to write notes about their application of active reading strategies to a story or an article they read independently.

READING FICTION

Fiction comes in different forms. **Realistic fiction** has characters and settings that are believable, although the story is made up. In **fantasy,** things happen that could not happen in real life. When you read fiction, you can use strategies to increase your enjoyment and understanding. Follow Alana as she uses strategies before and during her reading of "Election Day."

I don't understand why Cricket is saying this. I think I'd better reread the last few paragraphs to see what's going on.

I wonder what kind of "Election Day" this is. The title of the book is Class President, so it must be a school election. I wonder if this election day is anything like the one we had in our class.

The introduction tells what happened earlier in the book. Now I know where I am in the story.

I think Cricket and Lucas will be important characters because they both are running for president.

Julio seems smart! What he says makes sense to me. I wonder if anyone will listen to him.

★ Election Day ★

from *Class President*

by Johanna Hurwitz

Julio's new teacher, Mr. Flores, has announced that there will be an election for class president. At first, it seems like a contest between Cricket Kaufman and Lucas Cott, two of the most popular students. But although Julio has promised to help Lucas campaign, he wonders what qualities a president should have besides popularity.

Before lunch, Mr. Flores read an announcement from the principal. "From now on, there is to be no more soccer playing in the schoolyard at lunchtime."

"No more soccer playing?" Julio called out. "Why not?"

Mr. Flores looked at Julio. "If you give me a moment, I'll explain. Mr. Herbertson is concerned about accidents. Last week, Arthur broke his glasses. Another time, someone might be injured more seriously."

Julio was about to call out again, but he remembered just in time and raised his hand.

"Yes, Julio," said Mr. Flores.

"It's not fair to make us stop playing soccer just because someone *might* get hurt. Someone might fall down walking to school, but we still have to come to school every day."

Julio didn't mean to be funny, but everyone started to laugh. Even Mr. Flores smiled.

"There must be other activities to keep you fellows busy at lunchtime," he said. "Is soccer the only thing you can do?"

Lucas raised his hand. "I don't like jumping rope," he said when the teacher called on him. All the girls giggled at that.

"You could play jacks," suggested Cricket. Everyone knew it wasn't a serious possibility, though.

"Couldn't we tell Mr. Herbertson that we want to play soccer?" asked Julio.

"You could make an appointment to speak to him, if you'd like," said Mr. Flores. "He might change his decision if you convince him that you are right."

"Lucas and I will talk to him," said Julio. "Right, Lucas?"

"Uh, sure," said Lucas, but he didn't look too sure.

The principal, Mr. Herbertson, spoke in a loud voice and had eyes that seemed to bore right into your head when he looked at you. Julio had been a little bit afraid of Mr. Herbertson since the very first day of kindergarten. Why had he offered to go to his office and talk to him?

Mr. Flores sent Julio and Lucas down to the principal's office with a note, but the principal was out of the office at a meeting.

"You can talk to him at one o'clock," the secretary said.

Julio is really determined. But this hasn't told me anything about the class election yet. I'll keep reading to see what I can find out.

Going to the principal can be scary! I wonder if Julio and Lucas will talk to the principal later and if this will help Lucas win the election.

(See pages 22–37 for the entire story of "Election Day.")

Reading Fiction

Exploring the Strategies   Have students read the introductory paragraph. You may want to explain that the words in italics at the side show what Alana, a successful reader, is thinking. Model one or more of her thoughts, along with the corresponding parts of the excerpt. Emphasize that no two readers will formulate exactly the same thoughts and questions, but that successful readers think about what is happening in the story as they read.

Following Up   You may use these suggestions with all of your students or with selected groups, as you think they apply.

- Have students work in small groups to create posters including the strategies for reading fiction. Display the finished posters.
- Encourage students to apply the rereading strategy used by Alana at the top of page 555, as needed, when they read the next selections.

READING NONFICTION

Nonfiction contains facts, or information that is true. Often illustrations and diagrams present facts or make them clearer. Headings and subheadings that show how the information is organized may also be included. A strategy that can help when you are reading nonfiction is **K-W-L.**

- **K** stands for "What I **K**now." As you preview the selection, think about what you already know about the topic. Read the headings and subheadings to see how the information is organized. Look at the illustrations and read the captions.
- **W** stands for "What I **W**ant to Know." After you preview, think of questions that you want to find the answers to as you read.
- **L** stands for "What I **L**earned." After you have read, review your questions to see whether you learned what you expected to.

Lance makes a chart before he reads "Running With the Pack." He goes through the **K** and **W** steps and makes notes in the first two columns. He keeps his questions in mind as he reads.

What I Know	What I Want to Know	What I Learned
The selection must be about wolves because I see wolves in the picture. Wolves are like wild dogs. They have some way to talk to each other.	What does the word pack in the title mean? How do wolves talk to each other? Why do wolves attack people?	

Those stories about wolves eating people aren't true at all!

It says that a pack is a group of wolves that live together.

I was right. Wolves are like dogs.

Well, wolves don't really talk, but they do have ways of telling each other things.

Running With the Pack

In a well-known fairy tale, the Big Bad Wolf to eat up Little Red Riding Hood. This story one of many that have caused people to misunderstand and fear wolves. The truth is tha healthy wolves do not attack people. Scienti say wolves tend to be intelligent and shy. Th live in groups called packs, and cooperate to survive.

Wolves are the largest wild members of t dog family. Gray wolves, shown on these pa live in parts of North America, Europe, and Asia—usually in packs with no more than ei members. A pack includes a head male and female, their young, and sometimes other ad The head male usually decides when and wh hunt, and he settles fights. The head female the other females, the young, and sometimes weaker males. The leaders and other pack me bers communicate by using facial expression body postures, and sounds. For example, by standing tall with its ears erect and tail held high, a leader says: "I'm boss." By crouchin lowering its ears and tail, a follower replies: know."

After Lance finishes reading, he thinks for a few minutes about what he has learned. Then he writes down the main points in the last column of his chart. Here is part of his list.

What I Learned
1. A pack is a group of about eight wolves that live together so they can survive.
2. Wolves use their faces, bodies, and sounds to communicate.
3. Healthy wolves don't attack people.
4. Wolves live in North America, Europe, and Asia.

(See pages 186–190 for the entire selection of "Running With the Pa

---

Reading Nonfiction

Exploring the K-W-L Strategy   Have pairs of students read the information on page 556. After discussing Lance's K-W-L chart at the bottom of the page, you may want to write on the board the heading *What I Learned*. Then, as partners read the excerpt on page 557 and Lance's thoughts in italics at the left, have them write their answers to Lance's questions. Students can then compare and evaluate what they wrote and what Lance wrote at the bottom of page 557.

Following Up   You might want to use these supplementary activities with some or all of your students.

- Have students apply the strategies for reading nonfiction to a chapter in their science or social studies textbook.
- As needed, suggest to students that they use the previewing and predicting strategies they learned on page 552 to help them focus on what to write in the second column of their charts.

VOCABULARY STRATEGIES

When you're reading and you meet an unfamiliar word, you may decide you don't need to know its exact meaning. The sentence or paragraph may become clear if you continue reading. When you do need to know the meaning of the word, there are several strategies to help you.

The following letter includes some words you may not know. On the next page you will see how you could use **context** and **structural clues** to figure out the meanings of the underlined words.

Dear Classmates,

As <u>director</u> of Jamal Turner's campaign, I ask you to vote for him. He is the best candidate for class president. Besides being hardworking, Jamal is <u>smart</u> and <u>enthusiastic</u>.

Because Jamal is quiet, people sometimes <u>misjudge</u> him. But he is just careful when he speaks. He wants to <u>clarify</u> issues, not confuse them.

Jamal gets things done. He met with the principal and her assistants — the school <u>administration</u> — about the mess in the cafeteria. Today our school is a cleaner place because of him. Vote for Jamal!

Sincerely,

Maria Vilan

The **context,** or words and sentences that surround the unfamiliar word, will often lead you to discover its meaning.

clarify   The word *not* tells you that *clarify* is the opposite, or **antonym,** of *confuse.* Sometimes a **synonym,** a word with a similar meaning, may help you.

administration   The **definition** of a word may appear close by it. The definition of *administration* comes right before the word.

The **structure** of a word may provide clues to its meaning also. When you understand the parts, you can often combine them to decode the whole word, as in these examples.

director   The suffix *-or,* meaning "one who," tells you that *director* means "one who directs."

misjudge   If you know that the prefix *mis-* means "incorrectly," you can figure out that *misjudge* means "judge incorrectly."

A glossary or dictionary will give definitions. Sometimes a word's dictionary meaning, or **denotation,** doesn't fit the way it is used. Words often suggest ideas, called **connotations,** that go beyond the dictionary definition.

smart, enthusiastic   The words *smart* and *enthusiastic* make you think well of Jamal. They have good **connotations.** His opponents might use the words *tricky* and *excitable.* The **denotations** would make you think Jamal is sneaky and acts without thinking. These words have negative connotations.

Keep a vocabulary notebook to record each word, its meaning, and a sentence that includes the word.

Vocabulary Strategies

Exploring the Strategies   Students may work in small groups to determine how the strategies presented on page 559 were applied to the underlined words in Maria's letter on page 558. You may want to help students formulate the idea that they can use more than one strategy as they try to figure out words in their own reading. You might ask students why they think it would be useful to keep a vocabulary notebook.

Following Up   You may want to use these activities with all of your students or with selected groups.

- Suggest that students apply the vocabulary strategies as they read the next selection. Have them make brief notes about their use of the strategies that they can later share in discussions with other students.
- Students may be encouraged to read in pairs and to work cooperatively to apply the strategies when they encounter unfamiliar words.

SPEAKING

Speaking in front of a group can be fun if you feel sure of yourself. Some strategies can help you feel more confident.

- Think carefully about your **purpose.** Decide what you want to say and why you think it's important. Do you want to share an idea or experience that you think others will appreciate?
- **Prepare** by writing down your ideas. This will help keep your thoughts organized. If you forget where you are or feel nervous, your notes will help you get back on track.
- **Practice** speaking. Concentrate on speaking clearly and loudly enough to be understood. Explain your ideas thoroughly and use examples when you can.

Dena wants to run for class president. She is nervous about speaking in front of her classmates. Her teacher suggests that she write out the speech and practice it.

When Dena gives her speech, she feels prepared and sure of herself. She knows what she wants to say so well that she only glances at her notes a couple of times.

During a class discussion about South America, Enrico's teacher asks him to tell about living in Colombia. At first Enrico is shy. But as he starts talking he becomes enthusiastic. His classmates ask him lots of questions. Enrico finds that he enjoys participating in discussions.

560

LISTENING

Being a good listener is as important as being a good speaker. Here are some helpful strategies you can use the next time you are listening.

- Think about the topic ahead of time. What do you know about it and what do you want to learn? What is your **purpose** for listening?
- Give your complete **attention** to the speaker. Save your reactions or questions until the speaker is finished.
- Decide which of the speaker's points are **facts** and which are the speaker's personal **opinions.**
- Think about whether you agree with the speaker's points.

Dena's classmates were interested in hearing plans for running for the class presidency. They listened carefully and thought about whether they agreed with her ideas. This helped them decide to vote for in the class election.

Enrico's classmates enjoyed hearing about what it's like to live in a different country. They were interested in hearing him talk. At first they were very quiet because he spoke softly. When Enrico told a funny story, his classmates enjoyed it and asked him more questions.

Speaking

Exploring Speaking Strategies Have students read the information on page 560. You may want to draw on students' experiences by asking how they would feel if they had to give a speech, as Dena did, or speak in class, as Enrico did. Have them identify the speaking strategies Dena and Enrico used and tell how each strategy helped the speaker. Guide students in seeing that, although Enrico had no opportunity to prepare or practice, he gained confidence by focusing on his purpose as he was speaking.

Listening

Exploring Listening Strategies After students have read page 561 and identified the listening strategies used by Dena's and Enrico's classmates, you may ask them to name other situations in which they could apply the listening strategies. You might ask students to tell why they would want an audience to use listening strategies if they were speaking. Similarly, have students consider why it is helpful for a listener if a speaker uses good speaking strategies.

THE WRITING PROCESS

The writing process is a plan that writers use. The steps involve choosing a **task,** or the kind of writing, choosing the **audience,** and deciding on the **purpose.** You might choose a personal narrative as your task. If your audience is your classmates, your purpose might be to entertain them. At any point during the writing process you can decide to move ahead or start again.

PREWRITING

Begin by choosing a topic. You might find ideas for a personal narrative in your personal journal—perhaps a time when you entered a contest or you helped an animal. Make a list of possible topics and choose one to write about.

After you have chosen your topic, organize your thoughts. List the details and then use a time line, an outline, or a chart to put the details in order. Now you are ready to go on to the next stage.

DRAFTING

Remember these strategies as you write your first draft.

- Write a strong first sentence to catch your audience's interest.
- Use your organizer to be sure the details are in order.
- Write your ideas quickly. You can revise your writing later.

RESPONDING AND REVISING

Good writers often ask other people to read their writing and tell them how it could be improved. The reader might recommend any or all of the following changes.

- Make the first sentence more interesting.
- Use more colorful words to make your writing come alive.
- Add dialogue to make your narrative seem more real.
- Take out unnecessary details.

If your partner did not understand your writing, reread your draft and decide whether to continue with it.

Imagine that you wrote about a time when you played a musical instrument in front of an audience. You might use Editor's Marks to make revisions like these on the first part of your draft.

EDITOR'S MARKS	
∧ Add something.	↻ Move something.
✂ Cut something.	⌒ Replace something.

Every time I thought about playing in front of an audience, my fingers ~~became tight~~ froze. There was no way that I ~~am~~ was going to play the piano at the school recital. My friend ∧Kelly said it would be exciting. I shook my head and said ~~that~~ I know I ~~knew~~ I will mess up and ~~they~~ everyone will laugh at me. I didn't want to play.

"You'll never know unless you try," ~~she~~ Kelly said.

The Writing Process

Prewriting/Drafting   Have students read pages 562–565 before discussing individual pages. You may want to discuss each stage of the writing process to be sure students understand why it is important, what strategies they can use, and how that stage fits into the overall plan. In summarizing, ask students for examples of times when they may not need to apply the entire process. Have them tell which stages they would use in each case and explain why.

Responding and Revising   You may want to discuss and evaluate with students the revisions shown in the sample on page 563. Ask students to offer reasons for the changes that are shown in red. Students may find it helpful to refer to the Editor's Marks shown in the box on page 563.

PROOFREADING

After you have decided what to revise, you are ready to correct your errors. Here are more Editor's Marks to use.

EDITOR'S MARKS	
☰ Capitalize.	∿ Transpose.
⊙ Add a period.	◯ Spell correctly.
⋀ Add a comma.	⌧ Indent paragraph.
⋁⋁ Add quotation marks.	⁄ Make a lowercase letter.

Use the following checklist as you proofread.

✓ Did you indent your paragraphs? Use this mark to show where to indent: ⌧ .

✓ Did you capitalize correctly? Mark a letter to be capitalized with three underlines: ☰ . Mark a letter to be made lowercase like this: ⁄ .

✓ Did you circle misspelled words and write the correct spelling above? Write correctly in your spelling notebook any words you misspelled. This way you can help yourself remember them.

✓ Did you check and correct your grammar? Use this symbol: ⌒ .

✓ Did you check punctuation? Add quotation marks like this: ⋁⋁ . Add a period with this mark: ⊙ . Add a comma with this mark: ⋀ .

I practiced for hours every day. then the day of the recital was finally here. I felt as if I had (butterflys) *butterflies* in my stomach. My knees shook *trembled*, and my hands were sweaty. ⋁I just can't do it,⋁I thought.

    Kelly tells *told* me not to be a coward. "The show must go on!" she said⌧After I played the first line of notes,I was surprised to find that my fingers weren't (num) *numb* and I wasn't messing up. I actually felt very calm⊙The audience clapped, which made me feel good. I can't wait until our next recital!

PUBLISHING

When you have corrected your writing and made a clean copy in your best handwriting, you can publish it by giving it to your classmates to read. Here are some other publishing ideas.

■ Dramatize your narrative as if it were a television program. Choose classmates to play the parts. You be the director.

■ Use your narrative as the introduction to a class book of experiences of your class. You may want to include artwork drawn by members of the class and musical compositions written by classmates.

Proofreading/Publishing As you review with students the proofreading sample on page 565, they may notice that, in addition to the proofreading changes made in red, some revising changes are also shown. You might want to take the opportunity to have students comment on the ongoing nature of the writing process. Then have students read about the different ways the finished work may be published.

Following Up You may want to have students think about the stages of the writing process and how completing each stage will help them in their writing.

• You might suggest to some students that they try to incorporate words from their vocabulary notebooks into their writing.

• As students complete writing assignments, challenge them to explore different ways to publish their work. Encourage them to consult with others and to share their publishing ideas.

RESEARCHING INFORMATION

The first step in doing research is to **define your topic.** Are you writing a biography about the famous aviator Amelia Earhart, making a class presentation about the settling of the American West, or writing a research report about wolves? After you have defined your topic, you need to **gather information** about it. Look for **reference sources** that are likely to have information about the topic. Then you can begin to **search for facts.** Helpful strategies include **skimming, scanning,** and **taking notes.**

SKIMMING: Skimming means looking over a book or reference source quickly to find out what it is about and how it is organized. When you skim, look mainly at the headings and subheadings.

SCANNING: Scanning means looking quickly through a passage to find certain key words or facts.

Subject • • • • • •

Division • • • • • •
heading

Subheading • • •

Key words • • •
and phrases • • •

> **Wolf** is one of the largest members of the dog family. Wolves are expert hunters and prey chiefly on large hoofed animals, such as caribou, deer, elk, and moose. Many people fear wolves. They believe wolves attack human beings, and the animal's eerie howl frightens them. But wolves avoid people as much as possible.

> **The life of a wolf**
> Wolves live in family groups called *packs.* Most packs have about 8 members, but some may have more than 20. Zoologists believe the members of a pack remain together because they have strong affection for one another.

> **Young**. Wolves mate during the winter. The female carries her young inside her body for about 65 days. She then gives birth to 1 to 11 pups in a sheltered area called a *den.* The den may be in a cave, a hollow log, an abandoned beaver lodge, or underground.

"Wolf" from *The World Book Encyclopedia.* © 1991 by World Book, Inc. Reprinted by permission of World Book, Inc.

TAKING NOTES: Take notes on the information you find as you skim and scan. Notes are important because you will use them when you write your report.

Write the topic at the top of your page. • • • • • • • • • • •

Write in short phrases instead of sentences. • •

Use your own words. • • •

Write only what you need to remember.

Write the name of the source, including the author's name if it • • • • • • • • is given.

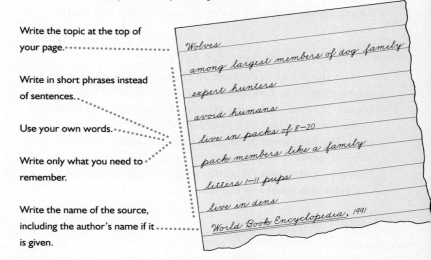

Wolves
among largest members of dog family
expert hunters
avoid humans
live in packs of 8–20
pack members like a family
litters 1–11 pups
live in dens
World Book Encyclopedia, 1991

Remember that skimming, scanning, and taking notes are strategies that can save you time and help you when writing your report. You can also use these strategies to improve your studying and to become a faster, more efficient reader.

Researching Information

Exploring the Strategies   After students have read pages 566 and 567, you may want to suggest that they make a flowchart of the steps for doing a research report. Then students might work in small groups to discuss the example of scanning shown at the bottom of page 566 and the example of note taking on page 567. Encourage students to pay close attention to the words at the left of each example to be sure they understand what each phrase or sentence means.

Following Up   You may want to use either of these activities with some or all of your students.

- When students begin taking notes, they often focus more on finding the information than on stating it briefly and in their own words. It may be helpful for students to work in pairs to reduce the volume of their notes and to reword them.

- Have students practice researching information, using a nonfiction book rather than an encyclopedia article.

THE LIBRARY

A library contains information in books, magazines and newspapers, reference materials, and video and audio materials.

CARD CATALOG

The library is organized so that it is easy to locate information. The **card catalog** is the first place to look for books. The card catalog is a set of cards that lists every book in the library in alphabetical order by the first word on the card. The three kinds of cards are **title card, author card,** and **subject card.** The cards are usually filed in drawers. However, today many libraries keep the information on a computer data base or on microfilm.

The subject card lists the subject of the book first.

The author card lists the author's last name first.

The title card lists the title of the book first.

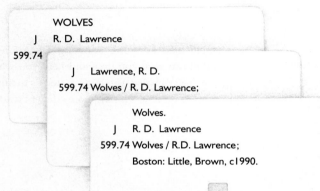

WOLVES

J   R. D. Lawrence

599.74

    J   Lawrence, R. D.

    599.74 Wolves / R. D. Lawrence;

          Wolves.

        J   R. D. Lawrence

        599.74 Wolves / R.D. Lawrence;

           Boston: Little, Brown, c1990.

COMPUTERIZED CATALOG

The computerized card catalog contains the same information as the card catalog that is found in drawers. There are three ways to find a book in the computerized catalog: by title, by author, or by subject. Suppose you want to use the computerized catalog to find information on wolves. First, you type the subject command and the word *wolves* on the computer keyboard, according to the instructions in the printed guide. The printed guide explains on the screen the options and steps as you go along. For example, the instructions on the screen may tell you to type a command such as *S = wolves.* The computer then gives you a list of titles and call numbers of books on the subject *Wolves.* The call numbers help you find the books on the library shelves.

CALL NUMBERS

Each nonfiction book has a **call number** that appears on its three cards or on the computer screen. This call number is also on the book itself. Each fiction book is identified by the first letters of the author's last name instead of by a call number. The library shelves are labeled with the call letters or call numbers of the books they contain.

The Library

Exploring the Library As students read and discuss the information about the card catalog, you may want to ask them to give examples of times when they would look for each kind of card in the card catalog. Similarly, you might ask for examples of other ways students might use the computerized catalog besides typing in the subject. In addition, display some library books with call numbers and call letters on them to give students a better idea of what to look for in the library.

Following Up You may want to provide additional opportunities for students to learn about the library.

- You might set aside some time for students to find materials in the school library for projects or independent reading, using the card catalog or the computerized catalog. Pairs of students can work together to formulate and carry out their plans.
- Challenge students to discover what the Dewey Decimal System is and how it works.

Introducing the Glossary

Explain to students that a glossary is often included in a book so that readers can find information about words used in the book. Model looking up one or more words, pointing out how you rely on alphabetical order and the guide words at the top of the glossary pages to help you locate an entry. Then demonstrate how to use the pronunciation key on page 571 to determine the correct pronunciation of the word.

As students look over the Glossary, point out that illustrations accompany some definitions, such as those of *accordion* and *appliqué* on page 572. Use the same page to indicate that some words, such as *ad lib,* have a more complete explanation and background information about them presented in the margin.

Have students locate several words in the Glossary, identifying the correct page and guide words. Ask them to tell which words are accompanied by illustrations or additional information in the margin. Students may recall that one of the vocabulary strategies they learned on page 559 involved using a dictionary or a glossary.

GLOSSARY

The **pronunciation** of each word in this glossary is shown by a phonetic respelling in brackets; for example, [ad′vər·tīz′mənt]. An accent mark (′) follows the syllable with the most stress: [ik·splōd′]. A secondary, or lighter, accent mark (′) follows a syllable with less stress: [ek′splə·nā′shən]. The key to other pronunciation symbols is below. You will find a shortened version of this key on alternate pages of the glossary.

Pronunciation Key*

a	add, map	m	move, seem	u	up, done
ā	ace, rate	n	nice, tin	û(r)	burn, term
â(r)	care, air	ng	ring, song	yōō	fuse, few
ä	palm, father	o	odd, hot	v	vain, eve
b	bat, rub	ō	open, so	w	win, away
ch	check, catch	ô	order, jaw	y	yet, yearn
d	dog, rod	oi	oil, boy	z	zest, muse
e	end, pet	ou	pout, now	zh	vision, pleasure
ē	equal, tree	ōō	took, full	ə	the schwa,
f	fit, half	ōō	pool, food		an unstressed
g	go, log	p	pit, stop		vowel representing
h	hope, hate	r	run, poor		the sound spelled
i	it, give	s	see, pass		a in *above*
ī	ice, write	sh	sure, rush		e in *sicken*
j	joy, ledge	t	talk, sit		i in *possible*
k	cool, take	th	thin, both		o in *melon*
l	look, rule	th	this, bathe		u in *circus*

*Adapted entries, the Pronunciation Key, and the Short Key that appear on the following pages are reprinted from *HBJ School Dictionary.* Copyright © 1990 by Harcourt Brace Jovanovich, Inc. Reprinted by permission of Harcourt Brace Jovanovich, Inc.

571

---

accordion

A

accordion

ac·cor·di·on [ə·kôr′dē·ən] *n.* A musical instrument that is played by fingering keys and squeezing the instrument at the same time.

ac·cus·ing·ly [ə·kyōōz′ing·lē] *adv.* In a way that blames someone for something.

a·chieve·ment [ə·chēv′mənt] *n.* Something that a person has done very well: **Learning to ride a horse was a special *achievement* for Felipe.**

ac·knowl·edge [ak·nol′ij] *v.* To look at someone and speak to him or her.

a·cre [ā′kər] *n.* A large amount of land.

ad lib [ad′lib′] *v.* To make up words or actions at the moment, not before.

ad·ver·tise·ment [ad′vər·tīz′mənt *or* ad·vûr′tis·mənt] *n.* A printed or spoken statement whose purpose is to sell something. *syn.* notice

ad·vise [ad·vīz′] *v.* To tell someone what to do. *syn.* recommend

ag·ile [aj′əl] *adj.* Able to move easily.

a·light [ə·līt′] *v.* To land: **Vern saw a robin *alight* on a tree branch.**

ad lib *Ad lib* is a shortened form of the Latin phrase *ad libitum,* which means "at pleasure." So speakers and comedians who *ad lib* say whatever gives them pleasure instead of following a set script.

appliqué

an·ces·tor [an′ses·tər] *n.* A family member who lived a long time ago.

an·ni·ver·sa·ry [an′ə·vûr′sə·rē] *n.* The day of the year when people remember something of importance from the past.

anx·ious [angk′shəs] *adj.* Worried or nervous: **Tom felt *anxious* and concerned about his sick uncle in the hospital.** *syn.* uneasy

ap·pli·qué [ap′li·kā′] *v.* **ap·pli·quéd, ap·pli·qué·ing** To decorate by sewing one piece of cloth onto another.

ar·gu·ment [är′gyə·mənt] *n.* A strong reason for or against something: **One of Jerome's *arguments* for getting a bike was that he could use it to run errands for the family.**

ar·ti·fi·cial [är′tə·fish′əl] *adj.* False; not natural or real: **The colored leaves in the store window were *artificial*, but the pumpkins were real.**

as·sem·bly [ə·sem′blē] *n.* A gathering or meeting of people; in school, a gathering of all students and teachers for entertainment or educational programs.

at·ten·tive [ə·ten′tiv] *adj.* Careful to notice things and pay attention. *syn.* aware

572

---

authority

au·thor·i·ty [ə·thôr′ə·tē] *n.* Someone who is in charge of doing things the right way: **The city *authorities* decide who will march in the front of the parade.**

av·a·lanche [av′ə·lanch′] *n.* The falling of objects suddenly in a heap.

a·void [ə·void′] *v.* **a·void·ed, a·void·ing** To stay away from something.

B

baf·fle [baf′əl] *v.* **baf·fled, baf·fling** To mix up. *syn.* confuse

bal·ance [bal′əns] *n.* The ability to move without leaning or falling.

be·have [bi·hāv′] *v.* To act.

be·wil·der·ment [bi·wil′dər·mənt] *n.* The feeling of not understanding something: **Oscar looked with *bewilderment* at the math problem because it did not make sense to him.** *syn.* confusion

board [bôrd] *n.* A colorful, flat piece of heavy paper or wood on which a game is played: **The *board* for checkers has squares of two colors.**

bored [bôrd] *adj.* Without interest or excitement: **The children were *bored* after the clown left the party.**

boun·ti·ful [boun′tə·fəl] *adj.* Plentiful; generous in size: **The crop was so *bountiful* that the farmer gave apples away.**

brand [brand] *v.* To make a permanent mark on an animal to identify it.

bro·cade [brō·kād′] *n.* A rich cloth that is embroidered with raised designs.

bur·den [bûr′dən] *n.* Something that causes people to worry or have extra work.

balance

---

carbon dioxide

C

cam·paign [kam·pān′] *n.* Activities organized to gain or win something.

can·di·date [kan′də·dāt′] *n.* A person being considered for a certain position.

can·vas [kan′vəs] *n.* A piece of heavy cloth stretched over a frame on which pictures are painted: **For his art project, Randy bought oil paints, special brushes, and a *canvas* to paint on.**

car·bon di·ox·ide [kär′bən dī·ok′sīd′] *n.* A gas that has no color or smell and that plants need.

candidate A candidate was originally someone dressed in white. To the ancient Romans, white symbolized purity and honesty. Our words *candid,* "honest," and *candor,* "honesty," go back to the same root, meaning "white."

canvas

a	add	ōō	took	
ā	ace	ōō	pool	
â	care	u	up	
ä	palm	û	burn	
e	end	yōō	fuse	
ē	equal	oi	oil	
i	it	ou	pout	
ī	ice	ng	ring	
o	odd	th	thin	
ō	open	th	this	
ô	order	zh	vision	

ə = { a in *above*   e in *sicken*   i in *possible*   o in *melon*   u in *circus* }

573

---

carnival | common

car·ni·val [kär'nə·vəl] *n.* **1** A festival with parades and dancing. **2** (*written* **Carnival**) A special holiday that comes a few weeks before Easter: **Maria is happy about the beautiful costume she will wear during *Carnival*.**

centimeter

cau·tious·ly [kô'shəs·lē] *adv.* Carefully: **Always cross a busy street *cautiously*.**

cel·e·brate [sel'ə·brāt'] *v.* To take part in special activities in honor of a holiday or special day: **Our town *celebrates* the Fourth of July with a parade, a huge picnic, and fireworks displays.**

cen·ti·me·ter [sen'tə·mē'tər] *n.* A measure of length somewhat less than half an inch: **Luis learned that one *centimeter* equals almost half an inch.**

cer·e·mo·ny [ser'ə·mō'nē] *n.* Actions done for the purpose of celebrating something.

char·coal [chär'kōl'] *n.* A black substance that is made from wood burned in a special way; often used in drawing.

collection

chem·i·cal [kem'i·kəl] *n.* One of many basic materials or elements found in nature and often combined by scientists to make medicines.

chemical In the Middle Ages, the Arabs who invaded Europe brought with them practices they called *al-kimia*. The Europeans changed the Arab word to *alchemy*. From the name for the practices of working with metals and medicines came our scientific words *chemical*, *chemistry*, and *chemist*.

cit·i·zen [sit'ə·zən] *n.* A person born in a country or legally made a member of it: **Mr. Kwan took tests to become an American *citizen* after he moved here from Korea.**

claim [klām] *n.* Something a person demands that rightfully belongs to him or her: **Pioneers established their *claim* to land by living on it.**

clam·or [klam'ər] *n.* A loud and constant noise.

clan [klan] *n.* A group of families who are all related to the same ancestor.

clum·sy [klum'zē] *adj.* Without much control or grace of movement.

col·lard greens [kol'ərd grēnz] *n.* The green leaves of a cabbagelike plant: **Our family's Thanksgiving dinner includes my two favorite vegetables, corn and *collard greens*.**

col·lec·tion [kə·lek'shən] *n.* A group of the same kind of things kept together: **Angela is proud of her *collection* of seashells.**

com·mon [kom'ən] *adj.* Usual; widely available or found: **Chickens, pigs, and cows are *common* farm animals.**

574

---

compete | custom

com·pete [kəm·pēt'] *v.* **com·pet·ed, com·pet·ing** To work at winning a contest: **The teams were *competing* for the first prize in the storytelling contest.**

com·pet·i·tive [kəm·pet'ə·tiv] *adj.* Fond of being in contests for the purpose of winning.

com·pli·ment [kom'plə·mənt] *n.* A nice thing that someone says about another person: **Carmen received a *compliment* when her teacher said that she was a very good painter.** *syn.* praise

con·cen·trate [kon'sən·trāt'] *v.* To think about one thing very hard.

con·clude [kən·klōod'] *v.* **con·clud·ed, con·clud·ing** To form an idea or opinion after thinking about something: **Nora saw the dark clouds and *concluded* that it was going to rain.**

con·fi·dence [kon'fə·dəns] *n.* Trust; the feeling that everything will turn out all right: **Ellen had *confidence* that she would do well on the spelling test.**

con·sid·er·ate [kən·sid'ər·it] *adj.* Caring about another person's feelings. *syns.* kind, polite

con·so·la·tion [kon'sə·lā'shən] *n.* Something given to someone to cheer him or her up: **Phil lost the drawing contest, but he felt better when he was given a small prize as a *consolation*.** *syn.* comfort

converse

con·tra·dict [kon'trə·dikt'] *v.* **con·tra·dict·ed, con·tra·dict·ing** To disagree or say the opposite. *syns.* deny, oppose

con·verse [kən·vûrs'] *v.* **con·versed, con·vers·ing** To talk: **Sometimes my mother and Mrs. Potter *converse* on the phone for an hour.** *syn.* speak

con·vince [kən·vins'] *v.* To cause someone to believe something. *syns.* persuade, prove

cor·ral [kə·ral'] *n.* A fenced area where animals are kept: **All the cattle were driven into the *corral* so that they could be kept together.**

cow·er [kou'ər] *v.* **cow·ered, cow·er·ing** To curl up with fear. *syns.* tremble, cringe

crys·tal·line [kris'tə·lin] *adj.* Clear and sparkling.

cus·tom [kus'təm] *n.* A practice followed by most people in a group, often for many years.

corral This word was added to the English language by the Spanish explorers, who brought horses and cattle to the southwestern part of the United States. They kept their animals in pens called *corrals*, where animals had room to run. The word can be traced all the way back to the Latin word *currere*, meaning "to run."

a	add	ŏŏ	took
ā	ace	ōō	pool
â	care	u	up
ä	palm	û	burn
e	end	yōō	fuse
ē	equal	oi	oil
i	it	ou	pout
ī	ice	ng	ring
o	odd	th	thin
ō	open	th	this
ô	order	zh	vision

ə = { a in *above* e in *sicken*
{ i in *possible*
{ o in *melon* u in *circus*

575

---

deadline | election

D

design

dead·line [ded'līn'] *n.* The time that something must be finished.

deed [dēd] *n.* A written note proving that someone owns a piece of land.

del·i·cate [del'ə·kit] *adj.* Very fine and not heavy: **The old curtains were made of very *delicate* lace.**

de·sign [di·zīn'] *n.* The shapes and colors that are on something, such as a piece of cloth. *syn.* pattern

dilemma A *dilemma* is a choice between two things. The word part *di-* is related to *dwo*, an ancient word for *two*.

des·ti·ny [des'tə·nē] *n.* Something that seems certain to happen to someone. *syn.* fate

de·vice [di·vīs'] *n.* Something designed for a certain purpose. *syn.* tool

di·lem·ma [di·lem'ə] *n.* The need to choose between two unpleasant things.

disguise

dis·ap·point·ment [dis'ə·point'mənt] *n.* A feeling of sadness because things did not happen as expected: **Regina's *disappointment* showed in her face when she wasn't allowed to go to the zoo.**

dis·cour·aged [dis·kûr'ijd] *adj.* Feeling bad about the way things happened. *syn.* disappointed

dugout

dis·guise [dis·gīz'] *n.* Something that changes the way someone usually looks. *syn.* costume

dis·qual·i·fy [dis·kwol'ə·fī'] *v.* **dis·qual·i·fied, dis·qual·i·fy·ing** To take someone out of a contest for some reason.

dis·solve [di·zolv'] *v.* **dis·solved, dis·solv·ing** To become a liquid or to melt: **The grease on the dirty frying pans will *dissolve* when Raymond washes them with detergent.**

dis·tinct [dis·tingkt'] *adj.* Very clear: **The *distinct* smell of cookies filled the bakery.** *syn.* sharp

dou·ble [dub'əl] *n.* A two-base hit in baseball.

dug·out [dug'out'] *n.* A home built by digging out a living space in the side of a hill or river bank.

E

ech·o [ek'ō] *n.* Sound reflected or bounced back: **The *echoes* in the empty room made it sound as if more than two people were talking.**

e·lec·tion [i·lek'shən] *n.* The choosing of a person for a position by voting.

576

---

embarrassed | exquisite

em·bar·rassed [im·bar'əst] *adj.* Ashamed: **Craig felt *embarrassed* because he made a mistake in front of his classmates.**

em·broi·dered [im·broi'dərd] *adj.* Decorated with fancy stitching: **The *embroidered* purse was covered with gold stitching.**

e·merge [i·mûrj'] *v.* To come out or become visible.

emp·ty [emp'tē] *adj.* Holding nothing; unfilled. *syn.* vacant

en·dan·gered [in·dān'jərd] *adj.* In danger of no longer existing.

en·dur·ance [in·d(y)ŏŏr'əns] *n.* The ability to work hard for a long time.

en·vi·ron·ment [in·vī'rən·mənt] *n.* The place where something lives, or its surroundings: **Peaches grow best in a warm, sunny *environment*.**

er·rand [er'ənd] *n.* A short trip for the purpose of doing something, usually for someone else.

e·rupt [i·rupt'] *v.* To suddenly burst out.

e·vap·o·rate [i·vap'ə·rāt'] *v.* **e·vap·o·rat·ed, e·vap·o·rat·ing** To dry up: **The hot sun had *evaporated* the puddles on the sidewalk, so we didn't get wet feet.**

e·vent·ful [i·vent'fəl] *adj.* Filled with important happenings: **Martin Luther King, Jr., was given many awards during his *eventful* life.** *syns.* noteworthy, significant

empty

ex·er·tion [ig·zûr'shən] *n.* Hard work.

ex·haus·tion [ig·zôs'chən] *n.* The feeling of being very tired.

ex·ot·ic [ig·zot'ik] *adj.* Strange and interesting.

ex·pen·sive [ik·spen'siv] *adj.* Costing a lot of money: **Even with a loan from his father, Luis decided the bicycle was too *expensive* to buy.**

ex·pe·ri·ence [ik·spir'ē·əns] *n.* What someone knows by watching or doing something.

ex·pla·na·tion [ek'splə·nā'shən] *n.* A reason given that makes something easier to understand: **The students learned from the teacher's *explanation* of the story.**

ex·plode [ik·splōd'] *v.* **ex·plod·ed, ex·plod·ing** To suddenly burst with great force.

ex·qui·site [eks'kwi·zit *or* ik·skwiz'it] *adj.* Very beautiful: **Bright yellow, blue, and green feathers made the bird look *exquisite*.**

explode

explode When we say that something exploded, we are describing a destructive blowup. The origins of *explode* are much less violent. *Explode* comes from two Latin words — *ex*, "out," and *plaudo*, "clap." If the ancient Romans disliked a theatrical performance, they would "explode," or clap the actors off the stage.

a	add	ŏŏ	took
ā	ace	ōō	pool
â	care	u	up
ä	palm	û	burn
e	end	yōō	fuse
ē	equal	oi	oil
i	it	ou	pout
ī	ice	ng	ring
o	odd	th	thin
ō	open	th	this
ô	order	zh	vision

ə = { a in *above* e in *sicken*
{ i in *possible*
{ o in *melon* u in *circus*

577

Page 578

fascinate

F

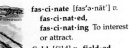

furrow

fas·ci·nate [fas′ə·nāt′] *v.* **fas·ci·nat·ed, fas·ci·nat·ing** To interest or attract.

field [fēld] *v.* **field·ed, field·ing** To catch or pick up a batted baseball and throw it to the proper player.

file [fīl] *v.* To register or record formally.

flu·ent [flōō′ənt] *adj.* Spoken smoothly and easily: **Maria spoke such *fluent* Spanish that no one believed she grew up in Chicago.**

fore·close [fôr·klōz′] *v.* **fore·closed, fore·clos·ing** To take away land from a person who owes money on it.

gaucho

fra·grant [frā′grənt] *adj.* Having a sweet smell: **Aurora's perfume smelled like *fragrant* roses.**

frail [frāl] *adj.* Very weak. *syn.* feeble

frame [frām] *v.* **framed, fram·ing** To trick someone into the appearance of being involved in a crime.

fur·row [fûr′ō] *n.* A groove in the ground where seeds are planted: **Andrew made a *furrow* for the flower seeds.**

fu·ry [fyŏŏr′ē] *n.* Great anger.

greenhorn You wouldn't want anyone to call you a greenhorn. It would mean that you are a beginner and lack the experience to do a good job. This word was first used in the days when people used oxen to do farm work. If a farmer had a beast whose horns were still *green* ("young" or "new"), it probably wouldn't have been trained to pull a plow.

G

gar·ment [gär′mənt] *n.* A piece of clothing: **Mr. Sa·wado sells shirts, jackets, suits, and other *garments*.**

gau·cho [gou′chō] *n.* A South American cowhand: *Gauchos* are workers who ride horses and take care of cattle.

gen·er·a·tion [jen′ə·rā′shən] *n.* A group of people born around the same time.

gen·er·ous [jen′ər·əs] *adj.* Eager to share: **Alma's *generous* grandparents bought new books for the school library.** *syns.* unselfish, giving

gin·ger ale [jin′jər āl] *n.* A bubbly drink flavored by the ginger plant: **Bradley liked *ginger ale* better than any other soda pop.**

glis·ten [glis′(ə)n] *v.* **glis·tened, glis·ten·ing** To shine. *syns.* sparkle, shimmer

green·horn [grēn′hôrn′] *n.* A person who is new at doing something: **I felt like a *greenhorn* as I tried with·out success to get on my horse.** *syn.* beginner

grieve [grēv] *v.* To be very upset and sorry about something lost: **Tony will *grieve* when his cousin Alonso moves to a faraway city.** *syn.* mourn

Page 579

grieve   herb   insulated

H

herb [(h)ûrb] *n.* A plant used for medicine or adding flavor to food.

hes·i·tant·ly [hez′ə·tənt·lē] *adv.* Doubtfully; undecidedly: **The princess wasn't sure whether to kiss the frog, so she did it *hesitantly*.** *syn.* uncertainly

hes·i·tate [hez′ə·tāt′] *v.* **hes·i·tat·ed, hes·i·tat·ing** To act slowly, as if in doubt. *syn.* pause

hon·ored [on′ərd] *adj.* Feeling loved and admired: **Grandfather felt *honored* on his birthday when his grandchildren spent the whole day with him.**

hoof [hŏŏf *or* hōōf] *n.; pl.* **hoofs** or **hooves** The hard cover on the foot of an animal such as a horse: **You can hear the *hooves* of a running horse beat the ground.**

ho·ri·zon [hə·rī′zən] *n.* The line where the sky and the earth seem to meet.

I

id·i·o·syn·cra·sy [id′ē·ō·sing′krə·sē] *n.* A way of acting that is odd or different.

im·me·di·ate·ly [i·mē′dē·it·lē] *adv.* Right away; without waiting; now.

im·mer·sion heat·er [i·mûr′shən hē′tər *or* i·mûr′zhən hē′tər] *n.* A tool heated electrically and put into liquid to warm it.

im·mi·grant [im′ə·grənt] *n.* A person who comes to live in a new country.

im·pa·tient [im·pā′shənt] *adj.* Not wanting to wait: **Tim was *impatient* for his favorite television show to begin.**

in·de·scrib·a·ble [in′di·skrī′bə·bəl] *adj.* Impossible to describe or tell about.

in·no·cent [in′ə·sənt] *adj.* Not to blame.

in·spec·tion [in·spek′shən] *n.* A careful look at something.

in·stinct [in′stingkt] *n.* A natural force that makes people or animals act in certain ways: **The mother duck's *instincts* were to provide food for and protect her babies.**

in·su·lat·ed [in′sə·lāt′əd] *adj.* Designed to keep contents hot or cold: **I have an *insulated* container in my lunch box that keeps my soup hot all day.**

hoof

instinct *Instinct* comes from the Latin word *instinguere*, meaning "to prod or force." Instincts are inner forces that cause animals to behave in certain ways. *Instinct* is also related to our word *stick*. Think of an instinct as something that sticks or prods a rabbit, forcing it to run away from danger.

insulated

a	add	ŏŏ	took
ā	ace	ōō	pool
â	care	u	up
ä	palm	û	burn
e	end	yōō	fuse
ē	equal	oi	oil
i	it	ou	pout
ī	ice	ng	ring
o	odd	th	thin
ō	open	ŧh	this
ô	order	zh	vision

ə = { a in *above*   e in *sicken*
i in *possible*
o in *melon*   u in *circus* }

Page 580

international *Inter·* means "between or among." An airplane that makes an *international* flight travels between two or more nations, such as the United States and France.

journalist

in·tel·li·gence [in·tel′ə·jəns] *n.* The ability to learn and to solve problems: **The clever monkey showed its *intelligence* by putting a puzzle together.**

in·ten·si·ty [in·ten′sə·tē] *n.* Great force in feelings or actions.

in·ten·tion [in·ten′shən] *n.* Plan or purpose: **Carla had no *intention* of going to the party because she was too busy.** *syn.* motive

in·tent·ly [in·tent′lē] *adv.* With full attention: **The children listened *intently* to the interesting story about dinosaurs.**

in·ter·na·tion·al [in′tər·nash′ən·əl] *adj.* In nations all over the world. *syn.* worldwide

in·ter·pret·er [in·tûr′prit·ər] *n.* Someone who understands several languages and helps people who speak different languages to understand each other: **The *interpreter* told the Russian visitor that the French woman wanted to thank him.** *syn.* translator

in·ter·rupt [in′tə·rupt′] *v.* **in·ter·rupt·ed, in·ter·rupt·ing** To start talking before someone else has finished.

J

jour·nal·ist [jûr′nəl·ist] *n.* Someone who writes or edits articles for newspapers or magazines: **The *journalist* wrote an article about recycling for the magazine.** *syn.* reporter

K

kin·ship [kin′ship′] *n.* A relationship or connection like that between family members.

L

lan·tern [lan′tərn] *n.* A kind of lamp used outdoors.

las·so [las′ō] *n.* A rope with a loop at the end, used for catching cattle.

laun·dry [lôn′drē] *n.* Clothes that need washing: **Donnie piled the family's *laundry* next to the washing machine.**

la·va [lä′və *or* lav′ə] *n.* Very hot melted rock that bursts out of a volcano.

league [lēg] *n.* A group of sports teams that usually play each other.

lasso

Page 581

logical   nominate

log·i·cal [loj′ə·kəl] *adj.* In a way that is orderly and makes sense: **The plan was so *logical* that it was easy to carry out.**

loom [lōōm] *n.* A machine used for weaving cloth.

loop·hole [lōōp′hōl′] *n.* A way of getting around a law or legal agreement.

lum·ber [lum′bər] *v.* **lum·bered, lum·ber·ing** To move along slowly and heavily. *syn.* plod

lu·nar [lōō′nər] *adj.* Having to do with the moon: **In the *lunar* calendar, one month equals the number of days from one full moon to another.**

M

mag·nif·i·cent [mag·nif′ə·sənt] *adj.* Wonderful; impressive: **The king wore a *magnificent* jeweled crown that we all admired.** *syn.* splendid

mane [mān] *n.* The long hair on the neck of an animal such as a horse.

mem·o·ry [mem′ər·ē] *n.* Something a person remembers: **Mr. White has happy *memories* of the times he went fishing with his sons.**

me·nag·er·ie [mə·naj′ər·ē] *n.* A group of different animals: **There was a *menagerie* of stuffed animals in the toy store.**

mi·grate [mī′grāt′] *v.* **mi·grat·ed, mi·grat·ing** To move from one place to another when the season changes: **The birds are *migrating* south to spend winter in a warmer part of the country.**

mis·chief [mis′chif] *n.* Harmful or tricky acts.

mon·o·tone [mon′ə·tōn′] *n.* A voice that never changes in highness or lowness.

mound [mound] *n.* In baseball, the small hill that the pitcher stands on when throwing the ball to the batter: **Derrick stood still on the *mound* before throwing the pitch.**

muf·fled [muf′əld] *adj.* Sounding as if wrapped or covered up. *syns.* quieted, deadened

N

nec·tar [nek′tər] *n.* A sweet liquid made by flowers.

nom·i·nate [nom′ə·nāt′] *v.* To name someone to run in an election.

loom The word *loom* comes from Old and Middle English words that mean "tool." Native Americans began weaving beautiful blankets and clothing, often using looms made of tree branches, as early as in the 700s.

mane

menagerie

a	add	ŏŏ	took
ā	ace	ōō	pool
â	care	u	up
ä	palm	û	burn
e	end	yōō	fuse
ē	equal	oi	oil
i	it	ou	pout
ī	ice	ng	ring
o	odd	th	thin
ō	open	ŧh	this
ô	order	zh	vision

ə = { a in *above*   e in *sicken*
i in *possible*
o in *melon*   u in *circus* }

O

pollen

oc·ca·sion [ə·kā′zhən] *n.* Event or situation: **We had a party for Enrico because his return home from Mexico was a special *occasion*.**

oc·cu·py [ok′yə·pī′] *v.* **oc·cu·pied, oc·cu·py·ing** To live in a place.

op·por·tu·ni·ty [op′ər·t(y)ōō′nə·tē] *n.* A chance to do something.

or·di·nar·y [ôr′də·ner′ē] *n.* Something usual.

ox·y·gen [ok′sə·jin] *n.* The part of air that animals and people need to stay alive.

principle Homophones are pairs of words that sound alike but have different spellings and meanings, such as *principle* and *principal*. Both are related to the Latin word *primus*, which means "first." A *principle* is a basic ("first") belief or idea, while *principal* means "major or first in importance."

property

P

pol·len [pol′ən] *n.* A powder made by flowers from which new seeds grow.

pos·ses·sion [pə·zesh′ən] *n.* Something that belongs to a person: **Almost all of Uncle Diego's *possessions* were saved before the fire burned the house down.**

prac·ti·cal [prak′ti·kəl] *adj.* Full of common sense. *syn.* sensible

praise [prāz] *v.* To say nice things about someone or something. *syn.* compliment

pre·cious [presh′əs] *adj.* Very special or valuable.

pre·serve [pri·zûrv′] *v.* To keep from harm. *syn.* save

pre·tend [pri·tend′] *v.* **pre·tend·ed, pre·tend·ing** To fake or make believe: **Steve knew his sister was only *pretending* to be asleep so she could listen to him talk to his friends.**

prey [prā] *n.* An animal used by another animal as food.

prin·ci·ple [prin′sə·pəl] *n.* An important idea or rule on which people's behavior is based: **One of the *principles* of American democracy is that all people are equal in the eyes of the law.**

probe [prōb] *v.* **probed, prob·ing** To explore with a pointed object or tool.

prop·er·ty [prop′ər·tē] *n.* Land belonging to someone: **Mr. Teng built a fence around his *property* to keep the neighbor's dog out.**

pros·per·i·ty [pros·per′ə·tē] *n.* Success that includes wealth.

pro·test [prə·test′] *v.* **pro·test·ed, pro·test·ing** To object: **Some people *protested* that a new airport would make their neighborhood too noisy.**

R

ran·sacked [ran′sakt′] *adj.* Torn apart during a search.

rare [râr] *adj.* Very uncommon; found in very few places.

re·cite [ri·sīt′] *v.* **re·cit·ed, re·cit·ing** To say something that has been memorized in front of an audience.

re·cov·er·y [ri·kuv′ər·ē] *n.* A return to good health: **Everyone hoped Alana would make a quick *recovery* from the flu and return to school soon.**

re·flec·tion [ri·flek′shən] *n.* Something seen because its image is bounced back from a shiny surface: **Robert looked at his *reflection* in the mirror.**

re·lief [ri·lēf′] *n.* A feeling of freedom from pain, discomfort, or worry.

re·morse [ri·môrs′] *n.* Sorrow for having done something: **After Rachel yelled at her little brother, she felt such *remorse* that she made him a card.** *syn.* regret

res·er·va·tion [rez′ər·vā′shən] *n.* An area of land set aside by the government for a certain group of people to live on.

res·i·dent [rez′ə·dənt] *n.* A person living in a certain place.

re·spon·si·bil·i·ty [ri·spon′sə·bil′ə·tē] *n.* Something someone must do or take care of; duty.

ri·dic·u·lous [ri·dik′yə·ləs] *adj.* Funny: **The puppet's green, fuzzy hair looked *ridiculous* and made us laugh.** *syns.* laughable, silly

roam [rōm] *v.* To wander around.

rook·ie [rook′ē] *n.* A person who is playing his or her first year in a professional sport.

reflection

senhor This Portuguese word for "Mr." traces its origins to the Latin word *senior*, which means "older." Only an adult man was considered worthy of this formal title. The Spanish word *señor* and the Italian *signor* have the same origin and meaning. Even our English word *sir* can be traced to *senior*.

S

sci·en·tist [sī′ən·tist] *n.* A person who learns by studying and experimenting with things in nature.

scrunch [skrunch] *v.* **scrunched, scrunch·ing** To sit with arms and legs pulled in close to the body. *syn.* crouch

se·nhor [si·nyō(ə)r′] *n.* Portuguese title for a man, the same as *Mr.* or *Sir*: **In Brazil, where they speak Portuguese, the people Mr. Mason met called him *senhor*.**

a	add	ōō	took
ā	ace	ōō	pool
â	care	u	up
ä	palm	û	burn
e	end	yōō	fuse
ē	equal	oi	oil
i	it	ou	pout
ī	ice	ng	ring
o	odd	th	thin
ō	open	th	this
ô	order	zh	vision

ə = { a in *above*, e in *sicken*, i in *possible*, o in *melon*, u in *circus* }

shield

silhouette This word comes from the name of Etienne de Silhouette, who was in charge of the treasury of France during the 1700s. We aren't exactly sure why his name was given to this kind of picture, which shows only an outline filled in with a solid color. Perhaps he was such a bad treasurer that his name seemed to fit these pictures that appeared so simple and unfinished.

stamen

sen·si·ble [sen′sə·bəl] *adj.* Smart; reasonable: **Mike knew that eating all that candy was not *sensible* because too many sweets are not healthy.** *syn.* wise

sheep·ish·ly [shē′pish·lē] *adv.* With a feeling of shame.

shel·ter [shel′tər] *v.* To provide a safe, covered place.

shield [shēld] *n.* Something held up in front of a person for protection: **The soldier held up his *shield* as he marched into battle.**

shriv·eled [shriv′əld] *adj.* Small and dried up. *syn.* shrunken

shut·tle [shut′(ə)l] *n.* In weaving, an object used to carry a thread over and under other threads.

si·es·ta [sē·es′tə] *n.* A nap in the afternoon.

sil·hou·ette [sil′ōō·et′] *v.* **sil·hou·et·ted, sil·hou·et·ting** To make a dark outline of a person or thing against a light background.

sliv·er [sliv′ər] *n.* A thin and sometimes sharp piece broken, split, or cut off from something: **When Alan slid down the pole, he got *slivers* in his hands from the rough wood.** *syn.* splinter

splen·did [splen′did] *adj.* Wonderful. *syn.* glorious

squan·der [skwon′dər] *v.* **squan·dered, squan·der·ing** To spend money in a wasteful way. *syn.* waste

sta·men [stā′mən] *n.* The part of the flower that sticks out from the center.

stam·pede [stam·pēd′] *v.* To rush wildly in a group.

star·tling [stär′tling] *adj.* Surprising; shocking. *syn.* amazing

sta·tion·er·y [stā′shən·er′ē] *n.* Paper used for writing letters: **Carmela wrote a letter on yellow *stationery* to send to her aunt.**

steer·age [stir′ij] *n.* The crowded area of a ship for passengers with the cheapest tickets.

stunned [stund] *adj.* Very surprised.

sub·stance [sub′stəns] *n.* Material that something is made of.

sur·vive [sər·vīv′] *v.* To stay alive.

sus·pend [sə·spend′] *v.* **sus·pend·ed, sus·pend·ing** To hang: **The swing was *suspended* from a tree branch.**

sus·pi·cious [sə·spish′əs] *adj.* Having a feeling that something is wrong. *syn.* untrusting

sym·pa·thy [sim′pə·thē] *n.* The understanding of another person's feelings: **Because Kendra was crying, Gloria hugged her in *sympathy*.**

T

tech·nique [tek·nēk′] *n.* A way of doing something. *syns.* method, procedure, strategy

tem·per [tem′pər] *n.* Mood.

ter·ri·to·ry [ter′ə·tôr′ē] *n.* An open area of land that has not been settled or claimed by anyone.

tes·ti·fy [tes′tə·fī] *v.* To speak under oath in a court of law.

ther·a·py [ther′ə·pē] *n.* Treatment to help a person do something better.

thick·et [thik′it] *n.* A group of trees growing very close together. *syn.* grove

tra·di·tion [trə·dish′ən] *n.* An idea or way of doing things that is passed down among people over many years.

trans·late [trans·lāt′] *v.* **trans·lat·ed, trans·lat·ing** To explain the meaning of words or actions. *syn.* interpret

trans·par·ent [trans·pâr′ənt] *adj.* Able to be seen through: **We could see the cat sleeping behind the *transparent* curtains.**

trim [trim] *v.* **trimmed, trim·ming** To decorate something: **We *trimmed* the tree with lights.**

tri·um·phant·ly [trī·um′fənt·lē] *adv.* With joy and pride.

tu·ber [t(y)ōō′bər] *n.* A thick part of the stem of some plants that grows underground.

tur·moil [tûr′moil] *n.* Loud fussing: **The crowd at the baseball game was in a *turmoil* because of the shortstop's error.**

twi·light [twī′līt′] *n.* The light as the sun sets.

transparent

tuber *Tuber* and *thumb* are both related to the same ancient root word. They both refer to something swollen or fat. A *tuber* such as a potato or peanut is a swelling on a plant. Compared to your other fingers, your *thumb* is fat.

U

UFO [yōō′ef·ō′] *n.* Unidentified *Flying Object*; something seen in the sky that seems too strange to be real.

un·doubt·ed·ly [un·dou′tid·lē] *adv.* Certainly: **The sun is *undoubtedly* important to growing plants.** *syn.* surely

a	add	ōō	took
ā	ace	ōō	pool
â	care	u	up
ä	palm	û	burn
e	end	yōō	fuse
ē	equal	oi	oil
i	it	ou	pout
ī	ice	ng	ring
o	odd	th	thin
ō	open	th	this
ô	order	zh	vision

ə = { a in *above*, e in *sicken*, i in *possible*, o in *melon*, u in *circus* }

unity   yoke

violinist

u·ni·ty [yōō′ni·tē] *n.* The quality of being together and sharing: **The** *unity* **among the people of the village helped them choose and work together on their goals.**

ur·gent·ly [ûr′jənt·lē] *adv.* In a way calling for quick action.

 W

weird [wird] *adj.* Very strange.

wil·der·ness [wil′dər·nis] *n.* Land where people do not usually live.

wound [wōōnd] *v.* **wound·ed, wound·ing** To injure or hurt. *syn.* harm

V

vain [vān] *adj.* Too proud of the way one looks: **The** *vain* **beauty queen thought she was the prettiest woman in the world.**

vig·or·ous·ly [vig′ər·əs·lē] *adv.* With strength and energy: **The girls played basketball so** *vigorously* **that they were worn out after the game.**

vi·o·lin·ist [vī′ə·lin′ist] *n.* A person who plays a musical instrument called a violin: **The** *violinist* **broke a string on her instrument as she was playing it.**

vol·ca·no [vol·kā′nō] *n.* A kind of mountain from which melted rock, stones, and ashes sometimes explode.

Y

yoke [yōk] *v.* **yoked, yok·ing** To join together by a wooden frame.

volcano *Volcano* comes from the name Vulcan, the Roman god of fire and metalworking. The Romans believed that Vulcan's workshop and fiery furnace were buried under Mt. Etna, a volcano on the island of Sicily near Italy. When Vulcan and his helpers were heating and hammering, the mountain rumbled and shook, and sometimes fire and smoke came from the top.

yoke

Using the Index of Titles and Authors

Explain to students that an index is often found at the back of a book and usually consists of an alphabetical listing of topics covered in that particular book. Tell students that sometimes books have special kinds of indexes, such as the Index of Titles and Authors at the back of their anthologies.

While reviewing with students the first page of the Index, page 588, you may want to point out that all of the entries are in alphabetical order and that authors are listed with last names first. Ask students how they can tell at a glance which entries are selection titles and which are authors' names. Then call attention to the references to page numbers in light print. You may want to select several index entries and have students predict what they will find when they turn to the page or pages listed.

INDEX OF TITLES AND AUTHORS

Page numbers in light print refer to biographical information.

588

589

Acknowledgments continued

HarperCollins Publishers: "Pearls" from *Hey World, Here I Am!* by Jean Little. Text copyright © 1986 by Jean Little. "Is It Waiting Just for Me" from *Flower Moon Snow: A Book of Haiku* (Retitled: "Wildflower") by Kazue Mizumura. Text copyright © 1977 by Kazue Mizumura. Cover illustration by Pat Cummings from *Go Fish* by Mary Stolz. Illustration copyright © 1991 by Pat Cummings. From *Charlotte's Web* by E. B. White, illustrated by Garth Williams. Copyright 1952 by E. B. White. Text copyright renewed © 1980 by E. B. White; illustrations copyright renewed © 1980 by Garth Williams. "Runaway" from *On the Banks of Plum Creek* by Laura Ingalls Wilder, illustrated by Garth Williams. Text copyright 1937 by Laura Ingalls Wilder, renewed © 1963 by Roger L. MacBride; illustrations copyright 1953 by Garth Williams, renewed © 1981 by Garth Williams.

Holiday House: From *Totem Pole* by Diane Hoyt-Goldsmith. Text copyright © 1990 by Diane Hoyt-Goldsmith. Cover photograph by Lawrence Migdale from *Pueblo Storyteller* by Diane Hoyt-Goldsmith. Photograph copyright © 1991 by Lawrence Migdale.

Henry Holt and Company, Inc.: On the Pampas by María Cristina Brusca. Copyright © 1991 by María Cristina Brusca.

Houghton Mifflin Company: Jumanji by Chris Van Allsburg. Copyright © 1981 by Chris Van Allsburg.

Georgeanne Irvine: Cover photograph by Ron Garrison from *Raising Gordy Gorilla at the San Diego Zoo* by Georgeanne Irvine. Copyright © 1990 by Zoological Society of San Diego and Georgeanne Irvine.

Lerner Publications Company, 241 First Avenue, Minneapolis, MN 55401: From *Carnivorous Plants* by Cynthia Overbeck. Text copyright © 1982 by Lerner Publications Company.

Little, Brown and Company: "Philippe and the Blue Parrot" from *Light: Stories of a Small Kindness* by Nancy White Carlstrom. Text copyright © 1990 by Nancy White Carlstrom.

Little, Brown and Company, in conjunction with Sierra Club Books: Cover illustration from *Urban Roosts: Where Birds Nest in the City* by Barbara Bash. Copyright © 1990 by Barbara Bash.

Lodestar Books, an affiliate of Dutton Children's Books, a division of Penguin USA Inc.: Cover photograph by Richard Hewett from *Getting Elected: The Diary of a Campaign* by Joan Hewett. Photograph copyright © 1989 by Richard Hewett. "The Case of the Million Pesos" from *Encyclopedia Brown Gets His Man* by Donald J. Sobol. Text copyright © 1967 by Donald J. Sobol.

Lothrop, Lee and Shepard Books, a division of William Morrow & Company, Inc.: Cover illustration from *The Discovery of the Americas* by Betsy and Giulio Maestro. Illustration copyright © 1991 by Giulio Maestro. Cover photographs by George Ancona from *Making a New Home in America* by Maxine B. Rosenberg. Photographs copyright © 1986 by George Ancona. *Mufaro's Beautiful Daughters* by John Steptoe. Copyright © 1987 by John Steptoe. Used with the approval of the Estate of John Steptoe.

Macmillan Publishing Company: Cover illustration by Diane deGroat from *Jace the Ace* by Joanne Rocklin. Illustration copyright © 1990 by Diane deGroat. Cover illustration by Karl Swanson from *Carver* by Ruth Yaffe Radin. Illustration copyright © 1990 by Karl Swanson. Cover illustration by Jerry Pinkney from *Turtle in July* by Marilyn Singer. Illustration copyright © 1989 by Jerry Pinkney. From pp. 67-77 in *Grasshopper Summer* (Retitled: "Sailing") by Ann Turner. Text copyright © 1989 by Ann Turner.

Margaret K. McElderry Books, an imprint of Macmillan Publishing Company: "Apple Tree" from *Remembering and Other Poems* by Myra Cohn Livingston. Text copyright © 1989 by Myra Cohn Livingston. *Chin Chiang and the Dragon's Dance* by Ian Wallace. Copyright © 1984 by Ian Wallace.

McIntosh and Otis, Inc.: "The Case of the Locked Room" from *Two-Minute Mysteries* by Donald J. Sobol. Text copyright © 1967 by Donald J. Sobol. Published by Scholastic Book Services.

Morrow Junior Books, a division of William Morrow & Company, Inc.: Cover illustration by Sheila Hamanaka from *School's Out* by Johanna Hurwitz. Illustration copyright © 1991 by Sheila Hamanaka.

William Morrow & Company, Inc.: From *Aldo Ice Cream* (Retitled: "Muddy Sneakers") by Johanna Hurwitz. Text copyright © 1981 by Johanna Hurwitz. From *Class President* (Retitled: "Election Day") by Johanna Hurwitz, cover illustration by Sheila Hamanaka. Text copyright © 1990 by Johanna Hurwitz; cover illustration copyright © 1990 by Sheila Hamanaka. Cover illustration by Gail Owens from *Encyclopedia Brown and the Case of the Treasure Hunt* by Donald J. Sobol. Illustration copyright © 1988 by William Morrow & Company, Inc. and Bantam Books, Inc.

National Geographic Society: "Running With the Pack" from *National Geographic World* Magazine, February 1987. Text copyright © 1987 by National Geographic Society.

Philomel Books: "Far, Far Will I Go" from *Beyond the High Hills* by Knud Rasmussen. Text copyright © 1961 by The World Publishing Company; copyright renewed © 1989 by Guy Mary Rousseliere. Cover illustration by Ed Young from *Yeh-Shen: A Cinderella Story from China,* retold by Ai-Ling Louie. Illustration copyright © 1982 by Ed Young.

Plays, Inc.: "Close Encounter of a Weird Kind" by A. F. Bauman from *Space and Science Fiction Plays for Young People,* edited by Sylvia E. Kamerman. Text copyright © 1981 by Plays, Inc.

Pleasant Company: Cover illustration by Renée Graef from *Meet Kirsten: An American Girl* by Janet Shaw. Illustration copyright © 1986 by Pleasant Company.

Prentice Hall, a division of Simon & Schuster, Inc.: From *Alexander the Grape: Fruit and Vegetable Jokes* (Retitled: "Fruit and Vegetable Stew") by Charles Keller. Text © 1982 by Charles Keller.

Random House Inc.: Cover illustration by Sheila Hamanaka from *The Skates of Uncle Richard* by Carol Fenner. Illustration copyright © 1990 by Sheila Hamanaka.

Roberts Rinehart Publishers, Post Office Box 666, Niwot, CO 80544: Cover illustration by Birgitta Säflund from *The People Who Hugged the Trees* by Deborah Lee Rose. Illustration copyright © 1990 by Birgitta Säflund.

Scholastic, Inc.: Cover illustration by Deborah Haeffele from *The Ring and the Window Seat* by Amy Hest. Illustration copyright © 1990 by Deborah Haeffele. "How Many Spots Does A Leopard Have?" from *How Many Spots Does A Leopard Have? and Other Tales* by Julius Lester, illustrated by David Shannon. Text copyright © 1989 by Julius Lester; illustration copyright © 1989 by David Shannon. *With Love From Koko* by Faith McNulty. Text copyright © 1990 by Faith McNulty. From *Jim Abbott: Against All Odds* (Retitled: "Growing Up") by Ellen Emerson White. Text copyright © 1990 by Ellen Emerson White.

Charles Scribner's Sons, an imprint of Macmillan Publishing Company: From pp. 45-66 in *The Cat Who Escaped from Steerage* (Retitled: "Chanah's Journey") by Evelyn Wilde Mayerson, cover illustration by Ronald Himler. Text copyright © 1990 by Evelyn Wilde Mayerson; cover illustration copyright © 1990 by Ronald Himler.

Viking Penguin, a division of Penguin Books USA Inc.: From *The Midnight Fox* (Retitled: "The Stormy Rescue") by Betsy Byars. Text copyright © 1968 by Betsy Byars. From *The Weaving of a Dream* by Marilee Heyer. Copyright © 1986 by Marilee Heyer.

Walker and Company: Cover illustration by Barbara Lavallee from *This Place Is Wet* by Vicki Cobb. Illustration © 1989 by Barbara Lavallee. Text and illustrations from *Tiger Lilies and Other Beastly Plants* by Elizabeth Ring, illustrated by Barbara Bash. Text copyright © 1984 by Elizabeth Ring; illustrations copyright © 1984 by Barbara Bash.

Sharon Wooding: Cover illustration by Sharon Wooding from *I'll Meet You at the Cucumbers* by Lilian Moore. Illustration copyright © 1988 by Sharon Wooding.

Handwriting models in this program have been used with permission of the publisher, Zaner-Bloser, Inc., Columbus, OH.

Photograph Credits

KEY: (t) top, (b) bottom, (l) left, (r) right, (c) center.

UNIT 1
20, HBJ/Britt Runion; 38(t), HBJ/Lisa Quinones for Black Star; 38–39(background), HBJ Photo; 74–75, HBJ/Britt Runion; 76, HBJ Photo; 89(t), Karl Bissinger; 96(t), The Granger Collection; 96(bl), Mark E. Gibson; 96(br), Chip & Rosa Maria Peterson.

UNIT 2
104, HBJ Photo; 117, Sara L. Stubbins; 120–134, Ronald H. Cohn/The Gorilla Foundation; 136–137, HBJ/Maria Paraskevas; 160–161, Courtesy Betsy Byars; 176, HBJ Photo; 186–189, Jim Brandenburg; 190, L. David Mech/U.S. Fish and Wildlife Service; 192(t), © SOUTHERN LIVING, INC. March 1991. Photo by Dianne Young; 192(b), M & E Bernstein/Woodfin Camp & Assoc.

UNIT 3
198, HBJ/Maria Paraskevas; 220–233, Kiyoshi Shimizu; 238, HBJ Photo; 251, HBJ Photo; 252, *Flower Garden and Bungalow, Bermuda,* 1889. Winslow Homer, The Metropolitan Museum of Art, Amelia B. Lazarus Fund, 1910; 253, *Still Life with Apples on a Pink Tablecloth,* 1924. Henri Matisse, National Gallery of Art, Washington, D.C., Chester Dale Collection; 254, HBJ Photo; 264, HBJ/Britt Runion; 286, HBJ/Ken Rogers for Black Star; 288(br), Rochester Museum & Science Center.

UNIT 4
294–295, HBJ/Britt Runion; 296–297, HBJ Photo; 316–317, Jack Graber; 317, Karen Kuehn/Matrix International; 336–337, HBJ/Debi Harbin; 338(background), HBJ Photo; 338(t), HBJ/Len Kaufman for Black Star; 342(t), HBJ/Len Kaufman for Black Star; 342-343 (background), HBJ Photo; 354, HBJ Photo; 372, D. Donne Bryant; 373, Kjell B. Sandved/Photo Researchers.

UNIT 5
378–379, HBJ/Debi Harbin; 380–381, HBJ Photo; 386–387 (background), John Bova/Photo Researchers; 387(b), HBJ Photo; 400–401, HBJ/Maria Paraskevas; 440–456, © 1990 by Lawrence Migdale. All rights reserved. Reprinted from TOTEM POLE by permission of Holiday House; 458(t), Ben Simmons/The Stock Market; 458(b), Bill Campbell/Picture Group; 459(t), HBJ /Rodney Jones; 459(b), HBJ/Rob Downey.

UNIT 6
464–465, HBJ/Britt Runion; 466, HBJ Photo; 481, James Ropiequet Schmidt; 482, HBJ Photo; 526–527, HBJ/Maria Paraskevas; 536, HBJ/Maria Paraskevas; 546(t), HBJ/Maria Paraskevas; 546(b), HBJ/Maria Paraskevas; 552, HBJ/Britt Runion; 553, HBJ/Britt Runion; 557, Jim Brandenburg; 560, HBJ/Debi Harbin; 561, HBJ/Debi Harbin; 564, HBJ/Britt Runion; 573, Gail Denham/PP/FA; 574, Murray Alcosser/Image Bank; 575, Janeart, Ltd/Image Bank; 576, Chuck Kahn/Image Bank.

Illustration Credits

KEY: (t) top, (b) bottom, (l) left, (r) right, (c) center.

Table of Contents Art
Abby Carter, 9 (tr), 11 (br), 12–13 (c); Regan Dunnick, 5 (br), 6–7 (c), 10 (tl), 12 (bl), 15 (tr); Cameron Eagle, 4 (tl), 7 (br), 8–9 (c), 12 (tl), 14 (bl); Jennifer Hewitson, 4 (bl), 7 (tr), 9 (br), 10–11 (c), 14 (tl); Tracy Sabin, 4–5 (c), 8 (tl), 10 (bl), 13 (tr), 15 (br); Rhonda Voo, 6 (far l), 8 (bl), 11 (tr), 13 (br), 14–15 (c).

Unit Opening Patterns
Tracy Sabin

Bookshelf Art
Alex Boies, 100–101; Gerald Bustamente, 18–19; Callie Butler, 196–197; David Diaz, 292–293; Armen Kojoyian, 462–463; Randy Verougstraete, 376–377.

Theme Opening Art
Barbara Banthien, 166–167; Seymour Cwast, 58–59; Bradley Clark, 20–21, 352–353; John Craig, 378–379; Cameron Eagle, 102–103; Tuko Fujisaki, 264–265; Chris Lam, 526–527; Ross Mac Donald, 336–337; Amanda Schaffer, 198–199, 504–505; Joel Spector, 74–75; Jean and Mou-sien Tseng, 426–427; Dale Verzaal, 236–237.

Theme Closing Art
Linda Bleck, 371, 457, 525; Cameron Eagle, 191, 263, 503; Tuko Fujisaki, 57, 165, 351; Edward Martinez, 95; Tim Raglin, 73, 135, 235, 425; Walter Stuart, 335, 399, 547.

Connections Art
Linda Bleck, 97; Mark Frueh, 193; William Maughan, 548–549; Clarence Porter, 458–459; Amanda Schaffer, 288–289, 372–373.

Selection Art
Barbara Bash, 254–262; Jamie Bennett, 318–321; Christoph Blumrich, 70–72; María Cristina Brusca, 536–545; Lynne Cherry, 238–251; Albert Co, 200–218; Sylvie Daigneault, 118–119; Lambert Davis, 90–93; Donna Diamond, 508–524; Mike Dooling, 404–424; Jack Garber, 316–317; Jan Spivey Gilchrist, 506–507; Paul Goble, 176–185; Brian Haynes, 402–403; Carie Henrie, 94; Marilee Heyer, 482–502; Denise Hilton Putnam, 370; Michael Koelsch, 22–37, 40–56; Jeffrey Mangiat, 322–334; Steven Meyers, 339–341, 344–350; Carol Norby, 546; Doug Panton 268–286; Alice and Martin Provensen, 162–163; Melodye Rosales, 61–69; David Shannon, 168–175; John Steptoe, 466–480; Dugald Stermer, 164; Doug Suma, 528–535; Jeffrey Terreson, 138–161; Chris Van Allsburg, 296–315; Neil Waldman, 354–369; Ian Wallace, 428–439; Garth Williams, 104–117, 380–385; Vera B. Williams, 76–89.

590

R20 / *FEAST YOUR EYES*

Integrated Instruction

We believe that through a more holistic approach to teaching reading and language arts, students will discover the connection between reading, writing, listening, and speaking.

Why Authentic Literature Has Replaced the Old Standards

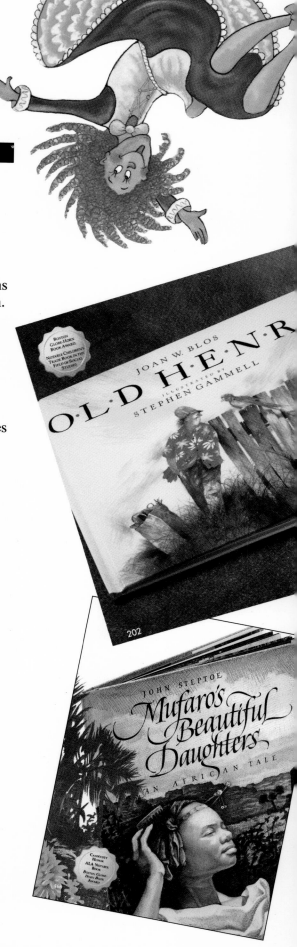

DR. DOROTHY S. STRICKLAND

The State of New Jersey Professor of Reading at Rutgers University and Senior Author, HBJ Treasury of Literature

Shared Reading! Literature Response Groups! Author Studies! Genre Studies! Response Logs!

Literature-Based Reading!

These terms are finding their way into the lesson plan books of an increasing number of teachers throughout the United States and the world. Their use is just one of the signs that literature-based reading is receiving widespread attention, acceptance, and acclaim.

Interest in the use of literature to teach reading and writing has increased as more and more teachers and administrators seek to re-examine the way literacy is taught in their schools. Many, having moved toward teaching writing as process, have sought to make their reading programs more process oriented, too. The use of strategies such as shared reading and literature response groups seemed to fit in well with their writing programs. Some were attracted to the idea by the wealth of quality books now available to children. Still others were influenced by the potential for linking content themes in social studies and science with literary studies typically associated with learning to read and write.

Children not only read and respond to a rich variety of literature, they also learn about many of the authors and poets...

The move toward literature-based reading may occur in a single classroom, a single school, or in many cases, an entire school district. Whether such a program is launched on a large scale or on a small one, certain instructional elements are evident. Each is an essential part of *HBJ Treasury of Literature*.

1. "Real literature" predominates in the reading program throughout the grade levels.

2. Reading, writing, and oral language are closely linked.

3. In-depth studies are made of authors and their craft.

4. Students respond to literature through discussion, writing, art, drama, and more reading.

5. Self-selected independent reading is valued, and student choice is respected.

6. Students read and respond to a wide variety of literary forms and genres.

7. Literature is integrated with content areas across the entire curriculum.

8. Students are helped to use their experiences with literature to learn the strategies and skills required to become competent readers, writers, and thinkers.

HBJ Treasury of Literature is filled with the works of award-winning poets and authors. Newbery and Caldecott Medal winners are represented, as are writers whose nonfiction works are listed among the Outstanding Science Trade Books.

Children not only read and respond to a rich variety of literature, they also learn about many of the authors and poets, discovering how these writers go about their craft. Through frequent discussion and daily opportunities to write, students link what they learn to their own writing development as well.

The literature selections are arranged in interesting themes that help to unify activities and to make connections with other curriculum areas such as social studies and science. This makes learning "real," the way it is outside of school.

Through varied experiences with literature, students are helped to see the naturally occurring patterns in text. It is through wide exposure to these patterns that the strategies and skills needed to read and write effectively are developed. These literacy strategies are made explicit through continued, varied exposure and through specific teacher-guided activities.

The goals of literature-based reading extend well beyond simply teaching children to read and write. As exemplified in *HBJ Treasury of Literature*, the primary goal of literature-based reading is to foster the development of *readers* and *writers*—students who are not only competent readers and writers, but who view reading and writing as an integral part of their lives. ●

Why Shouldn't Young Readers Read Great Writers?

DR. BERNICE E. CULLINAN

Professor of Early Childhood and Elementary Education at New York University and Senior Consultant, HBJ Treasury of Literature

It was survival of the greatest as books were selected for

HBJ Treasury of Literature.

The foundation of any successful literature-based reading program is, of course, great literature. Great literature does many things. It enriches children's lives and makes them aware of the pluralistic nature of our world. It allows children to savor experience and to experience life. As we selected literature for *HBJ Treasury of Literature*, we looked for these qualities and more. We looked for literature that

● stimulates the reader's imagination.

● contains sparkling language and natural dialogue.

● provides heroes, role models, and memorable characters.

● evokes deep emotion, tickles the funny bone, or tingles the spine.

● gives new information and deepens understanding.

● sparks a love of reading through many literary genres.

● elicits high praise from children and adults alike.

Some people spend their entire lives collecting great works. And sometimes, we, as teachers, are fortunate to discover that someone has done the work for us—that a treasury of great literature has already been assembled—that a program like *HBJ Treasury of Literature* exists. ●

Look for
· Authentic literature

· How the best books survive HBJ's screening process

· *HBJ Treasury of Literature* Library Books linked with every literary theme

· Numerous opportunities for self-selected independent reading

· In-depth studies of authors and their craft

Truth Is Stranger than Fiction
Or at least more interesting

DR. RICHARD F. ABRAHAMSON

Professor of Education at the University of Houston and Author, HBJ Treasury of Literature

Nonfiction's surprising appeal among young readers

Across the country, teachers of literature-based reading programs are discovering the powerful role that nonfiction plays in the reading lives of today's children and young adults—tomorrow's leaders.

America is a country of nonfiction readers. Our interest in nonfiction starts in elementary school and increases steadily as we move through middle school and high school. Within the pages of *HBJ Treasury of Literature,* our students can find some of the most interesting nonfiction pieces by the finest authors in the field.

Research tells us that between forty and fifty percent of all the books students check out of elementary and middle-school libraries are nonfiction. And they are read, often for pleasure. In a study of ten years of Children's Choice lists compiled by the International Reading Association and the Children's Book Council, forty-three percent of the titles were nonfiction.

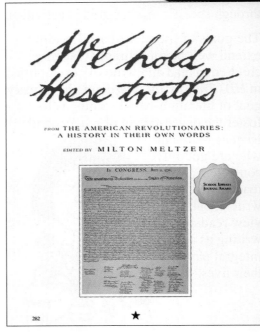

Much has been written recently about that growing segment of the student population called aliterate readers — those youngsters who can read but choose not to. Research has shown that even readers with the most negative attitudes toward reading do read some things. What they read is nonfiction— magazine selections about natural disasters, books about sports and sports heroes, math and science games, and fascinating discoveries about dinosaurs.

...a special book in your life... may well have been nonfiction.

What better way to welcome many aliterate readers back into the reading club than by using the inviting nonfiction pieces found in *HBJ Treasury of Literature*!

Good nonfiction writing is not just a collection of facts. It can move us deeply. Think back to a special book in your life, one that challenged you or even moved you to tears. It may well have been nonfiction.

Among the many quality nonfiction pieces offered in *HBJ Treasury of Literature* are selections from Alex Haley's *Roots,* Gary Paulsen's autobiographical account of competing in a grueling dogsled race, and many interviews with authors such as Chris Van Allsburg, Lois Lowry, Gary Soto, and James Michener. This is the kind of nonfiction that spells reading motivation for today's young readers. ●

Look for
- The most interesting nonfiction pieces by the finest authors in the field
- Great poetry that opens up a world of feeling for children

DR. LEE BENNETT HOPKINS

Poet, author, anthologist, and Consultant,
HBJ Treasury of Literature

The Gift of Poetry

Opening a world of feeling to children

I have said it many times; I shall say it again and again: Poetry should flow freely in the lives of children; it should come to them as naturally as breathing, for nothing—no thing—can ring and rage throughout hearts and minds as does this genre of literature.

As a classroom teacher, I quickly learned the value of poetry—how it can enhance every area of the curriculum—from mathematics to science. More important, I soon realized that poetry was an effective force with above-average, average, and reluctant readers on every grade level. And, oh, what poetry can do to bolster the self-esteem of children everywhere.

Every day is a great day for poetry—the kind of great poetry that can be found in *HBJ Treasury of Literature*. Poets such as Eve Merriam, Nikki Giovanni, John Ciardi, Teresa Paloma Acosta, and Aileen Fisher open up a world of feelings to children.

> *And, oh, what poetry can do to bolster the self-esteem of children everywhere.*

As educators we must lead children into poetry—ignite the spark for them to appreciate it, love it. This is one of the greatest gifts we can give to our students, whether they are pre-schoolers or young adult readers.

There is a place for poetry—every day—everywhere—all of the time.

For me, any day without a poem is just another day on the calendar. I hope it will be for you, too, and for the children you nurture, reach, touch. ●

Putting the Thinking Back into Reading

Developing strategic reader

DR. DONNA M. OGLE

Chair, Reading and Language Arts Department of National-Louis University, Evanston, Illinois, and Author, HBJ Treasury of Literature

Good readers are confident. They know they are in charge of the reading process and can adjust their reading behaviors if necessary to achieve their purpose. They have a repertoire of strategies they know will work for them in a variety of reading situations.

Reading is not a passive activity involving the eyes scanning a page. Each reading situation is an encounter between an absent author and a reader who is trying to construct a clear understanding from the available written message. Good readers, like athletes, set goals and plan for how they will achieve them. They make adjustments and alterations to their plan as necessary.

We know from much research with active readers that certain kinds of behaviors are common across all reading situations. These include anticipating meaning and linking the text to what the reader already knows, making predictions and altering them as information unfolds, constructing interpretations by making inferences

...good readers confidently adjust their reading and thinking behaviors to meet their own needs and those of the situation.

and elaborating on the ideas presented by the author, visualizing, asking questions of the text, and monitoring one's understanding so that alterations can be made and fix-up strategies employed.

Look for
- Preview and predict strategy employed in every fiction selection
- KWL or SQ3R strategy employed in every nonfiction selection
- Strategy lessons
- Vocabulary strategies
- Strategy conferences
- Critical thinking activities

DR. ROBERT J. STERNBERG

IBM Professor of Psychology and Education at Yale University and Consultant, HBJ Treasury of Literature

New Ways of Thinking About Thinking

Building critical and creative thinking

I don't understand why Cricket is saying this. I think I'd better reread the last few paragraphs to see what's going on.

Other behaviors are more situation specific. For example, if a reader needs to retain information for a specific purpose for school or personal learning, more active retention strategies will be employed. One of these might be filling out a K-W-L chart. Another might be following the SQ3R procedure. No matter what the task or how difficult the material, good readers confidently adjust their reading and thinking behaviors to meet their own needs and those of the situation.

Reading strategies don't develop automatically. A recent study of middle-school readers (LaZansky and Tierney) revealed that there was little variety in the strategies they used.

However, students who use the kind of strategy instruction provided in *HBJ Treasury of Literature* come to realize that there are options for dealing with unfamiliar text.

Instruction in strategic reading begins early in *HBJ Treasury of Literature*. Even first-grade readers employ strategies they have learned. As readers mature, they build a rich repertoire of strategies that empowers them so that they *want* to read and *do* read successfully. The program builds an understanding of the reading process. Young readers are given clear information about active reading-thinking behavior and direct modeling of each process. This scaffolded instruction produces confident readers who choose reading for their own pleasure and learning. ●

Critical thinking involves analyzing arguments, making judgments, drawing conclusions. Creative thinking involves such activities as inventing scenes, speculating, and solving problems.

A story from *Hatchet,* by Gary Paulsen, appears in *HBJ Treasury of Literature.* The story is about a boy who flies a plane when the pilot has a deadly heart attack. A comprehension question asks:

> What are the problems that Brian Robeson faces in this story?

Note that this question measures true understanding, not merely factual recall. A Critical Thinking Activity reads:

> Think about Brian's behavior throughout the story. Write a report that praises some of his actions and criticizes others.

Here students make judgments that critically evaluate Brian's response.

Finally, consider an activity from the lesson that explores creative thinking.

> What would have helped Brian during the emergency? Write a list of the supplies, information, and skills that might have made his ordeal more bearable.

These kinds of critical and creative thinking activities are an integral part of *HBJ Treasury of Literature.* They invite children to think by presenting them with challenges that are intriguing and that touch their lives. ●

Integrating the Language Arts

DR. BARBARA BOWEN COULTER

Director, Communication Arts for the Detroit Public School District and Author, HBJ Treasury of Literature

New insights on linking the language arts

As an information revolution sweeps us into the twenty-first century, we realize that we are teaching more than reading, more than writing, more than listening, and more than speaking. We are teaching communication. We recognize the need to teach skills, but we want children to do this at the same time that they are discovering the joys of reading, the power of writing, and the roles that listening and speaking play in those processes.

HBJ Treasury of Literature...*teaches reading within the context of the integrated language arts.*

HBJ Treasury of Literature embodies a teaching approach that contains the tools to achieve this goal. It teaches reading within the context of the integrated language arts. As students participate in the diverse activities that are available in *HBJ Treasury of Literature*, they build a foundation that makes them adept communicators. The teacher is empowered to structure their learning experience in ways that allow them to develop the confidence, the skills, and the knowledge to solve problems and become independent thinkers and learners. ●

Don't Underestimate the Power of the Pencil

DR. TIMOTHY SHANAHAN

Professor of Urban Education at the University of Illinois at Chicago and Author, HBJ Treasury of Literature

How writing builds better readers and writers

During the fifth grade, I decided to become a writer—a peculiar choice, as my school experiences offered no opportunity to put my thoughts to paper. Now, years later, it is finally widely recognized that we must provide children with an abundant heritage of literature while celebrating their voices.

We have, in *HBJ Treasury of Literature*, also a treasury of writing experiences carefully designed to help children become better readers. First, writing activities deepen their understanding of the processes of reading and the structures of text. After reading a mystery, for example, children might be asked to try their hand at creating their own mysteries—complete with suspense. Second, *HBJ Treasury of Literature* contains original interviews and specially commissioned personal reflections that reveal why authors write as they do. Throughout the program, children also use writing as a form of self-communication to help them participate in conversation with their classmates and others. Writer's Workshops involve children in the writing process. Finally, *HBJ Treasury of Literature* demonstrates how writing, when allied with reading, can become a more powerful avenue to learning. Toward this end, children are encouraged to do "quickwrites" to activate prior knowledge, to use writing to summarize and extend their understandings of text, and to write personal responses to literature.

This wonderful interplay between children's literature and the literature of children entices students to explore their world through the written word—to communicate, to create, to know. It almost makes me wish I were still in the fifth grade. ●

After reading a mystery, for instance, children might be asked to try their hand at creating their own mysteries—complete with suspense.

Look for
- Integrated Language Arts
- Reader/Writer Connections
- Writer's Workshops
- Quickwrites
- Personal journals
- Original interviews and personal reflections by authors

New Strategies Spell S-U-C-C-E-S-S with Students

DR. W. DORSEY HAMMOND

Professor of Education at Oakland University in Rochester, Michigan, and Senior Consultant, HBJ Treasury of Literature

Anything worth writing is worth spelling right.

Good readers and writers also become good spellers, or so the research indicates. However, the spelling abilities of elementary and middle school students will not develop or reach full potential if ignored or left to chance. All students, therefore, can benefit from an organized spelling curriculum.

Good spellers use strategies, conscious or unconscious. *HBJ Treasury of Literature Integrated Spelling* takes certain important strategies and makes them available to all students. Let's take a look at some of the strategies that super-spellers develop, seemingly by intuition.

Integrated Spelling teaches students to make spelling generalizations by taking key words directly from the reading selections. Students also receive explanations of unusual spellings and numerous opportunities to proofread for spelling. In addition, *Integrated Spelling* provides metacognitive strategies to help children develop their "spelling consciousness," including pattern recognition, going from the known to the unknown, and mnemonic devices. Perhaps most importantly for the concept of the reading and writing processes as systems, spelling is taught in the natural context of literature.

Most students want to be able to spell. It can be a source of pride to them as they learn other communication skills. The methods used in *HBJ Treasury of Literature Integrated Spelling* are designed to unlock the mysteries of good spelling and make the skill available to all students. ●

Integrated Spelling *provides metacognitive strategies to help students develop their "spelling consciousness"...*

PAT SMITH

Adjunct Professor of Education at the University of Houston at Clear Lake and Author, HBJ Treasury of Literature

Writing with Style

Teaching students to "read with a writer's eye"

"From that day forward, the generous king would frequently sort through the treasure chest looking for just the right jewel to offer as a gift. And they all lived happily ever after."

Just as the king in this traditional story had a cache from which to draw jewels, so, too, do the readers of *HBJ Treasury of Literature* have a source of beautifully crafted word usage. The literature serves as an exemplary language model for students. They are taught to "read with a writer's eye" in order to find and appreciate well-crafted passages.

Besides being generally immersed in a treasury of language-rich literature, students are explicitly instructed in effective language use. In each theme, Language/Literature Link offers explicit instruction on integrating language with literature. Elements of authors' craft such as elaboration through use of precise words, sensory language, examples, and

The literature serves as an exemplary language model for students.

dialogue are explained. Grammar elements such as vivid verb usage, sentences with compound predicates, and expanded sentences are integrated into the theme. Students always receive the dual invitation to return to the literature to experience the language technique and to reach forward to incorporate the language technique into their own writing.

For example, the precise word choice of Patricia MacLachlan exemplified in her *Sarah, Plain and Tall* becomes the model for student use of precise wording. The literature and language are linked together to form an integrated whole for effective reading and writing. Perhaps the result of the rich integration in *HBJ Treasury of Literature* would be this modern-day version of the traditional story ending.

"And so…from that day forward, the students called forth from the rich language of their literary experiences just the right techniques to present their thoughts. And they all lived happily ever after." ●

Look for
- Language/Literature Link
- Spelling-Vocabulary Connection
- *HBJ Treasury of Literature Integrated Spelling*

When Does Two Plus Two Equal Five?

DR. JUDITH L. IRVIN

Director, Center for the Study of Middle Level Education, and Author, HBJ Treasury of Literature

Making connections between different subjects can add up to greater learning.

Most teachers are humbled by their experience at one time or another. I was during a social studies lesson on pollution, years ago. A student asked me, "Is the environment we are studying in social studies the same environment we studied in science?"

Recent research on brain-based learning sheds valuable information on the reasons for integrating curriculum studies. It indicates that the brain recognizes, sorts, and organizes information according to large patterns. Information presented in context becomes meaningful to the learner while isolated bits of information seem to hinder this process.

...information presented in context becomes meaningful to the learner...

Set forth here are some general guidelines that *HBJ Treasury of Literature* followed to help you move toward an integrated curriculum.

- Each Anthology from grades 4 through 8 contains a unit of literature that focuses on science and a unit of literature that focuses on social studies.

- Integrated Curriculum activities appear in each lesson plan and Connections at the end of each unit.

- Within each level are eighteen themes—collections of literature related to a concept or idea.

Given these features from *HBJ Treasury of Literature* and the flexibility and ease-of-use of the program, reshaping curriculum has never been easier.

Of course, some students make connections between disciplines by themselves. For them, *HBJ Treasury of Literature* will validate these discoveries. For those who have not yet made their own internal learning "map," the cross-curricular activities in this series provide scaffolding for a skill that will serve them well throughout their lives. ●

Look for
- Literature arranged by themes
- Units focusing on science and on social studies
- Integrated curriculum in each lesson plan
- Cross-curriculum connections at the end of each unit

Classroom Management

We recognize that each classroom is a unique learning environment and that effectively managing the resources within that environment is a challenge. We are committed to helping teachers meet the needs of all students in a literature-based classroom.

Making Your Classroom Reading-Friendly

DR. ROGER C. FARR

Professor of Education and Director of the Center for Reading and Language Studies, Indiana University and Senior Author, HBJ Treasury of Literature

A checklist of management strategies for the literature-based classroom

There is no one best way to manage a literature-based classroom. However, good management grows out of good organization. When planning literature-based instruction, consider which of the many techniques for organizing the classroom will work best for you. Whatever technique you choose, consider these general guidelines:

- The instructional needs and interests of students are paramount in determining effective instructional strategies.

- The organization of the classroom provides students with many opportunities to share with you and with each other the things they are reading and writing.

- A variety of books, magazines, and writing materials are easily accessible to students. The classroom has comfortable reading "corners," which become havens where students can escape with a favorite book or magazine.

- The students are empowered. They are included in the planning and share in the responsibility to ensure that learning experiences are effective.

- The management plan is flexible. It allows the teacher to take advantage of student interests and motivation and to seize upon teachable moments.

The research-tested organizational patterns below have been used effectively by many teachers in literature-based reading programs. These are just a few of the options you will find support for in *HBJ Treasury of Literature.*

Good management grows out of good organization.

Popular Organizational Patterns

Organization	What is it?	Examples
Whole Class	Teacher works with the entire class at the same time. Variations may include times when the teacher is directing the entire group and times when individual class members are doing the same task at the same time.	Shared Reading Sustained Silent Reading Direct Whole-Class Instruction
Small-Group/ Cooperative Group	Groups of children work together toward a common goal. Often, the group determines how the task is divided among its members; other times the teacher directs the activity. Sometimes, as few as two students take turns reading a story or leading an activity.	Reader Response Groups Paired/Buddy Reading Small-Group Instruction Cooperative Reading Activity/Interest Groups
Individual	Each student functions independently and is responsible for his or her own work.	Independent Reading Self-Selected Reading Independent Projects Learning Centers

As you plan instruction for each new theme in *HBJ Treasury of Literature*, you will find specific suggestions given for managing a literature-based classroom. Here are a few general tips to help you start planning:

- Consider all of the factors that enter into planning: people, time, space, facilities, materials, and organization.

- Plan ahead in combining activities. As students work on a writing activity, you might pull out students for portfolio conferences.

- Be flexible. Develop plans that follow general guidelines.

- Continuously assess, revise, and modify your plans.

A significant factor in determining the success of a literature-based program is maintaining contact with students' families. Family Involvement Activities, such as those at the beginning of each *HBJ Treasury of Literature* lesson plan, can be used by parents to reinforce important concepts and themes. In addition, when Practice Book pages are assigned independently after small-group instruction, family members can help children build responsibility in completing and returning assignments.

Making family involvement flow smoothly also requires effective communication. Suggestions that might be included in a family information letter can be found in *HBJ Treasury of Literature* Family Involvement Activities. ●

Putting Literature Up for Discussion

DR. KAREN S. KUTIPER

Assistant Professor of Education at Southwest Texas State University and Author, HBJ Treasury of Literature

Finding shared and personal meanings in reader response groups

Reader response groups—small groups of students responding independently to literature selections in a non-threatening environment—offer teachers a new alternative in classroom management. Children in response groups hold a dialogue among themselves that is focused on elements of literature.

So why would teachers use reader response groups? Are they just one more classroom management option? Reader response groups are much more than a management technique.

Children working in response groups bring literature to life, find personal meanings in literature, and share the pleasure of reading. They begin to realize that each group member might have a differ-

ent yet valid response and that listening to these shared responses often helps them clarify or enrich their own understanding.

Children who participate in reader response groups see that their ideas can be received and valued by others. They are challenged to think critically by participating in discussions that seldom stay at the literal level. They learn to function in varying group roles. The teacher becomes a facilitator of learning, encouraging children to seek new depths of understanding by developing their own avenues of discussion. The reading of literature becomes a quest to discover personal and shared meanings.

Because of their flexibility, reader response groups fit well into many classroom-management plans. *HBJ Treasury of Literature* provides the teacher with many suggestions for using reader response groups. Appropriate places for their use are suggested in the lesson plans, along with management tips. Response Cards in the Teacher Resources section of the Teacher's Editions for grades 2–8 may be used to allow students to function independently from the teacher.

Reader response groups provide a means of encouraging a love of reading and of helping children build the communication and interpersonal skills that also affect self-esteem. No wonder so many teachers use them! ●

Reader response groups allow...students to respond to literature selections in a loosely-structured, non-threatening environment.

Look for
- Options for reading
- Management strategies for a literature-based classroom
- *HBJ Treasury of Literature* Family Involvement Activities
- Suggestions for using reader response groups
- Response Cards to copy and keep

Second-Language Support

DR. MARGARET A. GALLEGO

Assistant Professor of Education at Michigan State University and Author, HBJ Treasury of Literature

Tailoring teaching strategies for the linguistically diverse classroom

Millions of children are coming to school from homes where languages other than English are spoken, making it inevitable that all teachers will eventually teach students of various linguistic backgrounds. A classroom of diverse students can offer unlimited possibilities for creating a unique community of learners. However, addressing linguistically diverse students' individual reading instruction needs can be exceptionally challenging.

To meet the needs of linguistically diverse students, *HBJ Treasury of Literature* has integrated Second-Language Support throughout the program.

1. Second-Language Support notes in the Teacher's Editions are embedded throughout Vocabulary Strategies, Strategic Reading, and Learning Through Literature.

2. Suggestions for classroom management of Second-Language Support appear in each theme.

…unlimited possibilities for creating a unique community of learners.

3. Lessons in the Second-Language Support Manual give students the background and vocabulary needed to successfully participate in *HBJ Treasury of Literature*.

In addition, the *English as a Second Language (ESL) Manual* offers activities to help students develop English proficiency and the *Transition for ESL Students* provides support for those transferring into *HBJ Treasury of Literature* from Spanish or other language reading programs. ●

Are gifted children really worth all that extra attention?

Yes, but not at the expense of their classmates

DR. ROBERT J. STERNBERG

IBM Professor of Psychology and Education at Yale University and Consultant, HBJ Treasury of Literature

An ideal reading program for gifted and talented students offers diversity and challenge, stresses critical and creative thinking and offers opportunities for students to customize activities that result in concrete accomplishments. In addition, it provides a range of assessment instruments to meet the needs of all students.

Challenge activities help you customize the lesson plans.

How does *HBJ Treasury of Literature* compare to an ideal program for gifted and talented children? Meeting Individual Needs provides specific teaching strategies for gifted and talented students. Challenge activities help you customize the lesson plans. Critical and creative thinking questions and activities abound. Writer's Workshops, as well as other activities, invite students to create and customize tangible products. Also, a variety of assessment options helps teachers meet the needs of gifted and talented students.●

Look for
- Meeting Individual Needs section in every lesson plan
- Specific support for students with limited English proficiency, students at risk, special education students, and gifted and talented students
- Self-Assessment Notes, Strategy Conferences, and Portfolio Conferences
- Critical and creative thinking questions and activities
- Projects, activities, and Writer's Workshops
- Second-Language Support notes and manual
- *English as a Second Language (ESL) Manual*
- *Transition for ESL Students*

Special Education Without Special Classrooms

Meeting the individual needs of learning-disabled and other special pupils in a mainstream setting

More and more teachers are finding themselves teaching some children who, in the past, were taught in special education classes. Most teachers agree that this is a positive step in the education of special education students; however some teachers find it frustrating to meet the needs of an even wider variety of children than before.

Ideas are included for learning-disabled students, including those with dyslexia, as well as for students with physical, visual, and auditory disabilities.

The majority of special education students placed in mainstream classrooms have been learning-disabled students. For many of them, reading is a difficult process because of problems with visual or auditory acuity or perception. To be effective today, a reading program in a mainstream classroom must meet the needs of *all* students, including those with learning disabilities or other special needs.

HBJ Treasury of Literature was developed keeping special education students in mind. Meeting Individual Needs offers teachers specific strategies to help special students. Ideas are included for working with learning-disabled students, including those with dyslexia, as well as for students with physical, visual, and auditory disabilities. Flexibility in grouping throughout the program makes it especially easy to meet the needs of special students. ●

DR. ALONZO A. CRIM

Benjamin E. Mays Professor of Urban Educational Leadership at Georgia State University, Professor of Education at Spelman College and Consultant, HBJ Treasury of Literature

How to succeed with students at risk

There is no commonly agreed upon definition for "at risk." But although teachers may not agree on a definition, almost all will tell you they have students at risk sitting in their classrooms.

So who are students at risk? They can often be characterized by unsatisfactory academic achievement, performance below academic ability, poor self-concept, withdrawn behavior, or negative behavior not limited to a specific teacher or classroom situation.

While each student at risk would seem to have a dif-

No Risk of Failure

ferent profile, there are several strategies that research has shown to be effective for all students at risk.

1. Emphasize the positive.
2. Have high expectations.
3. Involve children in their own education.
4. Create opportunities for children to succeed.

Options within lesson plans allow all *students to meet common goals in a variety of ways.*

HBJ Treasury of Literature has embedded these strategies throughout the program. Meeting Individual Needs provides specific teaching strategies for students at risk. Options within lesson plans allow *all* students to meet common goals in a variety of ways. Self-Assessment Notes, Strategy Conferences, and Portfolio Conferences help students take an active part in their own education. Support, encouragement, and opportunities for individual successes fill every page of *HBJ Treasury of Literature*, and take the risk of failure out of teaching students at risk. ●

Pacing

A reading program that meets varied school schedules

A basic unit of instruction in *HBJ Treasury of Literature* takes from 4½ to 6 weeks to complete and is comprised of three themes.

A Typical Unit of Instruction / 4½ to 6 Weeks

Theme —	1	2	3
Weeks —	1½ – 2	1½ – 2	1½ – 2

While this model meets the needs of many teachers, we believe that classroom teachers must have the flexibility to make instructional pacing decisions based on their needs and the needs of their students. Special features, such as the following, have been embedded throughout the program to allow easy adjustment to meet any schedule:

- Managing the Literature-Based Classroom preceding each theme offers classroom-management suggestions that will vary the amount of time required to complete the theme. These range from the use of reader response groups for cooperative reading to suggestions for using additional literature to extend and enrich the themes.

- Sections labeled Teacher Choices are found throughout the lesson plans. Teachers will find many optional activities from which they may choose and that will help them adjust pacing.

Flexibility is the key component of the pacing of HBJ Treasury of Literature.

Reteach Lessons

When students have difficulty applying a strategy or skill, an array of multisensory teaching strategies is available to help you modify your methods and accommodate student needs.

Making Predictions

OBJECTIVE: *To use story evidence and prior knowledge to make predictions*

1. Focus

Share the following information with students:

When making a prediction, readers use clues from the story and what they already know to figure out what might happen next. Sometimes readers receive new information that makes them realize their predictions might need to be changed. Asking questions while reading helps readers make and revise their predictions.

2. Choose a Teaching Model

VISUAL MODEL Write the following paragraph on the board:

Ross has been campaigning for weeks. He really wants to be class treasurer. He already has three money-making ideas, and his classmates love them. Martin, his opponent, hasn't campaigned at all. Now, finally, it's election day.

Have a volunteer read the passage aloud. Ask students to predict who will win the election. Then discuss the passage with students, and underline the clues that helped lead them to the prediction. Invite students to suggest things they already knew that helped them make the prediction. (For example: To win an election, you have to work hard.) Then follow the suggestions in **Summarize/Reinforce.**

AUDITORY MODEL Read the passage in the Visual Model aloud. Ask students to predict who will win the election. Then read the passage again, and have students raise their hand each time they hear a clue that helped them make the prediction. Next, have volunteers state, in their own words, what they know from real-life experiences that helped them predict who will win. Then follow the suggestions in **Summarize/Reinforce.**

KINESTHETIC/MOTOR MODEL Have students form small groups. Duplicate the passage from the Visual Model, and give a copy to each group. Ask a volunteer to read the passage aloud while other volunteers role-play the parts of Ross and Martin. Encourage the other group members to predict who will win the election, and have them vote. Invite students to tell what clues in the passage or in the role-playing and what real-life experiences helped them predict who will win the election. Then follow the suggestions in **Summarize/ Reinforce.**

3. Summarize/Reinforce

Check students' understanding of the lesson by having them summarize what they learned. (Use story clues and what you already know to make predictions.) To reinforce the lesson, have students make predictions using other stories. Remind them to use the strategies in this lesson to help them make and revise predictions as they read.

Context Clues

OBJECTIVE: *To use contextual analysis to determine word meaning*

1. Focus

Share the following information with students:

When readers come across words they don't understand, they can sometimes figure out the words' meanings by thinking about what the other words in the sentence or paragraph mean.

2. Choose a Teaching Model

VISUAL MODEL Display or duplicate the following sentences in one column and definitions in another column:

1. Aldo walked through mud puddles to get his sneakers as dirty as possible so they would be <u>eligible</u> for the grubby-sneaker contest.
2. Thinking Aldo stood a fair chance to win, Aldo's mother <u>encouraged</u> him to enter the contest.
3. As his prize, Aldo selected a pair of blue suede sneakers that his mother had earlier <u>vetoed</u> buying because they were too expensive.
4. Trevor told the salesman he was sorry and that he didn't mean to be <u>dishonest</u>.

Definitions: said no to
untruthful
gave support to, urged
able to enter a contest

Read the first sentence aloud. Point to the underlined word, draw a line around the context clues (*mud puddles, as dirty as possible, grubby-sneaker contest*), and explain how they can help the reader figure out the meaning of the word *eligible*. Ask students to identify the correct definition for *eligible*. (*able to enter a contest*) Have students read the remaining sentences silently and look for clues to the meanings of the words *encouraged*, *vetoed*, and *dishonest*. Have volunteers read the sentences aloud and identify the correct definitions. Then ask students to draw a line around the context clues in each sentence and explain how the clues helped them figure out the meanings of the underlined words. Then follow the suggestions in **Summarize/Reinforce**.

AUDITORY MODEL Read aloud the first sentence from the examples in the Visual Model, and ask students to think about what they would do if they didn't know the meaning of the word *eligible*. Reread the sentence slowly and ask students to listen for clues that would help them figure out the meaning of *eligible*. Duplicate the three remaining example sentences and definitions from the Visual Model. Then have students work in pairs. Distribute the sentences and definitions to each pair. Have partners take turns reading each sentence aloud and choosing the correct definition for the underlined word. After all pairs have finished, ask volunteers to identify the context clues in each sentence and explain how the clues helped them figure out the meanings of the words. Then follow the suggestions in **Summarize/Reinforce**.

KINESTHETIC/MOTOR MODEL Display the sentences and definitions from the Visual Model. Have students work in pairs. Ask them to copy the sentences onto strips of paper and the definitions onto index cards. Then have pairs match each sentence with the correct definition, drawing a line around the context clues within the sentence. After partners have matched all four definitions with sentences, ask volunteers to discuss which clues in the sentences helped them arrive at their answers. Then follow the suggestions in **Summarize/Reinforce**.

3. Summarize/Reinforce

Check students' understanding of the lesson by having them summarize what they learned. (Readers can often figure out what an unfamiliar word means by examining the context clues in the sentence.) To reinforce this lesson, have students identify words they have recently learned while reading and explain how they figured out the words' meanings. Remind students to use the strategies from this lesson to help them understand unfamiliar words as they read.

Reference Sources

OBJECTIVE: *To understand why, when, and how to use an encyclopedia, an atlas, and a globe*

1. Focus

Share the following information with students:

Readers can use various reference sources to find more information on the topics about which they read. An *encyclopedia* is a set of books, or *volumes*, containing articles about a variety of topics. The volumes and the words within each volume are arranged in alphabetical order. Guide words at the top of each page in an encyclopedia help the reader find specific articles. Both an *atlas* and a *globe* provide information about the location of countries, cities, states, and bodies of water on the earth. An atlas is a book of maps; a globe is a three-dimensional model of the earth.

2. Choose a Teaching Model

VISUAL MODEL Write the word *sitar* on the board and explain that this is a musical instrument. Then have small groups of students locate information about the sitar in an encyclopedia. Have students work together to identify the guide words. Ask a volunteer to write on the board the letter or letters of the volume from which the article was taken. Then have students read the article to find out where the sitar originated. (India) Demonstrate locating India on a globe and in an atlas. Next, have students work in pairs to find in the encyclopedia other articles about instruments they play or know about. Help them develop a list of instruments, such as bagpipes, conga drums, and gongs. Ask volunteers to explain how they used the guide words to locate the articles. Have them tell where the instruments they chose originated and locate the country of origin on a globe and in an atlas. Then follow the suggestions in **Summarize/Reinforce.**

AUDITORY MODEL Write the word *sitar* on the board and explain to students that a sitar is a musical instrument. Ask a volunteer to say which letter or letters he or she would expect to find on the spine of an encyclopedia volume that contains an article on the sitar. Next, have a volunteer find an article on the sitar in an encyclopedia and identify the guide words. Then have another volunteer read the article aloud while students listen to find out in what country the sitar originated. (India) Demonstrate locating India on a globe and in an atlas. Then have students work in pairs to repeat the process for other instruments in which they are interested.

Suggest that pairs look for articles about such instruments as bagpipes, conga drums, and gongs, and encourage them to find the instruments' countries of origin. Have volunteers share the information they find. Then follow the suggestions in **Summarize/Reinforce.**

KINESTHETIC/MOTOR MODEL Write the word *sitar* on the board, and have students work in pairs to use the encyclopedia to find out what a sitar is and where it comes from. Invite a volunteer to pantomime a musician playing the sitar. Have partners write down the letter or letters of the volume in which they found the article, the guide words on the page, and what country the sitar comes from. (India) Help students find India on a globe and in an atlas. Next, ask them to use the encyclopedia to find information on another instrument in which they are interested, including its country of origin. Then encourage partners to locate that country on a globe or in an atlas and draw and label an outline map of the country. Have volunteers share their outlines with their classmates and explain how they used the various reference sources to find the information. Then follow the suggestions in **Summarize/Reinforce.**

3. Summarize/Reinforce

Check students' understanding of the lesson by having them summarize what they learned. (An encyclopedia provides information on a variety of subjects. An atlas or a globe can be used to find places on the earth.) To reinforce the lesson, have students use an encyclopedia, an atlas, and a globe to find information on styles of clothing worn or kinds of food eaten around the world. Remind students to use the strategies from this lesson to help them use reference sources to locate information.

Main Idea and Details

OBJECTIVE: *To understand how details in a paragraph or passage support a stated or unstated main idea*

1. Focus

Share the following information with students:

> The *main idea* is the one idea most of the sentences in a passage tell about. *Supporting details* give information about the main idea. The main idea may be stated or unstated. If it is unstated, the reader must use details in the passage to figure out the main idea.

2. Choose a Teaching Model

VISUAL MODEL   Recall with students what Koko has learned from Penny. Then draw the following web on the board, omitting the material in parentheses:

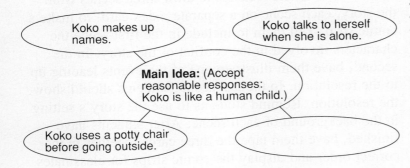

- Koko makes up names.
- Koko talks to herself when she is alone.
- **Main Idea:** (Accept reasonable responses: Koko is like a human child.)
- Koko uses a potty chair before going outside.

Help students use the three details listed to infer a main idea, and write it in the center of the diagram. Next, have volunteers suggest a fourth detail to write in the remaining space, and discuss with students how each detail supports the main idea. Then follow the suggestions in **Summarize/Reinforce.**

AUDITORY MODEL   Explain to students that you are going to list some facts about Koko. As you read aloud the three details listed in the web in the Visual Model, write them on the board. Have students use these details to suggest a main idea, and add their suggestion on the board. Next, have volunteers read aloud the main idea and identify and discuss other details from the story that support it. Then follow the suggestions in **Summarize/Reinforce.**

KINESTHETIC/MOTOR MODEL   Give each student four sentence strips. Read aloud the three details from the web in the Visual Model, and have students write each one on a separate strip. Then ask them to write a main idea that goes with these details on a separate piece of paper and arrange the detail strips to create a web as shown in the Visual Model. Next, have students find a fourth detail, write it on the remaining sentence strip, and place it on the web. Then follow the suggestions in **Summarize/Reinforce.**

3. Summarize/Reinforce

Check students' understanding by having them summarize what they learned. (Recognizing the important details in a passage helps readers identify the main idea. Knowing the main idea enables readers to better understand what they read.) You may want to reinforce the lesson by having students identify main ideas and supporting details in newspaper or magazine articles. Remind students to use the strategies from this lesson to recognize main ideas and details as they read.

Story Elements

OBJECTIVE: *To use setting, character, and plot to gain meaning*

1. Focus

Share the following information with students:

The basic elements of a story are the *major,* or the most important, *characters;* the *minor characters,* who reveal things about the major characters and help move the story along; the *setting,* which is the time and place in which a story happens; and the *plot,* which is usually a series of events that includes a conflict, or problem, and a resolution stating how the problem was solved. Readers understand better what they read by recognizing these elements.

2. Choose a Teaching Model

VISUAL MODEL   Have students recall "Election Day" from Unit One. Help them name the characters, identify the setting, and summarize the events of the story. Then display the following story map, and have volunteers fill in the details from "Election Day."

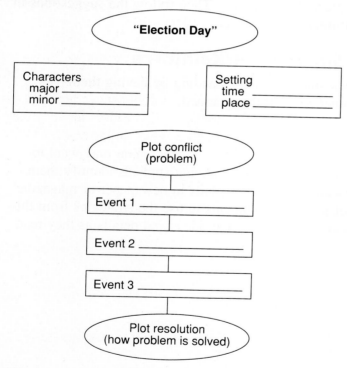

When the map is complete, point to its elements one at a time, and have students explain how each one is important to understanding the story. Then follow the suggestions in **Summarize/Reinforce.**

AUDITORY MODEL   Have students recall "Election Day" from Unit One and identify the characters, the setting, and the main events. Then display the story map from the Visual Model. Have students form pairs and take turns asking and answering questions based on the story map; for example: *Who are the major and minor characters? Where does the story take place?* After students have completed the activity, have volunteers describe how each element is important to understanding the story. Then follow the suggestions in **Summarize/ Reinforce.**

KINESTHETIC/MOTOR MODEL   Discuss "Election Day" with students. Help them identify the major and minor characters and the setting and summarize the main events. Then invite students to draw three scenes from the story, each scene on a separate index card, to make a comic strip. Tell them to include in the first scene the characters involved in the conflict of the story. In the second, have them illustrate one of the events leading up to the resolution. In the last scene, students should show the resolution. Remind students to use the story's setting in the background of each scene. After students have finished, have them tape the three cards together in the correct order and display the comic strips for classmates to enjoy. Then follow the suggestions in **Summarize/ Reinforce.**

3. Summarize/Reinforce

Check students' understanding of the lesson by having them summarize what they learned. (Knowing how to recognize the characters, setting, and plot of a story helps readers better understand what they read.) You may want to reinforce the lesson by having students create story maps for other stories they have read. Remind students to use the strategies from this lesson to help them identify story elements as they read.

Reference Sources

OBJECTIVE: *To locate information using a dictionary*

1. Focus

Share the following information with students:

> **Readers use dictionaries to find the definitions, pronunciations, or spellings of words they are unfamiliar with. Dictionary entries are listed in alphabetical order, with guide words at the top of each page to show the first and last entry on that page. A pronunciation key at the bottom of each page shows how to pronounce the respelling symbols.**

2. Choose a Teaching Model

VISUAL MODEL Write the following list of words on the board.

> muzzle
> haunches
> forepaw
> abdomen

Read the words aloud and ask volunteers to suggest possible guide words for the dictionary page on which each word would be found. Then have students use a dictionary to find the definitions of the words. Ask volunteers to pronounce each word and read aloud all of its definitions. Encourage students to draw a picture of a wolf on a sheet of paper and use the words from the list to label the appropriate parts. Then have students write four sentences, each containing one of the words and describing something about the wolf or something that happened to the wolf. Invite volunteers to read their sentences aloud. Then follow the suggestions in **Summarize/Reinforce.**

AUDITORY MODEL Have students work in pairs. Give each pair a dictionary and a copy of the list of words from the Visual Model. Ask one partner to read aloud one of the words and the other to suggest possible guide words for the dictionary page on which that word would be found. Then have partners locate the word in the dictionary, read the guide words at the top of the page, use the respellings and pronunciation key to help pronounce the word, and read the definition(s). Ask partners to alternate roles for the remaining words. Next, have partners orally compose and then write sentences on the topic of *wolves,* using each of the words at least once. Invite volunteers to read their sentences aloud. Then follow the suggestions in **Summarize/Reinforce.**

KINESTHETIC/MOTOR MODEL Write the words from the Visual Model on the board. Distribute four index cards to each student. Ask students to write each word on a separate index card and then look up the word in a dictionary. Have them write on the reverse side of the card the guide words from the dictionary page on which they found the word. Then ask students to write the definitions and a sentence using the word to tell something about a wolf. Next, have students draw a picture of a wolf. Explain to them that as you read aloud each word, they should place their word card over the appropriate part of the wolf in their drawings. Ask volunteers to read aloud their sentences using the words. Then follow the suggestions in **Summarize/Reinforce.**

3. Summarize/Reinforce

Check students' understanding of the lesson by having them summarize what they learned. (A reader can locate unfamiliar words in a dictionary by using the guide words. A reader can determine how to pronounce an unfamiliar word by using respellings and the pronunciation key.) You may want to reinforce the lesson by having students keep a list of new words they come across while reading and then look up those words in the dictionary. Remind students that dictionaries can help them better understand and enjoy what they read.

Sequence

OBJECTIVE: *To identify sequence of key story events*

1. Focus

Share the following information with students:

> **Events in a story usually happen in an order that makes sense. Authors include certain words, such as** *first, next, after, finally,* **and** *last,* **to signal the logical sequence of events. Recognizing the order in which events occur helps readers better understand what has happened and predict what might happen next in a story.**

2. Choose a Teaching Model

VISUAL MODEL   Refer students to the story "The Stormy Rescue" in Unit Two. Have them turn to the paragraph beginning *The rain was hard and slanting . . .* on Student Anthology page 155. Have students read the paragraph silently. Then ask volunteers to identify the time-order words in the paragraph. *(finally, then)* Next, have students work in pairs. Ask partners to read the next paragraph on the same page and identify the sequence terms. Then write on the board a numbered list, such as the one below, and fill in the first line as indicated.

1. It began to rain hard.
2. (I got up enough courage to turn my face out of the rain.)
3. (Then the lightning flashed.)
4. (I held the tree tightly.)
5. (After a while I began to slip.)
6. (Then I slowly went down.)

Have volunteers fill in the remaining lines (2–6) by summarizing in a sentence each event in the two paragraphs, taking care to include time-order words and phrases in the sentences. Then follow the suggestions in **Summarize/Reinforce.**

AUDITORY MODEL   Refer students to the story "The Stormy Rescue" in Unit Two. Have students work in pairs. Ask them to take turns reading the last two paragraphs on Student Anthology page 155 and the first two paragraphs on Student Anthology page 156. Ask students to note the words signaling sequence as they read or listen. When all have finished, write on the board the list of events from the first two paragraphs as indicated in the Visual Model. Ask partners to read the list and then work together to add to it from the next two paragraphs. Finally, have volunteers read aloud their lists. Encourage students to include their own time-order words in their retelling of the events. Then follow the suggestions in **Summarize/Reinforce.**

KINESTHETIC/MOTOR MODEL   Refer students to the story "The Stormy Rescue" in Unit Two, and instruct them to read the last two paragraphs on Student Anthology page 155. Then have students form small groups. Ask group members to work together to illustrate on separate sheets of paper each of the events mentioned in the two paragraphs. Then have them write at the top of each sheet some sentences, including time-order words, that describe the events. Finally, have volunteers order and display their drawings for their classmates and discuss the sentences they wrote. Then follow the suggestions in **Summarize/Reinforce.**

3. Summarize/Reinforce

Check students' understanding of the lesson by having them summarize what they learned. (Story events happen in a certain order and are usually signaled by time-order words or phrases.) To reinforce this lesson, have students use time-order words to retell another story they have read. Remind them to use the strategies from this lesson to help them follow the order of story events as they read.

Cause and Effect

OBJECTIVE: *To understand multiple effects of a single cause and to infer causes and effects*

1. Focus

Share the following information with students:

> *Effects* **are events that happen in a story.** *Causes* **explain why these events occur. An effect may have more than one cause and a cause may have more than one effect. Cause-and-effect relationships may either be implied or made obvious to readers by the use of certain words and phrases, such as** *because,* *since,* **and** *as a result.* **Sometimes causes and effects are not stated directly by the author, so readers must use story information and their own knowledge to figure out what the missing information might be. Recognizing causes and their effects in a story helps readers understand how story events fit together.**

2. Choose a Teaching Model

VISUAL MODEL   Have students turn to "The Amazing Beans" and reread the paragraph on Student Anthology page 208 beginning *They lay there in the dark waiting,* continuing through the paragraph on page 210 beginning *Since the beds were damp.* . . . Then display the following cause-and-effect chart on the board:

Effects (What happened?)	Cause (Why did it happen?)

Have students identify the effects of Norman and Michael's actions in this part of the story by asking them to tell the various things that happened as a result of Norman's shooting the Water Blaster. (Their room got wet; their parents woke up; they had to sleep on the couch.) Have volunteers write their suggestions on the board in the *Effects* column. Then ask students to name the cause of Norman and Michael's actions. Guide them to use clue words such as *because, since,* and *as a result* in their responses. Have volunteers write their suggestions on the board in the *Cause* column. Then follow the suggestions in **Summarize/Reinforce.**

AUDITORY MODEL   Display the chart headings from the Visual Model. Have students work in pairs, taking turns reading paragraphs of the passage indicated in the Visual Model. Ask students to think about the effects and the cause of the Water Blaster episode. Prompt them with the questions *What happened?* and *Why did it happen?* Remind students that sometimes authors do not state causes and effects directly, so readers must figure them out on their own by using story details and their own personal knowledge. Guide students to use clue words such as *because, since,* or *as a result* in their answers. Finally, ask volunteers to read aloud their responses. Then follow the suggestions in **Summarize/Reinforce.**

KINESTHETIC/MOTOR MODEL   Encourage students to work in pairs. Have them read the passage indicated in the Visual Model and write a sentence describing each of the story events in the Water Blaster episode on a separate index card. Then ask them to read each detail and ask themselves why this event happened. Tell partners to write on a separate index card a sentence stating the cause of each effect, using clue words such as *because, since,* or *as a result.* When partners are finished, invite them to shuffle the stack of cards and take turns drawing a card, reading the sentence, and telling whether it describes a cause or an effect. Then follow the suggestions in **Summarize/Reinforce.**

3. Summarize/Reinforce

Check students' understanding of the lesson by having them summarize what they learned. (To identify an effect, readers should ask themselves *What happened?* To identify a cause, readers should ask themselves *Why did it happen? A cause may have more than one effect.*) To reinforce this lesson, have students look for cause-and-effect relationships in favorite passages of a selection they have already read. Remind them to use the strategies from this lesson to help them identify effects and their causes as they read.

Structural Analysis

OBJECTIVE: *To use Greek and Latin roots for independent decoding of unfamiliar words*

1. Focus

Share the following information with students:

Many English words have roots that come from Greek and Latin. Readers who learn to recognize these roots can often use what they know about the roots' meanings to help them determine the meanings of words that contain them.

2. Choose a Teaching Model

VISUAL MODEL   Write the following lists on the board:

carnivorous	*caro:* "flesh" (Latin)
herbivorous	*herba:* "grass, herb" (Latin)
omnivorous	*omni:* "all, without restriction" (Latin)
botanist	*botanikos:* "plant" (Greek); *iste:* "a specialist in a science" (Greek)
biologist	*bios:* "life" (Greek); *logos:* "study or discourse" (Greek)

Remind students they have already learned that the word *carnivorous* comes from the Latin *caro*, meaning "flesh," and *vorus*, meaning "to eat." Point out that two of the other words in the first list also include the Latin root for "to eat." Then write the following context sentences on the board.

1. Biologists studying the behavior of deer have found that these animals are strictly herbivorous, feeding primarily on tree leaves and grass.
2. Because humans eat food that comes from both plants and animals, they are considered omnivorous creatures.
3. The Venus flytrap and other flesh-eating plants are the subjects of many studies done by botanists.

Help students determine the meanings of the underlined words from the context and from what they know about the meanings of the Greek and Latin roots. Then follow the suggestions in **Summarize/Reinforce**.

AUDITORY MODEL   Tell students that the Latin root *trans* means "across, beyond, or through." Write the following Latin roots on the board:

parere: "to be visible"   **portare: "to carry"**
mittere: "to send"   **lucere: "to shine"**

Then read aloud the following sentences and ask students to listen for the word that contains the Latin root *trans*:

1. Amy could see through the transparent tablecloth that the cat was hiding under the table.
2. The sun was shining so brightly that the translucence of the stained glass windows was very striking.
3. The telegraph was a remarkable invention, allowing people to transmit messages across great distances.
4. Trucks and trains are often used to transport goods from one area of the country to another.

After reading each sentence, write the underlined word on the board. Read the sentence again, and ask for volunteers to use the list of Latin roots, together with context clues from the sentence, to tell what they think the word means. Repeat the above process, using the roots and sentences from the Visual Model. Then follow the suggestions in **Summarize/Reinforce**.

KINESTHETIC/MOTOR MODEL   Have students work in small groups. Prepare sets of Greek and Latin root cards for each group by writing each of the following on a separate index card: *caro, omnis, herba, botanikos, iste, bios, logos, trans, parere, lucere, portare, mittere.* Write the meaning of each root on the back of its card. (These are listed in the Visual and Auditory models.) Then read aloud the seven context sentences from the Visual and Auditory models. For each sentence, have the groups first identify a word containing one or more of the roots, then find the correct root or roots from among their cards, and finally use them to figure out the meaning of the word. Then follow the suggestions in **Summarize/Reinforce.**

3. Summarize/Reinforce

Check students' understanding of the lesson by having them summarize what they learned. (Recognizing Greek and Latin roots can help readers figure out the meanings of unfamiliar words.) To reinforce the lesson, have students look in a dictionary to find other words with the roots presented here. Remind students to use the strategies from this lesson when they come across words with Greek and Latin roots.

Graphic Aids

OBJECTIVE: *To interpret information on maps and in tables*

1. Focus

Share the following information with students:

> **Graphic aids, such as maps and tables, help readers better understand information by showing it in a different way or by providing additional details.**

2. Choose a Teaching Model

VISUAL MODEL   Display the table below.

Table of California Forest Land	
Forest Type	**Total area (thousands of acres)**
Forest open to harvesting	17,944
Forest not open to harvesting	22,216

Remind students that a table is a chart of numbers in columns that allows readers to make comparisons—statistical information is often best presented in this form. Have students point to the information in the table that helps them answer the question.

- **How many acres of forest land are open to harvesting in California?** *(17,944)*
- **Is the amount of forest land that's open to harvesting in California greater or less than the amount not open to harvesting?** *(less than)*

Next, display a map of California and discuss the following map features: The compass rose shows directions on a map; the legend explains colors or symbols that appear on a map; the coordinates are letters and/or numbers on the sides of a map used to help locate places; the index lists the coordinates used to locate places on a map. Have students identify the following on the map:

1. The location of San Francisco
2. The location of the Trinity National Forest
3. The direction one travels to go from San Francisco to the Trinity National Forest
4. The symbol used to denote a city on the map

Then follow the suggestions in **Summarize/Reinforce.**

AUDITORY MODEL   Display the table from the Visual Model and describe it using the information given. Have volunteers orally answer the questions listed in the Visual Model. Then have students form pairs. Have partners ask each other additional questions about the information presented in the table. Next, display a map of California and discuss with students the map features listed in the Visual Model. Ask volunteers to locate each of these features on the map and describe which features they would use to find the locations of San Francisco and of the Trinity National Forest. Then follow the suggestions in **Summarize/Reinforce.**

KINESTHETIC/MOTOR MODEL   Duplicate the table from the Visual Model. Distribute the copies to pairs of students. Then have partners look at the table as you discuss its features and purpose using the information listed in the Visual Model. Ask students to draw a line around the number in the table that shows how many acres of forest are not open for harvesting.

Then provide partners with a map of California and discuss the map features mentioned in the Visual Model as they look it over. Ask partners to use the map to tell whether the Trinity National Forest is north or south of San Francisco. Next, have partners take turns tracing the route a bus would take to get from San Francisco to the Trinity National Forest. Then follow the suggestions in **Summarize/Reinforce.**

3. Summarize/Reinforce

Check students' understanding of the lesson by having them summarize what they learned. (Knowing how to read maps and tables helps readers understand information.) To reinforce the lesson, display other examples of graphic aids and discuss other uses for them. Remind students to use the strategies from this lesson to help them understand information presented graphically.

Following Directions

OBJECTIVE: *To follow written directions by using time-order words*

1. Focus

Share the following information with students:

Following directions in the correct order will help readers achieve the desired results. When the steps in a set of directions are not numbered, readers should look for time-order words that indicate the order in which the steps should be followed. Some examples of time-order words are *first, second, then, next, last,* and *finally*. Being able to identify these words will help readers follow directions successfully.

2. Choose a Teaching Model

VISUAL MODEL Distribute a copy of the following passage to each student. Have students follow along silently as you read the passage aloud.

How to Make Blackberry Pie

The first step in making a blackberry pie is to find some blackberry bushes and pick about a quart of berries. Next, rinse the berries in cool water. After the berries have been rinsed, put them in a ready-made pie crust and sprinkle a small amount of sugar over the berries. Then bake the pie at 350° for about 45 minutes. Finally, take the pie out of the oven and let it cool for at least an hour.

Ask students to circle the time-order words in the paragraph. Then have students work in pairs to create a numbered list of directions based on the passage. Remind them to use the time-order words to help them build their list. Next, develop a single set of numbered directions by having pairs share their lists. Discuss whether following the rewritten directions will achieve the desired result. Then follow the suggestions in **Summarize/Reinforce.**

AUDITORY MODEL Have students listen as you read aloud the passage from the Visual Model. Then reread the passage a second time, and ask students to raise their hand each time they hear a time-order word. Next, have students form pairs and retell the directions in their own words, using time-order words to show the sequence of the steps to be followed. Then follow the suggestions in **Summarize/Reinforce.**

KINESTHETIC/MOTOR MODEL Have students bring to school the label from a can of soup, a jar of instant coffee or hot chocolate, or any food or beverage item that has a set of simple directions on the label. Distribute an index card to each student, and have students rewrite the directions from the label onto the card using time-order words. Then ask students to write the name of the food or beverage at the top of the index card. Have students share the information on the index cards while classmates pantomime following the directions. Ask students to discuss whether following the rewritten directions would lead them to the desired result. After all students have shared their directions, have them put their cards into a file box labeled "Recipes." Then follow the suggestions in **Summarize/Reinforce.**

3. Summarize/Reinforce

Check students' understanding of the lesson by having them summarize what they learned. (Following directions in order helps one achieve the correct results. Time-order words indicate what the correct order is in a set of directions.) You may want to reinforce this lesson by having students write directions for accomplishing daily tasks, using time-order words. Remind students to use the strategies from this lesson to help them understand the order in which events occur in a story and the order in which directions should be followed.

Drawing Conclusions

OBJECTIVE: *To use story information and real-life experiences to draw valid conclusions*

1. Focus

Share the following information with students:

Because authors do not always explain everything that happens in a story, readers must sometimes combine what they already know with story details to draw valid conclusions. Knowing how to draw valid conclusions helps readers figure out the reasons behind story events and the behavior of characters.

2. Choose a Teaching Model

VISUAL MODEL   Direct students' attention to Student Anthology page 312 and read aloud the passage beginning with *Mother introduced them . . .* and ending with *Peter was interrupted by the adults' laughter.* Then write the following sentences on the board:

I conclude that the adults thought Peter was making up a silly story. Based on story evidence and my knowledge, I know this is a valid conclusion. I read that the adults laughed when Peter described the afternoon's events. I know that adults often laugh when a child tells a silly story as if it were something that had really happened.

As you discuss the sentences with students, underline the words that indicate prior knowledge and those that indicate a clue from the story. Next, have students work in pairs to write similar sentences to show how they would use story clues and what they already know to explain how to reach the following conclusion: *Daniel and Walter Budwing are going to have a wild and dangerous adventure playing Jumanji.* Ask a volunteer to write his or her sentences on the board, and invite students to discuss them. Then follow the suggestions in **Summarize/Reinforce.**

AUDITORY MODEL   Have students turn to the passage cited in the Visual Model. Have students work in pairs, and ask one partner to read aloud the passage. Then have partners work together to draw a valid conclusion about why the adults laughed, using details from the story and their own experiences. Model for students a possible conclusion using this format: I *conclude* that the adults thought Peter was making up a silly story because I

read _____ and I *know* _____. Ask partners to state their conclusions and explain how they drew them. Next, have partners repeat the process by reading the last three paragraphs of "Jumanji" to help them draw a valid conclusion about why Daniel and Walter Budwing will have a wild adventure when they play Jumanji. Then follow the suggestions in **Summarize/Reinforce.**

KINESTHETIC/MOTOR MODEL   Give each student three index cards labeled *Clues from the Story, What I Know,* and *Conclusion,* and have them fill in each card using one of the passages mentioned in the Auditory Model. Next, ask them to arrange the cards in a logical sequence (Clues + What I Know = Conclusion). Then follow the suggestions in **Summarize/Reinforce.**

3. Summarize/Reinforce

Check students' understanding of the lesson by having them summarize what they learned. (Sometimes readers need to draw conclusions because a writer does not always tell everything that happens in a story. Use story details and personal experience to draw valid conclusions.) To reinforce the lesson, have students review other selections they have read, identifying conclusions they drew and the clues and personal knowledge that led to those conclusions. Remind students to use strategies from this lesson to help them understand what they read.

Structural Analysis

OBJECTIVE: *To use base words, prefixes, and suffixes for independent decoding of words*

1. Focus

Share the following information with students:

> A *prefix,* such as *re-* or *un-,* is a group of letters added to the beginning of a base word to change the meaning of that word. A *suffix,* such as *-able* or *-ly,* is a group of letters added at the end of a word to change its meaning. Adding a suffix will also change how the word is used. Knowing how to recognize base words with prefixes and suffixes helps readers figure out the pronunciations and meanings of unfamiliar words.

2. Choose a Teaching Model

VISUAL MODEL Display the following sentences and chart:

1. **Tom reassured his mother that he, Jim, and Theresa could take care of themselves.**
2. **Jim proudly offered his thermos to the Letonian.**
3. **The Letonian was uninterested in the ice cubes because they already have ice on Leto.**
4. **At first, Mrs. Wilson found her children's story totally unbelievable.**

Prefix/Suffix	Meaning
re- un- -ly -able	"again" "not" "in a certain way" "capable of"

Read the first sentence, pointing to the word *reassured.* Ask a volunteer to identify the prefix and use the chart to tell what it means. Have students think about the meaning of *assured* and tell how adding the prefix *re-* changes that meaning. Then read the second sentence and point to the word *proudly.* Ask students to identify the suffix, tell its meaning, and explain how it changes the way in which *proud* is used. Have students read the remaining sentences. Ask volunteers to identify the word in each sentence that includes one of the listed prefixes and/or suffixes and tell how each of these affixes alters the meaning of the base word. Then follow the suggestions in **Summarize/Reinforce.**

AUDITORY MODEL Display the chart from the Visual Model. Have students work in pairs. Distribute a copy of the sentences to each pair. Have one partner read the first sentence slowly, while the other partner writes down the word or words containing a prefix and/or suffix. Next, have partners alternate roles and repeat the same process for the remaining sentences. After the words have been identified, have partners work together to underline the prefixes and draw a line around the suffixes in all four sentences. Have volunteers share their answers with their classmates, explaining how the meaning of the base word changed in each case. Then follow the suggestions in **Summarize/Reinforce.**

KINESTHETIC/MOTOR MODEL Display the chart from the Visual Model. Have students form two teams—the Prefixes and the Suffixes. Tell students that you are going to read four sentences. Explain that the Prefix team members should stand if they hear a word with a listed prefix, and the Suffix team members should stand if they hear a word with a listed suffix. Read aloud slowly the first sentence from the Visual Model. Ask a volunteer who's standing to identify the word with the prefix and its parts—base word and prefix. Encourage another team member to explain how the prefix added to the meaning of the base word. Repeat the process with the remaining sentences. Then follow the suggestions in **Summarize/Reinforce.**

3. Summarize/Reinforce

Check students' understanding of the lesson by having them summarize what they learned. (Recognizing base words, prefixes, and suffixes helps readers figure out the meanings and pronunciations of unfamiliar words.) To reinforce this lesson, have students find and decode unfamiliar words with prefixes and suffixes in the next selection. Remind them to use the strategies from this lesson to help them as they read.

Summarizing

OBJECTIVE: *To develop global meaning through summarizing*

1. Focus

Share the following information with students:

> **Summarizing is a way for readers to restate the logical sequence of events in a story in their own words. In a summary, one combines, or synthesizes, the author's most important ideas. Knowing how to summarize helps readers better understand and remember what they read.**

2. Choose a Teaching Model

VISUAL MODEL   Display the following questions:

- **Who or what is the story about?**
- **Where does the story take place?**
- **How does the story begin?**
- **What happens next in the story?**
- **How does the story end?**

Have students turn to the story "Jumanji," which begins on Student Anthology page 296. Review the story with them by asking the above questions. Have students write brief answers to each question on a sheet of paper. Next, have students work in pairs, allowing them time to reread the story if necessary. Ask partners to write a summary of the story, referring to the questions and answers as needed. Finally, have volunteers read their summaries aloud. Then follow the suggestions in **Summarize/ Reinforce.**

AUDITORY MODEL   Write on the board the questions from the Visual Model. Ask students to open their books to the story "Jumanji," which begins on Student Anthology page 296. Briefly review the story with students by reading aloud each question on the board, allowing time for students to take notes. Then have students work in pairs. Have one partner ask the first question on the board and the other partner answer the question, using his or her notes. Then tell partners to alternate roles in answering the remaining questions. Encourage pairs to summarize the story orally, and have volunteers share their oral summaries with their classmates. Then follow the suggestions in **Summarize/ Reinforce.**

KINESTHETIC/MOTOR MODEL   Write on the board the questions from the Visual Model. Have students work in pairs. Ask one partner to tell a favorite story or to recount something that recently happened to him or her. Encourage the student to pantomime key actions. Ask the other partner to take notes that contain the answers to the questions on the board and then write a summary of the story, thinking especially about what actions were pantomimed. Invite partners to reverse roles. When students have finished the activity, ask volunteers to share their summaries with their classmates. Then follow the suggestions in **Summarize/Reinforce.**

3. Summarize/Reinforce

Check students' understanding of the lesson by having them summarize what they learned. (To *summarize* a story, readers combine, or synthesize, only the most important ideas and retell them in their own words.) To reinforce this lesson, have students summarize newspaper articles they have read or television programs or movies they have seen. Remind them to use the strategies from this lesson to help them summarize as they read.

Paraphrasing

OBJECTIVE: *To develop global meaning through paraphrasing*

1. Focus

Share the following information with students:

When readers restate a passage or story in their own words, they are *paraphrasing*. A paraphrase should include the author's ideas only, not the reader's opinion of what the author says. Paraphrasing helps readers better understand and remember what they read.

2. Choose a Teaching Model

VISUAL MODEL   Refer students to the story "Muddy Sneakers," which begins on Student Anthology page 40. Review the story with them by writing on the board *Who? What? When? Where? Why?* and *How?* Have volunteers briefly answer the questions. Next, have students open to the last paragraph on page 44, which begins *Trevor's sneakers worried Aldo.* Have students work in pairs to write a paraphrased version of the paragraph. Encourage them to use time-order words, such as *then, next,* and *finally,* to make their statements read more smoothly. Suggest that they reread their completed paraphrases to make sure they used their own words and did not change the meaning of the original passage. Finally, have volunteers read their responses aloud. Then follow the suggestions in **Summarize/ Reinforce.**

AUDITORY MODEL   Briefly review the story "Muddy Sneakers" from Unit One with students by asking volunteers to answer the following questions: *Who is the main character in the story? When and where does the story take place? What happens in the story? Why does it happen? How does the story end?* Then read aloud the passage indicated in the Visual Model. Ask students to think about the main idea and details of the paragraph. Then reread the passage slowly, allowing time for students to take notes. Have students work in pairs to write a paraphrased version of the passage. Remind them to use time-order words in their statements. Suggest to students that they ask themselves the following questions: *Did I use my own words? Is the meaning of my paraphrase the same as the original passage?* Finally, have volunteers take turns reading aloud their paraphrases to their classmates. Then follow the suggestions in **Summarize/Reinforce.**

KINESTHETIC/MOTOR MODEL   Refer students to the story "Muddy Sneakers" in Unit One. Review the story with students by having them answer the questions *Who? What? When? Where? Why?* and *How?* Then ask students to read silently the passage indicated in the Visual Model. Have students form eight groups, and assign each group a sentence of the passage. Encourage group members to study their assigned sentence. Then have the first group pantomime the action in their sentence while a volunteer from that group writes a new sentence on the board that restates or explains the first idea in the passage. Instruct the other groups to pantomime and add their sentences to the board until the entire passage has been retold in the students' own words and with actions. Remind students to use time-order words as appropriate. Have the combined groups of students try to evaluate whether they successfully retold the paragraph in their own words while retaining the meaning of the original passage. Then follow the suggestions in **Summarize/Reinforce.**

3. Summarize/Reinforce

Check students' understanding of the lesson by having them summarize what they learned. (Readers are *paraphrasing* when they restate in their own words a passage or story.) To reinforce this lesson, have students paraphrase passages from other stories they have read. Remind them to use the strategies from this lesson to help them paraphrase as they read.

Fact and Opinion

OBJECTIVE: *To distinguish between facts and opinions*

1. Focus

Share the following information with students:

A *fact* is a statement that can be proved, and an *opinion* is a statement of feeling or belief. Words such as *probably, perhaps, often,* and *sometimes* are clues that a statement is an opinion. Knowing the difference between facts and opinions helps readers better understand and evaluate what they read.

2. Choose a Teaching Model

VISUAL MODEL   Duplicate for each student the following passage, omitting the words in parentheses:

> **Native American artists used materials provided by the land to create their work.** *(fact)* **The Algonquian people of the Northeastern woodlands in what is now New England used clay from the riverbanks to make pottery, and reeds from the plants to weave baskets.** *(fact)* **These artifacts may be among the most skillfully crafted of that region.** *(opinion)* **The Pueblo people of the Southwest also made use of the land.** *(fact)* **They developed a special technique for working with silver, used especially for making jewelry.** *(fact)* **The Pueblo necklaces and bracelets are probably the most ornate jewelry in the Southwestern area.** *(opinion)*

Write the headings *Fact* and *Opinion* on the board. Read the passage aloud with students, pausing after each statement, and have students tell whether it is a fact or an opinion. Have volunteers record under the appropriate headings any clue words that helped them identify the type of statement. Then follow the suggestions in **Summarize/Reinforce.**

AUDITORY MODEL   Read aloud the paragraph from the Visual Model, omitting the words in parentheses. Then have students work in pairs to discuss which statements are facts and which are opinions. Tell partners you are going to read the passage aloud slowly a second time and that one of them should stand when you read facts, and the other should stand when you read opinions. Next, read the passage aloud, one sentence at a time. The

appropriate partner should stand when you finish reading the sentence. Have a volunteer from the group that is standing explain how he or she arrived at the answer, pointing out any clue words that helped. Continue with the remaining sentences in the passage. Then follow the suggestions in **Summarize/Reinforce.**

KINESTHETIC/MOTOR MODEL   Duplicate the passage from the Visual Model, omitting the words in parentheses. Begin each sentence on a new line. Distribute copies of the passage to pairs of students and have them cut the sentences apart. Invite partners to shuffle the sentence strips and place them face down in a pile. Tell partners to take turns drawing a strip and reading aloud the sentence. Then ask partners to determine whether the statement is a fact or an opinion. Instruct students to separate the strips into two piles. Finally, have volunteers reread each sentence and explain how they figured out whether it was a fact or an opinion. Then follow the suggestions in **Summarize/Reinforce.**

3. Summarize/Reinforce

Check students' understanding of the lesson by having them summarize what they learned. (A *fact* is a statement that can be proved to find out whether it is true. An *opinion* is a statement of feeling or belief.) To reinforce the lesson, have students identify facts and opinions in a newspaper or magazine article. Remind students that knowing the difference between facts and opinions helps readers better understand and evaluate what they read.

Comparing and Contrasting

OBJECTIVE: *To determine likenesses and differences*

1. Focus

Share the following information with students:

> Writers show how two characters or things are alike by *comparing* them; they show how those characters or things are different by *contrasting* them. Writers often use characters' behavior and what they say to show differences and similarities. Sometimes writers will use words such as *but, yet, still,* and *although* to show that a contrast is being made, and *also, too,* and *similarly* to show that a comparison is being made. Identifying likenesses and differences between characters or things helps readers better understand what they read.

2. Choose a Teaching Model

VISUAL MODEL   Distribute copies of the following passage:

> I went to the shoe store to buy a pair of sneakers. I found two pairs I liked, Swifties and Quicksters, but I had only enough money for one pair. Both pairs were bright green, but the Swifties had orange stripes on the sides. The laces on the Quicksters were yellow-and-black checked, and the soles were purple. The salesperson said both pairs would help me run very fast. I decided to drop one shoe from each pair off the roof of the shoe store to find out which pair would help me jump the highest. The Quickster hit the pavement and bounced up about two feet, but the Swiftie bounced up over my head.

Have students read the passage. Then ask volunteers to tell what things are being compared and contrasted. Have students work in pairs to draw a line under the differences and draw a line around the likenesses. Then create a chart on the board like the one below to summarize the likenesses and differences.

Likenesses	Differences
(like them both; both bright green; both make a person run fast)	(Swifties—orange stripes on the sides; bounced high Quicksters—yellow-and-black checked laces; purple soles; didn't bounce as high)

Discuss with students any words that helped them figure out that a comparison or contrast was being made. Then follow the suggestions in **Summarize/Reinforce**.

AUDITORY MODEL   Ask students to keep the following questions in mind as you read aloud the passage from the Visual Model: *What things are being compared? What things are being contrasted?* Repeat the questions after reading the passage and ask volunteers to respond. Next, have students create a chart similar to the one in the Visual Model. Reread the passage and tell students to keep the following questions in mind as they use information from the passage to fill in the chart: *How are the two pairs of sneakers alike? How are they different?* Afterwards have volunteers summarize the passage orally. Ask students to share any words that helped them know a comparison or contrast was being made. Then follow the suggestions in **Summarize/Reinforce**.

KINESTHETIC/MOTOR MODEL   Distribute copies of the passage and the chart from the Visual Model. Have students work in pairs to read the passage and fill in the chart. Then have one partner draw a picture of the Swiftie sneakers and the other partner draw a picture of the Quickster sneakers. Partners should exchange drawings and check that all the details from the passage have been included and are accurate. Have volunteers share their charts and drawings with their classmates. Ask students to name any special words that helped them understand when a comparison or contrast was being made. Then follow the suggestions in **Summarize/ Reinforce**.

3. Summarize/Reinforce

Check students' understanding of the lesson by having them summarize what they learned. (To compare or contrast, a reader must ask how two or more characters or things are alike or how they are different.) You may want to reinforce the lesson by having students compare and contrast characters or things in selections they have read recently. Remind students to use this strategy to help them understand and enjoy what they read.

Multiculturalism

The literature and activities in *HBJ Treasury of Literature* celebrate cultural similarities and diversity, foster pride in cultural heritage and history, and open a world of possibilities for children.

Multiculturalism is most effective when it is infused throughout the curriculum.

Multicultural Literature:

A Celebration of Diversity

The widening scope of multicultural literature

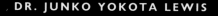

DR. JUNKO YOKOTA LEWIS

*Assistant Professor, Department
of Curriculum and Instruction
at the University of Northern
Iowa and Author,* HBJ
Treasury of Literature

DR. ROLANDO R. HINOJOSA-SMITH

*Ellen Clayton Garwood Professor
of English and the Mari Sabusawa
Michener Chair of Creative
Writing at the University of Texas
at Austin and Consultant*
HBJ Treasury of Literature

When one considers the increasing diversity of students in American schools today, the need for literature that reflects the multitude of their backgrounds becomes immediately obvious. All children benefit from having access to a multicultural body of literature. All children develop a sense of pride and increased self-concept by reading about characters with the same heritage as their own and with whom they can identify. And all children are able to develop an understanding of other cultures and see issues from the perspectives of various cultures by having vicarious experiences through multicultural literature. Allowing children to take part in a variety of cultural experiences such as those offered in *HBJ Treasury of Literature* opens the possibilities for future understandings.

The multicultural literature that children read in school must not only be of literary and aesthetic merit, but must portray a culturally-conscious view of the people represented. Without cultural accuracy, it is likely that stereotyped images of people will be perpetuated and that children will develop misinformed images of other cultures.

We are fortunate to be educating children in an age when an ever-increasing number of high-quality multicultural books such as the ones in *HBJ Treasury of Literature* can be found. These books provide a variety of perspectives for children. Some, such as folklore, give insights into the traditions and values of a cultural group. John Steptoe's *Mufaro's Beautiful Daughters* is an example of an African folktale endorsing the belief that greed and selfishness are bad and that kindness and generosity are rewarded.

HBJ Treasury of Literature also contains literature that tells about the experiences of people in other countries. For example, *Bringing the Rain to Kapiti Plain* by Verna Aardema is a cumulative tale that tells the story of a drought in Kenya. In *The Chalk Doll* by Charlotte Pomerantz, a mother shares with her daughter what it was like to grow up in Jamaica.

The multicultural literature found in *HBJ Treasury of Literature* can help children understand the experiences of a cultural group when they are located in the United States.

Books such as *Chin Chiang and the Dragon's Dance* reflect the experiences of Chinese Americans by telling about a dance from the Chinese culture that is popular in America today. *Fiesta!* tells of celebrating the Mexican American holiday Cinco de Mayo. Virginia Hamilton's *The House of Dies Drear* is set in a house where slaves once escaped to freedom through the tunnels. Hamilton shares historical information about slavery and the Underground Railroad. This book reflects experiences unique to African Americans. *Dream Wolf* is the story of a Plains Indian boy and a wolf. In it, Paul Goble shares the Native American viewpoint that we must have greater respect for wildlife or it will vanish.

While one role of the multicultural literature in *HBJ Treasury of Literature* is to help children appreciate the uniqueness of various cultures, another is to help children recognize values and experiences common to many cultures. For example, *My Friends* by Taro Gomi was originally written and illustrated in Japan and intended for a Japanese audience. The book was later translated and distributed in other countries because the concept of learning things from friends has a universal appeal. Likewise, the love between family members is a universal theme found in stories from many cultures. In Mildred Pitts Walter's "Spending Time with Grandpa," taken from *Justin and the Best Biscuits in the World*, we meet an African American family with strong love for one another. Carmen Lomas Garza's *Family Pictures* also reflects the theme of family bonding.

Allowing children to take part in a variety of cultural experiences...opens the possibilities for future understandings.

Including a variety of fine multicultural literature in *HBJ Treasury of Literature* does more than just delight children. It helps prepare them for their roles as global citizens. It allows them to see and appreciate the richness of the increasing diversity within their communities, their nation, and their world. ●

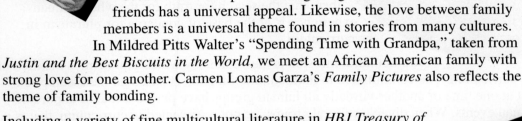

Look for
- Literature that allows children to take part in a variety of cultural experiences
- Literature that portrays a culturally conscious view of the people represented
- Literature that is consistently of the highest literary quality and aesthetic merit

Multicultural Infusion

A curriculum based on the truth of the whole human experience

As with any curriculum movement, the search for truth is the basis for change. It should not be surprising, then, that the search for truth for the whole human experience is at the base of concerns for pluralism in the curriculum.

Multicultural infusion is the vehicle by which pluralism is instilled in the curriculum. The commitment to multicultural infusion is based on the assumption that at one time or another virtually all human groups have played a role in important human events. When diverse cultural groups are not represented in curriculum, that is a relatively sure sign that important truths have been overlooked.

From its conception and throughout its development, the authors and consultants of *HBJ Treasury of Literature* have been committed to truth. The selection of literature for the program was governed by the principle of accurately reflecting diverse cultural groups. The same care went into creating each of the program's components. Multicultural advisors helped shape each phase of the program, acting on a mission to make *HBJ Treasury of Literature* truly represent the people of our nation.

In *HBJ Treasury of Literature*, Cultural Awareness Notes, Multicultural Perspectives, and Multicultural Connections reflect the truth of the human experience. They recognize the contributions of individuals from diverse cultures and the contributions of the cultures themselves. They cultivate in students an appreciation for diversity.

DR. ASA G. HILLIARD III

Fuller E. Callaway Professor of Urban Education, Department of Educational Foundations, Georgia State University and Senior Consultant, HBJ Treasury of Literature

> *When diverse cultural groups are not represented in curriculum, that is a relatively sure sign that important truths have been overlooked.*

We know that learners are more apt to be attracted to materials with which they can identify. However, it is not necessary to contrive situations where this would occur, since the truth of the human experience is that it reflects cultural pluralism. All school subjects should reflect this reality. In fact, pluralism in the curriculum should be seen as an enrichment to the school experience of all students.

HBJ Treasury of Literature offers teachers a socially responsible reading curriculum by helping children in their quest for knowledge and truth. ●

Look for

- Literature that accurately reflects diverse cultural groups

- Cultural Awareness Notes, Multicultural Perspectives, and Multicultural Connections that reflect the truth of the human experience

We believe in assessment that encourages students to share in the responsibility of assessing their learning. Assessment should help teachers and students understand what a student can do successfully rather than emphasize what a student can't do.

Some Old Ideas on Testing Flunk Out

New assessment tools measure what students really know.

DR. ROGER C. FARR

Professor of Education and Director of the Center for Reading and Language Studies at Indiana University and Senior Author, HBJ Treasury of Literature

An assessment program should help teachers and students understand what a student can do successfully rather than emphasize what a student can't do. Assessments should be positive experiences for students — a natural part of the learning process. In *HBJ Treasury of Literature,* assessment tools have been designed to enable every child to experience success.

An effective assessment program provides information not only about *how well* a student reads and writes, but also about *how.* No one improves from merely knowing a score on a test — or from having responses marked as acceptable or unacceptable. There must be an opportunity to review answer choices and drafts of reading and writing.

An effective assessment program encourages students to share in the responsibility of assessment, helping them to become reflective about their developing abilities. In *HBJ Treasury of Literature*, the assessment components include a variety of activities to involve students. These components include a Reading/Writing Portfolio, Portfolio Conferences, Strategy Conferences, and Student Self-Assessment Notes.

No one improves from merely knowing a score on a test....

The assessment activities in *HBJ Treasury of Literature* were developed out of the belief that assessment in a literature-based reading program should not interfere with the enjoyment and development of reading. Rather, it should be a thoughtful guide to help a child increase his or her understanding and appreciation of the power and beauty of literature. Assessment should do these things:

1. **Present Realistic Activities.** Assessments should engage students in activities that resemble ways they actually use reading and writing in everyday life.

2. **Reflect What Is Taught.** Assessment activities should use the skills and strategies that are taught.

3. **Consider Pupil Environment.** Assessment activities should provide opportunities for a student to select the work that he or she thinks is important as well as provide opportunities for the teacher and the student to discuss the student's abilities and interests.

4. **Integrate Language Behaviors.** Assessment should provide opportunities for students to use all of their language skills to accomplish literacy tasks.

5. **Be Ongoing and Congruent with Instruction.** Assessment should provide many opportunities for informal observations, or "kid watching," rather than just formal testing.

Assessment

Informal Assessment Options

Title	Key Features
Reading/Writing Portfolio	Each student is encouraged to save important examples of his or her writing in the Portfolio. Periodically, student and teacher discuss the Portfolio's contents and note the development of the student's literacy skills.
Informal Assessment Notes	These appear throughout each *HBJ Treasury of Literature* Teacher's Edition lesson plan and give the teacher suggestions for determining when students need help without waiting until the "teachable moment" has passed.
Strategy Conferences	Students are consistently given an opportunity to assess the effectiveness of the strategies they use when they read. The basis for metacognition must be student awareness.
Student Self-Assessment Notes	These appear throughout *HBJ Treasury of Literature* Teacher's Edition lesson plans and help students evaluate their own strategies for working effectively in reader response groups.
Running Records	The teacher keeps an informal account of skills and strategies students use as they read. Running Records provide a window on the reading process and help teachers understand how students are applying reading skills and strategies.

Formal Assessment Options

Title	Key Features
Integrated Performance Assessments	They provide realistic, integrated assessments that give students opportunities to use their reading and writing abilities to engage in authentic, performance activities.
Holistic Assessments	They provide a variety of interesting fiction and non-fiction selections with both multiple-choice and open-ended questions to determine how students are developing as total readers.
Skills Assessments	They provide activities that determine whether students can apply reading skills and strategies. The skills are assessed in the context of words, sentences, and paragraphs rather than in isolation.

An effective assessment program provides information not only about how well *a student* reads and writes, but also *about* how.

Look for

- Informal assessment guides
- Student self-assessment opportunities
- Strategy and Portfolio conferences
- Holistic Assessment
- Integrated reading and writing evaluation using authentic literature

The primary goal is to help the teacher plan an effective instructional program.

If assessment is to be effective, it must be linked to instructional planning. Each of the assessment components has been developed to serve teacher decision making. The specific interpretation and use of each test for instructional planning are discussed fully in either the *HBJ Treasury of Literature* Teacher's Edition or the manual accompanying the assessment component.

The table below provides an overview of how each of the components serves various teacher decisions. The emphasis is on providing teachers with information that empowers them to make decisions based on the assessment information as well as on their ongoing observations. The columns with two checks ✔✔ indicate a primary use of the assessment for that decision while a single check ✔ indicates a secondary use of the assessment for that decision.

Instructional Decisions

Component	Daily Planning	Unit Planning	Placement
Reading/Writing Portfolios	✔✔	✔	
Informal Assessment Notes	✔✔	✔	
Student Self-Assessment Notes	✔✔	✔	
Running Records	✔✔		
Integrated Performance Assessments		✔✔	
Holistic Assessments		✔✔	
Skills Assessments		✔✔	
Group Placement Test			✔✔
Individual Placement Test			✔✔

Each assessment component provides guidelines for the use and interpretation of that component. However, there are several general guidelines that will help to make the total assessment program more successful.

- Be observant every day. The best assessment tool is a classroom teacher.

- Get students involved in thinking and talking about their reading interests, habits, and development. Self-assessment is the most powerful instrument for bringing about change.

- Rely less often on single assessments and more often on a variety of literacy activities.

- Look for patterns in student responses. Just as a single test provides an incomplete picture, a single response reveals little about whether a student is developing particular reading strategies and skills. ●

Teacher Resources

The resources on these pages will help you customize your literature-based reading program. They include reproducible masters of Response Cards for the discussion of literature, Independent Reading Masters to help with self-selected reading, and Graphic Organizers for applying active reading strategies.

RESPONSE CARD

Characters

1 Who are the main characters? Who are the minor characters?

2 Do you like or dislike the characters? Why?

3 Does a character in this story remind you of anyone else you have read about? If so, how are they alike?

AFTER READING

4 Choose one character. Why was this character important in the story?

5 Did any of the characters change? If so, how?

6 If you could be any character in this story, who would you be? Why?

7 Suppose you had a chance to meet one of the characters. What would you say to him or her?

RESPONSE CARD 2

Setting

1 Where does the story take place?

2 Describe the place.

3 Have you ever been to a place like this? If you have, how was it like the place in the story?

4 When does this story take place—long ago, in the future, or in the present? How do you know?

5 How did the place affect what happened in the story?

6 How would the story be different if it were set in a different place?

7 How would the story be different if it were set in a different time?

8 If you could visit the place, would you go? Why or why not?

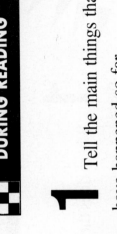

RESPONSE CARD

Plot

1 Tell the main things that have happened so far.

2 What is the problem in the story? How do you think it will be solved?

3 What do you think will happen next? What do you think will happen at the end?

4 Tell the main events that happened in the story.

5 What was the solution to the story problem?

6 Did you guess the ending? How else might the author have ended the story?

7 What do you think was the best part of the story? Why?

RESPONSE CARD

Theme/Mood

1 What do you think the author's message will be? Why do you think that?

2 From the title of the story, what did you think this story would be about?

3 How do you feel at this point in the story? Why?

4 What do you remember most about the story so far?

5 What was the author's message? Which story events helped you figure out the message?

6 If you wanted to suggest this story to a friend, what would you say it is mostly about?

7 How do you feel now that you have finished the story? Why?

8 What part was:
- the funniest?
- the saddest?
- the most exciting?

RESPONSE CARD

Author's Viewpoint

DURING READING

1 What do you know about the author?

2 What is the author trying to tell you? How do you know?

3 Can you tell what kinds of things (people, places, behavior, feelings) the author likes? If so, how do you know?

AFTER READING

4 Do you agree with the author? Why or why not?

5 What did the author have to know in order to write this article or story?

6 What else could the author have said to support his or her opinion?

RESPONSE CARD

Author's Craft

DURING READING

1 Have you noticed anything you think the author might bring up again later in the story? If so, what did you notice?

2 Tell about any pictures the author has left in your mind.

3 What special words has the author used so far to help you
- see things in the story?
- hear things in the story?
- feel things in the story?

4 What does the dialogue tell you about the characters? Do they talk the way people really talk? Why or why not?

AFTER READING

5 What is your favorite word, line, or paragraph in the story? Why is it your favorite?

6 What do you like about the way the author has written the story?

7 Would you like to read something else by this author? Why or why not?

8 What was the most important thing you learned from the dialogue in this story?

RESPONSE CARD

Responding Freely

1 Work with a partner. Look over the story, and decide whether you will read it silently or aloud.

2 Think about the way the story is organized. Decide with your partner how often you will stop to discuss it.

3 Each time you stop, talk about what you have read. Tell what you think, and listen to your partner.

You might talk about what you like or do not like.

- You might discuss things you do not understand.

- You might discuss what has happened so far or what might happen next.

4 Read the ne[xt] talk about it. Co[ntinue] until you finish [.]

5 Talk about the whole story. Tell what you think, and listen to what your partner says.

- You might talk about your favorite part of the story.

- You might discuss the author's writing.

- You might discuss whether what you thought would happen really did happen.

RESPONSE CARD

Written Conversation

DURING READING

1 Work with a partner. Silently read the pages your teacher suggests.

2 On a sheet of paper, write a comment about what you read. Then write a question about something you didn't understand.

3 Pass your paper to your partner.

4 Write the answer to your partner's question. Then add a new question to the paper.

5 Pass the paper back to your partner. Answer the new question your partner wrote.

6 Read the rest of the story. Repeat steps 2-5.

AFTER READING

7 Discuss the story. Use the questions and answers on your paper to help you.

COVER TO COVER

Clues from the inside and the outside can help you choose a book!

Outside   **Inside**

1 Look at the front and back covers of the book you are going to read. Does the book look interesting?

3 Are there illustrations? Do they spark your interest?

STORY
by JOE MOO

2 Who is the author? Have you or your friends read and liked other books by that author?

4 Preview the beginning of the book. Does it seem like a book you will understand and enjoy?

What book did you choose?

_____

Why do you think you will like it?

_____

NOTES AND QUOTES

Name: _____ **Date:** _____

The note pads below may help you keep track of some interesting or amazing things you'd like to remember from your book.

People / Animals / Characters

Places / Setting

Facts or Story Events

New or Interesting Words

RESPOND AND BEYOND

Name: _____   **Date:** _____

Title of Book: _____

> Check the box beside the activity you choose to do with your book. Activities with a double arrow (↔) may be done with a partner who has read the same book. Those with a circle (◯) may be done with a group.

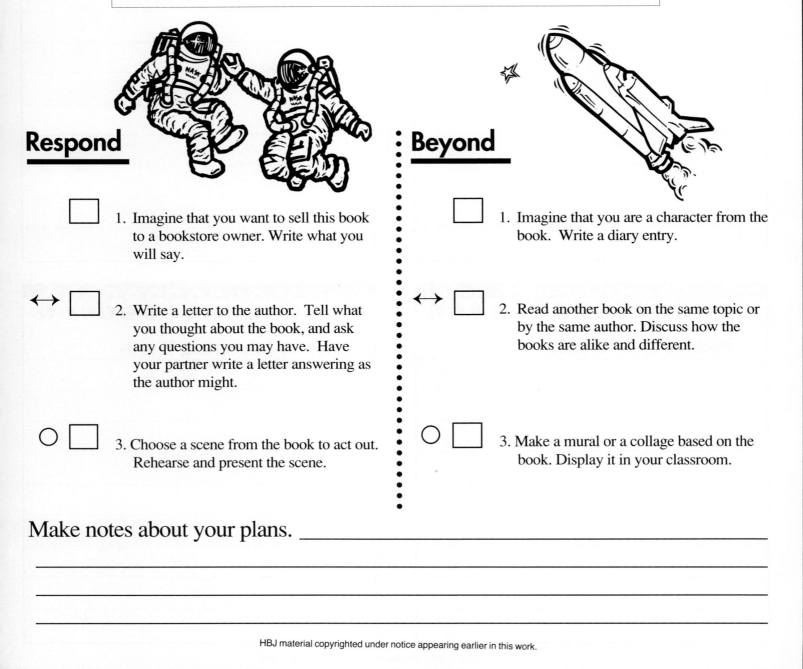

Respond

☐ 1. Imagine that you want to sell this book to a bookstore owner. Write what you will say.

↔ ☐ 2. Write a letter to the author. Tell what you thought about the book, and ask any questions you may have. Have your partner write a letter answering as the author might.

◯ ☐ 3. Choose a scene from the book to act out. Rehearse and present the scene.

Beyond

☐ 1. Imagine that you are a character from the book. Write a diary entry.

↔ ☐ 2. Read another book on the same topic or by the same author. Discuss how the books are alike and different.

◯ ☐ 3. Make a mural or a collage based on the book. Display it in your classroom.

Make notes about your plans. _____
_____
_____

READ ALL ABOUT IT!

Complete the newspaper page to tell about your book.

Weather: a good day for reading	**The Literary Ledger**	" Turning pages into ideas"

Date: _____

Today's Top Story:

_____
(your name)

Reviews

_____
(book title)

Some of the most interesting things about this book are listed below:

_____
_____
_____
_____

_____
_____
_____
_____
_____

A Scene from the Book

Critic's

C
o
r
n
e
r

I thought this book was

_____

because _____

_____

_____

_____

_____

_____

_____

This picture shows _____

_____

_____

_____

_____

_____

ORGANIZING IDEAS

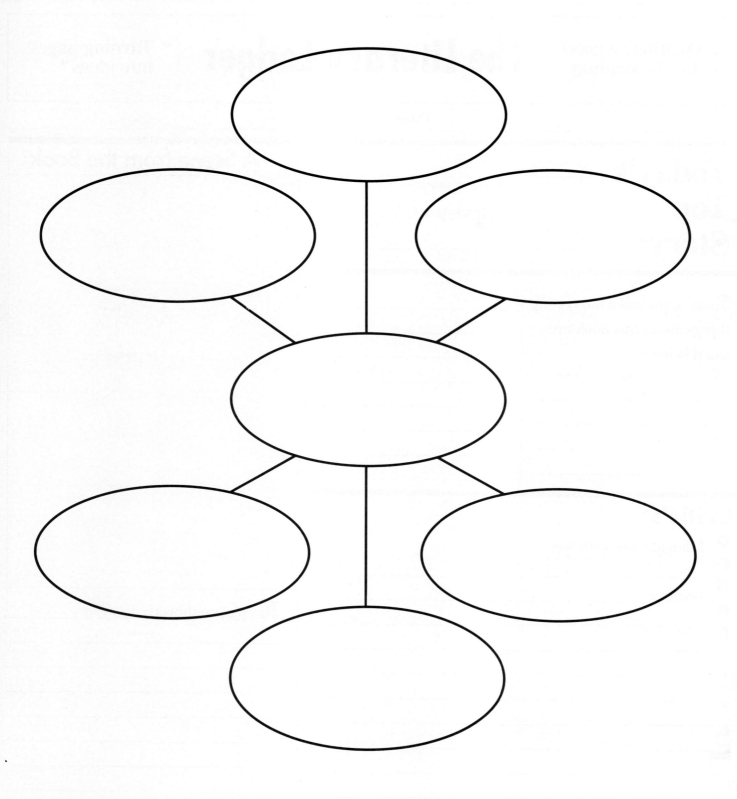

STORY MAP

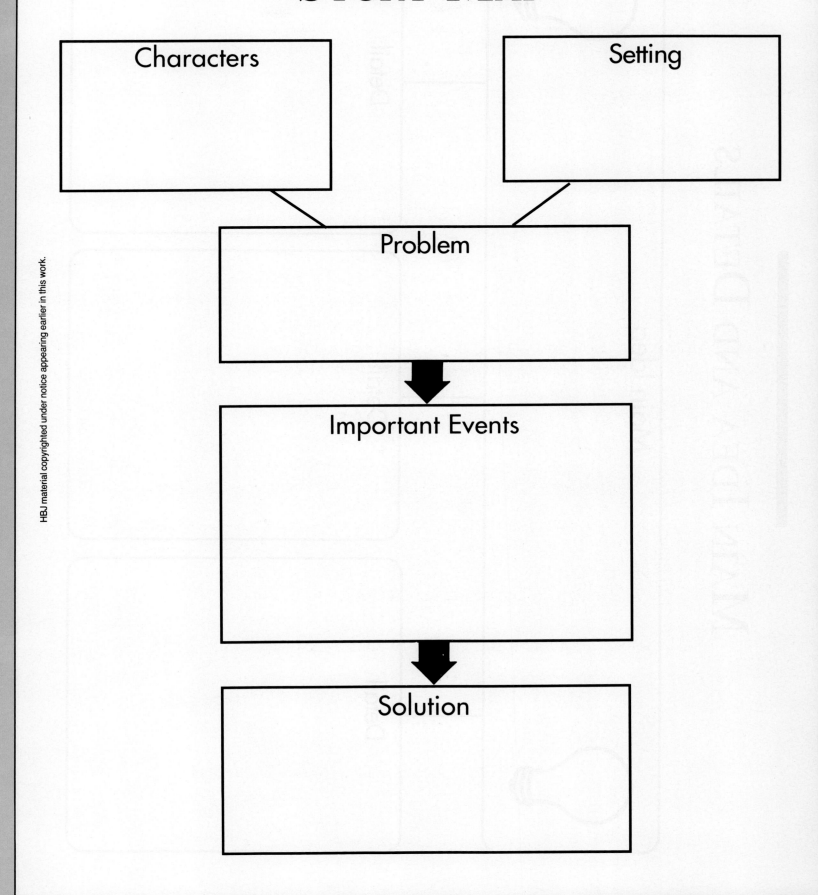

Characters

Setting

Problem

Important Events

Solution

MAIN IDEA AND DETAILS

Main Idea

Detail

Detail

Detail

DRAWING CONCLUSIONS

What I Already Know

Evidence in
the Selection

Conclusion

Making Predictions

Information from the Selection

What I Already Know

Prediction

What Actually Happens in the Selection

COMPARING AND CONTRASTING

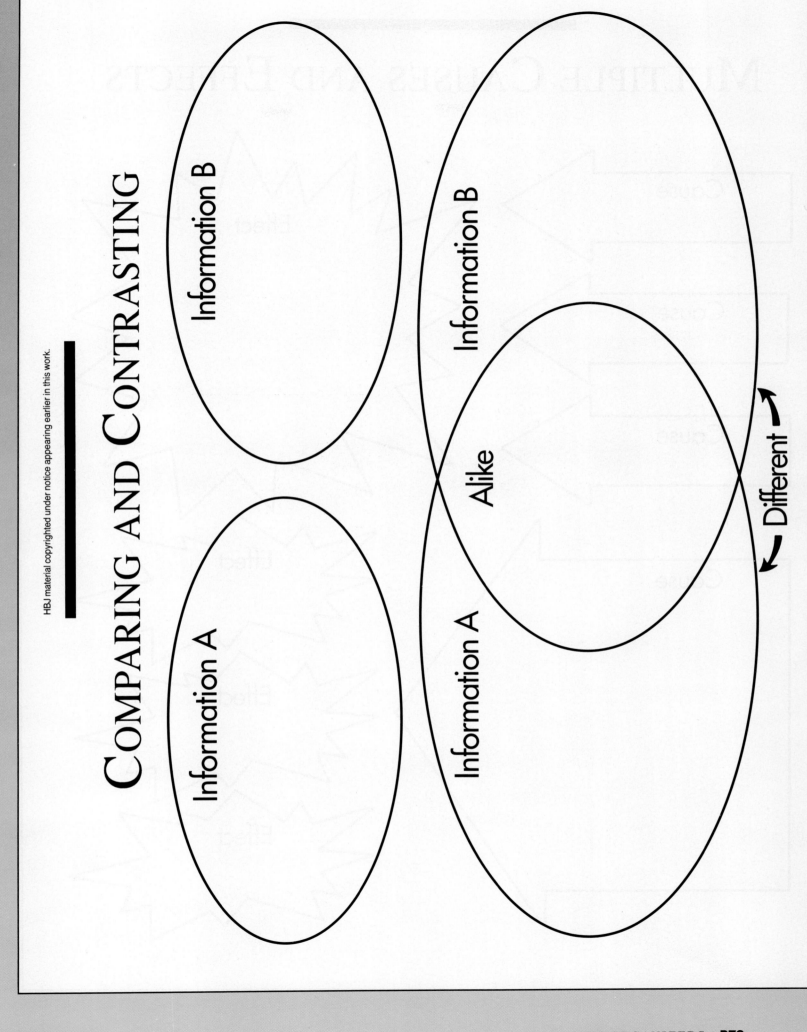

Information A

Information B

Information A

Alike

Information B

Different

MULTIPLE CAUSES AND EFFECTS

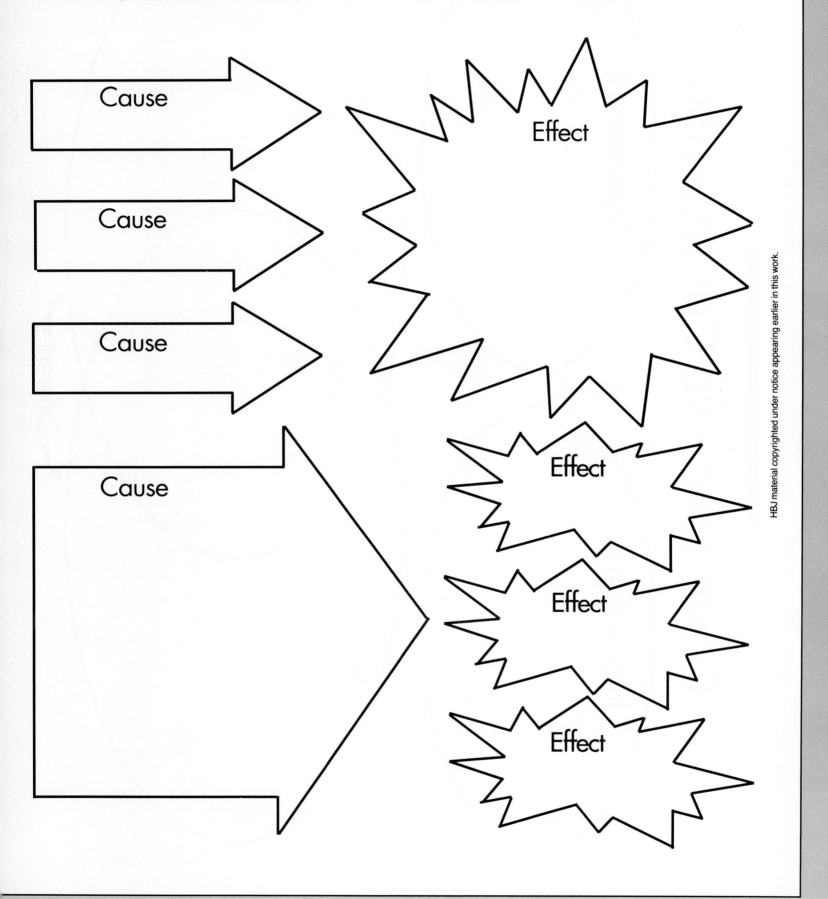

Cause

Cause

Cause

Cause

Effect

Effect

Effect

Effect

HBJ Treasury of Literature
Scope and Sequence

Legend: █ = Modeling/Instruction/Application ♦ = Tested

Grade/Level	1–1	1–2	1–3	1–4	1–5	1–6	2	3	4	5	6	7	8
STRATEGIC READING													
Active Reading Strategies	█	█	█	█	█	█	█	█	█	█	█	█	█
Read Fiction (Narrative Text)	█	█	█	█	█	█	█	█	█	█	█	█	█
Read Nonfiction (Expository Text)				█	█	█	█	█	█	█	█	█	█
Analyze Details	█	█	█	█	█	█	█	█	█	█	█	█	█
Synthesize Ideas/Information	█	█	█	█	█	█	█	█	█	█	█	█	█
Make Inferences	█	█	█	█	█	█	█	█	█	█	█	█	█
Decoding Strategy: Use phonetic/structural analysis plus context to unlock pronunciation	█	█	█	█	█	█	█	█	█	█	█	█	█
Vocabulary Strategy: Use phonetic/structural/contextual clues to determine meanings	█	█	█	█	█	█	█	█	█	█	█	█	█
Use Self-Assessment Strategies	█	█	█	█	█	█	█	█	█	█	█	█	█
COMPREHENSION													
Cause-Effect							♦	♦	♦	♦	♦	♦	♦
Classify/Categorize		♦					♦	█	█	█	█	█	█
Compare and Contrast								♦	♦	♦	♦	♦	♦
Draw Conclusions					♦		♦	♦	♦	♦	♦	♦	♦
Fact-Fantasy/Nonfact				♦			♦	█	█	█	█	█	█
Author's Purpose									♦	♦	♦	♦	♦
Author's Viewpoint									♦	♦	♦	♦	♦
Fact-Opinion								♦	♦	♦	♦	♦	♦
Main Idea (Global Meaning)/Details						♦	♦	♦	♦	♦	♦	♦	♦
Make Generalizations									♦	♦	♦	♦	♦
Make Judgments									♦	♦	♦	♦	♦
Paraphrase								♦	♦	♦	♦	♦	♦
Make Predictions					♦		♦	♦	♦	♦	♦	♦	♦
Referents	█	█	█	█	█	█	█	█	█	█	█	█	█
Sequence			♦				♦	♦	♦	♦	♦	♦	♦
Summarize								♦	♦	♦	♦	♦	♦
VOCABULARY													
Key Words/Selection Vocabulary	♦	♦	♦	♦	♦	♦	♦	♦	♦	♦	█	█	█
Synonyms/Antonyms							█	█	█	█	█	█	█
Multiple-Meaning Words							█	█	█	█	♦	♦	♦
Homophones/Homographs							█	█	█	█	█	█	█
Context Clues					♦		♦	♦	♦	♦	♦	♦	♦
Vocabulary Strategy: Use phonetic/structural/contextual clues to determine meanings	█	█	█	█	█	█	█	█	█	█	█	█	█
Analogies									█	█	█	█	█
Connotation/Denotation										█	█	█	█
Glossary							█	█	█	█	█	█	█
Dictionary (for Word Meaning)											♦	♦	█
DECODING													
Phonics													
Initial/Medial/Final Consonants	♦	♦	♦	♦	█	█	█						
Phonograms	█	█	█	█	█	█	█						
Short Vowels/Long Vowels		♦	♦	♦	♦	♦	█						
Consonant Clusters/Digraphs (Initial/Final)			♦	♦	♦	♦	█						
R-Controlled Vowels							♦						
Vowel Diphthongs/Vowel Digraphs/Variant Vowels							♦						
Schwa							█						
Decoding Strategy: Use phonetic/structural analysis plus context to unlock pronunciation	█	█	█	█	█	█	█	█	█	█	█	█	█
Structural Analysis													
Inflected Forms Nouns; Verbs With and Without Spelling Changes		♦	♦		♦		♦	█	█	█	█	█	█
Possessives, Comparatives, Superlatives							█	█	█	█	█	█	█
Contractions			♦	♦	█	█	█	█	█	█	█	█	█
Compound Words					█	█	█	█	█	█	█		█
Syllabication							█	█	█	█	█	█	█
Suffixes/Prefixes								♦	♦	♦	♦	♦	♦
Greek and Latin Roots										♦	♦	♦	♦
Spelling Patterns						█	█	█	█	█	█	█	█

█ **Modeling/Instruction/Application**   ♦ **Tested**
Testing options include Unit Skills Assessment, Unit Holistic Assessment, and Unit Integrated Performance Assessment.
For a complete scope and sequence of the kindergarten program, see the Teacher's Edition for that level.

Grade/Level	1–1	1–2	1–3	1–4	1–5	1–6	2	3	4	5	6	7	8
STUDY SKILLS													
Locate Sources of Information													
Use the Library (Parts of, Card Catalog, Computerized Card Catalog, Call Numbers, Database Searching Strategies, *Books in Print, Readers' Guide*)							▓	▓	▓	▓	▓	▓	▓
Alphabet/Alphabetical Order	▓	▓	▓	▓	♦	▓							
Use Sources of Information													
Book Parts	▓	▓	▓	▓	▓	▓	▓						
Graphic Aids (Maps, Charts, Graphs, Tables/Schedules, Diagrams, Timelines)	▓	▓	▓	▓	▓	▓	▓	♦	♦	♦	♦	♦	♦
Compare Information from More Than One Source											♦		♦
Use Reference Sources (Glossary/Dictionary, Thesaurus, Specialized Dictionary, Atlas/Globe, Encyclopedia, Newspaper, *Books in Print, Readers' Guide*)	▓	▓	▓	▓	▓	▓	▓		♦	♦	♦	♦	♦
Study Strategies (K-W-L, SQ3R, How to Study)							▓	▓	▓	▓	▓	▓	▓
Content-Area Reading							▓	▓	▓	▓	▓	▓	▓
Adjust Method/Rate of Reading							▓	▓	▓	▓	▓	▓	▓
Test-Taking Strategies							▓	▓	▓	▓	▓	▓	▓
Outlining/Notetaking Strategies							▓	▓	▓	▓	▓	▓	▓
Follow Directions				♦			♦	♦	♦	♦	♦	♦	♦
Forms/Applications													
LITERARY APPRECIATION													
Select Books for Individual Needs and Interests	▓	▓	▓	▓	▓	▓	▓	▓	▓	▓	▓	▓	▓
Read Full-length Books	▓	▓	▓	▓	▓	▓	▓	▓	▓	▓	▓	▓	▓
Literary Elements													
Plot Development													
Storyline	▓	▓	▓	▓	▓	▓	▓	♦	♦	♦	♦	♦	♦
Conflict (Internal/External)											♦	♦	♦
Climax													
Flashback/Foreshadowing													
Theme	▓	▓	▓	▓	▓	▓	▓	▓	▓	▓	▓	▓	♦
Character (Emotions, Types, Development, Traits)	▓	▓	▓	▓	▓	▓	▓	♦	♦	♦	♦	♦	♦
Setting	▓	▓	▓	▓	▓	▓	▓	♦	♦	♦	♦	♦	♦
Point of View													
Narration													
Dialogue	▓	▓	▓	▓	▓	▓	▓		♦				
Reader Response Groups/Strategies													
Author's Craft													
Figurative Language		▓	▓	▓	▓	▓	▓			♦	♦	♦	♦
Characterization		▓	▓	▓	▓	▓	▓						
Imagery	▓	▓	▓	▓	▓	▓	▓						
Mood/Tone	▓	▓	▓	▓	▓	▓	▓					♦	♦
Sound Devices (Rhythm/Rhyme/Alliteration/Onomatopoeia)	▓	▓	▓	▓	▓	▓	▓						
Author's Technique *See Appreciating Literature in each lesson plan.*													
Literary Forms/Genre													
Fiction													
Realistic Fiction		▓	▓	▓	▓	▓	▓	▓	▓	▓	▓	▓	▓
Historical Fiction									▓	▓	▓	▓	▓
Mystery								▓	▓	▓	▓	▓	▓
Fantasy	▓	▓	▓	▓	▓	▓	▓		▓	▓	▓	▓	▓
Science Fiction								▓	▓		▓	▓	▓
Full-length Book	▓	▓	▓	▓	▓	▓	▓	▓	▓	▓	▓	▓	▓
Riddle	▓	▓	▓	▓	▓	▓	▓						
Drama/Play	▓	▓	▓	▓	▓	▓	▓	▓	▓	▓	▓	▓	▓
Poetry/Song	▓	▓	▓	▓	▓	▓	▓	▓	▓	▓	▓	▓	▓
Nonfiction													
Biography/Autobiography								▓	▓	▓	▓	▓	▓
Journal/Diary/Letters	▓	▓	▓	▓	▓	▓	▓	▓	▓	▓	▓	▓	▓
Essay									▓	▓	▓	▓	▓
Informational Article				▓	▓	▓	▓	▓	▓	▓	▓	▓	▓
How-To Article								▓	▓	▓	▓	▓	▓
Interview								▓	▓	▓	▓	▓	▓
Speech								▓	▓	▓	▓	▓	▓
Personal Narrative							▓	▓	▓	▓	▓	▓	▓
Folklore (Folktale, Fairy Tale, Fable, Myth, Tall Tale, Legend, Nursery Rhyme)	▓	▓	▓	▓	▓	▓	▓	▓	▓	▓	▓	▓	▓

■ **Modeling/Instruction/Application**   ♦ **Tested**

Testing options include Unit Skills Assessment, Unit Holistic Assessment, and Unit Integrated Performance Assessment. For a complete scope and sequence of the kindergarten program, see the Teacher's Edition for that level.

Grade/Level	1–1	1–2	1–3	1–4	1–5	1–6	2	3	4	5	6	7	8
MULTICULTURALISM													
Respond to Literature Representing Our Pluralistic Culture	▓	▓	▓	▓	▓	▓	▓	▓	▓	▓	▓	▓	▓
View Concepts/Issues from Diverse Perspectives	▓	▓	▓	▓	▓	▓	▓	▓	▓	▓	▓	▓	▓
Understand the concept that all groups have contributed to society	▓	▓	▓	▓	▓	▓	▓	▓	▓	▓	▓	▓	▓
Acquire attitudes/skills/knowledge to interact successfully with members of diverse groups	▓	▓	▓	▓	▓	▓	▓	▓	▓	▓	▓	▓	▓
LANGUAGE													
Composition													
Writing Process (Prewriting, Drafting, Responding/Revising, Proofreading, Publishing)	▓	▓	▓	▓	▓	▓	▓	▓	▓	▓	▓	▓	▓
Writer's Craft													
Identifying Audience and Purpose	♦	♦	♦	♦	♦	♦	♦	♦	♦	♦	♦	♦	♦
Selecting, Narrowing, Expanding Topics/Gathering Information							♦	♦	♦	♦	♦	♦	♦
Choosing Effective Language							♦	♦	♦	♦	♦	♦	♦
Forms of Writing													
Expository Writing (Comparison/Contrast, Explanation, Letter, News Story, Report, Essay, Directions/Instructions)				▓	▓	▓	♦	♦	♦	♦	♦	♦	♦
Narrative Writing (Stories, Paragraph/s, Personal Narrative, Personal Journal, Play, Poetry)	▓	▓	▓	▓	♦	♦	♦	♦	♦	♦	♦	♦	♦
Descriptive Writing/Spatial Order (Titles, Captions, Paragraphs, Stories, Poetry)	♦	♦	♦	♦	♦	♦	♦	♦	♦	♦	♦	♦	♦
Persuasive Writing (Paragraph, Essay, Business Letter)							♦	♦	♦	♦	♦	♦	♦
Cross-Curricular Writing	▓	▓	▓	▓	▓	▓	▓	▓	▓	▓	▓	▓	▓
Skills of Revision													
Correcting Sentence Fragments/Run-Ons								♦	♦	♦	♦	♦	♦
Adding/Deleting/Rearranging Information							♦	♦	♦	♦	♦	♦	♦
Sentence/Word Variety								♦	♦	♦	♦	♦	♦
Unity and Coherence							♦	♦	♦	♦	♦	♦	♦
Using the Conventions of English				♦	♦	♦	♦	♦	♦	♦	♦	♦	♦
Listening													
Participate in Cooperative Groups	▓	▓	▓	▓	▓	▓	▓	▓	▓	▓	▓	▓	▓
Receive Direction/Gain Information/Enhance Appreciation of Language	▓	▓	▓	▓	▓	▓	▓	▓	▓	▓	▓	▓	▓
Respond to a speaker by retelling what was heard, asking questions, and/or contributing information	▓	▓	▓	▓	▓	▓	▓	▓	▓	▓	▓	▓	▓
Analyze/Evaluate Intent and Content of Speaker's Message							▓	▓	▓	▓	▓	▓	▓
Note Details	▓	▓	▓	▓	▓	▓	▓	▓	▓	▓	▓	▓	▓
Visualize	▓	▓	▓	▓	▓	▓	▓	▓	▓	▓	▓	▓	▓
Determine Problem/Solution	▓	▓	▓	▓	▓	▓	▓	▓	▓	▓	▓	▓	▓
Make Justifiable Inferences	▓	▓	▓	▓	▓	▓	▓	▓	▓	▓	▓	▓	▓
Identify Supporting Details	▓	▓	▓	▓	▓	▓	▓	▓	▓	▓	▓	▓	▓
Recognize Persuasion							▓	▓	▓	▓	▓	▓	▓
Identify Mood/Tone							▓	▓	▓	▓	▓	▓	▓
Recognize Bias/Prejudice/Propaganda/Emotional Appeals												▓	▓
Speaking													
Participate in Cooperative Groups	▓	▓	▓	▓	▓	▓	▓	▓	▓	▓	▓	▓	▓
Identify Audience/Purpose			▓	▓	▓	▓	▓	▓	▓	▓	▓	▓	▓
Use a Variety of Words to Convey Meaning	▓	▓	▓	▓	▓	▓	▓	▓	▓	▓	▓	▓	▓
Describe Personal Ideas, Feelings, and Expressions	▓	▓	▓	▓	▓	▓	▓	▓	▓	▓	▓	▓	▓
Orally Retell/Summarize Stories	▓	▓	▓	▓	▓	▓	▓	▓	▓	▓	▓	▓	▓
Entertain Others with Stories, Poems, Dramatic Activities	▓	▓	▓	▓	▓	▓	▓	▓	▓	▓	▓	▓	▓
Give Directions	▓	▓	▓	▓	▓	▓	▓	▓	▓	▓	▓	▓	▓
Share Information	▓	▓	▓	▓	▓	▓	▓	▓	▓	▓	▓	▓	▓
Compare/Contrast							▓	▓	▓	▓	▓	▓	▓
Persuade Others							▓	▓	▓	▓	▓	▓	▓
Develop Skill in Using the Conventions of English	▓	▓	▓	▓	▓	▓	▓	▓	▓	▓	▓	▓	▓
Integrated Spelling													
Apply Spelling Generalizations					♦	♦	♦	♦	♦	♦	♦	♦	♦
Apply Spelling Strategies					▓	▓	▓	▓	▓	▓	▓	▓	▓
Master Frequently Misspelled Words					▓	▓	▓	▓	▓	▓	▓	▓	▓

▓ **Modeling/Instruction/Application**   ♦ **Tested**
Testing options include Unit Skills Assessment, Unit Holistic Assessment, and Unit Integrated Performance Assessment.
For a complete scope and sequence of the kindergarten program, see the Teacher's Edition for that level.

UNIT ONE CELEBRATIONS

ADDITIONAL READING

The following list is a compilation of the additional reading selections taken from the lesson plans.

CONTESTS

Banana Blitz
by Florence Perry Heide. Holiday House, 1983.

Benny and the Crazy Contest
by Cheryl Zach. Bradbury, 1991.

Chocolate-Covered Ants
by Stephen Manes. Scholastic, 1990.

The Cold and Hot Winter
by Johanna Hurwitz. William Morrow, 1988.

The Fourth Grade Wizards
by Barthe DeClements. Viking Penguin, 1988.

The Luck of Pokey Bloom
by Ellen Conford. Little, Brown, 1975.

Teacher's Pet
by Johanna Hurwitz. William Morrow, 1988.

HOLIDAYS

America's Birthday: The Fourth of July
by Tom Shachtman. Macmillan, 1986.

HOLIDAYS (cont.)

Festivals Around the World
by Philip Steele. Dillon, 1986.

Have a Happy . . .
by Mildred Pitts Walter. Lothrop, Lee & Shepard, 1989.

Hoang Anh: A Vietnamese American Boy
by Diane Hoyt-Goldsmith. Holiday House, 1992.

The Story of Hanukkah
told by Amy Ehrlich. Dial, 1989.

Tree of Cranes
by Allen Say. Houghton Mifflin, 1991.

PERFORMANCES

Cynthia Gregory Dances Swan Lake
by Cynthia Gregory. Simon and Schuster, 1990.

Dancing Is . . .
by George Ancona. E. P. Dutton, 1981.

Mozart Tonight
by Julie Downing. Bradbury, 1991.

Nicholas Cricket
by Joyce Maxner. HarperCollins, 1989.

A Very Young Musician
by Jill Krementz. Simon and Schuster, 1991.

UNIT TWO ANIMAL·TALES

ADDITIONAL READING

The following list is a compilation of the additional reading selections taken from the lesson plans.

ANIMAL TALK

Chester the Worldly Pig
written and illustrated by Bill Peet. Houghton Mifflin, 1980.

The Chimpanzee Family Book
by Jane Goodall. Picture Book Studio, 1989.

Crazy About German Shepherds
by Brent Ashabranner. Cobblehill, 1990.

The Drugstore Cat
by Ann Petry. Beacon, 1988.

Gorilla, Gorilla
by Carol Fenner. Random House, 1973.

A Guide Dog Puppy Grows Up
by Caroline Arnold. Harcourt Brace Jovanovich, 1991.

How Animals Talk
by Susan McGrath. National Geographic, 1987.

Koko's Story
by Francine Patterson. Scholastic, 1987.

The Lady and the Spider
by Faith McNulty. HarperCollins, 1986.

Singing Birds and Flashing Fireflies: How Animals Talk to Each Other
by Dorothy Hinshaw Patent. Franklin Watts, 1989.

Stuart Little
by E. B. White. HarperCollins, 1970.

The Trumpet of the Swan
by E. B. White. HarperCollins, 1970.

CREATURE CARE

Baseball and Butterflies
by Karen Lynn Williams. Lothrop, Lee & Shepard, 1990.

Bird Watch
by Jane Yolen. Philomel, 1990.

The Computer Nut
by Betsy Byars. Viking, 1984.

CREATURE CARE (cont.)

House of Wings

by Betsy Byars. Viking, 1972.

The Midnight Fox

by Betsy Byars. Puffin, 1981.

Rats

by Pat Hutchins. Greenwillow, 1989.

Stranded

by Ann Coleridge. Delacorte, 1987.

Wanted . . . Mud Blossom

by Betsy Byars. Delacorte, 1991.

WILD WONDERS

Buffalo Woman

by Paul Goble. Bradbury, 1984.

Death of the Iron Horse

by Paul Goble. Bradbury, 1987.

Deputy Shep

by Mary Stolz. HarperCollins, 1991.

Dog Days

by Colby Rodowsky. Farrar, Straus & Giroux, 1990.

The First Dog

by Jan Brett. Harcourt Brace Jovanovich, 1988.

The Girl Who Loved Wild Horses

by Paul Goble. Bradbury, 1978.

Gray Wolf, Red Wolf

by Dorothy Hinshaw Patent. Clarion, 1990.

Great Northern Diver: The Loon

by Barbara Juster Esbensen. Little, Brown, 1990.

Lost and Found

by Jean Little. Viking, 1985.

Mission Rhino

by Jill Bailey. Steck-Vaughn, 1990.

Sterling: The Rescue of a Baby Harbor Seal

by Sandra Verrill White and Michael Filisky. Crown, 1989.

Were You a Wild Duck, Where Would You Go?

by George Mendoza. Stewart, Tabori & Chang, 1990.

ADDITIONAL READING

The following list is a compilation of the additional reading selections taken from the lesson plans.

MAIN COURSE

Cactus
by Cynthia Overbeck. Lerner, 1982.

A Flower Grows
by Ken Robbins. Dial, 1990.

Flowers
by Terry Jennings. Childrens Press, 1981.

Flowers for Everyone
by Dorothy Hinshaw Patent. Cobblehill, 1990.

Flowers, Fruits, Seeds
by Jerome Wexler. Prentice Hall, 1987.

The Fruit Book
by Cynthia Overbeck. Lerner, 1975.

How Seeds Travel
by Cynthia Overbeck. Lerner, 1982.

The Plant That Ate Dirty Socks
by Nancy McArthur. Avon, 1988.

Plants in Action
by Robin Kerrod. Marshall Cavendish, 1989.

The Return of the Plant That Ate Dirty Socks
by Nancy McArthur. Avon, 1990.

Rosy's Garden
by Elizabeth Laird. G. P. Putnam's/Philomel, 1990.

Sunflowers
by Cynthia Overbeck. Lerner, 1981.

Top Secret
by John Reynolds Gardiner. Little, Brown, 1985.

GARDEN VARIETY

Agave Blooms Just Once
by Gisela Jernigan. Harkinger, 1989.

The Almond Orchard
by Laura Jane Coats. Macmillan, 1991.

GARDEN VARIETY (cont.)

A Brighter Garden
> poetry by Emily Dickinson, collected by Karen Ackerman. Philomel, 1990.

Fir Trees
> by Heiderose Fischer-Nagel and Andreas Fischer-Nagel. Carolrhoda, 1989.

Linnea's Windowsill Garden
> by Christina Bjork and Lena Anderson. Raben & Sjogren, 1990.

Rain Forest Secrets
> by Arthur Dorros. Scholastic, 1990.

Sugaring Time
> by Kathryn Lasky. Macmillan, 1983.

Tree Trunk Traffic
> by Bianca Lavies. E. P. Dutton, 1989.

The World That Jack Built
> by Ruth Brown. E. P. Dutton, 1991.

HARVEST HUMOR

An Apple a Day
> by Dorothy Hinshaw Patent. Cobblehill, 1990.

Elliot's Extraordinary Cookbook
> by Christina Bjork and translated by Joan Sandin. Raben & Sjogren, 1990.

Everybody Cooks Rice
> by Norah Dooley. Carolrhoda, 1991.

The Mare's Egg
> by Carole Spray. Camden House, 1981.

McBroom and the Big Wind
> by Sid Fleischman. Little, Brown, 1982.

McBroom and the Great Race
> by Sid Fleischman. Little, Brown, 1980.

McBroom Tells a Lie
> Sid Fleischman. Little, Brown, 1976.

Vegetables
> by Susan Wake. Carolrhoda, 1990.

UNIT FOUR DISCOVERIES

ADDITIONAL READING

The following list is a compilation of the additional reading selections taken from the lesson plans.

FUN AND GAMES

Across Town
by Sara. Orchard, 1991.

Balloons: Building and Experimenting with Inflatable Toys
by Bernie Zubrowski. William Morrow, 1990.

The Chocolate Touch
by Patrick S. Catling. William Morrow, 1952.

Flatfoot Fox and the Case of the Missing Eye
by Eth Clifford. Houghton Mifflin, 1990.

Fourth Grade Rats
by Jerry Spinelli. Scholastic, 1991.

The Garden of Abdul Gasazi
by Chris Van Allsburg. Houghton Mifflin, 1979.

George and His Good Wife Elsie in *Plays, the Drama Publication for Children*
by A. F. Bauman. Plays, Inc. 1979.

Outdoor Fun
edited by Catherine Ripley. Joy, 1990.

The Shrinking of Treehorn
by Florence P. Heide, Holiday House, 1971.

The Stranger
by Chris Van Allsburg. Houghton Mifflin, 1986.

The Third Knot in *Children's Classics*
edited by Janet L. Bolinske. Milliken, 1987.

Travel Tips from Harry: A Guide to Family Vacations in the Sun
by Amy Hest. William Morrow, 1989.

FUN AND GAMES (cont.)

The True Story of the Three Little Pigs! by A. Wolfe
as told to Jon Scieszka. Viking, 1989.

SOLVE IT!

Encyclopedia Brown and the Case of the Disgusting Sneakers
by Donald J. Sobol. William Morrow, 1990.

Encyclopedia Brown's Book of the Wacky Outdoors
by Donald J. Sobol. William Morrow, 1987.

How Much Is a Million?
by David M. Schwartz. Lothrop, Lee & Shepard, 1985.

Lost In the Amazon: A Miss Mallard Mystery
by Robert Quackenbush. Pippin, 1990.

Sebastian (Super Sleuth) and the Mystery Patient
by Mary Blount Christian. Macmillan, 1991.

The Wright Brothers at Kitty Hawk
by Donald J. Sobol. Scholastic, 1987.

HIDDEN RICHES

As: A Surfeit of Similes
by Norton Juster. William Morrow, 1989.

The Eleventh Hour
by Graeme Base. Abrams, 1989.

Flat Stanley
by Jeff Brown. Harper, 1964.

Punching the Clock: Funny Action Idioms
by Marvin Terban. Clarion, 1990.

Tuesday
by David Wiesner. Clarion, 1991.

UNIT FIVE
TRAVELERS

ADDITIONAL READING

The following list is a compilation of the additional reading selections taken from the lesson plans.

PIONEERS

Cassie's Journey: Going West in the 1860s
by Brett Harvey. Holiday House, 1988.

Dakota Dugout
by Ann Turner. Macmillan, 1985.

Farmer Boy
by Laura Ingalls Wilder. HarperCollins, 1933/1961.

Heron Street
by Ann Turner. HarperCollins, 1989.

The Little House Cookbook: Frontier Foods from Laura Ingalls Wilder's Classic Stories
by Barbara M. Walker. HarperCollins, 1979.

Little House in the Big Woods
by Laura Ingalls Wilder. HarperCollins, 1932/1959.

The Pony Express: Hoofbeats in the Wilderness
by Joseph J. DiCerto. Franklin Watts, 1989.

The Tea Squall
by Ariane Dewey. Greenwillow, 1988.

Where the Buffaloes Begin
by Olaf Baker. Warne, 1981.

IMMIGRANTS

Ellis Island: New Hope in a New Land
by William Jay Jacobs. Charles Scribner's, 1990.

IMMIGRANTS (cont.)

The King of Prussia and a Peanut Butter Sandwich
by Alice Fleming. Charles Scribner's, 1988.

Mr. Blue Jeans: A Story about Levi Strauss
by Maryann N. Weidt. Carolrhoda, 1990.

A Portrait of Me
by Barbara Aiello and Jeffrey Shulman. 21st Century, 1989.

TRADITIONS

The American Family Farm
by Joan Anderson. Harcourt Brace Jovanovich, 1989.

Bird Life
by Ian Wallace, Rob Hume, and Rick Morris. Usborne, 1984.

Friendship Across Arctic Waters
by Claire Rudolf Murphy. Lodestar, 1991.

Hoang Anh: A Vietnamese American Boy
by Diane Hoyt-Goldsmith. Holiday House, 1992.

Morgan the Magnificent
by Ian Wallace. McElderry/Macmillan, 1987.

Penny in the Road
by Katharine Wilson Precek. Macmillan, 1989.

Pioneer Children of Appalachia
by Joan Anderson. Clarion, 1986.

The President's Cabinet and How It Grew
by Nancy Winslow Parker. HarperCollins, 1978/1991.

Pueblo Boy: Growing Up in Two Worlds
by Marcia Keegan. Cobblehill, 1991.

The Remembering Box
by Eth Clifford. Houghton Mifflin, 1985.

When I Was Young in the Mountains
by Cynthia Rylant. E. P. Dutton, 1982.

ADDITIONAL READING

The following list is a compilation of the additional reading selections taken from the lesson plans.

ACHIEVERS

The Little Lame Prince
by Rosemary Wells. Dial, 1990.

Love You, Soldier
by Amy Hest. Four Winds, 1991.

My Sister, My Science Report
by Margaret Bechard. Viking, 1990.

Nothing's Fair in Fifth Grade
by Barthe DeClements. Viking, 1981.

People Who Make a Difference
by Brent Ashabranner. Cobblehill, 1989.

The Present
by Michael Emberley. Little, Brown, 1991.

The Sailor Who Captured the Sea: A Story of the Book of Kells
by Deborah Nourse Lattimore. HarperCollins, 1991.

The Secret Language of the SB
by Elizabeth Scarboro. Viking, 1990.

The Talking Eggs
by Robert D. San Souci. Dial, 1989.

YOUNG AT HEART

And the Winner Is. . .
by Stephen Roos. Atheneum, 1989.

Eight Hands Round: A Patchwork Alphabet
by Ann Whitford Paul. HarperCollins, 1991.

YOUNG AT HEART (cont.)

The House on Walenska Street
by Charlotte Herman. E. P. Dutton, 1990.

Sachiko Means Happiness
by Kimiko Sakai. Childrens Press, 1990.

The Wild Horses of Sweetbriar
by Natalie Kinsey-Warnock. Cobblehill, 1990.

STARGAZERS

Child of the Silent Night
by Edith Fisher Hunter. Houghton Mifflin, 1963.

Follow the Dream: The Story of Christopher Columbus
by Peter Sis. Alfred A. Knopf, 1991.

Hannah
by Gloria Whelan. Alfred A. Knopf, 1991.

The Hundred Dresses
by Eleanor Estes. Harcourt Brace Jovanovich, 1944/1971.

Jobs for Kids: The Guide to Having Fun and Making Money
by Carol Barkin and Elizabeth James. Lothrop, Lee & Shepard, 1990.

Make-Believe Ball Player
by Alfred Slote. J. B. Lippincott, 1989.

Max Malone Makes a Million
by Charlotte Herman. Henry Holt, 1991.

True Stories About Abraham Lincoln
by Ruth Belov Gross. Lothrop, Lee & Shepard, 1973/1990.

Women in Space: Reaching the Last Frontier
by Carole S. Briggs. Lerner, 1988.

A Young Painter: The Life and Paintings of Wang Yani—China's Extraordinary Young Artist
by Zheng Zhensun and Alice Lowe. New China/Scholastic, 1991.

INDEX

"Hurt No Living Thing," T265–268
Hurwitz, Johanna, T19, T43–44

I . . . .

Idiom, T189, T319, T490–491
Illustrators
  Bash, Barbara, T437
  Diamond, Donna, T895
  Rosales, Melodye, T83
  Williams, Garth, T173, T197–198
Imagery
  introduce, T878–879
Independent reading, T22, T50, T86,
  T122, T176, T206, T238, T286,
  T310, T350, T378, T410, T440,
  T474, T522, T556, T594, T622,
  T668, T692, T724, T762, T786,
  T832, T860, T898, T932, T954,
  R70–73
  See also Additional reading.
Index, R19–20
Informal assessment
  informal assessment notes, T24, T52,
    T88, T110, T159, T178, T251,
    T280, T381, T412, T476, T505,
    T524, T533, T550, T586, T596,
    T599, T624, T670, T699, T726,
    T737, T764, T788, T797, T862,
    T900, T908
  options for, T8, T162, T336, T508,
    T654, T818
  portfolio conference, T159, T333,
    T505, T651, T815, T981
  running records, T8, T162, T336,
    T508, T654, T818
  strategy conference, T31, T60, T92,
    T130, T184, T215, T250, T292,
    T314, T361, T387, T418, T446,
    T484, T533, T564, T599, T631,
    T672, T699, T736, T769, T796,
    T840, T872, T908, T960
  student self-assessment, T32, T61,
    T93, T131, T150, T185, T216,
    T293, T315, T362, T388, T419,
    T447, T565, T600, T632, T673,
    T700, T737, T770, T797, T961
  summarizing, T37, T39, T60, T67,
    T69, T71, T99, T101, T102,
    T103, T137, T139, T140, T141,
    T191, T193, T221, T223, T257,
    T258, T259, T292, T299, T301,
    T314, T321, T322, T323, T361,
    T367, T369, T387, T393, T395,
    T418, T425, T426, T427, T446,
    T453, T455, T456, T457, T484,
    T491, T492, T493, T533, T539,

T540, T541, T571, T572, T573,
T605, T606, T607, T637, T638,
T639, T679, T680, T681, T705,
T707, T743, T745, T746, T747,
T769, T775, T776, T777, T803,
T805, T847, T848, T849, T879,
T880, T881, T915, T916, T917,
T937, T943, T944, T945, T967,
T969
Integrated curriculum
  art, T40, T72, T105, T142, T195,
    T225, T260, T303, T325, T370,
    T397, T429, T458, T459, T574,
    T609, T641, T683, T749, T779,
    T806, T807, T851, T882, T883,
    T918, T919, T947, T970
  dance, T748, T971
  health/safety, T104, T225
  language arts, T261, T303, T325
  mathematics, T41, T72, T73, T104,
    T142, T194, T195, T224, T260,
    T302, T324, T371, T396, T428,
    T458, T494, T542, T575, T608,
    T640, T682, T709, T748, T778,
    T807, T851, T882, T918, T946,
    T971
  music, T41, T324, T397, T494, T708,
    T748, T883, T946, T971
  physical education, T143, T779
  science, T73, T104, T143, T194,
    T195, T224, T225, T261, T302,
    T324, T325, T371, T396, T397,
    T428, T429, T459, T495, T542,
    T543, T574, T575, T609, T640,
    T682, T708, T749, T779, T806,
    T850, T883, T919, T946, T971
  social studies, T40, T41, T72, T73,
    T104, T105, T142, T194, T195,
    T224, T260, T302, T370, T371,
    T396, T428, T429, T458, T494,
    T495, T542, T543, T575, T608,
    T609, T640, T641, T682, T683,
    T708, T709, T748, T749, T778,
    T779, T806, T807, T850, T851,
    T882, T918, T919, T946, T947,
    T970
  "When Does Two Plus Two Equal
    Five?" R28
Integrated language arts
  "Integrating the Language Arts," R26
  listening, T35, T64, T96, T135, T189,
    T219, T254, T297, T318, T365,
    T391, T422, T450, T489, T504,
    T537, T568, T569, T603, T635,
    T677, T703, T740, T741, T773,
    T800, T844, T877, T913, T941,
    T964

reading, T34, T35, T63, T65, T95,
  T96, T97, T133, T134, T135,
  T187, T188, T218, T219, T253,
  T295, T317, T364, T390, T421,
  T449, T487, T536, T567, T602,
  T634, T675, T702, T739, T772,
  T799, T801, T843, T875, T876,
  T911, T940, T941, T963
speaking, T35, T64, T65, T97, T134,
  T188, T189, T219, T254, T255,
  T296, T297, T318, T319, T365,
  T391, T422, T423, T450, T451,
  T488, T537, T568, T603, T635,
  T676, T677, T703, T741, T773,
  T800, T801, T844, T845, T876,
  T912, T913, T941, T964, T965
spelling, T34, T63, T95, T133, T158,
  T187, T218, T253, T295, T317,
  T332, T364, T390, T421, T449,
  T487, T504, T536, T567, T602,
  T634, T650, T675, T702, T739,
  T772, T799, T814, T843, T875,
  T911, T940, T963, T980
writing, T34, T35, T63, T64, T65,
  T95, T96, T97, T133, T134, T135,
  T187, T188, T218, T253, T254,
  T255, T295, T296, T297, T317,
  T318, T319, T364, T365, T390,
  T391, T421, T422, T423, T449,
  T450, T451, T487, T488, T489,
  T536, T537, T567, T568, T569,
  T602, T603, T634, T635, T675,
  T676, T677, T702, T703, T739,
  T740, T741, T772, T773, T799,
  T800, T801, T843, T844, T845,
  T875, T876, T877, T911, T912,
  T913, T940, T941, T963, T964,
  T965
Integrated performance assessment
  See Formal assessment.
Integrated spelling
  See Spelling, integrated.
Interview with the author, T545–546,
  T587–588
Irvin, Dr. Judith L., R28
Irving, Patricia, T151

J . . . .

Japanese Children's Day, T107
Jim Abbott: Against All Odds, T927–948
Josefowitz, Natasha, T12
Journal, personal, T22, T32, T50, T61,
  T86, T93, T122, T131, T176, T185,
  T216, T238, T251, T286, T293,
  T315, T350, T362, T388, T410,

reporting facts, T319
retelling stories, T297
riddles, T451
role-playing, T255, T676
sales pitch, T365
science fiction tale, T374
show and tell, T579, T913
sign language, T219
skit, T188
speech on contests, T65
sportscast, T941
story ending, T635
storytelling, T423, T501
teaching a dance, T773
telling about a treasure, T647
thank-you speech, T801
TV commercial, T488
voice mail, T613
Special education students, T16, T80,
　　T116, T170, T232, T274, T344,
　　T404, T466, T516, T582, T662,
　　T716, T756, T826, T890, T926
"Special Education Without Special
　　Classrooms," R33
Specialized vocabulary, T674
Spelling
　　integrated, T21, T34, T49, T63, T85,
　　　T95, T121, T133, T158, T175,
　　　T187, T205, T218, T237, T253,
　　　T285, T295, T309, T317, T332,
　　　T349, T364, T377, T390, T409,
　　　T421, T439, T449, T473, T487,
　　　T504, T521, T536, T555, T567,
　　　T593, T602, T621, T634, T650,
　　　T667, T675, T691, T702, T723,
　　　T739, T761, T772, T785, T799,
　　　T814, T831, T843, T859, T875,
　　　T897, T911, T931, T940, T953,
　　　T963, T980
"New Strategies Spell S-U-C-C-E-S-S
　　with Students," R27A
　　review, T34, T63, T95, T133, T187,
　　　T218, T253, T295, T317, T364,
　　　T390, T421, T449, T487, T536,
　　　T567, T602, T634, T675, T702,
　　　T739, T772, T799, T843, T875,
　　　T911, T940, T963
　　spelling-vocabulary connection, T21,
　　　T49, T63, T85, T95, T121, T175,
　　　T205, T218, T237, T285, T309,
　　　T349, T377, T409, T439, T473,
　　　T521, T555, T593, T621, T667,
　　　T691, T723, T761, T785, T831,
　　　T859, T897, T931, T953
SQ3R strategy, T440, T786
　　introduce, T394–395
Steptoe, John, T829, T853–854

Sternberg, Dr. Robert J., R25, R32
"Stormy Rescue, The," from *The*
　　Midnight Fox, T233–262
Story elements
　　introduce, T256–257
　　review, T572, T638
　　test, T651
　　reteach, R40
Story follow-up, T31, T60, T92, T130,
　　T150, T184, T215, T250, T280,
　　T292, T314, T361, T387, T418,
　　T446, T484, T533, T550, T564,
　　T586, T599, T631, T672, T699,
　　T736, T769, T796, T840, T872,
　　T908, T937, T960
Strategic reading, T22, T50, T86, T122,
　　T147, T176, T206, T238, T275,
　　T286, T310, T350, T378, T410,
　　T440, T474, T522, T547, T556,
　　T583, T594, T622, T668, T692,
　　T724, T762, T786, T832, T860,
　　T898, T932, T954
"Putting the Thinking Back into
　　Reading," R24
See also Analyzing details; Author's
　　purpose; Cause and effect;
　　Comparing and contrasting;
　　Drawing conclusions; Fact and
　　opinion; Main idea and details;
　　Making generalizations; Making
　　inferences; Making predictions;
　　Paraphrasing; Point of view;
　　Preview and predict; Purpose for
　　reading; Sequence; Summarizing;
　　Synthesizing ideas.
Strategies
　　See Active reading strategies;
　　Comprehension strategies; Decoding
　　strategies; Handbook for Readers
　　and Writers; Listening strategies;
　　Thinking strategies; Vocabulary
　　strategies.
Strategy conference
　　See Informal assessment.
Strickland, Dr. Dorothy S., R22–23
Structural analysis
　　introduce, T392–393, T570–571
　　review, T639, T848
　　maintain, T777
　　reteach, R44, R48
Structural and contextual clues
　　introduce, T138–139
Structural clues
　　introduce, T298–299
Students at risk, T16, T80, T116, T170,
　　T232, T274, T344, T404, T466,
　　T516, T582, T662, T716, T756,

T826, T890, T926
"Students at Risk," R32
Student self-assessment
　　See Informal assessment.
Study skills
　　See Following directions; Graphic aids;
　　Note-taking strategies; Outlining;
　　Reference sources; Sources of
　　information; SQ3R strategy;
　　Test-taking strategies; Book parts.
Sugaring Time, T340–341
Summarizing
　　introduce, T678–679
　　review, T746, T776
　　test, T815
　　maintain, T916
　　reteach, R49
　　See also Informal assessment;
　　Summarizing the literature.
Summarizing the literature, T31, T60,
　　T92, T130, T184, T215, T250, T292,
　　T314, T361, T387, T418, T446,
　　T484, T533, T564, T599, T631,
　　T672, T699, T736, T769, T796,
　　T840, T872, T908, T937, T960
　　See also Informal assessment;
　　Summarizing.
"Sun Dancers," T151–152
Synonyms/antonyms, T217, T363
Synthesizing ideas
　　introduce, T190–191

T . . . .

"Talk To The Animals," T199–200
Tall tale, T469–496
　　writing, T489
"Tapping Time," from *Sugaring Time,*
　　T340–341
Teacher resources
　　graphic organizers, R74–80
　　independent reading, R70–73
　　response cards, R62–69
Testing and management
　　See Formal assessment; Informal
　　assessment.
Test-taking strategies
　　introduce, T454–455
Theme
　　discussing, T15, T79, T115, T169,
　　　T231, T273, T343, T403, T465,
　　　T515, T581, T615, T661, T715,
　　　T755, T825, T889, T925
　　introducing, T8, T162, T336, T508,
　　　T654, T818

REVIEWERS

FIELD TEST SITES, MULTICULTURAL ADVISORS, CRITICAL REVIEWERS

Field Test Sites

Vinemont, Alabama
Phoenix, Arizona
Cabot, Arkansas
Conway, Arkansas
Moreno Valley, California
Riverside, California
Sacramento, California
San Diego, California
Bridgeport, Connecticut
Lisbon, Connecticut
New Haven, Connecticut
Land O'Lakes, Florida
Pocatello, Idaho
Mahomet, Illinois
Naperville, Illinois
Gosport, Indiana
Spencer, Indiana
Donnellson, Iowa
Kansas City, Kansas
Mount Sterling, Kentucky
Bossier City, Louisiana
Bridgman, Michigan
Detroit, Michigan
Robbinsdale, Minnesota
Billings, Montana
Nashua, New Hampshire
North Bergen, New Jersey
Chaparral, New Mexico
Brooklyn, New York
Cincinnati, Ohio
New Carlisle, Ohio
Toledo, Ohio
University Heights, Ohio
Beaverton, Oregon
Eugene, Oregon
Portland, Oregon
Fairless Hills, Pennsylvania
N. Huntingdon, Pennsylvania
Philadelphia, Pennsylvania
Estill, South Carolina
Greer, South Carolina
Aberdeen, South Dakota
Nashville, Tennessee
Corsicana, Texas
Dallas, Texas
Grand Prairie, Texas
Harlingen, Texas
Houston, Texas
Katy, Texas
Lewisville, Texas
Lockhart, Texas
McAllen, Texas
Palestine, Texas
Plano, Texas
San Antonio, Texas
Dry Fork, Virginia
Everett, Washington
Vancouver, Washington
Green Bay, Wisconsin

Multicultural Advisors

Dr. James E. Anderson
Associate Professor, Department of
    Educational Leadership and
    Cultural Studies
College of Education
University of Houston
Houston, Texas

Dr. Mario Benitez
Professor, Department of Curriculum
    and Instruction
The University of Texas at Austin
Austin, Texas

Dr. Pat Browne
Director, African-American
    History/Multicultural Education
Indianapolis Public Schools
Indianapolis, Indiana

Dr. Jacob Carruthers
Associate Director and Professor
Northeastern Illinois University
    Center for Inner City Studies
Chicago, Illinois

Dr. Nancy Mayeda
Principal
Rooftop Alternative School
San Francisco, California

Dr. Maria E. Morales
Associate Professor and Director of
    Undergraduate Bilingual
    Education Program
Undergraduate Teacher Preparation
    Program
Texas A & I University
Kingsville, Texas

Dr. Cornel Pewewardy
Principal
Mounds Park All-Nations Magnet
    School
St. Paul, Minnesota

Dr. Rudy Rodriguez
Professor and Chair, Department of
    Reading and Bilingual Education
College of Education and Human
    Ecology
Texas Woman's University
Denton, Texas

Sherry Sellers
Librarian and Multicultural Specialist
Detroit, Michigan

Dr. Barbara Shin
Principal
Andersen Contemporary School
Minneapolis, Minnesota

Virginia Driving Hawk Sneve
Secondary Counselor
Indian Education and District
    Resource for Native-American
    Culture
Rapid City, South Dakota

Charlotte Stokes
Teacher Specialist - Social Studies
Alexandria City Public Schools
Alexandria, Virginia

Dr. Bernida Thompson
Principal
Roots Activity Learning Center
Washington, District of Columbia

Marilys Tognetti
Director of Instruction
Dixon Unified School District
Dixon, California

Critical Reviewers

Ginger Abel
Teacher
Peoria Public Schools
Peoria, Illinois

C. Gloria Akers
Principal
James Rhoads School
Philadelphia, Pennsylvania

Claudia Anderson
Teacher
Hawthorne Elementary
Fargo, North Dakota

Margo Angleton
Teacher
Indialantic Elementary
Melbourne, Florida

Karyn Aulwurm
Administrative Specialist
Clark County School District
Las Vegas, Nevada

Hilda Barrett
Teacher
Harper's Choice Middle School
Columbia, Maryland

Diana Bauske
Teacher
Richland Elementary
Richardson, Texas

Florence T. Carter
Teacher
Campbell School
Metuchen, New Jersey

Cicely Cerqui
Coordinator for Elementary
    Curriculum
Shoreline Public Schools
Seattle, Washington

Lenore Croudy
Coordinator of Language Arts and
    Humanities
Flint Community Schools
Flint, Michigan

Carol DeRita
Teacher
Porter Elementary
Mesquite, Texas

Judee DeStefano-Anen
Assistant Principal/Reading Specialist
Ella G. Clarke School
Lakewood, New Jersey

Marilyn Dickey
Language Arts Specialist
Shelton View Elementary
Bothell, Washington

Sheila Durante, RSM
Assistant Superintendent for
    Elementary Schools
Diocese of Providence
Providence, Rhode Island

Mary Ellen Everitt
Teacher
Antheil Elementary
Trenton, New Jersey

Lisa Fast
Teacher
Escola Americana do Rio de Janeiro
Rio de Janeiro, Brazil

Shirley Fields
District Reading Coordinator
Region III
Miami, Florida

Bettie Fitzhenry
Reading Consultant
Killeen Independent School District
Killeen, Texas

Ann Carol Franco
Teacher
American School Foundation
Tacubaya, Mexico

Janet Green
Teacher
Whitehouse Primary School
Whitehouse, Ohio

Rilla Hardgrove
Principal
Orchard School
Billings, Montana

Sister Patricia Healey, IHM
Elementary Supervisor
Sisters of the Immaculate Heart of
    Mary
Philadelphia, Pennsylvania

Don Hillyard
Reading Coordinator
Evansville-Vanderburgh Schools
Evansville, Indiana

Sandra Horst
Teacher
Solheim Elementary
Bismarck, North Dakota

Daisy Howard-Douglas
Teacher
Fairfield Court Elementary
Richmond, Virginia

William James
Principal
Durrance Elementary
Orlando, Florida

Karen Jao
Teacher
Taipei American School
Taipei, Taiwan

Mary Jennings
Teacher
Tubman Elementary
Washington, D.C.

Beth Kealy
Teacher
Patterson Elementary
Eugene, Oregon

Jan Keese
District Reading Chair
Ankeny Community Schools
Ankeny, Iowa

Laressa Jane Kschinka
Teacher
American School of The Hague
Wassenaar, The Netherlands

Maya Lagbara, Ed.D.
Assistant Principal
Lida Hooe Elementary
Dallas, Texas

Elizabeth Lolli
Coordinator, Elementary Education
Middletown City Schools
Middletown, Ohio

Joyce London
Reading Specialist
Southard School
Howell, New Jersey

Bertha Long-Jackson
Teacher
Jesse Owens School
South Holland, Illinois

Ida Love, Ph.D.
Director of Elementary Schools
Kansas City, Missouri School District
Kansas City, Missouri

Constance Major
Reading Specialist
Shawmont School
Philadelphia, Pennsylvania

Jana McCarthy
Language Arts Coordinator
Meridian School District
Meridian, Idaho

Mary K. McCarthy
Reading Specialist
Owyhee Elementary
Boise, Idaho

Bonnie McIntyre
Curriculum Coordinator
Minneapolis Public Schools
Minneapolis, Minnesota

Carlton Mead
Teacher
Whitford Intermediate
Beaverton, Oregon

Hilda Medrano, Ph.D.
Associate Professor
The University of Texas - Pan
    American
Edinburg, Texas

Dr. Jacqueline Mossburg
Coordinator, Staff Development
Fort Wayne Community Schools
Fort Wayne, Indiana

Lawrence Ostopowicz
Reading/Language Arts Chairperson
School District of Waukesha
Waukesha, Wisconsin

Charlotte J. Parks
Teacher
Windsor Elementary
Des Moines Public School District
Des Moines, Iowa

Beth Peterson
Teacher
Mount Tabor Elementary
New Albany, Indiana

Evelyn Pittman
Supervisor of Language Arts
Paterson Public Schools
Paterson, New Jersey

Kaye Price-Hawkins
Consultant
Region XIV
Abilene, Texas

Tamara Jo Rhomberg
Reading Specialist
Garlin Kellison Elementary
Fenton, Missouri

David Rubin
Supervisor of Reading
Gateway Center
New Haven, Connecticut

Blanche Ryan
Supervisor of Reading
Indianapolis Public Schools
Indianapolis, Indiana

Janet Sawyer
Teacher
Highland Park Elementary
Austin, Texas

James F. Schindler, Ed.D.
Curriculum Consultant
Jordan School District
Sandy, Utah

Jan Scott
Curriculum Coordinator, K-3
Bossier Parish School System
Bossier City, Louisiana

Sheila Scott
Teacher
Gower Elementary
Nashville, Tennessee

Marsha Shortt
Teacher
Stewart Elementary
Kemah, Texas

Sheldon Shuch, Ph.D.
Director of Curriculum
Community School District Five
New York, New York

Richard Wagner
Language Arts Curriculum
    Coordinator
Paradise Valley School District
Phoenix, Arizona

Mona Warner
ESOL Teacher
Hillsboro Elementary Schools
Hillsboro, Oregon

**Sister Mary Leanne Welch,
    PBVM**
Curriculum Director
Archdiocese of Dubuque
Dubuque, Iowa

Jackie Williams
Instructional Supervisor
Loudon County Schools
Loudon, Tennessee

Lola Williams, Ph.D.
Bilingual Coordinator
Harlingen Consolidated Independent
    School District
Harlingen, Texas

Louverne Williams
Teacher
Holland School
Minneapolis, Minnesota

Sara Jane Wilson
Teacher
Landis Elementary
Alief, Texas

**Sister Marla Ann Yeck, RSM,
    Ph.D.**
Associate Superintendent for
    Curriculum
Archdiocese of Detroit
Detroit, Michigan

Parent Reviewers

Gail Adler
Ft. Worth, Texas

Linda Curry
Bloomfield Hills, Michigan

Ian Fingerman
Skokie, Illinois

Louis Guerrero
Dallas, Texas

Rachel Guerrero
Dallas, Texas

Patricia Hales
Salt Lake City, Utah

Randa Henry
Coeur d'Alene, Idaho

Jo A. Jorgenson
Phoenix, Arizona

Kay Morton
Dallas, Texas

Sandy Nickley
Dayton, Ohio

Sharon Wille
Highlands Ranch, Colorado

Acknowledgments

For permission to reprint copyrighted material, grateful acknowledgment is made to the following sources:

Harry N. Abrams, Inc., New York: Cover illustration from *The Eleventh Hour: A Curious Mystery* by Graeme Base. Published by Harry N. Abrams, Inc., 1989.

Atheneum Publishers, an imprint of Macmillan Publishing Company: From *The Gold Coin* by Alma Flor Ada. Text copyright © 1991 by Alma Flor Ada.

August House Publishers, Inc.: "The Wooden Horse" from *Spanish-American Folktales* by Teresa Pijoan de Van Etten. Text copyright © 1990 by Teresa Pijoan Van Etten.

Carolrhoda Books, Inc., Minneapolis, MN: Cover illustration by Lydia M. Anderson from *Mr. Blue Jeans: A Story about Levi Strauss* by Maryann N. Weidt. Illustration copyright © 1990 by Carolrhoda Books, Inc.

Clarion Books, a Houghton Mifflin Company imprint: Cover photograph by George Ancona from *Pioneer Children of Appalachia* by Joan Anderson. Photograph © 1986 by George Ancona. Cover illustration by Tom Huffman from *Punching the Clock: Funny Action Idioms* by Marvin Terban. Illustration copyright © 1990 by Tom Huffman. Cover illustration from *Tuesday* by David Wiesner. Copyright © 1991 by David Wiesner.

Cobblehill Books, an affiliate of Dutton Children's Books, a division of Penguin Books USA Inc.: Cover photograph by Paul Conklin from *People Who Make a Difference.* Photograph copyright © 1989 by Paul Conklin. Cover photograph from *Pueblo Boy: Growing Up in Two Worlds* by Marcia Keegan. Copyright © 1991 by Marcia Keegan. Cover illustration by Ted Rand from *The Wild Horses of Sweetbriar* by Natalie Kinsey-Warnock. Illustration copyright © 1990 by Ted Rand.

Dial Books for Young Readers, a division of Penguin Books USA Inc.: Cover illustration by Jerry Pinkney from *The Talking Eggs* by Robert D. San Souci. Illustration copyright © 1989 by Jerry Pinkney. Cover illustration by Gary Blythe from *The Whale's Song* by Dyan Sheldon. Illustration copyright © 1990 by Gary Blythe. Cover illustration from *The Little Lame Prince* by Rosemary Wells. Copyright © 1990 by Rosemary Wells.

GRM Associates, Inc.: Cover illustration by Tomie Arai from *Sachiko Means Happiness* by Kimiko Sakai. Illustration copyright © 1990 by Tomie Arai.

Harcourt Brace Jovanovich, Inc.: Cover photograph by George Ancona from *The American Family Farm* by Joan Anderson. Photograph copyright © 1989 by George Ancona. Cover illustration by Louis Slobodkin from *The Hundred Dresses* by Eleanor Estes. Copyright 1944 by Harcourt Brace Jovanovich, Inc., renewed 1971 by Eleanor Estes and Louis Slobodkin. Pronunciation Key from *HBJ School Dictionary,* Third Edition. Text copyright © 1990 by Harcourt Brace Jovanovich, Inc.

HarperCollins Publishers: Cover illustration from *The Sailor Who Captured the Sea: A Story of the Book of Kells* by Deborah Nourse Lattimore. Copyright © 1991 by Deborah Nourse Lattimore. Cover illustration from *The President's Cabinet and How It Grew* by Nancy Winslow Parker. Copyright © 1991 by Nancy Winslow Parker. Cover illustration by Garth Williams from *The Little House Cookbook* by Barbara M. Walker. Illustration copyright © 1953, 1971 by Garth Williams. Cover illustration by Garth Williams from *Farmer Boy* by Laura Ingalls Wilder. Illustration copyright 1953 by Garth Williams; illustration copyright renewed © 1981 by Garth Williams. Cover illustration by Garth Williams from *Little House in the Big Woods* by Laura Ingalls Wilder. Illustration copyright 1953 by Garth Williams; illustration copyright renewed © 1981 by Garth Williams. From *On the Way Home* by Laura Ingalls Wilder. Text copyright © 1962 by Roger Lea MacBride.

Houghton Mifflin Company: Cover illustration by Brian Lies from *Flatfoot Fox and the Case of the Missing Eye* by Eth Clifford. Illustration © 1990 by Brian Lies. Cover illustration by Donna Diamond from *The Remembering Box* by Eth Clifford. Illustration © 1985 by Donna Diamond. Cover illustration by Bea Holmes from *Child of the Silent Night: The Story of Laura Bridgman* by Edith Fisher Hunter. Copyright © 1963 by Edith Fisher Hunter. Cover illustration from *The Stranger* by Chris Van Allsburg. Copyright © 1986 by Chris Van Allsburg.

Alfred A. Knopf, Inc.: Cover illustration from *Follow the Dream: The Story of Christopher Columbus* by Peter Sis. Copyright © 1991 by Peter Sis. Cover illustration by Leslie Bowman from *Hannah* by Gloria Whelan. Illustration copyright © 1991 by Leslie Bowman.

Little, Brown and Company: Cover illustration from *Outdoor Fun,* edited by Catherine Ripley. Copyright © 1989 by Greey de Pencier Books.

Lothrop, Lee & Shepard Books, a division of William Morrow & Company, Inc.: Cover illustration by Roy Doty From *Jobs for Kids* by Carol Barkin and Elizabeth James. Illustration copyright © 1990 by Roy Doty.

Macmillan Publishing Company: Cover illustration by Lisa McCue from *Sebastian [Super Sleuth] and the Mystery Patient* by Mary Blount Christian. Illustration copyright © 1991 by Lisa McCue. Cover illustration by Patricia Cullen-Clark from *Penny in the Road* by Katharine Wilson Precek. Illustration copyright © 1989 by Patricia Cullen-Clark. Cover illustration by Ron Himler from *Dakota Dugout* by Ann Turner. Illustration copyright © 1985 by Ron Himler.

Viqui Maggio, Inc.: Cover illustration by Viqui Maggio from *Ellis Island: New Hope in a New Land* by William Jay Jacobs. Illustration copyright © 1990 by Viqui Maggio.

Morrow Junior Books, a division of William Morrow & Company, Inc.: Cover illustration by Sue Truesdell from *Travel Tips from Harry: A Guide to Family Vacations in the Sun* by Amy Hest. Illustration copyright © 1989 by Susan G. Truesdell. Cover illustration by Gail Owens from *Encyclopedia Brown and the Case of the Disgusting Sneakers* by Donald J. Sobol. Illustration © 1990 by Gail Owens. Cover illustration by Roy Doty from *Balloons: Building and Experimenting with Inflatable Toys* by Bernie Zubrowski. Illustration copyright © 1990 by Roy Doty.

Pippin Press: Cover illustration from *Lost in the Amazon: A Miss Mallard Mystery* by Robert Quackenbush. Copyright © 1990 by Robert Quackenbush.

Scholastic, Inc.: Cover illustration by Paul Casale from *Fourth Grade Rats* by Jerry Spinelli. Illustration © 1991 by Paul Casale.

Charles Scribner's Sons, an imprint of Macmillan Publishing Company: From *The Cat Who Escaped from Steerage* (Retitled: "Chanah's Journey") by Evelyn Wilde Mayerson. Text copyright © 1990 by Evelyn Wilde Mayerson.

Twenty-First Century Books: Cover illustration by Loel Barr from *A Portrait of Me* by Barbara Aiello and Jeffrey Shulman. Copyright © 1989 by The Kids on the Block, Inc.

Viking Penguin, a division of Penguin Books USA Inc.: Cover illustration by Stephen Gammell from *Where The Buffaloes Begin* by Olaf Baker. Illustration copyright © 1981 by Stephen Gammell. Cover illustration by Kathy Krantz from *Nothing's Fair in Fifth Grade* by Barthe DeClements. Illustration copyright © 1981 by Viking Penguin, Inc. Cover illustration by Dan Andreasen from *The Secret Language of the SB* by Elizabeth Scarboro. Illustration copyright © 1990 by Dan Andreasen. "The Flying Saucer People" from *Einstein Anderson, Science Sleuth* by Seymour Simon. Text copyright © 1980 by Seymour Simon.

Franklin Watts, Inc.: Cover illustration from *The Pony Express: Hoofbeats in the Wilderness* by Joseph J. DiCerto. Illustration courtesy of The Granger Collection.

Illustration Credits

Chuck Abraham, pp. T822, T823; Cary Austin, pp. T910, T912, T913, T918, T919; Keith Bendis, pp. T62, T64, T65, T962, T964, T965, T970, T971; Catharine Bennett, pp. T658, T659; Peter Bianco, pp. T33, T35, T40, T41, T72, T73; Greta Buchart, pp. T9, T163, T377, T509, T655, T819; Judith Cheng, pp. T874, T876, T877, T882, T883; Garry Colby, pp. T603, T608, T609; John Eggert, pp. T217, T219, T224, T225; Richard Erickson, pp. T798, T800, T801, T806, T807; Toko Fujisaki, p. T12; Annie Gusman, pp. T420, T422, T423, T428, T429; Chet Jerierski, pp. T703, T708, T709; Larry Johnson, pp. T842, T844, T845, T850, T851; Gayle Kabaker, pp. T294, T296, T297, T302, T303; Brian Karas, pp. T771, T773, T778, T779; Manuel King, p. T513; Barbara Kiwak, pp. T633, T635, T640, T641; Benton Mahan, pp. T252, T254, T255, T260, T261; Paul Meisel, pp. T132, T134, T135, T142, T143; Susan Miller, pp. T96, T97, T104, T105; Kevin Popo, pp. T316, T318, T319, T324, T325; Tim Raglin, pp. T389, T391, T396, T397; Michael Smollin, pp. T186, T188, T189, T194, T195; Patrick Soper, pp. T674, T676, T677, T682, T683; Steve Sullivan, pp. T488, T489, T494, T495; Blair Thornley, pp. T365, T370, T371, T537, T542, T543; Bonnie Timmons, pp. T568, T569, T574, T575; George Ulrich, pp. T450, T451, T458, T459; Daniel Vasconcellos, pp. T911, T946, T947; Randy Verougstraete, pp. T738, T740, T741, T748, T749

Photo Credits

Key: (t) top, (b) bottom, (l) left, (c) center, (r) right

T516, HBJ/E. Kogler; T519(t), Karen Kuehn/Matrix International; T519(b), HBJ Photo; T544(t), North Wind Picture Archives; T544(b), The Granger Collection; T553(t), HBJ/Chuck Kneyse/Black Star; T553(b), HBJ Photo; T576(t), The Granger Collection; T576(c), The Granger Collection; T576(b), Minnesota Historical Society; T578, HBJ Photo; T579, Tony Freeman/PhotoEdit; T580, HBJ/Earl Kogler; T582, HBJ/Earl Kogler; T591, HBJ/Len Kaufman/Black Star; T610, Brian Kurtis/Turtle Quarterly; T612, Michael Heron/Woodfin Camp & Associates; T613, Randy G. Taylor/Leo De Wys; T616, HBJ/E. Kogler; T619(t), Courtesy of Jorgen Voss & Alma Flor Ada; T619(b), HBJ Photo; T642(t), J. P. Laffont/Sygma; T642(b), Brown Brothers; T646, HBJ Photo; T647, The Image Works; T648, HBJ/Maria Paraskevas; T651, HBJ/Maria Paraskevas; T662, HBJ/Earl Kogler; T665(t), Courtesy HarperCollins Children's Books; T665(b), HBJ Photo; T678, HBJ/Maria Paraskevas; T684(tr), Comstock; T684(c), Stephen Frisch/Stock, Boston; T684(b), The Granger Collection; T689(t), HBJ/Rick Friedman/Black Star; T689(b), HBJ Photo; T710(c), The Granger Collection; T710(b), Bettmann; T712, Lisa Valder/TSW; T713, Mimi Forsyth/Monkmeyer Press; T716, HBJ/Earl Kogler; T721(t), Courtesy of Evelyn Wilde Mayerson; T721(b), HBJ Photo; T750(t), Courtesy NASA; T750(cl), Courtesy of Ileana Ros-Lehtinen; T750(cr), Yale University Library; T752, Bob Daemmrich/Stock, Boston; T753, Bill Losh/FPG; T756, HBJ/E. Kogler; T759(t), Courtesy Macmillan Publishing; T759(b), HBJ Photo; T780, Steve Vidler/Leo de Wys Inc.; T781, c1990 by Lawrence Migdale. All rights reserved. Reprinted from TOTEM POLE by permission of Holiday House; T783(t), Lawrence Migdale; T783(b), HBJ Photo; T808(t), AP/Wide World Photos; T808(bl), The Granger Collection; T808(bc), ESM/Art Resource, NY, Calder Two Moons, 1969; T808(br), UPI/Bettmann; T810, The Image Works; T811, Bob Daemmrich/TSW; T812, HBJ/Terry Sinclair; T815, HBJ/Maria Paraskevas; T819, HBJ Photo; T826, HBJ/Earl Kogler; T829(t), Ann A. White/Ropiequet Schmidt; T829(b), HBJ Photo; T852(tl), The Granger Collection; T852(tr), AP Wide World; T852(c), UPI/Bettmann; T852(b), Cavendish/Reflex/Picture Group; T854, HBJ/Maria Paraskevas; T857(t), Martin E. Klimek/Martin Independent Journal; T857(b), HBJ Photo; T884(tr), UPI/Bettmann; T884(cl), UPI/Bettmann; T884(cr), Robert Frerck/Odyssey; T884(b), Bettmann; T886, Tom Tracy/FPG; T887, Melchior Digiacomo/The Image Bank; T890, HBJ/Earl Kogler; T895(t), Courtesy of Natalie Kinsey-Warnock; T895(b), HBJ Photo; T920(t), The Granger Collection; T920(b), HBJ Photo; T922, Edward Lettau/Peter Arnold Inc.; T923, Arthur Tilley/TSW; T926, HBJ/Earl Kogler; T929(t), HBJ/Tom Sobolik/Black Star; T929(b), HBJ Photo; T948(t), AP/Wide World Photos; T948(c), AP/Wide World Photos; T948(b), UPI/Bettmann; T951(t), Courtesy Maria Brusca; T951(b), HBJ Photo; T972(t), Bettmann; T972(b), Wyeth-Ayerst Laboratories; T976, The Image Works; T977, Robert Brenner/PhotoEdit; T978, HBJ/Terry Sinclair; T981, HBJ/Maria Paraskevas; T1004, HBJ/Maria Paraskevas; T1007, HBJ/Maria Paraskevas; R21, HBJ/Daniel Borris; R22, HBJ/Lisa Quinones/Black Star; R23, HBJ/Lisa Quinones/Black Star; R23A, HBJ/Thomason Productions/Black Star; R23B, HBJ/Alan Orling/Black Star; R24, HBJ/Gary Sigman/Black Star; R24(background), HBJ/Daniel Borris; R25, HBJ/Alan Orling/ Black Star; R26, HBJ/Santa Fabio/Black Star; R27, HBJ/Gary Sigman/Black Star; R27(background), HBJ/Daniel Borris; R27A, HBJ/Santa Fabio/Black Star; R27B, HBJ/Thomason Productions/Black Star; R29, HBJ/Daniel Borris; R30, HBJ/Mary Ann Carter/Black Star; R31, HBJ/Kevin Vandivier/Black Star; R32, HBJ/Santa Fabio/Black Star; R32(background), HBJ/Daniel Borris; R33, HBJ/Rob Nelson/Black Star; R33(background), HBJ/Daniel Borris; R35, HBJ/Daniel Borris; R53, HBJ/Daniel Borris; R54(t), HBJ/Jeff Davis/Black Star; R54(b), HBJ/Kevin Vandivier/Black Star; R55, HBJ/Daniel Borris; R56(t), HBJ/Debbie Harbin; R56(b), HBJ/Rob Nelson/Black Star; R57, HBJ/Daniel Borris; R58, HBJ/Mary Ann Carter/Black Star; R59, HBJ/Daniel Borris; R60, HBJ/Daniel Borris; R111, HBJ/Daniel Borris;

WRITER'S JOURNAL

T573, HBJ/Les Stone.

PRACTICE BOOK

T39, HBJ/Terry Sinclair; T541, Scheler/Black Star.